WHAT THEY'RE SAYING ABOUT "*THEY SAY / I SAY*"

"The best book that's happened to teaching composition—
ever!"   —**Karen Gaffney**, *Raritan Valley Community College*

"A brilliant book. . . . It's like a membership card in the academic club."   —**Eileen Seifert**, *DePaul University*

"This book demystifies rhetorical moves, tricks of the trade that
many students are unsure about. It's reasonable, helpful, nicely
written . . . and hey, it's true. I would have found it immensely
helpful myself in high school and college."

—**Mike Rose**, *University of California, Los Angeles*

"The argument of this book is important—that there are
'moves' to academic writing . . . and that knowledge of them
can be generative. The template format is a good way to teach
and demystify the moves that matter. I like this book a lot."

—**David Bartholomae**, *University of Pittsburgh*

"A beautifully lucid way to approach argument—different from
any rhetoric I've ever seen."

—**Anne-Marie Thomas**, *Austin Community College, Riverside*

"Students need to walk a fine line between their work and that
of others, and this book helps them walk that line, providing
specific methods and techniques for introducing, explaining,
and integrating other voices with their own ideas."

—**Libby Miles**, *University of Rhode Island*

"'*They Say*' *with Readings* is different from other rhetorics and
readers in that it really engages students in the act of writing
throughout the book. It's   of
a 'do this with me' kind o

—**Kelly Ritter**, *Ur*   *n*

D0968061

"It offers students the formulas we, as academic writers, all carry in our heads." —**Karen Gardiner**, *University of Alabama*

"Many students say that it is the first book they've found that actually helps them with writing in all disciplines."
—**Laura Sonderman**, *Marshall University*

"As a WPA, I'm constantly thinking about how I can help instructors teach their students to make specific rhetorical moves on the page. This book offers a powerful way of teaching students to do just that." —**Joseph Bizup**, *Boston University*

"The best tribute to '*They Say / I Say*' I've heard is this, from a student: 'This is one book I'm not selling back to the bookstore.' Nods all around the room. The students love this book."
—**Christine Ross**, *Quinnipiac University*

"What effect has '*They Say*' had on my students' writing? They are finally entering the Burkean Parlor of the university. This book uncovers the rhetorical conventions that transcend disciplinary boundaries, so that even freshmen, newcomers to the academy, are immediately able to join in the conversation."
—**Margaret Weaver**, *Missouri State University*

"It's the anti-composition text: Fun, creative, humorous, brilliant, effective."
—**Perry Cumbie**, *Durham Technical Community College*

"Loved by students, reasonably priced, manageable size, readable."
—**Roxanne Munch**, *Joliet Junior College*

"This book explains in clear detail what skilled writers take for granted." —**John Hyman**, *American University*

"The ability to engage with the thoughts of others is one of the most important skills taught in any college-level writing course, and this book does as good a job teaching that skill as any text I have ever encountered." —**William Smith**, *Weatherford College*

THIRD EDITION

"THEY SAY / I SAY"

The Moves That Matter
in Academic Writing

WITH READINGS

Wake Technical Community College

THIRD EDITION

"THEY SAY / I SAY"

*The Moves That Matter
in Academic Writing*

WITH READINGS

GERALD GRAFF
CATHY BIRKENSTEIN

both of the University of Illinois at Chicago

RUSSEL DURST

University of Cincinnatti

Wake Technical Community College

W· W· NORTON & COMPANY

NEW YORK | LONDON

Materials may be included from the following:
They Say/I Say 3e (Gerald Graff and Cathy Birkenstein)
Copyright © 2017, 2014, 2010, 2009, 2006 by W. W. Norton & Company, Inc.
They Say/I Say with Readings 3e (Gerald Graff, Cathy Birkenstein,
and Russel Durst)
Copyright © 2017, 2015, 2014, 2012, 2010, 2009, 2006 by W. W. Norton &
Company Inc.
The Norton Mix for Composition (Elizabeth Rodriguez Kessler et. al.)
Copyright © 2012 by W. W. Norton & Company, Inc.

Permission to use copyrighted material is included in the credits section of this
book, which begins on page 747.

The Library of Congress has cataloged an earlier edition as follows:
Library of Congress Cataloging-in-Publication Data
Graff, Gerald, author.
    "They say/I say": the moves that matter in academic writing, with readings / Gerald
Graff, University of Illinois at Chicago; Cathy Birkenstein, University of Illinois at
Chicago; Russel Durst, University of Cincinnati.—Third Edition.
    p. cm
Previous edition: 3rd. ed. 2014.
Includes bibliographical references and index.
ISBN 978-0-393-93751-0 (pbk.)
1.   English language—Rhetoric—Handbooks, manuals, etc.   2. Persuasion
(Rhetoric)—Handbooks, manuals, etc.   3. Report writing—Handbooks, manuals,
etc.   4. Academic writing—Handbooks, manuals, etc.   5. College readers.
I. Birkenstein, Cathy, editor. II. Durst, Russel K., 1954- editor. III. Title.
PE1431.G73 2014
808'.042—dc23   2014033777

This edition: **ISBN 978-0-393-29326-5**

W. W. Norton & Company, Inc., 500 Fifth Avenue, New York, NY 10110
wwnorton.com

W. W. Norton & Company Ltd., 15 Carlisle Street, London W1D 3BS
3 4 5 6 7 8 9 0

To the great rhetorician Wayne Booth,
who cared deeply
about the democratic art
of listening closely to what others say.

CONTENTS

CONTENTS

Contents

CONTENTS

Contents

PREFACE
TO THE THIRD EDITION

—⊡—

WHEN WE FIRST SET OUT TO WRITE THIS BOOK, our goal was simple: to offer a version of *"They Say / I Say": The Moves That Matter in Academic Writing* with an anthology of readings that would demonstrate the rhetorical moves "that matter." And because *"They Say"* teaches students that academic writing is a means of entering a conversation, we looked for readings on topics that would engage students and inspire them to respond—and to enter the conversations.

The book has been more successful than we ever imagined possible, which we believe reflects the growing importance of academic writing as a focus of first-year writing courses, and the fact that students find practical strategies like the ones offered in this book to be particularly helpful. In addition, some teachers have told us that this book works well in courses that focus on argument and research because students find these strategies easier to grasp than those in the books that teach various kinds of formal argumentation.

Our purpose in writing *"They Say"* has always been to offer students a user-friendly model of writing that will help them put into practice the important principle that writing is a social activity. Proceeding from the premise that effective writers enter conversations of other writers and speakers, this book encourages students to engage with those around them—including those who disagree with them—instead of just expressing their ideas "logically." Our own experience teaching first-year writing students has led us to believe that to be persuasive, arguments need not only supporting evidence but also motivation and exigency, and that the surest way to achieve this motivation and exigency is to generate one's own arguments as a response to those of others—to something "they say." To help students write their way into the often daunting conversations of academia and the wider public sphere, the book provides templates to help them make sophisticated rhetorical moves that they might otherwise not think of attempting. And of course learning to make these rhetorical moves in writing also helps students become better readers of argument.

That the two versions of *"They Say / I Say"* are now being taught at more than 1,500 schools suggests that there is a widespread desire for explicit instruction that is understandable but not oversimplified, to help writers negotiate the basic moves necessary to "enter the conversation." Instructors have told us how much this book helps their students learn how to write academic discourse, and some students have written to us saying that it's helped them to "crack the code," as one student put it.

This third edition of *"They Say / I Say" with Readings* includes forty-three readings on five compelling and controversial issues. The readings provide a glimpse into some important conversations of our day—and will, we hope, provoke students to respond and thus to join in those conversations.

HIGHLIGHTS

Forty-three readings that will prompt students to think—and write. Taken from a wide variety of sources, including the *New York Times*, the *Wall Street Journal*, *Salon*, the *Atlantic*, the

Pew Research Center, the *New Yorker*, *Wired* magazine, best-selling trade books, celebrated speeches, and more, the readings represent a range of perspectives on five important issues:

- Is College the Best Option?
- Are We in a Race against the Machine?
- What Should We Eat?
- What's Up with the American Dream?
- What's Gender Got to Do with It?

The readings can function as sources for students' own writing, and the study questions that follow each reading focus students' attention on how each author uses the key rhetorical moves—and include one question that invites them to write, and often to respond with their own views.

A chapter on reading (Chapter 14) encourages students to think of reading as an act of entering conversations. Instead of teaching students merely to identify the author's argument, this chapter shows them how to read with an eye for what arguments the author is responding to—in other words, to think carefully about why the writer is making the argument in the first place, and thus to recognize (and ultimately become a part of) the larger conversation that gives meaning to reading the text.

Two books in one, with a rhetoric up front and readings in the back. The two parts are linked by cross-references in the margins, leading from the rhetoric to specific examples in the readings and from the readings to the corresponding writing instruction. Teachers can therefore begin with either the rhetoric or the readings, and the links will facilitate movement between one section and the other.

WHAT'S NEW

Two topics are new, two are updated—all addressing important conversations taking place today. The chapters on gender and technology are new. The food chapter now reaches beyond fast food to address a broader question: what should we eat? And the education chapter asks not just is college worth the price but whether it is even the best option.

Thirty-one new readings, including at least one documented piece and one essay written by a student in each chapter, added in response to requests from many teachers who wanted more complex and documented writing.

They Say / I Blog. Updated monthly, this blog provides up-to-the-minute readings on the issues covered in the book, along with questions that prompt students to literally join the conversation. Check it out at **theysayiblog.com.**

A new chapter on "Using the Templates to Revise," which grew out of our own teaching experience, where we found that the templates in this book had the unexpected benefit of helping students when they revise.

A new chapter on writing online, exploring the debate about whether digital technologies improve or degrade the way we think and write, and whether they foster or impede the meeting of minds.

A complete instructor's guide, with teaching tips for all the chapters, syllabi, summaries of the readings, and suggested answers to the study questions. Go to wwnorton.com/instructors to access these materials.

We hope that this new edition of *"They Say / I Say" with Readings* will spark students' interest in some of the most pressing conversations of our day and provide them with some of the tools they need to engage in those conversations with dexterity and confidence.

Gerald Graff
Cathy Birkenstein
Russel Durst

PREFACE

Demystifying Academic Conversation

—⌐回⌐—

EXPERIENCED WRITING INSTRUCTORS have long recognized that writing well means entering into conversation with others. Academic writing in particular calls upon writers not simply to express their own ideas, but to do so as a response to what others have said. The first-year writing program at our own university, according to its mission statement, asks "students to participate in ongoing conversations about vitally important academic and public issues." A similar statement by another program holds that "intellectual writing is almost always composed in response to others' texts." These statements echo the ideas of rhetorical theorists like Kenneth Burke, Mikhail Bakhtin, and Wayne Booth as well as recent composition scholars like David Bartholomae, John Bean, Patricia Bizzell, Irene Clark, Greg Colomb, Lisa Ede, Peter Elbow, Joseph Harris, Andrea Lunsford, Elaine Maimon, Gary Olson, Mike Rose, John Swales and Christine Feak, Tilly Warnock, and others who argue that writing well means engaging the voices of others and letting them in turn engage us.

Yet despite this growing consensus that writing is a social, conversational act, helping student writers actually participate in these conversations remains a formidable challenge. This book aims to meet that challenge. Its goal is to demystify academic writing by isolating its basic moves, explaining them clearly, and representing them in the form of templates.

In this way, we hope to help students become active participants in the important conversations of the academic world and the wider public sphere.

HIGHLIGHTS

- *Shows that writing well means entering a conversation*, summarizing others ("they say") to set up one's own argument ("I say").
- *Demystifies academic writing*, showing students "the moves that matter" in language they can readily apply.
- *Provides user-friendly templates* to help writers make those moves in their own writing.
- *Includes a chapter on reading*, showing students how the authors they read are part of a conversation that they themselves can enter—and thus to see reading as a matter not of passively absorbing information but of understanding and actively entering dialogues and debates.

HOW THIS BOOK CAME TO BE

The original idea for this book grew out of our shared interest in democratizing academic culture. First, it grew out of arguments that Gerald Graff has been making throughout his career that schools and colleges need to invite students into the conversations and debates that surround them. More specifically, it is a practical, hands-on companion to his recent book, *Clueless in Academe: How Schooling Obscures the Life of the Mind*, in which he looks at academic conversations from the perspective of those who find them mysterious and proposes ways in which such mystification can be overcome. Second, this book grew out of writing templates that Cathy Birkenstein developed in the 1990s, for use in writing and literature courses she was teaching. Many students, she found, could readily grasp what it meant to support a thesis with evidence, to entertain a counter-argument, to identify a textual contradiction, and ultimately to summarize and respond to challenging arguments, but they often had trouble putting these concepts into practice in their own writing. When Cathy sketched out templates on the board, however, giving her students some of the language and patterns that these sophisticated moves require, their writing—and even their quality of thought—significantly improved.

This book began, then, when we put our ideas together and realized that these templates might have the potential to open up and clarify academic conversation. We proceeded from the premise that all writers rely on certain stock formulas that they themselves didn't invent—and that many of these formulas are so commonly used that they can be represented in model templates that students can use to structure and even generate what they want to say.

As we developed a working draft of this book, we began using it in first-year writing courses that we teach at UIC. In classroom exercises and writing assignments, we found that students who otherwise struggled to organize their thoughts, or even to think of something to say, did much better when we provided them with templates like the following.

▶ **In discussions of _____, a controversial issue is whether _____. While some argue that _____, others contend that _____.**

▶ **This is not to say that _____.**

One virtue of such templates, we found, is that they focus writers' attention not just on what is being said, but on the *forms* that structure what is being said. In other words, they make students more conscious of the rhetorical patterns that are key to academic success but often pass under the classroom radar.

THE CENTRALITY OF "THEY SAY / I SAY"

The central rhetorical move that we focus on in this book is the "they say / I say" template that gives our book its title. In our view, this template represents the deep, underlying structure, the internal DNA as it were, of all effective argument. Effective persuasive writers do more than make well-supported claims ("I say"); they also map those claims relative to the claims of others ("they say").

Here, for example, the "they say / I say" pattern structures a passage from an essay by the media and technology critic Steven Johnson.

> For decades, we've worked under the assumption that mass culture follows a path declining steadily toward lowest-common-denominator standards, presumably because the "masses" want dumb, simple pleasures and big media companies try to give the masses what they want. But . . . the exact opposite is happening: the culture is getting more cognitively demanding, not less.
>
> STEVEN JOHNSON, "Watching TV Makes You Smarter"

In generating his own argument from something "they say," Johnson suggests *why* he needs to say what he is saying: to correct a popular misconception.

Even when writers do not explicitly identify the views they are responding to, as Johnson does, an implicit "they say" can often be discerned, as in the following passage by Zora Neale Hurston.

I remember the day I became colored.

ZORA NEALE HURSTON, "How It Feels to Be Colored Me"

In order to grasp Hurston's point here, we need to be able to reconstruct the implicit view she is responding to and questioning: that racial identity is an innate quality we are simply born with. On the contrary, Hurston suggests, our race is imposed on us by society—something we "become" by virtue of how we are treated.

As these examples suggest, the "they say/I say" model can improve not just student writing, but student reading comprehension as well. Since reading and writing are deeply reciprocal activities, students who learn to make the rhetorical moves represented by the templates in this book figure to become more adept at identifying these same moves in the texts they read. And if we are right that effective arguments are always in dialogue with other arguments, then it follows that in order to understand the types of challenging texts assigned in college, students need to identify the views to which those texts are responding.

Working with the "they say/I say" model can also help with invention, finding something to say. In our experience, students best discover what they want to say not by thinking about a subject in an isolation booth, but by reading texts, listening closely to what other writers say, and looking for an opening through which they can enter the conversation. In other words, listening closely to others and summarizing what they have to say can help writers generate their own ideas.

THE USEFULNESS OF TEMPLATES

Our templates also have a generative quality, prompting students to make moves in their writing that they might not otherwise make or even know they should make. The templates in this book can be particularly helpful for students who are unsure about what to say, or who have trouble finding enough to say, often because they consider their own beliefs so self-evident that they need not be argued for. Students like this are often helped, we've found, when we give them a simple template like the following one for entertaining a counterargument (or planting a naysayer, as we call it in Chapter 6).

▸ **Of course some might object that** _____ . **Although I concede that** _____ , **I still maintain that** _____ .

What this particular template helps students do is make the seemingly counterintuitive move of questioning their own beliefs, of looking at them from the perspective of those who disagree. In so doing, templates can bring out aspects of students' thoughts that, as they themselves sometimes remark, they didn't even realize were there.

Other templates in this book help students make a host of sophisticated moves that they might not otherwise make: summarizing what someone else says, framing a quotation in one's own words, indicating the view that the writer is responding to, marking the shift from a source's view to the writer's own view, offering evidence for that view, entertaining and answering counterarguments, and explaining what is at stake in the first place. In showing students how to make such moves, templates do more than organize students' ideas; they help bring those ideas into existence.

OKAY, BUT TEMPLATES?

We are aware, of course, that some instructors may have reservations about templates. Some, for instance, may object that such formulaic devices represent a return to prescriptive forms of instruction that encourage passive learning or lead students to put their writing on automatic pilot.

This is an understandable reaction, we think, to kinds of rote instruction that have indeed encouraged passivity and drained writing of its creativity and dynamic relation to the social world. The trouble is that many students will never learn on their own to make the key intellectual moves that our templates represent. While seasoned writers pick up these moves unconsciously through their reading, many students do not. Consequently, we believe, students need to see these moves represented in the explicit ways that the templates provide.

The aim of the templates, then, is not to stifle critical thinking but to be direct with students about the key rhetorical moves that it comprises. Since we encourage students to modify and adapt the templates to the particularities of the arguments they are making, using such prefabricated formulas as learning tools need not result in writing and thinking that are themselves formulaic. Admittedly, no teaching tool can guarantee that students will engage in hard, rigorous thought. Our templates do, however, provide concrete prompts that can stimulate and shape such thought: What do "they say" about my topic? What would a naysayer say about my argument? What is my evidence? Do I need to qualify my point? Who cares?

In fact, templates have a long and rich history. Public orators from ancient Greece and Rome through the European Renaissance studied rhetorical *topoi* or "commonplaces," model passages and formulas that represented the different strategies available to public speakers. In many respects, our templates echo this classical rhetorical tradition of imitating established models.

The journal *Nature* requires aspiring contributors to follow a guideline that is like a template on the opening page of their manuscript: "Two or three sentences explaining what the main result [of their study] reveals in direct comparison with what was thought to be the case previously, or how the main result adds to previous knowledge." In the field of education, a form designed by the education theorist Howard Gardner asks postdoctoral fellowship applicants to complete the following template: "Most scholars in the field believe _____. As a result of my study, _____." That these two examples are geared toward post-doctoral fellows and veteran researchers shows that it is not only struggling undergraduates who can use help making these key rhetorical moves, but experienced academics as well.

Templates have even been used in the teaching of personal narrative. The literary and educational theorist Jane Tompkins devised the following template to help student writers make the often difficult move from telling a story to explaining what it means: "X tells a story about _____ to make the point that _____. My own experience with _____ yields a point that is similar/different/both similar and different. What I take away from my own experience with _____ is _____. As a result, I conclude _____." We especially like this template because it suggests that "they say/I say" argument need not be mechanical, impersonal, or dry, and that telling a story and making an argument are more compatible activities than many think.

WHY IT'S OKAY TO USE "I"

But wait—doesn't the "I" part of "they say / I say" flagrantly encourage the use of the first-person pronoun? Aren't we aware that some teachers prohibit students from using "I" or "we," on the grounds that these pronouns encourage ill-considered, subjective opinions rather than objective and reasoned arguments? Yes, we are aware of this first-person prohibition, but we think it has serious flaws. First, expressing ill-considered, subjective opinions is not necessarily the worst sin beginning writers can commit; it might be a starting point from which they can move on to more reasoned, less self-indulgent perspectives. Second, prohibiting students from using "I" is simply not an effective way of curbing students' subjectivity, since one can offer poorly argued, ill-supported opinions just as easily without it. Third and most important, prohibiting the first person tends to hamper students' ability not only to take strong positions but to differentiate their own positions from those of others, as we point out in Chapter 5. To be sure, writers can resort to various circumlocutions—"it will here be argued," "the evidence suggests," "the truth is"—and these may be useful for avoiding a monotonous series of "I believe" sentences. But except for avoiding such monotony, we see no good reason why "I" should be set aside in persuasive writing. Rather than prohibit "I," then, we think a better tactic is to give students practice at using it well and learning its use, both by supporting their claims with evidence and by attending closely to alternative perspectives—to what "they" are saying.

HOW THIS BOOK IS ORGANIZED

Because of its centrality, we have allowed the "they say/I say" format to dictate the structure of this book. So while Part 1 addresses the art of listening to others, Part 2 addresses how to offer one's own response. Part 1 opens with a chapter on

"Starting with What Others Are Saying" that explains why it is generally advisable to begin a text by citing others rather than plunging directly into one's own views. Subsequent chapters take up the arts of summarizing and quoting what these others have to say. Part 2 begins with a chapter on different ways of responding, followed by chapters on marking the shift between what "they say" and what "I say," on introducing and answering objections, and on answering the all-important questions: "so what?" and "who cares?" Part 3 offers strategies for "Tying It All Together," beginning with a chapter on connection and coherence; followed by a chapter on formal and informal language, arguing that academic discourse is often perfectly compatible with the informal language that students use outside school; and concluding with a chapter on the art of metacommentary, showing students how to guide the way readers understand a text. Part 4 offers guidance for entering conversations in specific academic contexts, with chapters on entering class discussions, writing online, reading, and writing in literature courses, the sciences, and social sciences. Finally, we provide five readings and an index of templates.

WHAT THIS BOOK DOESN'T DO

There are some things that this book does not try to do. We do not, for instance, cover logical principles of argument such as syllogisms, warrants, logical fallacies, or the differences between inductive and deductive reasoning. Although such concepts can be useful, we believe most of us learn the ins and outs of argumentative writing not by studying logical principles in the abstract, but by plunging into actual discussions and debates, trying out different patterns of response, and in this way getting a sense of what works to persuade different audiences and what doesn't. In our view, people learn more about arguing from hearing someone say, "You miss my point. What I'm saying is not _____, but _____," or "I agree with you that _____, and would even add that _____," than they do from studying the differences between inductive and deductive reasoning. Such formulas give students an immediate sense of what it feels like to enter a public conversation in a way that studying abstract warrants and logical fallacies does not.

ENGAGING WITH THE IDEAS OF OTHERS

One central goal of this book is to demystify academic writing by returning it to its social and conversational roots. Although writing may require some degree of quiet and solitude, the "they say / I say" model shows students that they can best develop their arguments not just by looking inward but by doing what they often do in a good conversation with friends and family— by listening carefully to what others are saying and engaging with other views.

This approach to writing therefore has an ethical dimension, since it asks writers not simply to keep proving and reasserting what they already believe but to stretch what they believe by putting it up against beliefs that differ, sometimes radically, from their own. In an increasingly diverse, global society, this ability to engage with the ideas of others is especially crucial to democratic citizenship.

Gerald Graff
Cathy Birkenstein

THIRD EDITION

"THEY SAY / I SAY"

The Moves That Matter
in Academic Writing

WITH READINGS

INTRODUCTION

Entering the Conversation

THINK ABOUT AN ACTIVITY that you do particularly well: cooking, playing the piano, shooting a basketball, even something as basic as driving a car. If you reflect on this activity, you'll realize that once you mastered it you no longer had to give much conscious thought to the various moves that go into doing it. Performing this activity, in other words, depends on your having learned a series of complicated moves—moves that may seem mysterious or difficult to those who haven't yet learned them.

The same applies to writing. Often without consciously realizing it, accomplished writers routinely rely on a stock of established moves that are crucial for communicating sophisticated ideas. What makes writers masters of their trade is not only their ability to express interesting thoughts but their mastery of an inventory of basic moves that they probably picked up by reading a wide range of other accomplished writers. Less experienced writers, by contrast, are often unfamiliar with these basic moves and unsure how to make them in their own writing. This book is intended as a short, user-friendly guide to the basic moves of academic writing.

One of our key premises is that these basic moves are so common that they can be represented in *templates* that you can use right away to structure and even generate your own writing. Perhaps the most distinctive feature of this book is its presentation of many such templates, designed to help you successfully enter not only the world of academic thinking and writing, but also the wider worlds of civic discourse and work.

Instead of focusing solely on abstract principles of writing, then, this book offers model templates that help you put those principles directly into practice. Working with these templates can give you an immediate sense of how to engage in the kinds of critical thinking you are required to do at the college level and in the vocational and public spheres beyond.

Some of these templates represent simple but crucial moves like those used to summarize some widely held belief.

▶ **Many Americans assume that** _____ **.**

Others are more complicated.

▶ **On the one hand,** _____ **. On the other hand,** _____ **.**

▶ **Author X contradicts herself. At the same time that she argues** _____ **, she also implies** _____ **.**

▶ **I agree that** _____ **.**

▶ **This is not to say that** _____ **.**

It is true, of course, that critical thinking and writing go deeper than any set of linguistic formulas, requiring that you question assumptions, develop strong claims, offer supporting reasons and evidence, consider opposing arguments, and so on. But these deeper habits of thought cannot be put into practice unless you have a language for expressing them in clear, organized ways.

STATE YOUR OWN IDEAS AS A RESPONSE TO OTHERS

The single most important template that we focus on in this book is the "they say _____; I say _____" formula that gives our book its title. If there is any one point that we hope you will take away from this book, it is the importance not only of expressing your ideas ("I say") but of presenting those ideas as a *response to some other person or group* ("they say"). For us, the underlying structure of effective academic writing—and of responsible public discourse—resides not just in stating our own ideas but in listening closely to others around us, summarizing their views in a way that they will recognize, and responding with our own ideas in kind. Broadly speaking, academic writing is argumentative writing, and we believe that to argue well you need to do more than assert your own position. You need to enter a conversation, using what others say (or might say) as a launching pad or sounding board for your own views. For this reason, one of the main pieces of advice in this book is to write the voices of others into your text.

In our view, then, the best academic writing has one underlying feature: it is deeply engaged in some way with other people's views. Too often, however, academic writing is taught as a process of saying "true" or "smart" things in a vacuum, as if it were possible to argue effectively without being in conversation *with* someone else. If you have been taught to write a traditional five-paragraph essay, for example, you have learned how to develop a thesis and support it with evidence. This is good advice as far as it goes, but it leaves out the important fact that in the real world we don't make arguments without being provoked. Instead, we make arguments because someone has said or done something (or perhaps *not* said or done something) and we need to respond: "I can't see why you like the Lakers so much"; "I agree: it was a great film"; "That argument is contradictory." If it weren't for other people and our need to challenge, agree with, or otherwise respond to them, there would be no reason to argue at all.

To make an impact as a writer, you need to do more than make statements that are logical, well supported, and consistent. You must also find a way of entering a conversation with others' views—with something "they say." If your own argument doesn't identify the "they say" that you're responding to, it probably won't make sense. As the figure above suggests, *what* you are saying may be clear to your audience, but *why* you are saying it won't be. For it is what others are saying and thinking that motivates our writing and gives it a reason for being. It follows, then, as the figure on the next page suggests, that your own argument—the thesis or "I say" moment of your text—should always be a response to the arguments of others.

Many writers make explicit "they say / I say" moves in their writing. One famous example is Martin Luther King Jr.'s "Letter from Birmingham Jail," which consists almost entirely of King's eloquent responses to a public statement by eight clergymen deploring the civil rights protests he was leading. The letter—which was written in 1963, while King was in prison for leading a demonstration against racial injustice in Birmingham—is structured almost entirely around a framework of summary and response, in which King summarizes and then answers their criticisms. In one typical passage, King writes as follows.

> You deplore the demonstrations taking place in Birmingham. But your statement, I am sorry to say, fails to express a similar concern for the conditions that brought about the demonstrations.
>
> MARTIN LUTHER KING JR., "Letter from Birmingham Jail"

King goes on to agree with his critics that "It is unfortunate that demonstrations are taking place in Birmingham," yet he hastens to add that "it is even more unfortunate that the city's white power structure left the Negro community with no alternative." King's letter is so thoroughly conversational, in fact, that it could be rewritten in the form of a dialogue or play.

> King's critics:
> King's response:
> Critics:
> Response:

Clearly, King would not have written his famous letter were it not for his critics, whose views he treats not as objections to his already-formed arguments but as the motivating source of those arguments, their central reason for being. He quotes not only what his critics have said ("Some have asked: 'Why didn't you give the new city administration time to act?'"), but also things they *might* have said ("One may well ask: 'How can you advocate breaking some laws and obeying others?'")—all to set the stage for what he himself wants to say.

A similar "they say / I say" exchange opens an essay about American patriotism by the social critic Katha Pollitt, who uses her own daughter's comment to represent the national fervor of post-9/11 patriotism.

> My daughter, who goes to Stuyvesant High School only blocks from the former World Trade Center, thinks we should fly the American flag out our window. Definitely not, I say: The flag stands for jingoism and vengeance and war. She tells me I'm wrong—the flag means standing together and honoring the dead and saying no to terrorism. In a way we're both right. . . .
>
> KATHA POLLITT, "Put Out No Flags"

As Pollitt's example shows, the "they" you respond to in crafting an argument need not be a famous author or someone known to your audience. It can be a family member like Pollitt's daughter, or a friend or classmate who has made a provocative claim. It can even be something an individual or a group might say—or a side of yourself, something you once believed but no longer do, or something you partly believe but also doubt. The important thing is that the "they" (or "you" or "she") represent some wider group with which readers might identify—in Pollitt's case, those who patriotically believe in flying the flag. Pollitt's example also shows that responding to the views of others need not always involve unqualified opposition. By agreeing and disagreeing with her daughter, Pollitt enacts what we call the "yes and no" response, reconciling apparently incompatible views. See Chapter 4 for more on agreeing, but with a difference.

While King and Pollitt both identify the views they are responding to, some authors do not explicitly state their views but instead allow the reader to infer them. See, for instance, if you can identify the implied or unnamed "they say" that the following claim is responding to.

> I like to think I have a certain advantage as a teacher of literature because when I was growing up I disliked and feared books.
>
> Gerald Graff, "Disliking Books at an Early Age"

In case you haven't figured it out already, the phantom "they say" here is the common belief that in order to be a good teacher of literature, one must have grown up liking and enjoying books.

As you can see from these examples, many writers use the "they say / I say" format to agree or disagree with others, to challenge standard ways of thinking, and thus to stir up controversy. This point may come as a shock to you if you have always had the impression that in order to succeed academically you need to play it safe and avoid controversy in your writing, making statements that nobody can possibly disagree with. Though this view of writing may appear logical, it is actually a recipe for flat, lifeless writing and for writing that fails to answer what we call the "so what?" and "who cares?" questions. "William Shakespeare wrote many famous plays and sonnets" may be a perfectly true statement, but precisely because nobody is likely to disagree with it, it goes without saying and thus would seem pointless if said.

WAYS OF RESPONDING

Just because much argumentative writing is driven by disagreement, it does not follow that *agreement* is ruled out. Although argumentation is often associated with conflict and opposition, the type of conversational "they say / I say" argument that we focus on in this book can be just as useful when you agree as when you disagree.

▸ **She argues _____ , and I agree because _____ .**

▸ **Her argument that _____ is supported by new research showing that _____ .**

Nor do you always have to choose between either simply agreeing *or* disagreeing, since the "they say / I say" format also works to both agree and disagree at the same time, as Pollitt illustrates above.

▸ He claims that _____, and I have mixed feelings about it.
On the one hand, I agree that _____. On the other hand,
I still insist that _____.

This last option—agreeing and disagreeing simultaneously—is one we especially recommend, since it allows you to avoid a simple yes or no response and present a more complicated argument, while containing that complication within a clear "on the one hand / on the other hand" framework.

While the templates we offer in this book can be used to structure your writing at the sentence level, they can also be expanded as needed to almost any length, as the following elaborated "they say / I say" template demonstrates.

▸ In recent discussions of _____, a controversial issue has
been whether _____. On the one hand, some argue
that _____. From this perspective, _____. On the other
hand, however, others argue that _____. In the words of
_____, one of this view's main proponents, "_____."
According to this view, _____. In sum, then, the issue is
whether _____ or _____.
  My own view is that _____. Though I concede that
_____, I still maintain that _____. For example,
_____. Although some might object that _____, I would
reply that _____. The issue is important because _____.

If you go back over this template, you will see that it helps you make a host of challenging moves (each of which is taken up in forthcoming chapters in this book). First, the template helps you open your text by identifying an issue in some ongoing conversation or debate ("In recent discussions of _____, a controversial issue has been _____"), and then to map some of the voices in this controversy (by using the "on the one hand / on the other hand" structure). The template also helps you introduce a quotation ("In the words of"), to explain the quotation in your own words ("According to this view"), and—in a new paragraph—to state your own argument ("My own view is that"), to qualify your argument ("Though I concede that"), and then to support your argument with evidence ("For example"). In addition, the template helps you make one of the most crucial moves in argumentative writing, what we call "planting a naysayer in your text," in which you summarize and then answer a likely objection to your own central claim ("Although it might be objected that _____, I reply _____"). Finally, this template helps you shift between general, overarching claims ("In sum, then") and smaller-scale, supporting claims ("For example").

Again, none of us is born knowing these moves, especially when it comes to academic writing. Hence the need for this book.

DO TEMPLATES STIFLE CREATIVITY?

If you are like some of our students, your initial response to templates may be skepticism. At first, many of our students complain that using templates will take away their originality and creativity and make them all sound the same. "They'll turn us into writing robots," one of our students insisted. Another agreed, adding, "Hey, I'm a jazz musician. And we don't play by set forms. We create our own." "I'm in college now," another student asserted; "this is third-grade-level stuff."

In our view, however, the templates in this book, far from being "third-grade-level stuff," represent the stock in trade of sophisticated thinking and writing, and they often require a great deal of practice and instruction to use successfully. As for the belief that pre-established forms undermine creativity, we think it rests on a very limited vision of what creativity is all about. In our view, the above template and the others in this book will actually help your writing become *more* original and creative, not less. After all, even the most creative forms of expression depend on established patterns and structures. Most songwriters, for instance, rely on a time-honored verse-chorus-verse pattern, and few people would call Shakespeare uncreative because he didn't invent the sonnet or the dramatic forms that he used to such dazzling effect. Even the most avant-garde, cutting-edge artists (like improvisational jazz musicians) need to master the basic forms that their work improvises on, departs from, and goes beyond, or else their work will come across as uneducated child's play. Ultimately, then, creativity and originality lie not in the avoidance of established forms but in the imaginative use of them.

Furthermore, these templates do not dictate the *content* of what you say, which can be as original as you can make it, but only suggest a way of formatting *how* you say it. In addition, once you begin to feel comfortable with the templates in this book, you will be able to improvise creatively on them to fit new situations and purposes and find others in your reading. In other words, the templates offered here are learning tools to get you started, not structures set in stone. Once you get used to using them, you can even dispense with them altogether, for the rhetorical moves they model will be at your fingertips in an unconscious, instinctive way.

But if you still need proof that writing templates do not stifle creativity, consider the following opening to an essay on the fast-food industry that we've included at the back of this book.

If ever there were a newspaper headline custom-made for Jay Leno's monologue, this was it. Kids taking on McDonald's this week, suing the company for making them fat. Isn't that like middle-aged men suing Porsche for making them get speeding tickets? Whatever happened to personal responsibility?

I tend to sympathize with these portly fast-food patrons, though. Maybe that's because I used to be one of them.

DAVID ZINCZENKO, "Don't Blame the Eater"

Although Zinczenko relies on a version of the "they say / I say" formula, his writing is anything but dry, robotic, or uncreative. While Zinczenko does not explicitly use the words "they say" and "I say," the template still gives the passage its underlying structure: "*They say* that kids suing fast-food companies for making them fat is a joke; but *I say* such lawsuits are justified."

BUT ISN'T THIS PLAGIARISM?

"But isn't this plagiarism?" at least one student each year will usually ask. "Well, is it?" we respond, turning the question around into one the entire class can profit from. "We are, after all, asking you to use language in your writing that isn't your own—language that you 'borrow' or, to put it less delicately, steal from other writers."

Often, a lively discussion ensues that raises important questions about authorial ownership and helps everyone better understand the frequently confusing line between plagiarism and the legitimate use of what others say and how they say it. Students are quick to see that no one person owns a conventional formula like "on the one hand . . . on the other hand . . . " Phrases like "a controversial issue" are so commonly used and recycled that they are generic—community property that can be freely used without fear of committing plagiarism. It *is* plagiarism, however, if the words used to fill in the blanks of such formulas are borrowed from others without proper acknowledgment. In sum, then, while it is not plagiarism to recycle conventionally used formulas, it is a serious academic offense to take the substantive content from others' texts without citing the author and giving him or her proper credit.

PUTTING IN YOUR OAR

Though the immediate goal of this book is to help you become a better writer, at a deeper level it invites you to become a certain type of person: a critical, intellectual thinker who, instead of sitting passively on the sidelines, can participate in the debates and conversations of your world in an active and empowered way. Ultimately, this book invites you to become a critical thinker who can enter the types of conversations described eloquently by the philosopher Kenneth Burke in the following widely cited passage. Likening the world of intellectual exchange to a never-ending conversation at a party, Burke writes:

> You come late. When you arrive, others have long preceded you, and they are engaged in a heated discussion, a discussion too heated for them to pause and tell you exactly what it is about. . . . You listen for a while, until you decide that you have caught the tenor of the argument; then you put in your oar. Someone answers; you answer him; another comes to your defense; another aligns himself against you. . . . The hour grows late, you must depart. And you do depart, with the discussion still vigorously in progress.
>
> KENNETH BURKE, *The Philosophy of Literary Form*

What we like about this passage is its suggestion that stating an argument and "putting in your oar" can only be done in conversation with others; that we all enter the dynamic world of ideas not as isolated individuals but as social beings deeply connected to others who have a stake in what we say.

This ability to enter complex, many-sided conversations has taken on a special urgency in today's diverse, post-9/11 world, where the future for all of us may depend on our ability to put ourselves in the shoes of those who think very differently from us. The central piece of advice in this book—that we listen carefully to others, including those who disagree with us, and then engage with them thoughtfully and respectfully—can help us see beyond our own pet beliefs, which may not be shared by everyone. The mere act of crafting a sentence that begins "Of course, someone might object that _____ " may not seem like a way to change the world; but it does have the potential to jog us out of our comfort zones, to get us thinking critically about our own beliefs, and perhaps even to change our minds.

Exercises

1. Read the following paragraph from an essay by Emily Poe, a student at Furman University. Disregarding for the moment what Poe says, focus your attention on the phrases she uses to structure what she says (italicized here). Then write a new paragraph using Poe's as a model but replacing her topic, vegetarianism, with one of your own.

   The term "vegetarian" tends to be synonymous with "tree-hugger" in many people's minds. *They see* vegetarianism as a cult that brainwashes its followers into eliminating an essential part of their daily diets for an abstract goal of "animal welfare." *However,* few vegetarians choose their lifestyle just to follow the crowd. *On the contrary,* many of these supposedly brainwashed people are actually independent thinkers, concerned citizens, and compassionate human beings. *For the truth is* that there are many very good reasons for giving up meat. Perhaps the best reasons are to improve the environment, to encourage humane treatment of livestock, or to enhance one's own health. *In this essay, then,* closely examining a vegetarian diet as compared to a meat-eater's diet will show that vegetarianism is clearly the better option for sustaining the Earth and all its inhabitants.

2. Write a short essay in which you first summarize our rationale for the templates in this book and then articulate your own position in response. If you want, you can use the template below to organize your paragraphs, expanding and modifying it as necessary to fit what you want to say.

In the Introduction to *"They Say / I Say": The Moves That Matter in Academic Writing,* Gerald Graff and Cathy Birkenstein provide templates designed to _____. Specifically, Graff and Birkenstein argue that the types of writing templates they offer _____. As the authors themselves put it, "_____." Although some people believe _____, Graff and Birkenstein insist that _____. In sum, then, their view is that _____.

    I [agree/disagree/have mixed feelings]. In my view, the types of templates that the authors recommend _____. For instance, _____. In addition, _____. Some might object, of course, on the grounds that _____. Yet I would argue that _____. Overall, then, I believe _____ —an important point to make given _____.

1

"THEY SAY"

"THEY SAY"

ONE

"THEY SAY"

Starting with What Others Are Saying

NOT LONG AGO we attended a talk at an academic conference where the speaker's central claim seemed to be that a certain sociologist—call him Dr. X—had done very good work in a number of areas of the discipline. The speaker proceeded to illustrate his thesis by referring extensively and in great detail to various books and articles by Dr. X and by quoting long passages from them. The speaker was obviously both learned and impassioned, but as we listened to his talk we found ourselves somewhat puzzled: the argument—that Dr. X's work was very important—was clear enough, but why did the speaker need to make it in the first place? Did anyone dispute it? Were there commentators in the field who had argued against X's work or challenged its value? Was the speaker's interpretation of what X had done somehow novel or revolutionary? Since the speaker gave no hint of an answer to any of these questions, we could only wonder why he was going on and on about X. It was only after the speaker finished and took questions from the audience that we got a clue: in response to one questioner, he referred to several critics who had

The hypothetical audience in the figure on p. 4 reacts similarly.

vigorously questioned Dr. X's ideas and convinced many sociologists that Dr. X's work was unsound.

This story illustrates an important lesson: that to give writing the most important thing of all—namely, a point—a writer needs to indicate clearly not only what his or her thesis is, but also what larger conversation that thesis is responding to. Because our speaker failed to mention what others had said about Dr. X's work, he left his audience unsure about why he felt the need to say what he was saying. Perhaps the point was clear to other sociologists in the audience who were more familiar with the debates over Dr. X's work than we were. But even they, we bet, would have understood the speaker's point better if he'd sketched in some of the larger conversation his own claims were a part of and reminded the audience about what "they say."

This story also illustrates an important lesson about the *order* in which things are said: to keep an audience engaged, a writer needs to explain what he or she is responding to—either before offering that response or, at least, very early in the discussion. Delaying this explanation for more than one or two paragraphs in a very short essay or blog entry, three or four pages in a longer work, or more than ten or so pages in a book reverses the natural order in which readers process material—and in which writers think and develop ideas. After all, it seems very unlikely that our conference speaker first developed his defense of Dr. X and only later came across Dr. X's critics. As someone knowledgeable in his field, the speaker surely encountered the criticisms first and only then was compelled to respond and, as he saw it, set the record straight.

See how an essay about community college opens by quoting its critics, p. 255.

Therefore, when it comes to constructing an argument (whether orally or in writing), we offer you the following advice: remember that you are entering a conversation and therefore need to start with "what others are saying," as the title of this chapter recommends, and then introduce your own ideas as a response. Specifically, we suggest that you summarize what "they say" as soon as you can in your text, and remind readers of it at strategic points as your text unfolds. Though it's true that not all texts follow this practice, we think it's important for all writers to master it before they depart from it.

This is not to say that you must start with a detailed list of everyone who has written on your subject before you offer your own ideas. Had our conference speaker gone to the opposite extreme and spent most of his talk summarizing Dr. X's critics with no hint of what he himself had to say, the audience probably would have had the same frustrated "why-is-he-going-on-like-this?" reaction. What we suggest, then, is that as soon as possible you state your own position and the one it's responding to *together*, and that you think of the two as a unit. It is generally best to summarize the ideas you're responding to briefly, at the start of your text, and to delay detailed elaboration until later. The point is to give your readers a quick preview of what is motivating your argument, not to drown them in details right away.

Starting with a summary of others' views may seem to contradict the common advice that writers should lead with their own thesis or claim. Although we agree that you shouldn't keep readers in suspense too long about your central argument, we also believe that you need to present that argument as part of some larger conversation, indicating something about the arguments of others that you are supporting, opposing, amending, complicating, or qualifying. One added benefit of summarizing others' views as soon as you can: you let those others do some of the work of framing and clarifying the issue you're writing about.

Consider, for example, how George Orwell starts his famous essay "Politics and the English Language" with what others are saying.

Most people who bother with the matter at all would admit that the English language is in a bad way, but it is generally assumed that we cannot by conscious action do anything about it. Our civilization is decadent and our language—so the argument runs—must inevitably share in the general collapse. . . .

[But] the process is reversible. Modern English . . . is full of bad habits . . . which can be avoided if one is willing to take the necessary trouble.

GEORGE ORWELL, "Politics and the English Language"

Orwell is basically saying, "Most people assume that we cannot do anything about the bad state of the English language. But I say we can."

Of course, there are many other powerful ways to begin. Instead of opening with someone else's views, you could start with an illustrative quotation, a revealing fact or statistic, or—as we do in this chapter—a relevant anecdote. If you choose one of these formats, however, be sure that it in some way illustrates the view you're addressing or leads you to that view directly, with a minimum of steps.

In opening this chapter, for example, we devote the first paragraph to an anecdote about the conference speaker and then move quickly at the start of the second paragraph to the misconception about writing exemplified by the speaker. In the following opening, from an opinion piece in the *New York Times Book Review*, Christina Nehring also moves quickly from an anecdote illustrating something she dislikes to her own claim—that book lovers think too highly of themselves.

"I'm a reader!" announced the yellow button. "How about you?" I looked at its bearer, a strapping young guy stalking my town's Festival of Books. "I'll bet you're a reader," he volunteered, as though we were two geniuses well met. "No," I replied. "Absolutely not," I wanted to yell, and fling my Barnes & Noble bag at his feet. Instead, I mumbled something apologetic and melted into the crowd.

There's a new piety in the air: the self congratulation of book lovers.

CHRISTINA NEHRING, "Books Make You a Boring Person"

Nehring's anecdote is really a kind of "they say": book lovers keep telling themselves how great they are.

TEMPLATES FOR INTRODUCING WHAT "THEY SAY"

There are lots of conventional ways to introduce what others are saying. Here are some standard templates that we would have recommended to our conference speaker.

▸ **A number of sociologists have recently suggested <u>that X's work has several fundamental problems.</u>**

▸ **It has become common today to dismiss _____ .**

▸ **In their recent work, Y and Z have offered harsh critiques of _____ for _____ .**

TEMPLATES FOR INTRODUCING "STANDARD VIEWS"

The following templates can help you make what we call the "standard view" move, in which you introduce a view that has become so widely accepted that by now it is essentially the conventional way of thinking about a topic.

- Americans have always believed that <u>individual effort can triumph over circumstances</u>.

- Conventional wisdom has it that _____.

- Common sense seems to dictate that _____.

- The standard way of thinking about topic X has it that _____.

- It is often said that _____.

- My whole life I have heard it said that _____.

- You would think that _____.

- Many people assume that _____.

These templates are popular because they provide a quick and efficient way to perform one of the most common moves that writers make: challenging widely accepted beliefs, placing them on the examining table, and analyzing their strengths and weaknesses.

TEMPLATES FOR MAKING WHAT "THEY SAY" SOMETHING *YOU* SAY

Another way to introduce the views you're responding to is to present them as your own. That is, the "they say" that you respond to need not be a view held by others; it can be one that you yourself once held or one that you are ambivalent about.

- I've always believed that <u>museums are boring</u>.

- When I was a child, I used to think that _____.

▶ Although I should know better by now, I cannot help thinking that _____ .

▶ At the same time that I believe _____ , I also believe _____ .

TEMPLATES FOR INTRODUCING
SOMETHING IMPLIED OR ASSUMED

Another sophisticated move a writer can make is to summarize a point that is not directly stated in what "they say" but is implied or assumed.

▶ Although none of them have ever said so directly, my teachers have often given me the impression that <u>education will open doors.</u>

▶ One implication of X's treatment of _____ is that _____ .

▶ Although X does not say so directly, she apparently assumes that _____ .

▶ While they rarely admit as much, _____ often take for granted that _____ .

These are templates that can help you think analytically—to look beyond what others say explicitly and to consider their unstated assumptions, as well as the implications of their views.

TEMPLATES FOR INTRODUCING
AN ONGOING DEBATE

Sometimes you'll want to open by summarizing a debate that presents two or more views. This kind of opening demonstrates your awareness that there are conflicting ways to look at your subject, the clear mark of someone who knows the subject and therefore is likely to be a reliable, trustworthy guide. Furthermore, opening with a summary of a debate can help you explore the issue you are writing about before declaring your own view. In this way, you can use the writing process itself to help you discover where you stand instead of having to commit to a position before you are ready to do so.

Here is a basic template for opening with a debate.

▸ **In discussions of X, one controversial issue has been _____. On the one hand, _____ argues _____. On the other hand, _____ contends _____. Others even maintain _____. My own view is _____.**

The cognitive scientist Mark Aronoff uses this kind of template in an essay on the workings of the human brain.

> Theories of how the mind/brain works have been dominated for centuries by two opposing views. One, rationalism, sees the human mind as coming into this world more or less fully formed—preprogrammed, in modern terms. The other, empiricism, sees the mind of the newborn as largely unstructured, a blank slate.
>
> Mark Aronoff, "Washington Slept Here"

Another way to open with a debate involves starting with a proposition many people agree with in order to highlight the point(s) on which they ultimately disagree.

▸ **When it comes to the topic of _____, most of us will readily agree that _____. Where this agreement usually ends,** however, is on the question of _____ . Whereas some are convinced that _____ , others maintain that _____ .

The political writer Thomas Frank uses a variation on this move.

> That we are a nation divided is an almost universal lament of this bitter election year. However, the exact property that divides us—elemental though it is said to be—remains a matter of some controversy.
>
> THOMAS FRANK, "American Psyche"

KEEP WHAT "THEY SAY" IN VIEW

We can't urge you too strongly to keep in mind what "they say" as you move through the rest of your text. After summarizing the ideas you are responding to at the outset, it's very important to continue to keep those ideas in view. Readers won't be able to follow your unfolding response, much less any complications you may offer, unless you keep reminding them what claims you are responding to.

In other words, even when presenting your own claims, you should keep returning to the motivating "they say." The longer and more complicated your text, the greater the chance that readers will forget what ideas originally motivated it—no matter how clearly you lay them out at the beginning. At strategic moments throughout your text, we recommend that you include what we call "return sentences." Here is an example.

▸ In conclusion, then, as I suggested earlier, defenders of
_____ can't have it both ways. Their assertion that
_____ is contradicted by their claim that _____.

We ourselves use such return sentences at every opportunity in
this book to remind you of the view of writing that our book
questions—that good writing means making true or smart or
logical statements about a given subject with little or no reference to what others say about it.

By reminding readers of the ideas you're responding to,
return sentences ensure that your text maintains a sense of
mission and urgency from start to finish. In short, they help
ensure that your argument is a genuine response to others' views
rather than just a set of observations about a given subject. The
difference is huge. To be responsive to others and the conversation you're entering, you need to start with what others are
saying and continue keeping it in the reader's view.

Exercises

1. The following is a list of arguments that lack a "they say"—
   any sense of who needs to hear these claims, who might
   think otherwise. Like the speaker in the cartoon on page 4
   who declares that *The Sopranos* presents complex characters,
   these one-sided arguments fail to explain what view they
   are responding to—what view, in effect, they are trying to
   correct, add to, qualify, complicate, and so forth. Your job
   in this exercise is to provide each argument with such a
   counterview. Feel free to use any of the templates in this
   chapter that you find helpful.

a. Our experiments suggest that there are dangerous levels of chemical X in the Ohio groundwater.
b. Material forces drive history.
c. Proponents of Freudian psychology question standard notions of "rationality."
d. Male students often dominate class discussions.
e. The film is about the problems of romantic relationships.
f. I'm afraid that templates like the ones in this book will stifle my creativity.

2. Below is a template that we derived from the opening of David Zinczenko's "Don't Blame the Eater" (p. 462). Use the template to structure a passage on a topic of your own choosing. Your first step here should be to find an idea that you support that others not only disagree with but actually find laughable (or, as Zinczenko puts it, worthy of a Jay Leno monologue). You might write about one of the topics listed in the previous exercise (the environment, gender relations, the meaning of a book or movie) or any other topic that interests you.

> If ever there was an idea custom-made for a Jay Leno monologue, this was it: _____. Isn't that like _____? Whatever happened to _____?
>
> I happen to sympathize with _____, though, perhaps because _____.

TWO

"HER POINT IS"

The Art of Summarizing

—◻︎—

IF IT IS TRUE, as we claim in this book, that to argue persuasively you need to be in dialogue with others, then summarizing others' arguments is central to your arsenal of basic moves. Because writers who make strong claims need to map their claims relative to those of other people, it is important to know how to summarize effectively what those other people say. (We're using the word "summarizing" here to refer to any information from others that you present in your own words, including that which you paraphrase.)

Many writers shy away from summarizing—perhaps because they don't want to take the trouble to go back to the text in question and wrestle with what it says, or because they fear that devoting too much time to other people's ideas will take away from their own. When assigned to write a response to an article, such writers might offer their own views on the article's *topic* while hardly mentioning what the article itself argues or says. At the opposite extreme are those who do nothing *but* summarize. Lacking confidence, perhaps, in their own ideas, these writers so overload their texts with summaries of others' ideas that their own voice gets lost. And since these summaries are not animated by the writers' own interests, they often read like mere lists of things that X thinks or Y says—with no clear focus.

As a general rule, a good summary requires balancing what the original author is saying with the writer's own focus. Generally speaking, a summary must at once be true to what the original author says while also emphasizing those aspects of what the author says that interest you, the writer. Striking this delicate balance can be tricky, since it means facing two ways at once: both outward (toward the author being summarized) and inward (toward yourself). Ultimately, it means being respectful of others but simultaneously structuring how you summarize them in light of your own text's central argument.

See how Nicholas Carr summarizes the mission of Google on p. 323, ¶24.

ON THE ONE HAND,
PUT YOURSELF IN *THEIR* SHOES

To write a really good summary, you must be able to suspend your own beliefs for a time and put yourself in the shoes of someone else. This means playing what the writing theorist Peter Elbow calls the "believing game," in which you try to inhabit the world-view of those whose conversation you are joining—and whom you are perhaps even disagreeing with—and try to see their argument from their perspective. This ability to temporarily suspend one's own convictions is a hallmark of good actors, who must convincingly "become" characters whom in real life they may detest. As a writer, when you play the believing game well, readers should not be able to tell whether you agree or disagree with the ideas you are summarizing.

If, as a writer, you cannot or will not suspend your own beliefs in this way, you are likely to produce summaries that are so obviously biased that they undermine your credibility with readers. Consider the following summary.

> David Zinczenko's article, "Don't Blame the Eater," is nothing more than an angry rant in which he accuses the fast-food companies of an evil conspiracy to make people fat. I disagree because these companies have to make money. . . .

If you review what Zinczenko actually says (pp. 462–64), you should immediately see that this summary amounts to an unfair distortion. While Zinczenko does argue that the practices of the fast-food industry have the *effect* of making people fat, his tone is never "angry," and he never goes so far as to suggest that the fast-food industry conspires to make people fat with deliberately evil intent.

Another tell-tale sign of this writer's failure to give Zinczenko a fair hearing is the hasty way he abandons the summary after only one sentence and rushes on to his own response. So eager is this writer to disagree that he not only caricatures what Zinczenko says but also gives the article a hasty, superficial reading. Granted, there are many writing situations in which, because of matters of proportion, a one- or two-sentence summary is precisely what you want. Indeed, as writing professor Karen Lunsford (whose own research focuses on argument theory) points out, it is standard in the natural and social sciences to summarize the work of others quickly, in one pithy sentence or phrase, as in the following example.

> Several studies (Crackle, 2012; Pop, 2007; Snap, 2006) suggest that these policies are harmless; moreover, other studies (Dick, 2011; Harry, 2007; Tom, 2005) argue that they even have benefits.

But if your assignment is to respond in writing to a single author like Zinczenko, you will need to tell your readers enough about his or her argument so they can assess its merits on their own, independent of you.

When a writer fails to provide enough summary or to engage in a rigorous or serious enough summary, he or she often falls prey to what we call "the closest cliché syndrome," in which what gets summarized is not the view the author in question has actually expressed but a familiar cliché that the writer *mistakes* for the author's view (sometimes because the writer believes it and mistakenly assumes the author must too). So, for example, Martin Luther King Jr.'s passionate defense of civil disobedience in "Letter from Birmingham Jail" might be summarized not as the defense of political protest that it actually is but as a plea for everyone to "just get along." Similarly, Zinczenko's critique of the fast-food industry might be summarized as a call for overweight people to take responsibility for their weight.

Whenever you enter into a conversation with others in your writing, then, it is extremely important that you go back to what those others have said, that you study it very closely, and that you not confuse it with something you already believe. A writer who fails to do this ends up essentially conversing with imaginary others who are really only the products of his or her own biases and preconceptions.

ON THE OTHER HAND, KNOW WHERE *YOU* ARE GOING

Even as writing an effective summary requires you to temporarily adopt the worldview of another, it does not mean ignoring your own view altogether. Paradoxically, at the same time that summarizing another text requires you to represent fairly what it says, it also requires that your own response exert a quiet influence. A good summary, in other words, has a focus or spin that allows the summary to fit with your own agenda while still being true to the text you are summarizing.

Thus if you are writing in response to the essay by Zinczenko, you should be able to see that an essay on the fast-food industry in general will call for a very different summary than will an essay on parenting, corporate regulation, or warning labels. If you want your essay to encompass all three topics, you'll need to subordinate these three issues to one of Zinczenko's general claims and then make sure this general claim directly sets up your own argument.

For example, suppose you want to argue that it is parents, not fast-food companies, who are to blame for children's obesity. To set up this argument, you will probably want to compose a summary that highlights what Zinczenko says about the fast-food industry *and parents*. Consider this sample.

In his article "Don't Blame the Eater," David Zinczenko blames the fast-food industry for fueling today's so-called obesity epidemic, not only by failing to provide adequate warning labels on its high-calorie foods but also by filling the nutritional void in children's lives left by their overtaxed working parents. With many parents working long hours and unable to supervise what their children eat, Zinczenko claims, children today are easily victimized by the low-cost, calorie-laden foods that the fast-food chains are all too eager to supply. When he was a young boy, for instance, and his single mother was away at work, he ate at Taco Bell, McDonald's, and other chains on a regular basis, and ended up overweight. Zinczenko's hope is that with the new spate of lawsuits against the food industry, other children with working parents will have healthier choices available to them, and that they will not, like him, become obese.

In my view, however, it is the parents, and not the food chains, who are responsible for their children's obesity. While it is true that many of today's parents work long hours, there are still several things that parents can do to guarantee that their children eat healthy foods. . . .

The summary in the first paragraph succeeds because it points in two directions at once—both toward Zinczenko's own text *and* toward the second paragraph, where the writer begins to establish her own argument. The opening sentence gives a sense of Zinczenko's general argument (that the fast-food chains are to blame for obesity), including his two main supporting claims (about warning labels and parents), but it ends with an emphasis on the writer's main concern: parental responsibility. In this way, the summary does justice to Zinczenko's arguments while also setting up the ensuing critique.

This advice—to summarize authors in light of your own arguments—may seem painfully obvious. But writers often summarize a given author on one issue even though their text actually focuses on another. To avoid this problem, you need to make sure that your "they say" and "I say" are well matched. In fact, aligning what they say with what you say is a good thing to work on when revising what you've written.

Often writers who summarize without regard to their own interests fall prey to what might be called "list summaries," summaries that simply inventory the original author's various points but fail to focus those points around any larger overall claim. If you've ever heard a talk in which the points were connected only by words like "and then," "also," and "in addition,"

THE EFFECT OF A TYPICAL LIST SUMMARY

you know how such lists can put listeners to sleep—as shown in the figure above. A typical list summary sounds like this.

> The author says many different things about his subject. *First* he says. . . . *Then* he makes the point that. . . . *In addition* he says. . . . *And then* he writes. . . . *Also* he shows that. . . . *And then* he says. . . .

It may be boring list summaries like this that give summaries in general a bad name and even prompt some instructors to discourage their students from summarizing at all.

In conclusion, writing a good summary means not just representing an author's view accurately, but doing so in a way that fits your own composition's larger agenda. On the one hand, it means playing Peter Elbow's believing game and doing justice to the source; if the summary ignores or misrepresents the source, its bias and unfairness will show. On the other hand, even as it does justice to the source, a summary has to have a slant or spin that prepares the way for your own claims. Once a summary enters your text, you should think of it as joint property—reflecting both the source you are summarizing and your own views.

SUMMARIZING SATIRICALLY

Thus far in this chapter we have argued that, as a general rule, good summaries require a balance between what someone else has said and your own interests as a writer. Now, however, we want to address one exception to this rule: the satiric summary, in which a writer deliberately gives his or her own spin to someone else's argument in order to reveal a glaring shortcoming in it. Despite our previous comments that well-crafted summaries generally strike a balance between heeding what someone else has said and your own independent interests, the satiric mode can at times be a very effective form of critique because it lets the summarized argument condemn itself without overt editorializing by you, the writer. If you've ever watched *The Daily Show*, you'll recall that it often merely summarizes silly things political leaders have said or done, letting their words or actions undermine themselves.

Consider another example. In September 2001, then-President George W. Bush in a speech to Congress urged the nation's "continued participation and confidence in the American economy" as a means of recovering from the terrorist attacks of 9/11. The journalist Allan Sloan criticized this proposal simply by summarizing it, observing that the president had equated "patriotism with shopping. Maxing out your credit cards at the mall wasn't self indulgence, it was a way to get back at Osama bin Laden." Sloan's summary leaves no doubt where he stands—he considers Bush's proposal ridiculous, or at least too simple.

USE SIGNAL VERBS THAT FIT THE ACTION

In introducing summaries, try to avoid bland formulas like "she says," or "they believe." Though language like this is sometimes serviceable enough, it often fails to reflect accurately what's been said. In some cases, "he says" may even drain the passion out of the ideas you're summarizing.

We suspect that the habit of ignoring the action in what we summarize stems from the mistaken belief we mentioned earlier that writing is about playing it safe and not making waves, a matter of piling up truths and bits of knowledge rather than a dynamic process of doing things to and with other people. People who wouldn't hesitate to *say* "X totally misrepresented," "attacked," or "loved" something when chatting with friends will in their writing often opt for far tamer and even less accurate phrases like "X said."

But the authors you summarize at the college level seldom simply "say" or "discuss" things; they "urge," "emphasize," and "complain about" them. David Zinczenko, for example, doesn't just *say* that fast-food companies contribute to obesity; he *complains* or *protests* that they do; he *challenges*, *chastises*, and *indicts* those companies. The Declaration of Independence doesn't just *talk about* the treatment of the colonies by the British; it *protests against* it. To do justice to the authors you cite, we recommend that when summarizing—or when introducing a quotation—you use vivid and precise signal verbs as often as possible. Though "he says" or "she believes" will sometimes be the most appropriate language for the occasion, your text will often be more accurate and lively if you tailor your verbs to suit the precise actions you're describing.

TEMPLATES FOR INTRODUCING SUMMARIES AND QUOTATIONS

▸ She advocates <u>a radical revision of the juvenile justice system</u>.

▸ They celebrate the fact that _____.

▸ _____, he admits.

VERBS FOR INTRODUCING SUMMARIES AND QUOTATIONS

VERBS FOR MAKING A CLAIM

argue	insist
assert	observe
believe	remind us
claim	report
emphasize	suggest

VERBS FOR EXPRESSING AGREEMENT

acknowledge	endorse
admire	extol
agree	praise

VERBS FOR EXPRESSING AGREEMENT

celebrate the fact that	reaffirm
corroborate	support
do not deny	verify

VERBS FOR QUESTIONING OR DISAGREEING

complain	qualify
complicate	question
contend	refute
contradict	reject
deny	renounce
deplore the tendency to	repudiate

VERBS FOR MAKING RECOMMENDATIONS

advocate	implore
call for	plead
demand	recommend
encourage	urge
exhort	warn

Exercises

1. To get a feel for Peter Elbow's "believing game," write a summary of some belief that you strongly disagree with. Then write a summary of the position that you actually hold on this topic. Give both summaries to a classmate or two, and see if they can tell which position you endorse. If you've succeeded, they won't be able to tell.

2. Write two different summaries of David Zinczenko's "Don't Blame the Eater" (pp. 462–64). Write the first one for an essay arguing that, contrary to what Zinczenko claims, there *are* inexpensive and convenient alternatives to fast-food restaurants. Write the second for an essay that questions whether being overweight is a genuine medical problem rather than a problem of cultural stereotypes. Compare your two summaries: though they are about the same article, they should look very different.

THREE

"AS HE HIMSELF PUTS IT"

The Art of Quoting

———⬚———

A KEY PREMISE OF THIS BOOK is that to launch an effective argument you need to write the arguments of others into your text. One of the best ways to do so is by not only summarizing what "they say," as suggested in Chapter 2, but by quoting their exact words. Quoting someone else's words gives a tremendous amount of credibility to your summary and helps ensure that it is fair and accurate. In a sense, then, quotations function as a kind of proof of evidence, saying to readers: "Look, I'm not just making this up. She makes this claim and here it is in her exact words."

Yet many writers make a host of mistakes when it comes to quoting, not the least of which is the failure to quote enough in the first place, if at all. Some writers quote too little— perhaps because they don't want to bother going back to the original text and looking up the author's exact words, or because they think they can reconstruct the author's ideas from memory. At the opposite extreme are writers who so overquote that they end up with texts that are short on commentary of their own—maybe because they lack confidence in their ability to comment on the quotations, or because they don't fully understand what they've quoted and therefore have trouble explaining what the quotations mean.

But the main problem with quoting arises when writers assume that quotations speak for themselves. Because the meaning of a quotation is obvious to *them*, many writers assume that this meaning will also be obvious to their readers, when often it is not. Writers who make this mistake think that their job is done when they've chosen a quotation and inserted it into their text. They draft an essay, slap in a few quotations, and whammo, they're done.

Such writers fail to see that quoting means more than simply enclosing what "they say" in quotation marks. In a way, quotations are orphans: words that have been taken from their original contexts and that need to be integrated into their new textual surroundings. This chapter offers two key ways to produce this sort of integration: (1) by choosing quotations wisely, with an eye to how well they support a particular part of your text, and (2) by surrounding every major quotation with a frame explaining whose words they are, what the quotation means, and how the quotation relates to your own text. The point we want to emphasize is that quoting what "they say" must always be connected with what *you* say.

See how one author connects what "they say" to what he wants to say, pp. 401, 403, ¶7–8.

QUOTE RELEVANT PASSAGES

Before you can select appropriate quotations, you need to have a sense of what you want to do with them—that is, how they will support your text at the particular point where you insert them. Be careful not to select quotations just for the sake of demonstrating that you've read the author's work; you need to make sure they support your own argument.

However, finding relevant quotations is not always easy. In fact, sometimes quotations that were initially relevant to your argument, or to a key point in it, become less so as your text changes during the process of writing and revising. Given the evolving and messy nature of writing, you may sometimes think that you've found the perfect quotation to support your argument, only to discover later on, as your text develops, that your focus has changed and the quotation no longer works. It can be somewhat misleading, then, to speak of finding your thesis and finding relevant quotations as two separate steps, one coming after the other. When you're deeply engaged in the writing and revising process, there is usually a great deal of back-and-forth between your argument and any quotations you select.

FRAME EVERY QUOTATION

Finding relevant quotations is only part of your job; you also need to present them in a way that makes their relevance and meaning clear to your readers. Since quotations do not speak for themselves, you need to build a frame around them in which you do that speaking for them.

Quotations that are inserted into a text without such a frame are sometimes called "dangling" quotations for the way they're left dangling without any explanation. One teacher we've worked with, Steve Benton, calls these "hit-and-run" quotations, likening them to car accidents in which the driver speeds away and avoids taking responsibility for the dent in your fender or the smashed taillights, as in the figure that follows.

DON'T BE A HIT-AND-RUN QUOTER.

Here's a typical hit-and-run quotation by a writer responding to an essay by the feminist philosopher Susan Bordo, who laments that media pressures on young women to diet are spreading to previously isolated regions of the world like the Fiji islands.

> Susan Bordo writes about women and dieting. "Fiji is just one example. Until television was introduced in 1995, the islands had no reported cases of eating disorders. In 1998, three years after programs from the United States and Britain began broadcasting there, 62 percent of the girls surveyed reported dieting."
> I think Bordo is right. Another point Bordo makes is that. . . .

Since this writer fails to introduce the quotation adequately or explain why he finds it worth quoting, readers will have a hard time reconstructing what Bordo argued. Besides neglecting to say who Bordo is or even See how Anne-Marie Slaughter introduces a long quote on p. 682, ¶13. that the quoted words are hers, the writer does not explain how her words connect with anything he is saying or even what she says that he thinks is so "right." He simply abandons the quotation in his haste to zoom on to another point.

To adequately frame a quotation, you need to insert it into what we like to call a "quotation sandwich," with the statement introducing it serving as the top slice of bread and the explanation following it serving as the bottom slice. The introductory or lead-in claims should explain who is speaking and set up what the quotation says; the follow-up statements should explain why you consider the quotation to be important and what you take it to say.

TEMPLATES FOR INTRODUCING QUOTATIONS

▸ X states, "<u>not all steroids should be banned from sports.</u>"

▸ As the prominent philosopher X puts it, "_____."

▸ According to X, "_____."

▸ X himself writes, "_____."

▸ In her book, _____, X maintains that "_____."

▸ Writing in the journal *Commentary*, X complains that "_____."

▸ In X's view, "_____."

▸ X agrees when she writes, "_____."

▸ X disagrees when he writes, "_____."

▸ X complicates matters further when she writes, "_____."

TEMPLATES FOR EXPLAINING QUOTATIONS

The one piece of advice about quoting that our students say they find most helpful is to get in the habit of following every major quotation by explaining what it means, using a template like one of the ones below.

▸ **Basically, X is warning <u>that the proposed solution will only make the problem worse</u>.**

▸ **In other words, X believes _____ .**

▸ **In making this comment, X urges us to _____ .**

▸ **X is corroborating the age-old adage that _____ .**

▸ **X's point is that _____ .**

▸ **The essence of X's argument is that _____ .**

When offering such explanations, it is important to use language that accurately reflects the spirit of the quoted passage. It is quite serviceable to write "Bordo states" or "asserts" in introducing the quotation about Fiji. But given the fact that Bordo is clearly alarmed by the extension of the media's reach to Fiji, it is far more accurate to use language that reflects her alarm: "Bordo is alarmed that" or "is disturbed by" or "complains."

See pp. 39–40 for a list of action verbs for summarizing what others say.

Consider, for example, how the earlier passage on Bordo might be revised using some of these moves.

The feminist philosopher Susan Bordo deplores Western media's obsession with female thinness and dieting. Her basic complaint is that increasing numbers of women across the globe are being led to see themselves as fat and in need of a diet. Citing the islands of Fiji as a case in point, Bordo notes that "until television was introduced in 1995, the islands had no reported cases of eating disorders. In 1998, three years after programs from the United States and Britain began broadcasting there, 62 percent of the girls surveyed reported dieting" (149–50). Bordo's point is that the Western cult of dieting is spreading even to remote places across the globe. Ultimately, Bordo complains, the culture of dieting will find you, regardless of where you live.

Bordo's observations ring true to me because, now that I think about it, many women I know, regardless of where they are from, worry about their weight. . . .

This framing of the quotation not only better integrates Bordo's words into the writer's text, but also serves to demonstrate the writer's interpretation of what Bordo is saying. While "the feminist philosopher" and "Bordo notes" provide information that readers need to know, the sentences that follow the quotation build a bridge between Bordo's words and those of the writer. The reference to 62 percent of Fijian girls dieting is no longer an inert statistic (as it was in the flawed passage presented earlier) but a quantitative example of how "the Western cult of dieting is spreading . . . across the globe." Just as important, these sentences explain what Bordo is saying in the writer's own words—and thereby make clear that the quotation is being used purposefully to set up the writer's own argument and has not been stuck in just for padding the essay or the works-cited list.

BLEND THE AUTHOR'S WORDS
WITH YOUR OWN

The above framing material also works well because it accurately represents Bordo's words while giving those words the writer's own spin. Notice how the passage refers several times to the key concept of dieting, and how it echoes Bordo's references to "television" and to U.S. and British "broadcasting" by referring to "culture," which is further specified as "Western." Instead of simply repeating Bordo word for word, the follow-up sentences echo just enough of her language while still moving the discussion in the writer's own direction. In effect, the framing creates a kind of hybrid mix of Bordo's words and those of the writer.

CAN YOU OVERANALYZE A QUOTATION?

But is it possible to overexplain a quotation? And how do you know when you've explained a quotation thoroughly enough? After all, not all quotations require the same amount of explanatory framing, and there are no hard-and-fast rules for knowing how much explanation any quotation needs. As a general rule, the most explanatory framing is needed for quotations that may be hard for readers to process: quotations that are long and complex, that are filled with details or jargon, or that contain hidden complexities.

And yet, though the particular situation usually dictates when and how much to explain a quotation, we will still offer one piece of advice: when in doubt, go for it. It is better to risk being overly explicit about what you take a quotation to mean than to leave the quotation dangling and your readers in doubt. Indeed, we encourage you to provide such explanatory framing even when writing to an audience that you know to be familiar with the author being quoted and able to interpret your quotations on their own. Even in such cases, readers need to see how *you* interpret the quotation, since words—especially those of controversial figures—can be interpreted in various ways and used to support different, sometimes opposing, agendas. Your readers need to see what you make of the material you've quoted, if only to be sure that your reading of the material and theirs is on the same page.

HOW *NOT* TO INTRODUCE QUOTATIONS

We want to conclude this chapter by surveying some ways *not* to introduce quotations. Although some writers do so, you should not introduce quotations by saying something like "Orwell asserts an idea that" or "A quote by Shakespeare says." Introductory phrases like these are both redundant and misleading. In the first example, you could write either "Orwell asserts that" or "Orwell's assertion is that," rather than redundantly combining the two. The second example misleads readers, since it is the writer who is doing the quoting, not Shakespeare (as "a quote by Shakespeare" implies).

The templates in this book will help you avoid such mistakes. Once you have mastered templates like "as X puts it," or "in X's own words," you probably won't even have to think about them—and will be free to focus on the challenging ideas that templates help you frame.

Exercises

1. Find a published piece of writing that quotes something that "they say." How has the writer integrated the quotation into his or her own text? How has he or she introduced the quotation, and what, if anything, has the writer said to explain it and tie it to his or her own text? Based on what you've read in this chapter, are there any changes you would suggest?

2. Look at something you have written for one of your classes. Have you quoted any sources? If so, how have you integrated the quotation into your own text? How have you introduced it? Explained what it means? Indicated how it relates to *your* text? If you haven't done all these things, revise your text to do so, perhaps using the Templates for Introducing Quotations (p. 46) and Explaining Quotations (pp. 46–47). If you've not written anything with quotations, try revising some academic text you've written to do so.

2

—▣—

"I SAY"

"I SAY"

FOUR

"YES / NO / OKAY, BUT"

Three Ways to Respond

THE FIRST THREE CHAPTERS of this book discuss the "they say" stage of writing, in which you devote your attention to the views of some other person or group. In this chapter we move to the "I say" stage, in which you offer your own argument as a response to what "they" have said.

Moving to the "I say" stage can be daunting in academia, where it often may seem that you need to be an expert in a field to have an argument at all. Many students have told us that they have trouble entering some of the high-powered conversations that take place in college or graduate school because they do not know enough about the topic at hand, or because, they say, they simply are not "smart enough." Yet often these same students, when given a chance to study in depth the contribution that some scholar has made in a given field, will turn around and say things like "I can see where she is coming from, how she makes her case by building on what other scholars have said. Perhaps had I studied the situation longer *I* could have come up with a similar argument." What these students came to realize is that good arguments are based not on knowledge that only a special class of experts has access to, but on everyday habits of mind that can be isolated, identified, and used by almost anyone. Though there's certainly no substitute for expertise and for knowing as much as possible about one's topic, the arguments that finally win the day are built, as the title of this chapter suggests, on some very basic rhetorical patterns that most of us use on a daily basis.

There are a great many ways to respond to others' ideas, but this chapter concentrates on the three most common and recognizable ways: agreeing, disagreeing, or some combination of both. Although each way of responding is open to endless variation, we focus on these three because readers come to any text needing to learn fairly quickly where the writer stands, and they do this by placing the writer on a mental map consisting of a few familiar options: the writer agrees with those he or she is responding to, disagrees with them, or presents some combination of both agreeing and disagreeing.

When writers take too long to declare their position relative to views they've summarized or quoted, readers get frustrated, wondering, "Is this guy agreeing or disagreeing? Is he *for* what this other person has said, *against* it, or what?" For this reason, this chapter's advice applies to reading as well as to writing. Especially with difficult texts, you need not only to find the position the writer is responding to—the "they say"—but also to determine whether the writer is agreeing with it, challenging it, or some mixture of the two.

ONLY *THREE* WAYS TO RESPOND?

Perhaps you'll worry that fitting your own response into one of these three categories will force you to oversimplify your argument or lessen its complexity, subtlety, or originality. This is certainly a serious concern for academics who are rightly skeptical of writing that is simplistic and reductive. We would argue, however, that the more complex and subtle your argument is, and the more it departs from the conventional ways people think, the more your readers will need to be able to place it on their mental map in order to process the complex details you present. That is, the complexity, subtlety, and originality of your response are more likely to stand out and be noticed if readers have a baseline sense of where you stand relative to any ideas you've cited. As you move through this chapter, we hope you'll agree that the forms of agreeing, disagreeing, and both agreeing and disagreeing that we discuss, far from being simplistic or one-dimensional, are able to accommodate a high degree of creative, complex thought.

It is always a good tactic to begin your response not by launching directly into a mass of details but by stating clearly whether you agree, disagree, or both, using a direct, no-nonsense formula such as: "I agree," "I disagree," or "I am of two minds. I agree that _____, but I cannot agree that _____." Once you have offered one of these straightforward statements (or one of the many variations discussed below), readers will have a strong grasp of your position and then be able to appreciate the complications you go on to offer as your response unfolds.

See p. 21 for suggestions on previewing where you stand.

Still, you may object that these three basic ways of responding don't cover all the options—that they ignore interpretive or analytical responses, for example. In other words, you might think that when you interpret a literary work you don't necessarily agree or disagree with anything but simply explain the work's meaning, style, or structure. Many essays about literature and the arts, it might be said, take this form—they interpret a work's meaning, thus rendering matters of agreeing or disagreeing irrelevant.

We would argue, however, that the most interesting interpretations in fact tend to be those that agree, disagree, or
both—that instead of being offered solo, the best interpretations take strong stands relative to other interpretations. In fact,
there would be no reason to offer an interpretation of a work
of literature or art unless you were responding to the interpretations or possible interpretations of others. Even when you
point out features or qualities of an artistic work that others
have not noticed, you are implicitly disagreeing with what
those interpreters have said by pointing out that they missed
or overlooked something that, in your view, is important. In
any effective interpretation, then, you need not only to state
what you yourself take the work of art to mean but to do so
relative to the interpretations of other readers—be they professional scholars, teachers, classmates, or even hypothetical
readers (as in, "Although some readers might think that this
poem is about _____, it is in fact about _____").

DISAGREE—AND EXPLAIN WHY

Disagreeing may seem like one of the simpler moves a writer can
make, and it is often the first thing people associate with critical
thinking. Disagreeing can also be the easiest way to generate an
essay: find something you can disagree with in what has been
said or might be said about your topic, summarize it, and argue
with it. But disagreement in fact poses hidden challenges. You
need to do more than simply assert that you disagree with a particular view; you also have to offer persuasive reasons *why* you
disagree. After all, disagreeing means more than adding "not" to
what someone else has said, more than just saying, "Although
they say women's rights are improving, I say women's rights

are *not* improving." Such a response merely contradicts the view it responds to and fails to add anything interesting or new. To turn it into an argument, you need to give reasons to support what you say: because another's argument fails to take relevant factors into account; because it is based on faulty or incomplete evidence; because it rests on questionable assumptions; or because it uses flawed logic, is contradictory, or overlooks what you take to be the real issue. To move the conversation forward (and, indeed, to justify your very act of writing), you need to demonstrate that you have something to contribute. See p. 582, ¶2 to see two authors disagree and explain why.

You can even disagree by making what we call the "duh" move, in which you disagree not with the position itself but with the assumption that it is a new or stunning revelation. Here is an example of such a move, used to open an essay on the state of American schools.

> According to a recent report by some researchers at Stanford University, high school students with college aspirations "often lack crucial information on applying to college and on succeeding academically once they get there."
>
> Well, duh. . . . It shouldn't take a Stanford research team to tell us that when it comes to "succeeding academically," many students don't have a clue.
>
> GERALD GRAFF, "Trickle-Down Obfuscation"

Like all of the other moves discussed in this book, the "duh" move can be tailored to meet the needs of almost any writing situation. If you find the expression "duh" too brash to use with your intended audience, you can always dispense with the term itself and write something like "It is true that _____; but we already knew that."

TEMPLATES FOR DISAGREEING, WITH REASONS

- ▶ X is mistaken because she overlooks <u>recent fossil discoveries in the South</u>.

- ▶ X's claim that _____ rests upon the questionable assumption that _____.

- ▶ I disagree with X's view that _____ because, as recent research has shown, _____.

- ▶ X contradicts herself/can't have it both ways. On the one hand, she argues _____. On the other hand, she also says _____.

- ▶ By focusing on _____, X overlooks the deeper problem of _____.

You can also disagree by making what we call the "twist it" move, in which you agree with the evidence that someone else has presented but show through a twist of logic that this evidence actually supports your own, contrary position. For example:

> X argues for stricter gun control legislation, saying that the crime rate is on the rise and that we need to restrict the circulation of guns. I agree that the crime rate is on the rise, but that's precisely why I oppose stricter gun control legislation. We need to own guns to protect ourselves against criminals.

In this example of the "twist it" move, the writer agrees with X's claim that the crime rate is on the rise but then argues that this increasing crime rate is in fact a valid reason for *opposing* gun control legislation.

At times you might be reluctant to express disagreement, for any number of reasons—not wanting to be unpleasant, to hurt someone's feelings, or to make yourself vulnerable to being disagreed with in return. One of these reasons may in fact explain why the conference speaker we described at the start of Chapter 1 avoided mentioning the disagreement he had with other scholars until he was provoked to do so in the discussion that followed his talk.

As much as we understand such fears of conflict and have experienced them ourselves, we nevertheless believe it is better to state our disagreements in frank yet considerate ways than to deny them. After all, suppressing disagreements doesn't make them go away; it only pushes them underground, where they can fester in private unchecked. Nevertheless, disagreements do not need to take the form of personal put-downs. Furthermore, there is usually no reason to take issue with *every* aspect of someone else's views. You can single out for criticism only those aspects of what someone else has said that are troubling, and then agree with the rest—although such an approach, as we will see later in this chapter, leads to the somewhat more complicated terrain of both agreeing and disagreeing at the same time.

AGREE—BUT WITH A DIFFERENCE

Like disagreeing, agreeing is less simple than it may appear. Just as you need to avoid simply contradicting views you disagree with, you also need to do more than simply echo views you agree with. Even as you're agreeing, it's important to bring something new and fresh to the table, adding something that makes you a valuable participant in the conversation.

There are many moves that enable you to contribute something of your own to a conversation even as you agree with what someone else has said. You may point out some unnoticed evidence or line of reasoning that supports X's claims that X herself hadn't mentioned. You may cite some corroborating personal experience, or a situation not mentioned by X that her views help readers understand. If X's views are particularly challenging or esoteric, what you bring to the table could be an accessible translation—an explanation for readers not already in the know. In other words, your text can usefully contribute to the conversation simply by pointing out unnoticed implications or explaining something that needs to be better understood.

Whatever mode of agreement you choose, the important thing is to open up some difference or contrast between your position and the one you're agreeing with rather than simply parroting what it says.

TEMPLATES FOR AGREEING

▸ I agree that <u>diversity in the student body is educationally valuable</u> because my experience <u>at Central University</u> confirms it.

▸ X is surely right about _____ because, as she may not be aware, recent studies have shown that _____.

▸ X's theory of _____ is extremely useful because it sheds light on the difficult problem of _____.

▸ Those unfamiliar with this school of thought may be interested to know that it basically boils down to _____.

Some writers avoid the practice of agreeing almost as much as others avoid disagreeing. In a culture like America's that prizes originality, independence, and competitive individualism, writers sometimes don't like to admit that anyone else has made the same point, seemingly beating them to the punch. In our view, however, as long as you can support a view taken by someone else without merely restating what he or she has said, there is no reason to worry about being "unoriginal." Indeed, there is good reason to rejoice when you agree with others since those others can lend credibility to your argument. While you don't want to present yourself as a mere copycat of someone else's views, you also need to avoid sounding like a lone voice in the wilderness.

But do be aware that whenever you agree with one person's view, you are likely disagreeing with someone else's. It is hard to align yourself with one position without at least implicitly positioning yourself against others. The psychologist Carol Gilligan does just that in an essay in which she agrees with scientists who argue that the human brain is "hard-wired" for cooperation, but in so doing aligns herself against anyone who believes that the brain is wired for selfishness and competition.

These findings join a growing convergence of evidence across the human sciences leading to a revolutionary shift in consciousness. . . . If cooperation, typically associated with altruism and self-sacrifice, sets off the same signals of delight as pleasures commonly associated with hedonism and self-indulgence; if the opposition between selfish and selfless, self vs. relationship biologically makes no sense, then a new paradigm is necessary to reframe the very terms of the conversation.

Carol Gilligan, "Sisterhood Is Pleasurable:
A Quiet Revolution in Psychology"

In agreeing with some scientists that "the opposition between selfish and selfless . . . makes no sense," Gilligan implicitly disagrees with anyone who thinks the opposition *does* make sense. Basically, what Gilligan says could be boiled down to a template.

▶ I agree that _____, a point that needs emphasizing since so many people still believe _____.

▶ If group X is right that _____, as I think they are, then we need to reassess the popular assumption that _____.

What such templates allow you to do, then, is to agree with one view while challenging another—a move that leads into the domain of agreeing and disagreeing simultaneously.

AGREE AND DISAGREE SIMULTANEOUSLY

This last option is often our favorite way of responding. One thing we particularly like about agreeing and disagreeing simultaneously is that it helps us get beyond the kind of "is too" / "is not" exchanges that often characterize the disputes of young children and the more polarized shouting matches of talk radio and TV.

TEMPLATES FOR AGREEING
AND DISAGREEING SIMULTANEOUSLY

"Yes and no." "Yes, but . . . " "Although I agree up to a point, I still insist . . . " These are just some of the ways you can make your argument complicated and nuanced while maintaining a clear, reader-friendly framework. The parallel structure—"yes and no"; "on the one hand I agree, on the other I disagree"—enables readers to place your argument on that map of positions we spoke of earlier in this chapter while still keeping your argument sufficiently complex.

Clive Thompson says "yes, but" to an argument that technology rewires our brains for the worse, p. 355, ¶34.

Another aspect we like about this option is that it can be tipped subtly toward agreement or disagreement, depending on where you lay your stress. If you want to stress the disagreement end of the spectrum, you would use a template like the one below.

> ▶ **Although I agree with X up to a point, I cannot accept his overriding assumption that <u>religion is no longer a major force today.</u>**

Conversely, if you want to stress your agreement more than your disagreement, you would use a template like this one.

> ▶ **Although I disagree with much that X says, I fully endorse his final conclusion that _____ .**

The first template above might be called a "yes, but . . ." move, the second a "no, but . . . " move. Other versions include the following.

> ▶ **Though I concede that _____ , I still insist that _____ .**

> ▶ **X is right that _____ , but she seems on more dubious ground when she claims that _____ .**

> ▶ **While X is probably wrong when she claims that _____ , she is right that _____ .**

> ▶ **Whereas X provides ample evidence that _____ , Y and Z's research on _____ and _____ convinces me that _____ instead.**

Another classic way to agree and disagree at the same time is to make what we call an "I'm of two minds" or a "mixed feelings" move.

▶ **I'm of two minds about X's claim that _____. On the one hand, I agree that _____. On the other hand, I'm not sure if _____.**

▶ **My feelings on the issue are mixed. I do support X's position that _____, but I find Y's argument about _____ and Z's research on _____ to be equally persuasive.**

This move can be especially useful if you are responding to new or particularly challenging work and are as yet unsure where you stand. It also lends itself well to the kind of speculative investigation in which you weigh a position's pros and cons rather than come out decisively either for or against. But again, as we suggest earlier, whether you are agreeing, disagreeing, or both agreeing and disagreeing, you need to be as clear as possible, and making a frank statement that you are ambivalent is one way to be clear.

IS BEING UNDECIDED OKAY?

Nevertheless, writers often have as many concerns about expressing ambivalence as they do about expressing disagreement or agreement. Some worry that by expressing ambivalence they will come across as evasive, wishy-washy, or unsure of themselves. Others worry that their ambivalence will end up confusing readers who require decisive clear-cut conclusions.

The truth is that in some cases these worries are legitimate. At times ambivalence can frustrate readers, leaving them with the feeling that you failed in your obligation to offer the guidance they expect from writers. At other times, however, acknowledging that a clear-cut resolution of an issue is impossible can demonstrate your sophistication as a writer. In an academic culture that values complex thought, forthrightly declaring that you have mixed feelings can be impressive, especially after having ruled out the one-dimensional positions on your issue taken by others in the conversation. Ultimately, then, how ambivalent you end up being comes down to a judgment call based on different readers' responses to your drafts, on your knowledge of your audience, and on the challenges of your particular argument and situation.

Exercises

1. Read one of the essays in the back of this book or on **theysayiblog.com**, identifying those places where the author agrees with others, disagrees, or both.

2. Write an essay responding in some way to the essay that you worked with in the preceding exercise. You'll want to summarize and/or quote some of the author's ideas and make clear whether you're agreeing, disagreeing, or both agreeing and disagreeing with what he or she says. Remember that there are templates in this book that can help you get started; see Chapters 1–3 for templates that will help you represent other people's ideas, and Chapter 4 for templates that will get you started with your response.

FIVE

"AND YET"

Distinguishing What You Say from What They Say

—◻—

IF GOOD ACADEMIC WRITING involves putting yourself into dialogue with others, it is extremely important that readers be able to tell at every point when you are expressing your own view and when you are stating someone else's. This chapter takes up the problem of moving from what *they* say to what *you* say without confusing readers about who is saying what.

DETERMINE WHO IS SAYING WHAT IN THE TEXTS YOU READ

Before examining how to signal who is saying what in your own writing, let's look at how to recognize such signals when they appear in the texts you read—an especially important skill when it comes to the challenging works assigned in school. Frequently, when students have trouble understanding difficult texts, it is not just because the texts contain unfamiliar ideas or words, but because the texts rely on subtle clues to let readers know when a particular view should be attributed to the writer or to someone else. Especially with texts that present a true dialogue of perspectives, readers need to be alert to the often subtle markers that indicate whose voice the writer is speaking in.

Consider how the social critic and educator Gregory Mantsios uses these "voice markers," as they might be called, to distinguish the different perspectives in his essay on America's class inequalities.

> "We are all middle-class," or so it would seem. Our national consciousness, as shaped in large part by the media and our political leadership, provides us with a picture of ourselves as a nation of prosperity and opportunity with an ever expanding middle-class life-style. As a result, our class differences are muted and our collective character is homogenized.
>
> Yet class divisions are real and arguably the most significant factor in determining both our very being in the world and the nature of the society we live in.
>
> GREGORY MANTSIOS, "Rewards and Opportunities:
> The Politics and Economics of Class in the U.S."

Although Mantsios makes it look easy, he is actually making several sophisticated rhetorical moves here that help him distinguish the common view he opposes from his own position.

In the opening sentence, for instance, the phrase "or so it would seem" shows that Mantsios does not necessarily agree with the view he is describing, since writers normally don't present views they themselves hold as ones that only "seem" to be true. Mantsios also places this opening view in quotation marks to signal that it is not his own. He then further distances himself from the belief being summarized in the opening paragraph by attributing it to "our national consciousness, as shaped in large part by the media and our political leadership," and then further attributing to this "consciousness" a negative, undesirable "result": one in which "our class differences" get "muted" and "our collective character" gets "homogenized," stripped of its diversity and distinctness. Hence, even before Mantsios has declared his own position in the second paragraph, readers can get a pretty solid sense of where he probably stands.

Furthermore, the second paragraph opens with the word "yet," indicating that Mantsios is now shifting to his own view (as opposed to the common view he has thus far been describing). Even the parallelism he sets up between the first and second paragraphs—between the first paragraph's claim that class differences do not exist and the second paragraph's claim that they do—helps throw into sharp relief the differences between the two voices. Finally, Mantsios's use of a direct, authoritative, declarative tone in the second paragraph also suggests a switch in voice. Although he does not use the words "I say" or "I argue," he clearly identifies the view he holds by presenting it not as one that merely *seems* to be true or that *others tell us* is true, but as a view that *is* true or, as Mantsios puts it, "real."

Paying attention to these voice markers is an important aspect of reading comprehension. Readers who fail to notice these markers often take an author's summaries of what someone else believes to be an expression of what the author himself or herself believes. Thus when we teach Mantsios's essay, some students invariably come away thinking that the statement "we are all middle-class" is Mantsios's own position rather than the perspective he is opposing, failing to see that in writing these words Mantsios acts as a kind of ventriloquist, mimicking what others say rather than directly expressing what he himself is thinking.

To see how important such voice markers are, consider what the Mantsios passage looks like if we remove them.

> We are all middle-class. . . . We are a nation of prosperity and opportunity with an ever expanding middle-class life-style. . . .
>
> Class divisions are real and arguably the most significant factor in determining both our very being in the world and the nature of the society we live in.

In contrast to the careful delineation between voices in Mantsios's original text, this unmarked version leaves it hard to tell where his voice begins and the voices of others end. With the markers removed, readers cannot tell that "We are all middle-class" represents a view the author opposes, and that "Class divisions are real" represents what the author himself believes. Indeed, without the markers, especially the "Yet," readers might well miss the fact that the second paragraph's claim that "Class divisions are real" contradicts the first paragraph's claim that "We are all middle-class."

See how Marion Nestle begins with a view and then refutes it on p. 497, ¶2.

TEMPLATES FOR SIGNALING WHO IS SAYING WHAT IN YOUR OWN WRITING

To avoid confusion in your own writing, make sure that at every point your readers can clearly tell who is saying what. To do so, you can use as voice-identifying devices many of the templates presented in previous chapters.

▶ Although **X** makes the best possible case for <u>universal, government-funded health care</u>, I <u>am not persuaded</u>.

▶ My view, however, contrary to what **X** has argued, is that _____.

▶ Adding to **X**'s argument, I would point out that _____.

▶ According to both **X** and **Y**, _____.

▶ Politicians, **X** argues, should _____.

▶ Most athletes will tell you that _____.

BUT I'VE BEEN TOLD NOT TO USE "I"

Notice that the first three templates above use the first-person "I" or "we," as do many of the templates in this book, thereby contradicting the common advice about avoiding the first person in academic writing. Although you may have been told that the "I" word encourages subjective, self-indulgent opinions rather than well-grounded arguments, we believe that texts using "I" can be just as well supported—or just as self-indulgent—as those that don't. For us, well-supported arguments are grounded in persuasive reasons and evidence, not in the use or nonuse of any particular pronouns.

Furthermore, if you consistently avoid the first person in your writing, you will probably have trouble making the key move addressed in this chapter: differentiating your views from those of others, or even offering your own views in the first place. But don't just take our word for it. See for yourself how freely the first person is used by the writers quoted in this book, and by the writers assigned in your courses.

Nevertheless, certain occasions may warrant avoiding the first person and writing, for example, that "she is correct" instead of "I think that she is correct." Since it can be monotonous to read an unvarying series of "I" statements ("I believe . . . I think . . . I argue"), it is a good idea to mix first-person assertions with ones like the following.

▸ **X is right that <u>certain common patterns can be found in the communities</u>.**

▸ **The evidence shows that _____ .**

▸ **X's assertion that _____ does not fit the facts.**

▸ **Anyone familiar with _____ should agree that _____ .**

One might even follow Mantsios's lead, as in the following template.

▸ **But _____ are real, and are arguably the most significant factor in _____ .**

On the whole, however, academic writing today, even in the sciences and social sciences, makes use of the first person fairly liberally.

See pp. 361–71 for an example of the way a student essay uses the first person.

ANOTHER TRICK FOR IDENTIFYING WHO IS SPEAKING

To alert readers about whose perspective you are describing at any given moment, you don't always have to use overt voice markers like "X argues" followed by a summary of the argument. Instead, you can alert readers about whose voice you're speaking in by *embedding* a reference to X's argument in your own sentences. Hence, instead of writing:

> Liberals believe that cultural differences need to be respected. I have a problem with this view, however.

you might write:

> I have a problem with *what liberals call cultural differences.*
>
> There is a major problem with the liberal doctrine of *so-called cultural differences.*

You can also embed references to something you yourself have previously said. So instead of writing two cumbersome sentences like:

> Earlier in this chapter we coined the term "voice markers." We would argue that such markers are extremely important for reading comprehension.

you might write:

> We would argue that "voice markers," as we identified them earlier, are extremely important for reading comprehension.

Embedded references like these allow you to economize your train of thought and refer to other perspectives without any major interruption.

TEMPLATES FOR EMBEDDING VOICE MARKERS

▸ **X overlooks what I consider an important point about <u>cultural differences</u>.**

▸ **My own view is that what X insists is a _____ is in fact a _____ .**

▸ **I wholeheartedly endorse what X calls _____ .**

▸ **These conclusions, which X discusses in _____ , add weight to the argument that _____ .**

When writers fail to use voice-marking devices like the ones discussed in this chapter, their summaries of others' views tend to become confused with their own ideas—and vice versa. When readers cannot tell if you are summarizing your own views or endorsing a certain phrase or label, they have to stop and think: "Wait. I thought the author disagreed with this claim. Has she actually been asserting this view all along?" or "Hmmm, I thought she would have objected to this kind of phrase. Is she actually endorsing it?" Getting in the habit of using voice markers will keep you from confusing your readers and help alert you to similar markers in the challenging texts you read.

Exercises

1. To see how one writer signals when she is asserting her own views and when she is summarizing those of someone else, read the following passage by the social historian Julie Charlip. As you do so, identify those spots where Charlip refers to the views of others and the signal phrases she uses to distinguish her views from theirs.

Marx and Engels wrote: "Society as a whole is more and more split-ting up into two great hostile camps, into two great classes directly facing each other—the bourgeoisie and the proletariat" (10). If only that were true, things might be more simple. But in late twentieth-century America, it seems that society is splitting more and more into a plethora of class factions—the working class, the working poor, lower-middle class, upper-middle class, lower uppers, and upper uppers. I find myself not knowing what class I'm from.

In my days as a newspaper reporter, I once asked a sociology pro-fessor what he thought about the reported shrinking of the middle class. Oh, it's not the middle class that's disappearing, he said, but the working class. His definition: if you earn thirty thousand dollars a year working in an assembly plant, come home from work, open a beer and watch the game, you are working class; if you earn twenty thousand dollars a year as a school teacher, come home from work to a glass of white wine and PBS, you are middle class.

How do we define class? Is it an issue of values, lifestyle, taste? Is it the kind of work you do, your relationship to the means of production? Is it a matter of how much money you earn? Are we allowed to choose? In this land of supposed classlessness, where we don't have the tradition of English society to keep us in our places, how do we know where we really belong? The average American will tell you he or she is "middle class." I'm sure that's what my father would tell you. But I always felt that we were in some no man's land, suspended between classes, sharing similari-ties with some and recognizing sharp, exclusionary differences from others. What class do I come from? What class am I in now? As an historian, I seek the answers to these questions in the specificity of my past.

JULIE CHARLIP, "A Real Class Act: Searching
for Identity in the Classless Society"

2. Study a piece of your own writing to see how many perspectives you account for and how well you distinguish your own voice from those you are summarizing. Consider the following questions:

   a. How many perspectives do you engage?
   b. What other perspectives might you include?
   c. How do you distinguish your views from the other views you summarize?
   d. Do you use clear voice-signaling phrases?
   e. What options are available to you for clarifying who is saying what?
   f. Which of these options are best suited for this particular text?

   If you find that you do *not* include multiple views or clearly distinguish between others' views and your own, revise your text to do so.

SIX

"SKEPTICS MAY OBJECT"

Planting a Naysayer in Your Text

THE WRITER Jane Tompkins describes a pattern that repeats itself whenever she writes a book or an article. For the first couple of weeks when she sits down to write, things go relatively well. But then in the middle of the night, several weeks into the writing process, she'll wake up in a cold sweat, suddenly realizing that she has overlooked some major criticism that readers will surely make against her ideas. Her first thought, invariably, is that she will have to give up on the project, or that she will have to throw out what she's written thus far and start over. Then she realizes that "this moment of doubt and panic is where my text really begins." She then revises what she's written in a way that incorporates the criticisms she's anticipated, and her text becomes stronger and more interesting as a result.

This little story contains an important lesson for all writers, experienced and inexperienced alike. It suggests that even though most of us are upset at the idea of someone criticizing our work, such criticisms can actually work to our advantage. Although it's naturally tempting to ignore criticism of our ideas, doing so may in fact be a big mistake, since our writing improves when we not only listen to these objections but give them an explicit hearing in our writing. Indeed, no single device more quickly improves a piece of writing than planting a naysayer in the text—saying, for example, that "although some readers may object" to something in your argument, you "would reply that _____."

ANTICIPATE OBJECTIONS

But wait, you say. Isn't the advice to incorporate critical views a recipe for destroying your credibility and undermining your argument? Here you are, trying to say something that will hold up, and we want you to tell readers all the negative things someone might say against you?

Exactly. We *are* urging you to tell readers what others might say against you, but our point is that doing so will actually *enhance* your credibility, not undermine it. As we argue throughout this book, writing well does not mean piling up uncontroversial truths in a vacuum; it means engaging others in a dialogue or debate—not only by opening your text with a summary of what others *have* said, as we suggest in Chapter 1, but also by imagining what others *might* say against your argument as it unfolds. Once you see writing as an act of entering a conversation, you should also see how opposing arguments can work for you rather than against you.

Paradoxically, the more you give voice to your critics' objections, the more you tend to disarm those critics, especially if you go on to answer their objections in convincing ways. When you entertain a counterargument, you make a kind of preemptive strike, identifying problems with your argument before others can point them out for you. Furthermore, by entertaining counterarguments, you show respect for your readers, treating them not as gullible dupes who will believe anything you say but as independent, critical thinkers who are aware that your view is not the only one in town. In addition, by imagining what others might say against your claims, you come across as a generous, broad-minded person who is confident enough to open himself or herself to debate—like the writer in the figure on the following page.

Conversely, if you don't entertain counterarguments, you may very likely come across as closed-minded, as if you think your beliefs are beyond dispute. You might also leave important questions hanging and concerns about your arguments unaddressed. Finally, if you fail to plant a naysayer in your text, you may find that you have very little to say. Our own students often say that entertaining counterarguments makes it easier to generate enough text to meet their assignment's page-length requirements.

Planting a naysayer in your text is a relatively simple move, as you can see by looking at the following passage from a book by the writer Kim Chernin. Having spent some thirty pages complaining about the pressure on American women to be thin, Chernin inserts a whole chapter entitled "The Skeptic," opening it as follows.

At this point I would like to raise certain objections that have been inspired by the skeptic in me. She feels that I have been ignoring some of the most common assumptions we all make about our bodies and these she wishes to see addressed. For example: "You know perfectly well," she says to me, "that you feel better when you lose weight. You buy new clothes. You look at yourself more eagerly in the mirror. When someone invites you to a party you don't stop and ask yourself whether you want to go. You feel sexier. Admit it. You like yourself better."

KIM CHERNIN, *The Obsession:*
Reflections on the Tyranny of Slenderness

"YOU WILL PROBABLY OBJECT THAT I HAVE MISREPRESENTED X'S WORK HERE, AND I CONCEDE THAT X NEVER SAYS _____ IN SO MANY WORDS. NEVERTHELESS. ..."

The remainder of Chernin's chapter consists of her answers to this inner skeptic. In the face of the skeptic's challenge to her book's central premise (that the pressure to diet seriously harms women's lives), Chernin responds neither by repressing the skeptic's critical voice nor by giving in to it and relinquishing her own position. Instead, she embraces that voice and writes it into her text. Note too that instead of dispatching this naysaying voice quickly, as many of us would be tempted to do, Chernin stays with it and devotes a full paragraph to it. By borrowing some of Chernin's language, we can come up with templates for entertaining virtually any objection.

TEMPLATES FOR ENTERTAINING OBJECTIONS

▸ **At this point I would like to raise some objections that have been inspired by the skeptic in me. She feels that I have been ignoring <u>the complexities of the situation</u>.**

▸ **Yet some readers may challenge my view by insisting that _____.**

▸ **Of course, many will probably disagree on the grounds that _____.**

Note that the objections in the above templates are attributed not to any specific person or group, but to "skeptics," "readers," or "many." This kind of nameless, faceless naysayer is perfectly appropriate in many cases. But the ideas that motivate arguments and objections often can—and, where possible, should—be ascribed to a specific ideology or school of thought (for example, liberals, Christian fundamentalists, neopragmatists) rather than to anonymous anybodies. In other words, naysayers can be labeled, and you can add precision and impact to your writing by identifying what those labels are.

TEMPLATES FOR NAMING YOUR NAYSAYERS

▸ Here many *feminists* would probably object that <u>gender does influence language</u>.

▸ But *social Darwinists* would certainly take issue with the argument that _____.

▸ *Biologists*, of course, may want to question whether _____.

▸ Nevertheless, both *followers and critics of Malcolm X* will probably suggest otherwise and argue that _____.

To be sure, some people dislike such labels and may even resent having labels applied to themselves. Some feel that labels put individuals in boxes, stereotyping them and glossing over what makes each of us unique. And it's true that labels can be used inappropriately, in ways that ignore individuality and promote stereotypes. But since the life of ideas, including many of our most private thoughts, is conducted through groups and types rather than solitary individuals, intellectual exchange requires labels to give definition and serve as a convenient shorthand. If you categorically reject all labels, you give up an important resource and even mislead readers by presenting yourself and others as having no connection to anyone else. You also miss an opportunity to generalize the importance and relevance of your work to some larger conversation. When you attribute a position you are summarizing to liberalism, say, or historical materialism, your argument is no longer just about your own solitary views but about the intersection of broad ideas and habits of mind that many readers may already have a stake in.

The way to minimize the problem of stereotyping, then, is not to categorically reject labels but to refine and qualify their use, as the following templates demonstrate.

▸ Although not all *Christians* think alike, some of them will probably dispute my claim that _____.

▸ *Non-native English speakers* are so diverse in their views that it's hard to generalize about them, but some are likely to object on the grounds that _____.

Another way to avoid needless stereotyping is to qualify labels carefully, substituting "pro bono lawyers" for "lawyers" in general, for example, or "quantitative sociologists" for all "social scientists," and so on.

TEMPLATES FOR INTRODUCING OBJECTIONS INFORMALLY

Objections can also be introduced in more informal ways. For instance, you can frame objections in the form of questions.

▸ But is my proposal realistic? What are the chances of its actually being adopted?

▸ Yet is it necessarily true that _____? Is it always the case, as I have been suggesting, that _____?

▸ However, does the evidence I've cited prove conclusively that _____?

You can also let your naysayer speak directly.

> ▶ **"Impossible," some will say. "You must be reading the research selectively."**

Moves like this allow you to cut directly to the skeptical voice itself, as the singer-songwriter Joe Jackson does in the following excerpt from a *New York Times* article complaining about the restrictions on public smoking in New York City bars and restaurants.

> I like a couple of cigarettes or a cigar with a drink, and like many other people, I only smoke in bars or nightclubs. Now I can't go to any of my old haunts. Bartenders who were friends have turned into cops, forcing me outside to shiver in the cold and curse under my breath. . . . It's no fun. Smokers are being demonized and victimized all out of proportion.
>
> "Get over it," say the anti-smokers. "You're the minority." I thought a great city was a place where all kinds of minorities could thrive. . . . "Smoking kills," they say. As an occasional smoker with otherwise healthy habits, I'll take my chances. Health consciousness is important, but so are pleasure and freedom of choice.
>
> JOE JACKSON, "Want to Smoke? Go to Hamburg"

Jackson could have begun his second paragraph, in which he shifts from his own voice to that of his imagined naysayer, more formally, as follows: "Of course anti-smokers will object that since we smokers are in the minority, we should simply stop complaining and quietly make the sacrifices we are being called on to make for the larger social good." Or "Anti-smokers might insist, however, that the smoking minority

See the essay on *Family Guy* (p. 145) that addresses naysayers throughout.

should submit to the non-smoking majority." We think, though, that Jackson gets the job done in a far more lively way with the more colloquial form he chooses. Borrowing a standard move of playwrights and novelists, Jackson cuts directly to the objectors' view and then to his own retort, then back to the objectors' view and then to his own retort again, thereby creating a kind of dialogue or miniature play within his own text. This move works well for Jackson, but only because he uses quotation marks and other voice markers to make clear at every point whose voice he is in.

See Chapter 5 for more advice on using voice markers.

REPRESENT OBJECTIONS FAIRLY

Once you've decided to introduce a differing or opposing view into your writing, your work has only just begun, since you still need to represent and explain that view with fairness and generosity. Although it is tempting to give opposing views short shrift, to hurry past them, or even to mock them, doing so is usually counterproductive. When writers make the best case they can for their critics (playing Peter Elbow's "believing game"), they actually bolster their credibility with readers rather than undermine it. They make readers think, "This is a writer I can trust."

See pp. 31–32 for more on the believing game.

We recommend, then, that whenever you entertain objections in your writing, you stay with them for several sentences or even paragraphs and take them as seriously as possible. We also recommend that you read your summary of opposing views with an outsider's eye: put yourself in the shoes of someone who disagrees with you and ask if such a reader would recognize himself in your summary. Would that reader think you have taken his views seriously, as beliefs that reasonable people might hold? Or would he detect a mocking tone or an oversimplification of his views?

There will always be certain objections, to be sure, that you believe do not deserve to be represented, just as there will be objections that seem so unworthy of respect that they inspire ridicule. Remember, however, that if you do choose to mock a view that you oppose, you are likely to alienate those readers who don't already agree with you—likely the very readers you want to reach. Also be aware that in mocking another's view you may contribute to a hostile argument culture in which someone may ridicule you in return.

ANSWER OBJECTIONS

Do be aware that when you represent objections successfully, you still need to be able to answer those objections persuasively. After all, when you write objections into a text, you take the risk that readers will find those objections more convincing than the argument you yourself are advancing. In the editorial quoted above, for example, Joe Jackson takes the risk that readers will identify more with the anti-smoking view he summarizes than with the pro-smoking position he endorses.

This is precisely what Benjamin Franklin describes happening to himself in *The Autobiography of Benjamin Franklin* (1793), when he recalls being converted to Deism (a religion that exalts reason over spirituality) by reading *anti*-Deist books. When he encountered the views of Deists being negatively summarized by authors who opposed them, Franklin explains, he ended up finding the Deist position more persuasive. To avoid having this kind of unintentional reverse effect on readers, you need to do your best to make sure that any counter-arguments you address are not more convincing than your own claims. It is good to address objections in your writing, but only if you are able to overcome them.

One surefire way to *fail* to overcome an objection is to dismiss it out of hand—saying, for example, "That's just wrong." The difference between such a response (which offers no supporting reasons whatsoever) and the types of nuanced responses we're promoting in this book is the difference between bullying your readers and genuinely persuading them.

Often the best way to overcome an objection is not to try to refute it completely but to agree with part of it while challenging only the part you dispute. In other words, in answering counterarguments, it is often best to say "yes, but" or "yes See pp. 61–64 for more on agreeing, with a difference. and no," treating the counterview as an opportunity to revise and refine your own position. Rather than build your argument into an impenetrable fortress, it is often best to make concessions while still standing your ground, as Kim Chernin does in the following response to the counterargument quoted above. While in the voice of the "skeptic," Chernin writes: "Admit it. You like yourself better when you've lost weight." In response, Chernin replies as follows.

Can I deny these things? No woman who has managed to lose weight would wish to argue with this. Most people feel better about themselves when they become slender. And yet, upon reflection, it seems to me that there is something precarious about this well-being. After all, 98 percent of people who lose weight gain it back. Indeed, 90 percent of those who have dieted "successfully" gain back more than they ever lost. Then, of course, we can no longer bear to look at ourselves in the mirror.

In this way, Chernin shows how you can use a counterview to improve and refine your overall argument by making a concession. Even as she concedes that losing weight feels good in the short run, she argues that in the long run the weight always returns, making the dieter far more miserable.

TEMPLATES FOR MAKING CONCESSIONS
WHILE STILL STANDING YOUR GROUND

▸ Although I grant that <u>the book is poorly organized</u>, I still maintain that <u>it raises an important issue</u>.

▸ Proponents of X are right to argue that _____. But they exaggerate when they claim that _____.

▸ While it is true that _____, it does not necessarily follow that _____.

▸ On the one hand, I agree with X that _____. But on the other hand, I still insist that _____.

Templates like these show that answering naysayers' objections does not have to be an all-or-nothing affair in which you either definitively refute your critics or they definitively refute you. Often the most productive engagements among differing views end with a combined vision that incorporates elements of each one.

But what if you've tried out all the possible answers you can think of to an objection you've anticipated and you *still* have a nagging feeling that the objection is more convincing than your argument itself? In that case, the best remedy is to go back and make some fundamental revisions to your argument, even reversing your position completely if need be. Although finding out late in the game that you aren't fully convinced by your own argument can be painful, it can actually make your final text more intellectually honest, challenging, and serious. After all, the goal of writing is not to keep proving that whatever you initially said is right, but to stretch the limits of your thinking. So if planting a strong naysayer in your text forces you to change your mind, that's not a bad thing. Some would argue that that is what the academic world is all about.

Exercises

1. Read the following passage by the cultural critic Eric Schlosser. As you'll see, he hasn't planted any naysayers in this text. Do it for him. Insert a brief paragraph stating an objection to his argument and then responding to the objection as he might.

The United States must declare an end to the war on drugs. This war has filled the nation's prisons with poor drug addicts and small-time drug dealers. It has created a multibillion-dollar black market, enriched organized crime groups and promoted the corruption of government officials throughout the world. And it has not stemmed the widespread use of illegal drugs. By any rational measure, this war has been a total failure.

We must develop public policies on substance abuse that are guided not by moral righteousness or political expediency but by common sense. The United States should immediately decriminalize the cultivation and possession of small amounts of marijuana for personal use. Marijuana should no longer be classified as a Schedule I narcotic, and those who seek to use marijuana as medicine should no longer face criminal sanctions. We must shift our entire approach to drug abuse from the criminal justice system to the public health system. Congress should appoint an independent commission to study the harm-reduction policies that have been adopted in Switzerland, Spain, Portugal, and the Netherlands. The commission should recommend policies for the United States based on one important criterion: what works.

In a nation where pharmaceutical companies advertise powerful antidepressants on billboards and where alcohol companies run amusing beer ads during the Super Bowl, the idea of a "drug-free society" is absurd. Like the rest of American society, our drug policy would greatly benefit from less punishment and more compassion.

ERIC SCHLOSSER, "A People's Democratic Platform"

2. Look over something you've written that makes an argument. Check to see if you've anticipated and responded to any objections. If not, revise your text to do so. If so, have you anticipated all the likely objections? Who if anyone have you attributed the objections to? Have you represented the objections fairly? Have you answered them well enough, or do you think you now need to qualify your own argument? Could you use any of the language suggested in this chapter? Does the introduction of a naysayer strengthen your argument? Why, or why not?

SEVEN

"SO WHAT? WHO CARES?"

Saying Why It Matters

———◫———

BASEBALL IS THE NATIONAL PASTIME. Bernini was the best sculptor of the baroque period. All writing is conversational. So what? Who cares? Why does any of this matter?

How many times have you had reason to ask these questions? Regardless of how interesting a topic may be to you as a writer, readers always need to know what is at stake in a text and why they should care. All too often, however, these questions are left unanswered—mainly because writers and speakers assume that audiences will know the answers already or will figure them out on their own. As a result, students come away from lectures feeling like outsiders to what they've just heard, just as many of us feel left hanging after talks we've attended. The problem is not necessarily that the speakers lack a clear, well-focused thesis or that the thesis is inadequately supported with evidence. Instead, the problem is that the speakers don't address the crucial question of why their arguments matter.

That this question is so often left unaddressed is unfortunate since the speakers generally *could* offer interesting, engaging answers. When pressed, for instance, most academics will tell you that their lectures and articles matter because they address some belief that needs to be corrected or updated—and because their arguments have important, real-world consequences. Yet many academics fail to identify these reasons and consequences explicitly in what they say and write. Rather than assume that audiences will know why their claims matter, all writers need to answer the "so what?" and "who cares?" questions up front. Not everyone can claim to have a cure for cancer or a solution to end poverty. But writers who fail to show that others *should* care or already *do* care about their claims will ultimately lose their audiences' interest.

This chapter focuses on various moves that you can make to answer the "who cares?" and "so what?" questions in your own writing. In one sense, the two questions get at the same thing: the relevance or importance of what you are saying. Yet they get at this significance in different ways. Whereas "who cares?" literally asks you to identify a person or group who cares about your claims, "so what?" asks about the real-world applications and consequences of those claims—what difference it would make if they were accepted. We'll look first at ways of making clear who cares.

"WHO CARES?"

To see how one writer answers the "who cares?" question, consider the following passage from the science writer Denise Grady. Writing in the *New York Times*, she explains some of the latest research into fat cells.

> Scientists used to think body fat and the cells it was made of were pretty much inert, just an oily storage compartment. But within the past decade research has shown that fat cells act like chemical factories and that body fat is potent stuff: a highly active

tissue that secretes hormones and other substances with profound and sometimes harmful effects. . . .

In recent years, biologists have begun calling fat an "endocrine organ," comparing it to glands like the thyroid and pituitary, which also release hormones straight into the bloodstream.

DENISE GRADY, "The Secret Life of a Potent Cell"

Notice how Grady's writing reflects the central advice we give in this book, offering a clear claim and also framing that claim as a response to what someone else has said. In so doing, Grady immediately identifies at least one group with a stake in the new research that sees fat as "active," "potent stuff": namely, the scientific community, which formerly believed that body fat is inert. By referring to these scientists, Grady implicitly acknowledges that her text is part of a larger conversation and shows who besides herself has an interest in what she says.

Consider, however, how the passage would read had Grady left out what "scientists used to think" and simply explained the new findings in isolation.

> Within the past few decades research has shown that fat cells act like chemical factories and that body fat is potent stuff: a highly active tissue that secretes hormones and other substances. In recent years, biologists have begun calling fat an "endocrine organ," comparing it to glands like the thyroid and pituitary, which also release hormones straight into the bloodstream.

Though this statement is clear and easy to follow, it lacks any indication that anyone needs to hear it. Okay, one nods while reading this passage, fat is an active, potent thing. Sounds plausible enough; no reason to think it's not true. But does anyone really care? Who, if anyone, is interested?

TEMPLATES FOR INDICATING WHO CARES

To address "who cares?" questions in your own writing, we suggest using templates like the following, which echo Grady in refuting earlier thinking.

► <u>Parents</u> used to think <u>spanking was necessary</u>. But recently [or within the past few decades] <u>experts</u> suggest that <u>it can be counterproductive</u>.

► This interpretation challenges the work of those critics who have long assumed that _____.

► These findings challenge the work of earlier researchers, who tended to assume that _____.

► Recent studies like these shed new light on _____, which previous studies had not addressed.

Grady might have been more explicit by writing the "who cares?" question directly into her text, as in the following template.

► But who really cares? Who besides me and a handful of recent researchers has a stake in these claims? At the very least, the researchers who formerly believed _____ should care.

To gain greater authority as a writer, it can help to name specific people or groups who have a stake in your claims and to go into some detail about their views.

► Researchers have long assumed that _____. For instance, one eminent scholar of cell biology, _____, assumed in _____, her seminal work on cell structures and functions, that fat cells _____. As _____ herself put it, "_____" (2012). Another leading scientist, _____, argued that fat cells "_____" (2011). Ultimately, when it came to the nature of fat, the basic assumption was that _____.

But a new body of research shows that fat cells are far more complex and that _____.

In other cases, you might refer to certain people or groups who *should* care about your claims.

▸ If sports enthusiasts stopped to think about it, many of them might simply assume that the most successful athletes _____. However, new research shows _____.

▸ These findings challenge neoliberals' common assumption that _____.

▸ At first glance, teenagers might say _____. But on closer inspection _____.

As these templates suggest, answering the "who cares?" question involves establishing the type of contrast between what others say and what you say that is central to this book. Ultimately, such templates help you create a dramatic tension or clash of views in your writing that readers will feel invested in and want to see resolved.

"SO WHAT?"

Although answering the "who cares?" question is crucial, in many cases it is not enough, especially if you are writing for general readers who don't necessarily have a strong investment in the particular clash of views you are setting up. In the case of Grady's argument about fat cells, such readers may still wonder why it matters that some researchers think fat cells are active, while others think they're inert. Or, to move to a different field of study, American literature, *so what* if some scholars disagree about Huck Finn's relationship with the runaway slave Jim in Mark Twain's *Adventures of Huckleberry Finn?* Why should anyone besides a few specialists in the field care about such disputes? What, if anything, hinges on them?

The best way to answer such questions about the larger consequences of your claims is to appeal to something that your audience already figures to care about. Whereas the "who cares?" question asks you to identify an interested person or group, the "so what?" question asks you to link your argument to some larger matter that readers already deem important. Thus in analyzing *Huckleberry Finn*, a writer could argue that seemingly narrow disputes about the hero's relationship with Jim actually shed light on whether Twain's canonical, widely read novel is a critique of racism in America or is itself marred by it.

Let's see how Grady invokes such broad, general concerns in her article on fat cells. Her first move is to link researchers' interest in fat cells to a general concern with obesity and health.

> Researchers trying to decipher the biology of fat cells hope to find new ways to help people get rid of excess fat or, at least, prevent obesity from destroying their health. In an increasingly obese world, their efforts have taken on added importance.

Further showing why readers should care, Grady's next move is to demonstrate the even broader relevance and urgency of her subject matter.

> Internationally, more than a billion people are overweight. Obesity and two illnesses linked to it, heart disease and high blood pressure, are on the World Health Organization's list of the top 10 global health risks. In the United States, 65 percent of adults weigh too much,

compared with about 56 percent a decade ago, and government researchers blame obesity for at least 300,000 deaths a year.

What Grady implicitly says here is "Look, dear reader, you may think that these questions about the nature of fat cells I've been pursuing have little to do with everyday life. In fact, however, these questions are extremely important—particularly in our 'increasingly obese world' in which we need to prevent obesity from destroying our health."

Notice that Grady's phrase "in an increasingly _____ world" can be adapted as a strategic move to address the "so what?" question in other fields as well. For example, a sociologist analyzing back-to-nature movements of the past thirty years might make the following statement.

Ellen Ullman uses the "so what" move on p. 729, ¶13–15.

In a world increasingly dominated by cellphones and sophisticated computer technologies, these attempts to return to nature appear futile.

This type of move can be readily applied to other disciplines because no matter how much disciplines may differ from one another, the need to justify the importance of one's concerns is common to them all.

TEMPLATES FOR ESTABLISHING WHY YOUR CLAIMS MATTER

▶ *Huckleberry Finn* matters/is important because <u>it is one of the most widely taught novels in the American school system.</u>

▶ Although X may seem trivial, it is in fact crucial in terms of today's concern over _____ .

▸ Ultimately, what is at stake here is _____.

▸ These findings have important implications for the broader domain of _____.

▸ If we are right about _____, then major consequences follow for _____.

▸ These conclusions/This discovery will have significant applications in _____ as well as in _____.

Finally, you can also treat the "so what?" question as a related aspect of the "who cares?" question.

▸ Although X may seem of concern to only a small group of _____, it should in fact concern anyone who cares about _____.

All these templates help you hook your readers. By suggesting the real-world applications of your claims, the templates not only demonstrate that others care about your claims but also tell your readers why *they* should care. Again, it bears repeating that simply stating and proving your thesis isn't enough. You also need to frame it in a way that helps readers care about it.

WHAT ABOUT READERS WHO ALREADY KNOW WHY IT MATTERS?

At this point, you might wonder if you need to answer the "who cares?" and "so what?" questions in *everything* you write. Is it really necessary to address these questions if you're proposing something so obviously consequential as, say, a treatment for autism or a program to eliminate illiteracy? Isn't it obvious that everyone cares about such problems? Does it really need to be spelled out? And what about when you're writing for audiences who you know are already interested in your claims and who understand perfectly well why they're important? In other words, do you always need to address the "so what?" and "who cares?" questions?

As a rule, yes—although it's true that you can't keep answering them forever and at a certain point must say enough is enough. Although a determined skeptic can infinitely ask why something matters—"Why should I care about earning a salary? And why should I care about supporting a family?"—you have to stop answering at some point in your text. Nevertheless, we urge you to go as far as possible in answering such questions. If you take it for granted that readers will somehow intuit the answers to "so what?" and "who cares?" on their own, you may make your work seem less interesting than it actually is, and you run the risk that readers will dismiss your text as irrelevant and unimportant. By contrast, when you are careful to explain who cares and why, it's a little like bringing a cheerleading squad into your text. And though some expert readers might already know why your claims matter, even they need to be reminded. Thus the safest move is to be as explicit as possible in answering the "so what?" question, even for those already in the know. When you step back from the text and explain why it matters, you are urging your audience to keep reading, pay attention, and care.

See how Monica Potts explains why one woman's life reflects a greater societal problem on p. 593, ¶7.

Exercises

1. Find several texts (scholarly essays, newspaper articles, emails, memos, blogs, etc.) and see whether they answer the "so what?" and "who cares?" questions. Probably some do, some don't. What difference does it make whether they do or do not? How do the authors who answer these questions do so? Do they use any strategies or techniques that you could borrow for your own writing? Are there any strategies or techniques recommended in this chapter, or that you've found or developed on your own, that you'd recommend to these authors?

2. Look over something you've written yourself. Do you indicate "so what?" and "who cares"? If not, revise your text to do so. You might use the following template to get started.

   My point here (that _____) should interest those who _____. Beyond this limited audience, however, my point should speak to anyone who cares about the larger issue of _____.

3

TYING IT ALL TOGETHER

EIGHT

"AS A RESULT"

Connecting the Parts

—⌐▯⌐—

WE ONCE HAD A STUDENT named Bill, whose characteristic sentence pattern went something like this.

> Spot is a good dog. He has fleas.

"Connect your sentences," we urged in the margins of Bill's papers. "What does Spot being good have to do with his fleas?" "These two statements seem unrelated. Can you connect them in some logical way?" When comments like these yielded no results, we tried inking in suggested connections for him.

> Spot is a good dog, *but* he has fleas.
> Spot is a good dog, *even though* he has fleas.

But our message failed to get across, and Bill's disconnected sentence pattern persisted to the end of the semester.

And yet Bill did focus well on his subjects. When he mentioned Spot the dog (or Plato, or any other topic) in one sentence, we could count on Spot (or Plato) being the topic of the following sentence as well. This was not the case with some of Bill's classmates, who sometimes changed topic from sentence to sentence or even from clause to clause within a single sentence. But because Bill neglected to mark his connections, his writing was as frustrating to read as theirs. In all these cases, we had to struggle to figure out on our own how the sentences and paragraphs connected or failed to connect with one another.

What makes such writers so hard to read, in other words, is that they never gesture back to what they have just said or forward to what they plan to say. "Never look back" might be their motto, almost as if they see writing as a process of thinking of something to say about a topic and writing it down, then thinking of something else to say about the topic and writing that down too, and on and on until they've filled the assigned number of pages and can hand the paper in. Each sentence basically starts a new thought, rather than growing out of or extending the thought of the previous sentence.

When Bill talked about his writing habits, he acknowledged that he never went back and read what he had written. Indeed, he told us that, other than using his computer software to check for spelling errors and make sure that his tenses were all aligned, he never actually reread what he wrote before turning it in. As Bill seemed to picture it, writing was something one did while sitting at a computer, whereas reading was a separate activity generally reserved for an easy chair, book in hand. It had never occurred to Bill that to write a good sentence he had to think about how it connected to those that came before and after; that he had to think hard about how that sentence fit into the sentences that surrounded it. Each sentence for Bill existed in a sort of tunnel isolated from every other sentence on the page. He never bothered to fit all the parts of his essay together because he apparently thought of writing as a matter of piling up information or observations rather than building a sustained argument. What we suggest in this chapter, then, is that you converse not only with others in your writing but with yourself: that you establish clear relations between one statement and the next by connecting those statements.

This chapter addresses the issue of how to connect all the parts of your writing. The best compositions establish a sense of momentum and direction by making explicit connections among their different parts, so that what is said in one sentence (or paragraph) both sets up what is to come and is clearly informed by what has already been said. When you write a sentence, you create an expectation in the reader's mind that the next sentence will in some way echo and extend it, even if—*especially if*—that next sentence takes your argument in a new direction.

It may help to think of each sentence you write as having arms that reach backward and forward, as the figure below suggests. When your sentences reach outward like this, they establish connections that help your writing flow smoothly in a way readers appreciate. Conversely, when writing lacks such connections and moves in fits and starts, readers repeatedly have to go back over the sentences and guess at the connections on their own. To prevent such disconnection and make your writing flow, we advise following a "do it yourself" principle, which means that it is your job as a writer to do the hard work of making the connections rather than, as Bill did, leaving this work to your readers.

This chapter offers several strategies you can use to put this principle into action: (1) using transition terms (like "therefore" and "as a result"); (2) adding pointing words (like "this" or "such"); (3) developing a set of key terms and phrases for each text you write; and (4) repeating yourself, but with a difference—a move that involves repeating what you've said, but with enough variation to avoid being redundant. All these moves require that you always look back and, in crafting any one sentence, think hard about those that precede it.

Notice how we ourselves have used such connecting devices thus far in this chapter. The second paragraph of this chapter, for example, opens with the transitional "And yet," signaling a change in direction, while the opening sentence of the third includes the phrase "in other words," telling you to expect a restatement of a point we've just made. If you look through this book, you should be able to find many sentences that contain some word or phrase that explicitly hooks them back to something said earlier, to something about to be said, or both. And many sentences in *this* chapter repeat key terms related to the idea of connection: "connect," "disconnect," "link," "relate," "forward," and "backward."

USE TRANSITIONS

For readers to follow your train of thought, you need not only to connect your sentences and paragraphs to each other, but also to mark the kind of connection you are making. One of the easiest ways to make this move is to use *transitions* (from the Latin root *trans*, "across"), which help you cross from one point to another in your text. Transitions are usually placed at or near the start of sentences so they can signal to readers where your text is going: in the same direction it has been moving, or in a new direction. More specifically, transitions tell readers whether your text is echoing a previous sentence or paragraph ("in other words"), adding something to it ("in addition"), offering an example of it ("for example"), generalizing from it ("as a result"), or modifying it ("and yet").

The following is a list of commonly used transitions, categorized according to their different functions.

ADDITION

also	indeed
and	in fact
besides	moreover
furthermore	so too
in addition	

ELABORATION

actually	to put it another way
by extension	to put it bluntly
in other words	to put it succinctly
in short	ultimately
that is	

EXAMPLE

after all	for instance
as an illustration	specifically
consider	to take a case in point
for example	

CAUSE AND EFFECT

accordingly	so
as a result	then
consequently	therefore
hence	thus
since	

COMPARISON

along the same lines	likewise
in the same way	similarly

CONTRAST

although	nevertheless
but	nonetheless
by contrast	on the contrary
conversely	on the other hand
despite	regardless
even though	whereas
however	while yet
in contrast	

CONCESSION

admittedly	naturally
although it is true	of course
granted	to be sure

CONCLUSION

as a result	in sum
consequently	therefore
hence	thus
in conclusion	to sum up
in short	to summarize

Ideally, transitions should operate so unobtrusively in a piece of writing that they recede into the background and readers do not even notice that they are there. It's a bit like what happens when drivers use their turn signals before turning right or left: just as other drivers recognize such signals almost unconsciously, readers should process transition terms with a minimum of thought. But even though such terms should function unobtrusively in your writing, they can be among the most powerful tools in your vocabulary. Think how your heart sinks when someone, immediately after praising you, begins a sentence with "but" or "however." No matter what follows, you know it won't be good.

Notice that some transitions can help you not only to move from one sentence to another, but to combine two or more sentences into one. Combining sentences in this way helps prevent the choppy, staccato effect that arises when too many short sentences are strung together, one after the other. For instance, to combine Bill's two choppy sentences ("Spot is a good dog. He has fleas.") into one, better-flowing sentence, we suggested that he rewrite them as "Spot is a good dog, *even though* he has fleas."

Transitions like these not only guide readers through the twists and turns of your argument but also help ensure that you *have* an argument in the first place. In fact, we think of words like "but," "yet," "nevertheless," "besides," and others as argument words, since it's hard to use them without making some kind of argument. The word "therefore," for instance, commits you to making sure that the claims preceding it lead logically to the conclusion that it introduces. "For example" also assumes an argument, since it requires the material you are introducing to stand as an instance or proof of some preceding generalization. As a result, the more you use transitions, the more you'll be able not only to connect the parts of your text but also to construct a strong argument in the first place. And if you draw on them frequently enough, using them should eventually become second nature.

To be sure, it is possible to overuse transitions, so take time to read over your drafts carefully and eliminate any transitions that are unnecessary. But following the maxim that you need to learn the basic moves of argument before you can deliberately depart from them, we advise you not to forgo explicit transition terms until you've first mastered their use. In all our years of teaching, we've read countless essays that suffered from having few or no transitions, but cannot recall one in which the transitions were overused. Seasoned writers sometimes omit explicit transitions, but only because they rely heavily on the other types of connecting devices that we turn to in the rest of this chapter.

See how Mary Maxfield uses transitions on p. 443.

Before doing so, however, let us warn you about inserting transitions without really thinking through their meanings—using "therefore," say, when your text's logic actually requires "nevertheless" or "however." So beware. Choosing transition terms should involve a bit of mental sweat, since the whole point of using them is to make your writing *more* reader-friendly, not less. The only thing more frustrating than reading Bill-style passages like "Spot is a good dog. He has fleas" is reading mis-connected sentences like "Spot is a good dog. For example, he has fleas."

USE POINTING WORDS

Another way to connect the parts of your argument is by using pointing words—which, as their name implies, point or refer backward to some concept in the previous sentence. The most common of these pointing words include "this," "these," "that," "those," "their," and "such" (as in "these pointing words" near the start of this sentence) and simple pronouns like "his," "he," "her," "she," "it," and "their." Such terms help you create the flow we spoke of earlier that enables readers to move effortlessly through your text. In a sense, these terms are like an invisible hand reaching out of your sentence, grabbing what's needed in the previous sentences and pulling it along.

Like transitions, however, pointing words need to be used carefully. It's dangerously easy to insert pointing words into your text that don't refer to a clearly defined object, assuming that because the object you have in mind is clear to you it will also be clear to your readers. For example, consider the use of "this" in the following passage.

> Alexis de Tocqueville was highly critical of democratic societies, which he saw as tending toward mob rule. At the same time, he accorded democratic societies grudging respect. *This* is seen in Tocqueville's statement that . . .

When "this" is used in such a way it becomes an ambiguous or free-floating pointer, since readers can't tell if it refers to Tocqueville's critical attitude toward democratic societies, his grudging respect for them, or some combination of both. "This what?" readers mutter as they go back over such passages and try to figure them out. It's also tempting to try to cheat with pointing words, hoping that they will conceal or make up for conceptual confusions that may lurk in your argument. By referring to a fuzzy idea as "this" or "that," you might hope the fuzziness will somehow come across as clearer than it is.

You can fix problems caused by a free-floating pointer by making sure there is one and only one possible object in the vicinity that the pointer could be referring to. It also often helps to name the object the pointer is referring to at the same time that you point to it, replacing the bald "this" in the example above with a more precise phrase like "this ambivalence toward democratic societies" or "this grudging respect."

REPEAT KEY TERMS AND PHRASES

A third strategy for connecting the parts of your argument is to develop a constellation of key terms and phrases, including their synonyms and antonyms, that you repeat throughout your text. When used effectively, your key terms should be items that readers could extract from your text in order to get a solid sense of your topic. Playing with key terms also can be a good way to come up with a title and appropriate section headings for your text.

Notice how often Martin Luther King Jr. uses the key words "criticism," "statement," "answer," and "correspondence" in the opening paragraph of his famous "Letter from Birmingham Jail."

Dear Fellow Clergymen:

While confined here in the Birmingham city jail, I came across your recent *statement* calling my present activities "unwise and untimely." Seldom do I pause to *answer criticism* of my work and ideas. If I sought to *answer* all the *criticisms* that cross my desk, my secretaries would have little time for anything other than *such correspondence* in the course of the day, and I would have no time for constructive work. But since I feel that you are men of genuine good will and that your *criticisms* are sincerely set forth, I want to try to *answer* your *statement* in what I hope will be patient and reasonable terms.

MARTIN LUTHER KING JR., "Letter from Birmingham Jail"

Even though King uses the terms "criticism" and "answer" three times each and "statement" twice, the effect is not overly repetitive. In fact, these key terms help build a sense of momentum in the paragraph and bind it together.

For another example of the effective use of key terms, consider the following passage, in which the historian Susan Douglas develops a constellation of sharply contrasting key terms around the concept of "cultural schizophrenics": women like herself who, Douglas claims, have mixed feelings about the images of ideal femininity with which they are constantly bombarded by the media.

> In a variety of ways, the mass media helped make us the cultural schizophrenics we are today, women who rebel against yet submit to prevailing images about what a desirable, worthwhile woman should be. . . . [T]he mass media has engendered in many women a kind of cultural identity crisis. We are ambivalent toward femininity on the one hand and feminism on the other. Pulled in opposite directions—told we were equal, yet told we were subordinate; told we could change history but told we were trapped by history—we got the bends at an early age, and we've never gotten rid of them.
>
> When I open *Vogue*, for example, I am simultaneously infuriated and seduced. . . . I adore the materialism; I despise the materialism. . . . I want to look beautiful; I think wanting to look beautiful is about the most dumb-ass goal you could have. The magazine stokes my desire; the magazine triggers my bile. And this doesn't only happen when I'm reading *Vogue*; it happens all the time. . . . On the one hand, on the other hand—that's not just me—that's what it means to be a woman in America.
>
> To explain this schizophrenia . . .
>
> SUSAN DOUGLAS, *Where the Girls Are:*
> *Growing Up Female with the Mass Media*

In this passage, Douglas establishes "schizophrenia" as a key concept and then echoes it through synonyms like "identity crisis," "ambivalent," "the bends"—and even demonstrates it through a series of contrasting words and phrases:

rebel against / submit
told we were equal / told we were subordinate
told we could change history / told we were trapped by history
infuriated / seduced
I adore / I despise
I want / I think wanting . . . is about the most dumb-ass goal
stokes my desire / triggers my bile
on the one hand / on the other hand

These contrasting phrases help flesh out Douglas's claim that women are being pulled in two directions at once. In so doing, they bind the passage together into a unified whole that, despite its complexity and sophistication, stays focused over its entire length.

REPEAT YOURSELF—BUT WITH A DIFFERENCE

The last technique we offer for connecting the parts of your text involves repeating yourself, but with a difference—which basically means saying the same thing you've just said, but in a slightly different way that avoids sounding monotonous. To effectively connect the parts of your argument and keep it moving forward, be careful not to leap from one idea to a different idea or introduce new ideas cold. Instead, try to build bridges between your ideas by echoing what you've just said while simultaneously moving your text into new territory.

Several of the connecting devices discussed in this chapter are ways of repeating yourself in this special way. Key terms, pointing terms, and even many transitions can be used in a way that not only brings something forward from the previous sentence but in some way alters it. When Douglas, for instance, uses the key term "ambivalent" to echo her earlier reference to schizophrenics, she is repeating herself with a difference—repeating the same concept, but with a different word that adds new associations.

In addition, when you use transition phrases like "in other words" and "to put it another way," you repeat yourself with a difference, since these phrases help you restate earlier claims but in a different register. When you open a sentence with "in other words," you are basically telling your readers that in case they didn't fully understand what you meant in the last sentence, you are now coming at it again from a slightly different angle, or that since you're presenting a very important idea, you're not going to skip over it quickly but will explore it further to make sure your readers grasp all its aspects.

We would even go so far as to suggest that after your first sentence, almost every sentence you write should refer back to previous statements in some way. Whether you are writing a "furthermore" comment that adds to what you have just said or a "for example" statement that illustrates it, each sentence should echo at least one element of the previous sentence in some discernible way. Even when your text changes direction and requires transitions like "in contrast," "however," or "but," you still need to mark that shift by linking the sentence to the one just before it, as in the following example.

> Cheyenne loved basketball. Nevertheless, she feared her height would put her at a disadvantage.

These sentences work because even though the second sentence changes course and qualifies the first, it still echoes key concepts from the first. Not only does "she" echo "Cheyenne," since both refer to the same person, but "feared" echoes "loved" by establishing the contrast mandated by the term "nevertheless." "Nevertheless," then, is not an excuse for changing subjects radically. It too requires repetition to help readers shift gears with you and follow your train of thought.

Repetition, in short, is the central means by which you can move from point A to point B in a text. To introduce one last analogy, think of the way experienced rock climbers move up a steep slope. Instead of jumping or lurching from one handhold to the next, good climbers get a secure handhold on the position they have established before reaching for the next ledge. The same thing applies to writing. To move smoothly from point to point in your argument, you need to firmly ground what you say in what you've already said. In this way, your writing remains focused while simultaneously moving forward.

"But hold on," you may be thinking. "Isn't repetition precisely what sophisticated writers should avoid, on the grounds that it will make their writing sound simplistic—as if they are belaboring the obvious?" Yes and no. On the one hand, writers certainly can run into trouble if they merely repeat themselves and nothing more. On the other hand, repetition is key to creating continuity in writing. It is impossible to stay on track in a piece of writing if you don't repeat your points throughout the length of the text. Furthermore, writers would never make an impact on readers if they didn't repeat their main points often enough to reinforce those points and make them stand out above subordinate points. The trick therefore is not to avoid repeating yourself but to repeat yourself in varied and interesting enough ways that you advance your argument without sounding tedious.

Exercises

1. Read the following opening to Chapter 2 of *The Road to Wigan Pier*, by George Orwell. Annotate the connecting devices by underlining the transitions, circling the key terms, and putting boxes around the pointing terms.

Our civilisation . . . is founded on coal, more completely than one realises until one stops to think about it. The machines that keep us alive, and the machines that make the machines, are all directly or indirectly dependent upon coal. In the metabolism of the Western world the coal-miner is second in importance only to the man who ploughs the soil. He is a sort of grimy caryatid upon whose shoulders nearly everything that is not grimy is supported. For this reason the actual process by which coal is extracted is well worth watching, if you get the chance and are willing to take the trouble.

When you go down a coal-mine it is important to try and get to the coal face when the "fillers" are at work. This is not easy, because when the mine is working visitors are a nuisance and are not encouraged, but if you go at any other time, it is possible to come away with a totally wrong impression. On a Sunday, for instance, a mine seems almost peaceful. The time to go there is when the machines are roaring and the air is black with coal dust, and when you can actually see what the miners have to do. At those times the place is like hell, or at any rate like my own mental picture of hell. Most of the things one imagines in hell are there—heat, noise, confusion, darkness, foul air, and, above all, unbearably cramped space. Everything except the fire, for there is no fire down there except the feeble beams of Davy lamps and electric torches which scarcely penetrate the clouds of coal dust.

When you have finally got there—and getting there is a job in itself: I will explain that in a moment—you crawl through the last line of pit props and see opposite you a shiny black wall three or four feet high. This is the coal face. Overhead is the smooth ceiling made by the rock from which the coal has been cut; underneath is the rock again, so that the gallery you are in is only as high as the ledge of coal itself, probably not much more than a yard. The first impression of all, overmastering everything else for a while, is the frightful, deafening din from the conveyor belt which carries the coal away. You cannot see very far, because the fog of coal dust throws back the beam of your lamp, but you can see on either side of you the line of half-naked kneeling men, one to every four or five yards, driving their shovels under the fallen coal and flinging it swiftly over their left shoulders. . . .

GEORGE ORWELL, *The Road to Wigan Pier*

2. Read over something you've written with an eye for the devices you've used to connect the parts. Underline all the transitions, pointing terms, key terms, and repetition. Do you see any patterns? Do you rely on certain devices more than others? Are there any passages that are hard to follow—and if so, can you make them easier to read by trying any of the other devices discussed in this chapter?

NINE

"AIN'T SO / IS NOT"

Academic Writing Doesn't Always Mean Setting Aside Your Own Voice

HAVE YOU EVER gotten the impression that writing well in college means setting aside the kind of language you use in everyday conversation? That to impress your instructors you need to use big words, long sentences, and complex sentence structures? If so, then we're here to tell you that it ain't necessarily so. On the contrary, academic writing can—and in our view *should*—be relaxed, easy to follow, and even a little bit fun. Although we don't want to suggest that you avoid using sophisticated, academic terms in your writing, we encourage you to draw upon the kinds of expressions and turns of phrase that you use every day when texting or conversing with family and friends. In this chapter, we want to show you how you can write effective academic arguments while holding on to some of your own voice.

This point is important, since you may well become turned off from writing if you think your everyday language practices have to be checked at the classroom door. You may end up feeling like a student we know who, when asked how she felt about the writing she does in college, answered, "I do it because I have to, but it's just not me!"

This is not to suggest that *any* language you use among friends has a place in academic writing. Nor is it to suggest that you may fall back on colloquial usage as an excuse for not learning more rigorous forms of expression. After all, learning these more rigorous forms of expression and developing a more intellectual self is a major reason for getting an education. We do, however, wish to suggest that relaxed, colloquial language can often enliven academic writing and even enhance its rigor and precision. Such informal language also helps you connect with readers in a personal as well as an intellectual way. In our view, then, it is a mistake to assume that the academic and the everyday are completely separate languages that can never be used together.

MIX ACADEMIC AND COLLOQUIAL STYLES

Many successful writers blend academic, professional language with popular expressions and sayings. Consider, for instance, the following passage from a scholarly article about the way teachers respond to errors in student writing.

> Marking and judging formal and mechanical errors in student papers is one area in which composition studies seems to have a multiple-personality disorder. On the one hand, our mellow, student-centered, process-based selves tend to condemn marking formal errors at all. Doing it represents the Bad Old Days. Ms. Fidditch and Mr. Flutesnoot with sharpened red pencils, spilling innocent blood across the page. Useless detail work. Inhumane, perfectionist standards, making our students feel stupid, wrong,

trivial, misunderstood. Joseph Williams has pointed out how arbitrary and context-bound our judgments of formal error are. And certainly our noting of errors on student papers gives no one any great joy; as Peter Elbow says, English is most often associated *either* with grammar or with high literature—"two things designed to make folks feel most out of it."

Robert Connors and Andrea Lunsford,
"Frequency of Formal Errors in Current College Writing,
or Ma and Pa Kettle Do Research"

This passage blends writing styles in several ways. First, it places informal, relaxed expressions like "mellow," "the Bad Old Days," and "folks" alongside more formal, academic phrases like "multiple-personality disorder," "student-centered," "process-based," and "arbitrary and context-bound." Even the title of the piece, "Frequency of Formal Errors in Current College Writing, or Ma and Pa Kettle Do Research," blends formal, academic usage on the left side of the comma with a popular-culture reference to the fictional movie characters Ma and Pa Kettle on the right. Second, to give vivid, concrete form to their discussion of grading disciplinarians, Connors and Lunsford conjure up such archetypal, imaginary figures as the stuffy, old-fashioned taskmasters Ms. Fidditch and Mr. Flutesnoot. Through such imaginative uses of language, Connors and Lunsford inject greater force into what might otherwise have been dry, scholarly prose.

Formal/informal mixings like this can be found in countless other texts, though more frequently in the humanities than the sciences, and more frequently still in journalism. Notice how the food industry critic Eric Schlosser describes some changes in the city of Colorado Springs in his best-selling book on fast foods in the United States.

> The loopiness once associated with Los Angeles has come full blown to Colorado Springs—the strange, creative energy that crops up where the future's consciously being made, where people walk the fine line separating a visionary from a total nutcase.
>
> ERIC SCHLOSSER, *Fast Food Nation*

Schlosser could have played it safe and referred not to the "loopiness" but to the "eccentricity" associated with Los Angeles, or to "the fine line separating a visionary from a lunatic" instead of " . . . a total nutcase." His decision, however, to go with the more adventuresome, colorful terms gives a liveliness to his writing that would have been lacking with the more conventional terms.

Another example of writing that blends the informal with the formal comes from an essay on the American novelist Willa Cather by the literary critic Judith Fetterley. Discussing "how very successful Cather has been in controlling how we think about her," Fetterley, building on the work of another scholar, writes as follows.

> As Merrill Skaggs has put it, "She is neurotically controlling and self-conscious about her work, but she knows at all points what she is doing. Above all else, she is self-conscious."
>
> Without question, Cather was a control freak.
>
> JUDITH FETTERLEY, "Willa Cather and the Question of Sympathy: The Unofficial Story"

This passage demonstrates not only that specialized phrases from psychology like "self-conscious" and "neurotically controlling" are compatible with everyday, popular expressions like "control freak," but also that translating the one type of language into the other, the specialized into the everyday, can help drive home a point. By translating Skaggs's polysyllabic description of Cather as "neurotically controlling and self-conscious" into the succinct, if blunt, claim that "Without question, Cather was a control freak," Fetterley suggests that one need not choose between rarified, See p. 264 for an essay that mixes colloquial and academic styles. academic ways of talking and the everyday language of casual conversation. Indeed, her passage offers a simple recipe for blending the high and the low: first make your point in the language of a professional field, and then make it again in everyday language—a great trick, we think, for underscoring a point.

While one effect of blending languages like this is to give your writing more punch, another is to make a political statement— about the way, for example, society unfairly overvalues some dialects and devalues others. For instance, in the titles of two of her books, *Talkin and Testifyin: The Language of Black America* and *Black Talk: Words and Phrases from the Hood to the Amen Corner*, the language scholar Geneva Smitherman mixes African American vernacular phrases with more scholarly language in order to suggest, as she explicitly argues in these books, that black English vernacular is as legitimate a variety of language as "standard" English. Here are three typical passages.

In Black America, the oral tradition has served as a fundamental vehicle for gittin ovuh. That tradition preserves the Afro-American heritage and reflects the collective spirit of the race.

Blacks are quick to ridicule "educated fools," people who done gone to school and read all dem books and still don't know nothin!

. . . it is a socially approved verbal strategy for black rappers to talk about how bad they is.

GENEVA SMITHERMAN, *Talkin and Testifyin:*
The Language of Black America

In these examples, Smitherman blends the standard written English of phrases like "oral tradition" and "fundamental vehicle" with black oral vernacular like "gittin ovuh," "dem books," and "how bad they is." Indeed, she even blends standard English spelling with that of black English variants like "dem" and "ovuh," thus mimicking what some black English vernacular actually sounds like. Although some scholars might object to these unconventional practices, this is precisely Smitherman's point: that our habitual language practices need to be opened up, and that the number of participants in the academic conversation needs to be expanded.

Along similar lines, the writer and activist Gloria Anzaldúa mixes standard English with Tex-Mex, a hybrid blend of English, Castilian Spanish, a North Mexican dialect, and the Indian language Nahuatl, to make a political point about the suppression of the Spanish language in the United States.

> From this racial, ideological, cultural, and biological cross-pollinization, an "alien" consciousness is presently in the making—a new *mestiza* consciousness, *una conciencia de mujer.*
>
> GLORIA ANZALDÚA,
> *Borderlands / La Frontera: The New Mestiza*

Like Smitherman, Anzaldúa gets her point across not only through what she says but through the way she says it, literally showing that the new hybrid, or *mestiza*, consciousness that she describes is, as she puts it, "presently in the making." Ultimately, these passages suggest that blending languages— what Vershawn Ashanti Young calls "code meshing"—can call into question the very idea that the languages are distinct and separate.

WHEN TO MIX STYLES?
CONSIDER YOUR AUDIENCE AND PURPOSE

Because there are so many options in writing, you should never feel limited in your choice of words, as if such choices are set in stone. You can always experiment with your language and improve it. You can always dress it up, dress it down, or some combination of both. In dressing down your language, for example, you can make the claim that somebody "failed to notice" something by saying instead that it "flew under the radar." Or you can state that the person was "unaware" of something by saying that he was "out to lunch." You could even recast the title of this book, *"They Say / I Say,"* as a teenager might say it: "She Goes / I'm Like."

But how do you know when it is better to play things straight and stick to standard English, and when to be more adventuresome and mix things up? When, in other words, should you write "failed to notice" and when is it okay (or more effective) to write "flew under the radar"? Is it *always* appropriate to mix styles? And when you do so, how do you know when enough is enough?

In all situations, think carefully about your audience and purpose. When you write a letter applying for a job, for instance, or submit a grant proposal, where your words will be weighed by an official screening body, using language that's too colloquial or slangy may well jeopardize your chances of success. On such occasions, it is usually best to err on the safe side, conforming as closely as possible to the conventions of standard written English. In other situations for other audiences, however, there is room to be more creative—in this book, for example. Ultimately, your judgments about the appropriate language for the situation should always take into account your likely audience and your purpose in writing.

Although it may have been in the past, academic writing in most disciplines today is no longer the linguistic equivalent of a black-tie affair. To succeed as a writer in college, then, you need not always limit your language to the strictly formal. Although academic writing does rely on complex sentence patterns and on specialized, disciplinary vocabularies, it is surprising how often such writing draws on the languages of the street, popular culture, our ethnic communities, and home. It is by blending these languages that what counts as "standard" English changes over time and the range of possibilities open to academic writers continues to grow.

Exercises

1. Take a paragraph from this book and dress it down, rewriting it in informal colloquial language. Then rewrite the same paragraph again by dressing it up, making it much more formal. Then rewrite the paragraph one more time in a way that blends the two styles. Share your paragraphs with a classmate, and discuss which versions are most effective and why.

2. Find something you've written for a course, and study it to see whether you've used any of your own everyday expressions, any words or structures that are not "academic." If by chance you don't find any, see if there's a place or two where shifting into more casual or unexpected language would help you make a point, get your reader's attention, or just add liveliness to your text. Be sure to keep your audience and purpose in mind, and use language that will be appropriate to both.

TEN

"BUT DON'T GET ME WRONG"

The Art of Metacommentary

—⊡—

WHEN WE TELL PEOPLE that we are writing a chapter on the art of metacommentary, they often give us a puzzled look and tell us that they have no idea what "metacommentary" is. "We know what commentary is," they'll sometimes say, "but what does it mean when it's *meta?*" Our answer is that whether or not they know the term, they practice the art of metacommentary on a daily basis whenever they make a point of explaining something they've said or written: "What I meant to say was _____," "My point was not _____ , but _____," or "You're probably not going to like what I'm about to say, but _____." In such cases, they are not offering new points but telling an audience how to interpret what they have already said or are about to say. In short, then, metacommentary is a way of commenting on your claims and telling others how—and how not—to think about them.

It may help to think of metacommentary as being like the chorus in a Greek play that stands to the side of the drama unfolding on the stage and explains its meaning to the audience—or like a voice-over narrator who comments on and explains the action in a television show or movie. Think of metacommentary as a sort of second text that stands alongside your main text and explains what it means. In the main text you say something; in the metatext you guide your readers in interpreting and processing what you've said.

What we are suggesting, then, is that you think of your text as two texts joined at the hip: a main text in which you make your argument and another in which you "work" your ideas, distinguishing your views from others they may be confused with, anticipating and answering objections, connecting one point to another, explaining why your claim might be controversial, and so forth. The figure below demonstrates what we mean.

THE MAIN TEXT SAYS SOMETHING, THE METATEXT TELLS READERS HOW—AND HOW NOT—TO THINK ABOUT IT.

USE METACOMMENTARY TO CLARIFY
AND ELABORATE

But why do you need metacommentary to tell readers what you mean and guide them through your text? Can't you just clearly say what you mean up front? The answer is that, no matter how clear and precise your writing is, readers can still fail to understand it in any number of ways. Even the best writers can provoke reactions in readers that they didn't intend, and even good readers can get lost in a complicated argument or fail to see how one point connects with another. Readers may also fail to see what follows from your argument, or they may follow your reasoning and examples yet fail to see the larger conclusion you draw from them. They may fail to see your argument's overall significance, or mistake what you are saying for a related argument that they have heard before but that you want to distance yourself from. As a result, no matter how straightforward a writer you are, readers still need you to help them grasp what you really mean. Because the written word is prone to so much mischief and can be interpreted in so many different ways, we need metacommentary to keep misinterpretations and other communication misfires at bay.

Jonathan Safran Foer uses lots of metacommentary; see, e.g., p. 457, ¶45.

Another reason to master the art of metacommentary is that it will help you develop your ideas and generate more text. If you have ever had trouble producing the required number of pages for a writing project, metacommentary can help you add both length and depth to your writing. We've seen many students who try to produce a five-page paper sputter to a halt at two or three pages, complaining they've said everything they can think of about their topic. "I've stated my thesis and presented my reasons and evidence," students have told us. "What else is there to do?" It's almost as if such writers have generated a thesis and don't know what to do with it. When these students learn to use metacommentary, however, they get more out of their ideas and write longer, more substantial texts. In sum, metacommentary can help you extract the full potential from your ideas, drawing out important implications, explaining ideas from different perspectives, and so forth.

So even when you may think you've said everything possible in an argument, try inserting the following types of metacommentary.

▶ In other words, <u>she doesn't realize how right she is</u>.

▶ What _____ really means is _____.

▶ My point is not _____ but _____.

▶ Ultimately, then, my goal is to demonstrate that _____.

Ideally, such metacommentary should help you recognize some implications of your ideas that you didn't initially realize were there.

Let's look at how the cultural critic Neil Postman uses metacommentary in the following passage describing the shift in American culture when it began to move from print and reading to television and movies.

> It is my intention in this book to show that a great . . . shift has taken place in America, with the result that the content of much of our public discourse has become dangerous nonsense. With this in view, my task in the chapters ahead is straightforward. I must, first, demonstrate how, under the governance of the printing press, discourse in America was different from what it is now— generally coherent, serious and rational; and then how, under the

governance of television, it has become shriveled and absurd. *But to avoid the possibility that my analysis will be interpreted as* standard-brand academic whimpering, a kind of elitist complaint against "junk" on television, *I must first explain that* . . . I appreciate junk as much as the next fellow, *and I know full well that* the printing press has generated enough of it to fill the Grand Canyon to overflowing. Television is not old enough to have matched printing's output of junk.

Neil Postman, Amusing Ourselves to Death:
Public Discourse in the Age of Show Business

To see what we mean by metacommentary, look at the phrases above that we have italicized. With these moves, Postman essentially stands apart from his main ideas to help readers follow and understand what he is arguing.

> He previews what he will argue: *It is my intention in this book to show* . . .

> He spells out how he will make his argument: *With this in view, my task in these chapters* . . . *is.* . . . *I must, first, demonstrate* . . . *and then* . . .

> He distinguishes his argument from other arguments it may easily be confused with: *But to avoid the possibility that my analysis will be interpreted as* . . . *I must first explain that* . . .

TITLES AS METACOMMENTARY

Even the title of Postman's book, *Amusing Ourselves to Death: Public Discourse in the Age of Show Business,* functions as a form of metacommentary since, like all titles, it stands apart from the text itself and tells readers the book's main point: that the very pleasure provided by contemporary show business is destructive.

Titles, in fact, are one of the most important forms of metacommentary, functioning rather like carnival barkers telling passersby what they can expect if they go inside. Subtitles, too, function as metacommentary, further explaining or elaborating on the main title. The subtitle of this book, for example, not only explains that it is about "the moves that matter in academic writing," but indicates that "they say / I say" is one of these moves. Thinking of a title as metacommentary can actually help you develop sharper titles, ones that, like Postman's, give readers a hint of what your argument will be. Contrast such titles with unhelpfully open-ended ones like "Shakespeare" or "Steroids" or "English Essay," or essays with no titles at all. Essays with vague titles (or no titles) send the message that the writer has simply not bothered to reflect on what he or she is saying and is uninterested in guiding or orienting readers.

USE OTHER MOVES AS METACOMMENTARY

Many of the other moves covered in this book function as metacommentary: entertaining objections, adding transitions, framing quotations, answering "so what?" and "who cares?" When you entertain objections, you stand outside of your text and imagine what a critic might say; when you add transitions, you essentially explain the relationship between various claims. And when you answer the "so what?" and "who cares?" questions, you look beyond your central argument and explain who should be interested in it and why.

TEMPLATES FOR INTRODUCING METACOMMENTARY

TO WARD OFF POTENTIAL MISUNDERSTANDINGS

The following moves help you differentiate certain views from ones they might be mistaken for.

▸ Essentially, I am arguing not that <u>we should give up the policy</u>, but that we should monitor effects far more closely.

▸ This is not to say _____ , but rather _____ .

▸ X is concerned less with _____ than with _____ .

TO ELABORATE ON A PREVIOUS IDEA

The following moves elaborate on a previous point, saying to readers: "In case you didn't get it the first time, I'll try saying the same thing in a different way."

▸ In other words, _____ .

▸ To put it another way, _____ .

▸ What X is saying here is that _____ .

TO PROVIDE A ROADMAP TO YOUR TEXT

This move orients readers, clarifying where you have been and where you are going—and making it easier for them to process and follow your text.

▸ Chapter 2 explores _____ , while Chapter 3 examines _____ .

▸ Having just argued that _____ , I want now to complicate the point by _____ .

TO MOVE FROM A GENERAL CLAIM TO A SPECIFIC EXAMPLE

These moves help you explain a general point by providing a concrete example that illustrates what you're saying.

▶ For example, _____ .

▶ _____ , for instance, demonstrates _____ .

▶ Consider _____ , for example.

▶ To take a case in point, _____ .

TO INDICATE THAT A CLAIM IS MORE, LESS, OR EQUALLY IMPORTANT

The following templates help you give relative emphasis to the claim that you are introducing, showing whether that claim is of more or less weight than the previous one, or equal to it.

▶ Even more important, _____ .

▶ But above all, _____ .

▶ Incidentally, we will briefly note, _____ .

▶ Just as important, _____ .

▶ Equally, _____ .

▶ Finally, _____ .

TO EXPLAIN A CLAIM WHEN YOU ANTICIPATE OBJECTIONS

Here's a template to help you anticipate and respond to possible objections.

▶ Although some readers may object that _____ , I would answer that _____ .

TO GUIDE READERS TO YOUR MOST GENERAL POINT

These moves show that you are wrapping things up and tying up various subpoints previously made.

Chapter 6 has more templates for anticipating objections.

▸ **In sum, then, _____ .**

▸ **My conclusion, then, is that _____ .**

▸ **In short, _____ .**

In this chapter we have tried to show that the most persuasive writing often doubles back and comments on its own claims in ways that help readers negotiate and process them. Instead of simply piling claim upon claim, effective writers are constantly "stage managing" how their claims will be recieved. It's true of course that to be persuasive a text has to have strong claims to argue in the first place. But even the strongest arguments will flounder unless writers use metacommentary to prevent potential misreadings and make their arguments shine.

Exercises

1. Read an essay or article and annotate it to indicate the different ways the author uses metacommentary. Use the templates on pp. 135–37 as your guide. For example, you may want to circle transitional phrases and write "trans" in the margins, to put brackets around sentences that elaborate on earlier sentences and mark them "elab," or underline sentences in which the author sums up what he or she has been saying, writing "sum" in the margins.

   How does the author use metacommentary? Does the author follow any of the templates provided in this book word for word? Did you find any forms of metacommentary not discussed in this chapter? If so, can you identify them, name them, and perhaps devise templates based on them for use in your own writing? And finally, how do you think the author's use of metacommentary enhances (or harms) his or her writing?

2. Complete each of the following metacommentary templates in any way that makes sense.

- ▶ In making a case for the medical use of marijuana, I am not saying that _____.

- ▶ But my argument will do more than prove that one particular industrial chemical has certain toxic properties. In this article, I will also _____.

- ▶ My point about the national obsessions with sports reinforces the belief held by many _____ that _____.

- ▶ I believe, therefore, that the war is completely unjustified. But let me back up and explain how I arrived at this conclusion: _____. In this way, I came to believe that this war is a big mistake.

ELEVEN

"HE ~~SAYS~~ CONTENDS"

Using the Templates to Revise

—◻—

ONE OF THE MOST IMPORTANT stages of the writing process is revision, when you look at a draft with an eye for how well you've made your argument and what you need to do to make it better. The challenge is to figure out what needs work—and then what exactly you need to do.

Sometimes you'll have specific comments and suggestions from a teacher, noting that you need to state your position more explicitly, that your point is unclear, that you've misunderstood an author you're summarizing, and so forth. But what if you don't have any such guidance, or aren't sure what to do with it? The list of guidelines below offers help and points you back to relevant advice and templates in this book.

Do you present your argument as a response to what others say? Do you make reference to other views besides your own? Do you use voice markers to distinguish clearly for readers between your views and those of others? In order to make your argument as convincing as possible, would it help to add more concessions to opposing views, using "yes but" templates?

Asking yourself these large-scale revision questions will help you see how well you've managed the "they say / I say" framework and this in turn should help you see where further revisions are needed. The checklist below follows the order of chapters in this book.

How Do You Represent What Others Say?

Do you start with what others say? If not, try revising to do so. See pp. 23–26 for templates that can help.

Do you summarize or paraphrase what they've said? If so, have you represented their views accurately—and adequately?

Do you quote others? Do you frame each quotation successfully, integrating it into your text? Does the quotation support your argument? Have you introduced each quotation adequately, naming the person you're quoting (and saying who that person is if your readers won't know)? Do you explain in your own words what the quotation means? Do you then clearly indicate how the quotation bears on your own argument? See pp. 44–46 for tips on creating a "quotation sandwich."

Check the verbs you use to introduce any summaries and quotations: do they express accurately what was said? If you've used common signal phrases such as "X said" or "Y believes," is there a verb that reflects more accurately what was said? See pp. 39–40 for a list of verbs for introducing summaries and quotations.

Have you documented all summaries and quotations, both with parenthetical documentation in your text and a references or works cited list?

Do you remind readers of what others say at various points throughout your text? If not, see pp. 27–28 for help revising in order to do so.

What Do You Say?

Do you agree, disagree, or both with those you're responding to? Have you said so explicitly?

If you disagree, do you give reasons why you disagree? If you agree, what more have you added to the conversation? If you both agree and disagree, do you do so without confusing readers or seeming evasive?

Have you stated your position and the one it responds to as a connected unit?

What reasons and evidence do you offer to support your "I say"? In other words, do your argument and the argument you are responding to—your "I say" and "they say"—address the same topic or issue, or does a switch occur that takes you on a tangent that will confuse readers? One way to ensure that your "I say" and "they say" are aligned rather than seeming like ships passing in the night is to use the same key terms in both. See Chapter 8 for tips on how to do so.

Will readers be able to distinguish what you say from what others say? See Chapter 5 for advice about using voice markers to make that distinction clear, especially at moments when you are moving from your view to someone else's view or back.

Have You Introduced Any Naysayers?

Have you acknowledged likely objections to your argument? If so, have you represented these views fairly—and responded to them persuasively? See Chapter 6 for tips on how to do so.

If not, think about what other perspectives exist on your topic, and incorporate them into your draft.

Have You Used Metacommentary to Clarify What You Do or Don't Mean?

No matter how clearly you've explained your points, it's a good idea to explain what you mean—or *don't* mean—with phrases like "in other words" or "don't get me wrong." See Chapter 10 for examples of how to do so.

Do you have a title? If so, does it tell readers what your main point or issue is, and does it do so in a lively manner? Should you add a subtitle to elaborate on the title?

Have You Tied It All Together?

Can readers follow your argument from one sentence and paragraph to the next and see how each successive point supports your overall argument?

Check your use of transitions, words like "however" and "therefore." Such words make clear how your ideas relate to one another; if you need to add transitions, see pp. 109–10 for a complete list.

Check your use of pointing words. Do you use common pointers like "this" and "that," which help lead readers from one sentence to the next? If so, is it always clear what "this" and "that" refer to, or do you need to add nouns in order to avoid ambiguity? See pp. 112–14 for help working with pointing words.

Have you used what we call "repetition with a difference" to help connect parts of your argument? See pp. 114–18 for examples of how to do so.

Have You Shown Why Your Argument Matters?

Don't assume that readers will see why your argument is important—or why they should care. Be sure that you have told them why. See Chapter 7 if you need help.

A REVISED STUDENT ESSAY

Here is an example of how one student, Antonia Peacocke, used this book to revise an essay. Starting with an article she'd written for her high school newspaper, Peacocke then followed the advice in our book as she turned her article into a college level academic essay. Her original article was a brief account of why she liked *Family Guy*, and her first step in revising was to open with a "they say" and an "I say," previewing her overall argument in brief form at the essay's beginning. While her original version had acknowledged that many find the show "objectionable," she hadn't named these people or indicated why they didn't like the show. In her revised version, after doing further research, Peacocke identified those with whom she disagreed and responded to them at length, as the essay itself illustrates.

In addition, Peacocke strengthened existing transitions, added new ones, and clarified the stakes of her argument, saying more explicitly why readers should care about whether *Family Guy* is good or bad. In making these revisions she gave her own spin to several templates in this book.

We've annotated Peacocke's essay in the margins to point out particular rhetorical moves discussed in our book and the chapters in which those discussions appear. We hope studying her essay and our annotations will suggest how you might craft and revise your own writing.

Antonia Peacocke wrote this essay in the summer between high school and her first year at Harvard. She is now a PhD student in philosophy at the University of California at Berkeley.

Family Guy and Freud: Jokes and Their Relation to the Unconscious

ANTONIA PEACOCKE

WHILE SLOUCHING in front of the television after a long day, you probably don't think a lot about famous psychologists of the twentieth century. Somehow, these figures don't come up often in prime-time—or even daytime—TV programming. Whether you're watching *Living Lohan* or the *NewsHour*, the likelihood is that you are not thinking of Sigmund Freud, even if you've heard of his book *Jokes and Their Relation to the Unconscious*. I say that you should be.

What made me think of Freud in the first place, actually, was *Family Guy*, the cartoon created by Seth MacFarlane. (Seriously—stay with me here.) Any of my friends can tell you that this program holds endless fascination for me; as a matter of fact, my high school rag-sheet "perfect mate" was the baby Stewie Griffin, a character on the show (see Fig. 1). Embarrassingly enough, I have almost reached the point at which I can perform

> Starts with what others are saying (Chapter 1)

> Responds to what they say (Chapter 4)

> Metacomment-ary wards off potential skepticism (Chapter 10)

one-woman versions of several episodes. I know every website that streams the show for free, and I still refuse to return the five *Family Guy* DVDs a friend lent me in 2006. Before I was such a devotee, however, I was adamantly opposed to the program for its particular brand of humor.

It will come as no surprise that I was not alone in this view; many still denounce *Family Guy* as bigoted and crude. *New York Times* journalist Stuart Elliott claimed just this year that "the characters on the Fox television series *Family Guy* . . . purposely offen[d] just about every group of people

Quotes and summarizes what others say (Chapters 2 and 3)

Fig 1. Peter and Stewie Griffin (Everett Collection)

you could name." Likewise Stephen Dubner, co-author of *Freakonomics*, called *Family Guy* "a cartoon comedy that packs more gags per minute about race, sex, incest, bestiality, etc. than any other show [he] can think of." Comparing its level of offense to that of Don Imus's infamous comments about the Rutgers women's basketball team in the same year, comments that threw the popular CBS radio talk-show host off the air, Dubner said he wondered why Imus couldn't get away with as much as *Family Guy* could.

Dubner did not know about all the trouble *Family Guy* has had. In fact, it must be one of the few television shows in history that has been canceled not just once, but twice. After its premiere in April 1999, the show ran until August 2000, but was besieged by so many complaints, some of them from MacFarlane's old high school headmaster, Rev. Richardson W. Schell, that Fox shelved it until July 2001 (Weinraub). Still afraid of causing a commotion, though, Fox had the cartoon censored and irregularly scheduled; as a result, its ratings fell so low that 2002 saw its second cancellation (Weinraub). But then it came back with a vengeance—I'll get into that later.

Family Guy has found trouble more recently, too. In 2007, comedian Carol Burnett sued Fox for 6 million dollars, claiming that the show's parody of the Charwoman, a character that she had created for *The Carol Burnett Show*, not only violated copyright but also besmirched the character's name in revenge for Burnett's refusal to grant permission to use her theme song ("Carol Burnett Sues"). The suit came after MacFarlane had made the Charwoman into a cleaning woman for a pornography store in one episode of *Family Guy*. Burnett lost, but U.S. district judge Dean Pregerson agreed that he could "fully appreciate how distasteful and offensive the segment [was] to Ms. Burnett" (qtd. in Grossberg).

I must admit, I can see how parts of the show might seem offensive if taken at face value. Look, for example, at the mock fifties instructional video that features in the episode "I Am Peter, Hear Me Roar."

> Represents a naysayer's objections fairly (Chapter 6)

[The screen becomes black and white. Vapid music plays in the background. The screen reads "WOMEN IN THE WORKPLACE ca. 1956," *then switches to a shot of an office with various women working on typewriters. A businessman speaks to the camera.]*

BUSINESSMAN: Irrational and emotionally fragile by nature, female coworkers are a peculiar animal. They are very insecure about their appearance. Be sure to tell them how good they look every day, even if they're homely and unkempt. *[He turns to an unattractive female typist.]* You're doing a great job, Muriel, and you're prettier than Mamie van Doren! *[She smiles. He grins at the camera, raising one eyebrow knowingly, and winks.]*

And remember, nothing says "Good job!" like a firm open-palm slap on the behind. [*He walks past a woman bent over a file cabinet and demonstrates enthusiastically. She smiles, looking flattered. He grins at the camera again as the music comes to an end.*]

Laughing at something so blatantly sexist could cause anyone a pang of guilt, and before I thought more about the show this seemed to be a huge problem. I agreed with Dubner, and I failed to see how anyone could laugh at such jokes without feeling at least slightly ashamed.

Agrees, but with a difference (Chapter 4)

Soon, though, I found myself forced to give *Family Guy* a chance. It was simply everywhere: my brother and many of my friends watched it religiously, and its devoted fans relentlessly proselytized for it. In case you have any doubts about its immense popularity, consider these facts. On Facebook, the universal forum for my generation, there are currently 23 separate *Family Guy* fan groups with a combined membership of 1,669 people (compared with only 6 groups protesting against *Family Guy*, with 105 members total). Users of the well-respected Internet Movie Database rate the show 8.8 out of 10. The box-set DVDs were the best-selling television DVDs of 2003 in the United States (Moloney). Among the public and within the industry, the show receives fantastic acclaim; it has won eight awards, including three prime-time Emmys (IMDb). Most importantly, each time it was cancelled fans provided the brute force necessary to get it

Anticipates a naysayer's skepticism (Chapter 6)

back on the air. In 2000, online campaigns did the trick; in 2002, devotees demonstrated outside Fox Studios, refused to watch the Fox network, and boycotted any companies that advertised on it (Moloney). Given the show's high profile, both with my friends and family and in the world at large, it would have been more work for me to avoid the Griffin family than to let myself sink into their animated world.

With more exposure, I found myself crafting a more positive view of *Family Guy*. Those who don't often watch the program, as Dubner admits he doesn't, could easily come to think that the cartoon takes pleasure in controversial humor just for its own sake. But those who pay more attention and think about the creators' intentions can see that *Family Guy* intelligently satirizes some aspects of American culture.

> *Distinguishes between what others say and what she says (Chapter 5)*

Some of this satire is actually quite obvious. Take, for instance, a quip Brian the dog makes about Stewie's literary choices in a fourth-season episode, "PTV." (Never mind that a dog and a baby can both read and hold lengthy conversations.)

> *Mixes academic and colloquial styles (Chapter 9)*

[*The Griffins are in their car. Brian turns to Stewie, who sits reading in his car seat.*]

> *Uses a quotation sandwich to explicate this excerpt (Chapter 3)*

BRIAN: *East of Eden?* So you, you, you pretty much do whatever Oprah tells you to, huh?
STEWIE: You know, this book's been around for fifty years. It's a classic.

BRIAN: But you just got it last week. And there's a giant Oprah sticker on the front.

STEWIE: Oh—oh—oh, is that what that is? Oh, lemme just peel that right off.

BRIAN: So, uh, what are you gonna read after that one?

STEWIE: Well, she hasn't told us yet—damn!

Brian and Stewie demonstrate insightfully and comically how Americans are willing to follow the instructions of a celebrity blindly—and less willing to admit that they are doing so.

The more off-color jokes, though, those that give *Family Guy* a bad name, attract a different kind of viewer. Such viewers are not "rats in a behaviorist's maze," as *Slate* writer Dana Stevens labels modern American television consumers in her article "Thinking Outside the Idiot Box." They are conscious and critical viewers, akin to the "screenagers" identified by Douglas Rushkoff in an essay entitled "Bart Simpson: Prince of Irreverence" (294). They are not—and this I cannot stress enough, self-serving as it may seem—immoral or easily manipulated people.

> Distinguishes what others say from what she says (Chapter 5)

Rushkoff's piece analyzes the humor of *The Simpsons*, a show criticized for many of the same reasons as *Family Guy*. "The people I call 'screenagers,'" Rushkoff explains, ". . . speak the media language better than their parents do and they see through clumsy attempts to program them into submission" (294). He claims that gaming technology has made my generation realize that television is programmed for us with certain intentions; since we can control characters in the virtual world, we are more aware that characters on TV are similarly controlled. "Sure, [these 'screenagers'] might sit back and watch a program now and again," Rushkoff explains, "but they do so voluntarily, and with full knowledge of their complicity. It is not an involuntary surrender" (294). In his opinion, our critical eyes and our unwillingness to be programmed by the programmers make for an entirely new relationship with the shows we watch. Thus we enjoy *The Simpsons'* parodies of mass media culture since we are skeptical of it ourselves.

Rushkoff's argument about *The Simpsons* actually applies to *Family Guy* as well, except in one dimension: Rushkoff writes that *The Simpsons'* creators do "not comment on social issues as much as they [do on] the media imagery around a particular social issue" (296). MacFarlane and company seem to do the reverse. Trusting in their viewers' ability to analyze what they are watching, the creators of *Family Guy* point out the weaknesses and defects of US society in a mocking and sometimes intolerant way.

Taken in this light, the "instructional video" quoted above becomes not only funny but also insightful. In its satire, viewers can recognize the sickly sweet and falsely sensitive sexism of the 1950s in observing just how conveniently

> Uses transitions to connect the parts (Chapter 8)

self-serving the speaker of the video appears. The message of the clip denounces and ridicules sexism rather than condoning it. It is an excerpt that perfectly exemplifies the bold-faced candor of the show, from which it derives a lot of its appeal.

Making such comically outrageous remarks on the air also serves to expose certain prejudiced attitudes as outrageous themselves. Taking these comments at face value would be as foolish as taking Jonathan Swift's "Modest Proposal" seriously. Furthermore, while they put bigoted words into the mouths of their characters, the show's writers cannot be accused of portraying these characters positively. Peter Griffin, the "family guy" of the show's title, probably says and does the most offensive things of all—but as a lazy, overweight, and insensitive failure of a man, he is hardly presented as someone to admire. Nobody in his or her right mind would observe Peter's behavior and deem it worth emulation.

Family Guy has its own responses to accusations of crudity. In the episode "PTV," Peter sets up his own television station broadcasting from home and the Griffin family finds itself confronting the Federal Communications Commission directly (see Fig. 2 for a picture of the whole family). The episode makes many tongue-in-cheek jabs at the FCC, some of which are sung in a rousing musical number, but also sneaks in some of the creator's own

Fig 2. The Griffin Family Watches TV. (Everett Collection)

opinions. The plot comes to a climax when the FCC
begins to censor "real life" in the town of Quahog; officials
place black censor bars in front of newly showered Griffins
and blow foghorns whenever characters curse. MacFarlane
makes an important point: that no amount of television
censorship will ever change the harsh nature of reality—
and to censor reality is mere folly. Likewise, he puts explicit
arguments about censorship into lines spoken by his

characters, as when Brian says that "responsibility lies with the parents [and] there are plenty of things that are much worse for children than television."

It must be said too that not all of *Family Guy's* humor could be construed as offensive. Some of its jokes are more tame and insightful, the kind you might expect from *The New Yorker*. The following light commentary on the usefulness of high school algebra from "When You Wish Upon a Weinstein" could hardly be accused of upsetting anyone— except, perhaps, a few high school math teachers.

[*Shot of Peter on the couch and his son Chris lying at his feet and doing homework.*]

CHRIS: Dad, can you help me with my math? [My teacher] says if I don't learn it, I won't be able to function in the real world.

[*Shot of Chris standing holding a map in a run-down gas station next to an attendant in overalls and a trucker cap reading "PUMP THIS." The attendant speaks with a Southern accent and gestures casually to show the different road configurations.*]

ATTENDANT: Okay, now what you gotta do is go down the road past the old Johnson place, and you're gonna find two roads, one parallel and one perpendicular. Now keep going until you come to a highway that bisects it at a 45-degree angle. [*Crosses his arms.*] Solve for x.

[*Shot of Chris lying on the ground next to the attendant in fetal position, sucking his thumb. His map lies abandoned near him.*]

In fact, *Family Guy* does not aim to hurt, and its creators take certain measures to keep it from hitting too hard. In an interview on *Access Hollywood*, Seth MacFarlane plainly states that there are certain jokes too upsetting to certain groups to go on the air. Similarly, to ensure that the easily misunderstood show doesn't fall into the hands of those too young to understand it, Fox will not license *Family Guy* rights to any products intended for children under the age of fourteen (Elliott).

Uses transitions to connect the parts (Chapter 8)

However, this is not to say that MacFarlane's mission is corrective or noble. It is worth remembering that he wants only to amuse, a goal for which he was criticized by several of his professors at the Rhode Island School of Design (Weinraub). For this reason, his humor can be dangerous. On the one hand, I don't agree with George Will's reductive and generalized statement in his article "Reality Television: Oxymoron" that "entertainment seeking a mass audience is ratcheting up the violence, sexuality, and degradation, becoming increasingly coarse and trying to be . . . shocking in an unshockable society." I believe *Family Guy*

Agrees and disagrees; makes concessions while standing her ground (Chapters 4 and 6) has its intelligent points, and some of its seemingly "coarse" scenes often have hidden merit. I must concede, though, that a few of the show's scenes seem to be doing just what Will claims; sometimes the creators do seem to cross—or, perhaps, eagerly race past—the line of indecency. In one such crude scene, an elderly dog slowly races a paraplegic and Peter, who has just been hit by a car, to get to a severed finger belonging to Peter himself ("Whistle While Your Wife Works"). Nor do I find it particularly funny when Stewie physically abuses Brian in a bloody fight over gambling money ("Patriot Games").

Thus, while *Family Guy* can provide a sort of relief by breaking down taboos, we must still wonder whether or not these taboos exist for a reason. An excess of offensive jokes, especially those that are often misconstrued, can seem to grant tacit permission to think offensively if it's done for comedy— and laughing at others' expense can be cruel, no matter how funny. Jokes all have their origins, and the funniest ones are those that hit home the hardest; if we listen to Freud, these are the ones that let our animalistic and aggressive impulses surface from the unconscious. The distinction between a shamelessly candid but insightful joke and a merely shameless joke is a slight but important one. While I love *Family Guy* as much as any fan, it's important not to lose sight of what's truly unfunny in real life—even as we appreciate what is hilarious in fiction.

> Concludes by showing who cares and why her argument matters (Chapter 7)

Works Cited

"Carole Burnett Sues over *Family Guy* Parody." *CBC*, 16 Mar. 2007, www.cbc.ca/news/arts/carol-burnett-sues-over-family-guy-parody-1.693570. Accessed 14 July 2008.

Dubner, Stephen J. "Why Is *Family Guy* Okay When Imus Wasn't?" *Freakonomics Blog*, 3 Dec. 2007, freakonomics.com. Accessed 14 July 2008.

Elliott, Stuart. "Crude? So What? These Characters Still Find Work in Ads." *New York Times*, 19 June 2008, nyti.ms/2bZWSAs. Accessed 14 July 2008.

Facebook search for *Family Guy* under "Groups." www.facebook.com. Accessed 14 July 2008.

Freud, Sigmund. *Jokes and Their Relation to the Unconscious.* 1905. Translated by James Strachey, W. W. Norton, 1989.

Grossberg, Josh. "Carole Burnett Can't Stop Stewie." *E! News*, Entertainment Television, 5 June 2007, www.eonline.com. Accessed 14 July 2008.

"I Am Peter, Hear Me Roar." *Family Guy*, season 2, episode 8, 20th Century Fox, 28 Mar. 2000. *Hulu*, www.hulu.com/watch/171050. Accessed 14 July 2008.

"Family Guy." *IMDb*, IMDb, 1999–2016, www.imdb.com/title/tt0182576. Accessed 14 July 2008.

MacFarlane, Seth. Interview. *Access Hollywood*, NBC Universal, 8 May 2007. *YouTube*, www.youtube.com/watch?v=rKURWCicyQU. Accessed 14 July 2008.

Moloney, Ben Adam. "*Family Guy*." *BBC.com*, 30 Sept. 2004, www.bbc.com. Accessed 14 July 2008.

"Patriot Games." *Family Guy*, season 4, episode 20,
      20th Century Fox, 29 Jan. 2006. *Hulu*, www.hulu.com/
      watch/171089. Accessed 22 July 2008.

"PVT." *Family Guy*, season 4, episode 14, 20th Century Fox,
      6 Nov. 2005. *Hulu*, www.hulu.com/watch/171083.
      Accessed 14 July 2008.

Rushkoff, Douglas. "Bart Simpson: Prince of Irreverence."
      *Leaving Springfield: The Simpsons and the Possibility of
      Oppositional Culture*, edited by John Alberti, Wayne
      State UP, 2004, pp. 292–301.

Stevens, Dana. "Thinking Outside the Idiot Box." *Slate*,
      25 Mar. 2005, www.slate.com/articles/news_and_
      politics/surfergirl/2005/04/thinkingoutside_the_
      idiot_box.html. Accessed 14 July 2008.

Weinraub, Bernard. "The Young Guy of 'Family Guy': A
      30-Year-Old's Cartoon Hit Makes an Unexpected
      Comeback." *New York Times*, 7 July 2004, nyti.ms/
      1IEBiUA. Accessed 14 July 2008.

"When You Wish Upon a Weinstein." *Family Guy*, season 3,
      episode 22, 20th Century Fox, 9 Nov. 2003. *Hulu*,
      www.hulu.com/watch/171136. Accessed 22 July 2008.

"Whistle While Your Wife Works." *Family Guy*, season 5,
      episode 5, 20th Century Fox, 12 Nov. 2006. *Hulu*,
      www.hulu.com/watch/171160. Accessed 22 July 2008.

Will, George F. "Reality Television: Oxymoron." *Washington
      Post*, 21 June 2001, p. A25.

4

---◻---

IN SPECIFIC
ACADEMIC CONTEXTS

TWELVE

"I TAKE YOUR POINT"

Entering Class Discussions

HAVE YOU EVER been in a class discussion that feels less like a genuine meeting of the minds than like a series of discrete, disconnected monologues? You make a comment, say, that seems provocative to you, but the classmate who speaks after you makes no reference to what you said, instead going off in an entirely different direction. Then, the classmate who speaks next makes no reference either to you or to anyone else, making it seem as if everyone in the conversation is more interested in their own ideas than in actually conversing with anyone else.

We like to think that the principles this book advances can help improve class discussions, which increasingly include various forms of online communication. Particularly important for class discussion is the point that our own ideas become more cogent and powerful the more responsive we are to others, and the more we frame our claims not in isolation but as responses to what others before us have said. Ultimately, then, a good face-to-face classroom discussion (or online communication) doesn't just happen spontaneously. It requires the same sorts of disciplined moves and practices used in many writing situations, particularly that of identifying to what and to whom you are responding.

FRAME YOUR COMMENTS AS A RESPONSE
TO SOMETHING THAT HAS ALREADY BEEN SAID

The single most important thing you need to do when joining a class discussion is to link what you are about to say to something that has already been said.

- ▸ I really liked Aaron's point about <u>the two sides being closer than they seem</u>. I'd add that <u>both seem rather moderate</u>.

- ▸ I take your point, Nadia, that _____. Still . . .

- ▸ Though Sheila and Ryan seem to be at odds about _____, they may actually not be all that far apart.

In framing your comments this way, it is usually best to name both the person and the idea you're responding to. If you name the person alone ("I agree with Aaron because _____"), it may not be clear to listeners what part of what Aaron said you are referring to. Conversely, if you only summarize what Aaron said without naming him, you'll probably leave your classmates wondering whose comments you're referring to.

But won't you sound stilted and deeply redundant in class if you try to restate the point your classmate just made? After all, in the case of the first template above, the entire class will have just heard Aaron's point about the two sides being closer than they seem. Why then would you need to restate it?

We agree that in oral situations, it does often sound artificial to restate what others just said precisely because they just said it. It would be awkward if, on being asked to pass the salt at lunch, one were to reply: "If I understand you correctly, you have asked me to pass the salt. Yes, I can, and here it is." But in oral discussions about complicated issues that are open to multiple interpretations, we usually do need to resummarize what others have said to make sure that everyone is on the same page. Since Aaron may have made several points when he spoke and may have been followed by other commentators, the class will probably need you to summarize which point of his you are referring to. And even if Aaron made only one point, restating that point is helpful, not only to remind the group what his point was (since some may have missed or forgotten it) but also to make sure that he, you, and others have interpreted his point in the same way.

TO CHANGE THE SUBJECT, INDICATE EXPLICITLY THAT YOU ARE DOING SO

It is fine to try to change the conversation's direction. There's just one catch: you need to make clear to listeners that this is what you are doing. For example:

▸ **So far we have been talking about <u>the characters in the film</u>. But isn't the real issue here <u>the cinematography</u>?**

▸ **I'd like to change the subject to one that hasn't yet been addressed.**

You can try to change the subject without indicating that you are doing so. But you risk that your comment will come across as irrelevant rather than as a thoughtful contribution that moves the conversation forward.

BE EVEN MORE EXPLICIT
THAN YOU WOULD BE IN WRITING

Because listeners in an oral discussion can't go back and reread what you just said, they are more easily overloaded than are readers of a print text. For this reason, in a class discussion you will do well to take some extra steps to help listeners follow your train of thought. (1) When you make a comment, limit yourself to one point only though you can elaborate on this point, fleshing it out with examples and evidence. If you feel you must make two points, either unite them under one larger umbrella point, or make one point first and save the other for later. Trying to bundle two or more claims into one comment can result in neither getting the attention it deserves. (2) Use metacommentary to highlight your key point so that listeners can readily grasp it.

▶ In other words, what I'm trying to get at here is _____ .

▶ My point is this: _____ .

▶ My point, though, is not _____ , but _____ .

▶ This distinction is important because _____ .

THIRTEEN

"IMHO"

Is Digital Communication Good or Bad—or Both?

YOU MAY WONDER what our advice in this book about entering conversations and debates has to do with one of the major innovations in our society, the online technologies through which we now do much of our reading and writing. You may have heard parents and journalists complain that smartphones, iPads, and other electronic devices that seem almost wired into our brains are destroying our ability to think, communicate, and interact with others. At the same time, you've also probably heard counterarguments to the effect that, on the contrary, these digital technologies actually stretch the mind, bring people together, and even make us better writers.

These arguments are part of a set of interrelated debates that are taking place today, sometimes in the blogosphere itself, among journalists, academic researchers, and other commentators. In some of these debates, those who extol their virtues argue that today's new online technologies make us smarter by exposing us to a wide range of perspectives and giving us instant access to massive stores of new information. Whereas once we would have had to spend hours burrowing through dusty library shelves to find the information we need, today we can access the same information with a click of a mouse in the comfort of our homes. Thanks to the internet, our potential knowledge is now thousands of times greater than ever before. How could such a development not be a huge plus for any writer?

The critics, however, retort that, far from making us smarter, online technologies are actually making us dumber, even in our capacity as writers. According to these critics, many online researchers end their investigations at the first entry that comes up in a Google search (often in Wikipedia), and the constraints of email, text messaging, and tweeting force us to communicate in reductive sound bites and inane abbreviations (OMG! LOL! IMHO!). The critics also charge that the very volume of new information that the web makes so easily available overwhelms us and prevents us from thinking clearly. So much comes at us so fast from electronic sources that we can no longer think straight or organize our thoughts into clear writing. The greater the mountain of information we have at our fingertips, say the critics, the less chance there is that we will find the fraction of it that is most valuable and useful to focus on and respond to. As a result, according to one critic, researcher Clifford Nass, the multitasking encouraged by the web and other digital tech-nologies is making student writers less able to sustain a "big idea" in an essay and more prone to write in "little bursts and snippets."

Yet many challenge this pessimistic view. Rhetoric and composition professor Andrea Lunsford rejects the notion that "Google is making us stupid," that "Facebook is frying our brains," and that the web is depriving students of the ability to express ideas (qtd. in Haven). According to Lunsford, reporting on a five-year research project, the Stanford Study of Writing, student writers today are remarkably "adept at crafting messages that will reach their intended audience *because* of their constant use of social media" (Lunsford). That is, today's students are proficient "at what rhetoricians call *kairos*—assessing their audience and adapting their tone and technique to best get their point across" (Thompson).

There is also disagreement over whether online technologies create or undermine genuine conversation and community. On the one hand, some praise the web for its ability to bring people from distant places together who otherwise would remain strangers, enabling them to interact more easily with others through such mediums as email, blogs, videochat, and social networking sites. Those who make this argument might claim that our advice in this book to present your ideas as a response to the ideas of others lends itself well to online communication. After all, the internet allows us to post something and then get quick, even instantaneous responses. It also allows us more easily to access multiple perspectives on any topic and then directly insert the voices of others into our text in links that readers can click on.

Critics, on the other hand, question the quality of the conversations that take place online, arguing that these conversations are rarely genuine meetings of minds and noting that online writers often speak past rather than to or with one another. Because online writers can hit "send" before reflecting, as writers more likely would using slower and more deliberate print media, these critics charge that true debate in which the various parties really listen to one another is exceedingly rare on the web. In other words, communicating online tends to undermine true conversation because writers can too easily dismiss or ignore other points of view, and thus are more likely to engage in egotistical monologues in which they use what others say as a pretext for expounding their own already established opinions.

So go some of the arguments pro and con about the impact of online technologies on our thinking and our communicative habits, including our writing. Though we agree that the internet has given us access to previously unimaginable stores of information and greatly expanded our range of communication—and that it potentially broadens our perspectives—we think the critics have a point in noting that many conversations on the web are not exchanges so much as monologues in which writers pass one another without intersecting. We ourselves have been dismayed when our own online articles have drawn comments that begin, "I haven't read Graff and Birkenstein's article, but in my opinion. . . ." In our view, the best remedy for such failures of communication is to improve the listening and summarizing skills we emphasize in this book, whether these skills are practiced online, offline, or even on a stone tablet.

As for how these digital technologies have influenced student writing, our own view, based on the writing we have seen in our combined seventy years of teaching, is that that this influence is neither disastrous, as the critics fear, nor wonderfully revolutionary, as the proponents claim. Contrary to Nass, student writers found it challenging to sustain a "big idea" long before the advent of the worldwide web, and, contrary to Lunsford, we see no evidence that tweeting and posting have made writers more adept at reaching audiences. As we see it, online technologies only recycle any difficulties writers have reaching audiences; if a writer has trouble reaching audiences in one medium, he or she will have it in another. A student of ours, for example, writing to an audience of his classmates on a course listserv, began a post in the following way:

"Going off what Meg said, I would argue..."

His audience was mystified, since nobody, including Meg herself, could remember what she had said. As this incident illustrates, the immediacy of online writing—not just in course listservs, but in emails, social media, and so forth—makes it appear so much like oral communication that we are seduced into forgetting that it is still a form of writing and therefore very often requires the mastery of formal conventions, in this case that of summarizing what has previously been said. It is hard to imagine any writer, as we have already suggested, who does not struggle with the rhetorical moves of argument, from summarizing, explaining, and quoting what others say to responding to what they say, and the myriad other competencies covered in this book.

Our purpose in this brief chapter, however, is not to try to settle these debates, but to invite *you* to think about how digital technologies affect your work as a reader and writer. Do these technologies make it easier to join conversations? Do they improve or degrade your thinking and writing? What is your opinion and why? To help you answer these questions, we conclude, then, with a couple of exercises that invite you to pick up where we have left off—and, as Kenneth Burke said, to put in your own oar.

Works Cited

Haven, Cynthia. "The New Literacy: Stanford Study Finds Richness and Complexity in Students' Writing." *Stanford Report*, Stanford University, 12 Oct. 2009, news.stanford.edu/pr/2009/pr-lunsford-writing-101209.html. Accessed 14 Nov. 2013.

Lunsford, Andrea. "Everyone's an Author." W. W. Norton Sales Conference, 5 Aug. 2012, Park City.

Nass, Clifford. Interview. *Frontline*, WBGH, 1 Dec. 2009. *PBS*, www.pbs.org/wgbh/pages/frontline/digitalnation/interviews/nass.html. Accessed 14 Nov. 2013.

Thompson, Clive. "Clive Thompson on the New Literacy." *Wired*, 24 Aug. 2009, www.wired.com/2009/08/st-thompson-7. Accessed 14 Nov. 2013.

Exercises

1. Have we formulated the debatable issues above in a useful way? Have we left out anything important? Write an essay in which you summarize some of our commentary as your "they say" and offer your own response, whether to disagree, agree with a difference, or reframe the issues in some way.

2. As a test case for thinking about the questions raised in this chapter, go to the blog that accompanies this book, **theysayiblog.com**. Examine some of the exchanges that appear there and evaluate the quality of the responses. For example, how well do the participants in these exchanges summarize one another's claims before making their own responses? How would you characterize any discussion? Is there a true meeting of the minds or are writers sometimes caricatured or treated as straw men? How do these online discussions compare with the face-to-face discussions you have in class? What advantages does each offer? Go to other blogs on topics that interest you and ask these same questions.

FOURTEEN

"WHAT'S MOTIVATING THIS WRITER?"

Reading for the Conversation

—⌐◻⌐—

"WHAT IS THE AUTHOR'S ARGUMENT? What is he or she trying to say?" For many years, these were the first questions we would ask our classes in a discussion of an assigned reading. The discussion that resulted was often halting, as our students struggled to get a handle on the argument, but eventually, after some awkward silences, the class would come up with something we could all agree was an accurate summary of the author's main thesis. Even after we'd gotten over that hurdle, however, the discussion would often still seem forced, and would limp along as we all struggled with the question that naturally arose next: Now that we had determined what the author was saying, what did we ourselves have to say?

For a long time we didn't worry much about these halting discussions, justifying them to ourselves as the predictable result of assigning difficult, challenging readings. Several years ago, however, as we started writing this book and began thinking about writing as the art of entering conversations, we latched onto the idea of leading with some different questions: "What other argument(s) is the writer responding to?" "Is the writer disagreeing or agreeing with something, and if so what?" "What is motivating the writer's argument?" "Are there other ideas that you have encountered in this class or elsewhere that might be pertinent?" The results were often striking. The discussions that followed tended to be far livelier and to draw in a greater number of students. We were still asking students to look for the main argument, but we were now asking them to see that argument as a response to some other argument that provoked it, gave it a reason for being, and helped all of us see why we should care about it.

What had happened, we realized, was that by changing the opening question, we changed the way our students approached reading, and perhaps the way they thought about academic work in general. Instead of thinking of the argument of a text as an isolated entity, they now thought of that argument as one that responded to and provoked other arguments. Since they were now dealing not with *one* argument but at least *two* (the author's argument and the one[s] he or she was responding to), they now had alternative ways of seeing the topic at hand. This meant that, instead of just trying to understand the view presented by the author, they were more able to question that view intelligently and engage in the type of discussion and debate that is the hallmark of a college education. In our discussions, animated debates often arose between students who found the author's argument convincing and others who were more convinced by the view it was challenging. In the best of these debates, the binary positions would be questioned by other students, who suggested each was too simple, that both might be right or that a third alternative was possible. Still other students might object that the discussion thus far had missed the author's real point and suggest that we all go back to the text and pay closer attention to what it actually said.

We eventually realized that the move from reading for the author's argument in isolation to reading for how the author's argument is in conversation with the arguments of others helps readers become active, critical readers rather than passive recipients of knowledge. On some level, reading for the conversation is more rigorous and demanding than reading for what one author says. It asks that you determine not only what the author thinks, but how what the author thinks fits with what others think, and ultimately with what you yourself think. Yet on another level, reading this way is a lot simpler and more familiar than reading for the thesis alone, since it returns writing to the familiar, everyday act of communicating with other people about real issues.

DECIPHERING THE CONVERSATION

We suggest, then, that when assigned a reading, you imagine the author not as sitting alone in an empty room hunched over a desk or staring at a screen, but as sitting in a crowded coffee shop talking to others who are making claims that he or she is engaging with. In other words, imagine the author as participating in an ongoing, multisided conversation in which everyone is trying to persuade others to agree or at least to take his or her position seriously.

The trick in reading for the conversation is to figure out *what views the author is responding to* and *what the author's own argument is*—or, to put it in the terms used in this book, to determine the "they say" and how the author responds to it.

One of the challenges in reading for the "they say" and "I say" can be figuring out which is which, since it may not be obvious when writers are summarizing others and when they are speaking for themselves. Readers need to be alert for any changes in voice that a writer might make, since instead of using explicit road-mapping phrases like "although many believe," authors may simply summarize the view that they want to engage with and indicate only subtly that it is not their own.

Consider again the opening to the selection by David Zinczenko on p. 462.

> If ever there were a newspaper headline custom made for Jay Leno's monologue, this was it. Kids taking on McDonald's this week, suing the company for making them fat. Isn't that like middle-aged men suing Porsche for making them get speeding tickets? Whatever happened to personal responsibility?
>
> I tend to sympathize with these portly fast-food patrons, though. Maybe that's because I used to be one of them.
>
> DAVID ZINCZENKO, "Don't Blame the Eater"

Whenever we teach this passage, some students inevitably assume that Zinczenko must be espousing the view expressed in his first paragraph: that suing McDonald's is ridiculous. When their reading is challenged by their classmates, these students point to the page and reply, "Look. It's right here on the page. This is what Zinczenko wrote. These are his exact words." The assumption these students are making is that if something appears on the page, the author must endorse it. In fact, however, we ventriloquize views that we don't believe in, and may in fact passionately disagree with, all the time. The central clues that Zinczenko disagrees with the view expressed in his opening

See Chapter 6 for more discussion of naysayers.

paragraph come in the second paragraph, when he finally offers a first-person declaration and uses a contrastive transition, "though," thereby resolving any questions about where he stands.

WHEN THE "THEY SAY" IS UNSTATED

Another challenge can be identifying the "they say" when it is not explicitly identified. Whereas Zinczenko offers an up-front summary of the view he is responding to, other writers assume that their readers are so familiar with these views that they need not name or summarize them. In such cases, you the reader have to reconstruct the unstated "they say" that is motivating the text through a process of inference.

See, for instance, if you can reconstruct the position that Tamara Draut is challenging in the opening paragraph of her essay "The Growing College Gap."

> "The first in her family to graduate from college." How many times have we heard that phrase, or one like it, used to describe a successful American with a modest background? In today's United States, a four-year degree has become the all-but-official ticket to middle-class security. But if your parents don't have much money or higher education in their own right, the road to college—and beyond—looks increasingly treacherous. Despite a sharp increase in the proportion of high school graduates going on to some form of postsecondary education, socio-economic status continues to exert a powerful influence on college admission and completion; in fact, gaps in enrollment by class and race, after declining in the 1960s and 1970s, are once again as wide as they were thirty years ago, and getting wider, even as college has become far more crucial to lifetime fortunes.
>
> TAMARA DRAUT, "The Growing College Gap"

You might think that the "they say" here is embedded in the third sentence: They say (or we all think) that a four-year degree is "the all-but-official ticket to middle-class security," and you might assume that Draut will go on to disagree.

If you read the passage this way, however, you would be mistaken. Draut is not questioning whether a college degree has become "the ticket to middle-class security," but whether most Americans can obtain that ticket, whether college is within the financial reach of most American families. You may have been thrown off by the "but" following the statement that college has become a prerequisite for middle-class security. However, unlike the "though" in Zinczenko's opening, this "but" does not signal that Draut will be disagreeing with the view she has just summarized, a view that in fact she takes as a given. What Draut disagrees with is that this ticket to middle-class security is still readily available to the middle and working classes.

Were one to imagine Draut in a room talking with others with strong views on this topic, one would need to picture her challenging not those who think college is a ticket to financial security (something she agrees with and takes for granted), but those who think the doors of college are open to anyone willing to put forth the effort to walk through them. The view that Draut is challenging, then, is not summarized in her opening. Instead, she assumes that readers are already so familiar with this view that it need not be stated.

Draut's example suggests that in texts where the central "they say" is not immediately identified, you have to construct it yourself based on the clues the text provides. You have to start by locating the writer's thesis and then imagine some of the arguments that might be made against it. What would it look like to disagree with this view? In Draut's case, it is relatively easy to construct a counterargument: it is the familiar faith in the

American Dream of equal opportunity when it comes to access to college. Figuring out the counterargument not only reveals what motivated Draut as a writer but helps you respond to her essay as an active, critical reader. Constructing this counter-argument can also help you recognize how Draut challenges your own views, questioning opinions that you previously took for granted.

WHEN THE "THEY SAY" IS ABOUT SOMETHING "NOBODY HAS TALKED ABOUT"

Another challenge in reading for the conversation is that writers sometimes build their arguments by responding to a *lack* of discussion. These writers build their case not by playing off views that can be identified (like faith in the American Dream or the idea that we are responsible for our body weight), but by pointing to something others have overlooked. As the writing theorists John M. Swales and Christine B. Feak point out, one effective way to "create a research space" and "establish a niche" in the academic world is "by indicating a gap in . . . previous research." Much research in the sciences and humanities takes this "Nobody has noticed X" form.

In such cases, the writer may be responding to scientists, for example, who have overlooked an obscure plant that offers insights into global warming, or to literary critics who have been so busy focusing on the lead character in a play that they have overlooked something important about the minor characters.

READING PARTICULARLY CHALLENGING TEXTS

Sometimes it is difficult to figure out the views that writers are responding to not because these writers do not identify those views but because their language and the concepts they are dealing with are particularly challenging. Consider, for instance, the first two sentences of *Gender Trouble: Feminism and the Subversion of Identity*, a book by the feminist philosopher and literary theorist Judith Butler, thought by many to be a particularly difficult academic writer.

> Contemporary feminist debates over the meaning of gender lead time and again to a certain sense of trouble, as if the indeterminacy of gender might eventually culminate in the failure of feminism. Perhaps trouble need not carry such a negative valence.
>
> JUDITH BUTLER, *Gender Trouble:*
> *Feminism and the Subversion of Identity*

There are many reasons readers may stumble over this relatively short passage, not the least of which is that Butler does not explicitly indicate where her own view begins and the view she is responding to ends. Unlike Zinczenko, Butler does not use the first-person "I" or a phrase such as "in my own view" to show that the position in the second sentence is her own. Nor does Butler offer a clear transition such as "but" or "however" at the start of the second sentence to indicate, as Zinczenko does with "though," that in the second sentence she is questioning the argument she has summarized in the first. And finally, like many academic writers, Butler uses abstract, unfamiliar words that many readers may need to look up, like "gender" (sexual identity, male or female), "indeterminacy" (the quality of being impossible to define or pin down), "culminate" (finally result in), and "negative valence" (a term borrowed from chemistry, roughly denoting "negative significance" or "meaning"). For all these reasons, we can imagine many readers feeling intimidated before they reach the third sentence of Butler's book.

But readers who break down this passage into its essential parts will find that it is actually a lucid piece of writing that conforms to the classic "they say / I say" pattern. Though it can be difficult to spot the clashing arguments in the two sentences, close analysis reveals that the first sentence offers a way of looking at a certain type of "trouble" in the realm of feminist politics that is being challenged in the second.

To understand difficult passages of this kind, you need to translate them into your own words—to build a bridge, in effect, between the passage's unfamiliar terms and ones more familiar to you. Building such a bridge should help you connect what you already know to what the author is saying—and will then help you move from reading to writing, providing you with some of the language you will need to summarize the text. One major challenge in translating the author's words into your own, however, is to stay true to what the author is actually saying, avoiding what we call "the closest cliché syndrome," in which one mistakes a commonplace idea for an author's more complex one (mistaking Butler's critique of the concept of "woman," for instance, for the common idea that women must have equal rights). The work of complex writers like Butler, who frequently challenge conventional thinking, cannot always be collapsed into the types of ideas most of us are already familiar with. Therefore, when you translate, do not try to fit the ideas of such writers into your preexisting beliefs, but instead allow your own views to be challenged. In building a bridge to the writers you read, it is often necessary to meet those writers more than halfway.

For more on the closest cliché syndrome, see Chapter 2.

So what, then, does Butler's opening say? Translating Butler's words into terms that are easier to understand, we can see that the first sentence says that for many feminists today, "the indeterminacy of gender"—the inability to define the essence of sexual identity—spells the end of feminism; that for many feminists the inability to define "gender," presumably the building block of the feminist movement, means serious "trouble" for feminist politics. In contrast, the second sentence suggests that this same "trouble" need not be thought of in such "negative" terms, that the inability to define femininity, or "gender trouble" as Butler calls it in her book's title, may not be such a bad thing—and, as she goes on to argue in the pages that follow, may even be something that feminist activists can profit from. In other words, Butler suggests, highlighting uncertainties about masculinity and femininity can be a powerful feminist tool.

Pulling all these inferences together, then, the opening sentences can be translated as follows: "While many contemporary feminists believe that uncertainty about what it means to be a woman will undermine feminist politics, I, Judith Butler, believe that this uncertainty can actually help strengthen feminist politics." Translating Butler's point into our own book's basic move: "They say that if we cannot define 'woman,' feminism is in big trouble. But I say that this type of trouble is precisely what feminism needs." Despite its difficulty, then, we hope you agree that this initially intimidating passage does make sense if you stay with it.

We hope it is clear that critical reading is a two-way street. It is just as much about being open to the way that writers can challenge you, maybe even transform you, as it is about questioning those writers. And if you translate a writer's argument into your own words as you read, you should allow the text to take you outside the ideas that you already hold and to introduce you to new terms and concepts. Even if you end up disagreeing with an author, you first have to show that you have really listened to what he or she is saying, have fully grasped his or her arguments, and can accurately summarize those arguments. Without such deep, attentive listening, any critique you make will be superficial and decidedly *uncritical*. It will be a critique that says more about you than about the writer or idea you're supposedly responding to.

In this chapter we have tried to show that reading for the conversation means looking not just for the thesis of a text in isolation but for the view or views that motivate that thesis— the "they say." We have also tried to show that reading for the conversation means being alert for the different strategies writers use to engage the view(s) that are motivating them, since not all writers engage other perspectives in the same way. Some writers explicitly identify and summarize a view they are responding to at the outset of their text and then return to it frequently as their text unfolds. Some refer only obliquely to a view that is motivating them, assuming that readers will be able to reconstruct that view on their own. Other writers may not explicitly distinguish their own view from the views they are questioning in ways that all of us find clear, leaving some readers to wonder whether a given view is the writer's own or one that he or she is challenging. And some writers push off against the "they say" that is motivating them in a challenging academic language that requires readers to translate what they are saying into more accessible, everyday terms. In sum, then, though most persuasive writers do follow a conversational "they say / I say" pattern, they do so in a great variety of ways. What this means for readers is that they need to be armed with various strategies for detecting the conversations in what they read, even when those conversations are not self-evident.

FIFTEEN

"ANALYZE THIS"

Writing in the Social Sciences

ERIN ACKERMAN

SOCIAL SCIENCE is the study of people—how they behave and relate to one another, and the organizations and institutions that facilitate these interactions. People are complicated, so any study of human behavior is at best partial, taking into account some elements of what people do and why, but not always explaining those actions definitively. As a result, it is the subject of constant conversation and argument.

Consider some of the topics studied in the social sciences: minimum wage laws, immigration policy, health care, employment discrimination. Got an opinion on any of these topics? You aren't alone. But in the writing you do as a student of the social sciences, you need to write about more than just

ERIN ACKERMAN is the Social Sciences Librarian at the College of New Jersey and formerly taught political science at John Jay College, City University of New York. Her research and teaching interests include women and American law, the law and politics of reproductive health, and information literacy in the social sciences.

your opinions. Good writing in the social sciences, as in other academic disciplines, requires that you demonstrate that you have thought about what it is you think. The best way to do that is to bring your views into conversation with those expressed by others and to test what you and others think against a review of data. In other words, you'll need to start with what others say and then present what you say as a response.

Consider the following example from a book about contemporary American political culture:

> Claims of deep national division were standard fare after the 2000 elections, and to our knowledge few commentators have publicly challenged them. . . . In sum, contemporary observers of American politics have apparently reached a new consensus around the proposition that old disagreements about economics now pale in comparison to new divisions based on sexuality, morality, and religion, divisions so deep as to justify fears of violence and talk of war in describing them.
>
> This short book advocates a contrary thesis: the sentiments expressed in the previously quoted pronouncements of scholars, journalists, and politicos range from simple exaggeration to sheer nonsense. . . . Many of the activists in the political parties and various cause groups do, in fact, hate each other and regard themselves as combatants in a war. But their hatreds and battles are not shared by the great mass of the American people. . . .
>
> MORRIS P. FIORINA, Culture War?
The Myth of a Polarized America

In other words, "they" (journalists, pundits, other political scientists) say that the American public is deeply divided, whereas Fiorina replies that they have misinterpreted the evidence—specifically, that they have generalized from a few exceptional cases (activists). Even the title of the book calls into question an idea held by others, one Fiorina labels a "myth."

This chapter explores some of the basic moves social science writers make. In addition, writing in the social sciences generally includes several core components: a strong introduction and thesis, a literature review, and the writer's own analysis, including presentation of data and consideration of implications. Much of your own writing will include one or more of these components as well. The introduction sets out the thesis, or point, of the paper, briefly explaining what you will say in your text and how it fits into the preexisting conversation. The literature review summarizes what has already been said on your topic. Your analysis allows you to present data—the information about human behavior you are measuring or testing against what other people have said—and to explain the conclusions you have drawn based on your investigation. Do you agree, disagree, or some combination of both, with what has been said by others? What reasons can you give for why you feel that way? And so what? Who should be interested in what you have to say, and why?

THE INTRODUCTION AND THESIS: "THIS PAPER CHALLENGES . . ."

Your introduction sets forth what you plan to say in your essay. You might evaluate the work of earlier scholars or certain widely held assumptions and find them incorrect when measured against new data. Alternatively, you might point out that an author's work is largely correct, but that it could use some qualifications or be extended in some way. Or you might identify a gap in our knowledge—we know a great deal about topic X but almost nothing about some other closely related topic. In each of these instances, your introduction needs to cover both "they say" and "I say" perspectives. If you stop after the "they say," your readers won't know what you are bringing to the conversation. Similarly, if you were to jump right to the "I say" portion of your argument, readers might wonder why you need to say anything at all.

Sometimes you join the conversation at a point where the discussion seems settled. One or more views about a topic have become so widely accepted among a group of scholars or society at large that these views are essentially the conventional way of thinking about the topic. You may wish to offer new reasons to support this interpretation, or you may wish to call these standard views into question. To do so, you must first introduce and identify these widely held beliefs and then present your own view. In fact, much of the writing in the social sciences takes the form of calling into question that which we think we already know. Consider the following example from an article in *The Journal of Economic Perspectives*:

> Fifteen years ago, Milton Friedman's 1957 treatise *A Theory of the Consumption Function* seemed badly dated. Dynamic optimization theory had not been employed much in economics when Friedman wrote, and utility theory was still comparatively primitive, so his statement of the "permanent income hypothesis" never actually specified a formal mathematical model of behavior derived explicitly from utility maximization . . . [W]hen other economists subsequently found multiperiod maximizing models that could be solved explicitly, the implications of those models differed sharply from Friedman's intuitive description of his "model." Furthermore, empirical tests in the 1970s and 1980s often rejected these rigorous versions of the permanent income hypothesis in favor of an

alternative hypothesis that many households simply spent all of their current income.

Today, with the benefit of a further round of mathematical (and computational) advances, Friedman's (1957) original analysis looks more prescient than primitive . . .

CHRISTOPHER D. CARROLL, "A Theory of Consumption
Function, With and Without Liquidity Constraints,"
The Journal of Economic Perspectives

This introduction makes clear that Carroll will defend Milton Friedman against some major criticisms of his work. Carroll mentions what has been said about Friedman's work and then goes on to say that the critiques turn out to be wrong and to suggest that Friedman's work reemerges as persuasive. A template of Carroll's introduction might look something like this: Economics research in the last fifteen years suggested Friedman's 1957 treatise was _____ because _____. In other words, they say that Friedman's work is not accurate because of _____, _____, and _____. Recent research convinces me, however, that Friedman's work makes sense.

In some cases, however, there may not be a strong consensus among experts on a topic. You might enter the ongoing debate by casting your vote with one side or another or by offering an alternative view. In the following example, Shari Berman identifies two competing accounts of how to explain world events in the twentieth century and then puts forth a third view.

Conventional wisdom about twentieth-century ideologies rests on two simple narratives. One focuses on the struggle for dominance between democracy and its alternatives. . . . The other narrative focuses on the competition between free-market capitalism and its rivals. . . . Both of these narratives obviously contain some truth. . . . Yet both only tell part of the story, which is why their common conclusion—neoliberalism as the "end of History"—is unsatisfying and misleading.

SHARI BERMAN, "The Primacy of Economics versus the
Primacy of Politics: Understanding the Ideological Dynamics
of the Twentieth Century," *Perspectives on Politics*

What the two conventional narratives fail to mention is that a third struggle was also going on: between those ideologies that believed in the primacy of economics and those that believed in the primacy of politics.

After identifying the two competing narratives, Berman suggests a third view—and later goes on to argue that this third view explains current debates over globalization. A template for this type of introduction might look something like this: In recent discussions of _____, a controversial aspect has been _____. On the one hand, some argue that _____. On the other hand, others argue that _____. Neither of these arguments, however, considers the alternative view that _____.

Given the complexity of many of the issues studied in the social sciences, however, you may sometimes agree *and* disagree with existing views—pointing out things that you believe are correct or have merit, while disagreeing with or refining other points. In the example below, anthropologist Sally Engle Merry agrees with another scholar about something that is a key trait of modern society but argues that this trait has a different origin than the other author identifies.

For more on different ways of responding, see Chapter 4.

Although I agree with Rose that an increasing emphasis on governing the soul is characteristic of modern society, I see the transformation not as evolutionary but as the product of social mobilization and political struggle.

> SALLY ENGLE MERRY, "Rights, Religion, and Community:
> Approaches to Violence against Women in the
> Context of Globalization," *Law and Society Review*

Here are some templates for agreeing and disagreeing:

▸ **Although I agree with X up to a point, I cannot accept his overall conclusion that _____ .**

▸ **Although I disagree with X on _____ and _____ , I agree with her conclusion that _____ .**

▸ **Political scientists studying _____ have argued that it is caused by _____ . While _____ contributes to the problem, _____ is also an important factor.**

In the process of examining people from different angles, social scientists sometimes identify gaps—areas that have not been explored in previous research. In an article on African American neighborhoods, sociologist Mary Pattillo identifies such a gap.

The research on African Americans is dominated by inquiries into the lives of the black poor. Contemporary ethnographies and journalistic descriptions have thoroughly described deviance, gangs, drugs, intergender relations and sexuality, stymied aspiration, and family patterns in poor neighborhoods (Dash 1989; Hagedorn 1988; Kotlowitz 1991; Lemann 1991; MacLeod 1995; Sullivan 1989; Williams 1989). Yet, the majority of African Americans are not poor (Billingsley 1992). A significant part of the black experience, namely that of working and middle-class blacks, remains unexplored. We have little information about what black middle-class neighborhoods look like and how social life is organized within them. . . . this article begins to fill this empirical and theoretical gap using ethnographic data collected in Groveland, a middle-class black neighborhood in Chicago.

> Mary E. Pattillo,
> "Sweet Mothers and Gangbangers: Managing Crime
> in a Black Middle-Class Neighborhood," *Social Forces*

Pattillo explains that much has been said about poor African American neighborhoods. But, she says, we have little information about the experience of working-class and middle-class black neighborhoods—a gap that her article will address.

Here are some templates for introducing gaps in the existing research:

▸ **Studies of X have indicated _____. It is not clear, however, that this conclusion applies to _____.**

▸ **_____ often take for granted that _____. Few have investigated this assumption, however.**

▸ **X's work tells us a great deal about _____. Can this work be generalized to _____?**

Again, a good introduction indicates what you have to say in the larger context of what others have said. Throughout the rest of your paper, you will move back and forth between the "they say" and the "I say," adding more details.

THE LITERATURE REVIEW:
"PRIOR RESEARCH INDICATES . . ."

In the literature review, you explain what "they say" in more detail, summarizing, paraphrasing, or quoting the viewpoints to which you are responding. But you need to balance what they are saying with your own focus. You need to characterize someone else's work fairly and accurately but set up the points you yourself want to make by selecting the details that are relevant to your own perspective and observations.

It is common in the social sciences to summarize several arguments at once, identifying their major arguments or findings in a single paragraph.

How do employers in a low-wage labor market respond to an increase in the minimum wage? The prediction from conventional economic theory is unambiguous: a rise in the minimum wage leads perfectly competitive employers to cut employment (George J. Stigler, 1946). Although studies in the 1970's based on aggregate teenage employment rates usually confirmed this prediction, earlier studies based on comparisons of employment at affected and unaffected establishments often did not (e.g., Richard A. Lester, 1960, 1964). Several recent studies that rely on a similar comparative methodology have failed to detect a negative employment effect of higher minimum wages. Analyses of the 1990–1991 increases in the federal minimum wage (Lawrence F. Katz and Krueger, 1992; Card, 1992a) and of an earlier increase in the minimum wage in California (Card, 1992b) find no adverse employment impact.

DAVID CARD AND ALAN KRUEGER,
"Minimum Wages and Employment: A Case Study of the
Fast-Food Industry in New Jersey and Pennsylvania,"
The American Economic Review

Card and Krueger cite the key findings and conclusions of works that are relevant to the question they are investigating and the point they plan to address, asking "How do employers in a low-wage labor market respond to an increase in the minimum wage?" They go on, as good writers should, to answer the question they ask. And they do so by reviewing others who have answered that question, noting that this question has been answered in different, sometimes contradictory, ways.

Such summaries are brief, bringing together relevant arguments by several scholars to provide an overview of scholarly work on a particular topic. In writing such a summary, you need to ask yourself how the authors themselves might describe their positions and also consider what in their work is relevant for the point you wish to make. This kind of summary is especially appropriate when you have a large amount of research material on a topic and want to identify the major strands of a debate or to show how the work of one author builds on that of another. Here are some templates for overview summaries:

▸ **In addressing the question of _____, political scientists have considered several explanations for _____. X argues that _____. According to Y and Z, another plausible explanation is _____.**

▸ **What is the effect of _____ on _____? Previous work on _____ by X and by Y and Z supports _____.**

Sometimes you may need to say more about the works you cite. On a midterm or final exam, for example, you may need to demonstrate that you have a deep familiarity with a particular work. And in some disciplines of the social sciences, longer, more detailed literature reviews are the standard. Your instructor and the articles he or she has assigned are your best guides for the length and level of detail of your literature review. Other times, the work of certain authors is especially important for your argument, and therefore you need to provide more details to explain what these authors have said. See how Martha Derthick summarizes an argument that is central to her book about the politics of tobacco regulation.

> The idea that governments could sue to reclaim health care costs from cigarette manufacturers might be traced to "Cigarettes and Welfare Reform," an article published in the *Emory Law Journal* in 1977 by Donald Gasner, a law professor at the University of Southern Illinois. Garner suggested that state governments could get a cigarette manufacturer to pay the direct medical costs "of looking after patients with smoking diseases." He drew an analogy to the Coal Mine Health and Safety Act of 1969, under which coal mine operators are required to pay certain disability benefits for coal miners suffering from pneumoconiosis, or black lung disease.
>
> MARTHA DERTHICK, *Up In Smoke:*
> *From Legislation to Litigation in Tobacco Politics*

Note that Derthick identifies the argument she is summarizing, quoting its author directly and then adding details about a precedent for the argument.

You may want to include direct quotations of what others have said, as Derthick does. Using an author's exact words helps you demonstrate that you are representing him or her fairly. But you cannot simply insert a quotation; you need to explain to your readers what it means for your point. Consider the following example drawn from a political science book on the debate over tort reform.

> The essence of *agenda setting* was well enunciated by E. E. Schattschneider: "In politics as in everything else, it makes a great

difference whose game we play" (1960, 47). In short, the ability to define or control the rules, terms, or perceived options in a contest over policy greatly affects the prospects for winning.

WILLIAM HALTOM AND MICHAEL McCANN,
Distorting the Law: Politics, Media, and the Litigation Crisis

Notice how Haltom and McCann first quote Schattschneider and then explain in their own words how political agenda setting can be thought of as a game, with winners and losers.

Remember that whenever you summarize, quote, or paraphrase the work of others, credit must be given in the form of a citation to the original work. The words may be your own, but if the idea comes from someone else you must give credit to the original work. There are several formats for documenting sources. Consult your instructor for help choosing which citation style to use.

THE ANALYSIS

The literature review covers what others have said on your topic. The analysis allows you to present and support your own response. In the introduction you indicate whether you agree, disagree, or some combination of both with what others have said. You will want to expand on how you have formed your opinion and why others should care about your topic.

"The Data Indicate . . ."

The social sciences use data to develop and test explanations. Data can be quantitative or qualitative and can come from a number of sources. You might use statistics related to GDP growth, unemployment, voting rates, or demographics. Or you could use surveys, interviews, or other first-person accounts.

Regardless of the type of data used, it is important to do three things: define your data, indicate where you got the data, and then say what you have done with your data. In a journal article, political scientist Joshua C. Wilson examines a court case about protests at an abortion clinic and asks whether each side of the conflict acts in a way consistent with their general views on freedom of speech.

> [T]his paper relies on close readings of in-person, semi-structured interviews with the participants involved in the real controversy that was the *Williams* case.
>
> Thirteen interviews ranging in length from 40 minutes to 1 hour and 50 minutes were conducted for this paper. Of those interviewed, all would be considered "elites" in terms of political psychology / political attitude research—six were active members of Solano Citizens for Life . . . ; two were members of Planned Parenthood Shasta-Diablo management; one was the lawyer who obtained the restraining order, temporary injunction, and permanent injunction for Planned Parenthood; one was the lawyer for the duration of the case for Solano Citizens for Life; two were lawyers for Planned Parenthood on appeal; and one was the Superior Court judge who heard arguments for, and finally crafted, the restraining order and injunctions against Solano Citizens for Life. During the course of the interviews, participants were asked a range of questions about their experiences and thoughts in relation to the Williams case, as well as their beliefs about the interpretation and limits of the First Amendment right to free speech—both in general, and in relation to the Williams case.
>
> JOSHUA C. WILSON. "When Rights Collide:
Anti-Abortion Protests and the Ideological Dilemma
in Planned Parenthood Shasta-Diablo, Inc. v. Williams,"
Studies in Law, Politics, and Society

Wilson identifies and describes his qualitative data—interviews conducted with key parties in the conflict—and explains the nature of the questions he asked.

If your data are quantitative, you will need to explain them similarly. See how political scientist Brian Arbour explains the quantitative data he used to study for an article in *The Forum* how a change of rules might have affected the outcome of the 2008 Democratic primary contest between Hillary Clinton and Barack Obama.

> I evaluate these five concerns about the Democratic system of delegate allocation by "rerunning" the Obama-Clinton contest with a different set of allocation rules, those in effect for the 2008 Republican presidential contest. . . . Republicans allow each state to make their own rules, leading to "a plethora of selection plans" (Shapiro & Bello 2008, 5) . . . To "rerun" the Democratic primary under Republican rules, I need data on the results of the Democratic primary for each state and congressional district and on the Republican delegate allocation rules for each state. The Green Papers (www.thegreenpapers.com), a website that serves as an almanac of election procedures, rules, and results, provides each of these data sources. By "rerunning" the Democratic primaries and caucuses, I use the exact results of each contest.
>
> BRIAN ARBOUR, "Even Closer, Even Longer: What If the 2008 Democratic Primary Used Republican Rules?" *The Forum*

Note that Arbour identifies his data as primary voting results and the rules for Republican primaries. In the rest of the paper, Arbour shows how his use of these data suggests that political commentators who thought Republican rules would have clarified the close race between Clinton and Obama were wrong and the race would have been "even closer, even longer."

Here are some templates for discussing data:

- In order to test the hypothesis that _____, we assessed _____. Our calculations suggest _____.

- I used _____ to investigate _____. The results of this investigation indicate _____.

"But Others May Object . . ."

No matter how strongly your data support your argument, there are almost surely other perspectives (and thus other data) that you need to acknowledge. By considering possible objections to your argument and taking them seriously, you demonstrate that you've done your work and that you're aware of other perspectives—and most important, you present your own argument as part of an ongoing conversation.

See how economist Christopher Carroll acknowledges that there may be objections to his argument about how people allocate their income between consumption and savings.

> I have argued here that the modern version of the dynamically optimizing consumption model is able to match many of the important features of the empirical data on consumption and saving behavior. There are, however, several remaining reasons for discomfort with the model.
>
> CHRISTOPHER D. CARROLL, "A Theory of Consumption Function, With and Without Liquidity Constraints," *The Journal of Economic Perspectives*

Carroll then goes on to identify the possible limitations of his mathematical analysis.

Someone may object because there are related phenomena that your analysis does not explain or because you do not have the right data to investigate a particular question. Or perhaps someone may object to assumptions underlying your argument or how you handled your data. Here are some templates for considering naysayers:

▶ _____ might object that _____ .

▶ Is my claim realistic? I have argued _____ , but readers may question _____ .

▶ My explanation accounts for _____ but does not explain _____ . This is because _____ .

"Why Should We Care?"

Who should care about your research, and why? Since the social sciences attempt to explain human behavior, it is important to consider how your research affects the assumptions we make about human behavior. In addition, you might offer recommendations for how other social scientists might continue to explore an issue, or what actions policymakers should take.

In the following example, sociologist Devah Pager identifies the implications of her study of the way having a criminal record affects a person applying for jobs.

> [I]n terms of policy implications, this research has troubling conclusions. In our frenzy of locking people up, our "crime control" policies may in fact exacerbate the very conditions that lead to crime in the first place. Research consistently shows that finding

quality steady employment is one of the strongest predictors of desistance from crime (Shover 1996; Sampson and Laub 1993; Uggen 2000). The fact that a criminal record severely limits employment opportunities—particularly among blacks—suggests that these individuals are left with few viable alternatives.

DEVAH PAGER, "The Mark of a Criminal Record,"
The American Journal of Sociology

Pager's conclusion that a criminal record negatively affects employment chances creates a vicious circle, she says: steady employment discourages recidivism, but a criminal record makes it harder to get a job.

In answering the "so what?" question, you need to explain why your readers should care. Although sometimes the implications of your work may be so broad that they would be of interest to almost anyone, it's never a bad idea to identify explicitly any groups of people who will find your work important.

Templates for establishing why your claims matter:

▸ **X is important because _____.**

▸ **Ultimately, what is at stake here is _____.**

▸ **The finding that _____ should be of interest to _____ because _____.**

As noted at the beginning of this chapter, the complexity of people allows us to look at their behavior from many different viewpoints. Much has been, and will be, said about how and why people do the things they do. As a result, we can look at writing in the social sciences as an ongoing conversation.

When you join this conversation, the "they say / I say" framework will help you figure out what has already been said (they say) and what you can add (I say). The components of social science writing presented in this chapter are tools to help you join that conversation.

"ON CLOSER EXAMINATION"

Entering Conversations about Literature

—◻—

IN CHINUA ACHEBE'S NOVEL *Things Fall Apart*, Okonkwo, the main character, is a tragic hero.

So what? Who cares?

Why does this typical way of opening an essay on a literary work leave readers wondering, "Why are you telling me this?" Because, in our view, such statements leave it unclear who would say otherwise. Would anyone deny that the main character of Achebe's novel is a tragic hero? Is there some other view of the subject that this writer is responding to? Since no such alternative interpretation is indicated, the reader thinks, "OK, Okonkwo is a tragic hero—as opposed to what?"

Now compare this opening with another possible one:

> Several members of our class have argued that Okonkwo, the main character of *Things Fall Apart*, is a hateful villain. My own view, however, is that, while it is true that Okonkwo commits villainous acts, he is ultimately a tragic hero—a flawed but ultimately sympathetic figure.

We hope you agree that the second version, which responds to what someone else says about Okonkwo, makes for more engaging writing than the first. Since the first version fails to present itself as a response to any alternative view of its subject, it comes at readers out of the blue, leaving them wondering why it needs to be said at all.

As we stress in this book, it is the views of others and our desire to respond to these views that gives our writing its underlying motivation and helps readers see why what we say matters, why others should care, and why we need to say it in the first place. In this chapter we suggest that this same principle applies to writing about literature. Literary critics, after all, don't make assertions about literary works out of the blue. Rather, they contribute to discussions and debates about the meaning and significance of literary works, some of which may continue for years and even centuries.

Indeed, this commitment to discussion animates most literature courses, in which students discuss and debate assigned works in class before writing papers about them. The premise is that engaging with classmates and teachers enables us to make discoveries about the work that we might not arrive at in simply reading the work alone.

We suggest that you think of writing about literature as a natural extension of such in-class discussions, listening carefully to others and using what they say to set up and motivate what you have to say.

START WITH WHAT OTHERS ARE SAYING

But in writing about literature, where do views to respond to—"they says"—come from? Many sources. Published literary criticism is perhaps the most obvious:

▸ Critic X complains that Author Y's story is compromised by his _____ perspective. While there's some truth to this critique, I argue that Critic X overlooks _____.

▸ According to Critic A, novel X suggests _____. I agree, but would add that _____.

But the view that you respond to in writing about literature can be far closer to home than published literary criticism. As our opening example illustrates, it can be something said about the literary work by a classmate or teacher:

▸ Several members of our class have suggested that the final message of play X is _____. I agree up to a point, but I still think that _____.

Another tactic is to start with something you yourself thought about the work that on second thought you now want to revise:

▸ On first reading play Z, I thought it was an uncritical celebration of _____. After rereading the play and discussing it in class, however, I see that it is more critical of _____ than I originally thought.

You can even respond to something that hasn't actually been said about the work, but might hypothetically be said:

▸ It might be said that poem Y is chiefly about _____. But the problem with this reading, in my view, is _____.

▸ Though religious readers might be tempted to analyze poem X as a parable about _____, a closer examination suggests that the poem is in fact _____.

Sometimes, the "they say" that you respond to in writing about a literary work can be found in the work itself, as distinct from what some critic or other reader has said *about* the work. Much great literary criticism responds directly to the literary work, summarizing some aspect of the work's form or content and then assessing it, in much the same way you can do in response to a persuasive essay:

▸ **Ultimately, as I read it, *The Scarlet Letter* seems to say _____. I have trouble accepting this proposition, however, on the grounds that _____.**

One of the more powerful ways of responding to a literary work is to address any contradictions or inconsistencies:

▸ **At the beginning of the poem, we encounter the generalization, seemingly introducing the poem's message, that "_____." But this statement is then contradicted by the suggestion made later in the poem that "_____." This opens up a significant inconsistency in the text: is it suggesting _____ or, on the contrary, _____?**

▸ **At several places in novel X, Author Y leads us to understand that the story's central point is that _____. Yet elsewhere the text suggests _____, indicating that Y may be ambivalent on this issue.**

If you review the above templates, you'll notice that each does what a good discussion, lecture, or essay does: it makes an argument about some aspect of a work that can be interpreted in various ways. Instead of just making a claim about the work in isolation—character X is a tragic hero; sonnet Y is about the loss of a loved one—these templates put one claim as a response to another, making clear what motivated the argument to begin with. They thus act as conversation starters that can invite or even provoke other readers to respond with their own interpretations and judgments.

FIGURING OUT
WHAT A LITERARY WORK "MEANS"

In order to enter conversations and debates about literature, you need to meet the time-honored challenge of being able to read and make sense of literary works, understanding and analyzing what the text says. On the one hand, like the types of persuasive essays we focus on throughout this book, literary works make arguments their authors want to convey, things they are for and against, ideas they want to endorse or condemn. On the other hand, discovering "the argument" of a literary work—what it's "saying"—can be a special challenge because, unlike persuasive essays, literary works usually do not spell out their arguments explicitly. Though poets, novelists, and playwrights may have the same level of conviction as persuasive writers, rarely do they step out from behind the pages of their texts and say, "Okay, folks, this is what it all means. What I'm trying to say in a nutshell is _____." That is, since literary texts do not include an explicit thesis statement identifying their main point, it's left up to us as readers to figure it out.

Because literary works tend to avoid such explicitness, their meanings often need to be teased out from the clues they provide: from the dialogue between characters, the plot, the imagery and symbolism, and the kind of language the author uses. In fact, it is this absence of overt argument that makes literature so endlessly debatable—and explains why scholars and critics argue so much about what literary works mean in ways similar to the classroom discussions that you have likely participated in as a student.

The Elusive Literary Author

Indeed, not even the use of the first person "I" in a literary work is an indication that you have located the author's own position or stance, as it usually is in an essay. When David Zinczenko, for example, in his essay "Don't Blame the Eater" writes "I tend to sympathize with these portly fast-food patrons" who file lawsuits against the fast food industry, we can be confident that the "I" is Zinczenko himself, and that the position he expresses is his own and informs everything else in his essay. But we cannot assume that the "I" who addresses us in a work of fiction or poetry is necessarily the author, for he or she is a fictional character—and one who may be unreliable and untrustworthy.

Take, for example, the first sentence of Edgar Allan Poe's short story "The Cask of Amontillado":

> The thousand injuries of Fortunato I had borne as best I could, but when he ventured upon insult I vowed revenge.

As soon becomes clear in the story, the "I" who speaks as the narrator here is not Poe himself but an insanely vengeful murderer whose words must be seen through to get at the point of Poe's story.

Instead of a readily identifiable position, literary works often present the perspectives of a number of different characters and leave it to readers to determine which if any speaks for the author. Thus when we encounter the seemingly eloquent lines in *Hamlet*, "To thine own self be true / And thou shalt not be false to any man," we can't assume, as we might if we encountered this statement in an essay, that it represents the author's own view. For these words are uttered by Polonius, a character whom Shakespeare presents as a tedious, cliché-spouting bore—not someone he leads us to trust. After all, part of Hamlet's problem is that it's not clear to him what being "true" to his own self would require him to do.

This elusive quality of literary texts helps explain why some of our students complain about the challenge of finding the "hidden meaning," as they sometimes call it, let alone summarizing that meaning in the way assignments often require. Sure, some students say, they enjoy reading literature for pleasure. But analyzing literature in school for its "meaning" or "symbolism"—that's another matter. Some even say that the requirement that they hunt for meanings and symbols robs literature of its fun.

In fact, as most students come to recognize, analyzing meanings, symbols, and other elements should enhance rather than stifle the pleasure we get from reading literature. But it can indeed be hard to figure out what literary works mean. How do we determine the point of a story or poem when the author, unlike an essayist like Zinczenko, does not tell us explicitly what he or she is trying to say? How do you go from a fictional event or poetic image (an insane man committing murder, two roads that diverge in the woods) or from a dialogue between fictional characters ("Frankly, my dear, I don't give a damn.") to what these events, images, or lines of dialogue mean?

Look for Conflict *in* the Work

There is no simple recipe for figuring out what a literary work means, but one tactic that seems to help our own students is to look for the conflict or debate in the literary work itself and then ask what the text is leading us to think about that conflict. Asking these questions—what is the conflict in the work and which side, if any, should we favor?—will help you think about and formulate a position on what the work means. And since such claims are often ones that literary scholars argue about, thinking about the conflict *in* a literary work will often lead you to discussions and debates *about* the work that you can then respond to in your writing. Because literary authors don't tell us explicitly what the text means, it's always going to be *arguable*—and your task in writing about a literary work is to argue for what *you* think it means. Here are two templates to help get you started responding to other interpretations:

▸ It might be argued that in the clash between character **X** and **Y** in play **Z**, the author wants us to favor character **Y**, since she is presented as the play's heroine. I contend, however, that _____.

▸ Several critics seem to assume that poem **X** endorses the values of discipline and rationality represented by the image of _____ over those of play and emotion represented by the image of _____. I agree, but with the following caveat: that the poem ultimately sees both values as equally important and even suggests that ideally they should complement one another.

This tactic of looking for the conflicts in literary works is part of a long tradition of critical thought that sees conflict as central to literature. In ancient Greece, Aristotle argued that conflict between characters or forces underlies the plots of tragic dramas such as *Oedipus*. Indeed, the ancient Greek word *agon*, which means antagonism, conflict, or debate, leaves its traces in the term "protagonist," the hero or leading character of a narrative work who comes into conflict with other characters or with the fates. And Plato noted the pervasiveness of conflict in literature when he banished poets from his ideal community on the grounds that their works depict endless conflict and division.

This emphasis on the centrality of conflict in literature has been echoed by modern theorists like the New Critics of the 1940s and 50s, who focused on such tensions and paradoxes as good and evil or innocence and experience—and more recently by poststructuralists and political theorists who see literature, like society, as saturated by such polarities as male/female, gay/straight, white/black, and so on. Writers today continue to recognize conflict as the engine of good storytelling. As the Hollywood screenwriter Robert McKee puts it, "Nothing moves forward in a story except through conflict."

Building on this idea that conflict is central to literature, we suggest the following four questions to help you understand and formulate your own position on any literary work:

1. What is the central conflict?
2. Which side—if any—does the text seem to favor?
3. What's your evidence? How might others interpret the evidence differently?
4. What's your opinion of the text?

WHAT IS THE CENTRAL CONFLICT?

Conflicts tend to manifest themselves in different ways in different literary genres. In works that take a narrative or story form (novels, short stories, and plays), the central conflict will often be represented in an actual debate between characters. These debates between characters will often reflect larger questions and debates in the society or historical era in which they were written, over such issues as the responsibility of rulers, the consequences of capitalism and consumerism, or the struggle for gender equality. Sometimes these debates will be located within an individual character, appearing as a struggle in someone caught between conflicting or incompatible choices. Whatever form they may take, these debates can provide you with points of entry into the issues raised by the work, its historical context, and its author's vision of the world.

One narrative work that lends itself to such an approach is Flannery O'Connor's 1961 short story "Everything That Rises Must Converge." The story presents a running debate between a mother and her son Julian about the civil rights movement for racial equality that had erupted in the American South at the time the story was written, with Julian defending the outlook of this movement and his mother defending the South's traditional racial hierarchy. The story raises the debatable question of which character we should side with: Julian, his mother, both, or neither?

WHICH SIDE—IF ANY—DOES THE TEXT SEEM TO FAVOR?

When we teach this story, most of our students first assume the story sides with Julian's outlook, which to them as Northern, urban college students in the twenty-first century seems the obviously enlightened position. Who, after all, could fail to see that the mother's views are backward and racist? As our class discussions unfold, however, most students come to reject this view as a misreading, one based more on their own views than on what's in the text. Sooner or later, someone points out that at several points Julian is presented in highly critical ways—and that his apparently progressive sympathy for racial integration rests on arid intellectual abstractions and a hypocritical lack of self-knowledge, in contrast with his mother's heartfelt loyalty to her roots. Eventually another possible interpretation surfaces, that both characters suffer from a common malady, that they're living in a mental bubble that keeps them from being able to see themselves as they really are.

The writing assignment we often give builds on this class discussion by offering students the following template for thinking about which character, if any, the text leads them to favor:

▸ **Some might argue that when it comes to the conflict between Julian and his mother over _____, our sympathies should lie with _____. My own view is that _____.**

WHAT'S YOUR EVIDENCE?

In entering the types of discussions and debates modeled by the above template, how do you determine where your "sympathies should lie"? More generally, how do you arrive at and justify an interpretation of what a literary text says?

The answer lies in the *evidence* provided by the work: its images, dialogue, plot, historical references, tone, stylistic details, and so forth.

It is important to remember, however, that evidence is not set in stone. Students sometimes assume that there exists some fixed code that unlocks the meaning of literary works, symbols, images, and other evidence. A character dies? This must mean that he or she is being condemned. A stairway appears? A symbol for upward mobility. A garden? Must be something sexual.

But evidence itself is open to interpretation and thus to debate. The mother's death in O'Connor's story, for instance, *could* be seen as evidence that we are supposed to disapprove of her as someone whose racial views are regressive and on the way out. On the other hand, her death may instead be evidence that she is to be seen as a heroic martyr too good for this cruel, harsh world. What a character's death means, then, depends—on how he or she is treated in the work, positively or negatively, which in turn may be subject to debate.

As we've repeatedly emphasized in this book, others will often disagree with you and may even use the same evidence you do to support interpretations that are contrary to your own. Like other objects of study, literary works are like the famous ambiguous drawing that can be seen as either a duck or a rabbit, depending how one views it.

Since the same piece of evidence in a literary work will often support differing, even opposing interpretations, you need to argue for what you think the evidence shows—and to acknowledge that others may read that evidence differently.

In writing about literature, then, you need to show that the evidence you are citing supports your interpretation and to anticipate other alternative ones:

▸ **Although some might read the metaphor of _____ in this poem as evidence that, for Author X, modern technology undermines community traditions and values, I see it as _____.**

To present evidence in such a "they say / I say" way, you need to be alert for how others may read the work differently than you—and even use this very same evidence in support of an opposing interpretation:

▸ **Some might claim that evidence X suggests _____, but I argue that, on the contrary, it suggests _____.**

▸ **I agree with my classmate _____ that the image of _____ in novel Y is evidence of childhood innocence that has been lost. Unlike _____, however, I think this loss of innocence is to be read not as a tragic event but as a necessary, even helpful, stage in human development.**

Are Some Interpretations Simply Wrong?

No matter how flexible and open to debate evidence might be, not all interpretations we arrive at using that evidence are equally valid. And some interpretations are simply unsupported by that evidence. Let us illustrate.

As we noted earlier, some of our students first favored Julian over his mother. One student, let us call her Nancy, cited as evidence a passage early in the story in which Julian is compared to Saint Sebastian, a Christian martyr who is said to have exhibited exceptional faith under extreme suffering and persecution. As the mother stood preparing for Julian to take her to her weekly swimming class, Julian is described as standing "pinned to the door frame, waiting like Saint Sebastian for the arrows to begin piercing him."

Thinking this passage proves that Julian is the more sympathetic character, Nancy pointed to other evidence as well, including the following passage:

> [Julian] was free of prejudice and unafraid to face facts. Most miraculous of all, instead of being blinded by love for [his mother] as she was for him, he had cut himself emotionally free of her and could see her with complete objectivity. He was not dominated by his mother. (412)

Citing passages like this in her essay, Nancy concluded: "Julian represents the future of society, a nonracist and an educated thinker."

After rereading the story, however, and hearing other students' views, Nancy came to realize that the passages she had cited—comparing Julian to a saint, suggesting that he is racially progressive, and that he is "free of" his mother and "objective" about her—were all intended ironically. Julian congratulates *himself* for being saintlike, free of prejudice, and objective, but the story ultimately implies that he deludes himself.

How did the supporters of the ironic reading convince Nancy to revise her initial reading—to see it as wrong, unsupported by the evidence? First, they pointed to the glaring discrepancy between the situations and kinds of suffering endured by Julian and Saint Sebastian. Could anyone be serious, they asked, in comparing something as mundane as being forced to wait a few minutes to go to the YMCA to a martyr dying for his faith? No, they answered, and the jarring incongruity of the events being compared, they argued, suggests that Julian, far from saintlike, is presented in this passage as an impatient, ungrateful, undutiful son. In addition, students pointed out that the gap between Julian's self-image as a progressive man of "complete objectivity" and "facts," "free of [his mother]" and the blubbering young man crying "Mama, Mama!" with "guilt and sorrow" at the end of the story suggests that Julian's righteous, high-minded image of himself is not to be taken at face value.

At this point you may be wondering, how can we say that some interpretations of literature must be ruled out as *wrong*? Isn't the great thing about interpreting literary works—in contrast to scientific and historical texts—that there are no wrong answers? Are we saying that there is one "correct" way to read a literary work—the one way the work itself tells us we "should" read it?

No, we aren't saying that there is only one way to read a literary work. If we believed there were, we would not be offering a method of literary analysis based on multiple interpretations and debate. But yes, acknowledging that literary interpretations are open to debate is not to say that a work can mean anything we want it to mean, as if all interpretations are equally good. In our view, and that of most literature teachers, some interpretations are better than others—more persuasively reasoned and better grounded in the evidence of the text.

If we maintain that all interpretations are equally valid, we risk confusing the perspective of the work's author with our own, as did the students who confused their own views on the civil rights movement of the 1960s with Flannery O'Connor's. Such misreadings are reminiscent of what we call "the closest cliché syndrome," where what's summarized is not the view the author actually expresses but a familiar cliché—or, in

See p. 33 for more on the closest cliché syndrome.

O'Connor's case, a certain social belief—that the writer believes and mistakenly assumes the author must too. The view that there are no wrong answers in literary interpretation encourages a kind of solipsism that erases the difference between us and others and transforms everything we encounter into a version of ourselves.

As the literary theorist Robert Scholes puts it, reading, conceived "as a submission to the intentions of another is the first step" to understanding what a literary work is saying. For "if we do not postulate the existence of [an author] behind the verbal text," we will "simply project our own subjective modes of thought and desire upon the text." In other words, unless we do the best we can to get at what the author is saying, we will never truly recognize his or her ideas except as some version of our own. Scholes acknowledges that good reading often involves going beyond the author's intention, pointing out contradictions and ideological blind spots, but he argues that we must recognize the author's intention *before* we can try to see beyond it in these ways.

WHAT'S YOUR OPINION OF THE TEXT?

In accord with the principle that we must try to understand the text on its own terms before responding to it, we have thus far in this chapter focused on how to understand and unpack what literary texts say and do. Our approach to get at what they say involves looking for the central conflict in the work and then asking yourself how the author uses various types of evidence (characters, dialogue, imagery, events, plot, etc.) to guide you in thinking about that conflict. Ultimately, your job as a reader of literature is to be open to a work as its author presents it, or else your reading will fail to see what makes that work worth reading and thinking about.

But once you have reached a good understanding of the work, it is time to allow your own opinion to come into play. Offering your own interpretation of a work and opening that interpretation to response are crucial steps in any act of literary analysis, but they are not the end of the process. The final step involves offering your own insight into or critique of the work and its vision, assessing whether, as you see it, it is morally justified or questionable, unified or contradictory, historically regressive or progressive, and so forth. For example:

> Though she is one of the most respected Southern authors of the American literary canon, Flannery O'Connor continually denigrates the one character in her 1961 story who represents the civil rights movement, and in so doing disparages progressive ideas that I believe deserve a far more sympathetic hearing.

Offering a critique, however, doesn't necessarily mean finding fault:

> Some criticize O'Connor's story by suggesting that it has a politically regressive agenda. But I see the story as a laudable critique of politics as such. In my view, O'Connor's story rightly criticizes the polarization of political conflicts—North vs. South, liberal vs. conservative, and the like—and suggests that they need to come together: to "converge," as O'Connor's title implies, through religious love, understanding, and forgiveness.

We realize that the prospect of critiquing a literary work can be daunting. Indeed, simply stating what you think an author is saying can be intimidating, since it means going out on a limb, asserting something about highly respected figures—works that are often complex, contradictory, and connected to larger historical movements. Nevertheless, if you can master these challenges, you may find that figuring out what a literary work is saying, offering an opinion about it, and entering into conversation and debate with others about such questions is what makes literature matter. And if you do it well, what *you* say will invite its own response: your "I say" will become someone else's "they say," and the conversation will go on and on.

RAY BRADBURY { *There Will Come Soft Rains*

RAY BRADBURY (b. 1920) was born in Waukegan, Illinois, and lived with his family in Tuscon, Arizona, as well as Los Angeles, where he graduated from Los Angeles High School. Bradbury did not attend college, preferring to read during evenings at the public library after a day of writing and selling newspapers on the street. Known for his science fiction, fantasy, and mystery narratives, Bradbury wrote his acclaimed *Fahrenheit 451* (1953) at UCLA's Powell Library, on a rented typewriter. His works have been adapted into comic books, television shows (*Alfred Hitchcock Presents*), and films. For eight years Bradbury hosted his own television show, *Ray Bradbury Presents*, for which he adapted sixty-five of his stories.

"There Will Come Soft Rains," from Bradbury's story collection *The Martian Chronicles* (1950), exposes a postapocalyptic world: humans have been eradicated by a nuclear disaster, but their homes—completely powered by technology—linger. What kind of existence does Bradbury imagine, both pre- and postapocalypse? How is this story a cautionary tale about the effects of technology? Do you agree with Bradbury's stance?

———————————

IN THE LIVING ROOM THE voice-clock sang, *Tick-tock, seven o'clock, time to get up, time to get up, seven o'clock!* as if it were afraid that nobody would. The morning house lay empty. The clock ticked on, repeating and repeating its sounds into the emptiness. *Seven-nine, breakfast time, seven-nine!*

In the kitchen the breakfast stove gave a hissing sigh and ejected from its warm interior eight pieces of perfectly browned toast, eight eggs sunnyside up, sixteen slices of bacon, two coffees, and two cool glasses of milk.

"Today is August 4, 2057," said a second voice from the kitchen ceiling, "in the city of Allendale, California." It repeated the date three times for memory's sake. "Today is Mr. Featherstone's birthday. Today is the anniversary of Tilita's marriage. Insurance is payable, as are the water, gas, and light bills."

Somewhere in the walls, relays clicked, memory tapes glided under electric eyes.

Eight-one, tick-tock, eight-one o'clock, off to school, off to work, run, run, eight-one! But no doors slammed, no carpets took the soft tread of rubber heels. It was raining outside. The weather box on the front door sang quietly: "Rain, rain, go away; rubbers, raincoats for today . . ." And the rain tapped on the empty house, echoing. 5

Outside, the garage chimed and lifted its door to reveal the waiting car. After a long wait the door swung down again.

At eight-thirty the eggs were shriveled and the toast was like stone. An aluminum wedge scraped them into the sink, where hot water whirled them down a metal throat which digested and flushed them away to the distant sea. The dirty dishes were dropped into a hot washer and emerged twinkling dry.

Nine-fifteen, sang the clock, *time to clean.*

Out of warrens in the wall, tiny robot mice darted. The rooms were acrawl with the small cleaning animals, all rubber and metal. They thudded against chairs, whirling their mustached runners, kneading the rug nap, sucking gently at hidden dust. Then, like mysterious invaders, they popped into their burrows. Their pink electric eyes faded. The house was clean.

Ten o'clock. The sun came out from behind the rain. The house stood alone in a city of rubble and ashes. This was the one house left standing. At night the ruined city gave off a radioactive glow which could be seen for miles. 10

Ten-fifteen. The garden sprinklers whirled up in golden founts, filling the soft morning air with scatterings of brightness. The water pelted windowpanes, running down the charred west side where the house had been burned evenly free of its white paint. The entire west face of the house was black, save for five places. Here the silhouette in paint of a man mowing a lawn. Here, as in a photograph, a woman bent to pick flowers. Still farther over, their images burned on wood in one titanic instant, a small boy, hands flung into the air; higher up, the image of a thrown ball, and opposite him a girl, hands raised to catch a ball which never came down.

The five spots of paint—the man, the woman, the children, the ball—remained. The rest was a thin charcoaled layer.

The gentle sprinkler rain filled the garden with falling light.

Until this day, how well the house had kept its peace. How carefully it had inquired, "Who goes there? What's the password?" and, getting no answer from lonely foxes and whining cats, it had shut up its windows and drawn shades in an old-maidenly preoccupation with self-protection which bordered on a mechanical paranoia.

It quivered at each sound, the house did. If a sparrow brushed a window, the shade snapped up. The bird, startled, flew off! No, not even a bird must touch the house! 15

The house was an altar with ten thousand attendants, big, small, servicing, attending, in choirs. But the gods had gone away, and the ritual of the religion continued senselessly, uselessly.

Twelve noon.

A dog whined, shivering, on the front porch.

The front door recognized the dog voice and opened. The dog, once huge and fleshy, but now gone to bone and covered with sores, moved in and through the house, tracking mud. Behind it whirled angry mice, angry at having to pick up mud, angry at inconvenience.

For not a leaf fragment blew under the door but what the wall panels flipped open and the copper scrap rats flashed swiftly out. The offending dust, hair, or paper, seized in miniature steel jaws, was raced back to the burrows. There, down tubes which fed into the cellar, it was dropped into the sighing vent of an incinerator which sat like evil Baal in a dark corner. 20

The dog ran upstairs, hysterically yelping to each door, at last realizing, as the house realized, that only silence was here.

It sniffed the air and scratched the kitchen door. Behind the door, the stove was making pancakes which filled the house with a rich baked odor and the scent of maple syrup.

The dog frothed at the mouth, lying at the door, sniffing, its eyes turned to fire. It ran wildly in circles, biting at its tail, spun in a frenzy, and died. It lay in the parlor for an hour.

Two o'clock, sang a voice.

Delicately sensing decay at last, the regiments of mice hummed out 25 as softly as blown gray leaves in an electrical wind.

Two-fifteen.

The dog was gone.

In the cellar, the incinerator glowed suddenly and a whirl of sparks leaped up the chimney.

Two thirty-five.

Bridge tables sprouted from patio walls. Playing cards fluttered 30 onto pads in a shower of pips. Martinis manifested on an oaken bench with egg-salad sandwiches. Music played.

But the tables were silent and the cards untouched.

At four o'clock the tables folded like great butterflies back through the paneled walls.

Four-thirty.

The nursery walls glowed.

Animals took shape: yellow giraffes, blue lions, pink antelopes, 35 lilac panthers cavorting in crystal substance. The walls were glass. They looked out upon color and fantasy. Hidden films clocked through well-oiled sprockets, and the walls lived. The nursery floor was woven to resemble a crisp, cereal meadow. Over this ran aluminum roaches and iron crickets, and in the hot still air butterflies of delicate red tissue wavered among the sharp aroma of animal spoors! There was the sound like a great matted yellow hive of bees within a dark bellows, the lazy bumble of a purring lion. And there was the patter of okapi feet and the murmur of a fresh jungle rain, like other hoofs, falling upon the summer-starched grass. Now the walls dissolved into distances of parched weed, mile on mile, and warm endless sky. The animals drew away into thorn brakes and water holes.

It was the children's hour.

Five o'clock. The bath filled with clear hot water.

Six, seven, eight o'clock, The dinner dishes manipulated like magic tricks, and in the study a *click.* In the metal stand opposite the hearth where a fire now blazed up warmly, a cigar popped out, half an inch of soft gray ash on it, smoking, waiting.

Nine o'clock. The beds warmed their hidden circuits, for nights were cool here.

Nine-five. A voice spoke from the study ceiling: 40

"Mrs. McClellan, which poem would you like this evening?"

The house was silent.

The voice said at last, "Since you express no preference, I shall select a poem at random." Quiet music rose to back the voice. "Sara Teasdale. As I recall, your favorite. . . .

"There will come soft rains and the smell of the ground,
And swallows circling with their shimmering sound;

And frogs in the pools singing at night,
And wild plum trees in tremulous white;

Robins will wear their feathery fire,
Whistling their whims on a low fence-wire;

And not one will know of the war, not one
Will care at last when it is done.

Not one would mind, neither bird nor tree,
If mankind perished utterly;

And Spring herself, when she woke at dawn
Would scarcely know that we were gone."

The fire burned on the stone hearth and the cigar fell away into a mound of quiet ash on its tray. The empty chairs faced each other between the silent walls, and the music played.

At ten o'clock the house began to die.   45

The wind blew. A falling tree bough crashed through the kitchen window. Cleaning solvent, bottled, shattered over the stove. The room was ablaze in an instant!

"Fire!" screamed a voice. The house lights flashed, water pumps shot water from the ceilings. But the solvent spread on the linoleum, licking, eating, under the kitchen door, while the voices took it up in chorus: "Fire, fire, fire!"

The house tried to save itself. Doors sprang tightly shut, but the windows were broken by the heat and the wind blew and sucked upon the fire.

The house gave ground as the fire in ten billion angry sparks moved with flaming ease from room to room and then up the stairs. While scurrying water rats squeaked from the walls, pistoled their water, and ran for more. And the wall sprays let down showers of mechanical rain.

But too late. Somewhere, sighing, a pump shrugged to a stop. The   50
quenching rain ceased. The reserve water supply which had filled baths and washed dishes for many quiet days was gone.

The fire crackled up the stairs. It fed upon Picassos and Matisses in the upper halls, like delicacies, baking off the oily flesh, tenderly crisping the canvases into black shavings.

Now the fire lay in beds, stood in windows, changed the colors of drapes!

And then, reinforcements.

From attic trapdoors, blind robot faces peered down with faucet mouths gushing green chemical.

The fire backed off, as even an elephant must at the sight of a dead   55
snake. Now there were twenty snakes whipping over the floor, killing the fire with a clear cold venom of green froth.

But the fire was clever. It had sent flames outside the house, up through the attic to the pumps there. An explosion! The attic brain which directed the pumps was shattered into bronze shrapnel on the beams.

The fire rushed back into every closet and felt of the clothes hung there.

The house shuddered, oak bone on bone, its bared skeleton cringing from the heat, its wire, its nerves revealed as if a surgeon had torn the skin off to let the red veins and capillaries quiver in the scalded air. Help, help! Fire! Run, run! Heat snapped mirrors like the brittle winter ice. And the voices wailed Fire, fire, run, run, like a tragic nursery rhyme, a dozen voices, high, low, like children dying in a forest, alone, alone. And the voices fading as the wires popped their sheathings like hot chestnuts. One, two, three, four, five voices died.

In the nursery the jungle burned. Blue lions roared, purple giraffes bounded off. The panthers ran in circles, changing color, and ten million animals, running before the fire, vanished off toward a distant steaming river. . . .

Ten more voices died. In the last instant under the fire avalanche, other choruses, oblivious, could be heard announcing the time, playing music, cutting the lawn by remote-control mower, or setting an umbrella frantically out and in the slamming and opening front door, a thousand things happening, like a clock shop when each clock strikes the hour insanely before or after the other, a scene of maniac confusion, yet unity; singing, screaming, a few last cleaning mice darting bravely out to carry the horrid ashes away! And one voice, with sublime disregard for the situation, read poetry aloud in the fiery study, until all the film spools burned, until all the wires withered and the circuits cracked.

The fire burst the house and let it slam flat down, puffing out skirts of spark and smoke.

In the kitchen, an instant before the rain of fire and timber, the stove could be seen making breakfasts at a psychopathic rate, ten dozen eggs, six loaves of toast, twenty dozen bacon strips, which, eaten by fire, started the stove working again, hysterically hissing!

The crash. The attic smashing into kitchen and parlor. The parlor into cellar, cellar into sub-cellar. Deep freeze, armchair, film tapes, circuits, beds, and all like skeletons thrown in a cluttered mound deep under.

Smoke and silence. A great quantity of smoke.

Dawn showed faintly in the east. Among the ruins, one wall stood 65
alone. Within the wall, a last voice said, over and over again and again,
even as the sun rose to shine upon the heaped rubble and steam:

"Today is August 5, 2057, today is August 5, 2057, today is . . ."

STUDY QUESTIONS

1. What is the SETTING of this story—what has happened as the story opens?

2. If technological advancements are the CAUSE, what are their EFFECTS—both positive and negative—in this story?

3. Reread the poem by Sara Teasdale within the story. What does the poem predict will be Nature's reaction when mankind perishes? What does happen? Discuss the IRONY of the poem's relationship to the events in the story.

4. *For Writing.* In an essay, explore your own relationship to technology. Do you use a GPS? An MP3 player? Do you reach for your cell phone out of muscle memory? Consider all the ways in which you interact with technology on a daily basis and determine whether those interactions are ultimately helpful or could have negative consequences. Be sure to cite—and examine in detail—specific examples.

RALPH ELLISON { *Battle Royal*

RALPH ELLISON (1913–1994) published only one novel in his lifetime, yet he holds a spot as one of America's great writers. Though Ellison gave his birth year as 1914, recent biographers have determined that he was born March 1, 1913, in Oklahoma City, Oklahoma, just six years after statehood. A gifted trumpeter, Ellison attended Tuskegee Institute to study music composition. After three years, he moved to New York City, where he met author Richard Wright, who encouraged Ellison to begin writing. His National Book Award–winning novel, *Invisible Man,* was published in 1952. A coming-of-age story that deals with race and identity, it is frequently cited among the most important American books. Following his death, some two thousand pages of manuscript were edited down into the novel *Juneteenth* (1999).

"Battle Royal," the opening chapter of *Invisible Man,* explores the process of how a young black valedictorian attempts to make his speech to an audience of "upstanding" white male members of the community who prefer to see him fight other young black men in a "battle royal," a fight among more than two combatants in which the winner is the last person standing. What are the obstacles to his making his speech clearly and confidently? What does this story say about the power dynamics between black and white individuals?

IT GOES A LONG WAY back, some twenty years. All my life I had been looking for something, and everywhere I turned someone tried to tell me what it was. I accepted their answers too, though they were often

in contradiction and even self-contradictory. I was naïve. I was looking for myself and asking everyone except myself questions which I,
and only I, could answer. It took me a long time and much painful
boomeranging of my expectations to achieve a realization everyone
else appears to have been born with: That I am nobody but myself.
But first I had to discover that I am an invisible man!

And yet I am no freak of nature, nor of history. I was in the cards,
other things having been equal (or unequal) eighty-five years ago. I am
not ashamed of my grandparents for having been slaves. I am only
ashamed of myself for having at one time been ashamed. About eighty-
five years ago they were told that they were free, united with others
of our country in everything pertaining to the common good, and,
in everything social, separate like the fingers of the hand. And they
believed it. They exulted in it. They stayed in their place, worked hard,
and brought up *my* father to do the same. But my grandfather is the one.
He was an odd old guy, my grandfather, and I am told I take after him.
It was he who caused the trouble. On his deathbed he called my father
to him and said, "Son, after I'm gone I want you to keep up the good
fight. I never told you, but our life is a war and I have been a traitor all
my born days, a spy in the enemy's country ever since I give up my gun
back in the Reconstruction. Live with your head in the lion's mouth. I
want you to overcome 'em with yeses, undermine 'em with grins, agree
'em to death and destruction, let 'em swoller you till they vomit or bust
wide open." They thought the old man had gone out of his mind. He
had been the meekest of men. The younger children were rushed from
the room, the shades drawn and the flame of the lamp turned so
low that it sputtered on the wick like the old man's breathing. "Learn
it to the younguns," he whispered fiercely; then he died.

But my folks were more alarmed over his last words than over his
dying. It was as though he had not died at all, his words caused so
much anxiety. I was warned emphatically to forget what he had said
and, indeed, this is the first time it has been mentioned outside the
family circle. It had a tremendous effect upon me, however. I could
never be sure of what he meant. Grandfather had been a quiet old man
who never made any trouble, yet on his deathbed he had called himself
a traitor and a spy, and he had spoken of his meekness as a dangerous

activity. It became a constant puzzle which lay unanswered in the back of my mind. And whenever things went well for me I remembered my grandfather and felt guilty and uncomfortable. It was as though I was carrying out his advice in spite of myself. And to make it worse, everyone loved me for it. I was praised by the most lily-white men of the town. I was considered an example of desirable conduct— just as my grandfather had been. And what puzzled me was that the old man had defined it as *treachery*. When I was praised for my conduct I felt a guilt that in some way I was doing something that was really against the wishes of the white folks, that if they had understood they would have desired me to act just the opposite, that I should have been sulky and mean, and that that really would have been what they wanted, even though they were fooled and thought they wanted me to act as I did. It made me afraid that some day they would look upon me as a traitor and I would be lost. Still I was more afraid to act any other way because they didn't like that at all. The old man's words were like a curse. On my graduation day I delivered an oration in which I showed that humility was the secret, indeed, the very essence of progress. (Not that I believed this—how could I, remembering my grandfather?—I only believed that it worked.) It was a great success. Everyone praised me and I was invited to give the speech at a gathering of the town's leading white citizens. It was a triumph for our whole community.

It was in the main ballroom of the leading hotel. When I got there I discovered that it was on the occasion of a smoker, and I was told that since I was to be there anyway I might as well take part in the battle royal to be fought by some of my schoolmates as part of the entertainment. The battle royal came first.

All of the town's big shots were there in their tuxedoes, wolfing 5 down the buffet foods, drinking beer and whiskey and smoking black cigars. It was a large room with a high ceiling. Chairs were arranged in neat rows around three sides of a portable boxing ring. The fourth side was clear, revealing a gleaming space of polished floor. I had some misgivings over the battle royal, by the way. Not from a distaste for fighting, but because I didn't care too much for the other fellows who were to take part. They were tough guys who seemed to have no grandfather's curse worrying their minds. No one could mistake their toughness. And besides, I suspected that fighting a battle royal might detract from the dignity of my speech. In those pre-invisible days I visualized myself as a potential Booker T. Washington. But the other fellows didn't care too much for me either, and there were nine of them. I felt superior to them in my way, and I didn't like the manner in which we were all crowded together into the servants' elevator. Nor did they like my being there. In fact, as the warmly lighted floors flashed past the elevator we had words over the fact that I, by taking part in the fight, had knocked one of their friends out of a night's work.

We were led out of the elevator through a rococo hall into an anteroom and told to get into our fighting togs. Each of us was issued a pair of boxing gloves and ushered out into the big mirrored hall, which we entered looking cautiously about us and whispering, lest we might accidentally be heard above the noise of the room. It was foggy with cigar smoke. And already the whiskey was taking effect. I was shocked to see some of the most important men of the town quite tipsy. They were all there—bankers, lawyers, judges, doctors, fire chiefs, teachers, merchants. Even one of the more fashionable pastors. Something we could not see was going on up front. A clarinet was vibrating sensuously and the men were standing up and moving eagerly forward. We were a small tight group, clustered together, our bare upper bodies touching and shining with anticipatory sweat; while up front the big shots were becoming increasingly excited over something we still could not see. Suddenly I heard the school superintendent, who had told me to come, yell, "Bring up the shines, gentlemen! Bring up the little shines!"

We were rushed up to the front of the ballroom, where it smelled even more strongly of tobacco and whiskey. Then we were pushed into place. I almost wet my pants. A sea of faces, some hostile, some amused, ringed around us, and in the center, facing us, stood a magnificent blonde—stark naked. There was dead silence. I felt a blast of cold air chill me. I tried to back away, but they were behind me and around me. Some of the boys stood with lowered heads, trembling. I felt a wave of irrational guilt and fear. My teeth chattered, my skin turned to goose flesh, my knees knocked. Yet I was strongly attracted and looked in spite of myself. Had the price of looking been blindness,

I would have looked. The hair was yellow like that of a circus kewpie doll, the face heavily powdered and rouged, as though to form an abstract mask, the eyes hollow and smeared a cool blue, the color of a baboon's butt. I felt a desire to spit upon her as my eyes brushed slowly over her body. Her breasts were firm and round as the domes of East Indian temples, and I stood so close as to see the fine skin texture and beads of pearly perspiration glistening like dew around the pink and erected buds of her nipples. I wanted at one and the same time to run from the room, to sink through the floor, or go to her and cover her from my eyes and the eyes of the others with my body; to feel the soft thighs, to caress her and destroy her, to love her and murder her, to hide from her, and yet to stroke where below the small American flag tattooed upon her belly her thighs formed a capital V. I had a notion that of all in the room she saw only me with her impersonal eyes.

And then she began to dance, a slow sensuous movement; the smoke of a hundred cigars clinging to her like the thinnest of veils. She seemed like a fair bird-girl girdled in veils calling to me from the angry surface of some gray and threatening sea. I was transported. Then I became aware of the clarinet playing and the big shots yelling at us. Some threatened us if we looked and others if we did not. On my right I saw one boy faint. And now a man grabbed a silver pitcher from a table and stepped close as he dashed ice water upon him and stood him up and forced two of us to support him as his head hung and moans issued from his thick bluish lips. Another boy began to plead to go home. He was the largest of the group, wearing dark red fighting trunks much too small to conceal the erection which projected from him as though in answer to the insinuating low-registered moaning of the clarinet. He tried to hide himself with his boxing gloves.

And all the while the blonde continued dancing, smiling faintly at the big shots who watched her with fascination, and faintly smiling at our fear. I noticed a certain merchant who followed her hungrily, his lips loose and drooling. He was a large man who wore diamond studs in a shirtfront which swelled with the ample paunch underneath, and each time the blonde swayed her undulating hips he ran his hand through the thin hair of his bald head and, with his arms upheld, his posture clumsy like that of an intoxicated panda, wound his belly in a slow and obscene grind. This creature was completely hypnotized. The music had quickened. As the dancer flung herself about with a detached expression on her face, the men began reaching out to touch her. I could see their beefy fingers sink into the soft flesh. Some of the others tried to stop them and she began to move around the floor in graceful circles, as they gave chase, slipping and sliding over the polished floor. It was mad. Chairs went crashing, drinks were spilt, as they ran laughing and howling after her. They caught her just as she reached a door, raised her from the floor, and tossed her as college boys are tossed at a hazing, and above her red, fixed-smiling lips I saw the terror and disgust in her eyes, almost like my own terror and that which I saw in some of the other boys. As I watched, they tossed her twice and her soft breasts seemed to flatten against the air and her legs flung wildly as she spun. Some of the more sober ones helped her to escape. And I started off the floor, heading for the anteroom with the rest of the boys.

Some were still crying and in hysteria. But as we tried to leave we were stopped and ordered to get into the ring. There was nothing to do but what we were told. All ten of us climbed under the ropes and allowed ourselves to be blindfolded with broad bands of white cloth. One of the men seemed to feel a bit sympathetic and tried to cheer us up as we stood with our backs against the ropes. Some of us tried to grin. "See that boy over there?" one of the men said. "I want you to run across at the bell and give it to him right in the belly. If you don't get him, I'm going to get you. I don't like his looks." Each of us was told the same. The blindfolds were put on. Yet even then I had been going over my speech. In my mind each word was as bright as flame. I felt the cloth pressed into place, and frowned so that it would be loosened when I relaxed.

But now I felt a sudden fit of blind terror. I was unused to darkness. It was as though I had suddenly found myself in a dark room filled with poisonous cottonmouths. I could hear the bleary voices yelling insistently for the battle royal to begin.

"Get going in there!"

"Let me at that big nigger!"

I strained to pick up the school superintendent's voice, as though to squeeze some security out of that slightly more familiar sound.

"Let me at those black sonsabitches!" someone yelled.   15

"No, Jackson, no!" another voice yelled. "Here, somebody, help me hold Jack."

"I want to get at that ginger-colored nigger. Tear him limb from limb," the first voice yelled.

I stood against the ropes trembling. For in those days I was what they called ginger-colored, and he sounded as though he might crunch me between his teeth like a crisp ginger cookie.

Quite a struggle was going on. Chairs were being kicked about and I could hear voices grunting as with a terrific effort. I wanted to see, to see more desperately than ever before. But the blindfold was tight as a thick skin-puckering scab and when I raised my gloved hands to push the layers of white aside a voice yelled, "Oh, no you don't, black bastard! Leave that alone!"

"Ring the bell before Jackson kills him a coon!" someone boomed   20 in the sudden silence. And I heard the bell clang and the sound of the feet scuffing forward.

A glove smacked against my head. I pivoted, striking out stiffly as someone went past, and felt the jar ripple along the length of my arm to my shoulder. Then it seemed as though all nine of the boys had turned upon me at once. Blows pounded me from all sides while I struck out as best I could. So many blows landed upon me that I wondered if I were not the only blindfolded fighter in the ring, or if the man called Jackson hadn't succeeded in getting me after all.

Blindfolded, I could no longer control my motions. I had no dignity. I stumbled about like a baby or a drunken man. The smoke had become thicker, and with each new blow it seemed to sear and further restrict my lungs. My saliva became like hot bitter glue. A glove connected with my head, filling my mouth with warm blood. It was everywhere. I could not tell if the moisture I felt upon my body was sweat or blood. A blow landed hard against the nape of my neck. I felt myself going over, my head hitting the floor. Streaks of blue light filled the black world behind the blindfold. I lay prone, pretending that I was knocked out, but felt myself seized by hands and yanked to my feet. "Get going, black boy! Mix it up!" My arms were like lead, my head smarting from blows. I managed to feel my way to the ropes and held on, trying to catch my breath. A glove landed in my mid-section and I went over again, feeling as though the smoke had become a knife jabbed into my guts. Pushed this way and that by the legs milling around me, I finally pulled erect and discovered that I could see the black, sweat-washed forms weaving, in the smoky-blue atmosphere like drunken dancers weaving to the rapid drumlike thuds of blows.

Everyone fought hysterically. It was complete anarchy. Everybody fought everybody else. No group fought together for long. Two, three, four, fought one, then turned to fight each other, were themselves attacked. Blows landed below the belt and in the kidney, with the gloves open as well as closed, and with my eye partly opened now there was not so much terror. I moved carefully, avoiding blows, although not too many to attract attention, fighting from group to group. The boys groped about like blind, cautious crabs crouching to protect their mid-sections, their heads pulled in short against their shoulders, their arms stretched nervously before them, with their fists testing the smoke-filled air like the knobbed feelers of hypersensitive snails. In one corner I glimpsed a boy violently punching the air and heard him scream in pain as he smashed his hand against a ring post. For a second I saw him bent over holding his hand, then going down as a blow caught his unprotected head. I played one group against the other, slipping in and throwing a punch then stepping out of range while pushing the others into the melee to take the blows blindly aimed at me. The smoke was agonizing and there were no rounds, no bells at three-minute intervals to relieve our exhaustion. The room spun round me, a swirl of lights, smoke, sweating bodies surrounded by tense white faces. I bled from both nose and mouth, the blood spattering upon my chest.

The men kept yelling, "Slug him, black boy! Knock his guts out!"

"Uppercut him! Kill him! Kill that big boy!"   25

Taking a fake fall, I saw a boy going down heavily beside me as though we were felled by a single blow, saw a sneaker-clad foot shoot into his groin as the two who had knocked him down stumbled upon him. I rolled out of range, feeling a twinge of nausea.

The harder we fought the more threatening the men became. And yet, I had begun to worry about my speech again. How would it go? Would they recognize my ability? What would they give me?

I was fighting automatically when suddenly I noticed that one after another of the boys was leaving the ring. I was surprised, filled with panic, as though I had been left alone with an unknown danger. Then I understood. The boys had arranged it among themselves. It was the custom for the two men left in the ring to slug it out for the winner's prize. I discovered this too late. When the bell sounded two men in tuxedoes leaped into the ring and removed the blindfold. I found myself facing Tatlock, the biggest of the gang. I felt sick at my stomach. Hardly had the bell stopped ringing in my ears than it clanged again and I saw him moving swiftly toward me. Thinking of nothing else to do I hit him smash on the nose. He kept coming, bringing the rank sharp violence of stale sweat. His face was a black blank of a face, only his eyes alive—with hate of me and aglow with a feverish terror from what had happened to us all. I became anxious. I wanted to deliver my speech and he came at me as though he meant to beat it out of me. I smashed him again and again, taking his blows as they came. Then on a sudden impulse I struck him lightly and as we clinched, I whispered, "Fake like I knocked you out, you can have the prize."

"I'll break your behind," he whispered hoarsely.

"For *them*?"

"For *me*, sonofabitch!"

They were yelling for us to break it up and Tatlock spun me half around with a blow, and as a joggled camera sweeps in a reeling scene, I saw the howling red faces crouching tense beneath the cloud of blue-gray smoke. For a moment the world wavered, unraveled, flowed, then my head cleared and Tatlock bounced before me. That fluttering shadow before my eyes was his jabbing left hand. Then falling forward, my head against his damp shoulder, I whispered.

"I'll make it five dollars more."

"Go to hell!"

But his muscles relaxed a trifle beneath my pressure and I breathed, "Seven?"

"Give it to your ma," he said, ripping me beneath the heart.

And while I still held him I butted him and moved away. I felt myself bombarded with punches. I fought back with hopeless desperation. I wanted to deliver my speech more than anything else in

30

35

the world, because I felt that only these men could judge truly my ability, and now this stupid clown was ruining my chances. I began fighting carefully now, moving in to punch him and out again with my greater speed. A lucky blow to his chin and I had him going too— until I heard a loud voice yell, "I got my money on the big boy."

Hearing this, I almost dropped my guard. I was confused: Should I try to win against the voice out there? Would not this go against my speech, and was not this a moment for humility, for nonresistance? A blow to my head as I danced about sent my right eye popping like a jack-in-the-box and settled my dilemma. The room went red as I fell. It was a dream fall, my body languid and fastidious as to where to land, until the floor became impatient and smashed up to meet me. A moment later I came to. An hypnotic voice said FIVE emphatically. And I lay there, hazily watching a dark red spot of my own blood shaping itself into a butterfly, glistening and soaking into the soiled gray world of the canvas.

When the voice drawled TEN I was lifted up and dragged to a chair. I sat dazed. My eye pained and swelled with each throb of my pounding heart and I wondered if now I would be allowed to speak. I was wringing wet, my mouth still bleeding. We were grouped along the wall now. The other boys ignored me as they congratulated Tatlock and speculated as to how much they would be paid. One boy whimpered over his smashed hand. Looking up front, I saw attendants in white jackets rolling the portable ring away and placing a small square rug in the vacant space surrounded by chairs. Perhaps, I thought, I will stand on the rug to deliver my speech.

Then the M.C. called to us, "Come on up here boys and get your money." 40

We ran forward to where the men laughed and talked in their chairs, waiting. Everyone seemed friendly now.

"There it is on the rug," the man said. I saw the rug covered with coins of all dimensions and a few crumpled bills. But what excited me, scattered here and there, were the gold pieces.

"Boys, it's all yours," the man said. "You get all you grab."

"That's right, Sambo," a blond man said, winking at me confidentially.

I trembled with excitement, forgetting my pain. I would get the 45
gold and the bills, I thought. I would use both hands. I would throw
my body against the boys nearest me to block them from the gold.

"Get down around the rug now," the man commanded, "and don't
anyone touch it until I give the signal."

"This ought to be good," I heard.

As told, we got around the square rug on our knees. Slowly the man
raised his freckled hand as we followed it upward with our eyes.

I heard, "These niggers look like they're about to pray!"

Then, "Ready," the man said. "Go!" 50

I lunged for a yellow coin lying on the blue design of the carpet, touching it and sending a surprised shriek to join those rising around me. I
tried frantically to remove my hand but could not let go. A hot, violent
force tore through my body, shaking me like a wet rat. The rug was elec-
trified. The hair bristled up on my head as I shook myself free. My
muscles jumped, my nerves jangled, writhed. But I saw that this was not
stopping the other boys. Laughing in fear and embarrassment, some
were holding back and scooping up the coins knocked off by the painful
contortions of the others. The men roared above us as we struggled.

"Pick it up, goddamnit, pick it up!" someone called like a bass-
voiced parrot. "Go on, get it!"

I crawled rapidly around the floor, picking up the coins, trying to
avoid the coppers and to get greenbacks and the gold. Ignoring the
shock by laughing, as I brushed the coins off quickly, I discovered that
I could contain the electricity—a contradiction, but it works. Then the
men began to push us onto the rug. Laughing embarrassedly, we struggled out of their hands and kept after the coins. We were all wet and
slippery and hard to hold. Suddenly I saw a boy lifted into the air, glistening with sweat like a circus seal, and dropped, his wet back landing
flush upon the charged rug, heard him yell and saw him literally dance
upon his back, his elbows beating a frenzied tattoo upon the floor, his
muscles twitching like the flesh of a horse stung by many flies. When he
finally rolled off, his face was gray and no one stopped him when he ran
from the floor amid booming laughter.

"Get the money," the M.C. called. "That's good hard American
cash!"

And we snatched and grabbed, snatched and grabbed. I was careful   55
not to come too close to the rug now, and when I felt the hot whiskey
breath descend upon me like a cloud of foul air I reached out and
grabbed the leg of a chair. It was occupied and I held on desperately.

"Leggo, nigger! Leggo!"

The huge face wavered down to mine as he tried to push me free. But
my body was slippery and he was too drunk. It was Mr. Colcord, who
owned a chain of movie houses and "entertainment palaces." Each time
he grabbed me I slipped out of his hands. It became a real struggle.
I feared the rug more than I did the drunk, so I held on, surprising
myself for a moment by trying to topple *him* upon the rug. It was such
an enormous idea that I found myself actually carrying it out. I tried not
to be obvious, yet when I grabbed his leg, trying to tumble him out of
the chair, he raised up roaring with laughter, and, looking at me with
soberness dead in the eye, kicked me viciously in the chest. The chair
leg flew out of my hand and I felt myself going and rolled. It was as
though I had rolled through a bed of hot coals. It seemed a whole century would pass before I would roll free, a century in which I was seared
through the deepest levels of my body to the fearful breath within me
and the breath seared and heated to the point of explosion. It'll all be
over in a flash, I thought as I rolled clear. It'll all be over in a flash.

But not yet, the men on the other side were waiting, red faces swollen as though from apoplexy as they bent forward in their chairs. Seeing their fingers coming toward me I rolled away as a fumbled football
rolls off the receiver's fingertips, back into the coals. That time I luckily sent the rug sliding out of place and heard the coins ringing against
the floor and the boys scuffling to pick them up and the M.C. calling,
"All right, boys, that's all. Go get dressed and get your money."

I was limp as a dish rag. My back felt as though it had been beaten
with wires.

When we had dressed the M.C. came in and gave us each five dol-   60
lars, except Tatlock, who got ten for being last in the ring. Then he told
us to leave. I was not to get a chance to deliver my speech, I thought. I
was going out into the dim alley in despair when I was stopped and
told to go back. I returned to the ballroom, where the men were pushing back their chairs and gathering in groups to talk.

The M.C. knocked on a table for quiet. "Gentlemen," he said, "we almost forgot an important part of the program. A most serious part, gentlemen. This boy was brought here to deliver a speech which he made at his graduation yesterday . . ."

"Bravo!"

"I'm told that he is the smartest boy we've got out there in Greenwood. I'm told that he knows more big words than a pocket-sized dictionary."

Much applause and laughter.

"So now, gentlemen, I want you to give him your attention." 65

There was still laughter as I faced them, my mouth dry, my eye throbbing. I began slowly, but evidently my throat was tense, because they began shouting, "Louder! Louder!"

"We of the younger generation extol the wisdom of that great leader and educator," I shouted, "who first spoke these flaming words of wisdom: 'A ship lost at sea for many days suddenly sighted a friendly vessel. From the mast of the unfortunate vessel was seen a signal: "Water, water; we die of thirst!" The answer from the friendly vessel came back: "Cast down your bucket where you are." The captain of the distressed vessel, at last heeding the injunction, cast down his bucket, and it came up full of fresh sparkling water from the mouth of the Amazon River.' And like him I say, and in his words, 'To those of my race who depend upon bettering their condition in a foreign land, or who underestimate the importance of cultivating friendly relations with the southern white man, who is his next-door neighbor, I would say: "Cast down your bucket where you are"—cast it down in making friends in every manly way of the people of all races by whom we are surrounded . . .'"

I spoke automatically and with such fervor that I did not realize that the men were still talking and laughing until my dry mouth, filling up with blood from the cut, almost strangled me. I coughed, wanting to stop and go to one of the tall brass, sand-filled spittoons to relieve myself, but a few of the men, especially the superintendent, were listening and I was afraid. So I gulped it down, blood, saliva and all, and continued. (What powers of endurance I had during those days! What enthusiasm! What a belief in the rightness of things!) I spoke even louder in spite of the pain. But still they talked and still they laughed, as though deaf with cotton in dirty ears. So I spoke with greater emotional emphasis. I closed my ears and swallowed blood until I was nauseated. The speech seemed a hundred times as long as before, but I could not leave out a single word. All had to be said, each memorized nuance considered, rendered. Nor was that all. Whenever I uttered a word of three or more syllables a group of voices would yell for me to repeat it. I used the phrase "social responsibility" and they yelled:

"What's that word you say, boy?"

"Social responsibility," I said.   70

"What?"

"Social . . ."

"Louder."

". . . responsibility."

"More."   75

"Respon—"

"Repeat!"

"—sibility."

The room filled with the uproar of laughter until, no doubt distracted by having to gulp down my blood, I made a mistake and yelled a phrase I had often seen denounced in newspaper editorials, heard debated in private.

"Social . . ."   80

"What?" they yelled.

". . . equality—"

The laughter hung smokelike in the sudden stillness. I opened my eyes, puzzled. Sounds of displeasure filled the room. The M.C. rushed forward. They shouted hostile phrases at me. But I did not understand.

A small dry mustached man in the front row blared out, "Say that slowly, son!"

"What, sir?"   85

"What you just said!"

"Social responsibility, sir," I said.

"You weren't being smart, were you, boy?" he said, not unkindly.

"No, sir!"

"You sure that about 'equality' was a mistake?" 90

"Oh, yes, sir," I said. "I was swallowing blood."

"Well, you had better speak more slowly so we can understand. We mean to do right by you, but you've got to know your place at all times. All right, now, go on with your speech."

I was afraid. I wanted to leave but I wanted also to speak and I was afraid they'd snatch me down.

"Thank you, sir," I said, beginning where I had left off, and having them ignore me as before.

Yet when I finished there was a thunderous applause. I was sur- 95 prised to see the superintendent come forth with a package wrapped in white tissue paper, and, gesturing for quiet, address the men.

"Gentlemen, you see that I did not overpraise this boy. He makes a good speech and some day he'll lead his people in the proper paths. And I don't have to tell you that that is important in these days and times. This is a good, smart boy, and so to encourage him in the right direction, in the name of the Board of Education I wish to present him a prize in the form of this . . ."

He paused, removing the tissue paper and revealing a gleaming calfskin brief case.

". . . in the form of this first-class article from Shad Whitmore's shop."

"Boy," he said, addressing me, "take this prize and keep it well. Consider it a badge of office. Prize it. Keep developing as you are and some day it will be filled with important papers that will help shape the destiny of your people."

I was so moved that I could hardly express my thanks. A rope of 100 bloody saliva forming a shape like an undiscovered continent drooled upon the leather and I wiped it quickly away. I felt an importance that I had never dreamed.

"Open it and see what's inside," I was told.

My fingers a-tremble, I complied, smelling the fresh leather and finding an official-looking document inside. It was a scholarship to the state college for Negroes. My eyes filled with tears and I ran awkwardly off the floor.

I was overjoyed; I did not even mind when I discovered that the gold pieces I had scrambled for were brass pocket tokens advertising a certain make of automobile.

When I reached home everyone was excited. Next day the neighbors came to congratulate me. I even felt safe from grandfather, whose deathbed curse usually spoiled my triumphs. I stood beneath his photograph with my brief case in hand and smiled triumphantly into his stolid black peasant's face. It was a face that fascinated me. The eyes seemed to follow everywhere I went.

That night I dreamed I was at a circus with him and that he refused to laugh at the clowns no matter what they did. Then later he told me to open my brief case and read what was inside and I did, finding an official envelope stamped with the state seal; and inside the envelope I found another and another, endlessly, and I thought I would fall of weariness. "Them's years," he said. "Now open that one." And I did and in it I found an engraved document containing a short message in letters of gold. "Read it," my grandfather said. "Out loud!"

"To Whom It May Concern," I intoned. "Keep This Nigger-Boy Running."

I awoke with the old man's laughter ringing in my ears.

(It was a dream I was to remember and dream again for many years after. But at that time I had no insight into its meaning. First I had to attend college.)

STUDY QUESTIONS

1. Why does the mild-mannered, passive grandfather say that he has been a "traitor in enemy country"? How can the grandfather's advice to both "live with your head in the lion's mouth" and "overcome 'em with yeses" be followed?

2. The NARRATOR'S speech borrows directly from Booker T. Washington's "Atlanta Exposition Address." Locate a copy of Washington's speech and COMPARE AND CONTRAST it to what the narrator says. How are the SETTINGS for the two speeches different? What is the EFFECT of the narrator's using Washington's conciliatory rhetoric after a battle royal?

3. This story depicts the narrator's reflection on the PROCESS of giving his valedictory speech. What do the blindfolds that the young men wear during the battle royal SYMBOLIZE? How do they prevent the fighters from recognizing truths about themselves and others around them? Does the narrator see clearly by the end of the process? Why or why not?

4. *For Writing.* Consider some of the elements of the traditional American dream: healthy competition, financial success, a good education, an attractive, loving spouse, being respected among one's peers in the community. In an essay, explore how Ellison's story twists these elements. Why and how does the American dream become an American nightmare for this young, African American protagonist?

JOYCE CAROL OATES 〈 *Where Are You Going,*
Where Have You Been?

Joyce Carol Oates (b. 1938) is a prolific and versatile writer whose work is popular both with the general reading public (her 1996 novel *We Were the Mulvaneys* was featured on Oprah's Book Club) and in academia, where her fiction and poetry often appear on the syllabi of college courses. Oates was raised in a rural area near Lockport, New York, and earned her BA at Syracuse University; as a student there, she won a fiction contest sponsored by *Mademoiselle* magazine. She went on to obtain an MA in English at the University of Wisconsin. She has taught at the University of Windsor and is currently a professor of creative writing at Princeton. The author of more than one hundred novels, novellas, and short story collections, as well as many books of poetry, plays, and essays, Oates received the National Book Award in 1970 for her novel *them*, which, like much of her fiction, reimagines historical events in fictional form. Her other novels include *Black Water* (1993), *What I Lived For* (1994), *Blonde* (2000), and *The Gravedigger's Daughter* (2007).

"Where Are You Going, Where Have You Been?" (1966) is Oates's most anthologized short story. It presents a vivid picture of the seemingly conventional life of its teenaged protagonist, Connie, and describes what happens when an element of danger is introduced. As you read, consider how the story both reflects and undercuts the popular culture of the early 1960s.

for Bob Dylan[1]

HER NAME WAS CONNIE. SHE was fifteen and she had a quick, nervous giggling habit of craning her neck to glance into mirrors or checking other people's faces to make sure her own was all right. Her mother, who noticed everything and knew everything and who hadn't much reason any longer to look at her own face, always scolded Connie about it. "Stop gawking at yourself. Who are you? You think you're so pretty?" she would say. Connie would raise her eyebrows at these familiar old complaints and look right through her mother, into a shadowy vision of herself as she was right at that moment: she knew she was pretty and that was everything. Her mother had been pretty once too, if you could believe those old snapshots in the album, but now her looks were gone and that was why she was always after Connie.

"Why don't you keep your room clean like your sister? How've you got your hair fixed—what the hell stinks? Hair spray? You don't see your sister using that junk."

Her sister June was twenty-four and still lived at home. She was a secretary in the high school Connie attended, and if that wasn't bad enough—with her in the same building—she was so plain and chunky and steady that Connie had to hear her praised all the time by her mother and her mother's sisters. June did this, June did that, she saved money and helped clean the house and cooked and Connie couldn't do a thing, her mind was all filled with trashy daydreams. Their father was away at work most of the time and when he came home he wanted supper and he read the newspaper at supper and after supper he went to bed. He didn't bother talking much to them, but around his bent head Connie's mother kept picking at her until Connie wished her mother was dead and she herself was dead and it was all over. "She makes me want to throw up sometimes," she complained to her friends. She had a high, breathless, amused voice that made everything she said sound a little forced, whether it was sincere or not.

---

[1] The mood and tone of this story was inspired by American folk and rock singer and songwriter Bob Dylan (b. 1941).

There was one good thing: June went places with girl friends of hers, girls who were just as plain and steady as she, and so when Connie wanted to do that her mother had no objections. The father of Connie's best girl friend drove the girls the three miles to town and left them at a shopping plaza so they could walk through the stores or go to a movie, and when he came to pick them up again at eleven he never bothered to ask what they had done.

They must have been familiar sights, walking around the shopping plaza in their shorts and flat ballerina slippers that always scuffed the sidewalk, with charm bracelets jingling on their thin wrists; they would lean together to whisper and laugh secretly if someone passed who amused or interested them. Connie had long dark blond hair that drew anyone's eye to it, and she wore part of it pulled up on her head and puffed out and the rest of it she let fall down her back. She wore a pull-over jersey blouse that looked one way when she was at home and another way when she was away from home. Everything about her had two sides to it, one for home and one for anywhere that was not home: her walk, which could be childlike and bobbing, or languid enough to make anyone think she was hearing music in her head; her mouth, which was pale and smirking most of the time, but bright and pink on these evenings out; her laugh, which was cynical and drawling at home—"Ha, ha, very funny,"—but high-pitched and nervous anywhere else, like the jingling of the charms on her bracelet.

Sometimes they did go shopping or to a movie, but sometimes they went across the highway, ducking fast across the busy road, to a drive-in restaurant where older kids hung out. The restaurant was shaped like a big bottle, though squatter than a real bottle, and on its cap was a revolving figure of a grinning boy holding a hamburger aloft. One night in midsummer they ran across, breathless with daring, and right away someone leaned out a car window and invited them over, but it was just a boy from high school they didn't like. It made them feel good to be able to ignore him. They went up through the maze of parked and cruising cars to the bright-lit, fly-infested restaurant, their faces pleased and expectant as if they were entering a sacred building that loomed up out of the night to give them what haven and blessing they yearned for.

They sat at the counter and crossed their legs at the ankles, their thin shoulders rigid with excitement, and listened to the music that made everything so good: the music was always in the background, like music at a church service; it was something to depend upon.

A boy named Eddie came in to talk with them. He sat backwards on his stool, turning himself jerkily around in semicircles and then stopping and turning back again, and after a while he asked Connie if she would like something to eat. She said she would and so she tapped her friend's arm on her way out—her friend pulled her face up into a brave, droll look—and Connie said she would meet her at eleven, across the way. "I just hate to leave her like that," Connie said earnestly, but the boy said that she wouldn't be alone for long. So they went out to his car, and on the way Connie couldn't help but let her eyes wander over the windshields and faces all around her, her face gleaming with a joy that had nothing to do with Eddie or even this place; it might have been the music. She drew her shoulders up and sucked in her breath with the pure pleasure of being alive, and just at that moment she happened to glance at a face just a few feet from hers. It was a boy with shaggy black hair, in a convertible jalopy painted gold. He stared at her and then his lips widened into a grin. Connie slit her eyes at him and turned away, but she couldn't help glancing back and there he was, still watching her. He wagged a finger and laughed and said, "Gonna get you, baby," and Connie turned away again without Eddie noticing anything.

She spent three hours with him, at the restaurant where they ate hamburgers and drank Cokes in wax cups that were always sweating, and then down an alley a mile or so away, and when he left her off at five to eleven only the movie house was still open at the plaza. Her girl friend was there, talking with a boy. When Connie came up, the two girls smiled at each other and Connie said, "How was the movie?" and the girl said, "*You* should know." They rode off with the girl's father, sleepy and pleased, and Connie couldn't help but look back at the darkened shopping plaza with its big empty parking lot and its signs that were faded and ghostly now, and over at the drive-in restaurant where cars were still circling tirelessly. She couldn't hear the music at this distance.

Next morning June asked her how the movie was and Connie said, "So-so."

She and that girl and occasionally another girl went out several ¹⁰ times a week, and the rest of the time Connie spent around the house—it was summer vacation—getting in her mother's way and thinking, dreaming about the boys she met. But all the boys fell back and dissolved into a single face that was not even a face but an idea, a feeling, mixed up with the urgent insistent pounding of the music and the humid night air of July. Connie's mother kept dragging her back to the daylight by finding things for her to do or saying suddenly, "What's this about the Pettinger girl?"

And Connie would say nervously, "Oh, her. That dope." She always drew thick clear lines between herself and such girls, and her mother was simple and kind enough to believe it. Her mother was so simple, Connie thought, that it was maybe cruel to fool her so much. Her mother went scuffling around the house in old bedroom slippers and complained over the telephone to one sister about the other, then the other called up and the two of them complained about the third one. If June's name was mentioned her mother's tone was approving, and if Connie's name was mentioned it was disapproving. This did not really mean she disliked Connie, and actually Connie thought that her mother preferred her to June just because she was prettier, but the two of them kept up a pretense of exasperation, a sense that they were tugging and struggling over something of little value to either of them. Sometimes, over coffee, they were almost friends, but something would come up—some vexation that was like a fly buzzing suddenly around their heads—and their faces went hard with contempt.

One Sunday Connie got up at eleven—none of them bothered with church—and washed her hair so that it could dry all day long in the sun. Her parents and sister were going to a barbecue at an aunt's house and Connie said no, she wasn't interested, rolling her eyes to let her mother know just what she thought of it. "Stay home alone then," her mother said sharply. Connie sat out back in a lawn chair and watched them drive away, her father quiet and bald, hunched around so that he could back the car out, her mother with a look that was still angry and not at all softened through the windshield, and in the back seat poor old June, all dressed up as if she didn't know what a barbecue was, with all the running yelling kids and the flies. Connie sat with her eyes closed in the sun, dreaming and dazed with the warmth about her as if this were a kind of love, the caresses of love, and her mind slipped over onto thoughts of the boy she had been with the night before and how nice he had been, how sweet it always was, not the way someone like June would suppose but sweet, gentle, the way it was in movies and promised in songs; and when she opened her eyes she hardly knew where she was, the back yard ran off into weeds and a fence-like line of trees and behind it the sky was perfectly blue and still. The asbestos "ranch house" that was now three years old startled her—it looked small. She shook her head as if to get awake.

It was too hot. She went inside the house and turned on the radio to drown out the quiet. She sat on the edge of her bed, barefoot, and listened for an hour and a half to a program called XYZ Sunday Jamboree, record after record of hard, fast, shrieking songs she sang along with, interspersed by exclamations from "Bobby King": "An' look here, you girls at Napoleon's—Son and Charley want you to pay real close attention to this song coming up!"

And Connie paid close attention herself, bathed in a glow of slow-pulsed joy that seemed to rise mysteriously out of the music itself and lay languidly about the airless little room, breathed in and breathed out with each gentle rise and fall of her chest.

After a while she heard a car coming up the drive. She sat up at once, startled, because it couldn't be her father so soon. The gravel kept crunching all the way in from the road—the driveway was long—and Connie ran to the window. It was a car she didn't know. It was an open jalopy, painted a bright gold that caught the sunlight opaquely. Her heart began to pound and her fingers snatched at her hair, checking it, and she whispered, "Christ. Christ," wondering how bad she looked. The car came to a stop at the side door and the horn sounded four short taps, as if this were a signal Connie knew.

She went into the kitchen and approached the door slowly, then hung out the screen door, her bare toes curling down off the step. There were two boys in the car and now she recognized the driver: he had shaggy, shabby black hair that looked crazy as a wig and he was grinning at her.

15

"I ain't late, am I?" he said.

"Who the hell do you think you are?" Connie said.

"Toldja I'd be out, didn't I?"

"I don't even know who you are."   20

She spoke sullenly, careful to show no interest or pleasure, and he spoke in a fast, bright monotone. Connie looked past him to the other boy, taking her time. He had fair brown hair, with a lock that fell onto his forehead. His sideburns gave him a fierce, embarrassed look, but so far he hadn't even bothered to glance at her. Both boys wore sunglasses. The driver's glasses were metallic and mirrored everything in miniature.

"You wanta come for a ride?" he said.

Connie smirked and let her hair fall loose over one shoulder.

"Don'tcha like my car? New paint job," he said. "Hey."

"What?"   25

"You're cute."

She pretended to fidget, chasing flies away from the door.

"Don'tcha believe me, or what?" he said.

"Look, I don't even know who you are," Connie said in disgust.

"Hey, Ellie's got a radio, see. Mine broke down." He lifted his   30 friend's arm and showed her the little transistor radio the boy was holding, and now Connie began to hear the music. It was the same program that was playing inside the house.

"Bobby King?" she said.

"I listen to him all the time. I think he's great."

"He's kind of great," Connie said reluctantly.

"Listen, that guy's *great*. He knows where the action is."

Connie blushed a little, because the glasses made it impossible for   35 her to see just what this boy was looking at. She couldn't decide if she liked him or if he was just a jerk, and so she dawdled in the doorway and wouldn't come down or go back inside. She said, "What's all that stuff painted on your car?"

"Can'tcha read it?" He opened the door very carefully, as if he were afraid it might fall off. He slid out just as carefully, planting his feet firmly on the ground, the tiny metallic world in his glasses slowing down like gelatine hardening, and in the midst of it Connie's bright green blouse. "This here is my name, to begin with," he said. ARNOLD

FRIEND was written in tarlike black letters on the side, with a drawing of a round, grinning face that reminded Connie of a pumpkin, except it wore sunglasses. "I wanta introduce myself, I'm Arnold Friend and that's my real name and I'm gonna be your friend, honey, and inside the car's Ellie Oscar, he's kinda shy." Ellie brought his transistor radio up to his shoulder and balanced it there. "Now, these numbers are a secret code, honey," Arnold Friend explained. He read off the numbers 33, 19, 17 and raised his eyebrows at her to see what she thought of that, but she didn't think much of it. The left rear fender had been smashed and around it was written, on the gleaming gold background: DONE BY CRAZY WOMAN DRIVER. Connie had to laugh at that. Arnold Friend was pleased at her laughter and looked up at her. "Around the other side's a lot more—you wanta come and see them?"

"No."

"Why not?"

"Why should I?"

"Don'tcha wanta see what's on the car? Don'tcha wanta go for a ride?"   40

"I don't know."

"Why not?"

"I got things to do."

"Like what?"

"Things."   45

He laughed as if she had said something funny. He slapped his thighs. He was standing in a strange way, leaning back against the car as if he were balancing himself. He wasn't tall, only an inch or so taller than she would be if she came down to him. Connie liked the way he was dressed, which was the way all of them dressed: tight faded jeans stuffed into black, scuffed boots, a belt that pulled his waist in and showed how lean he was, and a white pull-over shirt that was a little soiled and showed the hard small muscles of his arms and shoulders. He looked as if he probably did hard work, lifting and carrying things. Even his neck looked muscular. And his face was a familiar face, somehow: the jaw and chin and cheeks slightly darkened because he hadn't shaved for a day or two, and the nose long and hawklike, sniffing as if she were a treat he was going to gobble up and it was all a joke.

"Connie, you ain't telling the truth. This is your day set aside for a ride with me and you know it," he said, still laughing. The way he straightened and recovered from his fit of laughing showed that it had been all fake.

"How do you know what my name is?" she said suspiciously.

"It's Connie."

"Maybe and maybe not." 50

"I know my Connie," he said, wagging his finger. Now she remembered him even better, back at the restaurant, and her cheeks warmed at the thought of how she had sucked in her breath just at the moment she passed him—how she must have looked to him. And he had remembered her. "Ellie and I come out here especially for you," he said. "Ellie can sit in back. How about it?"

"Where?"

"Where what?"

"Where're we going?"

He looked at her. He took off the sunglasses and she saw how pale 55 the skin around his eyes was, like holes that were not in shadow but instead in light. His eyes were like chips of broken glass that catch the light in an amiable way. He smiled. It was as if the idea of going for a ride somewhere, to someplace, was a new idea to him.

"Just for a ride, Connie sweetheart."

"I never said my name was Connie," she said.

"But I know what it is. I know your name and all about you, lots of things," Arnold Friend said. He had not moved yet but stood still leaning back against the side of his jalopy. "I took a special interest in you, such a pretty girl, and found out all about you—like I know your parents and sister are gone somewhere and I know where and how long they're going to be gone, and I know who you were with last night, and your best girl friend's name is Betty. Right?"

He spoke in a simple lilting voice, exactly as if he were reciting the words to a song. His smile assured her that everything was fine. In the car Ellie turned up the volume on his radio and did not bother to look around at them.

"Ellie can sit in the back seat," Arnold Friend said. He indicated his 60 friend with a casual jerk of his chin, as if Ellie did not count and she should not bother with him.

"How'd you find out all that stuff?" Connie said.

"Listen: Betty Schultz and Tony Fitch and Jimmy Pettinger and Nancy Pettinger," he said in a chant. "Raymond Stanley and Bob Hutter—"

"Do you know all those kids?"

"I know everybody."

"Look, you're kidding. You're not from around here." 65

"Sure."

"But—how come we never saw you before?"

"Sure you saw me before," he said. He looked down at his boots, as if he were a little offended. "You just don't remember."

"I guess I'd remember you," Connie said.

"Yeah?" He looked up at this, beaming. He was pleased. He began to 70 mark time with the music from Ellie's radio, tapping his fists lightly together. Connie looked away from his smile to the car, which was painted so bright it almost hurt her eyes to look at it. She looked at that name, ARNOLD FRIEND. And up at the front fender was an expression that was familiar—MAN THE FLYING SAUCERS. It was an expression kids had used the year before but didn't use this year. She looked at it for a while as if the words meant something to her that she did not yet know.

"What're you thinking about? Huh?" Arnold Friend demanded. "Not worried about your hair blowing around in the car, are you?"

"No."

"Think I maybe can't drive good?"

"How do I know?"

"You're a hard girl to handle. How come?" he said. "Don't you 75 know I'm your friend? Didn't you see me put my sign in the air when you walked by?"

"What sign?"

"My sign." And he drew an X in the air, leaning out toward her. They were maybe ten feet apart. After his hand fell back to his side the X was still in the air, almost visible. Connie let the screen door close and stood perfectly still inside it, listening to the music from her radio and the boy's blend together. She stared at Arnold Friend. He stood there so stiffly relaxed, pretending to be relaxed, with one hand idly on the door handle as if he were keeping himself up that way and had no intention of ever moving again. She recognized most things about him, the tight jeans that showed his thighs and buttocks and the greasy leather boots and the tight shirt, and even that slippery friendly smile of his, that sleepy dreamy smile that all the boys used to get across ideas they didn't want to put into words. She recognized all this and also the singsong way he talked, slightly mocking, kidding, but serious and a little melancholy, and she recognized the way he tapped one fist against the other in homage to the perpetual music behind him. But all these things did not come together.

She said suddenly, "Hey, how old are you?"

His smiled faded. She could see then that he wasn't a kid, he was much older—thirty, maybe more. At this knowledge her heart began to pound faster.

"That's a crazy thing to ask. Can'tcha see I'm your own age?" 80

"Like hell you are."

"Or maybe a coupla years older. I'm eighteen."

"Eighteen?" she said doubtfully.

He grinned to reassure her and lines appeared at the corners of his mouth. His teeth were big and white. He grinned so broadly his eyes became slits and she saw how thick the lashes were, thick and black as if painted with a black tarlike material. Then, abruptly, he seemed to become embarrassed and looked over his shoulder at Ellie. "*Him,* he's crazy," he said. "Ain't he a riot? He's a nut, a real character." Ellie was still listening to the music. His sunglasses told nothing about what he was thinking. He wore a bright orange shirt unbuttoned halfway to show his chest, which was a pale, bluish chest and not muscular like Arnold Friend's. His shirt collar was turned up all around and the very tips of the collar pointed out past his chin as if they were protecting him. He was pressing the transistor radio up against his ear and sat there in a kind of daze, right in the sun.

"He's kinda strange," Connie said. 85

"Hey, she says you're kinda strange! Kinda strange!" Arnold Friend cried. He pounded on the car to get Ellie's attention. Ellie turned for the first time and Connie saw with shock that he wasn't a kid either— he had a fair, hairless face, cheeks reddened slightly as if the veins grew too close to the surface of his skin, the face of a forty-year-old baby.

Connie felt a wave of dizziness rise in her at this sight and she stared at him as if waiting for something to change the shock of the moment, make it all right again. Ellie's lips kept shaping words, mumbling along with the words blasting in his ear.

"Maybe you two better go away," Connie said faintly.

"What? How come?" Arnold Friend cried. "We come out here to take you for a ride. It's Sunday." He had the voice of the man on the radio now. It was the same voice, Connie thought. "Don'tcha know it's Sunday all day? And honey, no matter who you were with last night, today you're with Arnold Friend and don't you forget it! Maybe you better step out here," he said, and this last was in a different voice. It was a little flatter, as if the heat was finally getting to him.

"No. I got things to do."

"Hey." 90

"You two better leave."

"We ain't leaving until you come with us."

"Like hell I am—"

"Connie, don't fool around with me. I mean—I mean, don't fool *around*," he said, shaking his head. He laughed incredulously. He placed his sunglasses on top of his head, carefully, as if he were indeed wearing a wig, and brought the stems down behind his ears. Connie stared at him, another wave of dizziness and fear rising in her so that for a moment he wasn't even in focus but was just a blur standing there against his gold car, and she had the idea that he had driven up the driveway all right but had come from nowhere before that and belonged nowhere and that everything about him and even about the music that was so familiar to her was only half real.

"If my father comes and sees you—" 95

"He ain't coming. He's at a barbecue."

"How do you know that?"

"Aunt Tillie's. Right now they're—uh—they're drinking. Sitting around," he said vaguely, squinting as if he were staring all the way to town and over to Aunt Tillie's back yard. Then the vision seemed to get clear and he nodded energetically. "Yeah. Sitting around. There's your sister in a blue dress, huh? And high heels, the poor sad bitch—

nothing like you, sweetheart! And your mother's helping some fat woman with the corn, they're cleaning the corn—husking the corn—"

"What fat woman?" Connie cried.

"How do I know what fat woman, I don't know every goddamn fat woman in the world!" Arnold Friend laughed. 100

"Oh, that's Mrs. Hornsby. . . . Who invited her?" Connie said. She felt a little lightheaded. Her breath was coming quickly.

"She's too fat. I don't like them fat. I like them the way you are, honey," he said, smiling sleepily at her. They stared at each other for a while through the screen door. He said softly, "Now, what you're going to do is this: you're going to come out that door. You're going to sit up front with me and Ellie's going to sit in the back, the hell with Ellie, right? This isn't Ellie's date. You're my date. I'm your lover, honey."

"What? You're crazy—"

"Yes, I'm your lover. You don't know what that is but you will," he said. "I know that too. I know all about you. But look: it's real nice and you couldn't ask for nobody better than me, or more polite. I always keep my word. I'll tell you how it is, I'm always nice at first, the first time. I'll hold you so tight you won't think you have to try to get away or pretend anything because you'll know you can't. And I'll come inside you where it's all secret and you'll give in to me and you'll love me—"

"Shut up! You're crazy!" Connie said. She backed away from the 105 door. She put her hands up against her ears as if she'd heard something terrible, something not meant for her. "People don't talk like that, you're crazy," she muttered. Her heart was almost too big now for her chest and its pumping made sweat break out all over her. She looked out to see Arnold Friend pause and then take a step toward the porch, lurching. He almost fell. But, like a clever drunken man, he managed to catch his balance. He wobbled in his high boots and grabbed hold of one of the porch posts.

"Honey?" he said. "You still listening?"

"Get the hell out of here!"

"Be nice, honey. Listen."

"I'm going to call the police—"

He wobbled again and out of the side of his mouth came a fast spat   110
curse, an aside not meant for her to hear. But even this "Christ!"
sounded forced. Then he began to smile again. She watched this smile
come, awkward as if he were smiling from inside a mask. His whole
face was a mask, she thought wildly, tanned down to his throat but then
running out as if he had plastered make-up on his face but had forgotten about his throat.

"Honey—? Listen, here's how it is. I always tell the truth and I
promise you this: I ain't coming in that house after you."

"You better not! I'm going to call the police if you—if you don't—"

"Honey," he said, talking right through her voice, "honey, I'm not
coming in there but you are coming out here. You know why?"

She was panting. The kitchen looked like a place she had never seen
before, some room she had run inside but that wasn't good enough,
wasn't going to help her. The kitchen window had never had a curtain, after three years, and there were dishes in the sink for her to do—
probably—and if you ran your hand across the table you'd probably
feel something sticky there.

"You listening, honey? Hey?"   115

"—going to call the police—"

"Soon as you touch the phone I don't need to keep my promise and
can come inside. You won't want that."

She rushed forward and tried to lock the door. Her fingers were
shaking. "But why lock it," Arnold Friend said gently, talking right into
her face. "It's just a screen door. It's just nothing." One of his boots was
at a strange angle, as if his foot wasn't in it. It pointed out to the left,
bent at the ankle. "I mean, anybody can break through a screen door
and glass and wood and iron or anything else if he needs to, anybody
at all, and specially Arnold Friend. If the place got lit up with a fire,
honey, you'd come runnin' out into my arms, right into my arms an'
safe at home—like you knew I was your lover and'd stopped fooling
around. I don't mind a nice shy girl but I don't like no fooling around."
Part of those words were spoken with a slight rhythmic lilt, and Connie
somehow recognized them—the echo of a song from last year, about a
girl rushing into her boy friend's arms and coming home again—

Connie stood barefoot on the linoleum floor, staring at him. "What do you want?" she whispered.

"I want you," he said. 120

"What?"

"Seen you that night and thought, that's the one, yes sir. I never needed to look anymore."

"But my father's coming back. He's coming to get me. I had to wash my hair first—" She spoke in a dry, rapid voice, hardly raising it for him to hear.

"No, your daddy is not coming and yes, you had to wash your hair and you washed it for me. It's nice and shining and all for me. I thank you, sweetheart," he said with a mock bow, but again he almost lost his balance. He had to bend and adjust his boots. Evidently his feet did not go all the way down; the boots must have been stuffed with something so that he would seem taller. Connie stared out at him and behind him at Ellie in the car, who seemed to be looking off toward Connie's right, into nothing. This Ellie said, pulling the words out of the air one after another as if he were just discovering them, "You want me to pull out the phone?"

"Shut your mouth and keep it shut," Arnold Friend said, his face 125 red from bending over or maybe from embarrassment because Connie had seen his boots. "This ain't none of your business."

"What—what are you doing? What do you want?" Connie said. "If I call the police they'll get you, they'll arrest you—"

"Promise was not to come in unless you touch that phone, and I'll keep that promise," he said. He resumed his erect position and tried to force his shoulders back. He sounded like a hero in a movie, declaring something important. But he spoke too loudly and it was as if he were speaking to someone behind Connie. "I ain't made plans for coming in that house where I don't belong but just for you to come out to me, the way you should. Don't you know who I am?"

"You're crazy," she whispered. She backed away from the door but did not want to go into another part of the house, as if this would give him permission to come through the door. "What do you . . . you're crazy, you. . . ."

"Huh? What're you saying, honey?"

Her eyes darted everywhere in the kitchen. She could not remem- 130
ber what it was, this room.

"This is how it is, honey: you come out and we'll drive away, have a
nice ride. But if you don't come out we're gonna wait till your people
come home and then they're all going to get it."

"You want that telephone pulled out?" Ellie said. He held the radio
away from his ear and grimaced, as if without the radio the air was too
much for him.

"I toldja shut up, Ellie," Arnold Friend said, "you're deaf, get a hearing aid, right? Fix yourself up. This little girl's no trouble and's gonna
be nice to me, so Ellie keep to yourself, this ain't your date—right?
Don't hem in on me, don't hog, don't crush, don't bird dog, don't trail
me," he said in a rapid, meaningless voice, as if he were running
through all the expressions he'd learned but was no longer sure which
of them was in style, then rushing on to new ones, making them up
with his eyes closed. "Don't crawl under my fence, don't squeeze in my
chipmunk hole, don't sniff my glue, suck my Popsicle, keep your own
greasy fingers on yourself!" He shaded his eyes and peered in at
Connie, who was backed against the kitchen table. "Don't mind him,
honey, he's just a creep. He's a dope. Right? I'm the boy for you and
like I said, you come out here nice like a lady and give me your hand,
and nobody else gets hurt, I mean, your nice old bald-headed daddy
and your mummy and your sister in her high heels. Because listen: why
bring them in this?"

"Leave me alone," Connie whispered.

"Hey, you know that old woman down the road, the one with the 135
chickens and stuff—you know her?"

"She's dead!"

"Dead? What? You know her?" Arnold Friend said.

"She's dead—"

"Don't you like her?"

"She's dead—she's—she isn't here any more—" 140

"But don't you like her, I mean, you got something against her?
Some grudge or something?" Then his voice dipped as if he were con-

scious of a rudeness. He touched the sunglasses perched up on top of his head as if to make sure they were still there. "Now, you be a good girl."

"What are you going to do?"

"Just two things, or maybe three," Arnold Friend said. "But I promise it won't last long and you'll like me the way you get to like people you're close to. You will. It's all over for you here, so come on out. You don't want your people in any trouble, do you?"

She turned and bumped against a chair or something, hurting her leg, but she ran into the back room and picked up the telephone. Something roared in her ear, a tiny roaring, and she was so sick with fear that she could do nothing but listen to it—the telephone was clammy and very heavy and her fingers groped down to the dial but were too weak to touch it. She began to scream into the phone, into the roaring. She cried out, she cried for her mother, she felt her breath start jerking back and forth in her lungs as if it were something Arnold Friend was stabbing her with again and again with no tenderness. A noisy sorrowful wailing rose all about her and she was locked inside it the way she was locked inside this house.

After a while she could hear again. She was sitting on the floor with   145
her wet back against the wall.

Arnold Friend was saying from the door, "That's a good girl. Put the phone back."

She kicked the phone away from her.

"No, honey. Pick it up. Put it back right."

She picked it up and put it back. The dial tone stopped.

"That's a good girl. Now, you come outside."   150

She was hollow with what had been fear but what was now just an emptiness. All that screaming had blasted it out of her. She sat, one leg cramped under her, and deep inside her brain was something like a pinpoint of light that kept going and would not let her relax. She thought, I'm not going to see my mother again. She thought, I'm not going to sleep in my bed again. Her bright green blouse was all wet.

Arnold Friend said, in a gentle-loud voice that was like a stage voice, "The place where you came from ain't there any more, and where you had in mind to go is cancelled out. This place you are now—inside your daddy's house—is nothing but a cardboard box I can knock down any time. You know that and always did know it. You hear me?"

She thought, I have got to think. I have got to know what to do.

"We'll go out to a nice field, out in the country here where it smells so nice and it's sunny," Arnold Friend said. "I'll have my arms tight around you so you won't need to try to get away and I'll show you what love is like, what it does. The hell with this house! It looks solid all right," he said. He ran a fingernail down the screen and the noise did not make Connie shiver, as it would have the day before. "Now, put your hand on your heart, honey. Feel that? That feels solid too but we know better. Be nice to me, be sweet like you can because what else is there for a girl like you but to be sweet and pretty and give in?—and get away before her people come back?"

She felt her pounding heart. Her hand seemed to enclose it. She 155 thought for the first time in her life that it was nothing that was hers, that belonged to her, but just a pounding, living thing inside this body that wasn't really hers either.

"You don't want them to get hurt," Arnold Friend went on. "Now, get up, honey. Get up all by yourself."

She stood.

"Now, turn this way. That's right. Come over here to me.—Ellie, put that away, didn't I tell you? You dope. You miserable creepy dope," Arnold Friend said. His words were not angry but only part of an incantation. The incantation was kindly. "Now, come out through the kitchen to me, honey, and let's see a smile, try it, you're a brave, sweet little girl and now they're eating corn and hot dogs cooked to bursting over an outdoor fire, and they don't know one thing about you and never did and honey, you're better than them because not a one of them would have done this for you."

Connie felt the linoleum under her feet; it was cool. She brushed her hair back out of her eyes. Arnold Friend let go of the post tentatively and opened his arms for her, his elbows pointing in toward each other and his wrists limp, to show that this was an embarrassed embrace and a little mocking, he didn't want to make her self-conscious.

She put out her hand against the screen. She watched herself push 160 the door slowly open as if she were back safe somewhere in the other doorway, watching this body and this head of long hair moving out into the sunlight where Arnold Friend waited.

"My sweet little blue-eyed girl," he said in a half-sung sigh that had nothing to do with her brown eyes but was taken up just the same by the vast sunlit reaches of the land behind him and on all sides of him— so much land that Connie had never seen before and did not recognize except to know that she was going to it.

STUDY QUESTIONS

1. Where does Connie first encounter Arnold Friend? What does he do when he sees her?

2. One of the techniques that Oates uses to add DESCRIPTION to this story is to include many COMPARISONS (e.g., "as if" statements). Select one of these comparisons that you find interesting. ANALYZE what that comparison adds to the story and provide an updated version of it, using contemporary language.

3. This story is commonly discussed as a coming-of-age NARRATIVE that takes an unexpected turn. Where does the story include the expected components of a coming-of-age story? At what point does its turn to the unexpected take place? How is the story's outcome different from what you would expect from a conventional coming-of-age narrative?

4. The DIALOGUE between Connie and Arnold Friend moves the PLOT forward in the second half of the story. How would you CHARACTERIZE Arnold Friend's language? How does it change as the story progresses? How does it help to establish Arnold Friend's character?

5. *For Writing.* Arnold Friend is a puzzling character, one who is often interpreted symbolically. In an essay, analyze Arnold Friend as a SYMBOL: what do you think he symbolizes? What EVIDENCE from the story supports your analysis?

TIM O'BRIEN { *How to Tell a True War Story*

Tim O'Brien (b. 1946) was born in Austin, Minnesota, and spent his teenage years in Worthington, two locales that inform the setting of much of his fiction. He graduated in 1968 from Macalester College, where he was president of the student body and earned a BA in political science. Following graduation, O'Brien was drafted into the U.S. Army and served in Vietnam from 1969 to 1970. He then entered a PhD program in government studies at Harvard, working as a reporter for the *Washington Post* during the summers; he left graduate school in 1976 to concentrate on his writing. He often writes about his wartime experiences, including in his memoir, *If I Die in a Combat Zone, Box Me Up and Ship Me Home* (1973), and in his critically acclaimed novel *The Things They Carried* (1990). He teaches in the creative writing program at the University of Texas at San Marcos.

"How to Tell a True War Story" is excerpted from *The Things They Carried*. In it, the narrator reflects on the death of Curt Lemon, a fellow soldier in Vietnam, through a series of stories. O'Brien plays with the tension between what he calls "story-truth," or fiction, and "happening-truth," or reality, as the line between the two blurs in the story. How do reality and fiction complicate each other as the narrator explains the process of how to tell a true war story?

THIS IS TRUE.

I had a buddy in Vietnam. His name was Bob Kiley, but everybody called him Rat.

A friend of his gets killed, so about a week later Rat sits down and writes a letter to the guy's sister. Rat tells her what a great brother she had, how together the guy was, a number one pal and comrade. A real soldier's soldier, Rat says. Then he tells a few stories to make the point, how her brother would always volunteer for stuff nobody else would volunteer for in a million years, dangerous stuff, like doing recon or going out on these really badass night patrols. Stainless steel balls, Rat tells her. The guy was a little crazy, for sure, but crazy in a good way, a real daredevil, because he liked the challenge of it, he liked testing himself, just man against gook. A great, great guy, Rat says.

Anyway, it's a terrific letter, very personal and touching. Rat almost bawls writing it. He gets all teary telling about the good times they had together, how her brother made the war seem almost fun, always raising hell and lighting up villes[1] and bringing smoke to bear every which way. A great sense of humor, too. Like the time at this river when he went fishing with a whole damn crate of hand grenades. Probably the funniest thing in world history, Rat says, all that gore, about twenty zillion dead gook fish. Her brother, he had the right attitude. He knew how to have a good time. On Halloween, this real hot spooky night, the dude paints up his body all different colors and puts on this weird mask and hikes over to a ville and goes trick-or-treating almost stark naked, just boots and balls and an M-16. A tremendous human being, Rat says. Pretty nutso sometimes, but you could trust him with your life.

And then the letter gets very sad and serious. Rat pours his heart out. He says he loved the guy. He says the guy was his best friend in the world. They were like soul mates, he says, like twins or something, they had a whole lot in common. He tells the guy's sister he'll look her up when the war's over.

So what happens?

[1] Villages.

Rat mails the letter. He waits two months. The dumb cooze[2] never writes back.

A true war story is never moral. It does not instruct, nor encourage virtue, nor suggest models of proper human behavior, nor restrain men from doing the things men have always done. If a story seems moral, do not believe it. If at the end of a war story you feel uplifted, or if you feel that some small bit of rectitude has been salvaged from the larger waste, then you have been made the victim of a very old and terrible lie. There is no rectitude whatsoever. There is no virtue. As a first rule of thumb, therefore, you can tell a true war story by its absolute and uncompromising allegiance to obscenity and evil. Listen to Rat Kiley. Cooze, he says. He does not say bitch. He certainly does not say woman, or girl. He says cooze. Then he spits and stares. He's nineteen years old—it's too much for him—so he looks at you with those big sad gentle killer eyes and says *cooze*, because his friend is dead, and because it's so incredibly sad and true: she never wrote back.

You can tell a true war story if it embarrasses you. If you don't care for obscenity, you don't care for the truth; if you don't care for the truth, watch how you vote. Send guys to war, they come home talking dirty.

Listen to Rat: "Jesus Christ, man, I write this beautiful fuckin' letter, I slave over it, and what happens? The dumb cooze never writes back."

The dead guy's name was Curt Lemon. What happened was, we crossed a muddy river and marched west into the mountains, and on the third day we took a break along a trail junction in deep jungle. Right away, Lemon and Rat Kiley started goofing. They didn't understand about the spookiness. They were kids; they just didn't know. A nature hike, they thought, not even a war, so they went off into the shade of some giant trees—quadruple canopy, no sunlight at all—and they were giggling and calling each other yellow mother and playing a silly game they'd invented. The game involved smoke grenades, which were harmless unless you did stupid things, and what they did

[2]Vagina, or a woman viewed as a sex object.

was pull out the pin and stand a few feet apart and play catch under the shade of those huge trees. Whoever chickened out was a yellow mother. And if nobody chickened out, the grenade would make a light popping sound and they'd be covered with smoke and they'd laugh and dance around and then do it again.

It's all exactly true.

It happened, to *me*, nearly twenty years ago, and I still remember that trail junction and those giant trees and a soft dripping sound somewhere beyond the trees. I remember the smell of moss. Up in the canopy there were tiny white blossoms, but no sunlight at all, and I remember the shadows spreading out under the trees where Curt Lemon and Rat Kiley were playing catch with smoke grenades. Mitchell Sanders sat flipping his yo-yo. Norman Bowker and Kiowa and Dave Jensen were dozing, or half dozing, and all around us were those ragged green mountains.

Except for the laughter things were quiet.

At one point, I remember, Mitchell Sanders turned and looked at me, not quite nodding, as if to warn me about something, as if he already *knew*, then after a while he rolled up his yo-yo and moved away.

It's hard to tell you what happened next.

They were just goofing. There was a noise, I suppose, which must've been the detonator, so I glanced behind me and watched Lemon step from the shade into bright sunlight. His face was suddenly brown and shining. A handsome kid, really. Sharp gray eyes, lean and narrow-waisted, and when he died it was almost beautiful, the way the sunlight came around him and lifted him up and sucked him high into a tree full of moss and vines and white blossoms.

In any war story, but especially a true one, it's difficult to separate what happened from what seemed to happen. What seems to happen becomes its own happening and has to be told that way. The angles of vision are skewed. When a booby trap explodes, you close your eyes and duck and float outside yourself. When a guy dies, like Curt Lemon, you look away and then look back for a moment and then look away again. The pictures get jumbled; you tend to miss a lot. And then afterward, when you go to tell about it, there is always that surreal seemingness, which makes the story seem untrue, but which in fact represents the hard and exact truth as it *seemed*.

• ○ •

In many cases a true war story cannot be believed. If you believe it, be skeptical. It's a question of credibility. Often the crazy stuff is true and the normal stuff isn't, because the normal stuff is necessary to make you believe the truly incredible craziness.

In other cases you can't even tell a true war story. Sometimes it's just beyond telling.

I heard this one, for example, from Mitchell Sanders. It was near dusk and we were sitting at my foxhole along a wide muddy river north of Quang Ngai. I remember how peaceful the twilight was. A deep pinkish red spilled out on the river, which moved without sound, and in the morning we would cross the river and march west into the mountains. The occasion was right for a good story.

"God's truth," Mitchell Sanders said. "A six-man patrol goes up into the mountains on a basic listening-post operation. The idea's to spend a week up there, just lie low and listen for enemy movement. They've got a radio along, so if they hear anything suspicious—anything—they're supposed to call in artillery or gunships, whatever it takes. Otherwise they keep strict field discipline. Absolute silence. They just listen."

Sanders glanced at me to make sure I had the scenario. He was playing with his yo-yo, dancing it with short, tight little strokes of the wrist.

His face was blank in the dusk.

"We're talking regulation, by-the-book LP. These six guys, they don't say boo for a solid week. They don't got tongues. *All* ears."

"Right," I said.

"Understand me?"

"Invisible."

Sanders nodded.

"Affirm," he said. "Invisible. So what happens is, these guys get themselves deep in the bush, all camouflaged up, and they lie down and wait and that's all they do, nothing else, they lie there for seven straight days and just listen. And man, I'll tell you—it's spooky. This is mountains. You don't *know* spooky till you been there. Jungle, sort of, except it's way up in the clouds and there's always this fog—like rain, except it's not raining—everything's all wet and swirly and tangled up and you can't see jack, you can't find your own pecker to piss with. Like you don't even have a body. Serious spooky. You just go with the vapors—the fog sort of takes you in . . . And the sounds, man. The sounds carry forever. You hear stuff nobody should *ever* hear."

Sanders was quiet for a second, just working the yo-yo, then he smiled at me.

"So after a couple days the guys start hearing this real soft, kind of wacked-out music. Weird echoes and stuff. Like a radio or something, but it's not a radio, it's this strange gook music that comes right out of the rocks. Faraway, sort of, but right up close, too. They try to ignore it. But it's a listening post, right? So they listen. And every night they keep hearing that crazyass gook concert. All kinds of chimes and xylophones. I mean, this is wilderness—no way, it can't be real—but there it *is*, like the mountains are tuned in to Radio fucking Hanoi. Naturally they get nervous. One guy sticks Juicy Fruit in his ears. Another guy almost flips. Thing is, though, they can't report music. They can't get on the horn and call back to base and say, 'Hey, listen, we need some firepower, we got to blow away this weirdo gook rock band.' They can't do that. It wouldn't go down. So they lie there in the fog and keep their mouths shut. And what makes it extra bad, see, is the poor dudes can't horse around like normal. Can't joke it away. Can't even talk to each other except maybe in whispers, all hush-hush, and that just revs up the willies. All they do is listen."

Again there was some silence as Mitchell Sanders looked out on the river. The dark was coming on hard now, and off to the west I could see the mountains rising in silhouette, all the mysteries and unknowns.

"This next part," Sanders said quietly, "you won't believe."

"Probably not," I said.

"You won't. And you know why?" He gave me a long, tired smile. "Because it happened. Because every word is absolutely dead-on true."

Sanders made a sound in his throat, like a sigh, as if to say he didn't care if I believed him or not. But he did care. He wanted me to feel the truth, to believe by the raw force of feeling. He seemed sad, in a way.

"These six guys," he said, "they're pretty fried out by now, and one night they start hearing voices. Like at a cocktail party. That's what it sounds like, this big swank gook cocktail party somewhere out there in the fog. Music and chitchat and stuff. It's crazy, I know, but they hear the champagne corks. They hear the actual martini glasses. Real hoity-toity, all very civilized, except this isn't civilization. This is Nam.

"Anyway, the guys try to be cool. They just lie there and groove, but after a while they start hearing—you won't believe this—they hear chamber music. They hear violins and cellos. They hear this terrific mama-san soprano. Then after a while they hear gook opera and a glee club and the Haiphong Boys Choir and a barbershop quartet and all kinds of weird chanting and Buddha-Buddha stuff. And the whole time, in the background, there's still that cocktail party going on. All these different voices. Not human voices, though. Because it's the mountains. Follow me? The rock—it's *talking*. And the fog, too, and the grass and the goddamn mongooses. Everything talks. The trees talk politics, the monkeys talk religion. The whole country. Vietnam. The place talks. It talks. Understand? Nam—it truly *talks*.

"The guys can't cope. They lose it. They get on the radio and report enemy movement—a whole army, they say—and they order up the firepower. They get arty[3] and gunships. They call in air strikes. And I'll tell you, they fuckin' crash that cocktail party. All night long, they just smoke those mountains. They make jungle juice. They blow away trees and glee clubs and whatever else there is to blow away. Scorch time. They walk napalm up and down the ridges. They bring in the Cobras and F-4s, they use Willie Peter and HE[4] and incendiaries. It's all fire. They make those mountains burn.

---

[3]That is, artillery.

[4]High explosive grenades. *Willie Peter*: white phosphorus, a chemical weapon often dropped in cans from jets during the Vietnam War.

"Around dawn things finally get quiet. Like you never even *heard* quiet before. One of those real thick, real misty days—just clouds and fog, they're off in this special zone—and the mountains are absolutely dead-flat silent. Like Brigadoon—pure vapor, you know? Everything's all sucked up inside the fog. Not a single sound, except they still *hear* it.

"So they pack up and start humping. They head down the mountain, back to base camp, and when they get there they don't say diddly. They don't talk. Not a word, like they're deaf and dumb. Later on this fat bird colonel comes up and asks what the hell happened out there. What'd they hear? Why all the ordnance? The man's ragged out, he gets down tight on their case. I mean, they spent six trillion dollars on firepower, and this fatass colonel wants answers, he wants to know what the fuckin' story is.

"But the guys don't say zip. They just look at him for a while, sort of funny like, sort of amazed, and the whole war is right there in that stare. It says everything you can't ever say. It says, man, you got *wax* in your ears. It says, poor bastard, you'll never know—wrong frequency—you don't *even* want to hear this. Then they salute the fucker and walk away, because certain stories you don't ever tell."

You can tell a true war story by the way it never seems to end. Not then, not ever. Not when Mitchell Sanders stood up and moved off into the dark.

It all happened.

Even now, at this instant, I remember that yo-yo. In a way, I suppose, you had to be there, you had to hear it, but I could tell how desperately Sanders wanted me to believe him, his frustration at not quite getting the details right, not quite pinning down the final and definitive truth.

And I remember sitting at my foxhole that night, watching the shadows of Quang Ngai, thinking about the coming day and how we would cross the river and march west into the mountains, all the ways I might die, all the things I did not understand.

Late in the night Mitchell Sanders touched my shoulder.

"Just came to me," he whispered. "The moral, I mean. Nobody listens. Nobody hears nothin'. Like that fatass colonel. The politicians, all the civilian types. Your girlfriend. My girlfriend. Everybody's sweet little virgin girlfriend. What they need is to go out on LP. The vapors, man. Trees and rocks—you got to *listen* to your enemy."

And then again, in the morning, Sanders came up to me. The platoon was preparing to move out, checking weapons, going through all the little rituals that preceded a day's march. Already the lead squad had crossed the river and was filing off toward the west.

"I got a confession to make," Sanders said. "Last night, man, I had to make up a few things."

"I know that."

"The glee club. There wasn't any glee club."

"Right."

"No opera."

"Forget it, I understand."

"Yeah, but listen, it's still true. Those six guys, they heard wicked sound out there. They heard sound you just plain won't believe."

Sanders pulled on his rucksack, closed his eyes for a moment, then almost smiled at me. I knew what was coming.

"All right," I said, "what's the moral?"

"Forget it."

"No, go ahead."

For a long while he was quiet, looking away, and the silence kept stretching out until it was almost embarrassing. Then he shrugged and gave me a stare that lasted all day.

"Hear that quiet, man?" he said. "That quiet—just listen. There's your moral."

In a true war story, if there's a moral at all, it's like the thread that makes the cloth. You can't tease it out. You can't extract the meaning without unraveling the deeper meaning. And in the end, really, there's nothing much to say about a true war story, except maybe "Oh."

True war stories do not generalize. They do not indulge in abstraction or analysis.

For example: War is hell. As a moral declaration the old truism seems perfectly true, and yet because it abstracts, because it generalizes, I can't believe it with my stomach. Nothing turns inside.

It comes down to gut instinct. A true war story, if truly told, makes the stomach believe.

● ○ ●

This one does it for me. I've told it before—many times, many versions—but here's what actually happened.

We crossed that river and marched west into the mountains. On the third day, Curt Lemon stepped on a booby-trapped 105 round. He was playing catch with Rat Kiley, laughing, and then he was dead. The trees were thick; it took nearly an hour to cut an LZ for the dustoff.

Later, higher in the mountains, we came across a baby VC water buffalo. What it was doing there I don't know—no farms or paddies—but we chased it down and got a rope around it and led it along to a deserted village where we set up for the night. After supper Rat Kiley went over and stroked its nose.

He opened up a can of C rations, pork and beans, but the baby buffalo wasn't interested.

Rat shrugged.

He stepped back and shot it through the right front knee. The animal did not make a sound. It went down hard, then got up again, and Rat took careful aim and shot off an ear. He shot it in the hindquarters and in the little hump at its back. He shot it twice in the flanks. It wasn't to kill; it was to hurt. He put the rifle muzzle up against the mouth and shot the mouth away. Nobody said much. The whole platoon stood there watching, feeling all kinds of things, but there wasn't a great deal of pity for the baby water buffalo. Curt Lemon was dead. Rat Kiley had lost his best friend in the world. Later in the week he would write a long personal letter to the guy's sister, who would not write back, but for now it was a question of pain. He shot off the tail. He shot away chunks of meat below the ribs. All around us there was the smell of smoke and filth and deep greenery, and the evening was humid and very hot. Rat went to automatic. He shot randomly, almost casually, quick little spurts in the belly and butt. Then he reloaded, squatted down, and shot it in the left front knee. Again the animal fell hard and tried to get up, but this time it couldn't quite make it. It wobbled and went down sideways. Rat shot it in the nose. He bent forward and whispered something, as if talking to a pet, then he shot it in the throat. All the while the baby buffalo was silent, or almost silent, just a light bubbling sound where the nose had been. It lay very still. Nothing moved except the eyes, which were enormous, the pupils shiny black and dumb.

Rat Kiley was crying. He tried to say something, but then cradled his rifle and went off by himself.

The rest of us stood in a ragged circle around the baby buffalo. For a time no one spoke. We had witnessed something essential, some-thing brand-new and profound, a piece of the world so startling there was not yet a name for it.

Somebody kicked the baby buffalo.

It was still alive, though just barely, just in the eyes.

"Amazing," Dave Jensen said. "My whole life, I never seen anything like it."

"Never?"

"Not hardly. Not once."

Kiowa and Mitchell Sanders picked up the baby buffalo. They hauled it across the open square, hoisted it up, and dumped it in the village well.

Afterward, we sat waiting for Rat to get himself together.

"Amazing," Dave Jensen kept saying. "A new wrinkle. I never seen it before."

Mitchell Sanders took out his yo-yo. "Well, that's Nam," he said. "Garden of Evil. Over here, man, every sin's real fresh and original."

How do you generalize?

War is hell, but that's not the half of it, because war is also mystery and terror and adventure and courage and discovery and holiness and pity and despair and longing and love. War is nasty; war is fun. War is thrilling; war is drudgery. War makes you a man; war makes you dead.

The truths are contradictory. It can be argued, for instance, that war is grotesque. But in truth war is also beauty. For all its horror, you can't help but gape at the awful majesty of combat. You stare out at tracer rounds unwinding through the dark like brilliant red ribbons. You crouch in ambush as a cool, impassive moon rises over the night-time paddies. You admire the fluid symmetries of troops on the move, the harmonies of sound and shape and proportion, the great sheets of metal-fire streaming down from a gunship, the illumination rounds, the white phosphorus, the purply orange glow of napalm, the rocket's red glare. It's not pretty, exactly. It's astonishing. It fills the eye. It commands you. You hate it, yes, but your eyes do not. Like a killer forest fire, like cancer under a microscope, any battle of bombing raid or artillery barrage has the aesthetic purity of absolute moral indifference—a powerful, implacable beauty—and a true war story will tell the truth about this, though the truth is ugly.

To generalize about war is like generalizing about peace. Almost everything is true. Almost nothing is true. At its core, perhaps, war is just another name for death, and yet any soldier will tell you, if he tells the truth, that proximity to death brings with it a corresponding proximity to life. After a firefight, there is always the immense pleasure of aliveness. The trees are alive. The grass, the soil—everything. All around you things are purely living, and you among them, and the aliveness makes you tremble. You feel an intense, out-of-the-skin awareness of your living self—your truest self, the human being you want to be and then become by the force of wanting it. In the midst of evil you want to be a good man. You want decency. You want justice and courtesy and human concord, things you never knew you wanted. There is a kind of largeness to it, a kind of godliness. Though it's odd, you're never more alive than when you're almost dead. You recognize what's valuable. Freshly, as if for the first time, you love what's best in yourself and in the world, all that might be lost. At the hour of dusk you sit at your foxhole and look out on a wide river turning pinkish red, and at the mountains beyond, and although in the morning you must cross the river and go into the mountains and do terrible things and maybe die, even so, you find yourself studying the fine colors on the river, you feel wonder and awe at the setting of the sun, and you are filled with a hard, aching love for how the world could be and always should be, but now is not.

Mitchell Sanders was right. For the common soldier, at least, war has the feel—the spiritual texture—of a great ghostly fog, thick and permanent. There is no clarity. Everything swirls. The old rules are no longer binding, the old truths no longer true. Right spills over into wrong. Order blends into chaos, love into hate, ugliness into beauty, law into anarchy, civility into savagery. The vapors suck you in. You can't tell where you are, or why you're there, and the only certainty is overwhelming ambiguity.

In war you lose your sense of the definite, hence your sense of truth itself, and therefore it's safe to say that in a true war story nothing is ever absolutely true.

Often in a true war story there is not even a point, or else the point doesn't hit you until twenty years later, in your sleep, and you wake up and shake your wife and start telling the story to her, except when you get to the end you've forgotten the point again. And then for a long time you lie there watching the story happen in your head. You listen to your wife's breathing. The war's over. You close your eyes. You smile and think, Christ, what's the *point?*

This one wakes me up.

In the mountains that day, I watched Lemon turn sideways. He laughed and said something to Rat Kiley. Then he took a peculiar half step, moving from shade into bright sunlight, and the booby-trapped 105 round blew him into a tree. The parts were just hanging there, so Dave Jensen and I were ordered to shinny up and peel him off. I remember the white bone of an arm. I remember pieces of skin and something wet and yellow that must've been the intestines. The gore was horrible, and stays with me. But what wakes me up twenty years later is Dave Jensen singing "Lemon Tree"[5] as we threw down the parts.

---

[5]Folk song recorded by Peter, Paul, and Mary in the 1960s. The lyrics run, in part, "Lemon tree, very pretty / And the lemon flower is sweet / But the fruit of the poor lemon is impossible to eat."

You can tell a true war story by the questions you ask. Somebody tells a story, let's say, and afterward you ask, "Is it true?" and if the answer matters, you've got your answer.

For example, we've all heard this one. Four guys go down a trail. A grenade sails out. One guy jumps on it and takes the blast and saves his three buddies.

Is it true?

The answer matters.

You'd feel cheated if it never happened. Without the grounding reality, it's just a trite bit of puffery, pure Hollywood, untrue in the way all such stories are untrue. Yet even if it did happen—and maybe it did, anything's possible—even then you know it can't be true, because a true war story does not depend upon that kind of truth. Absolute occurrence is irrelevant. A thing may happen and be a total lie; another thing may not happen and be truer than the truth. For example: Four guys go down a trail. A grenade sails out. One guy jumps on it and takes the blast, but it's a killer grenade and everybody dies anyway. Before they die, though, one of the dead guys says, "The fuck you do *that* for?" and the jumper says, "Story of my life, man," and the other guy starts to smile but he's dead.

That's a true story that never happened.

Twenty years later, I can still see the sunlight on Lemon's face. I can see him turning, looking back at Rat Kiley, then he laughed and took that curious half step from shade into sunlight, his face suddenly brown and shining, and when his foot touched down, in that instant, he must've thought it was the sunlight that was killing him. It was not the sunlight. It was a rigged 105 round. But if I could ever get the story right, how the sun seemed to gather around him and pick him up and lift him high into a tree, if I could somehow recreate the fatal whiteness of that light, the quick glare, the obvious cause and effect, then you would believe the last thing Curt Lemon believed, which for him must've been the final truth.

Now and then, when I tell this story, someone will come up to me afterward and say she liked it. It's always a woman. Usually it's an older woman of kindly temperament and humane politics. She'll explain that as a rule she hates war stories; she can't understand why people want to wallow in all the blood and gore. But this one she liked. The poor baby buffalo, it made her sad. Sometimes, even, there are little tears. What I should do, she'll say, is put it all behind me. Find new stories to tell.

I won't say it but I'll think it.

I'll picture Rat Kiley's face, his grief, and I'll think, *You dumb cooze.*

Because she wasn't listening.

It *wasn't* a war story. It was a *love* story.

But you can't say that. All you can do is tell it one more time, patiently, adding and subtracting, making up a few things to get at the real truth. No Mitchell Sanders, you tell her. No Lemon, no Rat Kiley. No trail junction. No baby buffalo. No vines or moss or white blossoms. Beginning to end, you tell her, it's all made up. Every goddamn detail—the mountains and the river and especially that poor dumb baby buffalo. None of it happened. *None* of it. And even if it did happen, it didn't happen in the mountains, it happened in this little village on the Batangan Peninsula, and it was raining like crazy, and one night a guy named Stink Harris woke up screaming with a leech on his tongue. You can tell a true war story if you just keep on telling it.

And in the end, of course, a true war story is never about war. It's about sunlight. It's about the special way that dawn spreads out on a river when you know you must cross the river and march into the mountains and do things you are afraid to do. It's about love and memory. It's about sorrow. It's about sisters who never write back and people who never listen.

STUDY QUESTIONS

1. Why does the NARRATOR suggest that Curt Lemon might have believed that the sunlight was killing him?

2. What are the challenges the narrator faces when attempting to tell a "true" war story?

3. How does the narrator attempt to ANALYZE THE PROCESS of telling a true war story? Where do you see both "story-truth" and "happening-truth" in the narrative? How are they both part of the narrator's process?

4. How do the stories told here intersect with one another? What is the effect of the narrator's telling the same story about Lemon in several different ways? Why does he open his story with "This is true," and why does he repeat some form of that idea throughout the story?

5. *For Writing.* Write down a story, about yourself and at least two other people, that you have told in the past. Then write it down again, from each of the other two individuals' perspectives. In an essay, explore how the different perspectives engage both story-truth and happening-truth. What, then, does the teller know and the reader learn about the truths of the story?

FLANNERY O'CONNOR $\Big\{$ *A Good Man Is Hard to Find*

Flannery O'Connor (1925–1964), novelist, short-story writer, and essayist, was born in Savannah, Georgia. She graduated from Georgia State College for Women in 1945 and earned an MFA from the Iowa Writers' Workshop in 1947. O'Connor, whose Catholicism figures prominently in her work, is considered a "Southern Gothic" writer; the genre is defined by disturbing and often grotesque incidents set in the southern United States. O'Connor wrote two novels—Wise Blood (1952) and The Violent Bear It Away (1960)—and six collections of stories, essays, and letters. Her Complete Short Stories, published posthumously in 1971, won the National Book Award.

The following is the title story from *A Good Man Is Hard to Find and Other Stories* (1955). It depicts a family's ill-fated vacation: a wrong turn, a road accident, a confrontation with three escaped convicts. Both humorous and horrifying, the story explores themes of good and evil, religious hypocrisy, and grace. As you read, notice the foreshadowing, the many instances of irony, and the detached narrative tone. Pay attention to the details that O'Connor uses to craft the personalities of each character.

─────────────────

THE GRANDMOTHER DIDN'T WANT TO go to Florida. She wanted to visit some of her connections in east Tennessee and she was seizing every chance to change Bailey's mind. Bailey was the son she lived with, her only boy. He was sitting on the edge of his chair at the table, bent over the orange sports section of the *Journal*. "Now look here, Bailey," she said, "see here, read this," and she stood with one hand on her thin hip and the other rattling the newspaper at his bald head. "Here this fellow that calls himself The Misfit is aloose from the Federal Pen and headed toward Florida and you read here what it says he did to these people. Just you read it. I wouldn't take my children in any direction with a criminal like that aloose in it. I couldn't answer to my conscience if I did."

Bailey didn't look up from his reading so she wheeled around then and faced the children's mother; a young woman in slacks, whose face was as broad and innocent as a cabbage and was tied around with a green headkerchief that had two points on the top like rabbit's ears. She was sitting on the sofa, feeding the baby his apricots out of a jar. "The children have been to Florida before," the old lady said. "You all ought to take them somewhere else for a change so they would see different parts of the world and be broad. They never have been to east Tennessee."

The children's mother didn't seem to hear her, but the eight-year-old boy, John Wesley, a stocky child with glasses, said, "If you don't want to go to Florida, why dontcha stay at home?" He and the little girl, June Star, were reading the funny papers on the floor.

"She wouldn't stay at home to be queen for a day," June Star said without raising her yellow head.

"Yes, and what would you do if this fellow, The Misfit, caught you?" the grandmother asked. 5

"I'd smack his face," John Wesley said.

"She wouldn't stay at home for a million bucks," June Star said. "Afraid she'd miss something. She has to go everywhere we go."

"All right, Miss," the grandmother said. "Just remember that the next time you want me to curl your hair."

June Star said her hair was naturally curly.

The next morning the grandmother was the first one in the car, ready to go. She had her big black valise that looked like the head of a hippopotamus in one corner, and underneath it she was hiding a basket with Pitty Sing,[1] the cat, in it. She didn't intend for the cat to be left 10

[1]The name of a character in Gilbert and Sullivan's comic opera *The Mikado* (1885).

alone in the house for three days because he would miss her too much and she was afraid he might brush against one of the gas burners and accidentally asphyxiate himself. Her son, Bailey, didn't like to arrive at a motel with a cat.

She sat in the middle of the back seat with John Wesley and June Star on either side of her. Bailey and the children's mother and the baby sat in the front and they left Atlanta at eight forty-five with the mileage on the car at 55890. The grandmother wrote this down because she thought it would be interesting to say how many miles they had been when they got back. It took them twenty minutes to reach the outskirts of the city.

The old lady settled herself comfortably, removing her white cotton gloves and putting them up with her purse on the shelf in front of the back window. The children's mother still had on slacks and still had her head tied up in a green kerchief, but the grandmother had on a navy blue straw sailor hat with a bunch of white violets on the brim and a navy blue dress with a small white dot in the print. Her collar and cuffs were white organdy trimmed with lace and at her neckline she had pinned a purple spray of cloth violets containing a sachet. In case of an accident, anyone seeing her dead on the highway would know at once that she was a lady.

She said she thought it was going to be a good day for driving, neither too hot nor too cold, and she cautioned Bailey that the speed limit was fifty-five miles an hour and that the patrolmen hid themselves behind billboards and small clumps of trees and sped out after you before you had a chance to slow down. She pointed out interesting details of the scenery: Stone Mountain;[2] the blue granite that in some places came up to both sides of the highway; the brilliant red clay banks slightly streaked with purple; and the various crops that made rows of green lace-work on the ground. The trees were full of silver-white sunlights and the meanest of them sparkled. The children were reading comic magazines and their mother had gone back to sleep.

---

[2]Memorial to the Confederate States of America near Atlanta, Georgia; it consists of large bas-relief images of generals Stonewall Jackson and Robert E. Lee, and Confederate President Jefferson Davis carved into an immense granite outcrop.

"Let's go through Georgia fast so we won't have to look at it much," John Wesley said.

"If I were a little boy," said the grandmother, "I wouldn't talk about my native state that way. Tennessee has the mountains and Georgia has the hills."

"Tennessee is just a hillbilly dumping ground," John Wesley said, "and Georgia is a lousy state too."

"You said it," June Star said.

"In my time," said the grandmother, folding her thin veined fingers, "children were more respectful of their native states and their parents and everything else. People did right then. Oh look at the cute little pickaninny!" she said and pointed to a Negro child standing in the door of a shack. "Wouldn't that make a picture, now?" she asked and they all turned and looked at the little Negro out of the back window. He waved.

"He didn't have any britches on," June Star said.

"He probably didn't have any," the grandmother explained. "Little niggers in the country don't have things like we do. If I could paint, I'd paint that picture," she said.

The children exchanged comic books.

The grandmother offered to hold the baby and the children's mother passed him over the front seat to her. She set him on her knee and bounced him and told him about the things they were passing. She rolled her eyes and screwed up her mouth and stuck her leathery thin face into his smooth bland one. Occasionally he gave her a faraway smile. They passed a large cotton field with five or six graves fenced in the middle of it, like a small island. "Look at the graveyard!" the grandmother said, pointing it out. "That was the old family burying ground. That belonged to the plantation."

"Where's the plantation?" John Wesley asked.

"Gone With the Wind,"[3] said the grandmother. "Ha. Ha."

When the children finished all the comic books they had brought, they opened the lunch and ate it. The grandmother ate a peanut but-

[3]Title of the best-selling 1936 novel by Margaret Mitchell about the Civil War and the passing of the old South, made into one of the most successful films of all time.

ter sandwich and an olive and would not let the children throw the box and the paper napkins out the window. When there was nothing else to do they played a game by choosing a cloud and making the other two guess what shape it suggested. John Wesley took one the shape of a cow and June Star guessed a cow and John Wesley said, no, an automobile, and June Star said he didn't play fair, and they began to slap each other over the grandmother.

The grandmother said she would tell them a story if they would keep quiet. When she told a story, she rolled her eyes and waved her head and was very dramatic. She said once when she was a maiden lady she had been courted by a Mr. Edgar Atkins Teagarden from Jasper, Georgia. She said he was a very good-looking man and a gentleman and that he brought her a watermelon every Saturday afternoon with his initials cut in it, E.A.T. Well, one Saturday, she said, Mr. Teagarden brought the watermelon and there was nobody at home and he left it on the front porch and returned in his buggy to Jasper, but she never got the watermelon, she said, because a nigger boy ate it when he saw the initials, E.A.T.! This story tickled John Wesley's funny bone and he giggled and giggled but June Star didn't think it was any good. She said she wouldn't marry a man that just brought her a watermelon on Saturday. The grandmother said she would have done well to marry Mr. Teagarden because he was a gentleman and had bought Coca-Cola stock when it first came out and that he had died only a few years ago, a very wealthy man.

They stopped at The Tower for barbecued sandwiches. The Tower was a part-stucco and part-wood filling station and dance hall set in a clearing outside of Timothy. A fat man named Red Sammy Butts ran it and there were signs stuck here and there on the building and for miles up and down the highway saying, TRY RED SAMMY'S FAMOUS BARBECUE. NONE LIKE FAMOUS RED SAMMY'S! RED SAM! THE FAT BOY WITH THE HAPPY LAUGH. A VETERAN! RED SAMMY'S YOUR MAN!

Red Sammy was lying on the bare ground outside The Tower with his head under a truck while a gray monkey about a foot high, chained to a small chinaberry tree, chattered nearby. The monkey sprang back into the tree and got on the highest limb as soon as he saw the children jump out of the car and run toward him.

Inside, The Tower was a long dark room with a counter at one end and tables at the other and dancing space in the middle. They all sat down at a broad table next to the nickelodeon[4] and Red Sam's wife, a tall burnt-brown woman with hair and eyes lighter than her skin, came and took their order. The children's mother put a dime in the machine and played "The Tennessee Waltz," and the grandmother said that tune always made her want to dance. She asked Bailey if he would like to dance but he only glared at her. He didn't have a naturally sunny disposition like she did and trips made him nervous. The grandmother's brown eyes were very bright. She swayed her head from side to side and pretended she was dancing in her chair. June Star said play something she could tap to so the children's mother put in another dime and played a fast number and June Star stepped out onto the dance floor and did her tap routine.

"Ain't she cute?" Red Sam's wife said, leaning over the counter. 30
"Would you like to come be my little girl?"

"No, I certainly wouldn't," June Star said. "I wouldn't live in a broken-down place like this for a million bucks!" and she ran back to the table.

"Ain't she cute?" the woman repeated, stretching her mouth politely.

"Aren't you ashamed?" hissed the grandmother.

Red Sam came in and told his wife to quit lounging on the counter and hurry up with these people's order. His khaki trousers reached just to his hip bones and his stomach hung over them like a sack of meal swaying under his shirt. He came over and sat down at a table nearby and let out a combination sigh and yodel. "You can't win," he said. "You can't win," and he wiped his sweating red face off with a gray handkerchief. "These days you don't know who to trust," he said. "Ain't that the truth?"

"People are certainly not nice like they used to be," said the grand- 35
mother.

"Two fellers come in here last week," Red Sammy said, "driving a Chrysler. It was an old beat-up car but it was a good one and these boys looked all right to me. Said they worked at the mill and you know I let them fellers charge the gas they bought? Now why did I do that?"

"Because you're a good man!" the grandmother said at once.

---

[4]Jukebox.

"Yes'm, I suppose so," Red Sam said as if he were struck with this answer.

His wife brought the orders, carrying the five plates all at once without a tray, two in each hand and one balanced on her arm. "It isn't a soul in this green world of God's that you can trust," she said. "And I don't count nobody out of that, not nobody," she repeated, looking at Red Sammy.

"Did you read about that criminal, The Misfit, that's escaped?" 40 asked the grandmother.

"I wouldn't be a bit surprised if he didn't attack this place right here," said the woman. "If he hears about it being here, I wouldn't be none surprised to see him. If he hears it's two cent in the cash register, I wouldn't be a tall surprised if he . . ."

"That'll do," Red Sam said. "Go bring these people their Co'-Colas," and the woman went off to get the rest of the order.

"A good man is hard to find," Red Sammy said. "Everything is getting terrible. I remember the day you could go off and leave your screen door unlatched. Not no more."

He and the grandmother discussed better times. The old lady said that in her opinion Europe was entirely to blame for the way things were now. She said the way Europe acted you would think we were made of money and Red Sam said it was no use talking about it, she was exactly right. The children ran outside into the white sunlight and looked at the monkey in the lacy chinaberry tree. He was busy catching fleas on himself and biting each one carefully between his teeth as if it were a delicacy.

They drove off again into the hot afternoon. The grandmother took 45 cat naps and woke up every few minutes with her own snoring. Outside of Toombsboro she woke up and recalled an old plantation that she had visited in this neighborhood once when she was a young lady. She said the house had six white columns across the front and that there was an avenue of oaks leading up to it and two little wooden trellis arbors on either side in front where you sat down with your suitor after a stroll in the garden. She recalled exactly which road to turn off to get to it. She knew that Bailey would not be willing to lose any time looking at an old house, but the more she talked about it, the more she wanted to see it once again and find out if the little twin arbors were still standing. "There was a secret panel in this house," she said craftily, not telling the truth but wishing that she were, "and the story went that all the family silver was hidden in it when Sherman[5] came through but it was never found . . ."

"Hey!" John Wesley said. "Let's go see it! We'll find it! We'll poke all the woodwork and find it! Who lives there? Where do you turn off at? Hey Pop, can't we turn off there?"

"We never have seen a house with a secret panel!" June Star shrieked. "Let's go to the house with the secret panel! Hey, Pop, can't we go see the house with the secret panel!"

"It's not far from here, I know," the grandmother said. "It wouldn't take over twenty minutes."

Bailey was looking straight ahead. His jaw was as rigid as a horseshoe. "No," he said.

The children began to yell and scream that they wanted to see the 50 house with the secret panel. John Wesley kicked the back of the front seat and June Star hung over her mother's shoulder and whined desperately into her ear that they never had any fun even on their vacation, that they could never do what THEY wanted to do. The baby began to scream and John Wesley kicked the back of the seat so hard that his father could feel the blows in his kidney.

"All right!" he shouted and drew the car to a stop at the side of the road. "Will you all shut up? Will you all just shut up for one second? If you don't shut up, we won't go anywhere."

"It would be very educational for them," the grandmother murmured.

"All right," Bailey said, "but get this. This is the only time we're going to stop for anything like this. This is the one and only time."

"The dirt road that you have to turn down is about a mile back," the grandmother directed. "I marked it when we passed."

"A dirt road," Bailey groaned. 55

After they had turned around and were headed toward the dirt road,

[5]In 1864 the Union army led by General William Tecumseh Sherman marched from Atlanta to Savannah, destroying civilian farms and houses along the way.

the grandmother recalled other points about the house, the beautiful glass over the front doorway and the candle lamp in the hall. John Wesley said that the secret panel was probably in the fireplace.

"You can't go inside this house," Bailey said. "You don't know who lives there."

"While you all talk to the people in front, I'll run around behind and get in a window," John Wesley suggested.

"We'll all stay in the car," his mother said.

They turned onto the dirt road and the car raced roughly along in a 60 swirl of pink dust. The grandmother recalled the times when there were no paved roads and thirty miles was a day's journey. The dirt road was hilly and there were sudden washes in it and sharp curves on dangerous embankments. All at once they would be on a hill, looking down over the blue tops of trees for miles around, then the next minute, they would be in a red depression with the dust-coated trees looking down on them.

"This place had better turn up in a minute," Bailey said, "or I'm going to turn around."

The road looked as if no one had traveled on it in months.

"It's not much farther," the grandmother said and just as she said it, a horrible thought came to her. The thought was so embarrassing that she turned red in the face and her eyes dilated and her feet jumped up, upsetting her valise in the corner. The instant the valise moved, the newspaper top she had over the basket under it rose with a snarl and Pitty Sing, the cat, sprang onto Bailey's shoulder.

The children were thrown to the floor and their mother, clutching the baby, was thrown out the door onto the ground; the old lady was thrown into the front seat. The car turned over once and landed right-side-up in a gulch on the side of the road. Bailey remained in the driver's seat with the cat—gray-striped with a broad white face and an orange nose—clinging to his neck like a caterpillar.

As soon as the children saw they could move their arms and legs, 65 they scrambled out of the car, shouting, "We've had an ACCIDENT!" The grandmother was curled up under the dashboard, hoping she was injured so that Bailey's wrath would not come down on her all at once. The horrible thought she had had before the accident was that the house she had remembered so vividly was not in Georgia but in Tennessee.

Bailey removed the cat from his neck with both hands and flung it out the window against the side of a pine tree. Then he got out of the car and started looking for the children's mother. She was sitting against the side of the red gutted ditch, holding the screaming baby, but she only had a cut down her face and a broken shoulder. "We've had an ACCIDENT!" the children screamed in a frenzy of delight.

"But nobody's killed," June Star said with disappointment as the grandmother limped out of the car, her hat still pinned to her head but the broken front brim standing up at a jaunty angle and the violet spray hanging off the side. They all sat down in the ditch, except the children, to recover from the shock. They were all shaking.

"Maybe a car will come along," said the children's mother hoarsely.

"I believe I have injured an organ," said the grandmother, pressing her side, but no one answered her. Bailey's teeth were clattering. He had on a yellow sport shirt with bright blue parrots designed in it and his face was as yellow as the shirt. The grandmother decided that she would not mention that the house was in Tennessee.

The road was about ten feet above and they could see only the tops of the trees on the other side of it. Behind the ditch they were sitting in there were more woods, tall and dark and deep. In a few minutes they saw a car some distance away on top of a hill, coming slowly as if the occupants were watching them. The grandmother stood up and waved both arms dramatically to attract their attention. The car continued to come on slowly, disappeared around a bend and appeared again, moving even slower, on top of the hill they had gone over. It was a big black battered hearselike automobile. There were three men in it.

It came to a stop over them and for some minutes, the driver looked down with a steady expressionless gaze to where they were sitting, and didn't speak. Then he turned his head and muttered something to the other two and they got out. One was a fat boy in black trousers and a red sweat shirt with a silver stallion embossed on the front of it. He moved around on the right side of them and stood staring, his mouth partly open in a kind of loose grin. The other had on khaki pants and

70

a blue striped coat and a gray hat pulled down very low, hiding most of his face. He came around slowly on the left side. Neither spoke.

The driver got out of the car and stood by the side of it, looking down at them. He was an older man than the other two. His hair was just beginning to gray and he wore silver-rimmed spectacles that gave him a scholarly look. He had a long creased face and didn't have on any shirt or undershirt. He had on blue jeans that were too tight for him and was holding a black hat and a gun. The two boys also had guns.

"We've had an ACCIDENT!" the children screamed.

The grandmother had the peculiar feeling that the bespectacled man was someone she knew. His face was as familiar to her as if she had known him all her life but she could not recall who he was. He moved away from the car and began to come down the embankment, placing his feet carefully so that he wouldn't slip. He had on tan and white shoes and no socks, and his ankles were red and thin. "Good afternoon," he said. "I see you all had you a little spill."

"We turned over twice!" said the grandmother. 75

"Oncet," he corrected. "We seen it happen. Try their car and see will it run, Hiram," he said quietly to the boy with the gray hat.

"What you got that gun for?" John Wesley asked. "Whatcha gonna do with that gun?"

"Lady," the man said to the children's mother, "would you mind calling them children to sit down by you? Children make me nervous. I want all you all to sit down right together there where you're at."

"What are you telling us what to do for?" June Star asked.

Behind them the line of woods gaped like a dark open mouth. 80 "Come here," said their mother.

"Look here now," Bailey began suddenly, "we're in a predicament! We're in . . ."

The grandmother shrieked. She scrambled to her feet and stood staring.

"You're The Misfit!" she said. "I recognized you at once!"

"Yes'm," the man said, smiling slightly as if he were pleased in spite of himself to be known, "but it would have been better for all of you, lady, if you hadn't of reckernized me."

Bailey turned his head sharply and said something to his mother 85 that shocked even the children. The old lady began to cry and The Misfit reddened.

"Lady," he said, "don't you get upset. Sometimes a man says things he don't mean. I don't reckon he meant to talk to you thataway."

"You wouldn't shoot a lady, would you?" the grandmother said and removed a clean handkerchief from her cuff and began to slap at her eyes with it.

The Misfit pointed the toe of his shoe into the ground and made a little hole and then covered it up again. "I would hate to have to," he said.

"Listen," the grandmother almost screamed, "I know you're a good man. You don't look a bit like you have common blood. I know you must come from nice people!"

"Yes mam," he said, "finest people in the world." When he smiled   90
he showed a row of strong white teeth. "God never made a finer woman than my mother and my daddy's heart was pure gold," he said. The boy with the red sweat shirt had come around behind them and was standing with his gun at his hip. The Misfit squatted down on the ground. "Watch them children, Bobby Lee," he said. "You know they make me nervous." He looked at the six of them huddled together in front of him and he seemed to be embarrassed as if he couldn't think of anything to say. "Ain't a cloud in the sky," he remarked, looking up at it. "Don't see no sun but don't see no cloud neither."

"Yes, it's a beautiful day," said the grandmother. "Listen," she said, "you shouldn't call yourself The Misfit because I know you're a good man at heart. I can just look at you and tell."

"Hush!" Bailey yelled. "Hush! Everybody shut up and let me handle this!" He was squatting in the position of a runner about to spring forward but he didn't move.

"I pre-chate that, lady," The Misfit said and drew a little circle in the ground with the butt of his gun.

"It'll take a half a hour to fix this here car," Hiram called, looking over the raised hood of it.

"Well, first you and Bobby Lee get him and that little boy to step   95
over yonder with you," The Misfit said, pointing to Bailey and John Wesley. "The boys want to ask you something," he said to Bailey. "Would you mind stepping back in them woods there with them?"

"Listen," Bailey began, "we're in a terrible predicament! Nobody realizes what this is," and his voice cracked. His eyes were as blue and intense as the parrots in his shirt and he remained perfectly still.

The grandmother reached up to adjust her hat brim as if she were going to the woods with him but it came off in her hand. She stood staring at it and after a second she let it fall on the ground. Hiram pulled Bailey up by the arm as if he were assisting an old man. John Wesley caught hold of his father's hand and Bobby Lee followed. They went off toward the woods and just as they reached the dark edge, Bailey turned and supporting himself against a gray naked pine trunk, he shouted, "I'll be back in a minute, Mamma, wait on me!"

"Come back this instant!" his mother shrilled but they all disappeared into the woods.

"Bailey Boy!" the grandmother called in a tragic voice but she found she was looking at The Misfit squatting on the ground in front of her. "I just know you're a good man," she said desperately. "You're not a bit common!"

"Nome, I ain't a good man," The Misfit said after a second as if he had considered her statement carefully, "but I ain't the worst in the world neither. My daddy said I was a different breed of dog from my brothers and sisters. 'You know,' Daddy said, 'it's some that can live their whole life out without asking about it and it's others has to know why it is, and this boy is one of the latters. He's going to be into everything!'" He put on his black hat and looked up suddenly and then away deep into the woods as if he were embarrassed again. "I'm sorry I don't have on a shirt before you ladies," he said, hunching his shoulders slightly. "We buried our clothes that we had on when we escaped and we're just making do until we can get better. We borrowed these from some folks we met," he explained.

"That's perfectly all right," the grandmother said. "Maybe Bailey has an extra shirt in his suitcase."

"I'll look and see terrectly," The Misfit said.

"Where are they taking him?" the children's mother screamed.

"Daddy was a card himself," The Misfit said. "You couldn't put anything over on him. He never got in trouble with the Authorities though. Just had the knack of handling them."

"You could be honest too if you'd only try," said the grandmother.   105
"Think how wonderful it would be to settle down and live a comfortable life and not have to think about somebody chasing you all the time."

The Misfit kept scratching in the ground with the butt of his gun as if he were thinking about it. "Yes'm, somebody is always after you," he murmured.

The grandmother noticed how thin his shoulder blades were just behind his hat because she was standing up looking down on him. "Do you ever pray?" she asked.

He shook his head. All she saw was the black hat wiggle between his shoulder blades. "Nome," he said.

There was a pistol shot from the woods, followed closely by another. Then silence. The old lady's head jerked around. She could hear the wind move through the tree tops like a long satisfied insuck of breath. "Bailey Boy!" she called.

"I was a gospel singer for a while," The Misfit said. "I been most   110 everything. Been in the arm service, both land and sea, at home and abroad, been twict married, been an undertaker, been with the railroads, plowed Mother Earth, been in a tornado, seen a man burnt alive oncet," and he looked up at the children's mother and the little girl who were sitting close together, their faces white and their eyes glassy; "I even seen a woman flogged," he said.

"Pray, pray," the grandmother began, "pray, pray . . ."

"I never was a bad boy that I remember of," The Misfit said in an almost dreamy voice, "but somewheres along the line I done something wrong and got sent to the penitentiary. I was buried alive," and he looked up and held her attention to him by a steady stare.

"That's when you should have started to pray," she said. "What did you do to get sent to the penitentiary that first time?"

"Turn to the right, it was a wall," The Misfit said, looking up again at the cloudless sky. "Turn to the left, it was a wall. Look up it was a ceiling, look down it was a floor. I forget what I done, lady. I set there and set there, trying to remember what it was I done and I ain't recalled it to this day. Oncet in a while, I would think it was coming to me, but it never come."

"Maybe they put you in by mistake," the old lady said vaguely.　115

"Nome," he said. "It wasn't no mistake. They had the papers on me."

"You must have stolen something," she said.

The Misfit sneered slightly. "Nobody had nothing I wanted," he said. "It was a head-doctor at the penitentiary said what I had done was kill my daddy but I known that for a lie. My daddy died in nineteen ought nineteen of the epidemic flu[6] and I never had a thing to do with it. He was buried in the Mount Hopewell Baptist churchyard and you can go there and see for yourself."

"If you would pray," the old lady said, "Jesus would help you."

"That's right," The Misfit said.　120

"Well then, why don't you pray?" she asked trembling with delight suddenly.

"I don't want no hep," he said. "I'm doing all right by myself."

Bobby Lee and Hiram came ambling back from the woods. Bobby Lee was dragging a yellow shirt with bright blue parrots in it.

"Throw me that shirt, Bobby Lee," The Misfit said. The shirt came flying at him and landed on his shoulder and he put it on. The grandmother couldn't name what the shirt reminded her of. "No, lady," The Misfit said while he was buttoning up, "I found out the crime don't matter. You can do one thing or you can do another, kill a man or take a tire off his car, because sooner or later you're going to forget what it was you done and just be punished for it."

The children's mother had begun to make heaving noises as if she　125 couldn't get her breath. "Lady," he asked, "would you and that little girl like to step off yonder with Bobby Lee and Hiram and join your husband?"

"Yes, thank you," the mother said faintly. Her left arm dangled helplessly and she was holding the baby, who had gone to sleep, in the other. "Hep that lady up, Hiram," The Misfit said as she struggled to climb out of the ditch, "and Bobby Lee, you hold onto that little girl's hand."

---

[6]The so-called "Spanish flu" spread through much of the world in 1918–19, killing millions.

"I don't want to hold hands with him," June Star said. "He reminds me of a pig."

The fat boy blushed and laughed and caught her by the arm and pulled her off into the woods after Hiram and her mother.

Alone with The Misfit, the grandmother found that she had lost her voice. There was not a cloud in the sky nor any sun. There was nothing around her but woods. She wanted to tell him that he must pray. She opened and closed her mouth several times before anything came out. Finally she found herself saying, "Jesus, Jesus," meaning, Jesus will help you, but the way she was saying it, it sounded as if she might be cursing.

"Yes'm," The Misfit said as if he agreed. "Jesus thrown everything off balance. It was the same case with Him as with me except He hadn't committed any crime and they could prove I had committed one because they had the papers on me. Of course," he said, "they never shown me my papers. That's why I sign myself now. I said long ago, you get you a signature and sign everything you do and keep a copy of it. Then you'll know what you done and you can hold up the crime to the punishment and see do they match and in the end you'll have something to prove you ain't been treated right. I call myself The Misfit," he said, "because I can't make what all I done wrong fit what all I gone through in punishment."

There was a piercing scream from the woods, followed closely by a pistol report. "Does it seem right to you, lady, that one is punished a heap and another ain't punished at all?"

"Jesus!" the old lady cried. "You've got good blood! I know you wouldn't shoot a lady! I know you come from nice people! Pray! Jesus, you ought not to shoot a lady. I'll give you all the money I've got!"

"Lady," The Misfit said, looking beyond her far into the woods, "there never was a body that give the undertaker a tip."

There were two more pistol reports and the grandmother raised her head like a parched old turkey hen crying for water and called, "Bailey Boy, Bailey Boy!" as if her heart would break.

"Jesus was the only One that ever raised the dead," The Misfit continued, "and He shouldn't have done it. He thrown everything off balance. If He did what He said, then it's nothing for you to do but throw away everything and follow Him, and if He didn't then it's nothing for you to do but enjoy the few minutes you got left the best way you can—by killing somebody or burning down his house or doing some other meanness to him. No pleasure but meanness," he said and his voice had become almost a snarl.

"Maybe He didn't raise the dead," the old lady mumbled, not knowing what she was saying and feeling so dizzy that she sank down in the ditch with her legs twisted under her.

"I wasn't there so I can't say He didn't," The Misfit said, "I wisht I had of been there," he said, hitting the ground with his fist. "It ain't right I wasn't there because if I had of been there I would of known. Listen lady," he said in a high voice, "if I had of been there I would of known and I wouldn't be like I am now." His voice seemed about to crack and the grandmother's head cleared for an instant. She saw the man's face twisted close to her own as if he were going to cry and she murmured, "Why, you're one of my babies. You're one of my own children!" She reached out and touched him on the shoulder. The Misfit sprang back as if a snake had bitten him and shot her three times through the chest. Then he put his gun down on the ground and took off his glasses and began to clean them.

Hiram and Bobby Lee returned from the woods and stood over the ditch, looking down at the grandmother who half sat and half lay in a puddle of blood with her legs crossed under her like a child's and her face smiling up at the cloudless sky.

Without his glasses, The Misfit's eyes were red-rimmed and pale and defenseless-looking. "Take her off and throw her where you thrown the others," he said, picking up the cat that was rubbing itself against his leg.

"She was a talker, wasn't she?" Bobby Lee said, sliding down the ditch with a yodel. 140

"She would of been a good woman," The Misfit said, "if it had been somebody there to shoot her every minute of her life."

"Some fun!" Bobby Lee said.

"Shut up, Bobby Lee," The Misfit said. "It's no real pleasure in life."

STUDY QUESTIONS

1. Examine paragraph 137, where the grandmother says to The Misfit, "Why, you're one of my babies. You're one of my own children!" Why does she say this? Why does she then touch him?

2. Consider the passage in which The Misfit has the entire family killed. What TONE is used to NARRATE the event? How appropriate is it? How effective is it? How does the tone help to shape your reaction to The Misfit and the murders?

3. While the phrase "a good man" is used six times in the story, the DEFINITION of "a good man" is implied rather than stated explicitly. With reference to the events and CHARACTERS in the story, formulate a definition of "a good man."

4. *For Writing.* Write an essay in which you explore the concept of a "good" man or woman. Think about how a "good man" is defined in O'Connor's story and use examples from your own experiences to support or refute that definition.

GWENDOLYN BROOKS { *We Real Cool*

GWENDOLYN BROOKS (1917–2000), a poet and the first African American to win a Pulitzer Prize, was born in Topeka, Kansas, but grew up in Chicago, the city with which she and her poetry are most closely identified. There she attended both segregated and integrated schools (including a primarily white high school) and graduated from Wilson Junior College in 1936. She published her first book of poetry, *A Street in Bronzeville* (its title referring to a historic African American neighborhood in the South Side of Chicago), in 1945. A dedicated chronicler of the urban experience, Brooks created strong characters, such as those in *Annie Allen* (1949), *Maud Martha* (1953), and *Bronzeville Boys and Girls* (1956). She was named poet laureate of Illinois in 1968 and used that position to reach out to people, holding workshops, readings, and contests for children.

Although the language and line length of "We Real Cool" are spare, the poem's narrative power is considerable. Note how Brooks develops a solid cause-and-effect argument about the place of "cool" in youth culture. How might her minimalist style/prose be more effective in this instance than a more complex poetic style?

"We Real Cool" from *Blacks*. Reprinted by consent of Brooks Permissions.

THE POOL PLAYERS,
SEVEN AT THE GOLDEN SHOVEL.

We real cool. We
Left school. We

Lurk late. We
Strike straight. We

Sing sin. We   5
Thin gin. We

Jazz June. We
Die soon.

STUDY QUESTIONS

1. **DESCRIBE**, in a paragraph, the scene and action of this poem—what is its **SETTING**? What do its **CHARACTERS** do and say?

2. Although this poem is brief—only eight short lines—it tells a complete story using **CAUSE AND EFFECT**. How does Brooks develop this cause-and-effect **NARRATIVE** from the first to the last line? How might these spare lines be even more effective than a longer narrative?

3. Each line of this poem, with the exception of the last, ends with "We," the beginning word of the following sentence. What effect does this form have on the printed version of the poem? Listen to Gwendolyn Brooks read "We Real Cool" (a recording is available on Poets.org) and respond again: how does Brooks's rhythmic reading of the line endings bring meaning to the poem?

4. *For Writing.* **REFLECT** on the quality of being "cool." In an essay, **ANA- LYZE** the ways the speaker and his buddies understand the concept as well as the way the poet understands both the pleasures and the dangers of act-ing "cool."

ROBERT FROST { *The Road Not Taken*

ROBERT FROST (1874–1963) was born in San Francisco, California, although reading his poetry might give you the impression he was born and reared in New England. In fact, Frost's father—who died in California—wished to be buried in his hometown of Lawrence, Massachusetts, a wish that prompted eleven-year-old Robert, his mother, and his sister to move there. After graduating from high school, Frost entered Dartmouth University but left without a degree to go into teaching as he continued writing. Except for a four-year stay in England just before the First World War, Frost and his wife and children lived on a series of farms in New Hampshire and Vermont. He is revered as the quintessential voice of rural New England and was awarded the Pulitzer Prize for Poetry four times. Frost recited his poem "The Gift Outright" (1942) at John F. Kennedy's presidential inauguration in 1961. After Frost's death, Kennedy praised him for his contribution to the arts.

"The Road Not Taken" is one of Frost's best-known poems. The narrator relates that a seemingly casual decision had to be made and only in retrospect did he come to understand what that decision really meant. In much the same way, at first this poem may seem artless and simple; careful rereading, though, reveals the poem's vivid imagery and formal structure. On rereading, consider whether the poem has the same message as you first thought.

Two roads diverged in a yellow wood,
And sorry I could not travel both
And be one traveler, long I stood
And looked down one as far as I could
To where it bent in the undergrowth;

Then took the other, as just as fair,
And having perhaps the better claim,
Because it was grassy and wanted wear;
Though as for that the passing there
Had worn them really about the same,   10

And both that morning equally lay
In leaves no step had trodden black.
Oh, I kept the first for another day!
Yet knowing how way leads on to way,
I doubted if I should ever come back.   15

I shall be telling this with a sigh
Somewhere ages and ages hence:
Two roads diverged in a wood, and I—
I took the one less traveled by,
And that has made all the difference.   20

STUDY QUESTIONS

1. The NARRATOR of the poem relates an incident about a choice that he or she once made. SUMMARIZE each stanza in one sentence, then create a paragraph from the four sentences and compare it to the poem. Does the prose paragraph convey the ideas and emotion of Frost's poem? Why or why not?

2. Read the poem again for meaning. Identify a possible THESIS of the poem and the parts of the poem that support this thesis. Can you know whether this is the meaning the poet had in mind or a meaning that you created for the poem? Explain.

3. ANALYZE the poem for the following elements: TONE, narrator's mood, DICTION, IMAGERY, structure, rhyme, and the title. How does each contribute to the poem's overall effect?

4. *For Writing.* Using your answers to the questions above, write a LITERARY ANALYSIS of the poem. You might want to summarize the poem, identify its thesis, and show how the NARRATOR supports it, breaks the poem down into literary elements, and then synthesizes the parts to arrive at an evaluative conclusion.

SEAMUS HEANEY ⎰ *Mid-Term Break*

SEAMUS HEANEY (b. 1939) was born in Northern Ireland, the eldest of nine children. At twelve, he enrolled in St. Columb's College, a Catholic boarding school located in Derry, on scholarship. He graduated from Queens University of Belfast in 1961 with a degree in English language and literature. During his first position as a teacher he began to publish poetry with the encouragement of his headmaster, the writer Michael McLaverty. He has achieved great critical and commercial success as a poet, lecturer, and translator, culminating in the Nobel Prize in Literature in 1995. Heaney often draws on his rural and working-class roots (his father was a farmer; his mother's family were linen millworkers) for his body of work, which includes *Death of a Naturalist* (1967), *Wintering Out* (1973), and *The Haw Lantern* (1987). He has taught at Harvard University and the University of Oxford. His lyrical translation of *Beowulf* (2000) brought the Anglo-Saxon epic to a contemporary audience, as Heaney melded modern language with Old English form.

"Mid-Term Break" is based on a true event: the death of Heaney's four-year-old brother while the poet was away at St. Columb's. Composed from the distance of time, the poem engages with memory as it addresses the speaker's process of gradually coming to terms with what has happened. How does memory act as a filter as well as a clear lens through which to view this sad occasion?

I sat all morning in the college sick bay
Counting bells knelling classes to a close.
At two o'clock our neighbours drove me home.

In the porch I met my father crying—
He had always taken funerals in his stride—   5
And Big Jim Evans saying it was a hard blow.

The baby cooed and laughed and rocked the pram
When I came in, and I was embarrassed
By old men standing up to shake my hand

And tell me they were "sorry for my trouble."   10
Whispers informed strangers I was the eldest,
Away at school, as my mother held my hand

In hers and coughed out angry tearless sighs.
At ten o'clock the ambulance arrived
With the corpse, stanched and bandaged by the nurses.   15

Next morning I went up into the room. Snowdrops
And candles soothed the bedside; I saw him
For the first time in six weeks. Paler now,

Wearing a poppy bruise on his left temple,
He lay in the four foot box as in his cot.   20
No gaudy scars, the bumper knocked him clear.

A four foot box, a foot for every year.

STUDY QUESTIONS

1. What is the occasion for this poem?

2. Consider the language in this poem. For instance, how does the title "Mid-Term Break" function on a literal and on a SYMBOLIC level? Choose two to three other examples and explore their multiple meanings. What do the different readings bring to the poem?

3. How does Heaney employ "memory" to help his speaker ANALYZE THE PROCESS of coming to terms with a death in the family? What is the effect?

4. How does Heaney use—and not use—emotion in this poem? How does Heaney employ both emotion and neutrality? What is the effect? Be sure to cite concrete language from the poem to support your points.

5. *For Writing.* Write a poem or an essay about a significant, highly emotional event in your life. Carefully choose the TONE that you feel will best convey your reaction to the event. Describe the event using details that appeal to the senses.

LANGSTON HUGHES (1902–1967) was born in Joplin, Missouri. He lived with his maternal grandmother in Lawrence, Kansas, after his parents divorced and then with family friends after her death before returning to his mother in Lincoln, Illinois. Hughes was elected class poet, though he suspected it was because of a stereotype in the largely white school that blacks had "rhythm." As a teen he was able to travel to Africa and Europe as a crewman on the *SS Malone.* Returning to the United States, he assisted the historian Carter G. Woodson before entering Lincoln University in Pennsylvania, earning a BA in 1929. He then moved to Harlem, in the midst of the Harlem Renaissance, a period when the African American community's artistic talent flourished. However, Hughes took issue with some of the shepherds of the Renaissance, such as W. E. B. Du Bois and Alain Locke, because he felt that their approach was too assimilationist. Instead, Hughes celebrated blackness unapologetically and focused his work on racial pride, employing rhythms from jazz and folk music. He also wrote fiction, nonfiction, plays, and children's books. His best-known works include *The Weary Blues* (1926), *The Big Sea* (1940), and *Mule Bone* (1931), the last written with Zora Neale Hurston.

"Theme for English B" depicts an African American student's reaction to being assigned an essay by a white instructor. The assignment seems simple enough, but as the speaker talks about himself, he

shows how it is loaded with cultural assumptions. Has the speaker
written something that's "true"?

The instructor said,

> *Go home and write*
> *a page tonight.*
> *And let that page come out of you—*
> *Then, it will be true.*   5

I wonder if it's that simple?
I am twenty-two, colored, born in Winston-Salem.
I went to school there, then Durham, then here
to this college on the hill above Harlem.
I am the only colored student in my class.   10
The steps from the hill lead down into Harlem,
through a park, then I cross St. Nicholas,
Eighth Avenue, Seventh, and I come to the Y,
the Harlem Branch Y, where I take the elevator
up to my room, sit down, and write this page: 15

It's not easy to know what is true for you or me
at twenty-two, my age. But I guess I'm what
I feel and see and hear, Harlem, I hear you:
hear you, hear me—we two—you, me, talk on this page.
(I hear New York, too.) Me—who?   20
Well, I like to eat, sleep, drink, and be in love.
I like to work, read, learn, and understand life.
I like a pipe for a Christmas present,
or records—Bessie, bop, or Bach.
I guess being colored doesn't make me *not* like   25
the same things other folks like who are other races.
So will my page be colored that I write?
Being me, it will not be white.
But it will be

a part of you, instructor.   30
You are white—
yet a part of me, as I am a part of you.
That's American.
Sometimes perhaps you don't want to be a part of me.
Nor do I often want to be a part of you.   35
But we are, that's true!
As I learn from you,
I guess you learn from me—
although you're older—and white—
and somewhat more free.   40

This is my page for English B.

STUDY QUESTIONS

1. Describe the SPEAKER of the poem. What do we know about his character and his situation?

2. Why does the speaker choose to reveal the things that he does about himself, such as his route home, his musical taste, his various likes? What do his DESCRIPTIVE choices say about him?

3. At first glance, the instructor's assignment appears generic: to write something that's "true." How does Hughes complicate the DEFINITION of what is "true" here?

4. Why do you think the speaker chooses to write his "page" in verse, rather than in prose? How is his choice of GENRE a response to his instructor?

5. *For Writing.* In an essay, analyze the ways the speaker COMPARES AND CONTRASTS himself with his white instructor, both implicitly and explicitly. Be sure to refer to specific language in the poem.

WILLIAM BUTLER YEATS { *The Second Coming*

WILLIAM BUTLER YEATS (1865–1939), Irish dramatist and poet, was born to a prosperous Protestant family of artists and merchants. He immersed himself in the complex politics of his time as Irish nationalists struggled to free Ireland from British rule, and though he was ambivalent about its factionalism, he embraced Ireland's cultural identity and incorporated Irish legends, mythology, and history into his poems and plays. Late in life he served two terms in the Senate of the newly independent Irish Republic. Although mainstream Christianity never held much interest for Yeats, he was fascinated by spiritualism and the occult, and much of his writing reflects religious themes. In 1923 Yeats was awarded the Nobel Prize in Literature for what the Nobel committee called his "inspired poetry, which in a highly artistic form gives expression to the spirit of a whole nation."

In "The Second Coming," one of his most anthologized poems, Yeats evokes an apocalyptic vision in which the modern world's turmoil ushers in an era not of Christian redemption but of "anarchy" and "darkness." As you read, pay particular attention to the way Yeats paces the poem to create first a sense of almost panicky urgency and then a slowly dawning awareness of what cannot be stopped.

> Turning and turning in the widening gyre[1]
> The falcon cannot hear the falconer;
> Things fall apart; the centre cannot hold;
> Mere anarchy is loosed upon the world,

---

[1] A vast circle or spiral, Yeats's image in many of his poems for the turnings and patterns of history.

The blood-dimmed tide is loosed, and everywhere   5
The ceremony of innocence is drowned;
The best lack all conviction, while the worst
Are full of passionate intensity.

Surely some revelation is at hand;
Surely the Second Coming[2] is at hand.   10
The Second Coming! Hardly are those words out
When a vast image out of Spiritus Mundi[3]
Troubles my sight: a waste of desert sand;
A shape with lion body and the head of a man,
A gaze blank and pitiless as the sun,   15
Is moving its slow thighs, while all about it
Wind shadows of the indignant desert birds.

The darkness drops again but now I know
That twenty centuries of stony sleep
Were vexed to nightmare by a rocking cradle,   20
And what rough beast, its hour come round at last,
Slouches towards Bethlehem to be born?

[2]That is, of Jesus Christ.
[3]The spirit of the world (Latin).

STUDY QUESTIONS

1. In one sentence, SUMMARIZE the poem.

2. How does the poem's IMAGERY underscore the message of the poem? How effective is it?

3. Find a DESCRIPTION of the prophecy of the Second Coming in the Bible's Book of Revelation, then COMPARE AND CONTRAST it with Yeats's description. What does Yeats's vision have in common with that of the Bible? How do they differ?

4. *For Writing.* Yeats wrote this poem in 1919, shortly after World War I ended. RESEARCH this war and then write an ANALYSIS of how the war might have influenced the dire, pessimistic mood of the poem. Focus on imagery, TONE, and other literary elements to support your THESIS.

"THE DATA SUGGEST"

Writing in the Sciences

CHRISTOPHER GILLEN

———

CHARLES DARWIN DESCRIBED *On the Origin of Species* as "one long argument." In *Dialogue Concerning the Two Chief World Systems*, Galileo Galilei cast his argument for a sun-centered solar system as a series of conversations. As these historical examples show, scientific writing is fundamentally argumentative. Like all academic writers, scientists make and defend claims. They address disagreements and explore unanswered questions. They propose novel mechanisms and new theories. And they advance certain explanations and reject others. Though their vocabulary may be more technical and their emphasis more numerical, science writers use the same

———

CHRISTOPHER GILLEN is a professor of biology at Kenyon College and the faculty director of the Kenyon Institute in Biomedical and Scientific Writing. He teaches courses in animal physiology, biology of exercise, and introductory biology, all stressing the critical reading of primary research articles.

rhetorical moves as other academic writers. Consider the following example from a book about the laws of physics.

> The common refrain that is heard in elementary discussions of quantum mechanics is that a physical object is in some sense both a wave and a particle, with its wave nature apparent when you measure a wave property such as wavelength, and its particle nature apparent when you measure a particle property such as position. But this is, at best, misleading and, at worst, wrong.
>
> V. J. STENGER, *The Comprehensible Cosmos*

The "they say / I say" structure of this passage is unmistakable: They say that objects have properties of both waves and particles; I say they are wrong. This example is not a lonely argumentative passage cherry-picked from an otherwise non-argumentative text. Rather, Stenger's entire book makes the argument that is foreshadowed by its title, *The Comprehensible Cosmos*: that although some might see the universe as hopelessly complex, it is essentially understandable.

Here's another argumentative passage, this one from a research article about the role of lactic acid in muscle fatigue:

> In contrast to the often suggested role for acidosis as a cause of muscle fatigue, it is shown that in muscles where force was depressed by high $[K^+]_o$, acidification by lactic acid produced a pronounced recovery of force.
>
> O. B. NIELSEN, F. DE PAOLI, AND K. OVERGAARD,
> "Protective Effects of Lactic Acid on Force Production in
> Rat Skeletal Muscle," *The Journal of Physiology*

In other words: Many scientists think that lactic acid causes muscle fatigue, but our evidence shows that it actually promotes recovery. Notice that the authors frame their claim with a version of the "they say / I say" formula: Although previous work suggests _____ , our data argue _____ . This basic move and its many variations are widespread in scientific writing. The essential argumentative moves taught in this book transcend disciplines, and the sciences are no exception. The examples in this chaper were written by professional scientists, but they show moves that are appropriate in any writing that addresses scientific issues.

Despite the importance of argument in scientific writing, newcomers to the genre often see it solely as a means for communicating uncontroversial, objective facts. It's easy to see how this view arises. The objective tone of scientific writing can obscure its argumentative nature, and many textbooks reinforce a nonargumentative vision of science when they focus on accepted conclusions and ignore ongoing controversies. And because science writers base their arguments on empirical data, a good portion of many scientific texts *does* serve the purpose of delivering uncontested facts.

However, scientific writing often does more than just report facts. Data are crucial to scientific argumentation, but they are by no means the end of the story. Given important new data, scientists assess their quality, draw conclusions from them, and ponder their implications. They synthesize the new data with existing information, propose novel theories, and design the next experiments. In short, scientific progress depends on the insight and creativity that scientists bring to their data. The thrill of doing science, and writing about it, comes from the ongoing struggle to use data to better understand our world.

START WITH THE DATA

Data are the fundamental currency of scientific argument. Scientists develop hypotheses from existing data and then test those by comparing their predictions to new experimental data. Summarizing data is therefore a basic move in science writing. Because data can often be interpreted in different ways, describing the data opens the door to critical analysis, creating opportunities to critique previous interpretations and develop new ones.

Describing data requires more than simply reporting numbers and conclusions. Rather than jumping straight to the punch line—to what X concluded—it is important first to describe the hypotheses, methods, and results that led to the conclusion: "To test the hypothesis that _____, X measured _____ and found that _____. Therefore, X concluded _____." In the following sections, we explore the three key rhetorical moves for describing the data that underpin a scientific argument: presenting the prevailing theories, explaining methodologies, and summarizing findings.

Present the Prevailing Theories

Readers must understand the prevailing theories that a study responds to before they can fully appreciate the details. So before diving into specifics, place the work in context by describing the prevailing theories and hypotheses. In the following passage from a journal article about insect respiration, the authors discuss an explanation for discontinuous gas exchange (DGC), a phenomenon where insects periodically close valves on their breathing tubes.

> Lighton (1996, 1998; see also Lighton and Berrigan, 1995) noted the prevalence of DGC in fossorial insects, which inhabit microclimates where CO_2 levels may be relatively high. Consequently, Lighton proposed the chthonic hypothesis, which suggests that

DGC originated as a mechanism to improve gas exchange while at the same time minimizing respiratory water loss.

> A. G. Gibbs and R. A. Johnson, "The Role of Discontinuous Gas Exchange in Insects: The Chthonic Hypothesis Does Not Hold Water," *The Journal of Experimental Biology*

Notice that Gibbs and Johnson not only describe Lighton's hypothesis but also recap the evidence that supports it. By presenting this evidence, Gibbs and Johnson set the stage for engaging with Lighton's ideas. For example, they might question the chthonic hypothesis by pointing out shortcomings of the data or flaws in its interpretation. Or they might suggest new approaches that could verify the hypothesis. The point is that by incorporating a discussion of experimental findings into their summary of Lighton's hypothesis, Gibbs and Johnson open the door to a conversation with Lighton.

Here are some templates for presenting the data that underpin prevailing explanations:

▸ **Experiments showing _____ and _____ have led scientists to propose _____ .**

▸ **Although most scientists attribute _____ to _____ , X's result _____ leads to the possibility that _____ .**

Explain the Methods

Even as we've argued that scientific arguments hinge on data, it's important to note that the quality of data varies depending on how they were collected. Data obtained with sloppy techniques or poorly designed experiments could lead to faulty conclusions. Therefore, it's crucial to explain the methods used to collect data. In order for readers to evaluate a method, you'll need to indicate its purpose, as the following passage from a journal article about the evolution of bird digestive systems demonstrates:

> To test the hypothesis that flowerpiercers have converged with hummingbirds in digestive traits, we compared the activity of intestinal enzymes and the gut nominal area of cinnamon-bellied flowerpiercers (Diglossa baritula) with those of eleven hummingbird species.
>
> J. E. SCHONDUBE AND C. MARTINEZ DEL RIO,
> "Sugar and Protein Digestion in Flowerpiercers and
> Hummingbirds: A Comparative Test of Adaptive Convergence,"
> *Journal of Comparative Physiology*

You need to indicate purpose whether describing your own work or that of others. Here are a couple of templates for doing so:

▸ **Smith and colleagues evaluated _____ to determine whether _____ .**

▸ **Because _____ does not account for _____ , we instead used _____ .**

Summarize the Findings

Scientific data often come in the form of numbers. Your task when presenting numerical data is to provide the context readers need to understand the numbers—by giving supporting information and making comparisons. In the following passage from a book about the interaction between organisms and their environments, Turner uses numerical data to support an argument about the role of the sun's energy on Earth.

> The potential rate of energy transfer from the Sun to Earth is prodigious—about 600 W m^{-2}, averaged throughout the year. Of this, only a relatively small fraction, on the order of 1–2 percent,

is captured by green plants. The rest, if it is not reflected back into space, is available to do other things. The excess can be considerable: although some natural surfaces reflect as much as 95% of the incoming solar beam, many natural surfaces reflect much less (Table 3.2), on average about 15–20 percent. The remaining absorbed energy is then capable of doing work, like heating up surfaces, moving water and air masses around to drive weather and climate, evaporating water, and so forth.

J. S. TURNER, *The Extended Organism*

Turner supports his point that a huge amount of the sun's energy is directly converted to work on Earth by quoting an actual value (600) with units of measurement ($W\ m^{-2}$, watts per square meter). Readers need the units to evaluate the value; 600 watts per square inch is very different from $600\ W\ m^{-2}$. Turner then makes comparisons using percent values, saying that only 1 to 2 percent of the total energy that reaches Earth is trapped by plants. Finally, Turner describes the data's variability by reporting comparisons as ranges—1 to 2 percent and 15 to 20 percent—rather than single values.

Supporting information—such as units of measurement, sample size (n), and amount of variability—helps readers assess the data. In general, the reliability of data improves as its sample size increases and its variability decreases. Supporting information can be concisely presented as:

▶ _____ ± _____ **(mean ± variability)** _____ **(units)**,
  n = _____ **(sample size)**.

For example: Before training, resting heart rate of the subjects was 56 ± 7 beats per minute, n = 12. Here's another way to give supporting information:

▶ We measured _____ (*sample size*) subjects, and the average response was _____ (*mean with units*) with a range of _____ (*lower value*) to _____ (*upper value*).

To help readers understand the data, make comparisons with values from the same study or from other similar work.

Here are some templates for making comparisons:

▶ Before training, average running speed was _____ ± _____ kilometers per hour, _____ kilometers per hour slower than running speed after training.

▶ We found athletes' heart rates to be _____ ± _____ % lower than nonathletes'.

▶ The subjects in X's study completed the maze in _____ ± _____ seconds, _____ seconds slower than those in Y's study.

You will sometimes need to present qualitative data, such as that found in some images and photographs, that cannot be reduced to numbers. Qualitative data must be described precisely with words. In the passage below from a review article about connections between cellular protein localization and cell growth, the author describes the exact locations of three proteins: Scrib, Dlg, and Lgl.

Epithelial cells accumulate different proteins on their apical (top) and basolateral (bottom) surfaces. . . . Scrib and Dlg are localized at the septate junctions along the lateral cell surface, whereas Lgl coats vesicles that are found both in the cytoplasm and "docked" at the lateral surface of the cell.

M. Peifer, "Travel Bulletin—Traffic Jams Cause Tumors," *Science*

EXPLAIN WHAT THE DATA MEAN

Once you summarize experiments and results, you need to say what the data mean. Consider the following passage from a study in which scientists fertilized plots of tropical rainforest with nitrogen (N) and / or phosphorus (P).

> Although our data suggest that the mechanisms driving the observed respiratory responses to increased N and P may be different, the large CO_2 losses stimulated by N and P fertilization suggest that knowledge of such patterns and their effects on soil CO_2 efflux is critical for understanding the role of tropical forests in a rapidly changing global C [carbon] cycle.
>
> C. C. CLEVELAND AND A. R. TOWNSEND, "Nutrient Additions to a Tropical Rain Forest Drive Substantial Soil Carbon Dioxide Losses to the Atmosphere," *Proceedings of the National Academy of Sciences*

Notice that in discussing the implications of their data, Cleveland and Townsend use language—including the verbs "suggest" and "may be"—that denotes their level of confidence in what they say about the data.

Whether you are summarizing what others say about their data or offering your own interpretation, pay attention to the verbs that connect data to interpretations.

To signify a moderate level of confidence:

▸ The data *suggest / hint / imply* _____ .

To express a greater degree of certainty:

▸ Our results *show / demonstrate* _____ .

Almost never will you use the verb "prove" in reference to a single study, because even very powerful evidence generally falls short of proof unless other studies support the same conclusion.

Scientific consensus arises when multiple studies point toward the same conclusion; conversely, contradictions among studies often signal research questions that need further work. For these reasons, you may need to compare one study's findings to those of another study. Here, too, you'll need to choose your verbs carefully.

- Our data *support / confirm / verify* the work of X by showing that _____ .

- By demonstrating _____ , X's work *extends* the findings of Y.

- The results of X *contradict / refute* Y's conclusion that _____ .

- X's findings *call into question* the widely accepted theory that _____ .

- Our data *are consistent with* X's hypothesis that _____ .

MAKE YOUR OWN ARGUMENTS

Now we turn toward the part of scientific writing where you express your own opinions. One challenge is that the statements of other scientists about their methods and results usually must be accepted. You probably can't argue, for example, that "X and Y claim to have studied 6 elephants, but I think they actually only studied 4." However, it might be fair to say, "X and Y studied only 6 elephants, and this small sample size casts doubts on their conclusions." The second statement doesn't question what the scientists did or found but instead examines how the findings are interpreted.

When developing your own arguments—the "I say"—you will often start by assessing the interpretations of other scientists. Consider the following example from a review article about the beneficial acclimation hypothesis (BAH), the idea that organisms exposed to a particular environment become better suited to that environment than unexposed animals.

> To the surprise of most physiologists, all empirical examinations of the BAH have rejected its generality. However, we suggest that these examinations are neither direct nor complete tests of the functional benefit of acclimation.
>
> R. S. WILSON AND C. E. FRANKLIN, "Testing the Beneficial Acclimation Hypothesis," *Trends in Ecology & Evolution*

Wilson and Franklin use a version of the "twist it" move: They acknowledge the data collected by other physiologists but question how those data have been interpreted, creating an opportunity to offer their own interpretation.

For more on the "twist it" move, see p. 60.

You might ask whether we should question how other scientists interpret their own work. Having conducted a study, aren't they in the best position to evaluate it? Perhaps, but as the above example demonstrates, other scientists might see the work from a different perspective or through more objective eyes. And in fact the culture of science depends on vigorous debate in which scientists defend their own findings and challenge those of others—a give and take that helps improve science's reliability. So expressing a critical view about someone else's work is an integral part of the scientific process. Let's examine some of the basic moves for entering scientific conversations: agreeing, with a difference; disagreeing and explaining why; simultaneously agreeing and disagreeing; anticipating objections; and saying why it matters.

Agree, But with a Difference

Scientific research passes through several levels of critical analysis before being published. Scientists get feedback when they discuss work with colleagues, present findings at conferences, and receive reviews of their manuscripts. So the juiciest debates may have been resolved before publication, and you may find little to disagree with in the published literature of a research field. Yet even if you agree with what you've read, there are still ways to join the conversation—and reasons to do so.

One approach is to suggest that further work should be done:

▸ **Now that _____ has been established, scientists will likely turn their attention toward _____.**

▸ **X's work leads to the question of _____. Therefore, we investigated _____.**

▸ **To see whether these findings apply to _____, we propose to _____.**

Another way to agree and at the same time jump into the conversation is to concur with a finding and then propose a mechanism that explains it. In the following sentence from a review article about dietary deficiencies, the author agrees with a previous finding and offers a probable explanation.

> Inadequate dietary intakes of vitamins and minerals are widespread, most likely due to excessive consumption of energy-rich, micronutrient-poor, refined food.
>
> B. AMES, "Low Micronutrient Intake
> May Accelerate the Degenerative Diseases of Aging through
> Allocation of Scarce Micronutrients by Triage,"
> *Proceedings of the National Academy of Sciences*

Here are some templates for explaining an experimental result.

▸ **One explanation for X's finding of _____ is that _____.**
   An alternative explanation is _____.

▸ **The difference between _____ and _____ is probably**
   due to _____.

Disagree—and Explain Why

Although scientific consensus is common, healthy disagreement is not unusual. While measurements conducted by different teams of scientists under the same conditions should produce the same result, scientists often disagree about which techniques are most appropriate, how well an experimental design tests a hypothesis, and how results should be interpreted. To illustrate such disagreement, let's return to the debate about whether or not lactic acid is beneficial during exercise. In the following passage, Lamb and Stephenson are responding to work by Kristensen and colleagues, which argues that lactic acid might be beneficial to resting muscle but not to active muscle.

The argument put forward by Kristensen and colleagues (12) . . . is not valid because it is based on observations made with isolated whole soleus muscles that were stimulated at such a high rate that >60% of the preparation would have rapidly become completely anoxic (4). . . . Furthermore, there is no reason to expect that adding more H+ to that already being generated by the muscle activity should in any way be advantageous. It is a bit like opening up the carburetor on a car to let in too much air or throwing gasoline over the engine and then concluding that air and gasoline are deleterious to engine performance.

G. D. LAMB AND D. G. STEPHENSON,
"Point: Lactic Acid Accumulation Is an Advantage during Muscle Activity," *Journal of Applied Physiology*

Lamb and Stephenson bring experimental detail to bear on their disagreement with Kristensen and colleagues. First, they criticize methodology, arguing that the high muscle stimulation rate used by Kristensen and colleagues created very low oxygen levels (anoxia). They also criticize the logic of the experimental design, arguing that adding more acid (H+) to a muscle that is already producing it isn't informative. It's also worth noting how they drive home their point, likening Kristensen and colleagues' methodology to flooding an engine with air or gasoline. Even in technical scientific writing, you don't need to set aside your own voice completely.

In considering the work of others, look for instances where the experimental design and methodology fail to adequately test a hypothesis.

▸ **The work of Y and Z appears to show that _____, but their experimental design does not control for _____.**

Also, consider the possibility that results do not lead to the stated conclusions.

▸ **While X and Y claim that _____, their finding of _____ actually shows that _____.**

Okay, But . . .

Science tends to progress incrementally. New work may refine or extend previous work but doesn't often completely overturn it. For this reason, science writers frequently agree up to a point and then express some disagreement. In the following example from a commentary about methods for assessing how proteins interact, the authors acknowledge the value of the two-hybrid studies, but they also point out their shortcomings.

> The two-hybrid studies that produced the protein interaction map for *D. melanogaster* (12) provide a valuable genome-wide view of protein interactions but have a number of shortcomings (13). Even if the protein-protein interactions were determined with high accuracy, the resulting network would still require careful interpretation to extract its underlying biological meaning. Specifically, the map is a representation of all possible interactions, but one would only expect some fraction to be operating at any given time.
>
> J. J. RICE, A. KERSHENBAUM, AND G. STOLOVITZKY,
> "Lasting Impressions: Motifs in Protein-Protein Maps
> May Provide Footprints of Evolutionary Events."
> *Proceedings of the National Academy of Sciences*

Delineating the boundaries or limitations of a study is a good way to agree up to a point. Here are templates for doing so.

▸ While X's work clearly demonstrates _____, _____ will be required before we can determine whether _____.

▸ Although Y and Z present firm evidence for _____, their data can not be used to argue that _____.

▸ In summary, our studies show that _____, but the issue of _____ remains unresolved.

Anticipate Objections

Skepticism is a key ingredient in the scientific process. Before an explanation is accepted, scientists demand convincing evidence and assess whether alternative explanations have been thoroughly explored, so it's essential that scientists consider possible objections to their ideas before presenting them. In the following example from a book about the origin of the universe, Tyson and Goldsmith first admit that some might doubt the existence of the poorly understood "dark matter" that physicists have proposed, and then they go on to respond to the skeptics.

> Unrelenting skeptics might compare the dark matter of today with the hypothetical, now defunct "ether," proposed centuries ago as the weightless, transparent medium through which light moved. . . . But dark matter ignorance differs fundamentally from ether ignorance. While ether amounted to a placeholder for our incomplete understanding, the existence of dark matter derives from not from mere presumption but from the observed effects of its gravity on visible matter.
>
> N. D. TYSON AND D. GOLDSMITH,
> *Origins: Fourteen Billion Years of Cosmic Evolution*

Anticipating objections in your own writing will help you clarify and address potential criticisms. Consider objections to your overall approach, as well as to specific aspects of your interpretations. Here are some templates for doing so.

▶ Scientists who take a _____ (*reductionist / integrative / biochemical / computational / statistical*) approach might view our results differently.

▸ This interpretation of the data might be criticized by X, who has argued that _____.

▸ Some may argue that this experimental design fails to account for _____.

Say Why It Matters

Though individual studies can be narrowly focused, science ultimately seeks to answer big questions and produce useful technologies. So it's essential when you enter a scientific conversation to say why the work—and your arguments about it—matter. The following passage from a commentary on a research article notes two implications of work that evaluated the shape of electron orbitals.

> The classic textbook shape of electron orbitals has now been directly observed. As well as confirming the established theory, this work may be a first step to understanding high-temperature superconductivity.
>
> C. J. Humphreys, "Electrons Seen in Orbit," *Nature*

Humphreys argues that the study confirms an established theory and that it may lead to better understanding in another area. When thinking about the broad significance of a study, consider both the practical applications and the impact on future scientific work.

▸ These results open the door to studies that _____.

▸ The methodologies developed by X will be useful for _____.

▸ Our findings are the first step toward _____.

▸ Further work in this area may lead to the development of
_____.

READING AS A WAY OF ENTERING
SCIENTIFIC CONVERSATIONS

In science, as in other disciplines, you'll often start with work done by others, and therefore you will need to critically evaluate their work. To that end, you'll need to probe how well their data support their interpretations. Doing so will lead you toward your own interpretations—your ticket into an ongoing scientific conversation. Here are some questions that will help you read and respond to scientific research.

How well do the methods test the hypothesis?

- Is the sample size adequate?
- Is the experimental design valid?
  Were the proper controls performed?
- What are the limitations of the methodology?
- Are other techniques available?

How fairly have the results been interpreted?

- How well do the results support the stated conclusion?
- Has the data's variability been adequately considered?
- Do other findings verify (or contradict) the conclusion?
- What other experiments could test the conclusion?

What are the broader implications of the work, and why does it matter?

- Can the results be generalized beyond the system that was studied?
- What are the work's practical implications?
- What questions arise from the work?
- Which experiments should be done next?

The examples in this chapter show that scientists do more than simply collect facts; they also interpret those facts and make arguments about their meaning. On the frontiers of science, where we are probing questions that are just beyond our capacity to answer, the data are inevitably incomplete and controversy is to be expected. Writing about science presents the opportunity to add your own arguments to the ongoing discussion.

NATALIE ANGIER
Men, Women, Sex and Darwin

NATALIE ANGIER (b. 1958) has built a career writing books and articles that explain the intricacies of science to the nonscientist. Born and raised in New York City, Angier graduated from Barnard College, where she studied physics, astronomy, and English. She began working as a science writer for *Discovery* magazine in 1980, and in 1990 she joined the staff of the *New York Times*, where she won a Pulitzer Prize for beat reporting in 1991. She has published four books, all of them bestsellers: *Natural Obsessions* (1988), *The Beauty of the Beastly* (1995), *Woman: An Intimate Geography* (2000), and *The Canon: A Whirligig Tour of the Beautiful Basics of Science* (2007).

In "Men, Women, Sex and Darwin," published in the *New York Times* in 1999, Angier examines the most common theories proposed by evolutionary psychologists to explain male and female sexual behavior—for instance, that men are naturally more promiscuous than women and that women are naturally more interested in marriage than men. Drawing on empirical evidence and the work of psychologists, anthropologists, and primatologists, Angier finds reason to doubt these theories and offers alternative explanations of her own. As you read, notice how Angier summarizes and synthesizes information from many different sources.

LIFE IS SHORT BUT JINGLES are forever. None more so, it seems, than the familiar ditty, variously attributed to William James, Ogden Nash and Dorothy Parker: "Hoggamus, higgamus,/Men are polygamous,/Higgamus, hoggamus,/Women monogamous."

Lately the pith of that jingle has found new fodder and new fans, through the explosive growth of a field known as evolutionary psychology. Evolutionary psychology professes to have discovered the fundamental modules of human nature, most notably the essential nature of man and of woman. It makes sense to be curious about the evolutionary roots of human behavior. It's reasonable to try to understand our impulses and actions by applying Darwinian logic to the problem. We're animals. We're not above the rude little prods and jests of natural and sexual selection. But evolutionary psychology as it has been disseminated across mainstream consciousness is a cranky and despotic Cyclops, its single eye glaring through an overwhelmingly masculinist lens. I say "masculinist" rather than "male" because the view of male behavior promulgated by hard-core evolutionary psychologists is as narrow and inflexible as their view of womanhood is.

I'm not interested in explaining to men what they really want or how they should behave. If a fellow chooses to tell himself that his yen for the fetching young assistant in his office and his concomitant disgruntlement with his aging wife make perfect Darwinian sense, who am I to argue with him? I'm only proposing here that the hard-core evolutionary psychologists have got a lot about women wrong—about some of us, anyway—and that women want more and deserve better than the cartoon Olive Oyl[1] handed down for popular consumption.

The cardinal premises of evolutionary psychology of interest to this discussion are as follows: 1. Men are more promiscuous and less sexually reserved than women are. 2. Women are inherently more interested in a stable relationship than men are. 3. Women are naturally attracted to high-status men with resources. 4. Men are naturally attracted to youth and beauty. 5. Humankind's core preferences and desires were hammered out long, long ago, a hundred thousand years or more, in the legendary Environment of Evolutionary Adaptation, or E.E.A., also known as the ancestral environment, also known as the Stone Age, and they have not changed appreciably since then, nor are they likely to change in the future.

---

[1] Popeye's long-suffering sweetheart in the *Popeye* comic strip and animations, first created by cartoonist Elzie Crisler Segar in 1929.

In sum: Higgamus, hoggamus, Pygmalionus, *Playboy* magazine, 5 eternitas. Amen.

Hard-core evolutionary psychology types go to extremes to argue in favor of the yawning chasm that separates the innate desires of women and men. They declare ringing confirmation for their theories even in the face of feeble and amusingly contradictory data. For example: Among the cardinal principles of the evo-psycho set is that men are by nature more polygamous than women are, and much more accepting of casual, even anonymous, sex. Men can't help themselves, they say: they are always hungry for sex, bodies, novelty and nubility. Granted, men needn't act on such desires, but the drive to sow seed is there nonetheless, satyric and relentless, and women cannot fully understand its force. David Buss, a professor of psychology at the University of Texas at Austin and one of the most outspoken of the evolutionary psychologists, says that asking a man not to lust after a pretty young woman is like telling a carnivore not to like meat.

At the same time, they recognize that the overwhelming majority of men and women get married, and so their theories must extend to different innate mate preferences among men and women. Men look for the hallmarks of youth, like smooth skin, full lips and perky breasts; they want a mate who has a long childbearing career ahead of her. Men also want women who are virginal and who seem as though they'll be faithful and not make cuckolds of them. The sexy, vampy types are fine for a Saturday romp, but when it comes to choosing a marital partner, men want modesty and fidelity.

Women want a provider, the theory goes. They want a man who seems rich, stable and ambitious. They want to know that they and their children will be cared for. They want a man who can take charge, maybe dominate them just a little, enough to reassure them that the man is genotypically, phenotypically, eternally, a king. Women's innate preference for a well-to-do man continues to this day, the evolutionary psychologists insist, even among financially independent and professionally successful women who don't need a man as a provider. It was adaptive in the past to look for the most resourceful man, they say, and adaptations can't be willed away in a generation or two of putative cultural change.

And what is the evidence for these male-female verities? For the difference in promiscuity quotas, the hard-cores love to raise the example of the differences between gay men and lesbians. Homosexuals are seen as a revealing population because they supposedly can behave according to the innermost impulses of their sex, untempered by the need to adjust to the demands and wishes of the opposite sex, as heterosexuals theoretically are. What do we see in this ideal study group? Just look at how gay men carry on! They are perfectly happy to have hundreds, thousands, of sexual partners, to have sex in bathhouses, in bathrooms, in Central Park. By contrast, lesbians are sexually sedate. They don't cruise sex clubs. They couple up and stay coupled, and they like cuddling and hugging more than they do serious, genitally based sex.

In the hard-core rendering of inherent male-female discrepancies in promiscuity, gay men are offered up as true men, real men, men set free to be men, while lesbians are real women, ultrawomen, acting out every woman's fantasy of love and commitment. Interestingly, though, in many neurobiology studies gay men are said to have somewhat feminized brains, with hypothalamic nuclei that are closer in size to a woman's than to a straight man's, and spatial-reasoning skills that are modest and ladylike rather than manfully robust. For their part, lesbians are posited to have somewhat masculinized brains and skills—to be sportier, more mechanically inclined, less likely to have played with dolls or tea sets when young—all as an ostensible result of exposure to prenatal androgens. And so gay men are sissy boys in some contexts and Stone Age manly men in others, while lesbians are battering rams one day and flower into the softest and most sexually divested girlish girls the next.

On the question of mate preferences, evo-psychos rely on surveys, most of them compiled by David Buss. His surveys are celebrated by some, derided by others, but in any event they are ambitious—performed in thirty-seven countries, he says, on six continents. His surveys, and others emulating them, consistently find that men rate youth and beauty as important traits in a mate, while women give comparatively greater weight to ambition and financial success. Surveys show that surveys never lie. Lest you think that women's mate prefer-

10

ences change with their own mounting economic clout, surveys assure us that they do not. Surveys of female medical students, according to John Marshall Townsend, of Syracuse University, indicate that they hope to marry men with an earning power and social status at least equal to and preferably greater than their own.

Perhaps all this means is that men can earn a living wage better, even now, than women can. Men make up about half the world's population, but they still own the vast majority of the world's wealth—the currency, the minerals, the timber, the gold, the stocks, the amber fields of grain. In her superb book *Why So Slow?* Virginia Valian, a professor of psychology at Hunter College, lays out the extent of lingering economic discrepancies between men and women in the United States. In 1978 there were two women heading Fortune 1000 companies; in 1994, there were still two; in 1996, the number had jumped all the way to four. In 1985, 2 percent of the Fortune 1000's senior-level executives were women; by 1992, that number had hardly budged, to 3 percent. A 1990 salary and compensation survey of 799 major companies showed that of the highest-paid officers and directors, less than one-half of 1 percent were women. Ask, and he shall receive. In the United States the possession of a bachelor's degree adds $28,000 to a man's salary but only $9,000 to a woman's. A degree from a high-prestige school contributes $11,500 to a man's income but subtracts $2,400 from a woman's. If women continue to worry that they need a man's money, because the playing field remains about as level as the surface of Mars, then we can't conclude anything about innate preferences. If women continue to suffer from bag-lady syndrome even as they become prosperous, if they still see their wealth as provisional and capsizable, and if they still hope to find a man with a dependable income to supplement their own, then we can credit women with intelligence and acumen, for inequities abound.

There's another reason that smart, professional women might respond on surveys that they'd like a mate of their socioeconomic status or better. Smart, professional women are smart enough to know that men can be tender of ego—is it genetic?—and that it hurts a man to earn less money than his wife, and that resentment is a noxious chemical in a marriage and best avoided at any price. "A woman who is more successful than her mate threatens his position in the male hierarchy," Elizabeth Cashdan, of the University of Utah, has written. If women could be persuaded that men didn't mind their being high achievers, were in fact pleased and proud to be affiliated with them, we might predict that the women would stop caring about the particulars of their mates' income. The anthropologist Sarah Blaffer Hrdy writes that "when female status and access to resources do not depend on her mate's status, women will likely use a range of criteria, not primarily or even necessarily prestige and wealth, for mate selection." She cites a 1996 *New York Times* story about women from a wide range of professions—bankers, judges, teachers, journalists—who marry male convicts. The allure of such men is not their income, for you can't earn much when you make license plates for a living. Instead, it is the men's gratitude that proves irresistible. The women also like the fact that their husbands' fidelity is guaranteed. "Peculiar as it is," Hrdy writes, "this vignette of sex-reversed claustration[2] makes a serious point about just how little we know about female choice in breeding systems where male interests are not paramount and patrilines[3] are not making the rules."

Do women love older men? Do women find gray hair and wrinkles attractive on men—as attractive, that is, as a fine, full head of pigmented hair and a vigorous, firm complexion? The evolutionary psychologists suggest yes. They believe that women look for the signs of maturity in men because a mature man is likely to be a comparatively wealthy and resourceful man. That should logically include baldness, which generally comes with age and the higher status that it often confers. Yet, as Desmond Morris points out, a thinning hairline is not considered a particularly attractive state.

Assuming that women find older men attractive, is it the men's alpha status? Or could it be something less complimentary to the male, something like the following—that an older man is appealing not because he is powerful but because in his maturity he has lost some of his power, has become less marketable and desirable and potentially   15

---

[2]Cloistering, enclosing.
[3]Groups of patrilineages, or lines of descent from a male ancestor.

more grateful and gracious, more likely to make a younger woman feel that there is a balance of power in the relationship? The rude little calculation is simple: He is male, I am female—advantage, man. He is older, I am younger—advantage, woman. By the same token, a woman may place little value on a man's appearance because she values something else far more: room to breathe. Who can breathe in the presence of a handsome young man, whose ego, if expressed as a vapor, would fill Biosphere II? Not even, I'm afraid, a beautiful young woman.

In the end, what is important to question, and to hold to the fire of alternative interpretation, is the immutability and adaptive logic of the discrepancy, its basis in our genome rather than in the ecological circumstances in which a genome manages to express itself. Evolutionary psychologists insist on the essential discordance between the strength of the sex drive in males and females. They admit that many nonhuman female primates gallivant about rather more than we might have predicted before primatologists began observing their behavior in the field—more, far more, than is necessary for the sake of reproduction. Nonetheless, the credo of the coy female persists. It is garlanded with qualifications and is admitted to be an imperfect portrayal of female mating strategies, but then, that little matter of etiquette attended to, the credo is stated once again.

"Amid the great variety of social structure in these species, the basic theme . . . stands out, at least in minimal form: males seem very eager for sex and work hard to find it; females work less hard," Robert Wright says in *The Moral Animal*. "This isn't to say the females don't like sex. They love it, and may initiate it. And, intriguingly, the females of the species most closely related to humans—chimpanzees and bonobos—seem particularly amenable to a wild sex life, including a variety of partners. Still, female apes don't do what male apes do: search high and low, risking life and limb, to find sex, and to find as much of it, with as many different partners, as possible; it has a way of finding them." In fact female chimpanzees do search high and low and take great risks to find sex with partners other than the partners who have a way of finding them. DNA studies of chimpanzees in West Africa show that half the offspring in a group of closely scrutinized chimpanzees turned out not to be the offspring of the resident males.

The females of the group didn't rely on sex "finding" its way to them; they proactively left the local environs, under such conditions of secrecy that not even their vigilant human observers knew they had gone, and became impregnated by outside males. They did so even at the risk of life and limb—their own and those of their offspring. Male chimpanzees try to control the movements of fertile females. They'll scream at them and hit them if they think the females aren't listening. They may even kill an infant they think is not their own. We don't know why the females take such risks to philander, but they do, and to say that female chimpanzees "work less hard" than males do at finding sex does not appear to be supported by the data.

Evo-psychos pull us back and forth until we might want to sue for whiplash. On the one hand we are told that women have a lower sex drive than men do. On the other hand we are told that the madonna-whore dichotomy is a universal stereotype. In every culture, there is a tendency among both men and women to adjudge women as either chaste or trampy. The chaste ones are accorded esteem. The trampy ones are consigned to the basement, a notch or two below goats in social status. A woman can't sleep around without risking terrible retribution, to her reputation, to her prospects, to her life. "Can anyone find a single culture in which women with unrestrained sexual appetites aren't viewed as more aberrant than comparably libidinous men?" Wright asks rhetorically.

Women are said to have lower sex drives than men, yet they are universally punished if they display evidence to the contrary—if they disobey their "natural" inclination toward a stifled libido. Women supposedly have a lower sex drive than men do, yet it is not low enough. There is still just enough of a lingering female infidelity impulse that cultures everywhere have had to gird against it by articulating a rigid dichotomy with menacing implications for those who fall on the wrong side of it. There is still enough lingering female infidelity to justify infibulation, purdah, claustration. Men have the naturally higher sex drive, yet all the laws, customs, punishments, shame, strictures, mystiques and antimystiques are aimed with full hominid fury at that tepid, sleepy, hypoactive creature, the female libido.

"It seems premature . . . to attribute the relative lack of female inter- 20 est in sexual variety to women's biological nature alone in the face of overwhelming evidence that women are consistently beaten for promiscuity and adultery," the primatologist Barbara Smuts has written. "If female sexuality is muted compared to that of men, then why must men the world over go to extreme lengths to control and contain it?"

Why indeed? Consider a brief evolutionary apologia for President Clinton's adulteries written by Steven Pinker, of the Massachusetts Institute of Technology. "Most human drives have ancient Darwinian rationales," he wrote. "A prehistoric man who slept with fifty women could have sired fifty children, and would have been more likely to have descendants who inherited his tastes. A woman who slept with fifty men would have no more descendants than a woman who slept with one. Thus, men should seek quantity in sexual partners; women, quality." And isn't it so, he says, everywhere and always so? "In our society," he continues, "most young men tell researchers that they would like eight sexual partners in the next two years; most women say that they would like one." Yet would a man find the prospect of a string of partners so appealing if the following rules were applied: that no matter how much he may like a particular woman and be pleased by her performance and want to sleep with her again, he will have no say in the matter and will be dependent on her mood and good graces for all future contact; that each act of casual sex will cheapen his status and make him increasingly less attractive to other women; and that society will not wink at his randiness but rather sneer at him and think him pathetic, sullied, smaller than life? Until men are subjected to the same severe standards and threat of censure as women are, and until they are given the lower hand in a so-called casual encounter from the start, it is hard to insist with such self-satisfaction that, hey, it's natural, men like a lot of sex with a lot of people and women don't.

Reflect for a moment on Pinker's philandering caveman who slept with fifty women. Just how good a reproductive strategy is this chronic, random shooting of the gun? A woman is fertile only five or six days a month. Her ovulation is concealed. The man doesn't know when she's fertile. She might be in the early stages of pregnancy when he gets to her; she might still be lactating and thus not ovulating. Moreover, even if our hypothetical Don Juan hits a day on which a woman is ovulating, the chances are around 65 percent that his sperm will fail to fertilize her egg; human reproduction is complicated, and most eggs and sperm are not up to the demands of proper fusion. Even if conception occurs, the resulting embryo has about a 30 percent chance of miscarrying at some point in gestation. In sum, each episode of fleeting sex has a remarkably small probability of yielding a baby—no more than 1 or 2 percent at best.

And because the man is trysting and running, he isn't able to prevent any of his casual contacts from turning around and mating with other men. The poor fellow. He has to mate with many scores of women for his wham-bam strategy to pay off. And where are all these women to be found, anyway? Population densities during that purportedly all-powerful psyche shaper the "ancestral environment" were quite low, and long-distance travel was dangerous and difficult.

There are alternatives to wantonness, as a number of theorists have emphasized. If, for example, a man were to spend more time with one woman rather than dashing breathlessly from sheet to sheet, if he were to feel compelled to engage in what animal behaviorists call mate guarding, he might be better off, reproductively speaking, than the wild Lothario, both because the odds of impregnating the woman would increase and because he'd be monopolizing her energy and keeping her from the advances of other sperm bearers. It takes the average couple three to four months of regular sexual intercourse to become pregnant. That number of days is approximately equal to the number of partners our hypothetical libertine needs to sleep with to have one encounter result in a "fertility unit," that is, a baby. The two strategies, then, shake out about the same. A man can sleep with a lot of women—the quantitative approach—or he can sleep with one woman for months at a time, and be madly in love with her—the qualitative tactic.

It's possible that these two reproductive strategies are distributed in discrete packets among the male population, with a result that some men are born philanderers and can never attach, while others are born romantics and perpetually in love with love; but it's also possible that men teeter back and forth from one impulse to the other, suffering an internal struggle between the desire to bond and the desire to retreat, with the circuits of attachment ever there to be toyed with, and their needs and desires difficult to understand, paradoxical, fickle, treacherous and glorious. It is possible, then, and for perfectly good Darwinian reason, that casual sex for men is rarely as casual as it is billed.

It needn't be argued that men and women are exactly the same, or that humans are meta-evolutionary beings, removed from nature and slaves to culture, to reject the perpetually regurgitated model of the coy female and the ardent male. Conflicts of interest are always among us, and the outcomes of those conflicts are interesting, more interesting by far than what the ultra-evolutionary psychology line has handed us. Patricia Gowaty, of the University of Georgia, sees conflict between males and females as inevitable and pervasive. She calls it sexual dialectics. Her thesis is that females and males vie for control over the means of reproduction. Those means are the female body, for there is as yet no such beast as the parthenogenetic[4] man.

Women are under selective pressure to maintain control over their reproduction, to choose with whom they will mate and with whom they will not—to exercise female choice. Men are under selective pressure to make sure they're chosen or, barring that, to subvert female choice and coerce the female to mate against her will. "But once you have this basic dialectic set in motion, it's going to be a constant push-me, pull-you," Gowaty says. That dynamism cannot possibly result in a unitary response, the caricatured coy woman and ardent man. Instead there are going to be some coy, reluctantly mating males and some ardent females, and any number of variations in between.

"A female will choose to mate with a male whom she believes, consciously or otherwise, will confer some advantage on her and her off-spring. If that's the case, then her decision is contingent on what she brings to the equation." For example, she says, "the 'good genes' model leads to oversimplified notions that there is a 'best male' out there, a top-of-the-line hunk whom all females would prefer to mate with if they had the wherewithal. But in the viability model, a female brings

[4]Created from an unfertilized egg.

her own genetic complement to the equation, with the result that what looks good genetically to one woman might be a clash of colors for another."

Maybe the man's immune system doesn't complement her own, for example, Gowaty proposes. There's evidence that the search for immune variation is one of the subtle factors driving mate selection, which may be why we care about how our lovers smell; immune molecules may be volatilized and released in sweat, hair, the oil on our skin. We are each of us a chemistry set, and each of us has a distinctive mix of reagents. "What pleases me might not please somebody else," Gowaty says. "There is no one-brand great male out there. We're not all programmed to look for the alpha male and only willing to mate with the little guy or the less aggressive guy because we can't do any better. But the propaganda gives us a picture of the right man and the ideal woman, and the effect of the propaganda is insidious. It becomes self-reinforcing. People who don't fit the model think, I'm weird, I'll have to change my behavior." It is this danger, that the ostensible "discoveries" of evolutionary psychology will be used as propaganda, that makes the enterprise so disturbing.

Variation and flexibility are the key themes that get set aside in the 30 breathless dissemination of evolutionary psychology. "The variation is tremendous, and is rooted in biology," Barbara Smuts said to me. "Flexibility itself is the adaptation." Smuts has studied olive baboons, and she has seen males pursuing all sorts of mating strategies. "There are some whose primary strategy is dominating other males, and being able to gain access to more females because of their fighting ability," she says. "Then there is the type of male who avoids competition and cultivates long-term relationships with females and their infants. These are the nice, affiliative guys. There's a third type, who focuses on sexual relationships. He's the consorter. . . . And as far as we can tell, no one reproductive strategy has advantages over the others."

Women are said to need an investing male. We think we know the reason. Human babies are difficult and time consuming to raise. Stone Age mothers needed husbands to bring home the bison. Yet the age-old assumption that male parental investment lies at the heart of human evolution is now open to serious question. Men in traditional foraging cultures do not necessarily invest resources in their offspring. Among the Hadza of Africa, for example, the men hunt, but they share the bounty of that hunting widely, politically, strategically. They don't deliver it straight to the mouths of their progeny. Women rely on their senior female kin to help feed their children. The women and their children in a gathering-hunting society clearly benefit from the meat that hunters bring back to the group. But they benefit as a group, not as a collection of nuclear family units, each beholden to the father's personal pound of wildeburger.

This is a startling revelation, which upends many of our presumptions about the origins of marriage and what women want from men and men from women. If the environment of evolutionary adaptation is not defined primarily by male parental investment, the bedrock of so much of evolutionary psychology's theories, then we can throw the door wide open and ask new questions, rather than endlessly repeating ditties and calling the female coy long after she has run her petticoats through the presidential paper shredder.

For example: Nicholas Blurton Jones, of the University of California at Los Angeles, and others have proposed that marriage developed as an extension of men's efforts at mate guarding. If the cost of philandering becomes ludicrously high, the man might be better off trying to claim rights to one woman at a time. Regular sex with a fertile woman is at least likely to yield offspring at comparatively little risk to his life, particularly if sexual access to the woman is formalized through a public ceremony—a wedding. Looked at from this perspective, one must wonder why an ancestral woman bothered to get married, particularly if she and her female relatives did most of the work of keeping the family fed from year to year. Perhaps, Blurton Jones suggests, to limit the degree to which she was harassed. The cost of chronic male harassment may be too high to bear. Better to agree to a ritualized bond with a male and to benefit from whatever hands-off policy that marriage may bring, than to spend all of her time locked in one sexual dialectic or another.

Thus marriage may have arisen as a multifaceted social pact: between man and woman, between male and male and between the couple and the tribe. It is a reasonable solution to a series of cultural challenges that arose in concert with the expansion of the human neocortex. But its roots may not be what we think they are, nor may our contemporary mating behaviors stem from the pressures of an ancestral environment as it is commonly portrayed, in which a woman needed a mate to help feed and clothe her young. Instead, our "deep" feelings about marriage may be more pragmatic, more contextual and, dare I say it, more egalitarian than we give them credit for being.

If marriage is a social compact, a mutual bid between man and 35 woman to contrive a reasonably stable and agreeable microhabitat in a community of shrewd and well-armed members, then we can understand why, despite rhetoric to the contrary, men are as eager to marry as women are. A raft of epidemiological studies have shown that marriage adds more years to the life of a man than it does to that of a woman. Why should that be, if men are so "naturally" ill suited to matrimony?

What do women want? None of us can speak for all women, or for more than one woman, really, but we can hazard a mad guess that a desire for emotional parity is widespread and profound. It doesn't go away, although it often hibernates under duress, and it may be perverted by the restrictions of habitat or culture into something that looks like its opposite. The impulse for liberty is congenital. It is the ultimate manifestation of selfishness, which is why we can count on its endurance.

STUDY QUESTIONS

1. What theories of evolutionary psychology does Angier call into question? What alternative theories does she propose?

2. List the people Angier quotes or cites. How does each contribute to her essay? What is the rhetorical effect of using these sources? How would the essay be different if she hadn't used sources?

3. *For Writing.* Write an essay in which you explain, in your own words, a theory of evolutionary psychology that Angier discusses. Then DESCRIBE the behavior of at least two people you know and explain how that behavior supports or refutes that theory.

DAVID DOBBS { *A Depression Switch?*

DAVID DOBBS (b. 1958) is a journalist who writes about science, medicine, and culture. His articles have been published in the *New York Times Magazine*, *Slate*, *Audubon*, and *Scientific American Mind*, where he is a contributing editor. Dobbs has also written several books: *The Northern Forest*, with Richard Ober (1995), *The Great Gulf: Fishermen, Scientists, and the Struggle to Revive the World's Greatest Fishery* (2000), and *Reef Madness* (2005).

The following essay, originally published in the *New York Times*, was featured in *The Best American Science Writing 2007*. In it, the author tells the story of a healthy woman who suddenly falls ill with severe depression. Dobbs analyzes the way a doctor applies a scientific discovery to alleviate the woman's illness through experimental brain surgery. As you read, take note of how Dobbs presents the step-by-step process of the procedure to the reader.

DEANNA COLE-BENJAMIN NEVER FIGURED to be a test case for a radical new brain surgery for depression. Her youth contained no traumas; her adult life, as she describes it, was blessed. At 22 she joined Gary Benjamin, a career financial officer in the Canadian Army, in a marriage that brought her happiness and, in the 1990s, three children. They lived in a comfortable house in Kingston, a pleasant university town on Lake Ontario's north shore, and Deanna, a public-health nurse, loved her work. But in the last months of 2000, apropos of nothing—no life changes, no losses—she slid into a depression of extraordinary depth and duration.

"It began with a feeling of not really feeling as connected to things as usual," she told me one evening at the family's dining-room table. "Then it was like this wall fell around me. I felt sadder and sadder and then just numb."

Her doctor prescribed progressively stronger antidepressants, but they scarcely touched her. A couple of weeks before Christmas, she stopped going to work. The simplest acts—deciding what to wear, making breakfast—required immense will. Then one day, alone in the house after Gary had taken the kids to school and gone to work, she felt so desperate to escape her pain that she drove to her doctor's office and told him she didn't think she could go on anymore.

"He took one look," she told me later, "and said that he wanted me to stay right there in the office. Then he called Gary, and Gary came to the office, and he told us he wanted Gary to take me straight to the hospital."

They drove to the Providence Continuing Care Center's mental-health hospital, still known locally as the Kingston Psychiatric Hospital, or K.P.H., its name when it was built in the 1950s. "It's a dingy, archaic place," Deanna said, "typical of older mental hospitals." There, in the locked ward that also contained psychotic patients, she would spend the next 10 months straight and about 85 percent of the three years after that. Her depression would prove resistant to every class of antidepressant, numerous combinations of antidepressants and anti-anxiety drugs, intensive psychotherapy, and about a hundred sessions of electroconvulsive therapy. Patients who have failed that many treatments usually don't emerge from their depressions.

Finally, in the spring of 2004, Deanna's psychiatrist at the hospital, Dr. Gebrehiwot Abraham, received a fax from a University of Toronto research team asking if he had an appropriate candidate for a clinical trial of a new, experimental surgery for treatment-resistant depression. The operation borrowed a procedure called deep brain stimulation, or D.B.S., which is used to treat Parkinson's.[1] It involves planting electrodes in a region near the center of the brain called Area 25 and sending in a steady stream of low voltage from a pacemaker in the chest.

[1] A degenerative disorder of the central nervous system.

One of the study's leaders, Dr. Helen Mayberg, a neurologist, had detected in depressed patients what she suspected was a crucial dysfunction in Area 25's activity. She hypothesized that the electrodes might modulate the area and ease the depression.

The procedure, Dr. Abraham told Deanna and Gary, had worked safely in thousands of Parkinson's patients. But it would carry some risk of neural complications (it was, after all, brain surgery), it would be uncomfortable and it might not work.

"We were in tears," said Deanna, who is now 41. "We felt we'd tried everything and nothing worked. But we talked about it and decided, 'Well, what have we got to lose?'"

What she hoped to lose, of course, was her depression. But depression, which 5 to 10 percent of Americans suffer in any given year and about 15 percent will suffer in their lifetimes, can be hard to lose. Drugs, as shown in a comprehensive study released last month by the National Institute of Mental Health, are effective in only half of patients with major depression. Psychotherapy does no better. For those people who are not helped by therapy or drugs, electroconvulsive therapy, or ECT, can bring relief. But few of those cures are complete. These therapies usually ease rather than cure depression while sometimes bringing side effects like insomnia or memory loss, and their potency often proves fleeting; as many as half to two-thirds of those successfully treated relapse within two years. Neither neuroscientists nor psychiatrists can say exactly what depression is. Neurologically and psychologically, what Hippocrates called the "black bile" and Susan Sontag[2] "melancholy minus its charms" presents an almost impossibly complicated puzzle.

The expectations for the Toronto team's D.B.S. study were accordingly modest. When I later asked Mayberg's collaborator Dr. Andres Lozano, the neurosurgeon who performed the operations, what he had expected, he replied, "Nothing."   10

As it turned out, 8 of the 12 patients he operated on, including Deanna, felt their depressions lift while suffering minimal side

---

[2]American novelist, essayist, and cultural critic (1933–2004). *Hippocrates* (c. 460–c. 370 BCE): ancient Greek physician revered as the "Father of Medicine."

effects—an incredible rate of effectiveness in patients so immovably depressed. Nor did they just vaguely recover. Their scores on the Hamilton depression scale, a standard used to measure the severity of depression, fell from the soul-deadening high 20s to the single digits— essentially normal. They've re-engaged their families, resumed jobs and friendships, started businesses, taken up hobbies old and new, replanted dying gardens. They've regained the resilience that distinguishes the healthy from the depressed.

These results brought a marvelous surprise to both the patients and the doctors involved—and nervous anticipation about whether their luck will hold. Though a few of the patients are more than two years out from the surgery, none completely trust their cure. No one can tell them for sure that it will last, and they worry. The study doctors and the wider medical community, meanwhile, are guarded about whether D.B.S. will prove so effective in larger trials. "I can't emphasize enough that we need a large, randomized study to confirm this as a treatment," says Valerie Voon, a University of Toronto psychiatrist who was with the team for the first six patients and who is now a research fellow at the National Institutes of Health.

Those caveats notwithstanding, many scientists following the trial say they believe it will change how psychiatrists define and treat mood disorders. Mayberg, who speaks of a "paradigm shift," notes that she developed the trial to evaluate not a treatment but a hypothesis. In that sense the trial succeeded. Mayberg's focus on Area 25 tests the emerging "network" model of mood disorders, a new way of looking at psychiatric conditions that isn't restricted by the neurochemical model of mood that has dominated over the past quarter century or so. Rather, it incorporates neurochemistry into the concept of the brain as a circuit board or wiring diagram. The network model carries profound implications for research and, ultimately, treatment. The Prozac revolution showed everyone that tweaking neurochemistry can dampen and sometimes extinguish depression—but only through a generalized approach, hitting the entire brain. ("Carpet-bombing," one neuroscientist calls it.) And the 50 percent success rate of antidepressant drugs suggests that they aren't hitting depression's central mechanism. The network approach, on the other hand, focuses on specific nodes, pathways and gateways that might be approached with various treatments—electrical, surgical or pharmacological. This small trial appears to confirm this model so emphatically that it's already changing the neuropsychiatric view of the brain and the direction of research.

"People often ask me about the significance of small first studies like this," says Dr. Thomas Insel, who as director of the National Institute of Mental Health enjoys an unparalleled view of the discipline. "I usually tell them: 'Don't bother. We don't know enough.' But this is different. Here we know enough to say this is something significant. I really do believe this is the beginning of a new way of understanding depression."

When she started her research in the late 1980's, Helen Mayberg, too, 15 looked at neurochemistry. "That's where biological psychiatry was then," she told me. "It was about the brain as a bowl of soup. You whip up a chemical, add it and stir. An alchemist's point of view. But I soon realized I wanted to find out where things were changing."

Lively, smart and quick-witted, Mayberg talks of brain science with contagious excitement. She possesses just the kind of presence someone having a hole drilled in his head would welcome—authoritative but warm. Mayberg originally considered becoming a psychiatrist, but she didn't like the discipline's resistance at the time (it was the 1970s) to neurological explanations of mood. So she became a behavioral neurologist, doing a residency at Columbia University and then moving to Johns Hopkins.

Setting aside the bowl-of-soup model did not mean deciding that neurochemicals weren't important. Rather it meant deciding that neurochemistry, and particularly the chemistry dictating how individual neurons communicate with one another, was probably driven by traffic between different brain areas, and that identifying the patterns in that traffic might yield new understanding. (Or, using another metaphor, if the brain is an orchestra, then the neurochemical approach focuses on how well individual players listen and respond to the players adjacent to them; the network approach, like a conductor, focuses on how the orchestra's sections—strings, winds, brass, etc.—coordinate and balance volume and tone. When both are working well, you've got music.)

Imaging tools for tracking these relationships, like PET scans and later functional magnetic resonance imagery,[3] were just maturing as Mayberg pursued her work. Neuroscientists were soon using these tools to help identify networks involved in mental processes ranging from distinguishing facial expressions to experiencing alarm or pleasure. Each of these networks engages different brain areas in different combinations. The areas active in recognizing a fearful expression, for instance, won't match those for recalling old memories, though some areas might overlap. Defining the network involved in any given process requires figuring out not just which parts are involved but also which parts are most vital and how one affects another.

By the 1990s, Mayberg was trying to define the network that goes awry in depression. She and other researchers soon established that depression involved abnormal patterns of activity in a network that includes limbic areas (a cluster of evolutionarily older brain areas around the top of the brain stem), which control basic emotions and drives like fear, lust, and hunger, and the newer cortex and subcortex responsible for thought, memory, motivation and reward.

Several researchers were working on this. But Mayberg, and, separately, Dr. Wayne Drevets, then at Washington University and now at the N.I.M.H., increasingly homed in on Area 25, which seemed crucial in both its behavior and its position in this network. They found that Area 25 was smaller in most depressed patients; that it lighted up in every form of depression and also in nondepressed people who intentionally pondered sad things; that it dimmed when depression was successfully treated; and that it was heavily wired to brain areas modulating fear, learning, memory, sleep, libido, motivation, reward and other functions that went fritzy in the depressed. It seemed to be a sort of junction box, in short, whose malfunction might be "necessary and sufficient," as Mayberg put it, to turn the world dim. Maybe it could provide a switch that would brighten the dark.

To work the switch, Mayberg needed a knife. In 1999 she moved from the University of Texas at San Antonio to the University of

20

---

[3]Positron emission tomography (PET) is a nuclear medicine imaging technique; magnetic resonance imagery is better known by its acronym, MRI.

Toronto, where she met Lozano, who had become expert at using deep brain stimulation for treating Parkinson's, the neurological affliction that causes tremors and rigidity as well as cognitive and emotional declines. By the time he and Mayberg met, he'd slipped electrodes into the brains of almost 300 patients.

Depression is more elusive than Parkinson's. But approaching Area 25 with D.B.S. allowed the researchers to use a known tool. Neurosurgeons found as early as the 1950s that they could treat Parkinson's by destroying a small portion of the hyperactive globus pallidus, a brain area that is crucial to movement. The treatment illustrated one of the brain's many oddities: some areas can cause more trouble when they are excessively active than when they have no activity at all. In the early 1990s, surgeons increasingly began to use D.B.S. to quiet the globus pallidus by sending it steady, rapid pulses of low voltage. Patients' tremors would instantly ease or cease; their rigidity and uncontrollable body movements would fade over a week or two. Killing the current revived the symptoms. Surgeons have now implanted D.B.S. electrodes in some 30,000 Parkinson's patients worldwide. The procedure is not a cure-all. It helps some patients less than others, does little to alleviate Parkinson's cognitive and emotional decay and occasionally creates complications including infection, bleeding and memory loss. Its biggest problem may be its success. So many medical centers now do it that some do it badly or on poorly qualified patients. But done well, it usually works.

Mayberg knew all this from the literature and learned more in conversations with Lozano. She grew increasingly convinced that applying D.B.S. to Area 25 might control depression.

"So one day," she told me, "I went to Lozano and said: 'I want to turn off Area 25. Can we put a stimulator there and see if that does it?' And he goes, 'Why not?'"

Occasionally, Deanna felt good enough to go home. This feeling seldom lasted more than a few days. "You could tell she was getting bad again when she couldn't sleep," Gary said. "That was the red flag. She'd be around the house all night, watching TV, up worried, cleaning. Then she'd get worse each day. Her eyes got that sunken look.

Those were the scariest times, when she was getting like that and I would drop the kids at school and go to work and know she was home alone."

During the bad periods, which was much of the time, Deanna thought about suicide almost constantly. Through the windows of the locked ward she could see Lake Ontario, cold and immense. While she was there, one patient managed to reach the lake, beyond the parking lot and a grove of trees, and drown himself. Deanna thought obsessively of doing the same.

"I imagined that all the time," she said. "That I would walk out there and walk into the lake and that would be it."

As the months and years passed and all treatments failed, it began to feel as if there were only one way out.

"It started to seem like, this is not going to stop," Gary said. "This is our life now. There were times I thought that it was going to end"—he looked across the table at Deanna—"only when you committed suicide."

"The worst part for me," Deanna said, "was not being able to feel anything for my children. To hug them, to have them hug me, and feel nothing. That was devastating. An awful, awful place to be."

The D.B.S. operation involves an intrusion that is delicate but brutal. The patients are kept awake so they can describe any changes, and the only drug administered is a local anesthetic. The surgical team shaves much of the patient's head and attaches to the skull, with four screws drilled through skin into bone, the stereotactic frame that will hold the head steady against the operating table and serve as a navigational aid. Mounting the frame takes only about ten minutes. But because it involves driving screws into the skull ("You can't truly feel it," as one patient said, "but you can hear it and see it and smell it"), and because it leaves you with a steel frame around the head, many patients find this the most distressing part of the whole business.

Gary found the frame more than he could take. He kissed his wife and went elsewhere, hoping she wouldn't be a vegetable when he next saw her. Then Deanna was rolled to an M.R.I. machine, where scans would be taken; the scans would help guide Lozano in placing the electrodes.

During the hour or so while the computer processed the scans, Deanna chatted with Mayberg. The day before, she told Mayberg, on video, that what she most wanted was to hold her children and feel it.

When the scans were ready, she went to the operating room. She was placed on a table, which was tilted back like a La-Z-Boy. Lozano and his team bolted the stereotactic frame to the table, as it was described to me later. There was some scrubbing on her head, some chitchat among the surgical team, much fiddling with sterile drapes and instruments. Then Lozano fit a half-inch burred bit into a drill, turned it on and started drilling. He drilled right into the top of Deanna's skull, which brought a rattling sensation and a sound like that made by an air wrench removing the lugs off a car's wheel. Then he did it again.

Now Lozano threaded a guide tube—"It's a straight shot," he said 35 later, "really quite easy"—down between crevices and seams to one side of Area 25, which is in two small lobes at the midline of the brain. He slid the first electrode and its lead down the tube, then repeated this for the other side. All this took nearly two hours. After he double-checked his locations, he wired the leads to a pacemaker and gave Mayberg a nod. They could turn it on anytime now.

Mayberg had squeezed into a spot at Deanna's side sometime before. She had told Deanna that if anything felt different, she should say so. Mayberg wasn't going to tell her when the device was activated. "Don't try to decide what's important," Mayberg told her. "If your nose itches, I want to know." Now and then the two would chat. But so far Deanna hadn't said much.

"So we turn it on," Mayberg told me later, "and all of a sudden she says to me, 'It's very strange,' she says, 'I know you've been with me in the operating room this whole time. I know you care about me. But it's not that. I don't know what you just did. But I'm looking at you, and it's like I just feel suddenly more connected to you.'"

Mayberg, stunned, signaled with her hand to the others, out of Deanna's view, to turn the stimulator off.

"And they turn it off," Mayberg said, "and she goes: 'God, it's just so odd. You just went away again. I guess it wasn't really anything.'

"It was subtle like a brick," Mayberg told me. "There's no reason 40 for her to say that. Zero. And all through those tapes I have of her, every time she's in the clinic beforehand, she always talks about this disconnect, this closeness and sense of affiliation she misses, that was so agonizingly painful for her to lose. And there it was. It was back in an instant."

Deanna later described it in similar terms. "It was literally like a switch being turned on that had been held down for years," she said. "All of a sudden they hit the spot, and I feel so calm and so peaceful. It was overwhelming to be able to process emotion on somebody's face. I'd been numb to that for so long."

It worked that way for other patients too. For those for whom it worked, the first surges of mood and sensation were peculiar to their natures. Patient 4, for instance, was fond of taking walks, and she had previously told Mayberg that she knew she was getting ill when whole landscapes turned dim, as if "half the pixels went dark." Her first comment when the stimulator went on was to ask what they'd done to the lights, for everything seemed much brighter. Patient 5, an elite bicycle racer before his depression, told me that a pulling that he had long felt in his legs and gut, "as if death were pulling me downward," had instantly ceased. Patient 1, who in predepression days was an avid gardener, amazed the operating room by announcing that she suddenly felt as if she were walking through a field of wildflowers. Two days after going home, she put a scarf over her shaved, stitched head, found her tools and went out to reclaim her long-neglected gardens.

Not all was light and flowers. On a purely biological level, the improvement made by D.B.S. sometimes amplified the side effects of the high doses of medication the patients had been taking. Doctors don't quite understand this phenomenon, but they see it happen in other instances too; it is as if the patient, deadened, is again made sensate. Deanna broke out in hives and felt nauseated; her hands shook. These symptoms eased when she (as several of the patients have done) reduced her meds—slowly, so as not to introduce new variables. She now takes standard doses of Effexor, an antidepressant, and Seroquel, an antipsychotic drug.

The cure also brought challenges at home. As with other disabilities, any partner turned caretaker gets used to calling the shots, and rearranging power, dependencies and expectations after a sudden recovery can prove hard. One patient, the cyclist, faced this challenge starkly, for he had started a relationship and married while he was depressed. "Frankly," he told me, "I'm not sure we've quite finished working this out." All the patients have benefited from coordinated assistance from psychiatrists, social workers and occupational therapists who try to smooth the transition.

"That help is crucial," says Mayberg, who is now a professor of psychiatry and neurology at Emory University in Atlanta. "We're just fixing the circuit. The patient's life still needs work. It's like fixing a knee. They need that high-quality physical and supportive therapy afterward if they're really going to move around again." 45

This transition is not back to a former self and family but to a new one. Gary Benjamin says he sees similar things in military families. "These soldiers get sent away for six months, they come back and all they want to do is return to their old home. But their old home isn't there, because everybody's changed. It takes some tough rearranging sometimes."

For a change so profound, these seem acceptable adjustments. And the treatment so far seems remarkably free of side effects. No one has suffered significant neural complications, probably because, unlike ECT, which sends 70 to 150 volts through the entire brain, these electrodes deliver only about 4 volts to an area about the size of a pea.

But what will happen when larger groups are treated? The team is continuing to operate on depressed patients, with a goal of 20. And would the successes stay high and the side effects low in a large, placebo-controlled trial? Neither Mayberg nor any of the other collaborators cares to guess. Other treatments have started this well and fizzled. For instance, vagus nerve stimulation, which sends a low current to the brain via a major nerve with connections to various brain areas, appeared to help about half of the patients in a small, initial, uncontrolled trial, but failed its only placebo-controlled trial. (In a controversial move, the

Food and Drug Administration overruled its own reviewers and approved the device as a depression treatment anyway.)

"What if you do a hundred patients," I asked Mayberg one day, "and they do no better than placebo?"

"I suppose that's possible," she said. But she doesn't think that will 50 be the case. The several authorities I talked to agree that the high success rate so far, along with the soundness of the theoretical base and D.B.S.'s track record with Parkinson's, suggests that this isn't just a lucky run.

"This just makes so much sense," says Dr. Antonio Damasio, director of the University of Southern California's Brain and Creativity Institute and a renowned neurologist, "and the weight of the results is so sizable. I would be surprised if they had no results with a larger body of patients."

On the other hand, even if it works, no one sees this becoming the new Prozac. The procedure costs too much (around $40,000) to use on anyone who hasn't tried everything else. The appropriate candidates for D.B.S. probably number in the thousands, not the millions. Perhaps the most sensible worry is that if the thing works, doctors might use it too freely, as they tend to do with successful new treatments; witness the problematic boom in D.B.S. for Parkinson's.

In the end, the procedure's greatest clinical value may lie in inspiring less-intrusive ways of tweaking key nodes—localized delivery of drug or gene therapies, or other means still to come. Such possibilities probably lie at least a decade away.

Regardless of how it pans out in the clinic, Mayberg and Lozano's D.B.S. study is already changing how neuroscientists and psychiatrists think about depression. One possibility, for instance, is that refining the networks that go awry in depression may reveal neurological subtypes of depression that can be diagnosed and treated differently. For example, Mayberg has already found that patients who respond well to Prozac usually show a change in their brain scans only a week after they start medication—even though they don't feel a difference for 3 to 10 weeks (a long and sometimes dangerous wait). She's done preliminary work suggesting she might be able to identify such

Prozac-friendly patients before they even start the drug. If she or others can replicate and elaborate on this diagnostic ability, doctors might be able to characterize a patient's depression and choose a best-odds therapy—Prozac for one patient, talk therapy for a second, both for a third—at the very beginning of treatment, saving weeks or months of trial and error.

The network model—which some scientists also call a "systems" model—also offers an organizing principle for research. Andreas Meyer-Lindenberg, a researcher with the N.I.M.H., points out that research on depression has so far followed clues left by drugs that were found to be effective only by chance. "We'd find a drug that helped depression, figure out how it works, and make hypotheses from that about how the brain works," he says. The effectiveness of selective serotonin reuptake inhibitors (S.S.R.I.'s) like Prozac, for instance, inspired piles of research showing that mood regulation depends heavily on the availability of the neurotransmitters serotonin. (Neurotransmitters are chemicals that help carry messages across the spaces between neurons; S.S.R.I.'s treat depression by making more serotonin available in those spaces.) 55

This focus on neurotransmitters is the "bowl of soup" approach that Mayberg speaks of, and it has formed the bulk of depression research for more than two decades. Defining the networks the neurotransmitters move within, however—and in particular identifying Area 25 as a key gateway within the depression network—will let researchers bring their neurochemical knowledge to bear on specific targets.

"With this D.B.S. work," Meyer-Lindenberg says, "they have characterized in detail a system"—or network—"underlying a major disorder. It's not a simplistic thing where you're saying it's all about this one area and you inject a current and everything's fine. It's a very complicated system. But this D.B.S. work shows us that amid this complicated system there is a place of overlap, a common denominator"—Area 25—"that's a very attractive treatment target." Here, Meyer-Lindenberg says, researchers can try to apply the knowledge they've gained about neurochemistry and genetics. The network theory presents a framework around which to apply these perspectives.

Meyer-Lindenberg's own work shows the power of this approach. Last June he published a study on the serotonin transporter gene, or sert gene, which helps determine serotonin availability. Other research had shown that people with the "short" version of the sert gene run more depression risk. Meyer-Lindenberg found a way to identify how various brain areas were affected by having that short version. Then he took 112 patients, half with the long version and half with the short, scanned their brains and asked the computer to find areas that scanned differently in the two groups. The area showing the most difference was Area 25. Along with redirecting research, the quieting of Area 25 may also change our conception of depression from a condition in which something is lacking—self-esteem, resilience, optimism, energy, serotonin, you name it—to one in which an active agent makes a person sick.

"Most people think of depression as a deficit state," Mayberg says. "You're low, you're negative. But in fact, talk to a depressed person, and you have this bizarre combination of numbness and what William James called 'an active anguish.' 'A sort of psychical neuralgia,' he said, 'wholly unknown to healthy life.' You're numb but you hurt. You can't think, but you are in pain. Now, how does your psyche hurt? What a weird choice of words. But it's not an arbitrary choice. It's there. These people are feeling a particular, indescribable kind of pain."

This anguish, Mayberg suggests, is the manifestation of a neural circuit run amok. For doctors, establishing this should focus research and care. For those of us who've never known depression, recognizing it may help us see depression not as a dead absence but as a live affliction. We might even stop indulging the romantic notion of depression as intrinsic to one's identity. For this notion, too, was tested by Mayberg's experiment. When a steady, 4-volt thrum calmed these patients' anguish, they did not lose their identities. They regained them, feeling again the engagements with the world that most define them: flowers for the gardener, lightness for the cyclist, and, for Deanna, a long-missed connection to others.

When Deanna, Gary and I finally finished talking, they insisted on driving me to my hotel. Halfway through town, Gary pulled off the main road, drove up a long, sinuous driveway and parked in a lot facing a dark, rambling building.

"This is the hospital," Gary said. "You see where Deanna stayed."

In the winter dark, the secure ward, off to the left, was easily discerned. It was a low wing, the only one with a few lights still on inside. Outside, bright flood lamps illuminated an exercise yard ringed by twenty-foot-tall cyclone fencing topped with razor wire.

"And there's the lake," Gary said, motioning behind us. Through trees I could make out its blackness.

We sat several minutes, but no one said much.

"Well," Gary said, putting the minivan in gear. "We'd better get home." 65

STUDY QUESTIONS

1. Why was Deanna Cole-Benjamin an ideal candidate for experimental brain surgery? Why might deep brain stimulation in Area 25 alleviate depression?

2. Explain the PROCESS that Dr. Helen Mayberg and her colleague, Dr. Andres Lozano, followed when designing this surgical treatment for depression. In ANALYZING their process, what does Dobbs, the author, focus on? Why?

3. Consider the METAPHOR that Dobbs introduces: depression is a switch that can be flipped on or off. How does adopting this metaphor change the way doctors and patients think about depression?

4. *For Writing.* RESEARCH established treatments for depression and write an essay in which you discuss how this new procedure COMPARES to its predecessors. How has this operation transformed the way doctors think about and treat depression? Consider both its advantages and its disadvantages.

STEPHEN JAY GOULD } *Sex, Drugs, Disasters, and the*
Extinction of Dinosaurs

STEVEN JAY GOULD (1941–2002) was born in New York City; he earned
his undergraduate degree at Antioch College in Ohio and his PhD at
Columbia University. For thirty-five years Gould was a professor at Harvard
University. However, he is best known for his ability to explain complex
scientific topics in ways that make them accessible to a general audience,
often by writing articles in popular magazines and by advising (and often
appearing in) television programs like PBS's *NOVA*. He collected his
columns from the magazine *Natural History* into several book-length
collections, including *Hen's Teeth and Horse's Toes* (1983), *The Flamingo's
Smile* (1985), and *Bully for Brontosaurus* (1991). The recipient of dozens
of honorary degrees, Gould was a finalist for the Pulitzer Prize for his book
Wonderful Life: The Burgess Shale and the Nature of History (1989).

The following essay, originally published in *Discover Magazine* in 1984,
presents three potential hypotheses for the extinction of the dinosaurs and
analyzes each for its scientific value. As you read, think about how the essay
is organized and how Gould incorporates humor into a serious discussion.
How might these qualities contribute to Gould's reputation as a writer who
excels at presenting scientific topics to a general audience?

SCIENCE, IN ITS MOST FUNDAMENTAL definition, is a fruitful mode
of inquiry, not a list of enticing conclusions. The conclusions are the
consequence, not the essence. My greatest unhappiness with most
popular presentations of science concerns their failure to separate fascinating claims from the methods that scientists use to establish the
facts of nature. Journalists, and the public, thrive on controversial and

stunning statements. But science is, basically, a way of knowing—in P. B. Medawar's apt words, "the art of the soluble." If the growing corps of popular science writers would focus on *how* scientists develop and defend those fascinating claims, they would make their greatest possible contribution to public understanding.

Consider three ideas, proposed in perfect seriousness to account for that greatest of all titillating puzzles—the extinction of dinosaurs. These three notions invoke the primarily fascinating themes of our culture—sex, drugs, and violence—and I want to show why two of them rank as silly speculation, and why the other represents science at its grandest and most useful.

Science works with testable hypotheses. If, after much compilation and scrutiny of data, new information continues to affirm a hypothesis, we may accept it provisionally and gain confidence as further evidence mounts. We can never be completely sure that a hypothesis is right, though we may be able to show with confidence that it is wrong. The best scientific hypotheses are also generous and expansive: they suggest extensions and implications that enlighten related, and even far distant, subjects. Simply consider how the idea of evolution has influenced virtually every intellectual field.

Useless speculation, on the other hand, is restrictive. It generates no testable hypothesis, proposes no way to obtain potentially refuting evidence. Please note that I am not speaking of truth or falsity. The speculation may well be true; still, if it provides, in principle, no material for affirmation or rejection, we can make nothing of it. It must simply stand forever as an intriguing idea. Useless speculation turns in on itself and leads nowhere; good science reaches out. But, enough preaching. Let's move on to dinosaurs, and the three proposed causes of their extinction.

1. Sex: Testes function only in a narrow range of temperature (those 5 of mammals hang externally in a scrotal sac because they need to be cooler than the body). A worldwide rise in temperature at the close of the Cretaceous period caused the testes of dinosaurs to stop functioning and led to their extinction by sterilization of males.

2. Drugs: Angiosperms (flowering plants) first evolved toward the end of the dinosaurs' reign. Many of these plants contain psychoactive

agents, avoided by mammals today because of their bitter taste. Dinosaurs had neither means to taste the bitterness, nor livers effective enough to detoxify the substances. They died of massive overdoses.

3. Disasters: A huge asteroid struck the earth some 65 million years ago, lofting a cloud of dust into the sky and blocking sunlight, thereby suppressing photosynthesis and so drastically lowering world temperatures that dinosaurs and hosts of other creatures became extinct.

Before analyzing these three tantalizing statements, we must establish a basic ground rule often violated in proposals for the dinosaurs' demise. *There is no separate problem of the extinction of dinosaurs.* Too often we divorce specific events from their wider contexts and systems of cause and effect. The fundamental fact of dinosaur extinction is that it coincided with the demise of many other groups across a wide range of habitats, from terrestrial to marine.

The history of life has been punctuated by brief episodes of mass extinction. A recent analysis by University of Chicago paleontologists Jack Sepkoski and Dave Raup, based on the best and most exhaustive tabulation of data ever assembled, shows clearly that five episodes of mass dying stand well above the "background" extinctions of normal times. The Cretaceous debacle, occurring 65 million years ago and separating the Mesozoic and Cenozoic eras of our geological time scale, ranks prominently among the five. Nearly all the marine plankton (single-celled floating creatures) died suddenly, at least in geological terms; among marine invertebrates, close to 15 percent of all families perished, including many previously dominant groups, especially the ammonites (relatives of squids in coiled shells). On land, the dinosaurs disappeared after more than 100 million years of unchallenged domination.

In this context, speculations limited to dinosaurs alone ignore the larger phenomenon. We need a coordinated explanation for a system of events that includes the extinction of dinosaurs as one component. Thus it makes little sense, though it may fuel our desire to view mammals as inevitable inheritors of the earth, to guess that dinosaurs died because small mammals ate their eggs (a perennial untestable speculation). It seems most unlikely that some disaster peculiar to dinosaurs befell these massive beasts—and that the debacle happened to strike

10

just when one of history's five great dyings had enveloped the earth for completely different reasons.

The testicular theory, an old favorite from the 1940s, had its root in an interesting and thoroughly respectable study of temperature tolerances in the American alligator, published in the staid *Bulletin of the American Museum of Natural History* in 1946 by three experts on living and fossil reptiles—E. H. Colbert, my own first teacher in paleontology, R. B. Cowles, and C. M. Bogert.

The first sentence of their summary reveals a purpose beyond alligators: "This report describes an attempt to infer the reactions of extinct reptiles, especially the dinosaurs, to high temperatures as based upon reactions observed in the modern alligator." They studied, by rectal thermometry, the body temperatures of alligators under changing conditions of heating and cooling. (Well, let's face it, you wouldn't want to try sticking a thermometer under a 'gator's tongue.) The predictions under test go way back to an old theory first stated by Galileo in the 1630s—the unequal scaling of surfaces and volumes. As an animal, or any object, grows (provided its shape doesn't change), surface areas must increase more slowly than volumes—since surfaces get larger as length squared, volumes much more rapidly, as length cubed. Therefore, small animals have high ratios of surface to volume, while large animals cover themselves with relatively little surface.

Among cold-blooded animals lacking any physiological mechanism for keeping their temperatures constant, small creatures have a hell of a time keeping warm—because they lose so much heat through their relatively large surfaces. On the other hand, large animals, with their relatively small surfaces, may lose heat so slowly that, once warm, they may maintain effectively constant temperatures against ordinary fluctuations of climate. (In fact, the resolution of the "hot-blooded dinosaur" controversy of a few years back may simply be that, while large dinosaurs possessed no physiological mechanism for constant temperature, and so were not warm-blooded in the technical sense, their size and relatively small surface area kept them warm.)

Colbert, Cowles, and Bogert compared the warming rates of small and large alligators. As predicted, the small fellows heated up (and cooled down) more quickly. When exposed to a warm sun, a tiny

50-gram (1.76-ounce) alligator heated up one degree Celsius every minute and a half, while a large alligator, 260 times bigger at 13,000 grams (28.7 pounds), took seven and a half minutes to gain a degree. Extrapolating up to an adult ten-ton dinosaur, they concluded that a one-degree rise in body temperature would take 86 hours. If large animals absorb heat so slowly (through their relatively small surfaces), they will also be unable to shed any excess heat gained when temperatures rise above a favorable level.

The authors then guessed that large dinosaurs lived at or near their 15 optimum temperatures; Cowles suggested that a rise in global temperatures just before the Cretaceous extinction caused the dinosaurs to heat up beyond their optimal tolerance—and, being so large, they couldn't shed the unwanted heat. (In a most unusual statement for a scientific paper, Colbert and Bogert explicitly disavowed this speculative extension of their empirical work on alligators.) Cowles conceded that this excess heat probably wasn't enough to kill or even to enervate the great beasts, but since testes often function only within a narrow range of temperature, he proposed that this global rise might have sterilized all the males, causing extinction by natural contraception.

The overdose theory has recently been supported by UCLA psychiatrist Ronald K. Siegel. Siegel has observed, he claims, more than 2,000 animals that can give themselves various drugs—from a swig of alcohol to massive doses of the big H.[1] Elephants will swill the equivalent of twenty beers at a time, but do not like alcohol in concentrations greater than 7 per cent. In a silly bit of anthropocentric speculation, Siegel states that "elephants drink, perhaps, to forget . . . the anxiety produced by shrinking rangeland and the competition for food."

Since fertile imaginations can apply almost any hot idea to the extinction of dinosaurs, Siegel found a way. Flowering plants did not evolve until late in the dinosaurs' reign. These plants also produced an array of aromatic, amino-acid-based alkaloids—the major group of psychoactive agents. Most mammals are "smart" enough to avoid these potential poisons. The alkaloids simply don't taste good (they are

[1]Slang term for heroin.

bitter), and in any case we mammals have livers happily supplied with the capacity to detoxify them. But, Siegel speculates, perhaps dinosaurs could neither taste the bitterness nor detoxify the substances once ingested. Speaking of their extinction, he recently told members of the American Psychological Association: "I'm not suggesting that all dinosaurs OD'd on plant drugs, but it certainly was a factor." He also argued that death by overdose may help explain why so many dinosaur fossils are found in contorted positions. (Do not go gentle into that good night.)[2]

Extraterrestrial catastrophes have long pedigrees in the popular literature of extinction, but the subject exploded again after a long lull three years ago when the father-son, physicist-geologist team of Luis and Walter Alvarez proposed that an asteroid, about six miles in diameter, struck the earth 65 million years ago. Most asteroids circle the sun in an orbit between Mars and Jupiter but some, the so-called Apollo objects, take a more eccentric route, actually crossing the earth's orbit in their path around the sun. The chance of a collision at any crossing is minuscule, but the number of Apollo objects and the immensity of geological time virtually guarantee that impacts will occur once in a great while.

The force of such a collision would be immense, greater by far than the megatonnage of all the world's nuclear weapons. In trying to reconstruct a scenario that would explain the simultaneous dying of dinosaurs on land and so many creatures in the sea, the Alvarezes proposed that a gigantic dust cloud, generated by particles blown aloft in the impact, would so darken the earth that photosynthesis would cease and temperatures drop precipitously. (Rage, rage against the dying of the light.)[3] The single-celled photosynthetic oceanic plankton, with life cycles measured in weeks, would perish outright, but land plants might survive through the dormancy of their seeds (land plants were not much affected by the Cretaceous extinction, and any adequate the-

---

[2]Repeated line (and title) of a poem by Welsh poet Dylan Thomas (1914–53).
[3]Another repeating line in Thomas's poem.

ory must account for the curious pattern of differential survival). Dinosaurs would die by starvation and freezing; small, warm-blooded mammals, with more modest requirements for food and better regulation of body temperature, would squeak through.

All three theories, testicular malfunction, psychoactive overdosing, and asteroidal zapping, grab our attention mightily. As pure statements, they rank about equally high on any hit parade of primal fascination. Yet one represents expansive science, the others restrictive and untestable speculation. 20

How could we possibly decide whether the hypothesis of testicular frying is right or wrong? We would have to know things that the fossil record cannot provide. What temperatures were optimal for dinosaurs? Could the beasts avoid the absorption of excess heat by staying in the shade, or in caves? At what temperatures did their testicles cease to function? Were late Cretaceous climates ever warm enough to drive the internal temperatures of dinosaurs close to this ceiling? Testicles simply don't fossilize, and how could we infer their temperature tolerances even if they did? In short, Cowles's hypothesis is simply an intriguing speculation leading nowhere. The most damning statement against it appeared right in the conclusion of Colbert, Cowles, and Bogert's paper, when they admitted: "It is difficult to advance any definite arguments against this hypothesis." My statement may seem paradoxical—isn't a hypothesis really good if you can't devise any arguments against it? Quite the contrary. It is simply untestable and unusable.

Siegel's overdosing has even less going for it. At least Cowles extrapolated his conclusion from some good data on alligators. And he didn't completely violate the primary guideline of explaining dinosaur extinction in the context of a general mass dying—for rise in temperature could be the root cause of a general catastrophe, zapping dinosaurs by testicular malfunction and different groups for other reasons. But Siegel's speculation cannot touch the extinction of ammonites or oceanic plankton (diatoms make their own food with good sweet sunlight; they don't OD on the chemicals of terrestrial plants). It is simply a gratuitous, attention-grabbing guess. It cannot be tested, for how can we know what dinosaurs tasted and what their livers could do?

The hypothesis doesn't even make any sense in its own context. Angiosperms were in full flower tens of millions of years before dinosaurs went the way of all flesh. Why did it take so long? As for the pains of a chemical death recorded in contortions of fossils, I regret to say (or rather I'm pleased to note for the dinosaurs' sake) that Siegel's knowledge of geology must be a bit deficient: muscles contract after death and geological strata rise and fall with motions of the earth's crust after burial—more than enough reason to distort a fossil's pristine appearance.

The asteroid story, on the other hand, has a basis in evidence. It can be tested, extended, refined and, if wrong, disproved. The Alvarezes did not just construct an arresting guess for public consumption. They proposed their hypothesis after laborious geochemical studies with Frank Asaro and Helen Michel had revealed a massive increase of iridium in rocks deposited right at the time of extinction. Iridium, a rare metal of the platinum group, is virtually absent from indigenous rocks of the earth's crust; most of our iridium comes from extraterrestrial objects that hit the earth.

The Alvarez hypothesis bore immediate fruit. Based originally on 25 evidence found in rocks at two sites in Europe, it led geochemists throughout the world to examine other sediments of the same age. They found abnormally high amounts of iridium everywhere—from continental rocks of the western United States to deep sea cores from the South Atlantic.

Cowles proposed his testicular hypothesis in the mid-1940s. Where has it gone since then? Absolutely nowhere, because scientists can do nothing with it. It merely stands as a curious appendage to a solid study of alligators. Siegel's overdose scenario will also win a few press notices and fade into oblivion. The Alvarezes' asteroid falls into a different category altogether, and much of the popular commentary has missed this essential distinction by focusing on the impact and its attendant results, and forgetting what is really important to a scientist—the iridium. If you talk just about asteroids, dust, and darkness, you simply tell stories no better and no more entertaining than fried testicles or terminal trips. It is the iridium—the source of testable evidence—that counts and forges the crucial distinction between speculation and science.

The proof, to twist a phrase, lies in the doing. In thirty-five years, Cowles's hypothesis led to no further advances toward our understanding of dinosaurian extinction. In three years, the Alvarez hypothesis has spawned hundreds of studies, a major conference, and attendant publications. Geologists are fired up. They are looking for iridium at all other extinction boundaries and, by the way, have not (with one exception) found any marked increases—thus proving that a good hypothesis also shows its worth by failing to work in other situations. Every week exposes a new wrinkle in the scientific press. In November a group of Yale scientists supported the hypothesis by finding a "cosmic signature" for isotopes of osmium in Cretaceous boundary rocks (a ratio of isotopes found in extraterrestrial material but not in crustal rocks produced on earth). Then, in December, chemists from the University of Maryland cast some doubt by reporting that volcanic eruptions of Kilauea on Hawaii had belched forth unexpectedly high levels of iridium; perhaps an extraterrestrial source need not be sought.

My point is simply this: whatever the eventual outcome (I suspect it will be positive), the Alvarez hypothesis is exciting, fruitful science because it generates tests, provides us with things to do, and expands outward. We are having fun, battling back and forth, moving toward a resolution, and extending the hypothesis beyond its original scope.

As just one example of the unexpected, distant cross-fertilization that good science engenders, the Alvarez hypothesis made a major contribution to a theme that has riveted public attention in the past few months—so-called nuclear winter. In a speech delivered in April 1982, Luis Alvarez calculated the energy that a six-mile asteroid would release on impact. He compared such an explosion with a full nuclear exchange and implied that all-out atomic war might unleash similar consequences.

This theme of impact leading to massive dust clouds and falling 30 temperatures was an important factor in the decision of Carl Sagan and a group of colleagues to model the climatic consequences of nuclear holocaust. We have, of course, long known that a full nuclear exchange could kill half of humanity outright and cannot be deemed acceptable on any grounds. But some of us still had lurking in our minds the hope that, if we hunkered down in our shelters and lived far from military sites or cities, at least we could survive after the initial fallout dropped.

Apparently, it is not necessarily so. Full nuclear exchange would probably generate the same kind of dust cloud and darkening that may have wiped out the dinosaurs. Temperatures would drop precipitously and agriculture might become impossible. Avoidance of nuclear war is fundamentally an ethical and political problem, but we must know the factual consequences to make firm judgments. Is this not a heartening thought: a recognition of the very phenomenon that made our evolution possible by exterminating the previously dominant dinosaurs and clearing a way for the evolution of large mammals, including us, might actually help to save us from joining those magnificent beasts in contorted poses among the strata of the earth.

STUDY QUESTIONS

1. Gould explores three possible explanations for the extinction of the dinosaurs. Which one of these does he think is best, and why?

2. What CRITERIA does Gould use to EVALUATE each of the three hypotheses? What other criteria might he have used? How would changing the criteria change the outcome of his evaluation? What makes for "good science," according to Gould?

3. Gould's writing is often praised as "accessible"—that is, he presents scientific information in a way that makes it understandable for nonscientists. The ORGANIZATION of this essay and its use of humor are two elements that help make it accessible; how is each suited for a general AUDIENCE? How would the essay have been different if it were written for an audience of scientists?

4. *For Writing.* Select a TOPIC for which there are multiple causes or explanations and do RESEARCH to uncover common ARGUMENTS for each explanation. In an essay, address a few of those causes or explanations and argue for the superiority of one of them. Be sure to DOCUMENT your sources using the CITATION style assigned.

TEMPLE GRANDIN

{

My Mind Is a Web Browser:
How People with Autism Think

TEMPLE GRANDIN (b. 1947) was born in Boston, Massachusetts, and was diagnosed with autism when she was three years old. She did not begin to speak until she was four, but later attended a boarding school for gifted children in New Hampshire, graduating in 1966. She earned a BS in psychology from Franklin Pierce College in 1970, an MS in animal science from Arizona State University in 1975, and a PhD in animal science from the University of Illinois at Urbana-Champaign in 1989. A professor at Colorado State University, Grandin designs livestock-handling facilities and is an advocate for animal welfare. She also advocates for autism rights and has been outspoken about this issue in the media. HBO made a dramatic film about her life, released in 2010, starring Claire Danes, which won five Emmys.

"My Mind Is a Web Browser: How People with Autism Think" analyzes Grandin's thought process: she thinks in images, not words; indeed, she has said that words are her second language. As you read, consider your own thought process. How do you think in words, images, or both?

SINCE WRITING *THINKING IN PICTURES*, which described my visual way of thinking, I have gained further insights into how my thought processes are different when compared to those of people who think in language. At autism meetings, I am often asked, "How can you be effective at public speaking when you think in pictures that are like video tapes in your imagination?" It is almost as though I have two levels of consciousness that operate separately. Only by interviewing people did I learn that many of them think primarily in words, and that their thoughts are linked to emotion. In my brain, words act as a narrator for the visual images in my imagination. I can see the pictures in my memory files.

To use a computer analogy: The language part of my brain is the computer operator, and the rest of my brain is the computer. In most people, the brain's computer operator and the computer are merged into one seamless consciousness; but in me they are separate. I hypothesize that the frontal cortex of my brain is the operator and the rest of my brain is the computer.

When I lecture, the language itself is mostly "downloaded" out of memory from files that are like tape recordings. I use slides or notes to trigger opening the different files. When I am talking about something for the first time, I look at the visual images on the "computer monitor" in my imagination, then the language part of me describes those images. After I have given the lecture several times, the new material in language is switched over into "audio tape-recording files." When I was in high school, other kids called me "tape recorder."

Non-autistic people seem to have a whole upper layer of verbal thinking that is merged with their emotions. By contrast, unless I panic, I use logic to make all decisions; my thinking can be done independently of emotion. In fact, I seem to lack a higher consciousness composed of abstract verbal thoughts that are merged with emotion. Researchers have learned that people with autism have a decreased metabolism in the area in the frontal cortex that connects the brain's emotional centers with higher thinking (the anterior cingulate).[1] The frontal cortex is the brain's senior executive, like the CEO of a corporation. Brain scans indicate that people with autism use problem-solving circuits in social situations. Unlike non-autistic people, the emotion center in their amygdala is not activated, for example, when they judge expressions in another person's eyes.[2]

---

[1]Haznedar MM, Buchsbaum MS, Metzer M, et al. Anterior cingulate gyrus volume and glucose metabolism in autistic disorder. *American Journal of Psychiatry.* 1997: 154:1047–1050.

[2]Baron-Cohen S, Ring HA, Wheelwright S. Social intelligence in the normal and autistic brain: an FMRI study. *European Journal of Neuroscience.* 1999: 11:1891–1898.

MY MIND IS A WEB BROWSER

Now let me explain how the language part of my brain and the "think- 5
ing in pictures" part of my brain seem to interact. My mind works just
like an Internet Web browser. A Web browser finds specific words; by
analogy, my mind looks for picture memories that are associated with
a word. It can also go off on a tangent in the same way as a Web browser,
because visual thinking is non-linear, associative thinking.

To demonstrate how my mind works, at an autism meeting I asked
a member of the audience to name a thing for me to invent. I wanted to
show how the visual part of my brain and the language part worked
separately. Somebody said, "invent a better paper clip." The language part of my brain said, "I can do that," and pictures immediately
started flashing into my imagination of all kinds of paper clips I have
seen. My "Web browser" searched the picture memory files; many
paper clip pictures flashed through my imagination like slides. I could
stop on any one picture and study it. I saw an odd, plastic paper clip
that was on a scientific paper from Europe. At this point, I got off the
subject and saw pictures of the first scientific meeting I had attended
in Spain. The language voice inside me said: "Get back on the subject
of paper clips." The language part of me is a manager who uses simple
non-descriptive language to tell the rest of my brain what to do.

Often, the best ideas for inventing things come just as I am drifting
off to sleep. The pictures are clearer then. It is as though I can access
the most concrete, vivid memory files with the most detailed images.
The language part of my brain is completely shut off at night.

To get ideas for new paper clip designs, I can pull up pictures of
clothes pins and other clip-like things, such as mouse traps and C
clamps used in woodworking. I start thinking that inventing a better
clip for holding a thick pile of papers together might be more marketable than a new paper clip design. Existing spring binder clips tend to
rip envelopes when papers are mailed, because the clips have protruding edges. When I think about this, I see ripped envelopes. The
language part of my mind says, "Design a flat binder clip for thick documents." When I say this, I see a mailed document in an undamaged
envelope. My visual imagination then sees a large plastic clip that I saw

in Japan. Japanese apartment dwellers who do not have clothes driers use large, plastic clips to hold blankets and other laundry on balcony railings. A small version of the Japanese balcony clip may make a better paper clip for holding many pages.

When I was responding to the paper clip inquiry, I knew that I could visually associate all day about paper clips. The language part of my mind then said, "That is enough," and I resumed my lecture. But as I corrected the first draft of this article, I saw a one-piece molded plastic binder clip that would lay flat on a thick bunch of papers.

I do have the ability to control the rate at which pictures come onto the "computer screen" in my imagination. Some people with autism are not able to do this. One person with autism told me that images explode into a web of a pictures that are interrelated. The decision-making process can become "locked up" and overloaded with pictures coming in all at once.

UNMASKING TALENT

I have been fascinated with research indicating that the detailed, realistic pictures that autistic savants—autistic individuals with extraordinary talent in a specific area—make may be created by directly accessing primary memory areas deep in the brain. Researchers in Australia hypothesize that autistic savants may have privileged access to lower levels of information.[3] A study with a non-autistic "human calculator," who could solve multiplication problems twice as quickly as a normal person, indicated that his brain had enhanced low-level processing.[4] EEG recordings of his brain waves showed that brain activity was greatest, as compared with a normal person, when the multiplication problem was first flashed on the screen.

I hypothesize that I am able to access primary visual files in my brain. When designing livestock equipment in my business, I can do

10

[3]Snyder AW, Mitchell JD. Is integer arithmetic fundamental to mental processing? The mind's secret arithmetic. *Proceedings of the Royal Society of London.* 1999:266: 587–592.

[4]Birbaumer N. Rain Man's revelations. *Nature.* 1999:399:211–212.

three-dimensional, full-motion videos of equipment and can test-run the equipment in my imagination. I can walk around it or fly over it. My ability to rotate the image is slow. I move my mind's eye around or over the image.

When I read an article in *Neurology* about frontal temporal lobe dementia, I became extremely excited. It provided a scientific foundation for the idea of hidden visual thinking under a layer of verbal thinking. Research on frontal temporal lobe dementia, an Alzheimer's-like condition that destroys language and social areas in the brain, demonstrated that, as the condition progressed, visual skills in art emerged in people who had no interest in art.[5] The increase in creativity was always visual, never verbal. Brain scans found the highest activity in the visual cortex. As the patient's cognitive abilities deteriorated, the art became more photo realistic. Artwork published with the journal article looks like the art of autistic savants.

I SEE THE DECISION PROCESS

I see the decision-making process in my mind in a way most people do not. When I tried to explain this to a person who thinks in language, he just didn't get it. How my decision-making works is most clearly seen in an emergency.

On a bright, sunny day, I was driving to the airport when an elk ran into the highway just ahead of my car. I had only three or four seconds to react. During those few seconds, I saw images of my choices. The first image was of a car rear-ending me. This is what would have happened if I had made the instinctive panic response and slammed on the brakes. The second image was of an elk smashing through my windshield. This is what would have happened if I had swerved. The last image showed the elk passing by in front of my car. The last choice was the one I could make if I inhibited the panic response and braked just a little to slow the car. I mentally "clicked" on slowing down and avoided an accident. It was like clicking a computer mouse on the desired picture.

15

---

[5]Miller BL, Cummings J, Mishkin F. Emergence of artistic talent in froniotemporal dementia. *Neurology*. 1998;51:978–982.

ANIMAL DECISION MAKING

I speculate that the decision-making process I used to avoid the accident may be similar to the process animals use. From my work with animals, I've come to believe that consciousness originally arose from the orienting response. When a deer sees a person, it will often freeze and look at him. This is the deer's orienting response. During this time, it decides either to run away or to keep grazing. It does not act as a programmed robot, governed by instinct or reflexes; it has the flexibility to make a decision. One of the things that has helped me to understand animals is that, more than most people, I think and feel like one. The more "animal" parts of the normal human brain may be covered by layers of language-based thinking.

THINKING IN AUDIO TAPES

In connection with my lectures, I have talked with autistic people who are not visual thinkers. They seem to think in audio tape clips. Audio tape thinking does not have to involve language; instead of using visual images to form memories, these people store very specific audio clips. I suspect that, for them, hearing is easier than seeing. Dr. John Stein and his colleagues at Oxford University have discovered that some people have difficulty seeing rapidly changing visual scenes. They find reading is difficult because the print appears jumbled.[6] This results from defects in brain circuits that process motion.[7] The eye is fine; the circuits between brain and eyes malfunction.

One person I know who is expert at training animals told me that she hears the animal's behavior instead of seeing it. She has audio tapes in her memory with little sound details. For example, she knows that the animal is relaxed or agitated by listening to its breathing or footsteps. She reads audio signals instead of body posture.

[6]Clayton J. Lost for Words. *New Scientist*. April 24, 1999. pp. 27–30.
[7]Eden GF, Van Meter JW, Ramsey J, et al. Abnormal processing of artistic talent in dyslexia revealed by functional brain imaging. *Nature*. 1996:382:66–69.

PIECING THE DETAILS TOGETHER

People with autism, and animals as well, pay more attention to details. As I described in *Thinking in Pictures*, all my thinking goes from the specific to the general. I look at lots of little details and piece them together to make a concept. The first step in forming an idea is to make categories. For example, the most primary level is sorting objects by color or shape. The next step is sorting things by less obvious features, as when we categorize cats and dogs. When I was five years old, I figured out that a miniature dachshund was not a cat because it had a dog's nose; all dogs had certain features that were visually recognizable.

My mind seeks these categories amidst an array of little details. In problem solving, my thinking process is like that of an epidemiologist tracking down a disease. The epidemiologist collects lots of little pieces of information and finally figures out the common factor that caused certain people to fall ill. For example, they may all have eaten strawberries from a certain place.

Also, I understand concepts visually. For example, all objects classified as keys will open locks. I realize that the word "key" can also be used metaphorically, when we say, "the key to success is positive thinking." When I think about that phrase, I see Norman Vincent Peale's book, *The Power of Positive Thinking*, and I see myself back at my aunt's ranch reading it. I then see a stage where a person is getting an award and I see a large cardboard key. Even in this situation, the key still unlocks the door to success. The ability to form categories is the beginning of the ability to form concepts. Keys in their physical form open physical locks but abstract keys can open many things, such as a scientific discovery or career success.

In teaching people to understand animal behavior, I have to help them to learn how to observe details that seem insignificant. Animals notice details in their environment that most people do not see, such as a branch that moves slightly or a shadow. In my work with livestock facilities, I try to get the language-based thinkers of the world to be more observant of little details that spook cattle. A cow may balk at entering a vaccinating chute because it sees a piece of jiggling chain that most people ignore, but which is significant in the cow's environment.

That little chain attracts the cow's attention because it moves quickly. Rapid movement activates the amygdala, the brain's emotion center.[8] In a prey species such as cattle, rapid movement elevates fear because, in the wild, things that move rapidly are often dangerous. Something moving quickly in the bushes may be a lion. On the other hand, a predatory animal, such as a dog, is attracted to rapid movement. This may explain why some dogs attack joggers. Rapid movement triggers chasing and attacking in a predatory animal, but it triggers flight in a prey species such as deer or cattle.

Objects that move rapidly also attract the attention of people with autism. When I was younger, I liked to play with automatic doors at supermarkets. I enjoyed watching the rapid opening movement. Elevator doors were not interesting; they did not move fast enough to be pleasurable to watch. Tests of my visual tracking indicate that I have a slight abnormality in my eye's ability to track a moving object. Children and adults with autism who never learn to speak have graver defects in their nervous system. The automatic doors that I liked to watch cause many nonverbal autistics to put their hands over their eyes. The rapid movement of the doors hurts their eyes. Possibly, a small defect in eye tracking makes rapidly moving things attractive to me, while a more serious neurological defect makes them unpleasant to other autistics. As a child, my favorite things all made rapid movements. I liked flapping flags, kites, and model airplanes that flew.

DISTURBING SOUNDS

I have always felt that my senses were more like those of an animal.   25
Does my brain have deeper access to the ancient anti-predator circuits that humans share with animals? At night, I cannot get to sleep if I hear high-pitched, intermittent noise such as a backup alarm on a truck or children yelling in the next hotel room; they make my heart

---

[8]LeDoux J. *The Emotional Brain.* Simon and Schuster; 1996.

race. Thunder or airport noise does not bother me, but the little high-pitched noises cannot be shut out. Recent research with pigs has confirmed that intermittent sounds are more disturbing to them than steady sounds.[9]

Why are high-pitched sounds disturbing to animals (and to me), while airport noises and thunder are not? I speculate that in nature the rumble of thunder is not dangerous but a high-pitched noise would be an animal's distress call. Beeping backup alarms and car alarms are electronic distress calls, which activate my nervous system even though I know they are harmless. It is almost as though these animal circuits in my brain have been laid bare.

PROPORTIONAL THINKING

A recent report in *Science* indicated that activities involving numbers are processed in at least two different parts of the brain.[1] Precise calculations are dependent on language and are processed in the frontal areas; proportional figuring is processed in visual areas. Proportional thinking is figuring out if one object is less or more than another. For example, three marbles are more than one marble. Animals can do proportional thinking. They can easily determine that 10 pieces of food are more than two. It is likely that proportional thinking is the kind of number processing that humans share with animals.

In school, math was a tough subject for me. Finding the precisely correct answer is difficult because I mix up numbers. On the other hand, I am very good at proportional thinking, coming up with an accurate approximate answer. In my scientific work, I often convert numerical differences between my control and experimental groups to percentage differences. Percentage differences can be visualized on a pie chart. When I present data, I like to use charts and graphs so I can see the proportional differences between different sets of data.

---

[9]Talling JC, Waran NK, Wathes CM. Sound avoidance by domestic pigs depends on the characteristics of the signal. *Applied Animal Behavior Science*. 1998: 58: 255–266.

[1]Dehaene S, Spelke E, Pinel P, Stanescu R, Tsivkin S. Sources of mathematical thinking: Behavioral and brain imaging evidence. *Science*. 1999: 284:970–973.

When I did cost estimating for cattle industry construction projects, I never tried to calculate projects to the penny. Instead, I estimated the cost of a new job by figuring out its proportional cost in relation to other finished projects. This was mainly a visual process. I would look at the drawing and build the entire project in my imagination. I then would put it up on the video screen in my imagination and compare it in size to other completed projects that had complete cost figures. In my mind, I could compare four or five completed projects with the drawing I was estimating. The project being estimated might be equal to two-thirds of a cattle-handling facility that I designed at Red River Feedlot and about 25 percent bigger than a corral I designed for Lone Mountain Ranch.

For money to have meaning to me, it must be related to something I 30 can buy with it, otherwise it is too abstract. For example, $3 is equal to lunch at McDonald's, $20 is a tank of gas, and $1000 can buy a computer. Big tables full of figures make little sense to me. Some more severely autistic people do not understand money at all. For me to understand a billion dollars, I have to have a picture in my mind of something that cost a billion dollars. One billion is one quarter of the cost of the new Denver Airport. When President Clinton announced part way through the war in Kosovo that it had cost $2 billion, I figured that half a Denver Airport worth of money had been spent. Different amounts of money have different visual values. It is interesting that proportional thinking for numbers is in the visual parts of the brain.

In proportional thinking, as in creating something new, making a decision, and forming concepts, my thinking relies on more direct access to the primary visual memory areas in my brain. There is a whole higher level of abstract thinking seamlessly linked to emotion that I do not have.

New York City, 2000

STUDY QUESTIONS

1. What is the difference between a verbal and a visual way of thinking? What role does emotion play in each? Why?

2. How effective is the METAPHOR of the web browser that Grandin uses for describing how her mind works?

3. What is the function of the subheadings in this essay? Are the subheadings effective? What other ways might Grandin have supplied TRANSITIONS and other signposts to the reader?

4. How does Grandin think in pictures? ANALYZE THE PROCESS of her "visual way of thinking."

5. *For Writing.* Consider your thought process by testing two of Grandin's examples. How would you go about designing a paper clip? How would you deal with an elk that suddenly entered your path? In an essay, explore the way that you would come to a solution. What does your process say about you?

RANDY PAUSCH $\Big\{$ *I Never Made It*
to the NFL

RANDY PAUSCH (1960–2008), professor of computer science and pioneer in the field of virtual reality, was born and raised in Maryland. He earned two degrees in computer science, a bachelor's at Brown University in 1982 and a PhD at Carnegie Mellon University in 1988. As a professor at Carnegie Mellon University, he developed the computer language Alice, which helps teach young people computer programming. In addition to publishing more than seventy scholarly articles and books, Pausch wrote *The Last Lecture* (2008), an expanded version of his inspirational speech delivered at Carnegie Mellon on September 18, 2007, as part of the "Last Lecture" series—a series in which top academics give a talk that captures the wisdom they would like to impart. Pausch's was especially poignant: he had been diagnosed with terminal pancreatic cancer a month earlier and had less than a year to live.

In this selection from the book, Pausch explains what he learned from playing youth football. Children who play sports, according to Pausch, learn far more than the skills and rules of the game. As you read, consider the role of Coach Graham in helping Pausch learn these important lessons.

I LOVE FOOTBALL. *TACKLE* FOOTBALL. I started playing when I was nine years old, and football got me through. It helped make me who I am today. And even though I did not reach the National Football League, I sometimes think I got more from pursuing that dream, and *not* accomplishing it, than I did from many of the ones I did accomplish.

My romance with football started when my dad dragged me, kicking and screaming, to join a league. I had no desire to be there. I was naturally wimpy, and the smallest kid by far. Fear turned to awe when I met my coach, Jim Graham, a hulking, six-foot-four wall-of-a-guy. He had been a linebacker at Penn State, and was seriously old-school. I mean, *really* old-school; like he thought the forward pass was a trick play.[1]

On the first day of practice, we were all scared to death. Plus he hadn't brought along any footballs. One kid finally spoke up for all of us. "Excuse me, Coach. There are no footballs."

And Coach Graham responded, "We don't need any footballs."

There was a silence, while we thought about that . . .   5

"How many men are on the football field at a time?" he asked us.

Eleven on a team, we answered. So that makes twenty-two.

"And how many people are touching the football at any given time?" One of them.

"Right!" he said. "So we're going to work on what those *other*   10 twenty-one guys are doing."

Fundamentals. That was a great gift Coach Graham gave us. Fundamentals, fundamentals, fundamentals. As a college professor, I've seen this as one lesson so many kids ignore, always to their detriment: You've *got* to get the fundamentals down, because otherwise the fancy stuff is not going to work.

●　○　●

Coach Graham used to ride me hard. I remember one practice in particular. "You're doing it all wrong, Pausch. Go back! Do it again!" I tried to do what he wanted. It wasn't enough. "You owe me, Pausch! You're doing push-ups after practice."

When I was finally dismissed, one of the assistant coaches came over to reassure me. "Coach Graham rode you pretty hard, didn't he?" he said.

I could barely muster a "yeah."

"That's a good thing," the assistant told me. "When you're screw-   15

---

[1] Football's forward pass become legal in 1906.

ing up and nobody says anything to you anymore, that means they've given up on you."

That lesson has stuck with me my whole life. When you see yourself doing something badly and nobody's bothering to tell you anymore, that's a bad place to be. You may not want to hear it, but your critics are often the ones telling you they still love you and care about you, and want to make you better.

There's a lot of talk these days about giving children self-esteem. It's not something you can *give;* it's something they have to build. Coach Graham worked in a no-coddling zone. Self-esteem? He knew there was really only one way to teach kids how to develop it: You give them something they can't do, they work hard until they find they can do it, and you just keep repeating the process.

When Coach Graham first got hold of me, I was this wimpy kid with no skills, no physical strength, and no conditioning. But he made me realize that if I work hard enough, there will be things I can do tomorrow that I can't do today. Even now, having just turned forty-seven, I can give you a three-point stance that any NFL lineman would be proud of.

I realize that, these days, a guy like Coach Graham might get thrown out of a youth sports league. He'd he too tough. Parents would complain.

I remember one game when our team was playing terribly. At half- 20 time, in our rush for water, we almost knocked over the water bucket. Coach Graham was livid: "Jeez! That's the most I've seen you boys move since this game started!" We were eleven years old, just standing there, afraid he'd pick us up one by one and break us with his bare hands. "Water?" he barked. "You boys want water?" He lifted the bucket and dumped all the water on the ground.

We watched him walk away and heard him mutter to an assistant coach: "You can give water to the first-string defense. They played OK."

Now let me be clear. Coach Graham would never endanger any kid. One reason he worked so hard on conditioning was he knew it reduces injuries. However, it was a chilly day, we'd all had access to water during the first half, and the dash to the water bucket was more about us being a bunch of brats than really needing hydration.

Even so, if that kind of incident happened today, parents on the sidelines would be pulling out their cell phones to call the league commissioner, or maybe their lawyer.

It saddens me that many kids today are so coddled. I think back to how I felt during that halftime rant. Yes, I was thirsty. But more than that, I felt humiliated. We had all let down Coach Graham, and he let us know it in a way we'd never forget. He was right. We had shown more energy at the water bucket than we had in the damn game. And getting chewed out by him meant something to us. During the second half, we went back on the field, and gave it our all.

I haven't seen Coach Graham since I was a teen, but he just keeps showing up in my head, forcing me to work harder whenever I feel like quitting, forcing me to be better. He gave me a feedback loop for life. 25

•   ○   •

When we send our kids to play organized sports—football, soccer, swimming, whatever—for most of us, it's not because we're desperate for them to learn the intricacies of the sport.

What we really want them to learn is far more important: teamwork, perseverance, sportsmanship, the value of hard work, an ability to deal with adversity. This kind of indirect learning is what some of us like to call a "head fake."

There are two kinds of head fakes. The first is literal. On a football field, a player will move his head one way so you'll think he's going in that direction. Then he goes the opposite way. It's like a magician using misdirection. Coach Graham used to tell us to watch a player's waist. "Where his belly button goes, his body goes," he'd say.

The second kind of head fake is the *really* important one—the one that teaches people things they don't realize they're learning until well into the process. If you're a head-fake specialist, your hidden objective is to get them to learn something you want them to learn.

This kind of head-fake learning is absolutely vital. And Coach Graham was the master. 30

STUDY QUESTIONS

1. What does the term "head fake" refer to in its original, literal sense? What does Pausch mean when he uses the term figuratively? How is this essay a "head fake"?

2. Notice how Pausch breaks this chapter into three sections. What is the main point of each section?

3. List some of Coach Graham's physical characteristics. Describe his personality. In what ways does Pausch create a DOMINANT IMPRESSION of his coach?

4. *For Writing.* What lessons have you learned that might be of value to others? Write an essay in which you use one or more ANECDOTES to illustrate how you learned a particular lesson. Be sure to include both specific details and the broader implications of your experience.

SCOTT RUSSELL SANDERS { *The Inheritance of Tools*

SCOTT RUSSELL SANDERS (b. 1945), born in Memphis, Tennessee, grew
up mainly in Ohio. He graduated from Brown University in 1967 and
received his PhD from Cambridge University in 1971. He has taught at
Indiana University since 1971. The author of eight novels and eleven works
of nonfiction, he has written widely on environmental issues, social justice,
and community.

In "The Inheritance of Tools," Sanders meditates on the proper use of
tools and the virtue and morality of building with one's hands, knowledge
that has been passed down through the generations of Sanders men. He
brings together past and present as he describes passing on his own knowledge to his children. By the end of his essay, Sanders has described not only
his tools and their history, but also what those tools represent—purpose,
timelessness, and love.

AT JUST ABOUT THE HOUR when my father died, soon after dawn one
February morning when ice coated the windows like cataracts, I
banged my thumb with a hammer. Naturally I swore at the hammer, the
reckless thing, and in the moment of swearing I thought of what my
father would say: "If you'd try hitting the nail it would go in a whole
lot faster. Don't you know your thumb's not as hard as that hammer?"
We both were doing carpentry that day, but far apart. He was building
cupboards at my brother's place in Oklahoma; I was at home in
Indiana putting up a wall in the basement to make a bedroom for my
daughter. By the time my mother called with news of his death—the

long-distance wires whittling her voice until it seemed too thin to bear the weight of what she had to say—my thumb was swollen. A week or so later a white scar in the shape of a crescent moon began to show above the cuticle, and month by month it rose across the pink sky of my thumbnail. It took the better part of a year for the scar to disappear, and every time I noticed it I thought of my father.

The hammer had belonged to him, and to his father before him. The three of us have used it to build houses and barns and chicken coops, to upholster chairs and crack walnuts, to make doll furniture and bookshelves and jewelry boxes. The head is scratched and pock-marked, like an old plowshare that has been working rocky fields, and it gives off the sort of dull sheen you see on fast creek water in the shade. It is a finishing hammer, about the weight of a bread loaf, too light really for framing walls, too heavy for cabinetwork, with a curved claw for pulling nails, a rounded head for pounding, a fluted neck for looks, and a hickory handle for strength.

The present handle is my third one, bought from a lumberyard in Tennessee down the road from where my brother and I were helping my father build his retirement house. I broke the previous one by try-ing to pull sixteen-penny nails out of floor joists—a foolish thing to do with a finishing hammer, as my father pointed out. "You ever hear of a crowbar?" he said. No telling how many handles he and my grandfa-ther had gone through before me. My grandfather used to cut down hickory trees on his farm, saw them into slabs, cure the planks in his hayloft, and carve handles with a drawknife. The grain in hickory is crooked and knotty, and therefore tough, hard to split, like the grain in the two men who owned this hammer before me.

After proposing marriage to a neighbor girl, my grandfather used this hammer to build a house for his bride on a stretch of river bottom in northern Mississippi. The lumber for the place, like the hickory for the handle, was cut on his own land. By the day of the wedding he had not quite finished the house, and so right after the ceremony he took his wife home and put her to work. My grandmother had worn her Sunday dress for the wedding, with a fringe of lace tacked on around the hem in honor of the occasion. She removed this lace and folded it away before going out to help my grandfather nail siding on the house.

"There she was in her good dress," he told me some fifty-odd years after that wedding day, "holding up them long pieces of clapboard while I hammered, and together we got the place covered up before dark." As the family grew to four, six, eight, and eventually thirteen, my grandfather used this hammer to enlarge his house room by room, like a chambered nautilus expanding his shell.

By and by the hammer was passed along to my father. One day he was up on the roof of our pony barn nailing shingles with it, when I stepped out the kitchen door to call him for supper. Before I could yell, something about the sight of him straddling the spine of that roof and swinging the hammer caught my eye and made me hold my tongue. I was five or six years old, and the world's commonplaces were still news to me. He would pull a nail from the pouch at his wrist, bring the hammer down, and a moment later the *thunk* of the blow would reach my ears. And that is what had stopped me in my tracks and stilled my tongue, that momentary gap between seeing and hearing the blow. Instead of yelling from the kitchen door, I ran to the barn and climbed two rungs up the ladder—as far as I was allowed to go—and spoke quietly to my father. On our walk to the house he explained that sound takes time to make its way through air. Suddenly the world seemed larger, the air more dense, if sound could be held back like any ordinary traveler.

By the time I started using this hammer, at about the age when I discovered the speed of sound, it already contained houses and mysteries for me. The smooth handle was one my grandfather had made. In those days I needed both hands to swing it. My father would start a nail in a scrap of wood, and I would pound away until I bent it over.

"Looks like you got ahold of some of those rubber nails," he would tell me. "Here, let me see if I can find you some stiff ones." And he would rummage in a drawer until he came up with a fistful of more cooperative nails. "Look at the head," he would tell me. "Don't look at your hands, don't look at the hammer. Just look at the head of that nail and pretty soon you'll learn to hit it square."

Pretty soon I did learn. While he worked in the garage cutting dovetail joints for a drawer or skinning a deer or tuning an engine, I would hammer nails. I made innocent blocks of wood look like porcupines.

He did not talk much in the midst of his tools, but he kept up a nearly ceaseless humming, slipping in and out of a dozen tunes in an afternoon, often running back over the same stretch of melody again and again, as if searching for a way out. When the humming did cease, I knew he was faced with a task requiring great delicacy or concentration, and I took care not to distract him.

He kept scraps of wood in a cardboard box—the ends of two-by-fours, slabs of shelving and plywood, odd pieces of molding—and everything in it was fair game. I nailed scraps together to fashion what I called boats or houses, but the results usually bore only faint resemblance to the visions I carried in my head. I would hold up these constructions to show my father, and he would turn them over in his hands admiringly, speculating about what they might be. My cobbled-together guitars might have been alien spaceships, my barns might have been models of Aztec temples, each wooden contraption might have been anything but what I had set out to make.

Now and again I would feel the need to have a chunk of wood shaped or shortened before I riddled it with nails, and I would clamp it in a vice and scrape at it with a handsaw. My father would let me lacerate the board until my arm gave out, and then he would wrap his hand around mine and help me finish the cut, showing me how to use my thumb to guide the blade, how to pull back on the saw to keep it from binding, how to let my shoulder do the work.

"Don't force it," he would say, "just drag it easy and give the teeth a chance to bite."

As the saw teeth bit down the wood released its smell, each kind with its own fragrance, oak or walnut or cherry or pine—usually pine, because it was the softest and the easiest for a child to work. No matter how weathered and gray the board, no matter how warped and cracked, inside there was this smell waiting, as of something freshly baked. I gathered every smidgen of sawdust and stored it away in coffee cans, which I kept in a drawer of the workbench. When I did not feel like hammering nails I would dump my sawdust on the concrete floor of the garage and landscape it into highways and farms and towns, running miniature cars and trucks along miniature roads. Looming as huge as a colossus, my father worked over and around me, now and again bending down to inspect my work, careful not to trample my creations. It was a landscape that smelled dizzyingly of wood. Even after a bath my skin would carry the smell, and so would my father's hair, when he lifted me for a bedtime hug.

I tell these things not only from memory but also from recent observation, because my own son now turns blocks of wood into nailed porcupines, dumps cans full of sawdust at my feet and sculpts highways on the floor. He learns how to swing a hammer from the elbow instead of the wrist, how to lay his thumb beside the blade to guide a saw, how to tap a chisel with a wooden mallet, how to mark a hole with an awl before starting a drill bit. My daughter did the same before him, and even now, on the brink of teenage aloofness, she will occasionally drag out my box of wood scraps and carpenter something. So I have seen my apprenticeship to wood and tools reenacted in each of my children, as my father saw his own apprenticeship renewed in me.

The saw I use belonged to him, as did my level and both of my squares, and all four tools had belonged to his father. The blade of the saw is the bluish color of gun barrels, and the maple handle, dark from the sweat of hands, is inscribed with curving leaf designs. The level is a shaft of walnut two feet long, edged with brass and pierced by three round windows in which air bubbles float in oil-filled tubes of glass. The middle window serves for testing whether a surface is horizontal, the others for testing whether it is plumb or vertical. My grandfather used to carry this level on the gun rack behind the seat in his pickup, and when I rode with him I would turn around to watch the bubbles dance. The larger of the two squares is called a framing square, a flat steel elbow so beat up and tarnished you can barely make out the rows of numbers that show how to figure the cuts on rafters. The smaller one is called a try square, for marking right angles, with a blued steel blade for the shank and a brass-faced block of cherry for the head.

I was taught early on that a saw is not to be used apart from a square: "If you're going to cut a piece of wood," my father insisted, "you owe it to the tree to cut it straight."

15

Long before studying geometry, I learned there is a mystical virtue in right angles. There is an unspoken morality in seeking the level and the plumb. A house will stand, a table will bear weight, the sides of a box will hold together only if the joints are square and the members upright. When the bubble is lined up between two marks etched in the glass tube of a level, you have aligned yourself with the forces that hold the universe together. When you miter the corners of a picture frame, each angle must be exactly forty-five degrees, as they are in the perfect triangles of Pythagoras, not a degree more or less. Otherwise the frame will hang crookedly, as if ashamed of itself and of its maker. No matter if the joints you are cutting do not show. Even if you are butting two pieces of wood together inside a cabinet, where no one except a wrecking crew will ever see them, you must take pains to insure that the ends are square and the studs are plumb.

I took pains over the wall I was building on the day my father died. Not long after that wall was finished—paneled with tongue-and-groove boards of yellow pine, the nail holes filled with putty and the wood all stained and sealed—I came close to wrecking it one afternoon when my daughter ran howling up the stairs to announce that her gerbils had escaped from their cage and were hiding in my brand-new wall. She could hear them scratching and squeaking behind her bed. Impossible! I said. How on earth could they get inside my drum-tight wall? Through the heating vent, she answered. I went downstairs, pressed my ear to the honey-colored wood, and heard the scritch scritch of tiny feet.

"What can we do?" my daughter wailed. "They'll starve to death, they'll die of thirst, they'll suffocate." "Hold on," I soothed. "I'll think of something."

While I thought and she fretted, the radio on her bedside table delivered us the headlines. Several thousand people had died in a city in India from a poisonous cloud that had leaked overnight from a chemical plant. A nuclear-powered submarine had been launched. Rioting continued in South Africa. An airplane had been hijacked in the Mediterranean. Authorities calculated that several thousand homeless people slept on the streets within sight of the Washington Monument. I felt my usual helplessness in face of all these calamities. But here was my daughter weeping because her gerbils were holed up in a wall. This calamity I could handle.

"Don't worry," I told her. "We'll set food and water by the heating   20 vent and lure them out. And if that doesn't do the trick, I'll tear the wall apart until we find them."

She stopped crying and gazed at me. "You'd really tear it apart? Just for my gerbils? The *wall*?" Astonishment slowed her down only for a second, however, before she ran to the workbench and began tugging at drawers, saying, "Let's see, what'll we need? Crowbar. Hammer. Chisels. I hope we don't have to use them—but just in case."

We didn't need the wrecking tools. I never had to assault my handsome wall, because the gerbils eventually came out to nibble at a dish of popcorn. But for several hours I studied the tongue-and-groove skin I had nailed up on the day of my father's death, considering where to begin prying. There were no gaps in that wall, no crooked joints.

I had botched a great many pieces of wood before I mastered the right angle with a saw, botched even more before I learned to miter a joint. The knowledge of these things resides in my hands and eyes and the webwork of muscles, not in the tools. There are machines for sale—powered miter boxes and radial arm saws, for instance—that will enable any casual soul to cut proper angles in boards. The skill is invested in the gadget instead of the person who uses it, and this is what distinguishes a machine from a tool. If I had to earn my keep by making furniture or building houses, I suppose I would buy powered saws and pneumatic nailers; the need for speed would drive me to it. But since I carpenter only for my own pleasure or to help neighbors or to remake the house around the ears of my family, I stick with hand tools. Most of the ones I own were given to me by my father, who also taught me how to wield them. The tools in my workbench are a double inheritance, for each hammer and level and saw is wrapped in a cloud of knowing.

All of these tools are a pleasure to look at and to hold. Merchants would never paste NEW NEW NEW! signs on them in stores. Their designs are old because they work, because they serve their purpose well. Like folksongs and aphorisms and the grainy bits of language, these tools have been pared down to essentials. I look at my claw hammer, the distillation of a hundred generations of carpenters, and consider that it holds up well beside those other classics—Greek vases, Gregorian chants, *Don Quixote,* barbed fishhooks, candles, spoons.

Knowledge of hammering stretches back to the earliest humans who squatted beside fires chipping flints. Anthropologists have a lovely name for those unworked rocks that served as the earliest hammers. "Dawn stones" they are called. Their only qualification for the work, aside from hardness, is that they fit the hand. Our ancestors used them for grinding corn, tapping awls, smashing bones. From dawn stones to this claw hammer is a great leap in time, but no great distance in design or imagination.

On that iced-over February morning when I smashed my thumb with the hammer, I was down in the basement framing the wall that my daughter's gerbils would later hide in. I was thinking of my father, as I always did whenever I built anything, thinking how he would have gone about the work, hearing in memory what he would have said about the wisdom of hitting the nail instead of my thumb. I had the studs and plates nailed together all square and trim, and was lifting the wall into place when the phone rang upstairs. My wife answered, and in a moment she came to the basement door and called down softly to me. The stillness in her voice made me drop the framed wall and hurry upstairs. She told me my father was dead. Then I heard the details over the phone from my mother. Building a set of cupboards for my brother in Oklahoma, he had knocked off work early the previous afternoon because of cramps in his stomach. Early this morning, on his way into the kitchen of my brother's trailer, maybe going for a glass of water, so early that no one else was awake, he slumped down on the linoleum and his heart quit.

For several hours I paced around inside my house, upstairs and down, in and out of every room, looking for the right door to open and knowing there was no such door. My wife and children followed me and wrapped me in arms and backed away again, circling and staring as if I were on fire. Where was the door, the door, the door? I kept wondering. My smashed thumb turned purple and throbbed, making me furious. I wanted to cut it off and rush outside and scrape away the snow and hack a hole in the frozen earth and bury the shameful thing.

I went down into the basement, opened a drawer in my workbench, and stared at the ranks of chisels and knives. Oiled and sharp, as my father would have kept them, they gleamed at me like teeth. I took up

25

a clasp knife, pried out the longest blade, and tested the edge on the hair of my forearm. A tuft came away cleanly, and I saw my father testing the sharpness of tools on his own skin, the blades of axes and knives and gouges and hoes, saw the red hair shaved off in patches from his arms and the backs of his hands. "That will cut bear," he would say. He never cut a bear with his blades, now my blades, but he cut deer, dirt, wood. I closed the knife and put it away. Then I took up the hammer and went back to work on my daughter's wall, snugging the bottom place against a chalkline on the floor, shimming the top plate against the joists overhead, plumbing the studs with my level, making sure before I drove the first nail that every line was square and true.

STUDY QUESTIONS

1. What advice did Sanders's father give him about hammering nails? What did Sanders make from the various chunks of wood his father gave him? What was Sanders's greatest achievement as a builder?

2. ANALYZE Sander's DESCRIPTION of his hammer (paragraphs 2–6). How does the hammer look, sound, and feel? How does this description contribute to Sander's overall NARRATIVE?

3. Sanders begins and ends his MEMOIR of his father by recounting what he is doing just before and just after he learns of his father's death. Why do you think he chose to frame the NARRATIVE in this way? What is the significance to this essay of using this rhetorical strategy? How does the word "frame" fit both the strategy and the subject?

4. *For Writing.* Choose a person who is special in your life, and make a list of some experiences that you have shared. Select the experience that stirs the most emotions, that best displays your relationship with this person, and that you can write about. Using DESCRIPTION, PATHOS, and any other rhetorical strategies that will give your AUDIENCE a full picture of your subject, write a memoir of this special person.

E. O. WILSON { *Apocalypse Now*

EDWARD O. WILSON (b. 1929), biologist, naturalist, and writer, was born
in Birmingham, Alabama. He earned three degrees in biology: a BS in 1949
and an MS in 1950, both from the University of Alabama, and a PhD in
1955 from Harvard University. He joined Harvard's faculty in 1956, where
he remained his entire career. Regarded as one of the most important scientists of the twentieth century, Wilson has discovered hundreds of new insect
species and has written extensively on biodiversity and sociobiology, the
study of how biology influences the behavior of organisms. Wilson won the
National Medal for Science in 1977 and has received two Pulitzer Prizes, for
On Human Nature (1979) and *The Ants* (1991).

"Apocalypse Now," Wilson's letter to a fictional Southern Baptist minister, originally appeared in *The New Republic*. Acknowledging their different
worldviews but highlighting the things they have in common, Wilson asks
the minister to join him in working to stop environmental destruction. Without an alliance between science and religion to "save the Creation," Wilson
argues, our survival as a species is in jeopardy. As you read, consider how—
and how effectively—Wilson establishes common ground with his fictional
minister and, more broadly, the evangelical Christian community he hopes
to reach.

DEAR PASTOR,

   We have not met, yet I feel I know you well enough to call you a
friend. First of all, we grew up in the same faith. As a boy, I, too,
answered the altar call; I went under the water. Although I no longer belong to that faith, I am confident that, if we met and spoke privately of

our deepest beliefs, it would be in a spirit of mutual respect and good-will. I know we share many precepts of moral behavior. Perhaps it also matters that we are both Americans and, insofar as it might still affect civility and good manners, we are both Southerners.

I write to you now for your counsel and help. Of course, in doing so, I see no way to avoid the fundamental differences in our worldviews. You are a strict interpreter of Christian Holy Scripture; I am a secular humanist. You believe that each person's soul is immortal, making this planet a waystation to a second, eternal life; I think heaven and hell are what we create for ourselves, on this planet. For you, the belief in God made flesh to save mankind; for me, the belief in Promethean fire seized to set men free.[1] You have found your final truth; I am still searching. You may be wrong; I may be wrong. We both may be partly right.

Do these differences in worldview separate us in all things? They do not. You and I and every other human being strive for the same imperatives of security, freedom of choice, personal dignity, and a cause to believe in that is larger than ourselves. Let us see, then, if we can meet on the near side of metaphysics in order to deal with the real world we share. You have the power to help solve a great problem about which I care deeply. I hope you have the same concern. I suggest that we set aside our differences in order to save the Creation. The defense of living nature is a universal value. It doesn't rise from, nor does it promote, any religious or ideological dogma. Rather, it serves without discrimination the interests of all humanity. Pastor, we need your help. The Creation—living nature—is in deep trouble.

Scientists estimate that, if habitat-conversion and other destructive human activities continue at their present rates, half the species of plants and animals on earth could be either gone or at least fated for early extinction by the end of the century. The ongoing extinction rate is calculated in the most conservative estimates to be about 100 times above that prevailing before humans appeared on earth, and it is expected to rise to at least 1,000 times greater (or more) in the next few

5

---

[1]Wilson refers to Jesus Christ, on the one hand, and Prometheus, the Titan who stole fire and gave it to mankind, on the other.

decades. If this rise continues unabated, the cost to humanity—in wealth, environmental security, and quality of life—will be catastrophic.

Surely we can agree that each species, however inconspicuous and humble it may seem to us at this moment, is a masterpiece of biology and well worth saving. Each species possesses a unique combination of genetic traits that fits it more or less precisely to a particular part of the environment. Prudence alone dictates that we act quickly to prevent the extinction of species and, with it, the pauperization of earth's ecosystems.

With all the troubles that humanity faces, why should we care about the condition of living nature? Homo sapiens is a species confined to an extremely small niche. True, our minds soar out to the edges of the universe and contract inward to subatomic particles—the two extremes encompassing 30 powers of ten in space. In this respect, our intellects are godlike. But, let's face it, our bodies stay trapped inside a proportionately microscopic envelope of physical constraints. Earth provides a self-regulating bubble that sustains us indefinitely without any thought or contrivance of our own. This protective shield is the biosphere, the totality of life, creator of all air, cleanser of all water, manager of all soil—but is itself a fragile membrane that barely clings to the face of the planet. We depend upon its razor-thin health for every moment of our lives. We belong in the biosphere, we were born here as species, we are closely suited to its exacting conditions—and not all conditions, either, but just those in a few of the climatic regimes that exist upon some of the land. Environmental damage can be defined as any change that alters our surroundings in a direction contrary to humanity's inborn physical and emotional needs. We must be careful with the environment upon which our lives ultimately depend.

In destroying the biosphere, we are destroying unimaginably vast sources of scientific information and biological wealth. Opportunity costs, which will be better understood by our descendants than by ourselves, will be staggering. Gone forever will be undiscovered medicines, crops, timber, fibers, soil-restoring vegetation, petroleum substitutes, and other products and amenities. Critics of environmentalism forget, if they ever knew, how the rosy periwinkle of Madagascar provided the alkaloids that cure most cases of Hodgkin's disease and acute childhood leukemia; how a substance from an obscure Norwegian fungus made possible the organ transplant industry; how a chemical from the saliva of leeches yielded a solvent that prevents blood clots during and after surgery; and so on through the pharmacopoeia that has stretched from the herbal medicines of Stone Age shamans to the magic-bullet cures of present-day biomedical science.

These are just a few examples of what could be lost if Homo sapiens pursue our current course of environmental destruction. Earth is a laboratory wherein nature—God, if you prefer, pastor—has laid before us the results of countless experiments. We damage her at our own peril.

You may well ask at this point, *Why me?* Simply because religion and science are the two most powerful forces in the world today and especially in the United States. If religion and science could be united on the common ground of biological conservation, the problem might soon be solved. [10]

It may seem far-fetched for a secular scientist to propose an alliance between science and religion. But the fact is that environmental activists cannot succeed without you and your followers as allies. The political process in American democracy, with rare exceptions, does not start at the top and work its way down to the voting masses. It proceeds in the opposite direction. Political leaders are compelled to calculate as precisely as they can what it will take to win the next election. The United States is an intensely religious nation. It is overwhelmingly Judeo-Christian, with a powerful undercurrent of evangelism. We secularists must face reality. The National Association of Evangelicals has 30 million members; the three leading American humanist organizations combined have, at best, a few thousand. Those who, for religious reasons, believe in saving the Creation, have the strength to do so through the political process; acting alone, secular environmentalists do not. An alliance between science and religion, forged in an atmosphere of mutual respect, may be the only way to protect life on earth, including, in the end, our own.

Yes, the gulf separating our worldviews is wide. The Abrahamic religions—Judaism, Christianity, and Islam—believe that the universe was constructed to be relevant to humanity. The discoveries of science, in unintended opposition, have reduced earth to an infinitesimal speck within an immensity of space unrelated to human destiny. The Abrahamic religions envisage a supreme ruler who, while existing outside the material universe, nevertheless oversees an agenda for each and every one of our immortal souls. Science can find no evidence of an agenda other than that fashioned by the complex interaction of genes and environment within parallel evolving cultures. Religious creation stories have a divinely engineered beginning and a divinely ordained ending. According to science, in contrast, humans descended from apish ancestors: our origin was basically no different from that of other animals, played out over geological time through a tortuous route of mutation and environmentally driven natural selection. In addition, all mainstream religious belief, whether fundamentalist or liberal, is predicated upon the assumption that humanity is not alone, and we are here for a life and purpose beyond our earthly existence. Science says that, as far as verifiable evidence tells, we are alone, and what significance we have is therefore of our own making. This is the heart of the agonizing conflict between science and religion that has persisted for the past 500 years.

I do not see how the difference in worldview between these two great productions of human striving can be closed. But, for the purposes of saving the Creation, I am not sure that it needs to be. To make the point in good gospel manner, let me tell the story of a young man, newly trained for the ministry and so fixed in his Christian faith that he referred all questions of morality to readings from the Bible. When he visited the Atlantic rainforest of Brazil, he saw the manifest hand of God, and in his notebook he wrote, "It is not possible to give an adequate idea of the higher feelings of wonder, admiration, and devotion which fill and elevate the mind." That was Charles Darwin in 1832, early into the voyage of the HMS *Beagle*, before he had given any thought to evolution. And here is Darwin, concluding *On the Origin of Species* in 1859, having first abandoned Christian dogma and then, with his newfound intellectual freedom, formulated the theory of evolution by natural selection: "There is grandeur in this view of life, with its several powers, having been originally breathed into a few forms or into one; and that, whilst this planet has gone cycling on according to the fixed law of gravity, from so simple a beginning endless forms most beautiful and most wonderful have been, and are being, evolved." Darwin's reverence for life remained the same as he crossed the seismic divide that separated his religious phase and his scientific one. And so it can be for the divide that, today, separates mainstream religion and scientific humanism. And that separates you and me.

Indeed, despite all that divides science from religion, there is good reason to hope that an alliance on environmental issues is possible. The spiritual reach of evangelical Christianity is nowadays increasingly extended to the environment. While the Old Testament God commands humanity to take dominion over the earth, the decree is not (as one evangelical leader recently affirmed) an excuse to trash the planet. The dominant theme in scripture as interpreted by many evangelicals is instead stewardship. Organizations like the Green Cross and the Evangelical Environmental Network (the latter a coalition of evangelical Christian agencies and institutions) are expanding their magisterium to include conservation—in religious terms, protection of the living Creation.

This evangelical interest in the environment is part of a worldwide 15
trend among religions. In the United States, the umbrella National Religious Partnership for the Environment works with evangelical groups and other prominent organizations, including the U.S. Conference of Catholic Bishops, the National Council of Churches of Christ, and the Coalition on the Environment and Jewish Life. In 2001, the Archbishop of Canterbury urged that "it may not be time to build an Ark like Noah, but it is high time to take better care of God's creation." Three years earlier, Bartholomew I, Patriarch of the Greek Orthodox Church, had gone further: "For humans to cause species to become extinct and to destroy the biological diversity of God's creation . . . these are sins." He and Pope John Paul II later issued a "Common Declaration" that "God has not abandoned the world. It is His will that His Design and our hope for it will be realized through our co-operation in

restoring its original harmony. In our own time we are witnessing a growth of an ecological awareness which needs to be encouraged, so that it will lead to practical programs and initiatives." Unfortunately, a corresponding magnitude of engagement has not yet occurred in Islam or the Eastern religions.

Every great religion offers mercy and charity to the poor. The poor of the world, of whom nearly a billion exist in the "poverty trap" of absolute destitution, are concentrated in the developing countries—the home of 80 percent of the world's population and most of Earth's biodiversity. The solution to the problems of both depends on the recognition that each depends on the other. The desperately poor have little chance to improve their lives in a devastated environment. Conversely, natural environments, where most of the Creation hangs on, cannot survive the press of land-hungry people who have nowhere else to go.

To be sure, some leaders of the religious right are reluctant to support biological conservation, an opposition sufficient to create a wedge within the evangelical movement. They may be partly afraid of paganism, by which worship of nature supplants worship of God. More realistically and importantly, opposition rises from the perceived association of environmental activism with the political left. For decades, conservatives have defined environmentalism as a movement bent on strangling the United States with regulations and bureaucratic power. This canard has dogged the U.S. environmental movement and helped keep it off the agenda of the past two presidential campaigns.

Finally, however, opinion may be changing. The mostly evangelical religious right, which, along with big business, has been the decisive source of power in the Republican Party, has begun to move care of the Creation back into the mainstream of conservative discourse. The opportunity exists to make the environment a universal concern and to render it politically nonpartisan.

Still, for all the positive signs, I remain puzzled that so many religious leaders have hesitated to make protection of the Creation an important part of their magisterium. Pastor, help me understand: Do they believe that human-centered ethics and preparation for the afterlife are the only things that matter? Do they believe that the Second Coming is imminent and that, therefore, the condition of the planet is of little consequence? These and other similar doctrines are not gospels of hope and compassion. They are gospels of cruelty and despair.

You and I are both humanists in the broadest sense: Human welfare 20 is at the center of our thought. So forget our disagreements, I say, and let us meet on common ground. That might not be as difficult as it first seems. When you think about it, our metaphysical differences have remarkably little effect on the conduct of our separate lives. My guess is that you and I are about equally ethical, patriotic, and altruistic. We are products of a civilization that rose from both religion and the science-based Enlightenment. We would gladly serve on the same jury, fight the same wars, and sanctify human life with the same intensity. Surely we also share a love of the Creation—and an understanding that, however the tensions play out between our opposing worldviews, however science and religion wax and wane in the minds of men, there remains the earthborn yet transcendental obligation we are both morally bound to share.

Warmly and respectfully,
Edward O. Wilson

STUDY QUESTIONS

1. What is Wilson's stated PURPOSE for writing "Apocalypse Now"? Why is he writing to a religious leader rather than, for instance, a political leader?

2. How does Wilson establish COMMON GROUND with the minister he addresses and with the evangelical Christian community in general? How effective are his efforts? Explain. Refer to specific passages in your response.

3. Wilson has in mind an AUDIENCE of evangelical Christians. What are some of the ways that he shapes his ARGUMENT to appeal to them? Cite passages from the text to support your RESPONSE. How successful do you think he is? Explain. What changes might he make if he were writing for a different audience?

4. *For Writing.* Pretend that you are the evangelical pastor whom Wilson is addressing and WRITE A LETTER responding to him. On what points do you agree with Wilson? On what points do you disagree? Do you believe science and religion can join hands on this issue? Why or why not? Before you begin drafting your letter, RESEARCH the REASONS that various religious groups have, as Wilson CLAIMS, opposed environmentalism, and address those reasons in your letter.

JESSICA MITFORD }
Behind the Formaldehyde
Curtain

JESSICA MITFORD (1917–1996) was born into an aristocratic English family
and moved in 1939 to the United States, where she became a naturalized
American citizen and pursued a career as an investigative reporter. A lifelong
activist, Mitford worked on behalf of pacifism and civil rights; when she and
her husband, Robert Treuhaft, a lawyer, became aware of funeral costs for
working-class families in the San Francisco Bay Area, she published *The
American Way of Death* (1963), which sold out on the day of publication.
While the work provoked queasiness in some readers and outrage in others
(mainly funeral directors), it has become a classic piece of expository prose,
anthologized in more than fifty textbooks. Mitford is the author of several
books, including *The American Way of Death Revisited* (1998).

    This chapter from *The American Way of Death* presents a critical look at
the process of embalming bodies and preparing them for burial. Mitford
uses an ironically breezy tone to convey her attitude toward the way funerals
are conducted in the United States as she describes the procedures used to
embalm the fictitious "Mr. Jones." Despite her gruesome subject matter (or
perhaps, for some readers, because of it), Mitford's understated sense of
humor has made "Behind the Formaldehyde Curtain" enduringly popular.

THE DRAMA BEGINS TO UNFOLD with the arrival of the corpse at the
mortuary.

    Alas, poor Yorick![1] How surprised he would be to see how his
counterpart of today is whisked off to a funeral parlor and is in short

---

[1]*Hamlet*, 5.1.171. Hamlet discovers the skull of an old friend in a graveyard.

order sprayed, sliced, pierced, pickled, trussed, trimmed, creamed, waxed, painted, rouged and neatly dressed—transformed from a common corpse into a Beautiful Memory Picture. This process is known in the trade as embalming and restorative art, and is so universally employed in the United States and Canada that the funeral director does it routinely, without consulting corpse or kin. He regards as eccentric those few who are hardy enough to suggest that it might be dispensed with. Yet no law requires embalming, no religious doctrine commends it, nor is it dictated by considerations of health, sanitation, or even of personal daintiness. In no part of the world but in Northern America is it widely used. The purpose of embalming is to make the corpse presentable for viewing in a suitably costly container; and here too the funeral director routinely, without first consulting the family, prepares the body for public display.

Is all this legal? The processes to which a dead body may be subjected are after all to some extent circumscribed by law. In most states, for instance, the signature of next of kin must be obtained before an autopsy may be performed, before the deceased may be cremated, before the body may be turned over to a medical school for research purposes; or such provision must be made in the decedent's will. In the case of embalming, no such permission is required nor is it ever sought. A textbook, *The Principles and Practices of Embalming*, comments on this: "There is some question regarding the legality of much that is done within the preparation room." The author points out that it would be most unusual for a responsible member of a bereaved family to instruct the mortician, in so many words, to *"embalm"* the body of a deceased relative. The very term "embalming" is so seldom used that the mortician must rely upon custom in the matter. The author concludes that unless the family specifies otherwise, the act of entrusting the body to the care of a funeral establishment carries with it an implied permission to go ahead and embalm.

Embalming is indeed a most extraordinary procedure, and one must wonder at the docility of Americans who each year pay hundreds of millions of dollars for its perpetuation, blissfully ignorant of what it is all about, what is done, how it is done. Not one in ten thousand has any idea of what actually takes place. Books on the subject are extremely hard to come by. They are not to be found in most libraries or bookshops.

In an era when huge television audiences watch surgical operations 5 in the comfort of their living rooms, when, thanks to the animated cartoon, the geography of the digestive system has become familiar territory even to the nursery school set, in a land where the satisfaction of curiosity about almost all matters is a national pastime, the secrecy surrounding embalming can, surely, hardly be attributed to the inherent gruesomeness of the subject. Custom in this regard has within this century suffered a complete reversal. In the early days of American embalming, when it was performed in the home of the deceased, it was almost mandatory for some relative to stay by the embalmer's side and witness the procedure. Today, family members who might wish to be in attendance would certainly be dissuaded by the funeral director. All others, except apprentices, are excluded by law from the preparation room.

A close look at what does actually take place may explain in large measure the undertaker's intractable reticence concerning a procedure that has become his major *raison d'être*. Is it possible he fears that public information about embalming might lead patrons to wonder if they really want this service? If the funeral men are loath to discuss the subject outside the trade, the reader may, understandably, be equally loath to go on reading at this point. For those who have the stomach for it, let us part the formaldehyde curtain. Others should skip to paragraph 20.

The body is first laid out in the undertaker's morgue—or rather, Mr. Jones is reposing in the preparation room—to be readied to bid the world farewell.

The preparation room in any of the better funeral establishments has the tiled and sterile look of a surgery, and indeed the embalmer-restorative artist who does his chores there is beginning to adopt the term "dermasurgeon" (appropriately corrupted by some mortician-writers as "demisurgeon") to describe his calling. His equipment, consisting of scalpels, scissors, augers, forceps, clamps, needles, pumps, tubes, bowls and basins, is crudely imitative of the surgeon's, as is his technique, acquired in a nine- or twelve-month post-high-school course in an embalming school. He is supplied by an advanced chemical industry with a bewildering array of fluids, sprays, pastes, oils, powders, creams, to fix or soften tissue, shrink or distend it as needed, dry it here, restore the moisture there. There are cosmetics, waxes and paints to fill and cover features, even plaster of Paris to replace entire limbs. There are ingenious aids to prop and stabilize the cadaver: a Vari-Pose Head Rest, the Edwards Arm and Hand Positioner, the Repose Block (to support the shoulders, during the embalming), and the Throop Foot Positioner, which resembles an old-fashioned stocks.

Mr. John H. Eckels, president of the Eckels College of Mortuary Science, thus describes the first part of the embalming procedure: "In the hands of a skilled practitioner, this work may be done in a comparatively short time and without mutilating the body other than by slight incision—so slight that it scarcely would cause serious inconvenience if made upon a living person. It is necessary to remove the blood, and doing this not only helps in the disinfecting, but removes the principal cause of disfigurements due to discoloration."

Another textbook discusses the all-important time element: "The 10 earlier this is done, the better, for every hour that elapses between death and embalming will add to the problems and complications encountered. . . ." Just how soon should one get going on the embalming? The author tells us, "On the basis of such scanty information made available to this profession through its rudimentary and haphazard system of technical research, we must conclude that the best results are to be obtained if the subject is embalmed before life is completely extinct—that is, before cellular death has occurred. In the average case, this would mean within an hour after somatic death." For those who feel that there is something a little rudimentary, not to say haphazard, about this advice, a comforting thought is offered by another writer. Speaking of fears entertained in early days of premature burial, he points out, "One of the effects of embalming by chemical injection, however, has been to dispel fears of live burial." How true; once the blood is removed, chances of live burial are indeed remote.

To return to Mr. Jones, the blood is drained out through the veins and replaced by embalming fluid pumped in through the arteries. As noted in *The Principles and Practices of Embalming*, "every operator has a favorite injection and drainage point—a fact which becomes a handicap only if he fails or refuses to forsake his favorites when conditions demand it." Typical favorites are the carotid artery, femoral artery, jugular vein, subclavian vein. There are various choices of embalming fluid. If Flextone is used, it will produce a "mild, flexible rigidity. The skin retains a velvety softness, the tissues are rubbery and pliable. Ideal for women and children." It may be blended with B. and G. Products Company's Lyf-Lyk tint, which is guaranteed to reproduce "nature's own skin texture . . . the velvety appearance of living tissue." Suntone comes in three separate tints: Suntan; Special Cosmetic Tint, a pink shade "especially indicated for young female subjects"; and Regular Cosmetic Tint, moderately pink.

About three to six gallons of a dyed and perfumed solution of formaldehyde, glycerin, borax, phenol, alcohol and water is soon circulating through Mr. Jones, whose mouth has been sewn together with a "needle directed upward between the upper lip and gum and brought out through the left nostril," with the corners raised slightly "for a more pleasant expression." If he should be bucktoothed, his teeth are cleaned with Bon Ami and coated with colorless nail polish. His eyes, meanwhile, are closed with flesh-tinted eye caps and eye cement.

The next step is to have at Mr. Jones with a thing called a trocar. This is a long, hollow needle attached to a tube. It is jabbed into the abdomen, poked around the entrails and chest cavity, the contents of which are pumped out and replaced with "cavity fluid." This done, and the hole in the abdomen sewn up, Mr. Jones's face is heavily creamed (to protect the skin from burns which may be caused by leakage of the chemicals), and he is covered with a sheet and left unmolested for a while. But not for long—there is more, much more, in store for him. He has been embalmed, but not yet restored, and the best time to start the restorative work is eight to ten hours after embalming, when the tissues have become firm and dry.

The object of all this attention to the corpse, it must be remembered, is to make it presentable for viewing in an attitude of healthy repose. "Our customs require the presentation of our dead in the semblance of normality . . . unmarred by the ravages of illness, disease, or mutilation," says Mr. J. Sheridan Mayer in his *Restorative Art*. This is rather a large order since few people die in the full bloom of health, unravaged by illness and unmarked by some disfigurement. The funeral industry is equal to the challenge: "In some cases the gruesome appearance of a mutilated or disease-ridden subject may be quite discouraging. The task of restoration may seem impossible and shake the confidence of the embalmer. This is the time for intestinal fortitude and determination. Once the formative work is begun and affected tissues are cleaned or removed, all doubts of success vanish. It is surprising and gratifying to discover the results which may be obtained."

The embalmer, having allowed an appropriate interval to elapse, 15 returns to the attack, but now he brings into play the skill and equipment of sculptor and cosmetician. Is a hand missing? Casting one in plaster of Paris is a simple matter. "For replacement purposes, only a cast of the back of the hand is necessary; this is within the ability of the average operator and is quite adequate." If a lip or two, a nose or an ear should be missing, the embalmer has at hand a variety of restorative waxes with which to model replacements. Pores and skin texture are simulated by stippling with a little brush, and over this cosmetics are laid on. Head off? Decapitation cases are rather routinely handled. Ragged edges are trimmed, and head joined to torso with a series of splints, wires and sutures. It is a good idea to have a little something at the neck—a scarf or high collar—when time for viewing comes. Swollen mouth? Cut out tissue as needed from inside the lips. If too much is removed, the surface contour can easily be restored by padding with cotton. Swollen necks and cheeks are reduced by removing tissue through vertical incisions made down each side of the neck. "When the deceased is casketed, the pillow will hide the suture incisions . . . as an extra precaution against leakage, the suture may be painted with liquid sealer."

The opposite condition is more likely to present itself—that of emaciation. His hypodermic syringe now loaded with massage cream, the embalmer seeks out and fills the hollowed and sunken areas by injection. In this procedure the backs of the hands and fingers and the under-chin area should not be neglected.

Positioning the lips is a problem that recurrently challenges the ingenuity of the embalmer. Closed too tightly, they tend to give a stern, even disapproving expression. Ideally, embalmers feel, the lips should give the impression of being ever so slightly parted, the upper lip protruding slightly for a more youthful appearance. This takes some engineering, however, as the lips tend to drift apart. Lip drift can sometimes be remedied by pushing one or two straight pins through the inner margin of the lower lip and then inserting them between the two front upper teeth. If Mr. Jones happens to have no teeth, the pins can just as easily be anchored in his Armstrong Face Former and Denture Replacer. Another method to maintain lip closure is to dislocate the lower jaw, which is then held in its new position by a wire run through holes which have been drilled through the upper and lower jaws at the midline. As the French are fond of saying, *il faut souffrir pour être belle.*[2]

If Mr. Jones has died of jaundice, the embalming fluid will very likely turn him green. Does this deter the embalmer? Not if he has intestinal fortitude. Masking pastes and cosmetics are heavily laid on, burial garments and casket interiors are color-correlated with particular care, and Jones is displayed beneath rose-colored lights. Friends will say, "How *well* he looks." Death by carbon monoxide, on the other hand, can be rather a good thing from the embalmer's viewpoint: "One advantage is the fact that this type of discoloration is an exaggerated form of a natural pink coloration." This is nice because the healthy glow is already present and needs but little attention.

The patching and filling completed, Mr. Jones is now shaved, washed and dressed. Cream-based cosmetic, available in pink, flesh, suntan, brunette and blond, is applied to his hands and face, his hair is shampooed and combed (and, in the case of Mrs. Jones, set), his hands manicured. For the horny-handed son of toil special care must be taken; cream should be applied to remove ingrained grime, and the nails cleaned. "If he were not in the habit of having them manicured in

---

[2]In 1963 *Mortuary Management* reports a new development: "Natural Expression Formers," an invention of Funeral Directors Research Company. "They may be used to replace one or both artificial dentures, or over natural teeth; have 'bite-indicator' lines as a closure guide . . . Natural Expression Formers also offer more control of facial expression" [Author's note]. *Il faut souffrir pour être belle:* One must suffer to be beautiful (French).

life, trimming and shaping is advised for better appearance—never questioned by kin."

Jones is now ready for casketing (this is the present participle of the verb "to casket"). In this operation his right shoulder should be depressed slightly "to turn the body a bit to the right and soften the appearance of lying flat on the back." Positioning the hands is a matter of importance, and special rubber positioning blocks may be used. The hands should be cupped slightly for a more lifelike, relaxed appearance. Proper placement of the body requires a delicate sense of balance. It should lie as high as possible in the casket, yet not so high that the lid, when lowered, will hit the nose. On the other hand, we are cautioned, placing the body too low "creates the impression that the body is in a box."

Jones is next wheeled into the appointed slumber room where a few last touches may be added—his favorite pipe placed in his hand or, if he was a great reader, a book propped into position. (In the case of little Master Jones a Teddy bear may be clutched.) Here he will hold open house for a few days, visiting hours 10 A.M. to 9 P.M.

All now being in readiness, the funeral director calls a staff conference to make sure that each assistant knows his precise duties. Mr. Wilber Krieger writes: "This makes your staff feel that they are a part of the team, with a definite assignment that must be properly carried out if the whole plan is to succeed. You never heard of a football coach who failed to talk to his entire team before they go on the field. They have drilled on the plays they are to execute for hours and days, and yet the successful coach knows the importance of making even the bench-warming third-string substitute feel that he is important if the game is to be won." The winning of *this* game is predicated upon glass-smooth handling of the logistics. The funeral director has notified the pallbearers whose names were furnished by the family, has arranged for the presence of clergyman, organist, and soloist, has provided transportation for everybody, has organized and listed the flowers sent by friends. In *Psychology of Funeral Service* Mr. Edward A. Martin points out: "He may not always do as much as the family thinks he is doing, but it is his helpful guidance that they appreciate in knowing they are proceeding as they should. . . . The important thing is how well his services can be used to make the family believe they are giving unlimited expression to their own sentiment."

The religious service may be held in a church or in the chapel of the funeral home; the funeral director vastly prefers the latter arrangement, for not only is it more convenient for him but it affords him the opportunity to show off his beautiful facilities to the gathered mourners. After the clergyman has had his say, the mourners queue up to file past the casket for a last look at the deceased. The family is *never* asked whether they want an open-casket ceremony; in the absence of their instruction to the contrary, this is taken for granted. Consequently well over 90 percent of all American funerals feature the open casket—a custom unknown in other parts of the world. Foreigners are astonished by it. An English woman living in San Francisco described her reaction in a letter to the writer:

> I myself have attended only one funeral here—that of an elderly fellow worker of mine. After the service I could not understand why everyone was walking towards the coffin (sorry, I mean casket), but thought I had better follow the crowd. It shook me rigid to get there and find the casket open and poor old Oscar lying there in his brown tweed suit, wearing a suntan makeup and just the wrong shade of lipstick. If I had not been extremely fond of the old boy, I have a horrible feeling that I might have giggled. Then and there I decided that I could never face another American funeral—even dead.

The casket (which has been resting throughout the service on a Classic Beauty Ultra Metal Casket Bier) is now transferred by a hydraulically operated device called Porto-Lift to a balloon-tired, Glide Easy casket carriage which will wheel it to yet another conveyance, the Cadillac Funeral Coach. This may be lavender, cream, light green—anything but black. Interiors, of course, are color-correlated, "for the man who cannot stop short of perfection."

At graveside, the casket is lowered into the earth. This office, once the prerogative of friends of the deceased, is now performed by a patented mechanical lowering device. A "Lifetime Green" artificial grass mat is at the ready to conceal the sere earth, and overhead, to conceal the sky, is a portable Steril Chapel Tent ("resists the intense heat and humidity of summer and the terrific storms of winter . . . available in Silver Grey, Rose or Evergreen"). Now is the time for the ritual scattering of earth over the coffin, as the solemn words "earth to earth, ashes to ashes, dust to dust" are pronounced by the officiating cleric. This can today be accomplished "with a mere flick of the wrist with the Gordon Leak-Proof Earth Dispenser. No grasping of a handful of dirt, no soiled fingers. Simple, dignified, beautiful, reverent! The modern way!" The Gordon Earth Dispenser (at $5) is of nickel-plated brass construction. It is not only "attractive to the eye and long wearing"; it is also "one of the 'tools' for building better public relations" if presented as "an appropriate non-commercial gift" to the clergyman. It is shaped something like a saltshaker.

Untouched by human hand, the coffin and the earth are now united.

It is in the function of directing the participants through this maze of gadgetry that the funeral director has assigned to himself his relatively new role of "grief therapist." He has relieved the family of every detail, he has revamped the corpse to look like a living doll, he has arranged for it to nap for a few days in a slumber room, he has put on a well-oiled performance in which the concept of *death* has played no part whatsoever—unless it was inconsiderately mentioned by the clergyman who conducted the religious service. He has done everything in his power to make the funeral a real pleasure for everybody concerned. He and his team have given their all to score an upset victory over death.

STUDY QUESTIONS

1. In paragraph 6, Mitford invites the reader to "part the formaldehyde curtain." What does she mean? How is the formaldehyde curtain like the "Iron Curtain" that divided western and eastern Europe during the Cold War era?

2. Mitford writes a PROCESS essay about embalming. However, rather than simply list each step, she DESCRIBES and EXPLAINS each part of the process. Identify two steps that are fully explained and discuss your reaction to them. Does this kind of process essay help you better understand the subject? Explain.

3. Consider the TOPIC and the TONE of the article. Do you think the two are consistent? Describe the tone that Mitford uses to explain the process of embalming. Who is her intended AUDIENCE? Rewrite one or two steps using a different tone for a different audience.

4. *For Writing.* Consider a process that you are familiar with. Write a process essay that explains the steps to complete the activity. Use Mitford's essay as a model—don't just list the steps, explain the steps and DESCRIBE the equipment needed to perform the activity. Write the paper for two different audiences: one that is familiar with the process and one that is unfamiliar with it.

WAKE TECH FACULTY ESSAYS

"We Say"

—▭—

Arguing Academically

In the following section, you'll find essays (by Wake Tech English faculty) that examine elements of academic argument. This material covers a wide range of intellectual history, from the Greek philosopher Aristotle, who lived 300 years before Christ, to the British philosopher Stephen Toulmin, who died in 2009. That argument—persuasion through reason—has been a concern of writers and thinkers for so long suggests its ongoing importance. The way we live—our pursuit of a college education, use of machines, consumption of food, conception of the American dream, perceptions of gender—has been shaped by academic argument and inquiry, the back-and-forth conversation between they say and I say.

When scholars argue academically, they enter into long-standing conversations, weighing their conclusions against those of experts in their field of study, modifying positions, and moving toward a truer claim based on facts. The standard research paper assigned in Freshman Composition mimics this process. Its goal is two-fold: to familiarize you with the kinds of essays you will write in other college classes and to help you develop your critical thinking skills, the ability to distinguish between true and false (or true and less true) claims. These skills were first understood and explained, as John Etheridge makes clear in his essay on classical argument, by the ancient Greeks, who recognized that the use of reason is essential to "creating civil and public discourse."

A skill required for succeeding in college (and, we believe, for being an educated citizen) is the ability to question others' arguments. You can't enter into an academic conversation without understanding what writers are persuading you to believe and how they are doing so. In her essay, Lisa Martin shows how to analyze and evaluate a writer's persuasive techniques. In learning how to critique others' techniques, you will improve your own rhetorical skills, your ability to persuade through written language. You will further develop these skills, as James Harr points out, by learning to recognize common logical flaws.

To make a persuasive claim, you need support, which is found through research. That's why teachers assign research papers. People use support all of the time to back up their claims. If you're arguing, for instance, that Tom Brady, not Joe Montana, is the best quarterback ever to play in the NFL, you'll compare quarterback ratings, touchdown to interception ratios, number of Super Bowls won—which requires research.

Frequently in our daily lives we use the internet for such research. Before buying something online, for instance, you're likely to read others' comments. And when you do, you're often evaluating the reliability of these reviewers. Who among them seems convincing because of their knowledge and use of specific details? You're also looking at overall ratings, since you realize a handful of negative or positive reviews is unrepresentative.

How many stars did this product receive? What is the consensus opinion? How recent are these comments? When you're asking these questions, you're doing just what scholars do when they evaluate the credibility of sources.

However, while in your daily life you may rely on the internet, instructors often limit your choice of sources, sometimes banishing internet sites entirely and forcing you to search in unfamiliar and hard-to-use library databases. Instructors do this to make sure your claims are supported by recent, credible sources. While the internet does provide a world of information, it also provides a world of false and distorted information. Conducting a thorough search of reliable sources, therefore, is essential for writing a well-supported argument. As Elena Fleggas explains in her essay on constructing effective academic arguments, the research process helps you discover what academic conversation to join and how to develop claims and organize your own argument.

When we think of argument, we tend to think of something contentious. The arguments that occur on cable news networks, for instance, often devolve into a he said/she said dead-end. Scott Dennis, in his essay on Rogerian argument, explains another model of argument, one that seeks consensus rather than contest. And in his discussion of the Toulmin model, Win Neagle explains the essence of academic arguments: how to construct a rational fact-based claim.

As individuals increasingly rely upon news gathered through social media, the ability to evaluate source credibility and truth claims grows ever more important. Some fear that we have entered the age of what comedian Stephen Colbert labelled "truthiness," which he defined as "something that seems like truth—the truth we want to exist." We believe, on the contrary, that there are such things as facts, that these are the basis of academic arguments, that when we enter into an academic conversation we seek to build upon an existing argument in order to reach a truer conclusion—and that the following selections will help you achieve these ends.

Works Cited

Colbert, Stephen. "The Word—Truthiness." *The Colbert Report.* 17 Oct. 2005, www.cc.com/video-clips/63ite2/the-colbert-report-the-word—truthiness.

ELENA FLEGGAS { *Constructing an Effective Academic Argument*

EFFECTIVE ACADEMIC ARGUMENTS differ from the biased ideas that surround us every day in advertisements, politics, and the news. For instance, a strong academic argument incorporates recent, credible research and engages respectfully with positions that oppose or differ from the author's. While you may encounter many types of argumentative assignments in college, the following techniques will help you develop a persuasive academic argument.

BEGIN BY CHOOSING A TOPIC

When you are assigned the task of writing an academic argument, your instructor may also assign the class a topic. You might be allowed to modify this topic to suit your own interests. In some cases, your instructor may provide students with a list of argumentative topics to choose from or allow students to come up with their own topics. In both of these instances, you have the freedom to pick which argumentative topic to explore. You should keep in mind that argumentative writing often comes easiest to writers when they choose a subject that interests them and that they actually *want* to learn more about, though you should be careful since being too personally invested in a topic can make argumentation and listening to opposing viewpoints more difficult. Often, too, college essays call for you to write on a topic you have little personal interest in. Learning the techniques of constructing an argument will help you succeed even on topics you may consider uninteresting.

If you are unsure which topic to research, you might begin by brainstorming. For example, you can make a list of tentative topics and then browse through articles and books that intrigue you on those topics. Often sources published within the last ten years will strengthen your argument the most—the conversations and realities surrounding debatable topics are always changing, so readers may question your credibility if you rely on texts that are out of date.

After doing a bit of research, you may find it easier to zero in on one or two subjects that speak to you the most and that allow you to meet the assignment criteria. You should always look to your assignment prompt and check with your instructor if you are unsure about the appropriateness of your topic or sources.

BECOME FAMILIAR WITH THE DISCUSSION SURROUNDING YOUR TOPIC AND ACTIVELY READ

Once you have decided on your topic, you should *actively* 5 engage with the texts you plan to use in your essay. Quickly reading your chosen materials will not help you fully understand how these will fit into your argument. Therefore, you should *actively read*. Use the following tips:

- Underline and highlight key phrases and words in your texts. This technique allows you to easily revisit important points. You should try to highlight and underline only *key* phrases and words—too much highlighting may confuse you later on.

- In the margins of your sources, briefly summarize key points, note any confusion you may have, and raise questions about these arguments. You can do this in printed books or Ebooks. Since annotating requires a bit more critical thinking than highlighting, it may help you remember the texts' key points better. You may also annotate on sticky notes if you prefer not to write in your texts.

- Ask questions about the text. Who is/are the author(s)? When was the text written? Also consider the purpose of the piece by asking what its goal is—is it a call to action? Does it attempt to explain something? Is it trying to persuade?

- Try to summarize what you have read to a friend. Without having read the piece, he or she should be able to understand its key points after hearing your synopsis (The Open University).

Although time consuming, active reading allows you to better understand the conversation surrounding your topic. You should understand what the key arguments are concerning your subject and who the most important figures are in this discussion. In other words, you should strive to understand the contours of and to join this academic conversation.

Remember, too, that, depending on your topic, you may need to gather research from a variety of sources or publications in order to engage a variety of perspectives.

FORM A NARROW CLAIM ABOUT YOUR TOPIC

As you conduct your research, you should be developing a claim you will argue and support. Generally speaking, the narrower your claim, the more persuasive your argument. A claim that is too broad may confuse your readers. Furthermore, broad claims require a great deal of support. One of the most consistent problems in student papers is an overly broad thesis. We believe that academic essays are stronger when they support narrowly focused claims. The narrower your claim, the more likely you are to effectively and convincingly support it.

Here is an example of a claim that is too broad:

> Smoking should be banned on college campuses.   10

There are quite a few issues with this claim. First, what does the writer mean by "smoking"? Is the writer referencing drug use or cigarettes? In addition, *why* does the author believe smoking should be banned on college campuses? How, in other words, is smoking harmful in this setting? Lastly, the writer references college campuses, but it is not clear to the audience which location(s) the writer will explore. Does the author plan to explore the United States or discuss other countries? On the whole, this claim is too general and likely leaves the audience with many unanswered questions.

For your claim to be strong and, most important, convincing, it must be narrow, arguable, and proveable with research. In addition, your claim should not leave the reader with questions about what the essay will explore or argue.

Here is an example of a narrow claim:

- Smoking cigarettes should be banned on America's college campuses since it is detrimental to the health of smokers and those around them.

This narrow claim manages detail well: it reveals who is harmed on college campuses by the act of smoking cigarettes. In addition, this claim is linked to a place—the United States. This statement can be supported with valid evidence, research, and reasoning. 15

Note that in order for your claim to be effective, you need to appropriately cite and reference written sources. What kinds of evidence might you incorporate? Facts, statistics, examples, visuals, expert opinions, all qualify. You should check with your instructor and review your assignment prompt to know which types of evidence are suitable.

USE AN APPROPRIATE TONE

If writing on a topic you feel strongly about, you may develop a tone that too aggressively expresses how you feel. You should avoid this aggressive tone. For example, if you were making an argument about who to blame for the obesity epidemic in the United States, you would not want to write:

> Of course, fast food companies are to blame for the obesity issue in the United States. They selfishly keep nutritional information from the public.

Here, the writer's tone reads as hostile and accusatory, potentially alienating the audience.

While an aggressive tone harms credibility, too passive a 20 tone risks weakening your argument:

> "I *might* be correct, but I think fast food companies are to blame for the obesity epidemic"

This statement suggests a lack of confidence in the writer's claim or even that he or she does not care enough to have done the research to support it.

The most appropriate tone for an effective academic argument is assertive. An assertive tone builds credibility and engages readers because it shows confidence in an ability to contribute to the conversation in a level-headed way:

> "Fast food companies often conceal nutritional information from the public, contributing to the obesity problem in the United States."

This statement is not too aggressive or passive—it is just asser- 25 tive enough. This type of language makes the writer seem level headed about the issue being discussed; therefore, the audience is more likely to take his or her argument seriously and be convinced by it.

CONSIDER YOUR AUDIENCE AND ADDRESS NAYSAYERS

Another way to convince your audience in an academic argument is to approach them as readers who do not or will not automatically agree with your claim. Instead, you should pretend your readers are skeptical about your argument and will only decide where they stand on your issue after hearing multiple sides of it—including the ideas of those who disagree with you. The most effective arguments, in other words, respectfully consider and carefully respond to opposing ideas

Responding to your naysayers strengthens your credibility because it shows you are open-minded and consider multiple points of view. While often it strengthens an essay to place the naysayer in the first or last body paragraphs, sometimes including your naysayer throughout the paper works best; where you place the naysayer ultimately depends on your assignment criteria and instructor's preferences.

Below are some easy-to-use templates from *They Say/I Say* that reveal how you may respond to your naysayer appropriately. These templates have been modified to remove the first person "I," as is sometimes required by academic disciplines:

> **X is mistaken because she overlooks _____ .**
>
> **X's claim that _____ rests upon the questionable assumption that _____ .**
>
> **X's view that _____ is flawed because, as recent research has shown, _____ .**
>
> **By focusing on _____ , X overlooks the deeper problem of _____ (Graff and Birkenstein 769).**

Although academic arguments take on different forms, this [30] genre of writing challenges you to accomplish more than just summarizing facts or research. You must consider and respond to ideas other than your own from recent resources with which you have actively engaged. Additionally, you must form a narrow claim about your topic, use an appropriate and assertive tone, and effectively address your naysayers.

Works Cited

Graff, Gerald, Cathy Birkenstein, and Russel Durst. *They Say I Say: The Moves That Matter in Academic Writing, with Readings.* 3rd ed., W.W. Norton & Company, 2015.

The Open University. "Skills for OU Study: Active Reading," 20 May 2013, http://www2.open.ac.uk/students/skillsforstudy/active-reading.php. Accessed 21 November 2016.

LISA MARTIN ⎰ *Rhetorical Analysis*

OFTEN IN A WRITING class, you may be asked to analyze someone else's written argument. This task typically involves analyzing the author's credibility, message, and audience. Why do instructors ask you to examine other people's arguments? Because you are surrounded by arguments everywhere you look, you need to be able to think critically about what you find persuasive—or not. You may not realize it but as you scroll through your social media page, you are bombarded by arguments; in fact, every website you view has an implicit argument: trust this website for this reason. Every commercial you watch makes an argument: buy this product for this reason. The ability to distinguish between credible evidence and sheer propaganda is a necessary skill in this digital age of media, fake news, blogs, memes, and tweets.

To avoid being manipulated, you need to determine who is making the argument, why the argument is being made, how well the argument is supported, and what rhetorical tactics are being employed to persuade you to think or believe a certain way. In fact, the same critical thinking skills used to analyze any argument are essential to your success in school and in the workplace as employers increasingly seek applicants with effective critical thinking skills. Before you can make your own effective arguments, you must first think critically about how arguments are constructed and why some arguments are more persuasive than others.

A rhetorical analysis—a common writing assignment in college English classes—looks to answer one central question: Did the arguer successfully persuade his or her intended audience to accept his or her claim as valid?

To begin a rhetorical analysis, you must first consider the time and place for the argument, what the ancient Greek philosophers called *kairos*. As Gregory Howard notes in his *Dictionary of Rhetorical Terms*, this term

> refers to the way a given context for communication both calls for and constrains one's speech. Thus, sensitive to *kairos*, a speaker or writer takes into account the contingencies of a given place and time, and considers the opportunities within this specific context for words to be effective and appropriate to that moment. (127)

The situational factors involved may also be part of the argument's constraints or demands. For example, writing an article for a magazine involves attention to the time and place (*kairos*), has restrictions on length and topic (constraints), and could be motivated by things like money, the need to get the word out, etc. (exigence).

You can examine an argument's context by answering the following questions:

1. Why did the author write the argument? What was his or her purpose?

2. What existing problem or argument is he or she responding to?

3. Where was the argument published? When was it published?

Thus, to analyze an argument, you first need to consider *the purpose* of the text:

- What was the author hoping to achieve?

- Is the writer trying to entertain you? Inform you? Something else?

- How does the author organize the argument and what types of evidence does he or she use?

- What does the author want you to do after reading or viewing the argument?

In addition, you will want to examine *the author's audience*, 10 the intended receiver of the argument. Who are they? What beliefs or values might they hold about the argument being made in the text? How does the author work to connect with the audience? When considering audience, you'll first need to identify the audiences the text is addressing and explain any assumptions, values, opinions, or beliefs they hold. You could also consider whether the audience is easily identifiable or not and evaluate how this impacts the argument's effectiveness.

Next, you might examine the specific rhetorical features of the argument by discussing whether or not the author uses *an appropriate tone and style* for the particular argument and the particular audience:

- Do the tone and style support the author's purpose?

- Does the author effectively address his or her reason for writing?

Here you might examine whether the argument's tone is optimistic, angry, sarcastic, condescending, serious, or calm. You might also look at the specific word choice the author uses to establish that tone.

In addition to looking at the author's purpose, the author's audience, and the author's tone and style, you might consider looking at three specific rhetorical appeals, first identified by Greek philosopher Aristotle: ethos, logos, and pathos. In fact, in his seminal work *The Art of Rhetoric,* Aristotle writes, "Of the modes of persuasion furnished by the spoken word there are three kinds. The first kind depends on the personal character of the speaker; the second on putting the audience into a certain frame of mind; the third on the proof, or apparent proof, provided by the words of the speech itself" (2155) Below is an explanation for analyzing arguments using those three appeals.

ETHOS

The word *ethos* is Greek for character. Greeks used the term to refer to the customs and characteristics of a people. Today, rhetoricians use *ethos* or *ethical appeal* to refer to the practice of convincing the reader of the credibility of the author (see also p. A-265). To analyze an argument's appeal to ethos, you want to examine how the author establishes that he or she is an ethical speaker both in terms of authority, trustworthiness, and credibility or believability on the subject of the argument **and** in terms of being an ethical person, a person of goodwill who respects the audience. To find appeals to ethos in any argument, you should ask these questions (some of which were prepared by the Brigham Young University Writing Center):

- How does the author demonstrate his or her expertise on the topic?

- What authority does the speaker want audience to trust? Is it the author him- or herself or someone the author is citing?

- How does the writer convince you that he or she is trustworthy?

- How does the author appeal to shared values, beliefs, or experiences to appear more relatable and thus more credible to the audience?

- How does the author demonstrate his or her goodwill for the audience?

LOGOS

Logos is a Greek word variously translated as word, speech, opinion, or thought, among others. In composition, it typically refers to an argument's logic (see also p. A-267). To analyze an argument's appeal to logos, you will need to examine how the author supports each claim with logic and reason. Sometimes those reasons can come in the form of hard evidence such as statistics or facts, but sometimes those reasons can come in the form of rational logic that appeals to the audience's brain. In other words, you should ask yourself these questions:

- What claims is the author making?

- How does the author support each claim?

- What types of evidence does the author use?

- How does the author assure readers that the evidence comes from credible sources?

- Does the author provide good, common-sense reasons to support each claim?

- Does the argument seem logical and rational or does the author make too many generalizations and leaps in logic?

- Does the argument contain any logical fallacies—gaps in logic—(see p. A-259) such as making false comparisons, oversimplifying objections, or mistaking sequence for cause?

PATHOS

The word "pathos" is Greek for suffering, experience, or emotion. To analyze an argument's appeal to pathos, you examine how the author appeals to the audience's emotions (see also p. A-266). Pathos, then, is about how the author wants the audience to feel in response to the arguments. Appeals to pathos are based not on how the author feels about the topic of the argument but rather on how the author evokes a specific emotion in the audience. To find appeals to pathos, you should ask the following:

- Where in the article does the author appeal to the emotions of his or her audience? 20

- Is the author arousing anger, pity, or hope in his or her audience? Why? For what purpose?

- What particular words, images, and analogies is the speaker using to manipulate or arouse these emotions? Does this strategy work? Why or why not?

- Once the speaker has created an emotion in listeners, how does he or she connect that emotion with the purpose of the argument? Is this strategy effective? Why or why not? In other words, how does establishing an emotional connection help persuade people to follow the speaker and accept his or her argument?

COMPARING WRITTEN ARGUMENTS

Occasionally, you may be asked to compare two or more written arguments, to evaluate how well two authors make a persuasive argument to different audiences. To generate those comparisons, you should ask the following:

1. Whose argument is effective given the constraints of the argument? Who does more to respond to an existing problem or argument?

2. Who does a better job of establishing trust and credibility with their audience? What exactly do they do to establish trust and credibility? In other words, do their appeals to ethos function the same way or are they different?

3. Who does a better job of presenting evidence to support their claim? Compare the types of evidence both authors present and examine why that evidence would be effective for that audience. Moreover, whose argument seems more

reasonable and logical? Why?. Do they both cite data? Do they both quote experts? Do they both use sound logic?

4. Who does a better job of arousing emotion in their audience? How are their emotional appeals similar or different? Which article contains more emotional appeals? Why?

SAMPLE RHETORICAL ANALYSIS ESSAY

Following is a sample rhetorical analysis written by a Wake Tech student for her English 112 course during the Fall 2016 semester. Note: this paper is formatted according to the MLA, 8th edition.

Works Cited

Aristotle. *The Art of Rhetoric.* Translated by Roberts, Rhys W., Megaphone eBooks, 2008.

Brigham Young University Writing Center. "Rhetorical Analysis: Prewriting." //writingcenter.byu.edu/sites/default/files/handouts/rhetorical_analysis_ prewriting_0.pdf

Howard, Gregory. *Dictionary of Rhetorical Terms.* Xlibris, 2010.

Brianna Paszko
ENG 112
Lisa Martin
12 October 2016

FOOD FOR THOUGHT

Obesity has become an increasingly complex issue over the years. Many disagree on how to effectively solve the obesity epidemic and exactly what causes it to be such a problem. One author who has entered the debate is Radley Balko, a former a policy analyst with the Cato Institute who now writes opinion articles for the Washington Post and holds degrees in journalism and political science from Indiana University. In his article "What You Eat Is Your Business," published on the Cato Institute's website in 2004, Radley Balko talks about how the government is trying to pass more anti-obesity initiatives and how those initiatives will affect his libertarian audience. The Cato Institute, which serves a primarily libertarian audience, is a public policy research organization dedicated to "the principles of individual liberty, limited government, free markets and peace" (466). Through his article, Balko is able to persuade his audience by establishing his credibility and a sense of trust, presenting facts to prove that the government is not helping to stop the obesity epidemic, and using a call to action to incite anger and fear in his audience.

In Balko's article, he establishes credibility with his audience by presenting detailed facts about the government's current plans for stopping the obesity epidemic saying that they are, "agitating for a panoply of government anti-obesity initiatives, including prohibiting junk food in school vending machines, federal funding for new bike trails and sidewalks, more demanding labels on foodstuffs, and prodding the food industry into more 'responsible' behavior" (466). This evidence proves to Balko's audience that he has an understanding of current government initiatives to stop the obesity epidemic. He also establishes trust with his readers by showing that he is looking out for their best interests by focusing on the financial effects of government intervention on the reader.

In addition, he appeals to logic by pointing out that, "President Bush earmarked $200 million in his budget for anti-obesity measures" (467). He uses this evidence to show his readers exactly how much government involvement there is in trying to stop the obesity epidemic. After presenting the amount of money put towards fighting obesity, he argues that the government getting involved in this matter presents no incentive for people to, "put down the cheeseburger" (467). He uses this incentive argument to show that if the government continues to be involved in the obesity epidemic there will be no incentive for people to stay healthy because there's no reason to. However, if the government steps away from the problem, there will be financial incentive for people to live a healthy lifestyle. Balko then discusses how government involvement is requiring people to be responsible for someone else's health. He uses all of this evidence to show his readers that government involvement in private healthcare is not helping to solve the obesity epidemic but is, in fact, making matters worse. Balko also uses his evidence for how much money is being put towards fighting obesity and the government's involvement in private healthcare to show that the government is not encouraging a sense of responsibility among consumers but is instead feeding the problem. All of Balko's evidence proves to his audience that the government should not be involved with the obesity epidemic as it will only make matters worse.

Furthermore, he tries to invoke discomfort and anger in his audience. He makes his audience uncomfortable by describing the government's involvement with the obesity epidemic as, "bringing government between you and your waistline" (466). He then invokes anger when he says, "Our lawmakers just enacted a huge entitlement that requires some people to pay for other people's medicine" (467). Balko uses these appeals to emotion because he knows that his audience of libertarians do not want the government involved with their private health matters. Balko is invoking anger over having to pay for someone else's medicine. He also attempts to make his audience angry by examining the intrusion of government into private healthcare. Balko knows that his audience will be very upset with the idea of paying for someone else's medicine and having the government involved with their private health matters.

Although Balko does a very good job of presenting his arguments, he does have a few gaps in logic. First, Balko makes a gap in logic known as a slippery slope. A slippery slope fallacy is when someone assumes that one action will lead to a continuous chain of actions. This fallacy occurs when Balko is describing how government involvement in private health, "paves the way for even more federal restrictions on consumer choice and civil liberties" (468). Although Balko has no evidence that this increase in federal restrictions will happen, he makes the assumption that government involvement will lead to more regulations. Balko also creates a non sequitur fallacy in his article, an argument that justifies something through irrelevant reasons, which occurs when he talks about how the, "largest organization of trial lawyers," are encouraging each other to, "weed jury pools of candidates who show 'personal responsibility bias'" (468). Although this information might be of interest to his audience, this point has nothing to do with the rest of his arguments. However, even though Balko had fallacies in his article, these fallacies would have no effect on his audience. In Balko's article, his gaps in logic would be completely overlooked by his audience. His audience already believes that government involvement will lead to more restrictions, so his Slippery Slope would only encourage their beliefs. His Non Sequitur would also have no effect on his arguments; it would only encourage his readers preconceived ideas regarding the industries attempt to cancel out personal responsibility.

Overall, Balko makes very convincing arguments for his specific audience. He is able to present detailed facts about the government's involvement in the obesity epidemic which ultimately builds his credibility and a sense of trust. Balko is also able to appeal to his audience's sense of logic by connecting the government's involvement to a lack of incentive for people to maintain healthy lifestyles. He is then able to incite a sense of anger and fear in his audience through the discussion of having to pay for someone else's poor choices and the government's involvement in private health matters. Finally, even though Balko does present two flaws in logic, he is still able to make very convincing arguments for his audience through ethos, logos, and pathos. Therefore, his argument is effective because he knows exactly how to connect with what his audience already values and believes.

Works Cited

Balko, Radley. "What You Eat Is Your Business." *They Say/I Say With Readings*, 3rd ed., edited by Cathy Birkenstein and Russel Durst, W.W. Norton, 2015, pp. 466–469.

JAMES B. HARR, III { *Logical Fallacies*

Fallacies are argumentative errors. They are often committed unknowingly, and to the unaware and unprepared audience, these erroneous arguments often appear valid. Fallacies tend to weaken or even undermine an argument by relying on misdirection and oversimplification. As children, we often hear and commit fallacies in arguments with friends, family, and authority figures: "But everyone else has one," "I know you are, but what am I?," "If you didn't take my toy, then who did?," "She got to do it, so why can't I?" Although most of us have progressed beyond these juvenile examples, more refined manifestations can be found in everyday arguments. Politicians, particularly, are guilty of committing fallacies to gain voter approval. Here are some of the more common logical fallacies:

- Slippery slope: One decision will lead to an exaggerated result (*If Wake Tech forbids the use of nicotine on campus, it is only a matter of time before they ban coffee because it contains caffeine.*)

- Ad hominem: Attacking the person rather than the argument (*My instructor is a Democrat, so I'm sure he knows nothing about business ethics.*)

- Non sequitur: Two ideas are falsely connected (*She goes to a community college, so she must have been a bad student in high school.*)

- Bandwagon: Accepting something because it is popular (*Everyone is skipping class this Friday. You should too.*)

- Straw Man: Redirecting an argument towards one which can easily be disputed (Speaker 1: *The state government should look into lowering college tuition costs.* Speaker 2: *So you're advocating taking money away from senior citizens and reallocating it to young people? Is that the way the state should treat the elderly?*)

- Post hoc (ergo propter hoc): Two ideas are related and thus directly affect each other (*Because I wear my socks inside out when I fly, I have never been in a plane crash.*)

- Scare tactics: Using fear as a way to manipulate (*This candidate wants to open up our borders, allowing terrorists free access to our nation.*)

- Either/Or or False Dichotomy: Presenting only two options when many could exist (*You either earn a degree or you work a menial job for the rest of your life.*)

Learning about the types of fallacies and their common uses is the best way to identify and refute them. It is also important to note that several fallacies can be committed at the same time. For example:

As the majority of Americans know, if you support a candidate who is nothing more than a self-indulging idiot, you vote for an individual who supports the 2nd amendment and ultimately will

drive us to martial law where no one will feel safe. Is that what 5
you want? Anarchy in the United States? You either support
anarchy or you support this candidate's opponent.

In this statement, we have committed bandwagon appeals
("as the majority of Americans know..."), ad hominem
("self-indulging idiot"), slippery slope (supporting the second amendment *will* lead to martial law), scare tactics/fear
mongering ("no one will feel safe"), and straw man (changing
the topic from a candidate's platform to wishing anarchy on
the United States). Studying and identifying the commonly
abused fallacies will strengthen your ability both to refute a
poorly structured argument and to avoid making those same
mistakes.

For additional information on logical fallacies, see Jane.
A. Aaron. *The Little, Brown Handbook, Brief Version.* 6th ed.,
Pearson, 2017, Section 11e, pp. 111–115.

JOHN ETHERIDGE { *Classical Argument*

THE CONTEXT

In the first year of the Peloponnesian War, with its citizens anxious about the fate of their city and full of sorrow over those many men already lost in battle, Athens held its traditional funeral for the fallen. The bodies of the war dead had been laid out in tents; offerings for the deceased had been made; the families of the fallen and all the war-weary citizens of Athens had processed to the Kerameikos, the section of the city that contained the honorary graveyard much like our own Arlington National Cemetery. Pericles, the esteemed Athenian leader, rose to deliver the traditional funeral oration for the dead.

What does one say in such a moment, when so many have died and the outcome of the conflict is unclear? *How* does one say it in a meaningful way that sounds neither trite nor dismissive?

The Athenian historian Thucydides was present that day at the Kerameikos, and in his work *The History of the Peloponnesian War,* he recalled the solemn scene. When Pericles rose to speak, his skill and training in the use of language and argument and his own personal character (his "ethos") allowed him to deliver a meaningful speech which honored the dead ("with life and limb [they] stood stoutly to their task…at the crowning moment not of fear but of glory" (335)), comforted the grieving ("be comforted by the fair fame of these your sons" (339)), exhorted the war-weary citizens ("for Athens alone among her contemporaries, when put to the test, is superior to the report of her" (331)), and honored the city of Athens ("when the vision of her greatness has inspired you, reflect that all this has been acquired by men of courage who knew their duty and in the hour of conflict were moved by a high sense of honour, who…were resolved that at least their country should not find herself deserted by their valour, but freely sacrificed to her the fairest offering it was in their power to give" (335-6)).

Classical Argument, such as Pericles's oration, is not merely a type of essay organization, as it is often presented in modern textbooks, nor is it a collection of Latinate terms to be memorized in a rote manner. Classical rhetoric (of which argument is the primary part) is a fundamental brick in the foundation of Western thinking, a vital yet increasingly forgotten effort to create civil and productive public discourse.

THE FIVE CANONS

Building on the work of Aristotle and Cicero, the Roman 5 rhetorician Quintilian codified classical rhetoric into five "canons" (e.g., categories) for creating, arranging, and presenting argument:

- *Inventio*—invention, creation, or discovery
- *Dispositio*—organization
- *Elocutio*—style

- *Pronuntiatio* or *actio*—delivery
- *Memoria*—memory

As ancient rhetoric revolved primarily around the spoken word, two of these canons (*memoria* and *pronuntiatio*) apply only to spoken rhetoric. Thus, the written rhetorical situation involves three canons (inventio, dispositio, and elocutio) Elocutio deals with competence in diction, grammar, and coherence, skills learned in foundational composition courses. Inventio and dispositio are therefore the two canons vital for the modern student's understanding of classical argument.

Canon 1: Inventio

For our purposes, the most important canon is inventio, the creation, discovery, or invention of an argument. Many of the techniques of inventio are not exclusive to classical argument, and so still prove useful in most rhetorical situations. We break down inventio into three "toolboxes" that you might go to as you think about how to effectively construct your argument.

TOOLBOX 1: A STRONG THESIS

Classical argument typically begins with a tentative thesis, usually, though not always, a one-sentence claim. It should be narrow, clear, and specific. The thesis should obviously be debatable, and it should be able to fit into a "should" or "should not" statement. This sentence does not need to include those words, but if you are having trouble creating a thesis statement, you might use one of those forms to help you produce a workable thesis.

TOOLBOX 2: THREE MODES OF PERSUASION

Teachers of rhetoric such as Aristotle, Cicero, and Quintilian 10
identify three primary ways to convince an audience to believe
or to act as we wish them to. It is by means of these three
"modes of persuasion" that we prove our thesis, and it is the
context of the situation which dictates how much of one or
the other we use.

Ethos

Quintilian, whose works on rhetoric formed the basis for
education for centuries, taught that the most foundational part
of an argument was the ethos of the speaker/writer: "he who
would have men trust his judgment as to what is expedient
and honorable should possess and be regarded as possessing
genuine wisdom and excellence of character" (485). If you
want to convince other people of what is just and necessary,
then you yourself must have and display good moral character
(*ethos*). Additionally, the appeal to ethos must show that the
writer is genuinely familiar with and concerned with the audience's real needs and desires (see also p. A-249).

Appeal by means of ethos may play out differently depending on the situation, but here are some possible ways to display ethos:

- Avoid fallacies and underhanded or lazy techniques;
- Properly integrate and cite testimony (source material);
- Apeal to the general welfare of the whole audience, not
  just a group;

- As appropriate, appeal directly to ethical standards (justice, temperance, fortitude, wisdom).

Why is ethos important? Manipulation by means of argument is as old as language itself. For example, in the Judeo-Christian story about the fall of man, it is not an act of violence or of lust or of injustice which brings evil into the created world. Rather, it is the serpent's manipulative argument in human language that leads to Adam and Eve's decision to sin against their Creator.

Pathos

The appeal to emotion (*pathos*) is the most powerful of the 15 modes of persuasion. Pathos requires no training or experience, and can be felt even by children completely unschooled in argumentative techniques. Its power and pervasiveness are the sources of its effectiveness (see also p. A-251).

To be sure, we ought not to reject pathos as a means of persuasion, as many situations exist in which pathos is a vital element. If we think again about the situation in which Pericles found himself delivering the Athenian funeral oration, we can see clearly that an appeal to pathos is, in fact, very necessary for that rhetorical context.

In deciding when and how to appeal to pathos, we must consider first what pathos does. To put it simply, our ethos establishes our trust and concern for the good; logos convinces the audience of the truth of our claim; and pathos moves our audience's will to action. To consider Pericles again, he appeals to the pathos of his audience so that (a) those grieving might be comforted and not consumed by their grief, and (b) that the citizenry might be inspired to continue their support of the war effort. In essence, pathos moves the audience to *do* something, not merely to *believe* something.

Consider the following tips for *how* and *where* to include appeals to pathos:

- Use powerful, vivid, descriptive diction and imagery
- Use personal anecdotes, examples, or narratives to engage the reader
- Use pathos in the introductory and concluding paragraphs, as emotion will help draw your reader in and can leave a strong final impression

Finally, the following two principles ought to be followed [20] when appealing to pathos:

- Appeal to pathos must be appropriate to the situation. For example, the Funeral Oration of Pericles requires emotional appeal, whereas an essay on the use of traffic cameras would likely not utilize much appeal to pathos.
- Appeal to pathos must be measured. Any fallacies of "loaded language" should be avoided.

Logos

While ethos is the most foundational means of persuasion and pathos the most powerful, logos is the most substantive. It is the primary tool used by writers, especially in the academic arena, and so it ought to be honed most sharply. Here we present the three most basic and most commonly used patterns of logic (see also p. A-250).

Pattern 1: Definition or Generalization

When we make an argument by definition, we draw a conclusion by saying what a thing actually is, or by placing it in a category. It is the most basic way we think about the world. We place an unknown item into a category of like things, or we divide it away from a category of unlike things. Thus, any time we use definitions, categorizations, or generalizations, we make an argument by *definition*.

Of course, there are shades of soundness to an argument by definition. This kind of argument is sound if (a) the unknown thing is placed (or excluded from) the appropriate category, or (b) the category is large and representative enough.

In his Funeral Oration, Pericles argues by definition when he attempts to place Athenians in a category distinct from other peoples. Thucydides records the Athenian leader's series of characteristics common to Athenians, saying, for example, that "we are lovers of the beauty" (327) and "for it is not by receiving kindness, but by conferring it, that we acquire our friends" (329). In offering these and other defining traits of the Athenian citizen, Pericles draws a precise picture of what he thinks an Athenian actually is.

We can also convince our audience by using the pattern of generalization, which categorizes in a way similar to definition. Pericles, after spending a good deal of time praising Athens itself, explains his purpose by saying, "for when I lauded the city, that was but the praise wherewith the brave deeds of these men and men like them have already adorned her" (Thucydides 333). Each of the dead is part of the Athenian whole, and so as Pericles praises the whole, he praises its parts—the praise belongs to the whole and to the parts of the whole.

Another notable example of a generalization would be a poll. Some polls are sound (not *certain*, but *sound*), and others are not. The soundness of a poll depends on how many people were polled, how representative the polled people were of the population as a whole, and how well-constructed the poll was. If all of those elements meet statistical and rhetorical standards, then the poll would be sound.

Pattern 2: Analogy (or Comparison/Contrast)

Our second basic pattern of thought is analogy. When we draw an analogy, we draw conclusions about one thing based on a comparison to a second thing. In some ways, this is like definition, but the distinction for analogy is that the comparison is a "one-to-one" analysis, whereas definition deals in categories.

When we make comparisons, we attempt to find two things that share properties. In order to constitute a sound analogy, those properties should be relevant to the conclusion drawn and as numerous as possible. The first criteria is much more important, as a comparison between two shared things that depends on two properties very relevant to the conclusion would be more sound than one that depends on a dozen properties that are not relevant to the conclusion.

To illustrate, consider Rev. Martin Luther King, Jr.'s 30 expression of disappointment in the church in his "Letter from Birmingham Jail":

> There was a time when the church was very powerful—in the time when the early Christians rejoiced at being deemed worthy

to suffer for what they believed. In those days the church was not merely a thermometer that recorded the ideas and principles of popular opinion; it was a thermostat that transformed the mores of society. . . . Things are different now. So often the contemporary church is a weak, ineffectual voice with an uncertain sound. So often it is an archdefender of the status quo. Far from being disturbed by the presence of the church, the power structure of the average community is consoled by the church's silent—and often even vocal—sanction of things as they are. (134)

Here, King creates an analogy between the church of the past and the church of the present. He does not need to expressly state why this analogy is legitimate, as it is understood that these two institutions share many relevant properties (because, of course, they are the same institution, just in different time periods). Instead, he develops the contrasts between the early church and the modern church to show the moral poverty of the modern church.

Specifically, he suggests the early church acted more bravely on principle and, in doing so, "transformed the mores of society." The modern church, however, not only acquiesces to the "status quo" of the modern world, but in fact offers "sanction of things as they are." Thus, using reasoning by analogy, King attempts to hold up the church of his day as inferior to the early church in its ability and desire to pursue justice. Considering his stated audience (the clergymen to whom the letter is addressed) and one of his implied audiences (the white moderate Southern Christian), King sees this analogy as both a stinging rebuke and an encouragement to action.

Pattern 3: Causal Relationship (Cause/Effect)

Causal reasoning means drawing conclusions based on causal relationships (i.e., cause and effect relationships). Good writers avoid drawing conclusions based on coincidental occurrences.

In "Letter from Birmingham Jail," King relies on causal 35 reasoning to illustrate that the form of nonviolent protest he advocates is far preferable to the alternative: "If this philosophy had not emerged, by now many streets of the South would, I am convinced, be flowing with blood. And I am further convinced that if our white brothers. . . . refuse to support our nonviolent efforts, millions of Negroes will, out of frustration and despair, seek solace and security in black-nationalist ideologies—a development that would inevitably lead to a frightening racial nightmare." (132)

The chain of reasoning is fairly easy to identify in this passage, with King forecasting a dire effect ("frightening racial nightmare") if the path of nonviolent protest is not supported, particularly by the white moderate and white church. Note that King *directly* links nonviolent protest to the avoidance of the "racial nightmare," arguing strongly that the *only* manner of producing a positive outcome (avoidance of racial nightmare) is support of nonviolent protest.

Causal reasoning is often the most easily identifiable and easiest to deploy in argument, so consideration of causes and effects ought to be at the forefront of your mind as you construct your ideas.

TOOLBOX 3: TESTIMONY

The final toolbox writers can deploy to prove a claim is what ancient thinkers called testimony and what we call research.

Aristotle called this the "non-artistic" means of persuasion, as research deals in objective evidence and witness testimony. Classical argument uses testimony in two primary ways:

- To confirm one's own claims using the claims of some other witness (a trusted expert);

- To refute one's opponent's claims by drawing attention especially to that opponent's fallacies or ineffective logic.

Canon 2: Dispositio

Dispositio is the organization of an argument. This method of organizing will likely seem familiar to students, since it has been the standard manner of presenting the order of an argument. In classical rhetoric, dispositio has five possible components: 40

- Introduction
- Statement of Facts (also called *narratio*)
- Confirmation
- Refutation
- Conclusion

In general practice in college essays, an argument requires at least an introduction, a conclusion, and either confirmation or refutation. Of course, an argument can contain all five of these elements or only one of them, depending on the topic and context. Techniques for constructing introductions and conclusions likely were covered in previous English courses, and those same tactics apply to (and are usually borrowed from) classical argument.

STATEMENT OF FACTS

The statement of facts is an explanation of the circumstances and details of the question at hand. It is an informative reminder, especially for an audience who may not be immediately familiar with the subject at hand. For placement, one option is to include the statement of facts in a single paragraph that comes after the introduction; it could also be scattered throughout the essay if the audience is already familiar with the topic.

If you choose to include a statement of facts, it should be lucid, brief, and objective.

CONFIRMATION AND REFUTATION

Confirmation and Refutation will make up the body of your 45 essay. Confirmation presents your supporting claims along with proof of those claims. It is the "positive" aspect of argumentation ("Here is why my argument is true."). It effectively deploys all three of the toolboxes mentioned in the inventio discussion above. The actual organization of the body paragraphs varies by circumstance, topic, requirements, and individual choice.

Refutation, as the name suggests, attempts to undercut the opposition argument, and could be seen as the "negative" form of argumentation ("here is why my opponent's argument is not true"). Refutation could be done in any one of several ways:

- Point out weak or poorly-used evidence (modes of persuasion or testimony);
- Present stronger, alternative evidence;

- Expose possible logical fallacies;
- Provide counter-examples or counter-consequences.

Classical argument is typically presented as a particular organizational model for argument. In reality, *dispositio* is treated by classical authors as a complement to *inventio*. Aristotle, for example, intended his treatment of organization in argument to be included in a different book than his material on *inventio*. Additionally, *dispositio* was consistently seen as being governed not by external form as is often presented, but rather as being governed by the necessities of the situation and the preferences of the writer, all in order to achieve maximum effect.

CONCLUSION

Ancient philosophers and rhetoricians—Socrates, Plato, Aristotle, Cicero, and Quintilian, among others—took seriously the role of words spoken or written for public consumption. To varying degrees, each was concerned with the frightful possibility of an immoral man skilled in oratorical style manipulating citizens untrained in logic and ethics. On the other hand, each also understood the potential beauty of a city skilled in the art of rhetoric—a citizenry moored in the virtues of justice, temperance, wisdom, and courage, engaging in rigorous yet civil public discourse in order to bring about what is good for the city and her citizens, a goal that historically has been central to a college education.

Works Cited

Aristotle. *On Rhetoric.* Translated by George Kennedy. Oxford UP, 2007.

King Jr., Martin Luther. "Letter from Birmingham Jail." *Wake Tech Reader.* Revised Edition. Cengage, 2015, pp.125–137.

Quintilian. *The Institutio Oratoria of Quintilian.* Translated by H.E. Butler. Vol. 1. New York, G.P. Putnam's Sons, 1920. *Google Books*, https://books.google.com/books?id=8AMdAAAAYAAJ&printsec=frontcover#v=onepage&q&f=true

Thucydides. *The History of the Peloponnesian War.* Translated by C.F. Smith. Book II. *Loeb Classical Library.* Harvard UP, 1928.

WIN NEAGLE { *Toulmin Model of Argument*

While humans have a distinguished record of incredible feats of reason, our individual perspectives tend to be formed more by instinct and emotion than by rational reflection. As we attempt to distinguish beliefs founded on sound, critical thought from those derived from less rational paths, clearly stating why we believe what we believe can be quite useful. The founder of formal logic, Aristotle, recognized this value more than 2,300 years ago when he proposed the use of syllogisms to present arguments for consideration. A syllogism is a deductive scheme constructed from premises (usually two or more) that lead to a conclusion, as in the following example:

> All humans are mortal.
> Jane is a human.
> Therefore, Jane is mortal.

To be sound, a syllogism must have factually accurate premises that lead to the eventual conclusion in a logically valid manner. The syllogism is a simple but powerful device for evaluating truthfulness, and British philosopher Stephen Toulmin (1922–2009) based his model for philosophical reasoning on this useful tool.

In the Toulmin model, a claim is supported by grounds (or data): *The county should implement a higher minimum wage because doing so would reduce homelessness and attract a pool of dedicated workers to the area.*

Warrants show that the grounds are, indeed, relevant to the claim: *Roughly 25% of the county's homeless hold full-time jobs.*

Backing answers any further questions regarding the rel- 5 evance of the grounds: *Availability of affordable housing has decreased in the county over the last decade.*

When putting forth an argument, we can anticipate counterarguments and respond to them. In the Toulmin model these responses are referred to as rebuttals: *While some claim that raising the minimum wage will lead to localized inflation, offsetting any potential gains, this has not proven to be the case in other communities where higher minimum wages have been implemented.*

Upon reflection, we may find that our claim needs to be refined. Toulmin referred to such equivocations as qualifiers: *The county should implement a higher minimum wage because doing so __might__ reduce homelessness and attract a pool of dedicated workers to the area.*

The power of the Toulmin argument, like the syllogism, lies in its simplicity, providing no room to hide irrational pleas and logical fallacies, thus forcing us to take a clear and honest look at our reasoning for accepting the claim that has been proposed.

DR. PHILLIP SCOTT DENNIS $\left\{\begin{array}{l} \textit{Rogerian} \\ \textit{Argument} \end{array}\right.$

Critical thinking means opening up our minds to diverse and unfamiliar points of view. The kinds of exploration we undertake in English 112 can also require us to test our own assumptions and sometimes reshape or reject ideas we may have previously held dear or even considered unquestionable. In addition, critical thinking often compels us to realize that issues, ideas, or circumstances we may have considered simple or straightforward are, in fact, complex, requiring more nuanced thought or a deeper consideration. The ability to recognize these complexities and use this recognition to cultivate more in-depth understanding will help us negotiate our complicated world in more informed, objective, and unprejudiced ways.

Carl Rogers was a famous twentieth-century psychologist who developed a method of mediation in which two people in a disagreement or conflict were each asked to state the positions of the other person prior to verbalizing their own positions. Rogers found that asking someone to first consider an opposite perspective led to better outcomes in negotiating conflicts or misunderstandings (86). By interweaving seemingly contradictory perspectives, opponents could often find workable compromises they had before been unable to reach.

Scholars quickly discovered that this technique might also help writers invent nuanced solutions to complex problems and developed the Rogerian argument as a tool for exploring such issues and reaching compromise solutions (Brent).

ROGERIAN STRUCTURE

Rogerian argument integrates multiple viewpoints in order to arrive at a middle ground, or compromise solution, rather than to produce a "winner" and "loser." This type of argument is often distinguished from "Classical" argument, which typically incorporates opposing or divergent viewpoints only to point out their weaknesses, or simply as a means to support the dominant thesis. Unlike Rogerian arguments, a "Classical" argument typically states a clear thesis near the beginning, including as support only that evidence which best reinforces or upholds that thesis, and airing carefully selected opposing viewpoints only for the purposes of counterargument. Rogerian arguments, on the other hand, incorporate multiple perspectives, not just to dissect or to oppose them, but rather to integrate diverse positions into a compromise, or middle ground, that also serves as the main thesis, or claim, of the essay.

Rogerian arguments also differ in structure from more traditional arguments. Instead of presenting the thesis in the introductory material, the Rogerian writer often chooses to defer the thesis statement until the *end* of the argument, waiting until many diverse perspectives have been explored *before* disclosing the main point of the essay. Rogerian writers typically capture the reader's attention with an engaging introduction, and then, rather than stating the thesis overtly, provide the audience with a general discussion of the issue. The object of this type of introduction is to "set the stage" before presenting a wide variety of viewpoints from diverse (and even diametrically opposed) perspectives, leading to a compromise, middle-ground conclusion.

A CONTEMPORARY EXAMPLE: IMMIGRATION POLICY

One function of the Rogerian approach is to reconcile extreme positions. This can be especially useful for exploring issues prone to "False Dichotomy" fallacies (also known as "False Dilemmas," "Either/Or," or "Black and White" fallacies), where potential arguments are falsely restricted to invite only binary "yes or no" or "pro or con" responses. Rogerian arguments are often used to illuminate these types of issues, extracting meaningful compromises from the integration of seemingly oppositional viewpoints.

U.S. immigration policy is one contemporary issue that can elicit polarized or even antagonistic stances. In order to persuade a broadly diverse audience, a well-reasoned Rogerian argument seeks to moderate between many possible positions to suggest a policy amenable to a wide audience. To most readers, for example, a policy position which prohibits immigration completely would seem extreme—so, too, would a position which advocates for free and unrestricted immigration. In between these two positions, however, lies a wide range of potential policies ripe for exploration. A Rogerian argument about immigration policy first considers a spectrum of divergent viewpoints, then creates a policy recommendation that incorporates differing concerns.

In such a case, an arguer might first engage the reader with an impactful, attention-getting introduction and then provide the reader with some background information demonstrating the importance of sound immigration policy or explaining briefly the history of the issue. Next, the arguer would integrate ideas backed by research exploring differing perspectives on the effects of immigration—on culture, economy, government, or health care, just to name a few possibilities. These divergent positions should be supported by evidence gathered from credible sources (and incorporated into the essay using correct documentation and citation). To avoid bias, and to convince the reader of his or her credibility, the author should make a deliberate effort to represent voices from multiple stakeholders; some examples might include immigrants, policymakers, workers, foreign governments, border and other law enforcement officials, health care employees, or social workers. This researched support might either be organized according to subtopic, or be divided roughly into "pro-immigration" and "anti-immigration" stances, with the idea that the final thesis will bring various perspectives together, presenting a compromise workable to all sides.

Finally, the conclusion would offer a detailed, nuanced policy argument (or *thesis*) that proposes a "middle-ground" policy or solution. In this case, for example, an author might offer a policy that encourages legal immigration, but with some carefully explained restrictions or exceptions. Based on this recommendation, the arguer would of course want to discuss how such a policy might affect the economy, employment, culture, health care, or governance, consistent with the issues discussed in the body of the essay. Though this policy may not satisfy all viewpoints regarding immigration, it is likely that such a compromise position would be acceptable to a broad diversity of readers—whose opinions would likely lie somewhere *in between* polar extremes.

CONCLUSION

Based on the belief that a combining of diverse perspectives leads to more equitable outcomes, Rogerian arguments are especially good for exploring complicated issues with diverse stakeholders and widely differing perspectives. Though not useful in all contexts or for all issues, Rogerian arguments are nonetheless an important tool for students of argumentation. The main elements of Rogerian argument—voicing, hearing, and considering differing viewpoints in search of compromise—are hallmarks of sophisticated critical thinking and a necessity for success in English 112 and beyond.

Works Cited

Brent, Douglas. "Rogerian Rhetoric: An Alternative to Traditional Rhetoric." University of Calgary Department of Communication and Culture. Web. 2-Jan-2017.

Rogers, Carl R. "Communication: its Blocking and its Facilitation." *ETC: A Review of General Semantics*, vol. 9, no. 2, 1952, pp. 83–88. Web. 2-Jan-2017.

READINGS

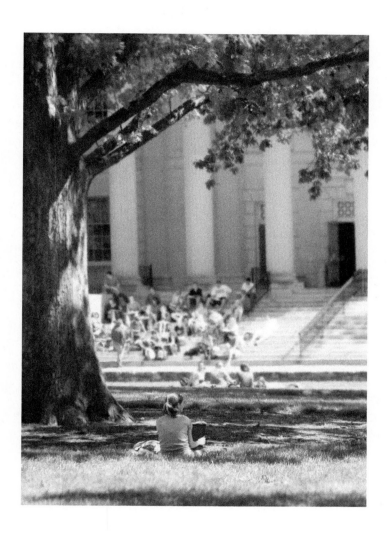

SIXTEEN

IS COLLEGE THE BEST OPTION?

AMERICAN SOCIETY MAY BE DIVIDED IN MANY WAYS, but not when it comes to college. From a very early age, we get the message that going to college is a crucial step in life. We hear this message regularly from our families, our schools, our communities. We see it constantly in the media: movies, television shows, sports broadcasts, newspapers, magazines, and websites all show the allure and advantages of going to college. Even on the highways, billboards portray attractive, smiling, confident, intelligent-looking students on tree-lined campuses promoting the virtues of particular colleges: strong academics, excellent career opportunities, affordable tuition. Indeed, most young people in the United States grow up to see college as inevitable.

But in addition to the success stories, we see occasional glimpses of another side of the college story: graduates unable to find good jobs, or any job at all; students with large college debts that can take years, even decades, to pay off; uncaring professors, huge classes, maze-like bureaucracies, distracted advisors; students who for a variety of reasons find themselves in academic trouble. As with all paths in life, it's possible to take a wrong turn in college, so it's advisable for anyone who's contemplating attending college to have specific, well-considered reasons for pursuing a so-called higher education, as well as a plan, regularly checked and updated, for how best to succeed.

The readings in this chapter focus on the present state of higher education in the United States and examine the potential benefits and pitfalls of going to college. The chapter begins with a report on a study showing that while college graduates on average make significantly more money than high-school graduates do, there is large variation in the return on investment based on such factors as college attended, major, whether or not the student graduates, and occupation. This report is followed by an essay by Sanford Ungar, a former college president, about the value of a college education steeped in the liberal arts, as opposed to the preprofessional training that many students now prefer. Political scientist Charles Murray advances the view that far too many American students currently go on to college but would be better off attending a vocational program or going right to work after high school. Liz Addison, drawing upon her own experience, articulates the often underappreciated value of a community college education.

Several other authors focus on ways that the faculty and the institution as a whole can support student success. College president Freeman Hrabowski argues that while it's easy to lament how expensive and dubious a college degree is, that degree ultimately prepares people not just for a career, but for life. And First Lady Michelle Obama pays tribute to the graduates of one university for their commitment to education and to helping others find opportunities to succeed.

Finally, two pieces argue that education can take place in settings other than college and about topics other than "academic" ones. Gerald Graff suggests that it matters less whether we read *Macbeth* or a Marvel comic book, as long as we approach what we read with a critical eye and question it in analytical, intellectual ways. And Mike Rose makes the case that people in blue-collar occupations who never attend college nonetheless develop sophisticated knowledge of how to do their work.

As a college student yourself, you'll find plenty to think about in this chapter—and on its companion blog, **theysayiblog.com.**

Should Everyone Go to College?

STEPHANIE OWEN AND ISABEL SAWHILL

—◻—

Summary

FOR THE PAST FEW DECADES, it has been widely argued that
a college degree is a prerequisite to entering the middle class
in the United States. Study after study reminds us that
higher education is one of the best investments we can
make, and President Obama has called it "an economic
imperative." We all know that, on average, college graduates
make significantly more money over their lifetimes than those
with only a high school education. What gets less attention

See pp. 25–27
on introducing
an ongoing
debate.

———

STEPHANIE OWEN AND ISABEL SAWHILL are the authors of *Should
Everyone Go to College?*, a report published in 2013 by the Brookings Institution, a centrist think tank in Washington, D.C. Owen
was a senior research assistant at Brookings' Center on Children
and Families at the time of the report's publication and currently
serves as a research associate at the Urban Institute, a nonpartisan
center for research on the problems of urban communities. Sawhill is
codirector of the Center on Children and Families and a senior fellow
in economic studies at Brookings.

is the fact that not all college degrees or college graduates are equal. There is enormous variation in the so-called return to education depending on factors such as institution attended, field of study, whether a student graduates, and post-graduation occupation. While the average return to obtaining a college degree is clearly positive, we emphasize that it is not universally so. For certain schools, majors, occupations, and individuals, college may not be a smart investment. By telling all young people that they should go to college no matter what, we are actually doing some of them a disservice.

The Rate of Return on Education

One way to estimate the value of education is to look at the increase in earnings associated with an additional year of schooling. However, correlation is not causation, and getting at the true causal effect of education on earnings is not so easy. The main problem is one of selection: if the smartest, most motivated people are both more likely to go to college and more likely to be financially successful, then the observed difference in earnings by years of education doesn't measure the true effect of college.

Researchers have attempted to get around this problem of causality by employing a number of clever techniques, including, for example, comparing identical twins with different levels of education. The best studies suggest that the return to an additional year of school is around 10 percent. If we apply this 10 percent rate to the median earnings of about $30,000 for a 25- to 34-year-old high school graduate working full time in 2010, this implies that a year of college increases earnings by $3,000, and four years increases them by $12,000. Notice that this amount is less than the raw differences in earnings between high school graduates and bachelor's degree holders of $15,000, but it is in the same ballpark. Similarly, the raw difference between high school graduates and associate's degree holders is about $7,000, but a return of 10% would predict the causal effect of those additional two years to be $6,000.

There are other factors to consider. The cost of college matters as well: the more someone has to pay to attend, the lower the net benefit of attending. Furthermore, we have to factor in the opportunity cost of college, measured as the foregone earnings a student gives up when he or she leaves or delays entering the workforce in order to attend school. Using average earnings for 18- and 19-year-olds and 20- and 21-year-olds with high school degrees (including those working part-time or not at all), Michael Greenstone and Adam Looney of Brookings' Hamilton Project calculate an opportunity cost of $54,000 for a four-year degree.

In this brief, we take a rather narrow view of the value of 5 a college degree, focusing on the earnings premium. However, there are many non-monetary benefits of schooling which are harder to measure but no less important. Research suggests that additional education improves overall wellbeing by affecting things like job satisfaction, health, marriage, parenting, trust, and social interaction. Additionally, there are social benefits to education, such as reduced crime rates and higher political participation. We also do not want to dismiss personal preferences, and we acknowledge that many people derive value from their careers in ways that have nothing to do with money. While beyond the scope of this piece, we do want to point out that these noneconomic factors can change the cost-benefit calculus.

As noted above, the gap in annual earnings between young high school graduates and bachelor's degree holders working full time is $15,000. What's more, the earnings premium associated with a college degree grows over a lifetime. Hamilton Project research shows that 23- to 25-year-olds with bachelor's degrees make $12,000 more than high school graduates but by age 50, the gap has grown to $46,500 (Figure 1). When we look at lifetime earnings—the sum of earnings over a career—the total premium is $570,000 for a bachelor's degree and $170,000 for an associate's degree. Compared to the average up-front cost of four years of college (tuition plus opportunity cost) of $102,000, the Hamilton Project is not alone in arguing that investing in college provides "a tremendous return."

It is always possible to quibble over specific calculations, but it is hard to deny that, on average, the benefits of a college degree far outweigh the costs. The key phrase here is "on average." The purpose of this brief is to highlight the reasons why,

Figure 1. Earning Trajectories by Educational Attainment

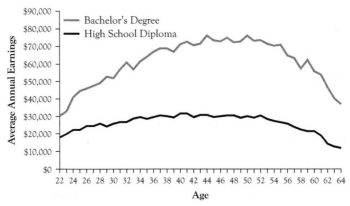

Source: Greenstone and Looney (2011).
Note: Sample includes all civilian U.S. citizens, excluding those in school. Annual earnings are averaged over the entire sample, including those without work. Source: March CPS 2007–2010.

for a given individual, the benefits may not outweigh the costs. We emphasize that a 17- or 18-year-old deciding whether and where to go to college should carefully consider his or her own likely path of education and career before committing a considerable amount of time and money to that degree. With tuitions rising faster than family incomes, the typical college student is now more dependent than in the past on loans, creating serious risks for the individual student and perhaps for the system as a whole, should widespread defaults occur in the future. Federal student loans now total close to $1 trillion, larger than credit card debt or auto loans and second only to mortgage debt on household balance sheets.

Variation in the Return to Education

It is easy to imagine hundreds of dimensions on which college degrees and their payoffs could differ. Ideally, we'd like to be able to look into a crystal ball and know which individual school will give the highest net benefit for a given student with her unique strengths, weaknesses, and interests. Of course, we are not able to do this. What we can do is lay out several key dimensions that seem to significantly affect the return to a college degree. These include school type, school selectivity level, school cost and financial aid, college major, later occupation, and perhaps most importantly, the probability of completing a degree.

Variation by School Selectivity

Mark Schneider of the American Enterprise Institute (AEI) and the American Institutes for Research (AIR) used longitudinal data from the Baccalaureate and Beyond survey to calculate lifetime earnings for bachelor's earners by type of institution attended, then compared them to the lifetime earnings of high school graduates. The difference (after accounting for tuition costs and discounting to a present value) is the value of a bachelor's degree. For every type of school (categorized by whether the school was a public institution or a nonprofit private institution and by its selectivity) this value is positive, but it varies widely. People who attended the most selective private schools have a lifetime earnings premium of over $620,000 (in 2012 dollars). For those who attended a minimally selective or open admission private school, the premium is only a third of that. Schneider performed a similar exercise with campus-level data on college graduates (compiled by the online salary information company PayScale), calculating the return on investment (ROI) of a bachelor's degree (Figure 2). These calculations suggest that public schools tend to have higher ROIs than private schools, and more selective schools offer higher returns than less selective ones. Even within a school type and selectivity category, the variation is striking. For example, the average ROI for a competitive public school in 2010 is 9 percent, but the highest rate within this category is 12 percent while the lowest is 6 percent.

Another important element in estimating the ROI on a college education is financial aid, which can change the expected return dramatically. For example, Vassar College is one of the most expensive schools on the 2012 list and has a relatively low annual ROI of 6%. But when you factor in its generous aid packages (nearly 60% of students receive aid, and the average amount is over $30,000), Vassar's annual ROI increases 50%, to a return of 9% (data available at http://www.payscale.com/college-education-value-2012).

FIGURE 2. RETURN ON INVESTMENT OF A BACHELOR'S
DEGREE BY INSTITUTION TYPE

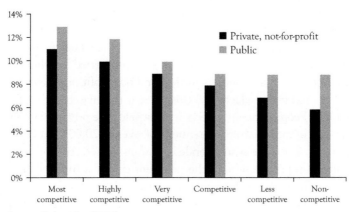

Source: Schneider (2010).
Note: Data uses PayScale return on investment data and Barron's index of
school selectivity.

One of the most important takeaways from the PayScale
data is that not every bachelor's degree is a smart investment.
After attempting to account for in-state vs. out-of-state tuition,
financial aid, graduation rates, years taken to graduate, wage
inflation, and selection, nearly two hundred schools on the
2012 list have negative ROIs. Students may want to think twice
about attending the Savannah College of Art and Design in
Georgia or Jackson State University in Mississippi. The problem is compounded if the students most likely to attend these
less selective schools come from disadvantaged families.

Variation by Field of Study and Career

Even within a school, the choices a student makes about his or
her field of study and later career can have a large impact on

what he or she gets out of her degree. It is no coincidence that the three schools with the highest 30-year ROIs on the 2012 PayScale list—Harvey Mudd, Caltech, and MIT—specialize in the STEM fields: science, technology, engineering, and math. Recent analysis by the Census Bureau also shows that the lifetime earnings of workers with bachelor's degrees vary widely by college major and occupation. The highest paid major is engineering, followed by computers and math. The lowest paid major, with barely half the lifetime earnings of engineering majors, is education, followed by the arts and psychology (Figure 3). The highest-earning

FIGURE 3. WORK-LIFE EARNINGS OF BACHELOR'S DEGREE HOLDERS BY COLLEGE MAJOR

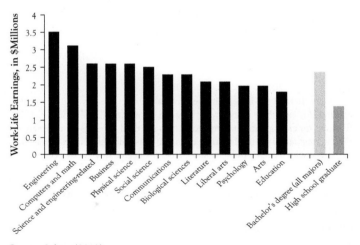

Source: Julian (2012).
Note: Synthetic work-life earnings estimates are calculated by finding median earnings for each 5-year age group between 25 and 64 (25–29, 30–34, etc.). Earnings for each group is multiplied by 5 to get total earnings for that period, then aggregated to get total lifetime earnings. This is done for high school graduates, bechelor's degree holders, and bachelor's degree holders by major.

FIGURE 4. WORK-LIFE EARNINGS OF BACHELOR'S DEGREE
HOLDERS BY OCCUPATION

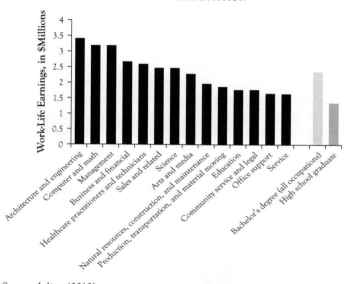

Source: Julian (2012).
Note: Synthetic work-life earnings estimates are calculated by finding median
earnings for each 5-year age group between 25 and 64 (25–29, 30–34, etc.).
Earnings for each group is multiplied by 5 to get total earnings for that period,
then aggregated to get total lifetime earnings. This is done for high school graduates, bechelor's degree holders, and bachelor's degree holders by occupation.

occupation category is architecture and engineering, with computers, math, and management in second place. The lowest-earning
occupation for college graduates is service (Figure 4). According
to Census's calculations, the lifetime earnings of an education or
arts major working in the service sector are actually lower than
the average lifetime earnings of a high school graduate.

When we dig even deeper, we see that just as not all college degrees are equal, neither are all high school diplomas.

Anthony Carnevale and his colleagues at the Georgetown Center on Education and the Workforce use similar methodology to the Census calculations but disaggregate even further, estimating median lifetime earnings for all education levels by occupation. They find that 14 percent of people with a high school diploma make at least as much as those with a bachelor's degree, and 17 percent of people with a bachelor's degree make more than those with a professional degree. The authors argue that much of this finding is explained by occupation. In every occupation category, more educated workers earn more.

But, for example, someone working in a STEM job with only a high school diploma can expect to make more over a lifetime than someone with a bachelor's degree working in education, community service and arts, sales and office work, health support, blue collar jobs, or personal services.

The numbers above are for full-time workers in a given field. 15 In fact, choice of major can also affect whether a college graduate can find a job at all. Another recent report from the Georgetown Center on Education and the Workforce breaks down unemployment rates by major for both recent (age 22–26) and experienced (age 30–54) college graduates in 2009–2010. People who majored in education or health have very low unemployment—even though education is one of the lowest-paying majors. Architecture graduates have particularly high unemployment, which may simply reflect the decline of the construction industry during the Great Recession. Arts majors don't fare too well, either. The expected earnings (median full-time earnings times the probability of being employed) of a young college graduate with a theater degree are about $6,000 more than the expected earnings of a young high school graduate. For a young person with a mechanical engineering degree, the expected earnings of the college graduate is a staggering $35,000 more than that of a typical high school graduate.

Variation in Graduation Rates

Comparisons of the return to college by highest degree attained include only people who actually complete college. Students who fail to obtain a degree incur some or all of the costs of a bachelor's degree without the ultimate payoff. This has major implications for inequalities of income and wealth, as the students least likely to graduate—lower-income students—are also the most likely to take on debt to finance their education.

Fewer than 60 percent of students who enter four-year schools finish within six years, and for low-income students it's even worse. Again, the variation in this measure is huge. Just within Washington, D.C., for example, six-year graduation rates range from a near-universal 93 percent at Georgetown University to a dismal 19 percent at the University of D.C. Of course, these are very different institutions, and we might expect high-achieving students at an elite school like Georgetown to have higher completion rates than at a less competitive school like UDC. In fact, Frederick Hess and his colleagues at AEI have documented that the relationship between selectivity and completion is positive, echoing other work that suggests that students are more likely to succeed in and graduate from college when they attend more selective schools (Figure 5). At the most selective schools, 88 percent of students graduate within six years; at non-competitive schools, only 35 percent do. Furthermore, the range of completion rates is negatively correlated with school ranking, meaning the least selective schools have the widest range. For example, one non-competitive school, Arkansas Baptist College, graduates 100 percent of its students, while only 8 percent of students at Southern University at New Orleans finish. Not every student can get into Harvard, where the likelihood of graduating is 97 percent, but students

FIGURE 5. AVERAGE SIX-YEAR GRADUATION RATES
BY SCHOOL SELECTIVITY

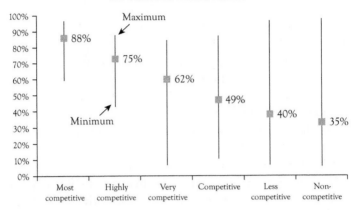

Source: Hess et al. (2009).

can choose to attend a school with a better track record within their ability level.

Unfortunately, recent evidence by Caroline Hoxby of Stanford and Christopher Avery of Harvard shows that most high-achieving low-income students never even apply to the selective schools that they are qualified to attend—and at which they would be eligible for generous financial aid. There is clearly room for policies that do a better job of matching students to schools.

Policy Implications

All of this suggests that it is a mistake to unilaterally tell young Americans that going to college—any college—is the best decision they can make. If they choose wisely and attend a school with generous financial aid and high expected earnings, and if they don't just enroll but graduate, they can greatly improve their lifetime prospects. The information needed to make a wise decision, however, can be difficult to find and hard to interpret.

One solution is simply to make the type of information discussed above more readily available. A study by Andrew Kelly and Mark Schneider of AEI found that when parents were asked to choose between two similar public universities in their state, giving them information on the schools' graduation rates caused them to prefer the higher-performing school. 20

The PayScale college rankings are a step in the right direction, giving potential students and their parents information with which to make better decisions. Similarly, the Obama Administration's new College Scorecard is being developed to increase transparency in the college application process. As it operates now, a prospective student can type in a college's name and learn its average net price, graduation rate, loan default rate, and median borrowed amount. The Department of Education is working to add information about the earnings of a given school's graduates. There is also a multi-dimensional search feature that allows users to find schools by location, size, and degrees and majors offered. The Student Right to Know Before You Go Act, sponsored by Senators Ron Wyden (D-OR) and Marco Rubio (R-FL), also aims to expand the data available on the costs and benefits of individual schools, as well as programs and majors within schools.

The College Scorecard is an admirable effort to help students and parents navigate the complicated process of choosing a college. However, it may not go far enough in improving transparency and helping students make the best possible decisions. A recent report by the Center for American Progress (CAP) showed a draft of the Scorecard to a focus group of college-bound high school students and found, among other things, that they are frequently confused about the term "net price" and give little weight to six-year graduation rates because they expect to graduate in four. It appears that the White House has responded to some of these critiques, for example showing median amount borrowed and default rates rather than the confusing "student loan repayment." Nevertheless, more information for students and their parents is needed.

There is also room for improvement in the financial aid system, which can seem overwhelmingly complex for families not familiar with the process. Studies have shown that students frequently underestimate how much aid they are eligible for, and don't claim the tax incentives that would save them money. Since 2009, the Administration has worked to simplify the FAFSA, the form that families must fill out to receive federal aid—but more could be done to guide low-income families through the process.

In the longer run, colleges need to do more to ensure that their students graduate, particularly the lower-income students who struggle most with persistence and completion. Research suggests that grants and loans increase enrollment but that aid must be tied to performance in order to affect persistence. Currently, we spend over $100 billion on Pell Grants and federal loans, despite a complete lack of evidence that this money leads to higher graduation rates. Good research on programs like Georgia's HOPE scholarships or West Virginia's PROMISE scholarships suggest that attaching strings to grant aid can improve college persistence and completion.

Finally, we want to emphasize that the personal characteristics and skills of each individual are equally important. It may be that for a student with poor grades who is on the fence [25] about enrolling in a four-year program, the most bang-for-the-buck will come from a vocationally-oriented associate's degree or career-specific technical training. Indeed, there are many well-paid job openings going unfilled because employers can't find workers with the right skills—skills that young potential workers could learn from training programs, apprenticeships, a vocational certificate, or an associate's degree. Policymakers should encourage these alternatives at the high school as well as the postsecondary level, with a focus on high-demand occupations and high-growth sectors. There has long been resistance to vocational education in American high schools, for fear that "tracking" students reinforces socioeconomic (and racial) stratification and impedes mobility. But if the default for many lower-achieving students was a career-focused training path rather than a path that involves dropping out of traditional college, their job prospects would probably improve. For example, Career Academies are high schools organized around an occupational or industry focus, and have partnerships with local employers and colleges. They have been shown by gold standard research to increase men's wages, hours worked, and employment stability after high school, particularly for those at high risk of dropping out.

Conclusions

In this brief, we have corralled existing research to make the point that while on average the return to college is highly positive, there is a considerable spread in the value of going to college. A bachelor's degree is not a smart investment for every student in every circumstance. We have outlined three important steps policymakers can take to make sure every person does make a smart investment in their choice of postsecondary education. First, we must provide more information in a comprehensible manner. Second, the federal government should lead the way on performance-based scholarships to incentivize college attendance and persistence. Finally, there should be more good alternatives to a traditional academic path, including career and technical education and apprenticeships.

ADDITIONAL READING

Anthony P. Carnevale, Ban Cheah, and Jeff Strohl, "Hard Times: College Majors, Unemployment, and Earnings: Not All College Degrees Are Created Equal," (Washington, D.C.: The Georgetown University Center on Education and the Workforce, January 2012).

Anthony P. Carnevale, Stephen J. Rose, and Ban Cheah, "The College Payoff: Education, Occupations, Lifetime Earnings," (Washington, D.C.: The Georgetown University Center on Education and the Workforce, August 2011).

Michael Greenstone and Adam Looney, "Where is the Best Place to Invest $102,000—In Stocks, Bonds, or a College Degree?" (Washington, D.C.: The Brookings Institution, June 2011).

Frederick M. Hess, Mark Schneider, Kevin Carey, and Andrew P. Kelly, "Diplomas and Dropouts: Which Colleges Actually Graduate Their Students (and Which Don't)," (Washington, D.C.: American Enterprise Institute for Public Policy Research, June 2009).

Harry J. Holzer and Robert I. Lerman, "The Future of Middle-Skill Jobs," (Washington, D.C.: The Brookings Institution, February 2009).

Caroline M. Hoxby and Christopher Avery, "The Missing 'One-Offs': The Hidden Supply of High-Achieving, Low Income Students," (Cambridge, MA, Working Paper, National Bureau of Economic Research, 2012).

Tiffany Julian, "Work-Life Earnings by Field of Degree and Occupation for People With a Bachelor's Degree: 2011," (Washington, D.C.: U.S. Census Bureau, October 2012).

Andrew P. Kelly and Mark Schneider, "Filling In the Blanks: How Information Can Affect Choice in Higher Education," (Washington, D.C.: American Enterprise Institute for Public Policy Research, January 2011).

Julie Margetta Morgan and Gadi Dechter, "Improving the College Scorecard: Using Student Feedback to Create an Effective Disclosure," (Washington, D.C.: Center for American Progress, November 2012).

Mark Schneider, "How Much Is That Bachelor's Degree Really Worth? The Million Dollar Misunderstanding," (Washington, D.C.: American Enterprise Institute for Public Policy Research, May 2009).

Mark Schneider, "Is College Worth the Investment?" (Washington, D.C.: American Enterprise Institute for Public Policy Research, October 2010).

Joining the Conversation

1. Stephanie Owen and Isabel Sawhill announce the "they say" in their second sentence—"Study after study reminds us that higher education is one of the best investments we can make"—and then proceed to report on how the return on that investment varies. What factors do they say make college a questionable investment?

2. This report draws upon quite a bit of quantitative data on the economic effects of graduating from college. Look carefully at one of the graphs that Owen and Sawhill provide, and explain in your own words what the data say.

3. Owen and Sawhill's analysis seems to favor baccalaureate degree programs as conferring the greatest advantages upon students. How might essayist Liz Addison, whose essay appears on pp. 255–58, respond to their argument?

4. In the essay's concluding paragraphs, the authors note information that students and parents should know before choosing a college. What information do they consider most important? What did you know and what did you not know about colleges you were considering as you were deciding

which school to attend? How might additional knowledge have helped you make a more informed choice?

5. The questions Owen and Sawhill explore are not new ones. Go to **theysayiblog.com** and read what Lawrence Mishel of the Economic Policy Institute wrote in 2012. (Enter Lawrence Mishel, "College and Then What?" in the search box and press "search" to access the article.) Read what he wrote and think about your own reasons for being in college. Then click on "Join the Conversation" and write out a response to Mishel.

6. According to Owen and Sawhill, "For certain schools, majors, occupations, and individuals, college may not be a smart investment." Taking this statement as a "they say," write a short essay responding with what you think. Discuss your own reasons for attending college, and refer to the authors' argument and data about the pros and cons of attending college.

The New Liberal Arts

SANFORD J. UNGAR

—▢—

HARD ECONOMIC TIMES inevitably bring scrutiny of all accepted ideals and institutions, and this time around liberal-arts education has been especially hard hit. Something that has long been held up as a uniquely sensible and effective approach to learning has come under the critical gaze of policy makers and the news media, not to mention budget-conscious families.

But the critique, unfortunately, seems to be fueled by reliance on common misperceptions. Here are a few of those misperceptions, from my vantage point as a liberal-arts college president, and my reactions to them:

SANFORD J. UNGAR was the president of Goucher College in Baltimore, Maryland, from 2001 to 2014. He is the author of *Fresh Blood: The New American Immigrants* (1998) and *Africa: The People and Politics of an Emerging Continent* (1986). Ungar has also worked in broadcast journalism both at National Public Radio and at the Voice of America, the U.S. government–funded broadcast network for a global audience. His extensive print journalism work includes articles in *Newsweek*, the *Economist*, and the *Washington Post*. This article first appeared in the *Chronicle of Higher Education*, a publication read by college faculty and administrators, on March 5, 2010.

Misperception No. 1: A liberal-arts degree is a luxury that most families can no longer afford. "Career education" is what we now must focus on. Many families are indeed struggling, in the depths of the recession, to pay for their children's college education. Yet one could argue that the traditional, well-rounded preparation that the liberal arts offer is a better investment than ever—that the future demands of citizenship will require not narrow technical or job-focused training, but rather a subtle understanding of the complex influences that shape the world we live in.

No one could be against equipping oneself for a career. But the "career education" bandwagon seems to suggest that short-cuts are available to students that lead directly to high-paying jobs—leaving out "frills" like learning how to write and speak well, how to understand the nuances of literary texts and scientific concepts, how to collaborate with others on research.

Many states and localities have officials or task forces in 5 charge of "work-force development," implying that business and industry will communicate their needs and educational institutions will dutifully turn out students who can head straight to the factory floor or the office cubicle to fulfill them. But history is filled with examples of failed social experiments that treated people as work units rather than individuals capable of inspiration and ingenuity. It is far wiser for students to prepare for change—and the multiple careers they are likely to have—than to search for a single job track that might one day become a dead end.

I recently heard Geoffrey Garin, president of Hart Research Associates, suggest that the responsibility of higher education today is to prepare people "for jobs that do not yet exist." It may be that studying the liberal arts is actually the best form of career education.

Misperception No. 2: College graduates are finding it harder to get good jobs with liberal-arts degrees. Who wants to hire somebody with an irrelevant major like philosophy or French? Yes, recent graduates have had difficulty in the job market, but the recession has not differentiated among major fields of study in its impact. A 2009 survey for the Association of American Colleges and Universities actually found that more than three-quarters of our nation's employers recommend that collegebound students pursue a "liberal education." An astounding 89 percent said they were looking for more emphasis on "the ability to effectively communicate orally and in writing," and almost as many urged the development of better "critical thinking and analytical reasoning skills." Seventy percent said they were on the lookout for "the ability to innovate and be creative."

See Chapter 4 for tips on explaining why you disagree.

It is no surprise, then, that a growing number of corporations, including some in highly technical fields, are headed by people with liberal-arts degrees. Plenty of philosophy and physics majors work on Wall Street, and the ability to analyze and compare literature across cultures is a skill linked to many other fields, including law and medicine. Knowledge of foreign languages is an advantage in all lines of work. What seemed a radical idea in business education 10 years or so ago—that critical and creative thinking is as "relevant" as finance or accounting—is now commonplace.

Misperception No. 3: The liberal arts are particularly irrelevant for low-income and first-generation college students. They, more than their more-affluent peers, must focus on something more practical and marketable. It is condescending to imply that those who have less cannot understand and appreciate the finer elements of knowledge—another way of saying, really, that the rich folks will do the important thinking, and the lower classes will simply carry out their ideas. That is just a form of prejudice and cannot be supported intellectually.

Perhaps students who come with prior acquaintance with certain fields and a reservoir of experience have an advantage at the start of college. But in my experience, it is often the people who are newest to certain ideas and approaches who are the most original and inventive in the discussion and application of those ideas. They catch up quickly.

We should respect what everyone brings to the table and train the broadest possible cross section of American society to participate in, and help shape, civil discourse. We cannot assign different socioeconomic groups to different levels or types of education. This is a country where a mixed-race child raised overseas by a struggling single mother who confronts impossible odds can grow up to be president. It is precisely a liberal education that allowed him to catch up and move ahead.

Misperception No. 4: One should not, in this day and age, study only the arts. The STEM fields—science, technology, engineering, and mathematics—are where the action is. The liberal arts encompass the broadest possible range of disciplines in the natural sciences, the humanities, and the social sciences. In fact, the historical basis of a liberal education is in the classical *artes liberales*, comprising the trivium (grammar, logic, and rhetoric) and the quadrivium (arithmetic, geometry, astronomy, and music). Another term sometimes substituted for liberal arts, for the sake of clarity, is "the arts and sciences." Thus, many universities have colleges, divisions, or schools of arts and sciences among their academic units.

To be sure, there is much concern about whether America is keeping up with China and other rising economies in the

STEM disciplines. No evidence suggests, however, that success in scientific and technical fields will be greater if it comes at the expense of a broad background in other areas of the liberal arts.

Misperception No. 5: It's the liberal Democrats who got this country into trouble in recent years, so it's ridiculous to continue indoctrinating our young people with a liberal education. A liberal education, as properly defined above, has nothing whatsoever to do with politics—except insofar as politics is one of the fields that students often pursue under its rubric. On the contrary, because of its inclusiveness and its respect for classical traditions, the liberal arts could properly be described as a conservative approach to preparation for life. It promotes the idea of listening to all points of view and not relying on a single ideology, and examining all approaches to solving a problem rather than assuming that one technique or perspective has all the answers. That calm and balanced sort of dialogue may be out of fashion in the American public arena today, when shouting matches are in vogue and many people seek information only from sources they know in advance they agree with. But it may be only liberal education that can help lead the way back to comity and respectful conversation about issues before us.

Misperception No. 6: America is the only country in the 15 world that clings to such an old-fashioned form of postsecondary education as the liberal arts. Other countries, with more practical orientations, are running way ahead of us. It is often difficult to explain the advantages of a liberal-arts education to people from other cultures, where it is common to specialize early. In many places, including Europe, the study of law or medicine often begins directly after high school, without any requirement to complete an undergraduate degree first. We should recognize, however, that a secondary education in some systems—say, those that follow the model of the German Gymnasium—often includes much that is left out of the typical high-school curriculum in America. One need only look in on a student preparing for the baccalaureat examination in France to understand the distinction: Mastery of philosophical and scientific concepts is mandatory.

Further, in recent years delegations from China have been visiting the United States and asking pointed questions about the liberal arts, seemingly because they feel there may be good reason to try that approach to education. The Chinese may be coming around to the view that a primary focus on technical training is not serving them adequately—that if they aspire to world leadership, they will have to provide young people with a broader perspective. Thus, it is hardly a propitious moment to toss out, or downgrade, one element of higher education that has served us so well.

Misconception No. 7: The cost of American higher education is spiraling out of control, and liberal-arts colleges are becoming irrelevant because they are unable to register gains in productivity or to find innovative ways of doing things. There is plenty wrong with American higher education, including the runaway costs. But the problem of costs goes beyond individual institutions. Government at all levels has come nowhere close to supporting colleges in ways that allow them to provide the kind of access and affordability that's needed. The best way to understand genuine national priorities is to follow the money, and by that standard, education is really not all that important to this country.

Many means exist to obtain a liberal education, including at some large universities, public and private. The method

I happen to advocate, for obvious reasons, is the small, residential liberal-arts college, usually independent, where there is close interaction between faculty members and students and, at its best, a sense of community emerges that prepares young people to develop high standards for themselves and others.

Efficiency is hardly the leading quality of liberal-arts colleges, and indeed, their financial model is increasingly coming into question. But because of their commitment to expand need-based financial aid, the net cost of attending a small liberal-arts college can be lower than that of a large public university. One can only hope that each institution will find ways to cut costs and develop distinguishing characteristics that help it survive through the tough times ahead.

The debate over liberal education will surely continue 20 through the recession and beyond, but it would be helpful to put these misperceptions aside. Financial issues cannot be ignored, but neither can certain eternal verities: Through immersion in liberal arts, students learn not just to make a living, but also to live a life rich in values and character. They come to terms with complexity and diversity, and otherwise devise means to solve problems—rather than just complaining about them. They develop patterns that help them understand how to keep learning for the rest of their days.

Joining the Conversation

1. Summarize in a few sentences the seven misperceptions that Sanford Ungar discusses. These of course are all things that "they say"—and that he uses to launch what he wants to say. How does calling them "misperceptions" affect the way you read his argument? Would you read it any differently if he instead called them "common assumptions"?

2. See paragraph 6, where Geoffrey Garin suggests that "the responsibility of higher education today is to prepare people 'for jobs that do not yet exist.'" Thus, according to Ungar, "It may be that studying the liberal arts is actually the best form of career education." How would you respond to this claim?

3. Misperception 5 relates liberal education to political affiliation. What does Ungar have to say on this issue, and what do you think about his response?

4. On what specific points do you think Ungar would agree with Charles Murray (pp. 234–54)? On what points would he be likely to disagree?

5. Write your own essay listing and explaining five assumptions about college education. Follow Ungar's essay as a model, and use the "they say / I say" pattern to organize your essay, with each assumption as a "they say" that sets up what you want to say.

Are Too Many People Going to College?

CHARLES MURRAY

—◫—

TO ASK WHETHER too many people are going to college requires
us to think about the importance and nature of a liberal education. "Universities are not intended to teach the knowledge
required to fit men for some special mode of gaining their
livelihood," John Stuart Mill told students at the University
of St. Andrews in 1867. "Their object is not to make skillful
lawyers, or physicians, or engineers, but capable and cultivated
human beings." If this is true (and I agree that it is), why say that
too many people are going to college? Surely a mass democracy
should encourage as many people as possible to become "capable
and cultivated human beings" in Mill's sense. We should not
restrict the availability of a liberal education to a rarefied intellectual elite. More people should be going to college, not fewer.

———

CHARLES MURRAY is the W. H. Brady Scholar at the American
Enterprise Institute, a conservative think tank in Washington, D.C.,
and describes himself as a libertarian. He is the coauthor, with Richard
Herrnstein, of *The Bell Curve* (1994) and author, most recently, of
Coming Apart (2012). This essay, adapted from his book, *Real Education: Four Simple Truths for Bringing America's Schools Back to Reality*
(2008), first appeared on September 8, 2008, in *The American*, the
journal of the American Enterprise Institute.

Yes and no. More people should be getting the basics of a liberal education. But for most students, the places to provide those basics are elementary and middle school. E. D. Hirsch Jr. is the indispensable thinker on this topic, beginning with his 1987 book *Cultural Literacy: What Every American Needs to Know.* Part of his argument involves the importance of a body of core knowledge in fostering reading speed and comprehension. With regard to a liberal education, Hirsch makes three points that are germane here:

See Chapter 4 for ways to agree, but with a difference.

Full participation in any culture requires familiarity with a body of core knowledge. To live in the United States and not recognize Teddy Roosevelt, Prohibition, the Minutemen, Wall Street, smoke-filled rooms, or Gettysburg is like trying to read without knowing some of the ten thousand most commonly used words in the language. It signifies a degree of cultural illiteracy about America. But the core knowledge transcends one's own country. Not to recognize Falstaff, Apollo, the Sistine Chapel, the Inquisition, the twenty-third Psalm, or Mozart signifies cultural illiteracy about the West. Not to recognize the solar system, the Big Bang, natural selection, relativity, or the periodic table is to be scientifically illiterate. Not to recognize the Mediterranean, Vienna, the Yangtze River, Mount Everest, or Mecca is to be geographically illiterate.

This core knowledge is an important part of the glue that holds the culture together. All American children, of whatever ethnic heritage, and whether their families came here 300 years ago or three months ago, need to learn about the Pilgrims, Valley Forge, Duke Ellington, Apollo 11, Susan B. Anthony, George C. Marshall, and the Freedom Riders. All students need to learn the iconic stories. For a society of immigrants such as ours, the core knowledge is our shared identity that makes us Americans together rather than hyphenated Americans.

K–8 are the right years to teach the core knowledge, and the effort should get off to a running start in elementary school. Starting early is partly a matter of necessity: There's a lot to learn, and it takes time. But another reason is that small children enjoy learning myths and fables, showing off names and dates they have memorized, and hearing about great historical figures and exciting deeds. The educational establishment sees this kind of curriculum as one that forces children to memorize boring facts. That conventional wisdom is wrong on every count. The facts can be fascinating (if taught right); a lot more than memorization is entailed; yet memorizing things is an indispensable part of education, too; and memorizing is something that children do much, much better than adults. The core knowledge is suited to ways that young children naturally learn and enjoy learning. Not all children will be able to do the reading with the same level of comprehension, but the fact-based nature of the core knowledge actually works to the benefit of low-ability students—remembering facts is much easier than making inferences and deductions. The core knowledge curriculum lends itself to adaptation for students across a wide range of academic ability.

In the 20 years since *Cultural Literacy* was published, Hirsch and his colleagues have developed and refined his original formulation into an inventory of more than 6,000 items that approximate the core knowledge broadly shared by literate Americans. Hirsch's Core Knowledge Foundation has also developed a detailed, grade-by-grade curriculum for K–8, complete with lists of books and other teaching materials.

The Core Knowledge approach need not stop with eighth grade. High school is a good place for survey courses in the humanities, social sciences, and sciences taught at a level below the demands of a college course and accessible to most students in the upper two-thirds of the distribution of academic ability. Some students will not want to take these courses, and it can be counterproductive to require them to do so, but high school can put considerable flesh on the liberal education skeleton for students who are still interested.

Liberal Education in College

Saying "too many people are going to college" is not the same as saying that the average student does not need to know about history, science, and great works of art, music, and literature. They do need to know—and to know more than they are currently learning. So let's teach it to them, but let's not wait for college to do it.

Liberal education in college means taking on the tough stuff. A high-school graduate who has acquired Hirsch's core knowledge will know, for example, that John Stuart Mill was an important 19th-century English philosopher who was associated with something called Utilitarianism and wrote a famous book called *On Liberty*. But learning philosophy in college, which is an essential component of a liberal education, means that the student has to be able to read and understand the actual text of *On Liberty*. That brings us to the limits set by the nature of college-level material. Here is the first sentence of *On Liberty*: "The subject of this essay is not the so-called liberty of the will, so unfortunately opposed to the misnamed doctrine of philosophical necessity; but civil, or social liberty:

the nature and limits of the power which can be legitimately exercised by society over the individual." I will not burden you with *On Liberty*'s last sentence. It is 126 words long. And Mill is one of the more accessible philosophers, and *On Liberty* is one of Mill's more accessible works. It would be nice if everyone could acquire a fully formed liberal education, but they cannot.

Specifically: When College Board researchers defined "col- 10 lege readiness" as the SAT score that is associated with a 65 percent chance of getting at least a 2.7 grade point average in college during the freshman year, and then applied those criteria (hardly demanding in an era of soft courses and grade inflation) to the freshmen in a sample of 41 major colleges and universities, the threshold "college readiness" score was found to be 1180 on the combined SAT math and verbal tests. It is a score that only about 10 percent of American 18-year-olds would achieve if they all took the SAT, in an age when more than 30 percent of 18-year-olds go to college.

Should all of those who do have the academic ability to absorb a college-level liberal education get one? It depends. Suppose we have before us a young woman who is in the 98th percentile of academic ability and wants to become a lawyer and eventually run for political office. To me, it seems essential that she spend her undergraduate years getting a rigorous liberal education. Apart from a liberal education's value to her, the nation will benefit. Everything she does as an attorney or as an elected official should be informed by the kind of wisdom that a rigorous liberal education can encourage. It is appropriate to push her into that kind of undergraduate program.

But the only reason we can get away with pushing her is that the odds are high that she will enjoy it. The odds are high because she is good at this sort of thing—it's no problem for her to read *On Liberty* or *Paradise Lost*. It's no problem for her to come up with an interesting perspective on what she's read and weave it into a term paper. And because she's good at it, she is also likely to enjoy it. It is one of Aristotle's central themes in his discussion of human happiness, a theme that John Rawls later distilled into what he called the Aristotelian Principle: "Other things equal, human beings enjoy the exercise of the irrealized capacities (their innate or trained abilities), and this enjoyment increases the more the capacity is realized, or the greater its complexity." And so it comes to pass that those who take the hardest majors and who enroll in courses that look most like an old fashioned liberal education are concentrated among the students in the top percentiles of academic ability. Getting a liberal education consists of dealing with complex intellectual material day after day, and dealing with complex intellectual material is what students in the top few percentiles are really good at, in the same way that other people are really good at cooking or making pottery. For these students, doing it well is fun.

Every percentile down the ability ladder—and this applies to all abilities, not just academic—the probability that a person will enjoy the hardest aspects of an activity goes down as well. Students at the 80th percentile of academic ability are still smart kids, but the odds that they will respond to a course that assigns Mill or Milton are considerably lower than the odds that a student in the top few percentiles will respond. Virtue has nothing to do with it. Maturity has nothing to do with it. Appreciation of the value of a liberal education has nothing to do with it. The probability that a student will enjoy *Paradise Lost* goes down as his linguistic ability goes down, but so does the probability that he works on double acrostic puzzles in his spare time or regularly plays online Scrabble, and for the identical reason. The lower down the linguistic ladder he is, the less fun such activities are.

And so we return to the question: Should all of those who have the academic ability to absorb a college-level liberal education get one? If our young woman is at the 80th percentile of linguistic ability, should she be pushed to do so? She has enough intellectual capacity, if she puts her mind to it and works exceptionally hard.

The answer is no. If she wants to, fine. But she probably won't, and there's no way to force her. Try to force her (for example, by setting up a demanding core curriculum), and she will transfer to another school, because she is in college for vocational training. She wants to write computer code. Start a business. Get a job in television. She uses college to take vocational courses that pertain to her career interests. A large proportion of people who are theoretically able to absorb a liberal education have no interest in doing so.

And reasonably so. Seen dispassionately, getting a traditional liberal education over four years is an odd way to enjoy spending one's time. Not many people enjoy reading for hour after hour, day after day, no matter what the material may be. To enjoy reading *On Liberty* and its ilk—and if you're going to absorb such material, you must in some sense enjoy the process—is downright peculiar. To be willing to spend many more hours writing papers and answers to exam questions about that material approaches masochism.

We should look at the kind of work that goes into acquiring a liberal education at the college level in the same way that we look at the grueling apprenticeship that goes into becoming a master chef: something that understandably attracts only a few people. Most students at today's colleges choose not to take the courses that go into a liberal education because the capabilities they want to develop lie elsewhere. These students are not lazy, any more than students who don't want to spend hours learning how to chop carrots into a perfect eighth-inch dice are lazy. A liberal education just doesn't make sense for them.

For Learning How to Make a Living, the Four-Year Brick-and-Mortar Residential College Is Increasingly Obsolete

We now go from one extreme to the other, from the ideal of liberal education to the utilitarian process of acquiring the knowledge that most students go to college to acquire— practical and vocational. The question here is not whether the traditional four-year residential college is fun or valuable as a place to grow up, but when it makes sense as a place to learn how to make a living. The answer is: in a sensible world, hardly ever.

Start with the time it takes—four years. Assuming a semester system with four courses per semester, four years of class work means 32 semester-long courses. The occupations for which "knowing enough" requires 32 courses are exceedingly rare. For some professions—medicine and law are the obvious examples—a rationale for four years of course work can be concocted (combining pre-med and pre-law undergraduate courses with three years of medical school and law school), but for every other occupation, the body of knowledge taught in classrooms can be learned more quickly. Even Ph.D.s don't require four years of course work. The Ph.D. is supposed to signify expertise, but that expertise comes from burrowing deep in to a specialty, not from dozens of courses.

Those are the jobs with the most stringent academic require- 20 ments. For the student who wants to become a good hotel manager, software designer, accountant, hospital administrator,

farmer, high-school teacher, social worker, journalist, optome-
trist, interior designer, or football coach, four years of class work
is ridiculous. Actually becoming good in those occupations
will take longer than four years, but most of the competence
is acquired on the job. The two-year community college and
online courses offer more flexible options for tailoring course
work to the real needs of the job.

A brick-and-mortar campus is increasingly obsolete. The
physical infrastructure of the college used to make sense for
three reasons. First, a good library was essential to higher learning, and only a college faculty and student body provided the
economies of scale that made good libraries affordable. Second,
scholarship flourishes through colleagueships, and the college
campus made it possible to put scholars in physical proximity
to each other. Third, the best teaching requires interaction
between teachers and students, and physical proximity was
the only way to get it. All three rationales for the brick-and-
mortar campus are fading fast.

The rationale for a physical library is within a few years of
extinction. Even now, the Internet provides access, for a price,
to all the world's significant technical journals. The books are
about to follow. Google is scanning the entire text of every
book in the libraries of Harvard, Princeton, Stanford, Oxford,
the New York Public Library, the Bavarian State Library,
Ghent University Library, Keio Library (Tokyo), the National
Library of Catalonia, University of Lausanne, and an expanding list of others. Collectively, this project will encompass close
to the sum total of human knowledge. It will be completely
searchable. Everything out of copyright will be free. Everything
still under copyright will be accessible for a fee. Libraries will
still be a selling point for colleges, but as a place for students
to study in pleasant surroundings—an amenity in the same

way that an attractive student union is an amenity. Colleges and universities will not need to exist because they provide libraries.

The rationale for colleges based on colleagueships has eroded. Until a few decades ago, physical proximity was important because correspondence and phone calls just weren't as good. As email began to spread during the 1980s, physical proximity became less important. As the capacity of the Internet expanded in the 1990s, other mechanisms made those interactions richer. Now, regular emails from professional groups inform scholars of the latest publications in their field of interest. Specialized chat groups enable scholars to bounce new ideas off other people working on the same problems. Drafts are exchanged effortlessly and comments attached electronically. Whether physical proximity still has any advantages depends mostly on the personality of the scholar. Some people like being around other people during the workday and prefer face-to-face conversations to emails. For those who don't, the value of being on a college campus instead of on a mountaintop in Montana is nil. Their electronic access to other scholars is incomparably greater than any scholar enjoyed even within the world's premier universities before the advent of the Internet. Like the library, face-to-face colleagueships will be an amenity that colleges continue to provide. But colleges and universities will not need to exist because they provide a community of scholars.

The third rationale for the brick-and-mortar college is that it brings teachers together with students. Working against that rationale is the explosion in the breadth and realism of what is known as distance learning. The idea of distance learning is surprisingly old—Isaac Pitman was teaching his shorthand system to British students through the postal service in the 1840s, and the University of London began offering degrees for correspondence students in 1858—but the technology of distance learning changed little for the next century. The advent of inexpensive videocassettes in the 1980s opened up a way for students to hear and see lectures without being in the classroom. By the early 1990s, it was possible to buy college-level courses on audio or videotape, taught by first-rate teaching professors, on a wide range of topics, for a few hundred dollars. But without easy interaction between teacher and student, distance learning remained a poor second-best to a good college seminar.

Once again, the Internet is revolutionizing everything. As 25 personal computers acquired the processing power to show high-definition video and the storage capacity to handle big video files, the possibilities for distance learning expanded by orders of magnitude. We are now watching the early expression of those possibilities: podcasts and streaming videos in real time of professors' lectures, online discussions among students scattered around the country, online interaction between students and professors, online exams, and tutorials augmented by computer-aided instruction software.

Even today, the quality of student-teacher interactions in a virtual classroom competes with the interactions in a brick-and-mortar classroom. But the technology is still in its early stages of development and the rate of improvement is breathtaking. Compare video games such as Myst and SimCity in the 1990s to their descendants today; the Walkman you used in the 1990s to the iPod you use today; the cell phone you used in the 1990s to the BlackBerry or iPhone you use today. Whatever technical limitations might lead you to say, "Yes, but it's still not the same as being there in the classroom," are probably within a few years of being outdated.

College Isn't All It's Cracked Up to Be

College looms so large in the thinking of both parents and students because it is seen as the open sesame to a good job. Reaping the economic payoff for college that shows up in econometric analyses is a long shot for large numbers of young people.

When high-school graduates think that obtaining a B.A. will help them get a higher-paying job, they are only narrowly correct. Economists have established beyond doubt that people with B.A.s earn more on average than people without them. But why does the B.A. produce that result? For whom does the B.A. produce that result? For some jobs, the economic premium for a degree is produced by the actual education that has gone into getting the degree. Lawyers, physicians, and engineers can earn their high incomes only by deploying knowledge and skills that take years to acquire, and degrees in law, medicine, and engineering still signify competence in those knowledges and skills. But for many other jobs, the economic premium for the B.A. is created by a brutal fact of life about the American job market: Employers do not even interview applicants who do not hold a B.A. Even more brutal, the advantage conferred by the B.A. often has nothing to do with the content of the education. Employers do not value what the student learned, just that the student has a degree.

Employers value the B.A. because it is a no-cost (for them) screening device for academic ability and perseverance. The more people who go to college, the more sense it makes for employers to require a B.A. When only a small percentage of people got college degrees, employers who required a B.A. would have been shutting themselves off from access to most of the talent. With more than a third of 23-year-olds now getting a B.A., many employers can reasonably limit their hiring pool to college graduates because bright and ambitious high-school graduates who can go to college usually do go to college. An employer can believe that exceptions exist but rationally choose not to expend time and money to identify them. Knowing this, large numbers of students are in college to buy their admission ticket—the B.A.

But while it is true that the average person with a B.A. 30 makes more than the average person without a B.A., getting a B.A. is still going to be the wrong economic decision for many high-school graduates. Wages within occupations form a distribution. Young people with okay-but-not-great academic ability who are thinking about whether to go after a B.A. need to consider the competition they will face after they graduate. Let me put these calculations in terms of a specific example, a young man who has just graduated from high school and is trying to decide whether to become an electrician or go to college and major in business, hoping to become a white-collar manager. He is at the 70th percentile in linguistic ability and logical mathematical ability—someone who shouldn't go to college by my standards, but who can, in today's world, easily find a college that will give him a degree. He is exactly average in interpersonal and intrapersonal ability. He is at the 95th percentile in the small-motor skills and spatial abilities that are helpful in being a good electrician.

He begins by looking up the average income of electricians and managers on the Bureau of Labor Statistics website, and finds that the mean annual income for electricians in 2005 was $45,630, only about half of the $88,450 mean for management occupations. It looks as if getting a B.A. will buy him a huge wage premium. Should he try to get the B.A. on economic grounds?

To make his decision correctly, our young man must start by throwing out the averages. He has the ability to become an excellent electrician and can reasonably expect to be near the top of the electricians' income distribution. He does not have it in him to be an excellent manager, because he is only average in interpersonal and intrapersonal ability and only modestly above average in academic ability, all of which are important for becoming a good manager, while his competitors for those slots will include many who are high in all of those abilities. Realistically, he should be looking at the incomes toward the bottom of the distribution of managers. With that in mind, he goes back to the Bureau of Labor Statistics website and discovers that an electrician at the 90th percentile of electricians' incomes made $70,480 in 2005, almost twice the income of a manager at the 10th percentile of managers' incomes ($37,800). Even if our young man successfully completes college and gets a B.A. (which is far from certain), he is likely to make less money than if he becomes an electrician.

Then there is job security to consider. A good way to make sure you always can find work is to be among the best at what you do. It also helps to have a job that does not require you to compete with people around the globe. When corporations downsize, they lay off mediocre managers before they lay off top electricians. When the economy gets soft, top electricians can find work when mediocre managers cannot. Low-level management jobs can often be outsourced to India, whereas electricians' jobs cannot.

What I have said of electricians is true throughout the American job market. The income for the top people in a wide variety of occupations that do not require a college degree is higher than the average income for many occupations that require a B.A. Furthermore, the range and number of such jobs are expanding rapidly. The need for assembly-line workers in factories (one of the most boring jobs ever invented) is falling, but the demand for skilled technicians of every kind—in healthcare, information technology, transportation networks, and every other industry that relies on high-tech equipment— is expanding. The service sector includes many low-skill, low-paying jobs, but it also includes growing numbers of specialized jobs that pay well (for example, in healthcare and the entertainment and leisure industries). Construction offers an array of high-paying jobs for people who are good at what they do. It's not just skilled labor in the standard construction trades that is in high demand. The increase in wealth in American society has increased the demand for all sorts of craftsmanship. Today's high-end homes and office buildings may entail the work of specialized skills in stonework, masonry, glazing, painting, cabinetmaking, machining, landscaping, and a dozen other crafts. The increase in wealth is also driving an increased demand for the custom-made and the exquisitely wrought, meaning demand for artisans in everything from pottery to jewelry to metalworking. There has never been a time in history when people with skills not taught in college have been in so much demand at such high pay as today, nor a time when the range of such jobs has been so wide. In today's America, finding a first-rate lawyer or physician is easy. Finding first-rate skilled labor is hard.

Intrinsic Rewards

The topic is no longer money but job satisfaction—intrinsic 35 rewards. We return to our high-school graduate trying to decide between going to college and becoming an electrician. He knows that he enjoys working with his hands and likes the idea of not being stuck in the same place all day, but he also likes the idea of being a manager sitting behind a desk in a big office, telling people what to do and getting the status that goes with it.

However, he should face facts that he is unlikely to know on his own, but that a guidance counselor could help him face. His chances of getting the big office and the status are slim. He is more likely to remain in a cubicle, under the thumb of the boss in the big office. He is unlikely to have a job in which he produces something tangible during the course of the day.

If he becomes a top electrician instead, he will have an expertise that he exercises at a high level. At the end of a workday, he will often be able to see that his work made a difference in the lives of people whose problems he has solved. He will not be confined to a cubicle and, after his apprenticeship, will be his own supervisor in the field. Top electricians often become independent contractors who have no boss at all.

The intrinsic rewards of being a top manager can be just as great as those of a top electrician (though I would not claim they are greater), but the intrinsic rewards of being a mediocre manager are not. Even as people in white-collar jobs lament the soullessness of their work, the intrinsic rewards of exercising technical skills remain undiminished.

Finally, there is an overarching consideration so important it is hard to express adequately: the satisfaction of being good at what one does for a living (and knowing it), compared to the melancholy of being mediocre at what one does for a living (and knowing it). This is another truth about living a human life that a 17-year-old might not yet understand on his own, but that a guidance counselor can bring to his attention. Guidance counselors and parents who automatically encourage young people to go to college straight out of high school regardless of their skills and interests are being thoughtless about the best interests of young people in their charge.

The Dark Side of the B.A. as Norm

It is possible to accept all that I have presented as fact and still 40
disagree with the proposition that too many people are going
to college. The argument goes something like this:

The meaning of a college education has evolved since the
19th century. The traditional liberal education is still available
for students who want it, but the curriculum is appropriately
broader now, and includes many courses for vocational preparation that today's students want. Furthermore, intellectual
requirements vary across majors. It may be true that few students can complete a major in economics or biology, but larger
proportions can handle the easier majors. A narrow focus on
curriculum also misses the important nonacademic functions of
college. The lifestyle on today's campuses may leave something
to be desired, but four years of college still give youngsters in
late adolescence a chance to encounter different kinds of people, to discover new interests, and to decide what they want to
make of their lives. And if it is true that some students spend
too much of their college years partying, that was also true of
many Oxford students in the 18th century. Lighten up.

If the only people we had to worry about were those who are
on college campuses and doing reasonably well, this position
would have something to be said for it. It does not address the
issues of whether four years makes sense or whether a residential
facility makes sense; nevertheless, college as it exists is not an
intrinsically evil place for the students who are there and are
coping academically. But there is the broader American society to worry about as well. However unintentionally, we have
made something that is still inaccessible to a majority of the
population—the B.A.—into a symbol of first-class citizenship.
We have done so at the same time that other class divisions are

becoming more powerful. Today's college system is implicated in the emergence of class-riven America.

The problem begins with the message sent to young people that they should aspire to college no matter what. Some politicians are among the most visible offenders, treating every failure to go to college as an injustice that can be remedied by increasing government help. American educational administrators reinforce the message by instructing guidance counselors to steer as many students as possible toward a college-prep track (more than 90 percent of high-school students report that their guidance counselors encouraged them to go to college). But politicians and educators are only following the lead of the larger culture. As long as it remains taboo to acknowledge that college is intellectually too demanding for most young people, we will continue to create crazily unrealistic expectations among the next generation. If "crazily unrealistic" sounds too strong, consider that more than 90 percent of high school seniors expect to go to college, and more than 70 percent of them expect to work in professional jobs.

One aspect of this phenomenon has been labeled misaligned ambitions, meaning that adolescents have career ambitions that are inconsistent with their educational plans. Data from the Sloan Study of Youth and Social Development conducted during the 1990s indicate that misaligned ambitions characterized more than half of all adolescents. Almost always, the misalignment is in the optimistic direction, as adolescents aspire to be attorneys or physicians without understanding the educational hurdles they must surmount to achieve their goals. They end up at a four-year institution not because that is where they can take the courses they need to meet their career goals, but because college is the place where B.A.s are handed out, and everyone knows that these days you've got to have a B.A. Many of them drop out. Of those who entered a four-year college in 1995, only 58 percent had gotten their B.A. five academic years later. Another 14 percent were still enrolled. If we assume that half of that 14 percent eventually get their B.A.s, about a third of all those who entered college hoping for a B.A. leave without one.

If these numbers had been produced in a culture where the 45 B.A. was a nice thing to have but not a big deal, they could be interpreted as the result of young adults deciding that they didn't really want a B.A. after all. Instead, these numbers were produced by a system in which having a B.A. is a very big deal indeed, and that brings us to the increasingly worrisome role of the B.A. as a source of class division. The United States has always had symbols of class, and the college degree has always been one of them. But through the first half of the 20th century, there were all sorts of respectable reasons a person might not go to college—not enough money to pay for college; needing to work right out of high school to support a wife, parents, or younger siblings; or the commonly held belief that going straight to work was better preparation for a business career than going to college. As long as the percentage of college graduates remained small, it also remained true, and everybody knew it, that the majority of America's intellectually most able people did not have B.A.s.

Over the course of the 20th century, three trends gathered strength. The first was the increasing proportion of jobs screened for high academic ability due to the advanced level of education they require—engineers, physicians, attorneys, college teachers, scientists, and the like. The second was the increasing market value of those jobs. The third was the opening up of college to more of those who had the academic ability to go to college, partly because the increase in American wealth meant that more parents could afford college for their children, and partly because the proliferation of scholarships and loans made it possible for most students with enough academic ability to go.

The combined effect of these trends has been to overturn the state of affairs that prevailed through World War II. Now the great majority of America's intellectually most able people do have a B.A. Along with that transformation has come a downside that few anticipated. The acceptable excuses for not going to college have dried up. The more people who go to college, the more stigmatizing the failure to complete college becomes. Today, if you do not get a B.A., many people assume it is because you are too dumb or too lazy. And all this because of a degree that seldom has an interpretable substantive meaning.

Let's approach the situation from a different angle. Imagine that America had no system of postsecondary education and you were made a member of a task force assigned to create one from scratch. Ask yourself what you would think if one of your colleagues submitted this proposal:

First, we will set up a common goal for every young person that represents educational success. We will call it a B.A. We will then make it difficult or impossible for most people to achieve this goal. For those who can, achieving the goal will take four years no matter what is being taught. We will attach an economic reward for reaching the goal that often has little to do with the content of what has been learned. We will lure large numbers of people who do not possess adequate ability or motivation to try to achieve the goal and then fail. We will then stigmatize everyone who fails to achieve it.

What I have just described is the system that we have in place. There must be a better way.

Joining the Conversation

1. The "I say" here is explicit: "too many people are going to college." We know what Charles Murray thinks. But why does he think this? In the rest of his essay, he tells us why. Summarize his argument, noting all the reasons and evidence he gives to support his claim.

2. Is Murray right—are too many people going to college? If you disagree, why? Whether or not you agree with him, do you find his argument persuasive?

3. In the middle of the essay is a lengthy narrative about someone who is trying to decide what to be when he grows up, an electrician or a manager. What does this narrative contribute to Murray's argument? Where would the argument be without the narrative?

4. Compare Murray's argument that college is a waste of time for many with Sanford J. Ungar's argument (pp. 226–33) that anyone can benefit from a college education. Which one do you find more convincing?

5. In one or two paragraphs, reflect on why you chose your current school. Did you consider, first and foremost, how your college would help you "learn how to make a living," as Murray would recommend? Did you consider other potential benefits of your college education? If you could have a well-paying job without a college education, would you go to college anyway?

Two Years Are Better than Four

LIZ ADDISON

—▢—

OH, THE HAND WRINGING. "College as America used to understand it is coming to an end," bemoans Rick Perlstein and his beatnik friend of fallen face. Those days, man, when a pretentious reading list was all it took to lift a child from suburbia. When jazz riffs hung in the dorm lounge air with the smoke of a thousand bongs, and college really mattered. Really mattered?

Rick Perlstein thinks so. It mattered so much to him that he never got over his four years at the University of Privilege. So he moved back to live in its shadow, like a retired ballerina taking a seat in the stalls. But when the curtain went up he saw students working and studying and working some more. Adults

———

LIZ ADDISON attended Piedmont Virginia Community College and Southern Maine Community College, where she graduated with a degree in biology in 2008. She received a graduate degree from the Royal Veterinary College in London in 2014 and now works as a veterinarian in Virginia. This essay, published in 2007, was a runner-up in a *New York Times Magazine* college essay contest. The essay responds to Rick Perlstein's opinion piece "What's the Matter With College?," in which he argues that universities no longer matter as much as they once did.

before their time. Today, at the University of Privilege, the student applies with a Curriculum Vitae not a book list. Shudder.

Thus, Mr. Perlstein concludes, the college experience—a rite of passage as it was meant it to be—must have come to an end. But he is wrong. For Mr. Perlstein, so rooted in his own nostalgia, is looking for himself—and he would never think to look for himself in the one place left where the college experience of self-discovery does still matter to those who get there. My guess, reading between the lines, is that Mr. Perlstein has never set foot in an American community college.

The philosophy of the community college, and I have been to two of them, is one that unconditionally allows its students to begin. Just begin. Implicit in this belief is the understanding that anything and everything is possible. Just follow any one of the 1,655 road signs, and pop your head inside—yes, they let anyone in—and there you will find discoveries of a first independent film, a first independent thought, a first independent study. This college experience remains as it should. This college brochure is not marketing for the parents—because the parents, nor grandparents, probably never went to college themselves.

Upon entry to my first community college I had but one 5 O'level to my name. These now disbanded qualifications once marked the transition from lower to upper high school in the Great British education system. It was customary for the average student to proceed forward with a clutch of O'levels, say eight or nine. On a score of one, I left school hurriedly at sixteen. Thomas Jefferson once wrote, "Everybody should have an education proportional to their life." In my case, my life became proportional to my education. But, in doing so, it had the good fortune to land me in an American community college and now, from that priceless springboard, I too seek admission to the University of Privilege. Enter on empty and leave with a head full of dreams? How can Mr. Perlstein say college does not matter anymore?

The community college system is America's hidden public service gem. If I were a candidate for office I would campaign from every campus. Not to score political points, but simply to make sure that anyone who is looking to go to college in this country knows where to find one. Just recently, I read an article in the *New York Times* describing a "college application essay" workshop for low-income students. I was strangely disturbed that those interviewed made no mention of community college. Mr. Perlstein might have been equally disturbed, for the thrust of the workshop was no different to that of an essay coach to the affluent. "Make Life Stories Shine," beams the headline. Or, in other words, prove yourself worldly, insightful, cultured, mature, before you get to college.

Yet, down at X.Y.C.C. it is still possible to enter the college experience as a rookie. That is the understanding—that you will grow up a little bit with your first English class, a bit more with your first psychology class, a whole lot more with your first biology, physics, chemistry. That you may shoot through the roof with calculus, philosophy, or genetics. "College is the key," a young African American student writes for the umpteenth torturous revision of his college essay, "as well as hope." Oh, I wanted desperately to say, please tell him about community college. Please tell him that hope can begin with just one placement test.

See Chapter 9 on mixing academic and colloquial styles.

When Mr. Perlstein and friends say college no longer holds importance, they mourn for both the individual and society. Yet, arguably, the community college experience is more critical to the nation than that of former beatnik types who, lest we forget, did not change the world. The community colleges of America cover this country college by college and community by community. They offer a network of affordable future, of accessible hope, and an option to dream. In the cold light of day, is it perhaps not more important to foster students with dreams rather than a building take-over?

I believe so. I believe the community college system to be one of America's uniquely great institutions. I believe it should be celebrated as such. "For those who find it necessary to go to a two-year college," begins one University of Privilege admissions paragraph. None too subtle in its implication, but very true. For some students, from many backgrounds, would never breathe the college experience if it were not for the community college. Yes, it is here that Mr. Perlstein will find his college years of self-discovery, and it is here he will find that college does still matter.

Joining the Conversation

1. What view is Liz Addison responding to? Write out a sentence or two summarizing the "they say."

2. Addison discusses her own educational experience as part of her argument. What role does this use of autobiographical narrative play in her argument?

3. How does Addison make clear that her topic is really important—and that it should matter to readers?

4. In closing, Addison writes of community colleges: "It is here that Mr. Perlstein will find his college years of self-discovery, and it is here he will find that college does still matter." Do you think college still matters? Write an essay responding to this point from your own perspective as a college student.

Colleges Prepare People for Life

FREEMAN HRABOWSKI

—◻—

Those Who Claim Education Is a Waste of Time
Are Missing the Bigger Picture

A RECENT NEW YORK TIMES illustration read, "*College Is
for Suckers.*"

The words were emblazoned across the sweatshirts of four
students, and the accompanying article made essentially that
point. It echoed an increasingly common refrain that college
is expensive, that students are taking on unmanageable debt
and that they too often graduate unprepared for the world of
work.

———

FREEMAN HRABOWSKI has been the president of the University of
Maryland, Baltimore County, since 1992. In 2012, President Obama
named him chair of the President's Advisory Commission on Educational Excellence for African Americans. Hrabowski is the coauthor
of the books *Beating the Odds: Raising Academically Successful African
American Males* (1998) and *Overcoming the Odds: Raising Academically
Successful African American Young Women* (2001). This article first
appeared in the *Baltimore Sun* on December 22, 2013.

In contrast, many economists and educators point to data showing that the fastest growing job categories require at least a college degree. College graduates are much more likely to be employed than those with only a high school diploma and earn substantially higher salaries. According to this viewpoint, college graduates aren't suckers; they're the winners in a globally competitive economy.

Both sides have points. However, the first argument treats colleges as monolithic, and the second turns individual students into averages. The reality is far more nuanced. Too often, our current system fails to help students identify the institutions best suited to them—based on their academic preparation, aspirations and resources. When we focus so heavily on monetary inputs and outputs, we ignore the question of what it truly means to be educated, such as contributing to the public good.

Yes, colleges prepare people for jobs, but more critically, they prepare people for life. A job may be the starting point for the good life, but it shouldn't be the end point.

One strength of American higher education is the diversity [5] of missions among our 4,700 colleges and universities. Students can find institutions—public and private, two-year and four-year—for just about any educational niche and budget. Students and families should learn as much as possible about each institution they are considering. They should also estimate the net costs, looking carefully at expenses and anticipated grants and loans.

Colleges and universities must also be more transparent. President Barack Obama has called on higher education to standardize the information given to students and families about costs, financial aid packages, students' debt at graduation and graduation rates. The University System of Maryland was one of the first systems to sign on to that initiative, and campuses now provide new details in a revised financial aid award letter sent to families.

Maryland families are fortunate. Thanks to the support of Gov. Martin O'Malley and the Maryland General Assembly, tuition at our public colleges and universities has increased only 3 percent each year for the past three years, following four years of tuition freezes. In addition, our public and private institutions have an impressive record of admitting and educating a broad range of students who have become leaders in Maryland and beyond. Enrollments at our institutions are healthy because families have seen that our graduates succeed.

Even so, students need strong counseling to identify the best possible options. Lack of counseling is one reason that fewer than 10 percent of Americans from the lowest income quartile have earned a college degree by age 24, compared to 80 percent of those in the top quartile.

My colleagues spend countless hours advising prospective students, some of whom ultimately choose UMBC, while others decide we're not the best fit. That type of counseling is critical, but it is time consuming and expensive for both colleges and high schools.

College preparatory initiatives such as Way2go Maryland, 10 led by the University System of Maryland, have proven promising. So, too, have programs run by such private organizations as the CollegeBound Foundation in Baltimore and CollegeTracks in Montgomery County. However, adequate funding continues to be a challenge, and much work remains in educating students about their options. Higher education must continue to partner with school systems to prepare more students for college. At stake isn't just a clearer path to financial stability, but the path to limitless possibilities.

I'm reminded of that each day when I walk past a statue of the late Walter Sondheim that stands in the heart of our campus and reminds us of the power of education each day. When Sondheim graduated from college, he took a job at Hochschild, Kohn & Company in Baltimore and had no idea what else he wanted to do with his life. Fortunately, college had given him a strong grounding in the liberal arts and the ability to think broadly. That uncertain young man became the most admired civic leader in Maryland. He advised mayors and governors, led desegregation of the city schools, and was an active leader for decades.

Sondheim's education helped him get a job. More important, it helped him change Maryland—and we all are the beneficiaries.

Joining the Conversation

1. After reading Freeman Hrabowski's essay carefully, pick the one sentence that you think expresses its main idea, and be prepared to explain your choice.
2. In what way does Hrabowski use a "they say / I say" format to structure his argument? What other points might he have included in his "I say"' response?
3. Hrabowski stresses the role of college in preparing leaders who help their communities. What counterarguments could you present to his emphasis on college as a place to learn how to help others?
4. How do you think Hrabowski might respond to Charles Murray's argument (pp. 234–54) that not everyone should go to college?

5. "Higher education as we know it is about to come to an end." That's the opening line of an article by two other college presidents. Go to **theysayiblog.com** and enter "Give Colleges More Credit" in the search box. How does this article's argument compare with Hrabowski's? Which piece do you find more persuasive, and why?

6. This piece appeared as an op-ed essay in the *Baltimore Sun*, a newspaper read primarily by people living in that city and its surrounding areas. In what ways did Hrabowski tailor his essay to this particular audience? How might he revise it to address a national audience?

Hidden Intellectualism

GERALD GRAFF

EVERYONE KNOWS SOME YOUNG PERSON who is impressively "street smart" but does poorly in school. What a waste, we think, that one who is so intelligent about so many things in life seems unable to apply that intelligence to academic work. What doesn't occur to us, though, is that schools and colleges might be at fault for missing the opportunity to tap into such street smarts and channel them into good academic work.

Nor do we consider one of the major reasons why schools and colleges overlook the intellectual potential of street smarts: the fact that we associate those street smarts with anti-intellectual concerns. We associate the educated life, the life of the mind, too narrowly and exclusively with subjects and texts that we consider inherently weighty and academic. We assume that it's possible to wax intellectual about Plato, Shakespeare,

---

GERALD GRAFF, one of the coauthors of this book, is a professor of English and education at the University of Illinois at Chicago. He is a past president of the Modern Language Association, the world's largest professional association of university scholars and teachers. This essay is adapted from his 2003 book, *Clueless in Academe: How Schooling Obscures the Life of the Mind.*

the French Revolution, and nuclear fission, but not about cars, dating, fashion, sports, TV, or video games.

The trouble with this assumption is that no necessary connection has ever been established between any text or subject and the educational depth and weight of the discussion it can generate. Real intellectuals turn any subject, however lightweight it may seem, into grist for their mill through the thoughtful questions they bring to it, whereas a dullard will find a way to drain the interest out of the richest subject. That's why a George Orwell writing on the cultural meanings of penny postcards is infinitely more substantial than the cogitations of many professors on Shakespeare or globalization (104–16).

See pp. 58–61 for tips on disagreeing, with reasons.

Students do need to read models of intellectually challenging writing—and Orwell is a great one—if they are to become intellectuals themselves. But they would be more prone to take on intellectual identities if we encouraged them to do so at first on subjects that interest them rather than ones that interest us.

I offer my own adolescent experience as a case in point. Until I entered college, I hated books and cared only for sports. The only reading I cared to do or could do was sports magazines, on which I became hooked, becoming a regular reader of *Sport* magazine in the late forties, *Sports Illustrated* when it began publishing in 1954, and the annual magazine guides to professional baseball, football, and basketball. I also loved the sports novels for boys of John R. Tunis and Clair Bee and autobiographies of sports stars like Joe DiMaggio's *Lucky to Be a Yankee* and Bob Feller's *Strikeout Story*. In short, I was your typical teenage anti-intellectual—or so I believed for a long time. I have recently come to think, however, that my preference for sports over schoolwork was not anti-intellectualism so much as intellectualism by other means.

In the Chicago neighborhood I grew up in, which had become a melting pot after World War II, our block was solidly middle class, but just a block away—doubtless concentrated there by the real estate companies—were African Americans, Native Americans, and "hillbilly" whites who had recently fled postwar joblessness in the South and Appalachia. Negotiating this class boundary was a tricky matter. On the one hand, it was necessary to maintain the boundary between "clean-cut" boys like me and working-class "hoods," as we called them, which meant that it was good to be openly smart in a bookish sort of way. On the other hand, I was desperate for the approval of the hoods, whom I encountered daily on the playing field and in the neighborhood, and for this purpose it was not at all good to be book-smart. The hoods would turn on you if they sensed you were putting on airs over them: "Who you lookin' at, smart ass?" as a leather-jacketed youth once said to me as he relieved me of my pocket change along with my self-respect.

I grew up torn, then, between the need to prove I was smart and the fear of a beating if I proved it too well; between the need not to jeopardize my respectable future and the need to impress the hoods. As I lived it, the conflict came down to a choice between being physically tough and being verbal. For a boy in my neighborhood and elementary school, only being "tough" earned you complete legitimacy. I still recall endless, complicated debates in this period with my closest pals over who was "the toughest guy in the school." If you were less than negligible as a fighter, as I was, you settled for the next best thing, which was to be inarticulate, carefully hiding telltale marks of literacy like correct grammar and pronunciation.

In one way, then, it would be hard to imagine an adolescence more thoroughly anti-intellectual than mine. Yet in retrospect, I see that it's more complicated, that I and the 1950s themselves were not simply hostile toward intellectualism, but divided and ambivalent. When Marilyn Monroe married the playwright Arthur Miller in 1956 after divorcing the retired baseball star

Joe DiMaggio, the symbolic triumph of geek over jock suggested the way the wind was blowing. Even Elvis, according to his biographer Peter Guralnick, turns out to have supported Adlai over Ike in the presidential election of 1956. "I don't dig the intellectual bit," he told reporters. "But I'm telling you, man, he knows the most" (327).

Though I too thought I did not "dig the intellectual bit," I see now that I was unwittingly in training for it. The germs had actually been planted in the seemingly philistine debates about which boys were the toughest. I see now that in the interminable analysis of sports teams, movies, and toughness that my friends and I engaged in—a type of analysis, needless to say, that the real toughs would never have stooped to—I was already betraying an allegiance to the egghead world. I was practicing being an intellectual before I knew that was what I wanted to be.

It was in these discussions with friends about toughness and sports, I think, and in my reading of sports books and magazines, that I began to learn the rudiments of the intellectual life: how to make an argument, weigh different kinds of evidence, move between particulars and generalizations, summarize the views of others, and enter a conversation about ideas. It was in reading and arguing about sports and toughness that I experienced what it felt like to propose a generalization, restate and respond to a counterargument, and perform other intellectualizing operations, including composing the kind of sentences I am writing now.

Only much later did it dawn on me that the sports world was more compelling than school because it was *more intellectual than school,* not less. Sports after all was full of challenging arguments, debates, problems for analysis, and intricate statistics that you could care about, as school conspicuously was not. I believe that street smarts beat out book smarts in our culture

10

not because street smarts are nonintellectual, as we generally suppose, but because they satisfy an intellectual thirst more thoroughly than school culture, which seems pale and unreal.

They also satisfy the thirst for community. When you entered sports debates, you became part of a community that was not limited to your family and friends, but was national and public. Whereas schoolwork isolated you from others, the pennant race or Ted Williams's .400 batting average was something you could talk about with people you had never met. Sports introduced you not only to a culture steeped in argument, but to a public argument culture that transcended the personal. I can't blame my schools for failing to make intellectual culture resemble the Super Bowl, but I do fault them for failing to learn anything from the sports and entertainment worlds about how to organize and represent intellectual culture, how to exploit its gamelike element and turn it into arresting public spectacle that might have competed more successfully for my youthful attention.

For here is another thing that never dawned on me and is still kept hidden from students, with tragic results: that the real intellectual world, the one that existed in the big world beyond school, is organized very much like the world of team sports, with rival texts, rival interpretations and evaluations of texts, rival theories of why they should be read and taught, and elaborate team competitions in which "fans" of writers, intellectual systems, methodologies, and -isms contend against each other.

To be sure, school contained plenty of competition, which became more invidious as one moved up the ladder (and has become even more so today with the advent of high-stakes testing). In this competition, points were scored not by making arguments, but by a show of information or vast reading, by grade-grubbing, or other forms of one-upmanship. School competition, in short, reproduced the less attractive features of sports culture without those that create close bonds and community.

And in distancing themselves from anything as enjoyable 15 and absorbing as sports, my schools missed the opportunity to capitalize on an element of drama and conflict that the intellectual world shares with sports. Consequently, I failed to see the parallels between the sports and academic worlds that could have helped me cross more readily from one argument culture to the other.

Sports is only one of the domains whose potential for literacy training (and not only for males) is seriously underestimated by educators, who see sports as competing with academic development rather than a route to it. But if this argument suggests why it is a good idea to assign readings and topics that are close to students' existing interests, it also suggests the limits of this tactic. For students who get excited about the chance to write about their passion for cars will often write as poorly and unreflectively on that topic as on Shakespeare or Plato. Here is the flip side of what I pointed out before: that there's no necessary relation between the degree of interest a student shows in a text or subject and the quality of thought or expression such a student manifests in writing or talking about it. The challenge, as college professor Ned Laff has put it, "is not simply to exploit students' nonacademic interests, but to get them to see those interests through academic eyes."

To say that students need to see their interests "through academic eyes" is to say that street smarts are not enough. Making students' nonacademic interests an object of academic study is useful, then, for getting students' attention and overcoming their boredom and alienation, but this tactic won't in itself necessarily move them closer to an academically rigorous treatment of those interests. On the other hand, inviting students to write about cars, sports, or clothing fashions does not have to be a pedagogical cop-out as long as students are required to see these interests "through academic eyes," that is, to think and write about cars, sports, and fashions in a reflective, analytical way, one that sees them as microcosms of what is going on in the wider culture.

If I am right, then schools and colleges are missing an opportunity when they do not encourage students to take their nonacademic interests as objects of academic study. It is self-defeating to decline to introduce any text or subject that figures to engage students who will otherwise tune out academic work entirely. If a student cannot get interested in Mill's *On Liberty* but will read *Sports Illustrated* or *Vogue* or the hip-hop magazine *Source* with absorption, this is a strong argument for assigning the magazines over the classic. It's a good bet that if students get hooked on reading and writing by doing term papers on *Source*, they will eventually get to *On Liberty*. But even if they don't, the magazine reading will make them more literate and reflective than they would be otherwise. So it makes pedagogical sense to develop classroom units on sports, cars, fashions, rap music, and other such topics. Give me the student anytime who writes a sharply argued, sociologically acute analysis of an issue in *Source* over the student who writes a lifeless explication of *Hamlet* or Socrates' *Apology*.

Works Cited

Cramer, Richard Ben. *Joe DiMaggio: The Hero's Life*. Simon & Schuster, 2000.

DiMaggio, Joe. *Lucky to Be a Yankee*. Bantam, 1949.

Feller, Bob. *Strikeout Story*. Bantam, 1948.

Guralnick, Peter. *Last Train to Memphis: The Rise of Elvis Presley*. Little, Brown, 1994.

Orwell, George. *A Collection of Essays*. Harcourt, 1953.

Joining the Conversation

1. Gerald Graff begins his essay with the view that we generally associate "book smarts" with intellectualism and "street smarts" with anti-intellectualism. Graff then provides an extended example from his early life to counter this viewpoint. What do you think of his argument that boyhood conversations about sports provided a solid foundation for his later intellectual life? What support does he provide, and how persuasive is it?

2. Graff argues in paragraph 13 that the intellectual world is much like the world of team sports, with "rival texts . . . , rival theories . . . , and elaborate team competitions." Can you think of any examples from your own experience that support this assertion? In what ways do you think "the real intellectual world" is different from the world of team sports?

3. Imagine a conversation between Graff and Mike Rose (pp. 272–84) on the intellectual skills people can develop outside the realm of formal education and the benefits of these skills.

4. So what? Who cares? Graff does not answer these questions explicitly. Do it for him: write a brief paragraph saying why his argument matters, and for whom.

5. Graff argues that schools should encourage students to think critically, read, and write about areas of personal interest such as cars, fashion, or music—as long as they do so in an intellectually serious way. What do you think? Write an essay considering the educational merits of such a proposal, taking Graff's argument as a "they say."

Blue-Collar Brilliance

MIKE ROSE

——□——

MY MOTHER, Rose Meraglio Rose (Rosie), shaped her adult identity as a waitress in coffee shops and family restaurants. When I was growing up in Los Angeles during the 1950s, my father and I would occasionally hang out at the restaurant until her shift ended, and then we'd ride the bus home with her. Sometimes she worked the register and the counter, and we sat there; when she waited booths and tables, we found a booth in the back where the waitresses took their breaks.

There wasn't much for a child to do at the restaurants, and so as the hours stretched out, I watched the cooks and waitresses and listened to what they said. At mealtimes, the pace of the kitchen staff and the din from customers picked up. Weaving in and out around the room, waitresses warned behind you in impassive but urgent voices. Standing at the service window

MIKE ROSE is a professor at the UCLA Graduate School of Education and Information Studies. He is well known for his writing on issues of literacy, including the books *Lives on the Boundary: The Struggles and Achievements of America's Underprepared* (1989) and *Back to School: Why Everyone Deserves a Second Chance at Education* (2012). This article originally appeared in 2009 in the *American Scholar*, a magazine published by the Phi Beta Kappa Society.

Rosie solved technical problems and human problems on the fly.

facing the kitchen, they called out abbreviated orders. Fry four on two, my mother would say as she clipped a check onto the metal wheel. Her tables were deuces, four-tops, or six-tops according to their size; seating areas also were nicknamed. The racetrack, for instance, was the fast-turnover front section. Lingo conferred authority and signaled know-how.

Rosie took customers' orders, pencil poised over pad, while fielding questions about the food. She walked full tilt through the room with plates stretching up her left arm and two cups of coffee somehow cradled in her right hand. She stood at a table or booth and removed a plate for this person, another for that person, then another, remembering who had the hamburger, who had the fried shrimp, almost always getting it right. She would haggle with the cook about a returned order and rush by us, saying, He gave me lip, but I got him. She'd take a minute to flop down in the booth next to my father. I'm all in, she'd say, and whisper something about a customer. Gripping the outer edge of the table with one hand, she'd watch the room and note, in the flow of our conversation, who needed a refill, whose order was taking longer to prepare than it should, who was finishing up.

I couldn't have put it in words when I was growing up, but what I observed in my mother's restaurant defined the world of adults, a place where competence was synonymous with physical work. I've since studied the working habits of blue-collar workers and have come to understand how much my mother's kind of work demands of both body and brain. A waitress acquires knowledge and intuition about the ways and the rhythms of the restaurant business. Waiting on seven to nine tables, each with two to six customers, Rosie devised memory strategies so that she could remember who ordered what. And because she knew the average time it took to prepare different dishes, she could monitor an order that was taking too long at the service station.

Like anyone who is effective at physical work, my mother ₅ learned to work smart, as she put it, to make every move count. She'd sequence and group tasks: What could she do first, then second, then third as she circled through her station? What tasks could be clustered? She did everything on the fly, and when problems arose—technical or human—she solved them within the flow of work, while taking into account the emotional state of her co-workers. Was the manager in a good mood? Did the cook wake up on the wrong side of the bed? If so, how could she make an extra request or effectively return an order?

And then, of course, there were the customers who entered the restaurant with all sorts of needs, from physiological ones, including the emotions that accompany hunger, to a sometimes complicated desire for human contact. Her tip depended on how well she responded to these needs, and so she became adept at reading social cues and managing feelings, both the customers' and her own. No wonder, then, that Rosie was intrigued by psychology. The restaurant became the place where she studied human behavior, puzzling over the problems of her regular customers and refining her ability to deal with people in a difficult world. She took pride in being among the public, she'd say. There isn't a day that goes by in the restaurant that you don't learn something.

My mother quit school in the seventh grade to help raise her brothers and sisters. Some of those siblings made it through high school, and some dropped out to find work in railroad yards, factories, or restaurants. My father finished a grade or two in primary school in Italy and never darkened the schoolhouse door again. I didn't do well in school either. By high school I had accumulated a spotty academic record and many hours of hazy disaffection. I spent a few years on the vocational track, but in my senior year I was inspired by my English teacher and managed to squeak into a small college on probation.

My freshman year was academically bumpy, but gradually I began to see formal education as a means of fulfillment and as a road toward making a living. I studied the humanities and later the social and psychological sciences and taught for ten years in a range of situations—elementary school, adult education courses, tutoring centers, a program for Vietnam veterans who wanted to go to college. Those students had socioeconomic and educational backgrounds similar to mine. Then I went back to graduate school to study education and cognitive psychology and eventually became a faculty member in a school of education.

Intelligence is closely associated with formal education—the type of schooling a person has, how much and how long—and most people seem to move comfortably from that notion to a belief that work requiring less schooling requires less intelligence. These assumptions run through our cultural history, from the post-Revolutionary War period, when mechanics were characterized by political rivals as illiterate and therefore incapable of participating in government, until today. More than once I've heard a manager label his workers as "a bunch of dummies." Generalizations about intelligence, work, and social class deeply affect our assumptions about ourselves and each other, guiding the ways we use our minds to learn, build knowledge, solve problems, and make our way through the world.

See Chapter 1 for ways to introduce something implied or assumed.

Although writers and scholars have often looked at the work-   10 ing class, they have generally focused on the values such workers exhibit rather than on the thought their work requires—a subtle but pervasive omission. Our cultural iconography promotes the muscled arm, sleeve rolled tight against biceps, but no brightness behind the eye, no image that links hand and brain.

One of my mother's brothers, Joe Meraglio, left school in the ninth grade to work for the Pennsylvania Railroad. From there he joined the Navy, returned to the railroad, which was already in decline, and eventually joined his older brother at General Motors where, over a 33-year career, he moved from working on the assembly line to supervising the paint-and-body department. When I was a young man, Joe took me on a tour of the factory. The floor was loud—in some places deafening—and when I turned a corner or opened a door, the smell of chemicals knocked my head back. The work was repetitive and taxing, and the pace was inhuman.

Still, for Joe the shop floor provided what school did not; it was like schooling, he said, a place where you're constantly learning. Joe learned the most efficient way to use his body by acquiring a set of routines that were quick and preserved energy. Otherwise he would never have survived on the line.

As a foreman, Joe constantly faced new problems and became a consummate multi-tasker, evaluating a flurry of demands quickly, parceling out physical and mental resources, keeping a number of ongoing events in his mind, returning to whatever task had been interrupted, and maintaining a cool head under the pressure of grueling production schedules. In the midst of all this, Joe learned more and more about the auto industry, the technological and social dynamics of the shop floor, the machinery and production processes, and the basics of paint chemistry and of plating and baking. With further promotions, he not only solved problems but also began to find problems to solve: Joe initiated the redesign of the nozzle on a paint sprayer, thereby eliminating costly and unhealthy over-spray. And he found a way to reduce energy costs on the baking ovens without affecting the quality of the paint. He lacked formal knowledge of how the machines under his supervision worked, but he had direct experience with them, hands-on knowledge, and was savvy about their quirks and operational capabilities. He could experiment with them.

In addition, Joe learned about budgets and management. Coming off the line as he did, he had a perspective of workers' needs and management's demands, and this led him to think of ways to improve efficiency on the line while relieving some of the stress on the assemblers. He had each worker in a unit learn his or her co-workers' jobs so they could rotate across stations to relieve some of the monotony. He believed that rotation would allow assemblers to get longer and more frequent breaks. It was

With an eighth-grade education, Joe (hands together) advanced to supervisor of a G.M. paint-and-body department.

an easy sell to the people on the line. The union, however, had to approve any modification in job duties, and the managers were wary of the change. Joe had to argue his case on a number of fronts, providing him a kind of rhetorical education.

Eight years ago I began a study of the thought processes 15 involved in work like that of my mother and uncle. I catalogued the cognitive demands of a range of blue-collar and service jobs, from waitressing and hair styling to plumbing and welding. To gain a sense of how knowledge and skill develop, I observed experts as well as novices. From the details of this close examination, I tried to fashion what I called "cognitive biographies" of blue-collar workers. Biographical accounts of the lives of scientists, lawyers, entrepreneurs, and other professionals are rich with detail about the intellectual dimension of their work.

But the life stories of working-class people are few and are typically accounts of hardship and courage or the achievements wrought by hard work.

Our culture—in Cartesian fashion—separates the body from the mind, so that, for example, we assume that the use of a tool does not involve abstraction. We reinforce this notion by defining intelligence solely on grades in school and numbers on IQ tests. And we employ social biases pertaining to a person's place on the occupational ladder. The distinctions among blue, pink, and white collars carry with them attributions of character, motivation, and intelligence. Although we rightly acknowledge and amply compensate the play of mind in white-collar and professional work, we diminish or erase it in considerations about other endeavors—physical and service work particularly. We also often ignore the experience of everyday work in administrative deliberations and policymaking.

But here's what we find when we get in close. The plumber seeking leverage in order to work in tight quarters and the hair stylist adroitly handling scissors and comb manage their bodies strategically. Though work-related actions become routine with experience, they were learned at some point through observation, trial and error, and, often, physical or verbal assistance from a co-worker or trainer. I've frequently observed novices talking to themselves as they take on a task, or shaking their head or hand as if to erase an attempt before trying again. In fact, our traditional notions of routine performance could keep us from appreciating the many instances within routine where quick decisions and adjustments are made. I'm struck by the thinking-in-motion that some work requires, by all the mental activity that can be involved in simply getting from one place to another: the waitress rushing back through her station to the kitchen or the foreman walking the line.

The use of tools requires the studied refinement of stance, grip, balance, and fine-motor skills. But manipulating tools is intimately tied to knowledge of what a particular instrument can do in a particular situation and do better than other similar tools. A worker must also know the characteristics of the material one is engaging—how it reacts to various cutting or compressing devices, to degrees of heat, or to lines of force. Some of these things demand judgment, the weighing of options, the consideration of multiple variables, and, occasionally, the creative use of a tool in an unexpected way.

In manipulating material, the worker becomes attuned to aspects of the environment, a training or disciplining of perception that both enhances knowledge and informs perception. Carpenters have an eye for length, line, and angle; mechanics troubleshoot by listening; hair stylists are attuned to shape, texture, and motion. Sensory data merge with concept, as when an auto mechanic relies on sound, vibration, and even smell to understand what cannot be observed.

Planning and problem solving have been studied since the 20 earliest days of modern cognitive psychology and are considered core elements in Western definitions of intelligence. To work is to solve problems. The big difference between the psychologist's laboratory and the workplace is that in the former the problems are isolated and in the latter they are embedded in the real-time flow of work with all its messiness and social complexity.

Much of physical work is social and interactive. Movers determining how to get an electric range down a flight of stairs require coordination, negotiation, planning, and the establishing of incremental goals. Words, gestures, and sometimes a quick pencil sketch are involved, if only to get the rhythm right. How important it is, then, to consider the social and communicative dimension of physical work, for it provides the medium for so much of work's intelligence.

Given the ridicule heaped on blue-collar speech, it might seem odd to value its cognitive content. Yet, the flow of talk at work provides the channel for organizing and distributing tasks, for troubleshooting and problem solving, for learning new information and revising old. A significant amount of teaching, often informal and indirect, takes place at work. Joe Meraglio saw that much of his job as a supervisor involved instruction. In some service occupations, language and communication are central: observing and interpreting behavior and expression, inferring mood and motive, taking on the perspective of others, responding appropriately to social cues, and knowing when you're understood. A good hair stylist, for instance, has the ability to convert vague requests (I want something light and summery) into an appropriate cut through questions, pictures, and hand gestures.

Verbal and mathematical skills drive measures of intelligence in the Western Hemisphere, and many of the kinds of work I studied are thought to require relatively little proficiency in either. Compared to certain kinds of white-collar occupations, that's true. But written symbols flow through physical work.

Numbers are rife in most workplaces: on tools and gauges, as measurements, as indicators of pressure or concentration or temperature, as guides to sequence, on ingredient labels, on lists and spreadsheets, as markers of quantity and price. Certain jobs require workers to make, check, and verify calculations, and to collect and interpret data. Basic math can be involved, and some workers develop a good sense of numbers and patterns. Consider, as well, what might be called material mathematics: mathematical functions embodied in materials and actions, as when a carpenter builds a cabinet or a flight of stairs. A simple mathematical act can extend quickly beyond itself. Measuring, for example, can involve more than recording the dimensions of an object. As I watched a cabinetmaker measure a long strip of wood, he read a number off the tape out loud, looked back over his shoulder to the kitchen wall, turned back to his task, took another measurement, and paused for a moment in thought. He was solving a problem involving the molding, and the measurement was important to his deliberation about structure and appearance.

In the blue-collar workplace, directions, plans, and refer- 25 ence books rely on illustrations, some representational and others, like blueprints, that require training to interpret. Esoteric symbols—visual jargon—depict switches and receptacles, pipe fittings, or types of welds. Workers themselves often make sketches on the job. I frequently observed them grab a pencil to sketch something on a scrap of paper or on a piece of the material they were installing.

Though many kinds of physical work don't require a high literacy level, more reading occurs in the blue-collar workplace than is generally thought, from manuals and catalogues to work orders and invoices, to lists, labels, and forms. With routine tasks, for example, reading is integral to understanding production quotas, learning how to use an instrument, or applying a product. Written notes can initiate action, as in restaurant orders or reports of machine malfunction, or they can serve as memory aids.

True, many uses of writing are abbreviated, routine, and repetitive, and they infrequently require interpretation or analysis. But analytic moments can be part of routine activities, and seemingly basic reading and writing can be cognitively rich. Because workplace language is used in the flow of other activities, we can overlook the remarkable coordination of words, numbers, and drawings required to initiate and direct action.

If we believe everyday work to be mindless, then that will affect the work we create in the future. When we devalue the full range of everyday cognition, we offer limited educational opportunities and fail to make fresh and meaningful instructional connections among disparate kinds of skill and knowledge. If we think that whole categories of people—identified by class or occupation—are not that bright, then we reinforce social separations and cripple our ability to talk across cultural divides.

Affirmation of diverse intelligence is not a retreat to a softhearted definition of the mind. To acknowledge a broader range of intellectual capacity is to take seriously the concept of cognitive variability, to appreciate in all the Rosies and Joes the thought that drives their accomplishments and defines who they are. This is a model of the mind that is worthy of a democratic society.

Joining the Conversation

1. This essay begins with a fairly detailed description of Mike Rose's mother at her work as a waitress in the 1950s, when he was a child. How is this description related to his argument? Is it an effective opening? Why or why not?
2. How would you summarize Rose's overall argument? What evidence does he offer as support? How convincing is his argument?
3. Where does Rose mention differing views, and what is his reason for bringing them up? What are these other views, and who holds them?

4. How do you think Rose would respond to Charles Murray's argument (pp. 234–54) that many students lack the intellectual potential to succeed in college?

5. Write an essay in which you consider the intellectual demands of a kind of work that you have done or are interested in.

Bowie State University
Commencement Speech

MICHELLE OBAMA

WELL, THANK YOU. (Applause.) Oh, my goodness. Thank you so much. (Applause.) Oh, my goodness. It is such a—you all, rest yourselves. You've got a long day ahead. It is beyond a pleasure and an honor for me to be here with all of you today.

Of course, I want to start by thanking President Bernim for that very kind introduction, for this wonderful degree, and for his outstanding leadership here at Bowie State University. I also want to recognize Chancellor Kirwan, Provost Jackson,

---

MICHELLE OBAMA, First Lady of the United States, has been assistant commissioner of planning and development in Chicago, dean of student services at the University of Chicago, and vice president of community and external affairs for the University of Chicago Medical Center. In 2014, Obama started the "Reach Higher" initiative, which encourages young people to continue their education after high school by completing another degree, whether through vocational training, community college, or a four-year college or university. This text comes from a commencement speech Obama made in 2013 at Bowie State University in Maryland.

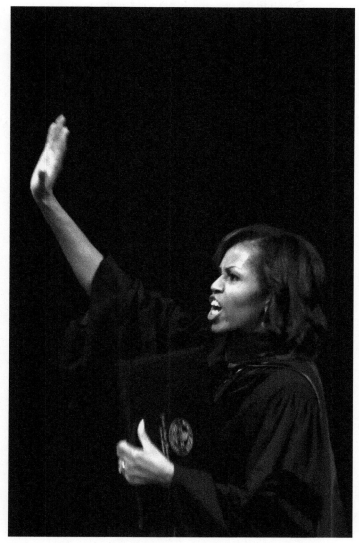

Michelle Obama delivering the commencement speech at Bowie State.

Executive Vice President and General Counsel Karen Johnson Shaheed, Vice Chair Barry Gossett. And of course, I want to thank the BSU Madrigal Singers—they did a great job—the university choir, and DeMarcus Franklin for their wonderful performances here today. You all are amazing. I just wish I could sing. Can't sing a lick.

I also want to recognize today's Presidential Medal of Excellence recipient, Professor Freeman Hrabowski, who's a for-real brother as well. (Applause.) And I want to thank him for his tremendous work as the Chair of the President's Advisory Commission on Educational Excellence for African Americans. He has done some magnificent work, but we have so much more work to do.

And let's take another moment to thank all of the beautiful people sitting all around us today—the folks who have loved you and pushed you and put up with you every step of the way. (Applause.) Give another round of applause to all the family members who are here today. (Applause.) Yes, indeed. This is your day, too.

But most of all, to the Bowie State University class of 2013, congratulations. (Applause.) Oh, congratulations. You don't know how proud we all are of you. Just look at you. We're so proud of how hard you worked, all those long hours in the classroom, in the library. Oh, yeah. Amen. (Laughter.) All those jobs you worked to help pay your tuition. Many of you are the first in your families to get a college degree. (Applause.) Some of you are balancing school with raising families of your own. (Applause.) So I know this journey hasn't been easy. I know you've had plenty of moments of doubt and frustration and just plain exhaustion.

See Chapter 9 for tips on considering your audience.

But listen, you dug deep and you kept pushing forward to make it to this magnificent day. (Applause.) And in doing so, you didn't just complete an important chapter in your own story, you also became part of the story of this great university—a story that began nearly 150 years ago, not far from where we all sit today. As you all know, this school first opened its doors in January of 1865, in an African Baptist church in Baltimore. And by 1866, just a year later, it began offering education courses to train a new generation of African American teachers.

Now, just think about this for a moment: For generations, in many parts of this country, it was illegal for black people to get an education. Slaves caught reading or writing could be beaten to within an inch of their lives. Anyone—black or white—who dared to teach them could be fined or thrown into jail. And yet, just two years after the Emancipation Proclamation was signed, this school was founded not just to educate African Americans, but to teach them how to educate others. It was in many ways an act of defiance, an eloquent rebuttal to the idea that black people couldn't or shouldn't be educated. And since then, generations of students from all backgrounds have come to this school to be challenged, inspired, and empowered. And they have gone on to become leaders here in Maryland and across this country, running businesses, educating young people, leading the high-tech industries that will power our economy for decades to come.

That is the story of Bowie State University, the commitment to educating our next generation and building ladders of opportunity for anyone willing to work for it. All of you are now part of that story. And with that tremendous privilege comes an important set of responsibilities—responsibilities that you inherit the moment you leave this stadium with that diploma in your hand.

And that's what I want to talk with you about today. I want to talk about the obligations that come with a Bowie State education, and how you can fulfill those obligations by how you live your lives.

So let's return, for a moment, to the time when the school 10 and others like it were founded. Many of these schools were little more than drafty log cabins with mud floors, leaky roofs and smoke-wood stoves in the corner. Blackboards, maps, and even books were considered luxuries. And both students and teachers faced constant threats from those who refused to accept freedom for African Americans.

In one Eastern Shore town, a teacher reported to work one morning to find that someone had smashed the windows of her schoolhouse. Other black schools across Maryland were burned to the ground. Teachers received death threats. One was even beaten by an angry mob. But despite the risks, understand, students flocked to these schools in droves, often walking as many as eight to ten miles a day to get their education. In fact, the educational association that founded Bowie State wrote in their 1864 report that—and this is a quote—"These people are coming in beyond our ability to receive them." Desperately poor communities held fundraisers for these schools, schools which they often built with their own hands. And folks who were barely scraping by dug deep into their own pockets to donate money.

You see, for these folks, education was about more than just learning to read or write. As the abolitionist Frederick Douglass put it, "Education means emancipation," he said. He said, "It means light and liberty. It means the uplifting of the soul of man into the glorious light of truth, the only light by which men can be free." You hear that? The only light by which men can be free. (Applause.)

So to the folks who showed up to your school on that January day back in 1865, education meant nothing less than freedom. It meant economic independence, a chance to provide for their families. It meant political empowerment, the chance to read the newspaper and articulate an informed opinion and take their rightful place as full citizens of this nation.

So back then, people were hungry to learn. Do you hear me? Hungry to get what they needed to succeed in this country. And that hunger did not fade over time. If anything, it only grew stronger. I mean, think about the century-long battle that so many folks waged to end the evil of segregation. Think about civil rights icons like Thurgood Marshall, Dr. King, who argued groundbreaking school integration cases, led historic marches, protests, and boycotts. As you know, Dr. King's house was bombed. A police chief pulled a gun on Thurgood Marshall. They both received piles of hate mail and countless death threats, but they kept on fighting.

Think about those nine young men and women who faced 15 down an angry mob just to attend school in Little Rock, Arkansas. And that was just the first day. For months afterwards, they were spat on, jeered at, punched, and tripped as they walked down the halls. Their classmates threw food at them in the cafeteria and hurled ink at them during class. But they kept on showing up. They kept claiming their rightful place at that school.

And think about little Ruby Bridges, who was just six years old when she became one of the first black children in New Orleans to attend an all-white school. Parents actually pulled their children out of that school in protest. People retaliated against her family. Her father lost his job. And only one teacher at that entire school would agree to teach her. But the Bridges family refused to back down. So for an entire year, little Ruby sat all alone, a class of one, dutifully learning her lessons.

See, that is the sacrifice that those folks and so many others have made. That is the hunger they felt. For them and so many others, getting an education was literally a matter of life or death.

But today, more than 150 years after the Emancipation Proclamation, more than 50 years after the end of "separate but equal," when it comes to getting an education, too many of our young people just can't be bothered. Today, instead of walking miles every day to school, they're sitting on couches for hours playing video games, watching TV. Instead of dreaming of being a teacher or a lawyer or a business leader, they're fantasizing about being a baller or a rapper. (Applause.) Right now, one in three African American students are dropping out of high school. Only one in five African Americans between the ages of twenty-five and twenty-nine has gotten a college degree—one in five.

But let's be very clear. Today, getting an education is as important if not more important than it was back when this university was founded. Just look at the statistics. (Applause.) People who earn a bachelor's degree or higher make nearly three times more money than high school dropouts, and they're far less likely to be unemployed. A recent study even found that African American women with a college degree live an average of six-and-a-half years longer than those without. And for men, it's nearly ten years longer. So yes, people who are more educated actually live longer.

So I think we can agree, and we need to start feeling that 20 hunger again, you know what I mean? (Applause.) We need to once again fight to educate ourselves and our children like our lives depend on it, because they do.

We need to dig deep and find the same kind of grit and determination that drove those first students at this school and generations of students who came after them. I am talking about the kind of grit and determination displayed by folks right here at Bowie State. Folks like Ariel Williams-Edwards, one of today's graduates. (Applause.) Yeah, Ariel!

Ariel's mother struggled with substance abuse, and Ariel and her sister were removed from her care and sent to live with their grandmother.

But Ariel decided to draw inspiration from her struggle—she majored in social work so she could help families like hers. (Applause.) Yes! She became a member of the Phi Alpha national honor society. And she's been accepted to graduate school to get her master's degree in social work starting in September. Yes, indeed. (Applause.)

And then there's Audrey Marie Lugmayer, another one of this year's graduates. Audrey is the daughter of a single father, and her dad has struggled with some serious health issues. So after graduating from high school, Audrey worked full time for a year, because she couldn't bear the thought of putting any more financial burdens on her father. She kept on working here at Bowie State, even while juggling a full course load. And today, she is graduating with a perfect 4.0 GPA. (Applause.) Yes. God is very good.

It is that kind of unwavering determination—that relentless focus on getting an education in the face of obstacles—that's what we need to reclaim, as a community and as a nation. That was the idea at the very heart of the founding of this school.

It's even in the words of your school song: "Oh Bowie State, 25 dear Bowie State, may you forever be the flame of faith, the torch of truth to guide the steps of youth." And that's not just a lyric—it is a call to action. Many of you will answer that call by carrying on the proud Bowie State tradition of serving as teachers, devoting your careers to guiding the steps of the next generation.

But for those of you who aren't going into education, you're not off the hook. Oh, no. Oh, no. No matter what career you pursue, every single one of you has a role to play as educators for our young people. So if you have friends or cousins or siblings who are not taking their education seriously, shake them up. Go talk some sense into them. Get them back on track. (Applause.)

If the school in your neighborhood isn't any good, don't just accept it. Get in there, fix it. Talk to the parents. Talk to the teachers. Get business and community leaders involved as well, because we all have a stake in building schools worthy of our children's promise.

And when it comes to your own kids, if you don't like what they're watching on TV, turn it off. (Applause.) If you don't like the video games they're playing, take them away. (Applause.) Take a stand against the media that elevates today's celebrity gossip instead of the serious issues of our time. Take a stand against the culture that glorifies instant gratification instead of hard work and lasting success.

And as my husband has said often, please stand up and reject the slander that says a black child with a book is trying to act white. Reject that. (Applause.)

In short, be an example of excellence for the next genera- 30 tion and do everything you can to help them understand the power and purpose of a good education. See, that's what my own parents did for me and my brother.

See, my parents didn't go to college, but they were determined to give us that opportunity. My dad was a pump operator at the city water plant, diagnosed with MS in his early thirties. And every morning I watched him struggle to get out of bed and inch his way to his walker, and painstakingly button his uniform, but never once did I hear him complain. Not once. He just kept getting up, day after day, year after year, to do whatever he could to give our family a better shot at life.

So when it came time for my brother and I to go to college, most of our tuition came from student loans and grants. But my dad still had to pay a small portion of that tuition each semester, and he was always determined to pay his share right on time—even taking out loans when he fell short, because he couldn't bear the thought of us missing a registration deadline because his check was late.

And there is not a day that goes by when I don't think about the sacrifices that my mom and dad made for me. There is not a day that goes by when I don't think about living up to the example they set, and how I must do everything in my power to make them proud of the daughter they raised. (Applause.)

And today, I am thinking about all the mothers and fathers just like my parents, all the folks who dug into their pockets for that last dime, the folks who built those schools brick by brick, who faced down angry mobs just to reach those schoolhouse doors. I am thinking about all the folks who worked that extra shift and took that extra job, and toiled and bled and prayed so that we could have something better. (Applause.)

The folks who, as the poet Alice Walker once wrote, "Knew 35 what we must know without knowing a page of it themselves." Their sacrifice is your legacy. Do you hear me? And now it is up to all of you to carry that legacy forward, to be that flame of fate, that torch of truth to guide our young people toward a better future for themselves and for this country.

And if you do that, and I know that you will, if you uphold that obligation, then I am confident we will build an even better future for the next generation of graduates from this fine school and for all of the children in this country—because our lives depend on it.

I wish you Godspeed, good luck. I love you all. Do good things. God bless. (Applause.)

Joining the Conversation

1. One purpose of this speech was to celebrate the achievements of the graduates. But at the same time, Michelle Obama is making an argument about some things she hopes those graduates will do. What's her main point, and how does she support that point?

2. Throughout her address, Obama explains why her argument matters, but she does not, as this book advises, start with what others are saying and then introduce her own ideas as a response. What do you think her "they say" would be?

3. Obama addresses much of the speech to the graduates and their families. Find some specific examples of her references to this audience, and discuss the ways in which she tries to make a connection with them.

4. Obama refers to college president Freeman Hrabowski in paragraph 3 of her speech. What parallels, if any, can you find between her speech and Hrabowski's op-ed (pp. 259–63)?

5. Imagine you were in the audience that day at Bowie State. Write a tweet summarizing something Obama said—and then responding in some way. You may need to write two tweets.

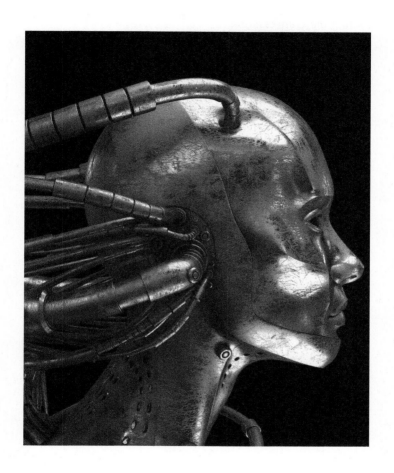

SEVENTEEN

ARE WE IN A RACE
AGAINST THE MACHINE?

Do we need to worry about technology? Many commentators worry that constant technological changes have serious repercussions for our brains, our bodies, and our societies. Neuroscientist Susan Greenfield argues that our brains are "under threat" from "an ever-expanding world of new technology: multichannel television, video games, MP3 players, the Internet, wireless networks, Bluetooth links" and that "attention spans are shorter, personal communication skills are reduced and there's a marked reduction in the ability to think abstractly." Scientists used to believe that the human brain changed up through adolescence but was relatively stable after that until it began to decline in old age. Now, however, there is strong evidence for what Greenfield calls "the malleability of the adult brain," with alterations in brain structure caused by the devices we have come to rely upon—and even some indications that we are losing important mental skills.

A number of experts argue that such claims are seriously overstated. In their view, as we adapt to new technologies, we are actually becoming smarter, happier, and more productive. Clive Thompson, for example, highlights the growing role of computers in chess playing in arguing that technology is changing our minds—and our lives—for the better. Similarly, Kevin Kelly asserts that robots will inevitably take over virtually all work now done by people but, at the same time, will allow us to develop rewarding careers that we presently can't even imagine. Using a graphic format, Brooke Gladstone and Josh Neufeld show that new technologies have been a source of anxiety since at least the fourth century BCE, when Greek philosopher Plato warned in the *Phaedrus* that reading and writing would harm people's memories. Responding to concerns that digital communication is leading to a decline in face-to-face interaction, Jenna Wortham writes about several smartphone applications that she claims can actually enhance relationships. Along these same lines, college student Michaela Cullington discusses her own research study, which found that, contrary to widespread belief, text messaging is a practical form of communication and does not weaken students' academic writing skills.

These optimistic views are countered by those of several other commentators. Nicholas Carr, for example, believes that extensive use of the internet is hurting our capacity for deep thought. Once a strong proponent of digital technologies, Sherry Turkle now argues that they are leading to a decline in intimacy and a move away from self-reflection. Malcolm Gladwell questions the potential of Twitter and other social media to play more than a superficial role in fostering political activism.

The readings in this chapter give us much to think about, raising a number of complex problems and providing no easy solutions. And while some commentators may paint a rosy picture of technology while others contemplate doomsday scenarios, there's a little bit of optimism and pessimism in each piece, which is one of the factors that make this conversation one worth joining.

Better than Human:
Why Robots Will—and Must—Take Our Jobs

KEVIN KELLY

—▭—

Imagine that 7 out of 10 working Americans got fired
tomorrow. What would they all do?

IT'S HARD TO BELIEVE you'd have an economy at all if you
gave pink slips to more than half the labor force. But that—
in slow motion—is what the industrial revolution did to the
workforce of the early 19th century. Two hundred years ago,
70 percent of American workers lived on the farm. Today automation has eliminated all but 1 percent of their jobs, replacing them (and their work animals) with machines. But the
displaced workers did not sit idle. Instead, automation created
hundreds of millions of jobs in entirely new fields. Those who

KEVIN KELLY was a founding member of *Wired* and served as its executive editor for six years. He is now "senior maverick" at *Wired* and
the editor of the *Cool Tools* website. His books include *Cool Tools:
A Catalog of Possibilities* (2013), *What Technology Wants* (2010), and
New Rules for the New Economy (1998). This essay first appeared on
the *Wired* website on December 24, 2012.

once farmed were now manning the legions of factories that churned out farm equipment, cars, and other industrial products. Since then, wave upon wave of new occupations have arrived—appliance repairman, offset printer, food chemist, photographer, web designer—each building on previous automation. Today, the vast majority of us are doing jobs that no farmer from the 1800s could have imagined.

For more on ways to address a skeptical reader, see Chapter 6.
It may be hard to believe, but before the end of this century, 70 percent of today's occupations will likewise be replaced by automation. Yes, dear reader, even you will have your job taken away by machines. In other words, robot replacement is just a matter of time. This upheaval is being led by a second wave of automation, one that is centered on artificial cognition, cheap sensors, machine learning, and distributed smarts. This deep automation will touch all jobs, from manual labor to knowledge work.

First, machines will consolidate their gains in already-automated industries. After robots finish replacing assembly line workers, they will replace the workers in warehouses. Speedy bots able to lift 150 pounds all day long will retrieve boxes, sort them, and load them onto trucks. Fruit and vegetable picking will continue to be robotized until no humans pick outside of specialty farms. Pharmacies will feature a single pill-dispensing robot in the back while the pharmacists focus on patient consulting. Next, the more dexterous chores of cleaning in offices and schools will be taken over by late-night robots, starting with easy-to-do floors and windows and eventually getting to toilets. The highway legs of long-haul trucking routes will be driven by robots embedded in truck cabs.

All the while, robots will continue their migration into white-collar work. We already have artificial intelligence in many of our machines; we just don't call it that. Witness one piece of software by Narrative Science . . . that can write newspaper stories about sports games directly from the games' stats or generate a synopsis of a company's stock performance each day from bits of text around the web. Any job dealing with reams of paperwork will be taken over by bots, including much of medicine. Even those areas of medicine not defined by paperwork, such as surgery, are becoming increasingly robotic. The rote tasks of any information-intensive job can be automated. It doesn't matter if you are a doctor, lawyer, architect, reporter, or even programmer: The robot takeover will be epic.

And it has already begun.   5

Here's why we're at the inflection point: Machines are acquiring smarts.

We have preconceptions about how an intelligent robot should look and act, and these can blind us to what is already happening around us. To demand that artificial intelligence be humanlike is the same flawed logic as demanding that artificial flying be birdlike, with flapping wings. Robots will think different. To see how far artificial intelligence has penetrated our lives, we need to shed the idea that they will be humanlike.

Consider Baxter, a revolutionary new workbot from Rethink Robotics. Designed by Rodney Brooks, the former MIT professor who invented the best-selling Roomba vacuum cleaner and its descendants, Baxter is an early example of a new class of industrial robots created to work alongside humans. Baxter does not look impressive. It's got big strong arms and a flatscreen display like many industrial bots. And Baxter's hands perform repetitive manual tasks, just as factory robots do. But it's different in three significant ways.

First, it can look around and indicate where it is looking by shifting the cartoon eyes on its head. It can perceive humans

Baxter, a workbot created to work alongside humans.

working near it and avoid injuring them. And workers can see whether it sees them. Previous industrial robots couldn't do this, which means that working robots have to be physically segregated from humans. The typical factory robot is imprisoned within a chain-link fence or caged in a glass case. They are simply too dangerous to be around, because they are oblivious to others. This isolation prevents such robots from working in a small shop, where isolation is not practical. Optimally, workers should be able to get materials to and from the robot or to tweak its controls by hand throughout the workday; isolation makes that difficult. Baxter, however, is aware. Using force-feedback technology to feel if it is colliding with a person or another bot, it is courteous. You can plug it into a wall socket in your garage and easily work right next to it.

Second, anyone can train Baxter. It is not as fast, strong, or precise as other industrial robots, but it is smarter. To train the bot you simply grab its arms and guide them in the correct motions and sequence. It's a kind of "watch me do this" routine. Baxter learns the procedure and then repeats it. Any worker is capable of this show-and-tell; you don't even have to be literate. Previous workbots required highly educated engineers and crack programmers to write thousands of lines of code (and then debug them) in order to instruct the robot in the simplest change of task. The code has to be loaded in batch mode, i.e., in large, infrequent batches, because the robot cannot be reprogrammed while it is being used. Turns out the real cost of the typical industrial robot is not its hardware but its operation. Industrial robots cost $100,000-plus to purchase but can require four times that amount over a lifespan to program, train, and maintain. The costs pile up until the average lifetime bill for an industrial robot is half a million dollars or more.

The third difference, then, is that Baxter is cheap. Priced at $22,000, it's in a different league compared with the $500,000 total bill of its predecessors. It is as if those established robots, with their batch-mode programming, are the mainframe computers of the robot world, and Baxter is the first PC robot. It is likely to be dismissed as a hobbyist toy, missing key features like sub-millimeter precision, and not serious enough. But as with the PC, and unlike the mainframe, the user can interact with it directly, immediately, without waiting for experts to mediate— and use it for nonserious, even frivolous things. It's cheap enough that small-time manufacturers can afford one to package up their wares or custom paint their product or run their 3-D printing machine. Or you could staff up a factory that makes iPhones.

Baxter was invented in a century-old brick building near the Charles River in Boston. In 1895 the building was a manufacturing marvel in the very center of the new manufacturing world. It even generated its own electricity. For a hundred years the factories inside its walls changed the world around us. Now the capabilities of Baxter and the approaching cascade of superior robot workers spur Brooks to speculate on how these robots will shift manufacturing in a disruption greater than the last revolution. Looking out his office window at the former industrial neighborhood, he says, "Right now we think of manufacturing as happening in China. But as manufacturing costs sink because of robots, the costs of transportation become a far greater factor than the cost of production. Nearby will be cheap. So we'll get this network of locally franchised factories, where most things will be made within 5 miles of where they are needed."

That may be true of making stuff, but a lot of jobs left in the world for humans are service jobs. I ask Brooks to walk with me through a local McDonald's and point out the jobs that his kind of robots can replace. He demurs and suggests it might be 30 years before robots will cook for us. "In a fast food place you're not doing the same task very long. You're always changing things on the fly, so you need special solutions. We are not trying to sell a specific solution. We are building a general-purpose machine that other workers can set up themselves and work alongside." And once we can cowork with robots right next to us, it's inevitable that our tasks will bleed together, and soon our old work will become theirs—and our new work will become something we can hardly imagine.

To understand how robot replacement will happen, it's useful to break down our relationship with robots into four categories, as summed up in this chart:

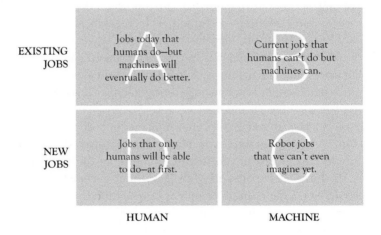

	HUMAN	MACHINE
EXISTING JOBS	Jobs today that humans do—but machines will eventually do better.	Current jobs that humans can't do but machines can.
NEW JOBS	Jobs that only humans will be able to do—at first.	Robot jobs that we can't even imagine yet.

The rows indicate whether robots will take over existing jobs 15 or make new ones, and the columns indicate whether these jobs seem (at first) like jobs for humans or for machines.

Let's begin with quadrant A: jobs humans can do but robots can do even better. Humans can weave cotton cloth with great effort, but automated looms make perfect cloth, by the mile, for a few cents. The only reason to buy handmade cloth today is because you want the imperfections humans introduce. We no longer value irregularities while traveling 70 miles per hour, though—so the fewer humans who touch our car as it is being made, the better.

And yet for more complicated chores, we still tend to believe computers and robots can't be trusted. That's why we've been slow to acknowledge how they've mastered some conceptual routines, in some cases even surpassing their mastery of physical routines. A computerized brain known as the autopilot can fly a 787 jet unaided, but irrationally we place human pilots in the cockpit to babysit the autopilot "just in case." In the 1990s, computerized mortgage appraisals replaced human appraisers wholesale. Much tax preparation has gone to computers, as well as routine x-ray analysis and pretrial evidence-gathering— all once done by highly paid smart people. We've accepted utter reliability in robot manufacturing; soon we'll accept it in robotic intelligence and service.

Next is quadrant B: jobs that humans can't do but robots can. A trivial example: Humans have trouble making a single brass screw unassisted, but automation can produce a thousand exact ones per hour. Without automation, we could not make a single computer chip—a job that requires degrees of precision, control, and unwavering attention that our animal bodies don't possess. Likewise no human, indeed no group of humans, no matter their education, can quickly search through all the web pages in the world to uncover the one page revealing the price of eggs in Katmandu yesterday. Every time you click on the search button you are employing a robot to do something we as a species are unable to do alone.

While the displacement of formerly human jobs gets all the headlines, the greatest benefits bestowed by robots and automation come from their occupation of jobs we are unable to do. We don't have the attention span to inspect every square millimeter of every CAT scan looking for cancer cells. We don't have the millisecond reflexes needed to inflate molten glass into the shape of a bottle. We don't have an infallible memory to keep track of every pitch in Major League Baseball and calculate the probability of the next pitch in real time.

We aren't giving "good jobs" to robots. Most of the time we are giving them jobs we could never do. Without them, these jobs would remain undone.

Now let's consider quadrant C, the new jobs created by automation—including the jobs that we did not know we wanted done. This is the greatest genius of the robot takeover: With the assistance of robots and computerized intelligence, we already can do things we never imagined doing 150 years ago. We can remove a tumor in our gut through our navel, make a talking-picture video of our wedding, drive a cart on Mars, print a pattern on fabric that a friend mailed to us through the air. We are doing, and are sometimes paid for doing, a million new activities that would have dazzled and shocked the farmers of 1850. These new accomplishments are not merely chores that were difficult before. Rather they are dreams that are created chiefly by the capabilities of the machines that can do them. They are jobs the machines make up.

Before we invented automobiles, air-conditioning, flatscreen video displays, and animated cartoons, no one living in ancient Rome wished they could watch cartoons while riding to Athens in climate-controlled comfort. Two hundred years ago not a single citizen of Shanghai would have told you that they would buy a tiny slab that allowed them to talk to faraway friends before they would buy indoor plumbing. Crafty AIs embedded in first-person-shooter games have given millions of teenage boys the urge, the need, to become professional game designers—a dream that no boy in Victorian times ever had. In a very real way our inventions assign us our jobs. Each successful bit of automation generates new occupations—occupations we would not have fantasized about without the prompting of the automation.

To reiterate, the bulk of new tasks created by automation are tasks only other automation can handle. Now that we have search engines like Google, we set the servant upon a thousand new errands. Google, can you tell me where my phone is? Google, can you match the people suffering depression with the doctors selling pills? Google, can you predict when the next viral epidemic will erupt? Technology is indiscriminate this way, piling up possibilities and options for both humans and machines.

It is a safe bet that the highest-earning professions in the year 2050 will depend on automations and machines that have not been invented yet. That is, we can't see these jobs from here, because we can't yet see the machines and technologies that will make them possible. Robots create jobs that we did not even know we wanted done.

Finally, that leaves us with quadrant D, the jobs that only humans can do—at first. The one thing humans can do that robots can't (at least for a long while) is to decide what it is that humans want to do. This is not a trivial trick; our desires are inspired by our previous inventions, making this a circular question.

When robots and automation do our most basic work, mak- 25
ing it relatively easy for us to be fed, clothed, and sheltered,
then we are free to ask, "What are humans for?" Industrializa-
tion did more than just extend the average human lifespan.
It led a greater percentage of the population to decide that
humans were meant to be ballerinas, full-time musicians, math-
ematicians, athletes, fashion designers, yoga masters, fan-fiction
authors, and folks with one-of-a-kind titles on their business
cards. With the help of our machines, we could take up these
roles; but of course, over time, the machines will do these as
well. We'll then be empowered to dream up yet more answers
to the question "What should we do?" It will be many generations before a robot can answer that.

This postindustrial economy will keep expanding, even
though most of the work is done by bots, because part of
your task tomorrow will be to find, make, and complete new
things to do, new things that will later become repetitive
jobs for the robots. In the coming years robot-driven cars and
trucks will become ubiquitous; this automation will spawn
the new human occupation of trip optimizer, a person who
tweaks the traffic system for optimal energy and time usage.
Routine robo-surgery will necessitate the new skills of keeping machines sterile. When automatic self-tracking of all your
activities becomes the normal thing to do, a new breed of
professional analysts will arise to help you make sense of the
data. And of course we will need a whole army of robot nannies, dedicated to keeping your personal bots up and running.
Each of these new vocations will in turn be taken over by
robots later.

The real revolution erupts when everyone has personal
workbots, the descendants of Baxter, at their beck and call.

Imagine you run a small organic farm. Your fleet of worker bots do all the weeding, pest control, and harvesting of produce, as directed by an overseer bot, embodied by a mesh of probes in the soil. One day your task might be to research which variety of heirloom tomato to plant; the next day it might be to update your custom labels. The bots perform everything else that can be measured.

Right now it seems unthinkable: We can't imagine a bot that can assemble a stack of ingredients into a gift or manufacture spare parts for our lawn mower or fabricate materials for our new kitchen. We can't imagine our nephews and nieces running a dozen workbots in their garage, churning out inverters for their friend's electric-vehicle startup. We can't imagine our children becoming appliance designers, making custom batches of liquid-nitrogen dessert machines to sell to the millionaires in China. But that's what personal robot automation will enable.

Everyone will have access to a personal robot, but simply 30 owning one will not guarantee success. Rather, success will go to those who innovate in the organization, optimization, and customization of the process of getting work done with bots and machines. Geographical clusters of production will matter, not for any differential in labor costs but because of the differential in human expertise. It's human-robot symbiosis. Our human assignment will be to keep making jobs for robots—and that is a task that will never be finished. So we will always have at least that one "job."

In the coming years our relationships with robots will become ever more complex. But already a recurring pattern is emerging. No matter what your current job or your salary, you will progress through these Seven Stages of Robot Replacement, again and again:

1. A robot/computer cannot possibly do the tasks I do.

[*Later.*]

2. OK, it can do a lot of them, but it can't do everything I do.

[*Later.*]

3. OK, it can do everything I do, except it needs me when it breaks down, which is often.

[*Later.*]

4. OK, it operates flawlessly on routine stuff, but I need to train it for new tasks.

[*Later.*]

5. OK, it can have my old boring job, because it's obvious that was not a job that humans were meant to do.

[*Later.*]

6. Wow, now that robots are doing my old job, my new job is much more fun and pays more!

[*Later.*]

7. I am so glad a robot/computer cannot possibly do what I do now.

This is not a race against the machines. If we race against them, we lose. This is a race with the machines. You'll be paid in the future based on how well you work with robots. Ninety percent of your coworkers will be unseen machines. Most of what you do will not be possible without them. And there will be a blurry line between what you do and what they do. You might no longer think of it as a job, at least at first, because anything that seems like drudgery will be done by robots.

We need to let robots take over. They will do jobs we have been doing, and do them much better than we can. They will do jobs we can't do at all. They will do jobs we never imagined even needed to be done. And they will help us discover new jobs for ourselves, new tasks that expand who we are. They will let us focus on becoming more human than we were.

Let the robots take the jobs, and let them help us dream up new work that matters.

Joining the Conversation

1. Kevin Kelly argues that machines will eventually take over many of the jobs that we now perform. This scenario may seem dire, yet he doesn't appear at all worried. To the contrary, in fact. Why not? Find statements in the article that explain his attitude.

2. This article appeared in *Wired*, a magazine for people who know and care about digital technology. How is the article geared toward a pro-technology audience? How might Kelly have presented his argument for a readership that was less enthusiastic about technology?

3. Though he acknowledges that some of his ideas are "hard to believe," Kelly does not begin by saying explicitly what other ideas or assumptions he's responding to. How does he begin, and how does that beginning set the stage for his argument?

4. Nicholas Carr (pp. 313–29) is less optimistic than Kelly about the future impact of technology. Who do you find more persuasive, and why?

5. Kelly concludes by saying that robots will help us find "new work that matters." Does that outcome seem likely? Write an essay responding to that assertion, perhaps focusing on one profession that interests you.

Is Google Making Us Stupid?

NICHOLAS CARR

—◻—

"DAVE, STOP. STOP, WILL YOU? Stop, Dave. Will you stop, Dave?" So the supercomputer HAL pleads with the implacable astronaut Dave Bowman in a famous and weirdly poignant scene toward the end of Stanley Kubrick's *2001: A Space Odyssey*. Bowman, having nearly been sent to a deep-space death by the malfunctioning machine, is calmly, coldly disconnecting the memory circuits that control its artificial "brain." "Dave, my mind is going," HAL says, forlornly. "I can feel it. I can feel it."

I can feel it, too. Over the past few years I've had an uncomfortable sense that someone, or something, has been tinkering with my brain, remapping the neural circuitry, reprogramming the memory. My mind isn't going—so far as I can tell—but it's changing. I'm not thinking the way I used to think. I can

---

NICHOLAS CARR writes frequently on issues of technology and culture. His books include *Does IT Matter?* (2004), *The Big Switch: Rewiring the World, from Edison to Google* (2008), *The Shallows: What the Internet Is Doing to Our Brains* (2010), and *The Glass Cage: Automation and Us* (2014). Carr also has written for periodicals including the *Guardian*, the *New York Times*, the *Wall Street Journal*, and *Wired*, and he blogs at roughtype.com. This essay appeared originally as the cover article in the July/August 2008 issue of the *Atlantic*.

Dave (Keir Dullea) removes HAL's "brain" in *2001: A Space Odyssey*.

feel it most strongly when I'm reading. Immersing myself in a book or a lengthy article used to be easy. My mind would get caught up in the narrative or the turns of the argument, and I'd spend hours strolling through long stretches of prose. That's rarely the case anymore. Now my concentration often starts to drift after two or three pages. I get fidgety, lose the thread, begin looking for something else to do. I feel as if I'm always dragging my wayward brain back to the text. The deep reading that used to come naturally has become a struggle.

I think I know what's going on. For more than a decade now, I've been spending a lot of time online, searching and surfing and sometimes adding to the great databases of the Internet. The Web has been a godsend to me as a writer. Research that once required days in the stacks or periodical rooms of libraries can now be done in minutes. A few Google searches, some quick clicks on hyperlinks, and I've got the telltale fact or pithy quote I was after. Even when I'm not working, I'm as likely as not to be foraging in the Web's info-thickets reading and writing e-mails, scanning headlines and blog posts, watching videos and listening to podcasts, or just tripping from link to link to link. (Unlike footnotes, to which they're sometimes likened, hyperlinks don't merely point to related works; they propel you toward them.)

For me, as for others, the Net is becoming a universal medium, the conduit for most of the information that flows through my eyes and ears and into my mind. The advantages of having immediate access to such an incredibly rich store of information are many, and they've been widely described and duly applauded. "The perfect recall of silicon memory," *Wired*'s Clive Thompson has written, "can be an enormous boon to thinking." But that boon comes at a price. As the media theorist Marshall McLuhan pointed out in the 1960s, media are not just passive channels of information. They supply the stuff of thought, but they also shape the process of thought. And what the Net seems to be doing is chipping away my capacity for concentration and contemplation. My mind now expects to take in information the way the Net distributes it: in a swiftly moving stream of particles. Once I was a scuba diver in the sea of words. Now I zip along the surface like a guy on a Jet Ski.

I'm not the only one. When I mention my troubles with 5 reading to friends and acquaintances—literary types, most of them—many say they're having similar experiences. The more they use the Web, the more they have to fight to stay focused on long pieces of writing. Some of the bloggers I follow have also begun mentioning the phenomenon. Scott Karp, who writes a blog about online media, recently confessed that he has stopped reading books altogether. "I was a lit major in college, and used to be [a] voracious book reader," he wrote. "What happened?" He speculates on the answer: "What if I do all my reading on the web not so much because the way I read has changed, i.e. I'm just seeking convenience, but because the way I *think* has changed?"

Bruce Friedman, who blogs regularly about the use of computers in medicine, also has described how the Internet has altered his mental habits. "I now have almost totally lost the ability to read and absorb a longish article on the web or in print," he wrote earlier this year. A pathologist who has long been on the faculty of the University of Michigan Medical School, Friedman elaborated on his comment in a telephone conversation with me. His thinking, he said, has taken on a "staccato" quality, reflecting the way he quickly scans short passages of text from many sources online. "I can't read *War and Peace* anymore," he admitted. "I've lost the ability to do that. Even a blog post of more than three or four paragraphs is too much to absorb. I skim it."

Anecdotes alone don't prove much. And we still await the long-term neurological and psychological experiments that will provide a definitive picture of how Internet use affects cognition. But a recently published study of online research habits, conducted by scholars from University College London, suggests that we may well be in the midst of a sea change in the way we read and think. As part of the five-year research program, the scholars examined computer logs documenting the behavior of visitors to two popular research sites, one operated by the British Library and one by a U.K. educational consortium, that provide access to journal articles, e-books, and other sources of written information. They found that people using the sites exhibited "a form of skimming activity," hopping from one source to another and rarely returning to any source they'd already visited. They typically read no more than one or two pages of an article or book before they would "bounce" out to another site. Sometimes they'd save a long article, but there's no evidence that they ever went back and actually read it. The authors of the study report:

> It is clear that users are not reading online in the traditional sense; indeed there are signs that new forms of "reading" are emerging as users "power browse" horizontally through titles, contents pages and abstracts going for quick wins. It almost seems that they go online to avoid reading in the traditional sense.

Thanks to the ubiquity of text on the Internet, not to mention the popularity of text-messaging on cell phones, we may well be reading more today than we did in the 1970s or 1980s, when television was our medium of choice. But it's a different kind of reading, and behind it lies a different kind of thinking—perhaps even a new sense of the self. "We are not only *what* we read," says Maryanne Wolf, a developmental psychologist at Tufts University and the author of *Proust and the Squid: The Story and Science of the Reading Brain*. "We are *how* we read." Wolf worries that the style of reading promoted by the Net, a style that puts "efficiency" and "immediacy" above all else, may be weakening our capacity for the kind of deep reading that emerged when an earlier technology, the printing press, made long and complex works of prose commonplace. When we read online, she says, we tend to become "mere decoders of information." Our ability to interpret text, to make the rich mental connections that form when we read deeply and without distraction, remains largely disengaged.

Reading, explains Wolf, is not an instinctive skill for human beings. It's not etched into our genes the way speech is. We have to teach our minds how to translate the symbolic characters we see into the language we understand. And the media or other technologies we use in learning and practicing the craft of reading play an important part in shaping the neural circuits inside our brains. Experiments demonstrate that readers of ideograms, such as the Chinese, develop a mental circuitry for reading that is very different from the circuitry found in those of us whose written language employs an alphabet. The variations extend across many regions of the brain, including those that govern such essential cognitive functions as memory and the interpretation of visual and auditory stimuli. We can expect as well that the circuits woven by our use of the Net will be different from those woven by our reading of books and other printed works.

Sometime in 1882, Friedrich Nietzsche bought a typewriter— 10 a Malling-Hansen Writing Ball, to be precise. His vision was failing, and keeping his eyes focused on a page had become exhausting and painful, often bringing on crushing headaches. He had been forced to curtail his writing, and he feared that he would soon have to give it up. The typewriter rescued him, at least for a time. Once he had mastered touch-typing, he was

Friedrich Nietzsche and his Malling-Hansen Writing Ball.

able to write with his eyes closed, using only the tips of his fingers. Words could once again flow from his mind to the page.

But the machine had a subtler effect on his work. One of Nietzsche's friends, a composer, noticed a change in the style of his writing. His already terse prose had become even tighter, more telegraphic. "Perhaps you will through this instrument even take to a new idiom," the friend wrote in a letter, noting that, in his own work, his "'thoughts' in music and language often depend on the quality of pen and paper."

"You are right," Nietzsche replied, "our writing equipment takes part in the forming of our thoughts." Under the sway of the machine, writes the German media scholar Friedrich A. Kittler, Nietzsche's prose "changed from arguments to aphorisms, from thoughts to puns, from rhetoric to telegram style."

The human brain is almost infinitely malleable. People used to think that our mental meshwork, the dense connections formed among the 100 billion or so neurons inside our skulls, was largely fixed by the time we reached adulthood. But brain researchers have discovered that that's not the case. James Olds, a professor of neuroscience who directs the Krasnow Institute for Advanced Study at George Mason University, says that even the adult mind "is very plastic." Nerve cells routinely break old connections and form new ones. "The brain," according to Olds, "has the ability to reprogram itself on the fly, altering the way it functions."

As we use what the sociologist Daniel Bell has called our "intellectual technologies"—the tools that extend our mental rather than our physical capacities—we inevitably begin to take on the qualities of those technologies. The mechanical clock, which came into common use in the 14th century, provides a compelling example. In *Technics and Civilization*, the historian and cultural critic Lewis Mumford described how the clock "disassociated time from human events and helped create the belief in an independent world of mathematically measurable sequences." The "abstract framework of divided time" became "the point of reference for both action and thought."

The clock's methodical ticking helped bring into being the scientific mind and the scientific man. But it also took something away. As the late MIT computer scientist Joseph Weizenbaum observed in his 1976 book, *Computer Power and Human Reason: From Judgment to Calculation*, the conception of the world that emerged from the widespread use of timekeeping instruments "remains an impoverished version of the older one, for it rests on a rejection of those direct experiences that formed the basis for, and indeed constituted, the old reality." In deciding when to eat, to work, to sleep, to rise, we stopped listening to our senses and started obeying the clock.

The process of adapting to new intellectual technologies is reflected in the changing metaphors we use to explain ourselves to ourselves. When the mechanical clock arrived, people began thinking of their brains as operating "like clockwork." Today, in the age of software, we have come to think of them as operating "like computers." But the changes, neuroscience tells us, go much deeper than metaphor. Thanks to our brain's plasticity, the adaptation occurs also at a biological level.

The Internet promises to have particularly far-reaching effects on cognition. In a paper published in 1936, the British mathematician Alan Turing proved that a digital computer, which at the time existed only as a theoretical machine, could be programmed to perform the function of any other information-processing device. And that's what we're seeing today. The Internet, an immeasurably powerful computing system, is subsuming most of our other intellectual technologies. It's becoming our map and our clock, our printing press and our typewriter, our calculator and our telephone, and our radio and TV.

When the Net absorbs a medium, that medium is re-created in the Net's image. It injects the medium's content with hyperlinks, blinking ads, and other digital gewgaws, and it surrounds the content with the content of all the other media it has absorbed. A new e-mail message, for instance, may announce its arrival as we're glancing over the latest headlines at a newspaper's site. The result is to scatter our attention and diffuse our concentration.

The Net's influence doesn't end at the edges of a computer screen, either. As people's minds become attuned to the crazy quilt of Internet media, traditional media have to adapt to the audience's new expectations. Television programs add text crawls and pop-up ads, and magazines and newspapers shorten their articles, introduce capsule summaries, and crowd their pages with easy-to-browse info-snippets. When, in March of this year, the *New York Times* decided to devote the second and third pages of every edition to article abstracts, its design director, Tom Bodkin, explained that the "shortcuts" would give harried readers a quick "taste" of the day's news, sparing them the "less efficient" method of actually turning the pages and reading the articles. Old media have little choice but to play by the new-media rules.

Never has a communications system played so many roles in 20 our lives—or exerted such broad influence over our thoughts—as the Internet does today. Yet, for all that's been written about the Net, there's been little consideration of how, exactly, it's reprogramming us. The Net's intellectual ethic remains obscure.

About the same time that Nietzsche started using his typewriter, an earnest young man named Frederick Winslow Taylor carried a stopwatch into the Midvale Steel plant in Philadelphia and began a historic series of experiments aimed at improving the efficiency of the plant's machinists. With the approval of Midvale's owners, he recruited a group of factory hands, set them to work on various metalworking machines, and recorded and timed their every movement as well as the operations of the machines. By breaking down every job into a sequence of small, discrete steps and then testing different ways of performing each one, Taylor created a set of precise instructions—an "algorithm," we might say today—for how each worker should work. Midvale's employees grumbled about the strict new regime, claiming that it turned them into little more than automatons, but the factory's productivity soared.

More than a hundred years after the invention of the steam engine, the Industrial Revolution had at last found its philosophy

A testing engineer (possibly Taylor) observes a Midvale Steel worker c. 1885.

and its philosopher. Taylor's tight industrial choreography—his "system," as he liked to call it—was embraced by manufacturers throughout the country and, in time, around the world. Seeking maximum speed, maximum efficiency, and maximum output, factory owners used time-and-motion studies to organize their work and configure the jobs of their workers. The goal, as Taylor defined it in his celebrated 1911 treatise, *The Principles of Scientific Management*, was to identify and adopt, for every job, the "one best method" of work and thereby to effect "the gradual substitution of science for rule of thumb throughout the mechanic arts." Once his system was applied to all acts of manual labor, Taylor assured his followers, it would bring about a restructuring not only of industry but of society, creating a utopia of perfect efficiency. "In the past the man has been first," he declared; "in the future the system must be first."

Taylor's system is still very much with us; it remains the ethic of industrial manufacturing. And now, thanks to the growing power that computer engineers and software coders wield over our intellectual lives, Taylor's ethic is beginning to govern the realm of the mind as well. The Internet is a machine designed for the efficient and automated collection, transmission, and manipulation of information, and its legions of programmers are intent on finding the "one best method"— the perfect algorithm—to carry out every mental movement of what we've come to describe as "knowledge work."

Google's headquarters, in Mountain View, California—the Googleplex—is the Internet's high church, and the religion practiced inside its walls is Taylorism. Google, says its chief executive, Eric Schmidt, is "a company that's founded around the science of measurement," and it is striving to "systematize everything" it does. Drawing on the terabytes of behavioral data

The Googleplex.

it collects through its search engine and other sites, it carries out thousands of experiments a day, according to the *Harvard Business Review*, and it uses the results to refine the algorithms that increasingly control how people find information and extract meaning from it. What Taylor did for the work of the hand, Google is doing for the work of the mind.

The company has declared that its mission is "to organize the world's information and make it universally accessible and useful." It seeks to develop "the perfect search engine," which it defines as something that "understands exactly what you mean and gives you back exactly what you want." In Google's view, information is a kind of commodity, a utilitarian resource that can be mined and processed with industrial efficiency. The more pieces of information we can "access" and the faster we can extract their gist, the more productive we become as thinkers.

Where does it end? Sergey Brin and Larry Page, the gifted young men who founded Google while pursuing doctoral degrees in computer science at Stanford, speak frequently of their desire to turn their search engine into an artificial intelligence, a HAL-like machine that might be connected directly to our brains. "The ultimate search engine is something as smart as people—or smarter," Page said in a speech a few years back. "For us, working on search is a way to work on artificial intelligence." In a 2004 interview with *Newsweek*, Brin said, "Certainly if you had all the world's information directly attached to your brain, or an artificial brain that was smarter than your brain, you'd be better off." Last year, Page told a convention of scientists that Google is "really trying to build artificial intelligence and to do it on a large scale."

Such an ambition is a natural one, even an admirable one, for a pair of math whizzes with vast quantities of cash at their disposal and a small army of computer scientists in their employ. A fundamentally scientific enterprise, Google is motivated by a desire to use technology, in Eric Schmidt's words, "to solve problems that have never been solved before," and artificial intelligence is the hardest problem out there. Why wouldn't Brin and Page want to be the ones to crack it?

Still, their easy assumption that we'd all "be better off" if our brains were supplemented, or even replaced, by an artificial intelligence is unsettling. It suggests a belief that intelligence is the output of a mechanical process, a series of discrete steps that can be isolated, measured, and optimized. In Google's world, the world we enter when we go online, there's little place for the fuzziness of contemplation. Ambiguity is not an opening for insight but a bug to be fixed. The human brain is just an outdated computer that needs a faster processor and a bigger hard drive.

The idea that our minds should operate as high-speed data-processing machines is not only built into the workings of the Internet, it is the network's reigning business model as well. The faster we surf across the Web—the more links we click and pages we view—the more opportunities Google and other companies gain to collect information about us and to feed us advertisements. Most of the proprietors of the commercial Internet have a financial stake in collecting the crumbs of data we leave behind as we flit from link to link—the more crumbs, the better. The last thing these companies want is to encourage leisurely reading or slow, concentrated thought. It's in their economic interest to drive us to distraction.

Maybe I'm just a worrywart. Just as there's a tendency to glo- 30 rify technological progress, there's a countertendency to expect the worst of every new tool or machine. In Plato's *Phaedrus*, Socrates bemoaned the development of writing. He feared that, as people came to rely on the written word as a substitute for the knowledge they used to carry inside their heads, they would, in the words of one of the dialogue's characters, "cease to exercise their memory and become forgetful." And because they would be able to "receive a quantity of information without proper instruction," they would "be thought very knowledgeable when they are for the most part quite ignorant." They would be "filled with the conceit of wisdom instead of real wisdom." Socrates wasn't wrong—the new technology did often have the effects he feared—but he was shortsighted. He couldn't foresee the many ways that writing and reading would serve to spread information, spur fresh ideas, and expand human knowledge (if not wisdom).

The arrival of Gutenberg's printing press, in the 15th century, set off another round of teeth gnashing. The Italian humanist Hieronimo Squarciafico worried that the easy availability of books would lead to intellectual laziness, making men "less studious" and weakening their minds. Others argued that cheaply printed books and broadsheets would undermine religious authority, demean the work of scholars and scribes, and spread sedition and debauchery. As New York University professor

Clay Shirky notes, "Most of the arguments made against the printing press were correct, even prescient." But, again, the doomsayers were unable to imagine the myriad blessings that the printed word would deliver.

See p. 31 for tips on putting yourself in their shoes.

So, yes, you should be skeptical of my skepticism. Perhaps those who dismiss critics of the Internet as Luddites or nostalgists will be proved correct, and from our hyperactive, data-stoked minds will spring a golden age of intellectual discovery and universal wisdom. Then again, the Net isn't the alphabet, and although it may replace the printing press, it produces something altogether different. The kind of deep reading that a sequence of printed pages promotes is valuable not just for the knowledge we acquire from the author's words but for the intellectual vibrations those words set off within our own minds. In the quiet spaces opened up by the sustained, undistracted reading of a book, or by any other act of contemplation, for that matter, we make our own associations, draw our own inferences and analogies, foster our own ideas. Deep reading, as Maryanne Wolf argues, is indistinguishable from deep thinking.

If we lose those quiet spaces, or fill them up with "content," we will sacrifice something important not only in our selves but in our culture. In a recent essay, the playwright Richard Foreman eloquently described what's at stake:

> I come from a tradition of Western culture, in which the ideal (my ideal) was the complex, dense and "cathedral-like" structure of the highly educated and articulate personality—a man or woman who carried inside themselves a personally constructed and unique version of the entire heritage of the West. [But now] I see within us all (myself included) the replacement of complex inner density with a new kind of self—evolving under the pressure of information overload and the technology of the "instantly available."

As we are drained of our "inner repertory of dense cultural inheritance," Foreman concluded, we risk turning into "'pancake people'—spread wide and thin as we connect with that vast network of information accessed by the mere touch of a button."

I'm haunted by that scene in *2001*. What makes it so poignant, and so weird, is the computer's emotional response to the disassembly of its mind: its despair as one circuit after another goes dark, its childlike pleading with the astronaut— "I can feel it. I can feel it. I'm afraid"—and its final reversion to what can only be called a state of innocence. HAL's outpouring of feeling contrasts with the emotionlessness that characterizes the human figures in the film, who go about their business with an almost robotic efficiency. Their thoughts and actions feel scripted, as if they're following the steps of an algorithm. In the world of *2001*, people have become so machinelike that the most human character turns out to be a machine. That's the essence of Kubrick's dark prophecy: as we come to rely on computers to mediate our understanding of the world, it is our own intelligence that flattens into artificial intelligence.

Joining the Conversation

1. "Is Google making us stupid?" How does Nicholas Carr answer this question, and what evidence does he provide to support his answer?
2. What possible objections to his own position does Carr introduce—and why do you think he does so? How effectively does he counter these objections?

3. Carr begins this essay by quoting an exchange between HAL and Dave, a supercomputer and an astronaut in the film *2001: A Space Odyssey*—and he concludes by reflecting on that scene. What happens to HAL and Dave, and how does this outcome support his argument?

4. How does Carr use transitions to connect the parts of his text and to help readers follow his train of thought? (See Chapter 8 to help you think about how transitions help develop an argument.)

5. In his essay on pp. 340–60, Clive Thompson reaches a different conclusion than Carr does, saying that "At their best, today's digital tools help us see more, retain more, communicate more. At their worst, they leave us prey to the manipulation of the toolmakers. But on balance . . . what is happening is deeply positive." Write a paragraph or two discussing how Carr might respond. What would he agree with, and what would he disagree with?

6. This article sparked widespread debate and conversation when it first appeared in 2008, and the discussion continues today. Go to **theysayiblog.com** and click on "Are We in a Race against the Machine?" to read some of what's been written on the topic recently.

The Influencing Machines

BROOKE GLADSTONE AND JOSH NEUFELD

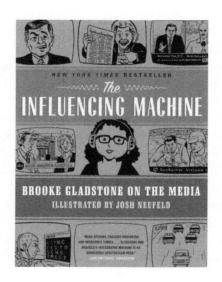

BROOKE GLADSTONE is a media analyst and host of NPR's *On the Media*. She has received two Peabody awards, and her work also has appeared in periodicals such as the *Boston Globe, London Observer,* and *Washington Post*. JOSH NEUFELD is a cartoonist whose work has appeared in the *New York Times, Washington Post,* and *Wall Street Journal*. He is the author of the graphic narrative *A.D.: New Orleans After the Deluge* (2009). This selection is from Gladstone and Neufeld's collaboration, *The Influencing Machine: Brooke Gladstone on the Media* (2011).

Many say that the Internet's ability to link like-minded souls everywhere fosters the creation of virtually impermeable echo chambers.

The echo chambers give rise to cybercascades: when a "fact" sent by one person spreads in a geometric progression to others until millions of people around the world potentially believe it.

GLOBAL WARMING IS BALONEY DRIVE THRU OPEN 24 HOURS

Cut off from dissenters, the chambers fill with an unjustified sense of certainty. It's called **incestuous amplification**, a term first applied to isolated military planners who base their strategies on flawed assumptions.

Incestuous amplification can occur in any sphere, even without the Internet. But it helps.

Real estate bubble? **Fuggedabboutit!**

Hint: When you hear a group of guys called "Masters of the Universe," **run!**

Cass Sunstein cites many studies showing how people who talk only to like-minded others grow more extreme. They **marginalize the moderates**...

...and **demonize** dissenters. The greatest danger of echo chambers is unjustified **extremism.** It's an ongoing **threat** to our **democracy.**

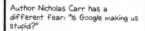

Author Nicholas Carr has a different fear: "Is Google making us stupid?"

Media are not just passive **channels** of information. They supply the **stuff** of thought, but they also shape the **process** of thought.

Over the past few years I've had an uncomfortable sense that someone, or something, has been tinkering with my brain, remapping the neural circuitry, reprogramming the memory.

Immersing myself in a book or a lengthy article used to be easy ... Now my concentration often starts to drift after two or three pages.

...Once I was a scuba diver in the sea of words. Now I zip along the surface like a guy on a Jet-Ski.

Technology does change our brains. Humanity's first use of handheld tools coincided with the growth of the prefrontal cortex, as well as grammatical language and more complex social networks.

So it's likely that our brains **will** process information differently in our increasingly interconnected environment. We'll also have the ability to rush ahead of evolution -- by **implanting** new technology.

Does that creep you out?

Actually, I'm **not** creeped out, and not because I'm especially optimistic about human nature. I just take my cues from history. And the history of communications is full of... histrionics.

People always see the future and despair that the latest gizmo will destroy our concentration, memory, communities, our mental and physical **health**...

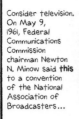

Consider television. On May 9, 1961, Federal Communications Commission chairman Newton N. Minow said **this** to a convention of the National Association of Broadcasters...

I invite each of you to sit down in front of your television set when your station goes on the air and stay there ... until the station signs off.

I can assure you that what you will observe is a vast wasteland.

Actually, the TV scares do have some very good data behind them.

Study after study has found strong links between excessive TV exposure and childhood obesity, smoking, and sexual activity.

But radio also was condemned. A 1936 issue of Gramophone cited research asserting that "children often lie awake in bed restless and fearful, or wake up screaming, as a result of nightmares brought on by mystery stories."

WELCOME, MY FRIENDS, TO THE INNER SANCTUM...!

Now we celebrate radio's golden age because "we had to use our imaginations."

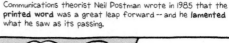

Communications theorist Neil Postman wrote in 1985 that the **printed word** was a great leap forward -- and he **lamented** what he saw as its passing.

Most of our modern ideas about the uses of the intellect were formed by the printed word, as were our ideas about education, knowledge, truth, and information...

"...as typography moves to the periphery of our culture ... the seriousness, clarity and, above all, value of public discourse dangerously declines."

But a century earlier, assiduous reading was itself suspect. Especially for girls.

"Foolish parents ... exhaust their children's brains ... with complex and multiple studies...The evils are becoming noticed in all quarters. Some of the prize girls soon find their way to **insane asylums**..."

THE SANITARIAN,

As Gutenberg's press took off, so did fears of information overload. In 1545, Conrad Gesner assembled a "Universal Library," while complaining of the...

...confusing and harmful abundance of books...

He decided to list only books written in Greek, Latin, and Hebrew.

Barnaby Rich, an English soldier, wrote in 1613 that books...

...so **overcharge** the world that it is not able to digest the abundance of **idle matter** that is every day hatched and brought forth into the world!

Rich himself authored some 26 books, including works on the military, manners, morals, and several romances.

In 1985, Tibor Braun coins the term "Barnaby Rich syndrome" -- the conviction that "it is always the other author who writes and publishes too much."

Ye Old Bookshoppe

In Plato's "Phaedrus," Socrates derides the invention of writing, with a story in which the Egyptian god who invented the alphabet brags to a king.

This will make the Egyptians **wiser** and give them better **memories.**

The inventor is not always the best judge of his own inventions. This discovery of yours will create **forgetfulness** in the learners' souls -- they will trust to the external written characters and **not remember** of themselves.

Which bring us 'round to the wisdom offered up by author Douglas Adams.

Anything that is in the world when you're born is normal and ordinary and is just a natural part of the way the world works.

Anything that's invented between when you're 15 and 35 is new and exciting and revolutionary.

Anything invented after you're 35 is against the natural order of things.

Adams offered the best advice for these terrifying times when, in 1979, he described his (then) imaginary "Hitchhiker's Guide to the Galaxy."

[It] had about 100 tiny flat press buttons and a screen about four inches square on which any one of a million "pages" could be summoned at a moment's notice.

It looked insanely complicated, and this was one of the reasons why ... it ... had the words "DON'T PANIC" printed on it in large friendly letters.

DON'T PANIC

Joining the Conversation

1. What is Brooke Gladstone and Josh Neufeld's argument, and how do they support their position?
2. What "they say" has motivated her argument? How do you know?
3. Gladstone quotes or paraphrases a number of writers across time. Some support her position and some do not, but she is very much in conversation with many thinkers on the subject of technology. Choose four and explain what they contribute to her argument.
4. See the "hint" Gladstone adds on p. 332. How does it function as metacommentary? (See Chapter 10 for a reminder about how writers use metacommentary.)
5. Write a response to Gladstone and Neufeld presenting your views in graphic form. Or if you prefer, choose one page of her piece and summarize it using words alone.

Smarter than You Think: How Technology Is Changing Our Minds for the Better

CLIVE THOMPSON

WHO'S BETTER AT CHESS—computers or humans?

The question has long fascinated observers, perhaps because chess seems like the ultimate display of human thought: the players sit like Rodin's *Thinker*, silent, brows furrowed, making lightning-fast calculations. It's the quintessential cognitive activity, logic as an extreme sport.

So the idea of a machine outplaying a human has always provoked both excitement and dread. In the eighteenth century, Wolfgang von Kempelen caused a stir with his clockwork Mechanical Turk—an automaton that played an eerily good game of chess, even beating Napoleon Bonaparte. The spectacle was so unsettling that onlookers cried out in astonishment

CLIVE THOMPSON is a freelance journalist and blogger who writes for the *New York Times Magazine* and *Wired*. He was awarded a 2002 Knight Science Journalism Fellowship at MIT. He blogs at collision-detection.net. This essay is adapted from his book, *Smarter Than You Think: How Technology Is Changing Our Minds for the Better* (2013).

The Thinker, by French sculptor Auguste Rodin (1840–1917).

when the Turk's gears first clicked into motion. But the gears, and the machine, were fake; in reality, the automaton was controlled by a chess savant cunningly tucked inside the wooden cabinet. In 1915, a Spanish inventor unveiled a genuine, honest-to-goodness robot that could actually play chess—a simple endgame involving only three pieces, anyway. A writer for *Scientific American* fretted that the inventor "Would Substitute Machinery for the Human Mind."

Eighty years later, in 1997, this intellectual standoff clanked to a dismal conclusion when world champion Garry Kasparov was defeated by IBM's Deep Blue supercomputer in a tournament of six games. Faced with a machine that could calculate two hundred million positions a second, even Kasparov's notoriously aggressive and nimble style broke down. In its final game, Deep Blue used such a clever ploy—tricking Kasparov into letting the computer sacrifice a knight—that it trounced him in nineteen moves. "I lost my fighting spirit," Kasparov said afterward, pronouncing himself "emptied completely." Riveted, the journalists announced a winner. The cover of *Newsweek* proclaimed the event "The Brain's Last Stand." Doom-sayers predicted that chess itself was over. If machines could out-think even Kasparov, why would the game remain interesting? Why would anyone bother playing? What's the challenge?

Then Kasparov did something unexpected.   5

The truth is, Kasparov wasn't completely surprised by Deep Blue's victory. Chess grand masters had predicted for years that computers would eventually beat humans, because they understood the different ways humans and computers play. Human chess players learn by spending years studying the world's best opening moves and endgames; they play thousands of games, slowly amassing a capacious, in-brain library of which strategies triumphed and which flopped. They analyze their opponents' strengths and weaknesses, as well as their moods. When they look at the board, that knowledge manifests as intuition—a eureka moment when they suddenly spy the best possible move.

In contrast, a chess-playing computer has no intuition at all. It analyzes the game using brute force; it inspects the pieces currently on the board, then calculates all options. It prunes away moves that lead to losing positions, then takes the promising ones and runs the calculations again. After doing this a few times—and looking five or seven moves out—it arrives at a few powerful plays. The machine's way of "thinking" is fundamentally unhuman. Humans don't sit around crunching every possible move, because our brains can't hold that much information at once. If you go eight moves out in a game of chess, there are more possible games than there are stars in our galaxy. If you total up every game possible? It outnumbers the atoms in the known universe. Ask chess grand masters, "How many moves can you see out?" and they'll likely deliver the answer attributed to the Cuban grand master José Raúl Capablanca: "One, the best one."

The fight between computers and humans in chess was, as Kasparov knew, ultimately about speed. Once computers could see all games roughly seven moves out, they would wear humans down. A person might make a mistake; the computer wouldn't. Brute force wins. As he pondered Deep Blue, Kasparov mused on these different cognitive approaches.

It gave him an audacious idea. What would happen if, instead of competing against one another, humans and computers *collaborated*? What if they played on teams together— one computer and a human facing off against another human and a computer? That way, he theorized, each might benefit from the other's peculiar powers. The computer would bring the lightning-fast—if uncreative—ability to analyze zillions of moves, while the human would bring intuition and insight, the ability to read opponents and psych them out. Together, they would form what chess players later called a centaur: a hybrid beast endowed with the strengths of each.

In June 1998, Kasparov played the first public game of human-computer collaborative chess, which he dubbed "advanced chess," against Veselin Topalov, a top-rated grand master. Each used a regular computer with off-the-shelf chess software and databases of hundreds of thousands of chess games, including some of the best ever played. They considered what moves the computer recommended, they examined historical databases to see if anyone had ever been in a situation like theirs before. Then they used that information to help plan. Each game was limited to sixty minutes, so they didn't have infinite time to consult the machines; they had to work swiftly.

Kasparov found the experience "as disturbing as it was exciting." Freed from the need to rely exclusively on his memory, he was able to focus more on the creative texture of his play. It was, he realized, like learning to be a race-car driver: He had to learn how to *drive* the computer, as it were—developing a split-second sense of which strategy to enter into the computer for assessment, when to stop an unpromising line of inquiry, and when to accept or ignore the computer's advice. "Just as a good Formula One driver really knows his own car, so did we have to learn the way the computer program worked," he later wrote. Topalov, as it turns out, appeared to be an even better Formula One "thinker" than Kasparov. On purely human terms, Kasparov was a stronger player; a month before, he'd trounced Topalov 4–0. But the centaur play evened the odds. This time, Topalov fought Kasparov to a 3–3 draw.

Garry Kasparov (right) plays Veselin Topalov (left) in Sofia, Bulgaria, on May 3, 1998.

In 2005, there was a "freestyle" chess tournament in which a team could consist of any number of humans or computers, in any combination. Many teams consisted of chess grand masters who'd won plenty of regular, human-only tournaments, achieving chess scores of 2,500 (out of 3,000). But the winning team didn't include any grand masters at all. It consisted of two young New England men, Steven Cramton and Zackary Stephen (who were comparative amateurs, with chess rankings down around 1,400 to 1,700), and their computers.

Why could these relative amateurs beat chess players with far more experience and raw talent? Because Cramton and Stephen were expert at collaborating with computers. They knew when to rely on human smarts and when to rely on the machine's advice. Working at rapid speed—these games, too, were limited to sixty minutes—they would brainstorm moves, then check to see what the computer thought, while also scouring databases to see if the strategy had occurred in previous games. They used three different computers simultaneously, running five different pieces of software; that way they could cross-check whether different programs agreed on the same move. But they wouldn't simply accept what the machine accepted, nor would they merely mimic old games. They selected moves that were low-rated by the computer if they thought they would rattle their opponents psychologically.

In essence, a new form of chess intelligence was emerging. You could rank the teams like this: (1) a chess grand master was good; (2) a chess grand master playing with a laptop was better. But even that laptop-equipped grand master could be beaten by (3) relative newbies, if the amateurs were extremely skilled at integrating machine assistance. "Human strategic guidance combined with the tactical acuity of a computer," Kasparov concluded, "was overwhelming."

Better yet, it turned out these smart amateurs could even 15 outplay a supercomputer on the level of Deep Blue. One of the entrants that Cramton and Stephen trounced in the freestyle chess tournament was a version of Hydra, the most powerful chess computer in existence at the time; indeed, it was probably faster and stronger than Deep Blue itself. Hydra's owners let it play entirely by itself, using raw logic and speed to fight its opponents. A few days after the advanced chess event, Hydra destroyed the world's seventh-ranked grand master in a man-versus-machine chess tournament.

But Cramton and Stephen beat Hydra. They did it using their own talents and regular Dell and Hewlett-Packard computers, of the type you probably had sitting on your desk in 2005, with software you could buy for sixty dollars. All of which brings us back to our original question here: Which is smarter at chess—humans or computers?

Neither.

It's the two together, working side by side.

We're all playing advanced chess these days. We just haven't learned to appreciate it.

Our tools are everywhere, linked with our minds, working 20 in tandem. Search engines answer our most obscure questions; status updates give us an ESP-like awareness of those around us; online collaborations let far-flung collaborators tackle problems too tangled for any individual. We're becoming less like Rodin's *Thinker* and more like Kasparov's centaurs. This transformation is rippling through every part of our cognition—how we learn, how we remember, and how we act upon that knowledge emotionally, intellectually, and politically. As with Cramton and Stephen, these tools can make even the amateurs among us radically smarter than we'd be on our own, assuming (and this is a big assumption) we understand how they work. At their best, today's digital tools help us see more, retain more, communicate more. At their worst, they leave us prey to the manipulation of the toolmakers. But on balance, I'd argue, what is happening is deeply positive. . . .

In a sense, this is an ancient story. The "extended mind" theory of cognition argues that the reason humans are so intellectually dominant is that we've always outsourced bits of cognition, using tools to scaffold our thinking into ever-more-rarefied realms. Printed books amplified our memory. Inexpensive paper and reliable pens made it possible to externalize our thoughts quickly. Studies show that our eyes zip around the page while performing long division on paper, using the handwritten digits as a form of prosthetic short-term memory. "These resources enable us to pursue manipulations and juxtapositions of ideas and data that would quickly baffle the unaugmented brain," as Andy Clark, a philosopher of the extended mind, writes.

Granted, it can be unsettling to realize how much thinking already happens outside our skulls. Culturally, we revere the Rodin ideal—the belief that genius breakthroughs come from our gray matter alone. The physicist Richard Feynman once got into an argument about this with the historian Charles Weiner. Feynman understood the extended mind; he knew that writing his equations and ideas on paper was crucial to his thought. But when Weiner looked over a pile of Feynman's notebooks, he called them a wonderful "record of his day-to-day work." No, no, Feynman replied testily. They weren't a record of his thinking process. They *were* his thinking process:

> "I actually did the work on the paper," he said.
> "Well," Weiner said, "the work was done in your head, but the record of it is still here."
> "No, it's not a *record*, not really. It's *working*. You have to work on paper and this is the paper. Okay?"

Every new tool shapes the way we think, as well as what we think about. The printed word helped make our cognition linear and abstract, along with vastly enlarging our stores of knowledge. Newspapers shrank the world; then the telegraph shrank it even more dramatically. With every innovation, cultural prophets bickered over whether we were facing a technological apocalypse or a utopia. Depending on which Victorian-age pundit you asked, the telegraph was either going usher in an era of world peace ("It is impossible that old prejudices and hostilities should longer exist," as Charles F. Briggs and Augustus Maverick intoned) or drown us in a Sargasso of idiotic trivia ("We are eager to tunnel under the

Atlantic . . . but perchance the first news that will leak through into the broad, flapping American ear will be that the Princess Adelaide has the whooping cough," as Thoreau opined). Neither prediction was quite right, of course, yet neither was quite wrong. The one thing that both apocalyptics and utopians understand and agree upon is that every new technology pushes us toward new forms of behavior while nudging us away from older, familiar ones. Harold Innis—the lesser-known but arguably more interesting intellectual midwife of Marshall McLuhan—called this the bias of a new tool. Living with new technologies means understanding how they bias everyday life.

What are the central biases of today's digital tools? There are many, but I see three big ones that have a huge impact on our cognition. First, they allow for prodigious external memory: smartphones, hard drives, cameras, and sensors routinely record more information than any tool before them. We're shifting from a stance of rarely recording our ideas and the events of our lives to doing it habitually. Second, today's tools make it easier for us to find connections—between ideas, pictures, people, bits of news—that were previously invisible. Third, they encourage a superfluity of communication and publishing. This last feature has many surprising effects that are often ill understood. Any economist can tell you that when you suddenly increase the availability of a resource, people do more things with it, which also means they do increasingly unpredictable things. As electricity became cheap and ubiquitous in the West, its role expanded from things you'd expect—like night-time lighting—to the unexpected and seemingly trivial: battery-driven toy trains, electric blenders, vibrators. The superfluity of communication today has produced everything from a rise in crowd-organized projects like Wikipedia to curious new forms of expression: television-show recaps, map-based storytelling, discussion threads that spin out of a photo posted to a smartphone app, Amazon product-review threads wittily hijacked for political satire. Now, none of these three digital biases is immutable, because they're the product of software and hardware, and can easily be altered or ended if the architects of today's tools (often corporate and governmental) decide to regulate the tools or find they're not profitable enough. But right now, these big effects dominate our current and near-term landscape.

In one sense, these three shifts—infinite memory, dot 25 connecting, explosive publishing—are screamingly obvious to anyone who's ever used a computer. Yet they also somehow constantly surprise us by producing ever-new "tools for thought" (to use the writer Howard Rheingold's lovely phrase) that upend our mental habits in ways we never expected and often don't apprehend even as they take hold. Indeed, these phenomena have already woven themselves so deeply into the lives of people around the globe that it's difficult to stand back and take account of how much things have changed and why. While [here I map] out what I call the future of thought, it's also frankly rooted in the *present*, because many parts of our future have already arrived, even if they are only dimly understood. As the sci-fi author William Gibson famously quipped: "The future is already here—it's just not very evenly distributed." This is an attempt to understand what's happening to us right now, the better to see where our augmented thought is headed. Rather than dwell in abstractions, like so many marketers and pundits—not to mention the creators of technology, who are often remarkably poor at predicting how people will use their tools—I focus more on the actual experiences of real people.

To provide a concrete example of what I'm talking about, let's take a look at something simple and immediate: my activities while writing the pages you've just read.

As I was working, I often realized I couldn't quite remember a detail and discovered that my notes were incomplete. So I'd zip over to a search engine. (*Which chess piece did Deep Blue sacrifice when it beat Kasparov? The knight!*) I also pushed some of my thinking out into the open: I blogged admiringly about the Spanish chess-playing robot from 1915, and within minutes commenters offered smart critiques. (One pointed out that the chess robot wasn't *that* impressive because it was playing an endgame that was almost impossible to lose: the robot started with a rook and a king, while the human opponent had only a mere king.) While reading Kasparov's book *How Life Imitates Chess* on my Kindle, I idly clicked on "popular highlights" to see what passages other readers had found interesting—and wound up becoming fascinated by a section on chess strategy I'd only lightly skimmed myself. To understand centaur play better, I read long, nuanced threads on chess-player discussion groups, effectively eavesdropping on conversations of people who know chess far better than I ever will. (Chess players who follow the new form of play seem divided—some think advanced chess is a grim sign of machines' taking over the game, and others think it shows that the human mind is much more valuable than computer software.) I got into a long instant-messaging session with my wife, during which I realized that I'd explained the gist of advanced chess better than I had in my original draft, so I cut and pasted that explanation into my notes. As for the act of writing itself? Like most writers, I constantly have to fight the procrastinator's urge to meander online, idly checking Twitter links and Wikipedia entries in a dreamy but pointless haze—until I look up in horror and realize I've lost two hours of work, a missing-time experience redolent of a UFO abduction. So I'd switch my word processor into full-screen mode, fading my computer desktop to black so

I could see nothing but the page, giving me temporary mental peace.

[Let's] explore each of these trends. First off, there's the emergence of omnipresent computer storage, which is upending the way we remember, both as individuals and as a culture. Then there's the advent of "public thinking": the ability to broadcast our ideas and the catalytic effect that has both inside and outside our minds. We're becoming more conversational thinkers—a shift that has been rocky, not least because everyday public thought uncorks the incivility and prejudices that are commonly repressed in face-to-face life. But at its best (which, I'd argue, is surprisingly often), it's a thrilling development, reigniting ancient traditions of dialogue and debate. At the same time, there's been an explosion of new forms of expression that were previously too expensive for everyday thought— like video, mapping, or data crunching. Our social awareness is shifting, too, as we develop ESP-like "ambient awareness," a persistent sense of what others are doing and thinking. On a social level, this expands our ability to understand the people we care about. On a civic level, it helps dispel traditional political problems like "pluralistic ignorance," catalyzing political action, as in the Arab Spring.

Are these changes good or bad for us? If you asked me twenty years ago, when I first started writing about technology, I'd have said "bad." In the early 1990s, I believed that as people migrated online, society's worst urges might be uncorked: pseudonymity would poison online conversation, gossip and trivia would dominate, and cultural standards would collapse. Certainly some of those predictions have come true, as anyone who's wandered into an angry political forum knows. But the truth is, while I predicted the bad stuff, I didn't foresee the good stuff. And what a torrent we have: Wikipedia, a

See p. 66 for ways to make the "I'm of two minds" move.

global forest of eloquent bloggers, citizen journalism, political fact-checking—or even the way status-update tools like Twitter have produced a renaissance in witty, aphoristic, haikuesque expression. If [I accentuate] the positive, that's in part because we've been so flooded with apocalyptic warnings of late. We need a new way to talk clearly about the rewards and pleasures of our digital experiences—one that's rooted in our lived experience and also detangled from the hype of Silicon Valley.

The other thing that makes me optimistic about our cog-30 nitive future is how much it resembles our cognitive past. In the sixteenth century, humanity faced a printed-paper wave of information overload—with the explosion of books that began with the codex and went into overdrive with Gutenberg's movable type. As the historian Ann Blair notes, scholars were alarmed: How would they be able to keep on top of the flood of human expression? Who would separate the junk from what was worth keeping? The mathematician Gottfried Wilhelm Leibniz bemoaned "that horrible mass of books which keeps on growing," which would doom the quality writers to "the danger of general oblivion" and produce "a return to barbarism." Thankfully, he was wrong. Scholars quickly set about organizing the new mental environment by clipping their favorite passages from books and assembling them into huge tomes—*florilegia*, bouquets of text—so that readers could sample the best parts. They were basically blogging, going through some of the same arguments modern bloggers go through. (Is it enough to clip a passage, or do you also have to verify that what the author wrote was true? It was debated back then, as it is today.) The past turns out to be oddly reassuring, because a pattern emerges. Each time we're faced with bewildering new thinking tools, we panic—then quickly set about deducing how they can be used to help us work, meditate, and create.

History also shows that we generally improve and refine our tools to make them better. Books, for example, weren't always as well designed as they are now. In fact, the earliest ones were, by modern standards, practically unusable—often devoid of the navigational aids we now take for granted, such as indexes, paragraph breaks, or page numbers. It took decades—centuries, even—for the book to be redesigned into a more flexible cognitive tool, as suitable for quick reference as it is for deep reading. This is the same path we'll need to tread with our digital tools. It's why we need to understand not just the new abilities our tools give us today, but where they're still deficient and how they ought to improve.

I have one caveat to offer. If you were hoping to read about the neuroscience of our brains and how technology is "rewiring" them, [I] will disappoint you.

This goes against the grain of modern discourse, I realize. In recent years, people interested in how we think have become obsessed with our brain chemistry. We've marveled at the ability of brain scanning—picturing our brain's electrical activity or blood flow—to provide new clues as to what parts of the brain are linked to our behaviors. Some people panic that our brains are being deformed on a physiological level by today's technology: spend too much time flipping between windows and skimming text instead of reading a book, or interrupting your conversations to read text messages, and pretty soon you won't be able to concentrate on anything—and if you can't concentrate on it, you can't understand it either. In his book *The Shallows*, Nicholas Carr eloquently raised this alarm, arguing that the quality of our thought, as a species, rose in tandem with the ascendance of slow-moving, linear print and began declining with the arrival of the zingy, flighty Internet. "I'm not thinking the way I used to think," he worried.

I'm certain that many of these fears are warranted. It has always been difficult for us to maintain mental habits of concentration and deep thought; that's precisely why societies have engineered massive social institutions (everything from universities to book clubs and temples of worship) to encourage us to keep it up. It's part of why only a relatively small subset of people become regular, immersive readers, and part of why an even smaller subset go on to higher education. Today's multitasking tools really do make it harder than before to stay focused during long acts of reading and contemplation. They require a high level of "mindfulness"—paying attention to your own attention. While I don't dwell on the perils of distraction [here], the importance of being mindful resonates throughout these pages. One of the great challenges of today's digital thinking tools is knowing when *not* to use them, when to rely on the powers of older and slower technologies, like paper and books.

That said, today's confident talk by pundits and journalists 35 about our "rewired" brains has one big problem: it is very premature. Serious neuroscientists agree that we don't really know how our brains are wired to begin with. Brain chemistry is particularly mysterious when it comes to complex thought, like memory, creativity, and insight. "There will eventually be neuroscientific explanations for much of what we do; but those explanations will turn out to be incredibly complicated," as the neuroscientist Gary Marcus pointed out when critiquing the popular fascination with brain scanning. "For now, our ability to understand how all those parts relate is quite limited, sort of like trying to understand the political dynamics of Ohio from an airplane window above Cleveland." I'm not dismissing brain scanning; indeed, I'm confident it'll be crucial in unlocking these mysteries in the decades to come. But right now the field is so new that it is rash to draw conclusions, either apocalyptic or Utopian, about how the Internet is changing our brains. Even Carr, the most diligent explorer in this area, cited only a single brain-scanning study that specifically probed how people's brains respond to using the Web, and those results were ambiguous.

The truth is that many healthy daily activities, if you scanned the brains of people participating in them, might appear outright dangerous to cognition. Over recent years, professor of psychiatry James Swain and teams of Yale and University of Michigan scientists scanned the brains of new mothers and fathers as they listened to recordings of their babies' cries. They found brain circuit activity similar to that in people suffering from obsessive-compulsive disorder. Now, these parents did not actually have OCD. They were just being temporarily vigilant about their newborns. But since the experiments appeared to show the brains of new parents being altered at a neural level, you could write a pretty scary headline if you wanted: BECOMING A PARENT ERODES YOUR BRAIN FUNCTION! In reality, as Swain tells me, it's much more benign. Being extra fretful and cautious around a newborn is a good thing for most parents: Babies are fragile. It's worth the tradeoff. Similarly, living in cities—with their cramped dwellings and pounding noise—stresses us out on a straightforwardly physiological level and floods our system with cortisol, as I discovered while researching stress in New York City several years ago. But the very urban density that frazzles us mentally also makes us 50 percent more productive, and more creative, too, as Edward Glaeser argues in *Triumph of the City*, because of all those connections between people. This is "the city's edge in producing ideas." The upside of creativity is tied to the downside of living in a sardine tin, or, as Glaeser puts it, "Density has costs as well as benefits." Our digital environments likely offer a similar push and pull. We tolerate their cognitive hassles and distractions for the enormous upside of being connected, in new ways, to other people.

I want to examine how technology changes our mental habits, but for now, we'll be on firmer ground if we stick to what's observably happening in the world around us: our cognitive behavior, the quality of our cultural production, and the social science that tries to measure what we do in everyday life. In any case, I won't be talking about how your brain is being "rewired." Almost everything rewires it. . . .

The brain you had before you read this paragraph? You don't get that brain back. I'm hoping the trade-off is worth it.

The rise of advanced chess didn't end the debate about man versus machine, of course. In fact, the centaur phenomenon only complicated things further for the chess world—raising questions about how reliant players were on computers and how their presence affected the game itself. Some worried that if humans got too used to consulting machines, they wouldn't be able to play without them. Indeed, in June 2011, chess master Christoph Natsidis was caught illicitly using a mobile phone during a regular human-to-human match. During tense moments, he kept vanishing for long bathroom visits; the referee, suspicious, discovered Natsidis entering moves into a piece of chess software on his smartphone. Chess had entered a phase similar to the doping scandals that have plagued baseball and cycling, except in this case the drug was software and its effect cognitive.

This is a nice metaphor for a fear that can nag at us in our everyday lives, too, as we use machines for thinking more and more. Are we losing some of our humanity? What happens if the Internet goes down: Do our brains collapse, too? Or is the question naive and irrelevant—as quaint as worrying about

40

whether we're "dumb" because we can't compute long division without a piece of paper and a pencil?

Certainly, if we're intellectually lazy or prone to cheating and shortcuts, or if we simply don't pay much attention to how our tools affect the way we work, then yes—we can become, like Natsidis, overreliant. But the story of computers and chess offers a much more optimistic ending, too. Because it turns out that when chess players were genuinely passionate about learning and being creative in their game, computers didn't degrade their own human abilities. Quite the opposite: it helped them internalize the game much more profoundly and advance to new levels of *human* excellence.

Before computers came along, back when Kasparov was a young boy in the 1970s in the Soviet Union, learning grand-master-level chess was a slow, arduous affair. If you showed promise and you were very lucky, you could find a local grand master to teach you. If you were one of the tiny handful who showed world-class promise, Soviet leaders would fly you to Moscow and give you access to their elite chess library, which contained laboriously transcribed paper records of the world's top games. Retrieving records was a painstaking affair; you'd contemplate a possible opening, use the catalog to locate games that began with that move, and then the librarians would retrieve records from thin files, pulling them out using long sticks resembling knitting needles. Books of chess games were rare and incomplete. By gaining access to the Soviet elite library, Kasparov and his peers developed an enormous advantage over their global rivals. That library was their cognitive augmentation.

But beginning in the 1980s, computers took over the library's role and bested it. Young chess enthusiasts could buy CD-ROMs filled with hundreds of thousands of chess games.

Chess-playing software could show you how an artificial opponent would respond to any move. This dramatically increased the pace at which young chess players built up intuition. If you were sitting at lunch and had an idea for a bold new opening move, you could instantly find out which historic players had tried it, then war-game it yourself by playing against software. The iterative process of thought experiments—"If I did *this*, then what would happen?"—sped up exponentially.

Chess itself began to evolve. "Players became more creative and daring," as Frederic Friedel, the publisher of the first popular chess databases and software, tells me. Before computers, grand masters would stick to lines of attack they'd long studied and honed. Since it took weeks or months for them to research and mentally explore the ramifications of a new move, they stuck with what they knew. But as the next generation of players emerged, Friedel was astonished by their unusual gambits, particularly in their opening moves. Chess players today, Kasparov has written, "are almost as free of dogma as the machines with which they train. Increasingly, a move isn't good or bad because it looks that way or because it hasn't been done that way before. It's simply good if it works and bad if it doesn't."

Most remarkably, it is producing players who reach grand master status younger. Before computers, it was extremely rare for teenagers to become grand masters. In 1958, Bobby Fischer stunned the world by achieving that status at fifteen. The feat was so unusual it was over three decades before the record was broken, in 1991. But by then computers had emerged, and in the years since, the record has been broken twenty times, as more and more young players became grand masters. In 2002, the Ukrainian Sergey Karjakin became one at the tender age of twelve.

So yes, when we're augmenting ourselves, we can be smarter. We're becoming centaurs. But our digital tools can also leave us smarter even when we're not actively using them.

Joining the Conversation

1. Clive Thompson lists three shifts—infinite memory, dot connecting, and explosive publishing—that he believes have strongly affected our cognition. What exactly does he mean by these three shifts, and in what ways does he think they have changed our thinking?

2. Thompson starts paragraph 20 by saying "Our tools are everywhere, linked with our minds, working in tandem." What do you think? Does his statement reflect your own experience with technology?

3. In paragraphs 33–35, Thompson cites Nicholas Carr, whose views about technology differ from his. How does he respond to Carr—and how does acknowledging views he disagrees with help support his own position?

4. So what? Has Thompson convinced you that his topic matters? If so, how and where does he do so?

5. Write an essay reflecting on the ways digital technologies have influenced your own intellectual development, drawing from Thompson's text and other readings in this chapter—and on your own experience as support for your argument. Be sure to acknowledge views other than your own.

Does Texting Affect Writing?

MICHAELA CULLINGTON

—▫—

IT'S TAKING OVER OUR LIVES. We can do it almost anywhere—walking to class, waiting in line at the grocery store, or hanging out at home. It's quick, easy, and convenient. It has become a concern of doctors, parents, and teachers alike. What is it? It's texting!

Text messaging—or texting, as it's more commonly called— is the process of sending and receiving typed messages via a cellular phone. It is a common means of communication among teenagers and is even becoming popular in the business world because it allows quick messages to be sent without people having to commit to a telephone conversation. A person is able to say what is needed, and the other person will receive the information and respond when it's convenient to do so.

In order to more quickly type what they are trying to say, many people use abbreviations instead of words. The language created by these abbreviations is called textspeak. Some people

---

MICHAELA CULLINGTON was a student at Marywood University in Pennsylvania when she wrote this essay, which originally appeared in *Young Scholars in Writing*, an undergraduate journal of writing published by the University of Missouri-Kansas City. She received a masters degree in speech and language pathology from Marywood in 2014.

Here's the
summary of
an ongoing
debate. For tips
on this move,
see Chapter 1.

believe that using these abbreviations is hindering the
writing abilities of students, and others argue that texting is actually having a positive effect on writing. In
fact, it seems likely that texting has no significant effect
on student writing.

Concerns about Textspeak

A September 2008 article in *USA Today* entitled "Texting, Testing Destroys Kids' Writing Style" summarizes many of the most
common complaints about the effect of texting. It states that
according to the National Center for Education Statistics, only
25% of high school seniors are "proficient" writers. The article
quotes Jacquie Ream, a former teacher and author of *K.I.S.S .—
Keep It Short and Simple*, a guide for writing more effectively.
Ream states, "[W]e have a whole generation being raised without communication skills." She blames the use of acronyms and
shorthand in text messages for students' inability to spell and ultimately to write well. Ream also points out that students struggle
to convey emotion in their writing because, as she states, in text
messages "emotions are always sideways smiley faces."

This debate became prominent after some teachers began 5
to believe they were seeing a decline in the writing abilities of
their students. Many attributed this perceived decline to the
increasing popularity of text messaging and its use of abbreviations. Naomi Baron, a linguistics professor at American University, blames texting for what she sees as the fact that "so much of
American society has become sloppy and laissez faire about the
mechanics of writing" ("Should We Worry or LOL?"). Teachers
report finding "2" for "to," "gr8" for "great," "dat" for "that,"
and "wut" for "what," among other examples of textspeak, in
their students' writing. A Minnesota teacher of the seventh

and ninth grades says that she has to spend extra time in class editing papers and must "explicitly" remind her students that it is not acceptable to use text slang and abbreviations in writing (Walsh). Another English teacher believes that text language has become "second nature" to her students (Carey); they are so used to it that they do not even catch themselves doing it.

Many also complain that because texting does not stress the importance of punctuation, students are neglecting it in their formal writing. Teachers say that their students are forgetting commas, apostrophes, and even capital letters to begin sentences. Another complaint is that text messages lack emotion. Many argue that texts lack feeling because of their tendency to be short, brief, and to the point. Because students are not able to communicate emotion effectively through texts, some teachers worry, they may lose the ability to do so in writing.

To get a more personal perspective on the question of how teachers perceive texting to be influencing student writing, I interviewed two of my former high school teachers—my junior-year English teacher and my senior-year theology teacher. Both teachers stress the importance of writing in their courses. They maintain that they notice text abbreviations in their students' writing often. To correct this problem, they point it out when it occurs and take points off for its use. They also remind their students to use proper sentence structure and complete sentences. The English teacher says that she believes texting inhibits good writing—it reinforces simplistic writing that may be acceptable for conversation but is "not so good for critical thinking or analysis." She suggests that texting tends to generate topic sentences without emphasizing the following explanation. According to these teachers, then, texting is inhibiting good writing. However, their evidence is limited, based on just a few personal experiences rather than on a significant amount of research.

Responses to Concerns about Textspeak

In response to these complaints that texting is having a negative impact on student writing, others insist that texting should be viewed as beneficial because it provides students with motivation to write, practice in specific writing skills, and an opportunity to gain confidence in their writing. For example, Sternberg, Kaplan, and Borck argue that texting is a good way to motivate students: teens enjoy texting, and if they frequently write through texts, they will be more motivated to write formally. Texting also helps to spark students' creativity, these authors argue, because they are always coming up with new ways to express their ideas (417).

In addition, because they are engaging in written communication rather than oral speech, texting teens learn how to convey their message to a reader in as few words as possible. In his book *Txtng: The Gr8 Db8*, David Crystal discusses a study that concludes that texting actually helps foster "the ability to summarize and express oneself concisely" in writing (168). Furthermore, Crystal explains that texting actually helps people to "sharpen their diplomatic skills . . . [because] it allows more time to formulate their thoughts and express them carefully" (168). One language arts teacher from Minnesota believes that texting helps students develop their own "individual voice" (qtd. in Walsh). Perfecting such a voice allows the writer to offer personal insights and express feelings that will interest and engage readers.

Supporters of texting also argue that it not only teaches 10 elements of writing but provides extra practice to those who struggle with the conventions of writing. As Crystal points out, children who struggle with literacy will not choose to use a technology that requires them to do something that is difficult for them. However, if they do choose to text, the experience will help them "overcome their awkwardness and develop their social and communication skills" (*Txtng* 171). Shirley Holm, a junior high school teacher, describes texting as a "comfortable form of communication" (qtd. in Walsh). Teenagers are used to texting, enjoy doing so, and as a result are always writing. Through this experience of writing in ways they enjoy, they can learn to take pleasure in writing formally. If students are continually writing in some form, they will eventually develop better skills.

Furthermore, those who favor texting explain that with practice comes the confidence and courage to try new things, which some observers believe they are seeing happen with writing as a result of texting. Teenagers have, for example, created an entirely new language—one that uses abbreviations and symbols instead of words, does not require punctuation, and uses short, incomplete phrases throughout the entire conversation. It's a way of speaking that is a language in and of itself. Crystal, among others, sees this "language evolution" as a positive effect of texting; he seems, in fact, fascinated that teenagers are capable of creating such a phenomenon, which he describes as the "latest manifestation of the human ability" (*Txtng* 175). David Warlick, a teacher and author of books about technology in the classroom, would agree with Crystal. He believes students should be given credit for "inventing a new language ideal for communicating in a high-tech world" (qtd. in Carey).

Methods

I decided to conduct my own research into this controversy. I wanted to get different, more personal, perspectives on the issue. First, I surveyed seven students on their opinions about the impact of texting on writing. Second, I questioned two high school teachers, as noted above. Finally, in an effort to compare what students are actually doing to people's perceptions of what they are doing, I analyzed student writing samples for instances of textspeak.[1]

To let students speak for themselves, I created a list of questions for seven high school and college students, some of my closest and most reliable friends. Although the number of respondents was small, I could trust my knowledge of them to help me interpret their responses. In addition, these students are very different from one another, and I believed their differences would allow for a wide array of thoughts and opinions on the issue. I was thus confident in the reliability and diversity of their answers but was cautious not to make too many assumptions because of the small sample size.

I asked the students how long they had been texting; how often they texted; what types of abbreviations they used most and how often they used them; and whether they noticed themselves using any type of textspeak in their formal writing. In analyzing their responses, I looked for commonalities to help me draw conclusions about the students' texting habits and if/how they believed their writing was affected.

I created a list of questions for teachers similar to the one for the students and asked two of my high school teachers to provide their input. I asked if they had noticed their students using textspeak in their writing assignments and, if so, how they dealt with it. I also asked if they believed texting had a positive or negative effect on writing. Next, I asked if they were texters themselves. And, finally, I solicited their opinions on what they believed should be done to prevent teens from using text abbreviations and other textspeak in their writing.

I was surprised at how different the students' replies and opinions were from the teachers'. I decided to find out for myself whose impressions were more accurate by comparing some students' actual writing with students' and teachers' perceptions of that writing. To do this I looked at twenty samples of student writing—end-of-semester research arguments written in two first-year college writing courses with different instructors. The topics varied from increased airport security after September 11 to the weapons of the Vietnam War to autism, and lengths ranged from eight to ten pages. To analyze the papers for the presence of textspeak, I looked closely for use of abbreviations and other common slang terms, especially those usages which the students had stated in their surveys were most common. These included "hbu" ("How about you?"); "gtg" ("Got to go"); and "cuz" ("because"). I also looked for the numbers 2 and 4 used instead of the words "to" and "for."

Discussion of Findings

My research suggests that texting actually has a minimal effect on student writing. It showed that students do not believe textspeak is appropriate in formal writing assignments. They recognize the difference between texting friends and writing formally and know what is appropriate in each situation. This was proven true in the student samples, in which no examples of textspeak were used. Many experts would agree that there is no harm in textspeak, as long as students continue to be taught and reminded that occasions where formal language is expected are not the place for it. As Crystal explains, the purpose of the abbreviations used in text messages is not to replace language but rather to make quick communications shorter and easier, since in a standard text message, the texter is allowed only 160 characters for a communication ("Texting" 81).

Dennis Baron, an English and linguistics professor at the University of Illinois, has done much research on the effect of technology on writing, and his findings are aligned with those of my own study. In his book *A Better Pencil: Readers, Writers, and the Digital Revolution,* he concludes that students do not use textspeak in their writing. In fact, he suggests students do not even use abbreviations in their text messages very often. Baron says that college students have "put away such childish things, and many of them had already abandoned such signs of middle-school immaturity in high school" (qtd. in Golden).

In surveying the high school and college students, I found that most have been texting for a few years, usually starting around ninth grade. The students said they generally text between thirty and a hundred messages every day but use abbreviations only occasionally, with the most common being "lol" ("Laugh out loud"), "gtg" ("Got to go"), "hbu" ("How about you?"), "cuz" ("because"), and "jk" ("Just kidding"). None of them believed texting abbreviations were acceptable in formal writing. In fact, research has found that most students report that they do not use textspeak in formal writing. As one Minnesota high school student says, "[T]here is a time and a place for everything," and formal writing is not the place for communicating the way she would if she were texting her friends (qtd. in Walsh). Another student admits that in writing for school she sometimes finds herself using these abbreviations. However, she notices and corrects them before handing in her final paper (Carey). One teacher reports that, despite texting, her students' "formal writing remains solid." She occasionally sees an abbreviation; however, it is in informal, "warm-up" writing. She believes that what students choose to use in everyday types of writing is up to them as long as they use standard English in formal writing (qtd. in Walsh).

Also supporting my own research findings are those from a 20 study which took place at a midwestern research university. This study involved eighty-six students who were taking an Introduction to Education course at the university. The participants were asked to complete a questionnaire that included questions about their texting habits, the spelling instruction they had received, and their proficiency at spelling. They also took a standardized spelling test. Before starting the study, the researchers had hypothesized that texting and the use of abbreviations would have a negative impact on the spelling abilities of the students. However, they found that the results did not support their hypothesis. The researchers did note that text messaging is continuing to increase in popularity; therefore, this issue should continue to be examined (Shaw et al.).

I myself am a frequent texter. I chat with my friends from home every day through texting. I also use texting to communicate with my school friends, perhaps to discuss what time we are going to meet for dinner or to ask quick questions about homework. According to my cell phone bill, I send and receive around 6,400 texts a month. In the messages I send, I rarely notice myself using abbreviations. The only time I use them is if I do not have time to write out the complete phrase. However, sometimes I find it more time-consuming to try to figure out how to abbreviate something so that my message will still be comprehensible.

Since I rarely use abbreviations in my texting, I never use them in my formal writing. I know that they are unacceptable and that it would make me look unintelligent if I included acronyms and symbols instead of proper and formal language. I also have not noticed an effect on my spelling as a result of texting. I am confident in my spelling abilities, and even when I use an abbreviation, I know how to spell the word(s) it stands for.

On the basis of my own research, expert research, and personal observations, I can confidently state that texting is not interfering with students' use of standard written English and has no effect on their writing abilities in general. It is interesting to look at the dynamics of the arguments over these issues. Teachers and parents who claim that they are seeing a decline in the writing abilities of their students and children mainly support the negative-impact argument. Other teachers and researchers suggest that texting provides a way for teens to practice writing in a casual setting and thus helps prepare them to write formally. Experts and students themselves, however, report that they see no effect, positive or negative. Anecdotal experiences should not overshadow the actual evidence.

NOTE

1. All participants in the study have given permission for their responses to be published.

WORKS CITED

Baron, Dennis. *A Better Pencil: Readers, Writers, and the Digital Revolution*. Oxford UP, 2009.

Carey, Bridget. "The Rise of Text, Instant Messaging Vernacular Slips into Schoolwork." *Miami Herald*, 6 Mar. 2007. *Academic Search Elite*, www .ebscohost.com/academic/academic-search-elite. Accessed 27 Oct. 2009.

Crystal, David. "Texting." *ELT Journal*, vol. 62, no. 1, Jan. 2008, pp. 77–83. *WilsonWeb*, doi: 10.1093/elt/ccm080. Accessed 8 Nov. 2009.

———. *Txting: The Gr8 Db8*. Oxford UP, 2008.

Golden, Serena. Review of *A Better Pencil*, by Dennis Baron. *Inside Higher Ed*, 18 Sept. 2009, www.insidehighered.com/news/2009/09/18/barron. Accessed 9 Nov. 2009.

Shaw, Donita M., et al. "An Exploratory Investigation into the Relationship between Text Messaging and Spelling." *New England Reading Association Journal*, vol. 43, no. 1, June 2007, pp. 57–62. *EbscoHOST*, connection .ebscohost.com/c/articles/25648081/exploratory-investigation-relationship-between-text-messaging-spelling. Accessed 8 Nov. 2009.

"Should We Worry or LOL?" *NEA Today*, vol. 22, no. 6, Mar. 2004, p. 12. *EbscoHOST*, connection.ebscohost.com/c/articles/12405267/should-we-worry-lol. Accessed 27 Oct. 2009.

Sternberg, Betty, et al. "Enhancing Adolescent Literacy Achievement through Integration of Technology in the Classroom." *Reading Research Quarterly*, vol. 42, no. 3, July–Sept. 2007, pp. 416–20. *ERIC*, eric.ed.gov/?id=EJ767777. Accessed 8 Nov. 2009.

"Texting, Testing Destroys Kids' Writing Style." *USA Today*, vol. 137, no. 2760, Sept. 2008, p. 8. *EbscoHOST*, connection.ebscohost.com/c/articles/34214935/texting-testing-destroys-kids-writing-style. Accessed 9 Nov. 2009.

Walsh, James. "Txt Msgs Creep in2 class—Some Say That's gr8." *Star Tribune*, 23 Oct. 2007. *Academic Search Elite*, www.ebscohost.com/academic/academic-search-elite. Accessed 27 Oct. 2009.

Joining the Conversation

1. Michaela Cullington makes clear in her first paragraph what viewpoint she's responding to. What is this view (her "they say"), and what is her view (her "I say")? What kinds of evidence does she offer in support of her argument?

2. Cullington acknowledges the views of quite a few naysayers, including teachers who believe that texting has a negative effect on their students' writing. How—and where in her essay—does she respond to this criticism? Is her response persuasive—and if not, why not?

3. What kinds of sources does Cullington cite, and how does she incorporate their ideas in her essay? Look at paragraph 18, for instance: how well does she introduce and explain Dennis Baron's ideas? (See pp. 44–48 on framing quotations.)

4. Cullington focuses on how texting affects writing, whereas Sherry Turkle is concerned with the way it affects communication more broadly (pp. 373–92). How do you think Cullington would respond to Turkle's concerns?

5. Cullington "send[s] and receive[s] around 6,400 texts a month" (paragraph 21). About how many do you send and receive? Write a paragraph reflecting on how your texting affects your other writing. First write it as a text, and then revise it to meet the standards of academic writing. How do the two differ?

No Need to Call

SHERRY TURKLE

—🔲—

"So many people hate the telephone," says Elaine, seventeen. Among her friends at Roosevelt High School, "it's all texting and messaging." She herself writes each of her six closest friends roughly twenty texts a day. In addition, she says, "there are about forty instant messages out, forty in, when I'm at home on the computer." Elaine has strong ideas about how electronic media "levels the playing field" between people like her—outgoing, on the soccer team, and in drama club—and the shy: "It's only on the screen that shy people open up." She explains why: "When you can think about what you're going to say, you can talk to someone you'd have trouble talking to. And it doesn't seem weird that you pause for two minutes to

———

SHERRY TURKLE teaches in the program in science, technology, and society at MIT and directs the MIT Initiative on Technology and Self. She has been described as the "Margaret Mead of digital culture." Her books include *Alone Together: Why We Expect More from Technology and Less from Each Other* (2011), *Life on the Screen: Identity in the Age of the Internet* (1995), and *The Second Self: Computers and the Human Spirit* (1984). This essay is from *Alone Together*.

think about what you're going to say before you say it, like it would be if you were actually talking to someone."

Elaine gets specific about the technical designs that help shy people express themselves in electronic messaging. The person to whom you are writing shouldn't be able to see your process of revision or how long you have been working on the message. "That could be humiliating." The best communication programs shield the writer from the view of the reader. The advantage of screen communication is that it is a place to reflect, retype, and edit. "It is a place to hide," says Elaine.

The notion that hiding makes it easier to open up is not new. In the psychoanalytic tradition, it inspired technique. Classical analysis shielded the patient from the analyst's gaze in order to facilitate free association, the golden rule of saying whatever comes to mind. Likewise, at a screen, you feel protected and less burdened by expectations. And, although you are alone, the potential for almost instantaneous contact gives an encouraging feeling of already being together. In this curious relational space, even sophisticated users who know that electronic communications can be saved, shared, and show up in court, succumb to its illusion of privacy. Alone with your thoughts, yet in contact with an almost tangible fantasy of the other, you feel free to play. At the screen, you have a chance to write yourself into the person you want to be and to imagine others as you wish them to be, constructing them for your purposes.[1] It is a seductive but dangerous habit of mind. When you cultivate this sensibility, a telephone call can seem fearsome because it reveals too much.

Elaine is right in her analysis: teenagers flee the telephone. Perhaps more surprisingly, so do adults. They claim exhaustion and lack of time; always on call, with their time highly leveraged through multitasking, they avoid voice communication outside of a small circle because it demands their full attention when they don't want to give it.

Technologies live in complex ecologies. The meaning of any one depends on what others are available. The telephone was once a way to touch base or ask a simple question. But once you have access to e-mail, instant messaging, and texting, things change. Although we still use the phone to keep up with those closest to us, we use it less outside this circle.[2] Not only do people say that a phone call asks too much, they worry it will be received as demanding too much. Randolph, a forty-six-year-old architect with two jobs, two young children, and a twelve-year-old son from a former marriage, makes both points. He avoids the telephone because he feels "tapped out. . . . It promises more than I'm willing to deliver." If he keeps his communications to text and e-mail, he believes he can "keep it together." He explains, "Now that there is e-mail, people expect that a call will be more complicated. Not about facts. A fuller thing. People expect it to take time—or else you wouldn't have called."

Tara, a fifty-five-year-old lawyer who juggles children, a job, and a new marriage, makes a similar point: "When you ask for a call, the expectation is that you have pumped it up a level. People say to themselves: 'It's urgent or she would have sent an e-mail.'" So Tara avoids the telephone. She wants to meet with friends in person; e-mail is for setting up these meetings. "That is what is most efficient," she says. But efficiency has its downside. Business meetings have agendas, but friends have unscheduled needs. In friendship, things can't always wait. Tara knows this; she feels guilty and she experiences a loss: "I'm at the point where I'm processing my friends as though they were items of inventory . . . or clients."

Leonora, fifty-seven, a professor of chemistry, reflects on her similar practice: "I use e-mail to make appointments to see friends, but I'm so busy that I'm often making an appointment one or two months in the future. After we set things up by e-mail, we do not call. Really. I don't call. They don't call. They feel that they have their appointment. What do I feel? I feel I have 'taken care of that person.'" Leonora's pained tone makes it clear that by "taken care of" she means that she has crossed someone off a to-do list. Tara and Leonora are discontent but do not feel they have a choice. This is where technology has brought them. They subscribe to a new etiquette, claiming the need for efficiency in a realm where efficiency is costly.

Audrey: A Life on the Screen

. . . Audrey, sixteen, a Roosevelt junior[,] talked about her Facebook profile as "the avatar of me." She's one of Elaine's shy friends who prefers texting to talking. She is never without her phone, sometimes using it to text even as she instant-messages at an open computer screen. Audrey feels lonely in her family. She has an older brother in medical school and a second, younger brother, just two years old. Her parents are divorced, and she lives half time with each of them. Their homes are about a forty-five-minute drive apart. This means that Audrey spends a lot of time on the road. "On the road," she says. "That's daily life." She sees her phone as the glue that ties her life together. Her mother calls her to pass on a message to her father. Her father does the same. Audrey says, "They call me to say, 'Tell your mom this. . . . Make sure your dad knows that.' I use the cell to pull it together." Audrey sums up the situation: "My parents use me and my cell like instant messenger. I am their IM."

Like so many other children who tell me similar stories, Audrey complains of her mother's inattention when she picks her up at school or after sports practice. At these times, Audrey says, her mother is usually focused on her cell phone, either texting or talking to her friends. Audrey describes the scene: she comes out of the gym exhausted, carrying heavy gear. Her mother sits in her beaten-up SUV, immersed in her cell, and doesn't even look up until Audrey opens the car door. Sometimes her mother will make eye contact but remain engrossed with the phone as they begin the drive home. Audrey says, "It gets between us, but it's hopeless. She's not going to give it up. Like, it could have been four days since I last spoke to her, then I sit in the car and wait in silence until she's done."[3]

Audrey has a fantasy of her mother, waiting for her, expectant, without a phone. But Audrey is resigned that this is not to be and feels she must temper her criticism of her mother because of her own habit of texting when she is with her friends. Audrey does everything she can to avoid a call.[4] "The phone, it's awkward. I don't see the point. Too much just a recap and sharing feelings. With a text . . . I can answer on my own time. I can respond. I can ignore it. So it really works with my mood. I'm not bound to anything, no commitment. . . . I have control over the conversation and also more control over what I say."

Texting offers protection:

Nothing will get spat at you. You have time to think and prepare what you're going to say, to make you appear like that's just the way you are. There's planning involved, so you can control how you're portrayed to this person, because you're choosing these words, editing it before you send it. . . . When you instant-message you can cross things out, edit what you say, block a person, or sign off. A phone conversation is a lot of pressure. You're always expected to uphold it, to keep it going, and that's too much pressure. . . . You have to just keep going . . . "Oh, how was your day?" You're trying to think of something else to say real fast so the conversation doesn't die out.

Then Audrey makes up a new word. A text, she argues, is better than a call because in a call "there is a lot less *boundness* to the person." By this she means that in a call, she could learn too much or say too much, and things could get "out of control." A call has insufficient boundaries. She admits that "later in life I'm going to need to talk to people on the phone. *But not now.*" When texting, she feels at a reassuring distance. If things start to go in a direction she doesn't like, she can easily redirect the conversation—or cut it off: "In texting, you get your main points off; you can really control when you want the conversation to start and end. You say, 'Got to go, bye.' You

Teenagers plugged into their devices but not each other.

just do it . . . much better than the long drawn-out good-byes, when you have no real reason to leave, but you want to end the conversation." This last is what Audrey likes least—the end of conversations. A phone call, she explains, requires the skill to end a conversation "when you have no real reason to leave. . . . It's not like there is a reason. You just want to. I don't know how to do that. *I don't want to learn.*"

Ending a call is hard for Audrey because she experiences separation as rejection; she projects onto others the pang of abandonment she feels when someone ends a conversation with her. Feeling unthreatened when someone wants to end a conversation may seem a small thing, but it is not. It calls upon a sense of self-worth; one needs to be at a place where Audrey has not arrived. It is easier to avoid the phone; its beginnings and endings are too rough on her.

Audrey is not alone in this. Among her friends, phone calls are infrequent, and she says, "Face-to-face conversations happen way less than they did before. It's always, 'Oh, talk to you online.'" This means, she explains, that things happen online that "should happen in person. . . . Friendships get broken. I've had someone ask me out in a text message. I've had someone break up with me online." But Audrey is resigned to such costs and focuses on the bounties of online life.

One of Audrey's current enthusiasms is playing a more social, even flirtatious version of herself in online worlds. "I'd like to be more like I am online," she says. As we've seen, for Audrey, building an online avatar is not so different from writing a social-networking profile. An avatar, she explains, "is a Facebook profile come to life." And avatars and profiles have a lot in common with the everyday experiences of texting and instant messaging. In all of these, as she sees it, the point is to do "a performance of you."

Making an avatar and texting. Pretty much the same. You're creating your own person; you don't have to think of things on the
spot really, which a lot of people can't really do. You're creating
your own little ideal person and sending it out. Also on the Internet, with sites like MySpace and Facebook, you put up the things
you like about yourself, and you're not going to advertise the bad
aspects of you.

You're not going to post pictures of how you look every day.
You're going to get your makeup on, put on your cute little outfit,
you're going to take your picture and post it up as your default, and
that's what people are going to expect that you are every day, when
really you're making it up for all these people. . . . You can write
anything about yourself; these people don't know. You can create
who you want to be. You can say what kind of stereotype mold you
want to fit in without . . . maybe in real life it won't work for you,
you can't pull it off. But you can pull it off on the Internet.

Audrey has her cell phone and its camera with her all day; all
day she takes pictures and posts them to Facebook. She boasts
that she has far more Facebook photo albums than any of her
friends. "I like to feel," she says, "that my life is up there." But,
of course, what is up on Facebook is her edited life. Audrey is
preoccupied about which photographs to post. Which put her
in the best light? Which show her as a "bad" girl in potentially
appealing ways? If identity play is the work of adolescence,
Audrey is at work all day: "If Facebook were deleted, I'd be
deleted. . . . All my memories would probably go along with
it. And other people have posted pictures of me. All of that
would be lost. If Facebook were undone, I might actually freak
out. . . . That is where I am. It's part of your life. It's a second
you." It is at this point that Audrey says of a Facebook avatar:
"It's your little twin on the Internet."

Since Audrey is constantly reshaping this "twin," she wonders what happens to the elements of her twin that she edits away. "What does Facebook do with pictures you put on and then take off?" She suspects that they stay on the Internet forever, an idea she finds both troubling and comforting. If everything is archived, Audrey worries that she will never be able to escape the Internet twin. That thought is not so nice. But if everything is archived, at least in fantasy, she will never have to give her up. That thought is kind of nice.

On Facebook, Audrey works on the twin, and the twin works on her. She describes her relationship to the site as a "give-and-take." Here's how it works: Audrey tries out a "flirty" style. She receives a good response from Facebook friends, and so she ramps up the flirtatious tone. She tries out "an ironic, witty" tone in her wall posts. The response is not so good, and she retreats. Audrey uses the same kind of tinkering as she experiments with her avatars in virtual worlds. She builds a first version to "put something out there." Then comes months of adjusting, of "seeing the new kinds of people I can hang with" by changing how she represents herself. Change your avatar, change your world.

. . .

Overwhelmed across the Generations

The teenagers I studied were born in the late 1980s and early 1990s. Many were introduced to the Internet through America Online when they were only a little past being toddlers. Their parents, however, came to online life as grown-ups. In this domain, they are a generation that, from the beginning, has been playing catch-up with their children. This pattern continues: the fastest-growing demographic on Facebook is adults from

"Conventional wisdom" is the "standard view." For more on this move, see pp. 23–24.

thirty-five to forty-four.[5] Conventional wisdom stresses how different these adults are from their children—laying out fundamental divides between those who migrated to digital worlds and those who are its "natives." But the migrants and natives share a lot: perhaps above all, the feeling of being overwhelmed. If teenagers, overwhelmed with demands for academic and sexual performance, have come to treat online life as a place to hide and draw some lines, then their parents, claiming exhaustion, strive to exert greater control over what reaches them. And the only way to filter effectively is to keep most communications online and text based.

So, they are always on, always at work, and always on call. [20] I remember the time, not many years ago, when I celebrated Thanksgiving with a friend and her son, a young lawyer, who had just been given a beeper by his firm. At the time, everyone at the table, including him, joked about the idea of his "legal emergencies." By the following year, he couldn't imagine not being in continual contact with the office. There was a time when only physicians had beepers, a "burden" shared in rotation. Now, we have all taken up the burden, reframed as an asset—or as just the way it is.

We are on call for our families as well as our colleagues. On a morning hike in the Berkshires, I fall into step with Hope, forty-seven, a real estate broker from Manhattan. She carries her BlackBerry. Her husband, she says, will probably want to be in touch. And indeed, he calls at thirty-minute intervals. Hope admits, somewhat apologetically, that she is "not fond" of the calls, but she loves her husband, and this is what he needs. She answers her phone religiously until finally a call comes in with spotty reception. "We're out of range, thank goodness," she says, as she disables her phone. "I need a rest."

Increasingly, people feel as though they must have a reason for taking time alone, a reason not to be available for calls. It is poignant that people's thoughts turn to technology when they imagine ways to deal with stresses that they see as having been brought on by technology. They talk of filters and intelligent agents that will handle the messages they don't want to see. Hope and Audrey, though thirty years apart in age, both see texting as the solution to the "problem" of the telephone. And both redefine "stress" in the same way—as pressure that happens in real time. With this in mind, my hiking partner explains that she is trying to "convert" her husband to texting. There will be more messages; he will be able to send more texts than he can place calls. But she will not have to deal with them "as they happen."

Mixed feelings about the drumbeat of electronic communication do not suggest any lack of affection toward those with whom we are in touch. But a stream of messages makes it impossible to find moments of solitude, time when other people are showing us neither dependency nor affection. In solitude we don't reject the world but have the space to think our own thoughts. But if your phone is always with you, seeking solitude can look suspiciously like hiding.

We fill our days with ongoing connection, denying ourselves time to think and dream. Busy to the point of depletion, we make a new Faustian* bargain. It goes something like this: if we are left alone when we make contact, we can handle being together.

. . .

The barrier to making a call is so high that even when people 25 have something important to share, they hold back. Tara, the lawyer who admits to "processing" her friends by dealing with

---

*Faustian** Relating to Faust, a character of German folklore, and used to describe something or someone that is concerned only with present gain and not future consequences.

them on e-mail, tells me a story about a friendship undermined. About four times a year, Tara has dinner with Alice, a classmate from law school. Recently, the two women exchanged multiple e-mails trying to set a date. Finally, after many false starts, they settled on a time and a restaurant. Alice did not come to the dinner with good news. Her sister had died. Though they lived thousands of miles apart, the sisters had spoken once a day. Without her sister, without these calls, Alice feels ungrounded.

At dinner, when Alice told Tara about her sister's death, Tara became upset, close to distraught. She and Alice had been e-mailing for months. Why hadn't Alice told her about this? Alice explained that she had been taken up with her family, with arrangements. And she said, simply, "I didn't think it was something to discuss over e-mail." Herself in need of support, Alice ended up comforting Tara.

As Tara tells me this story, she says that she was ashamed of her reaction. Her focus should have been—and should now be—on Alice's loss, not on her own ranking as a confidant. But she feels defensive as well. She had, after all, "been in touch." She'd e-mailed; she'd made sure that their dinner got arranged. Tara keeps coming back to the thought that if she and Alice had spoken on the telephone to set up their dinner date, she would have learned about her friend's loss. She says, "I would have heard something in her voice. I would have suspected. I could have drawn her out." But for Tara, as for so many, the telephone call is for family. For friends, even dear friends, it is close to being off the menu.

Tara avoids the voice but knows she has lost something. For the young, this is less clear. I talk with Meredith, a junior at Silver Academy who several months before had learned of a friend's death via instant message and had been glad that she didn't have to see or speak to anyone. She says, "It was a day off, so I was at home, and I hadn't seen anyone who lives around me, and then my friend Rosie IM'ed me and told me my friend died. I was shocked and everything, but I was more okay than I would've been if I saw people. I went through the whole thing not seeing anyone and just talking to people online about it, and I was fine. I think it would've been much worse if they'd told me in person."

I ask Meredith to say more. She explains that when bad news came in an instant message, she was able to compose herself. It would have been "terrible," she says, to have received a call. "I didn't have to be upset in front of someone else." Indeed, for a day after hearing the news, Meredith only communicated with friends by instant message. She describes the IMs as frequent but brief: "Just about the fact of it. Conversations like, 'Oh, have you heard?' 'Yeah, I heard.' And that's it." The IMs let her put her emotions at a distance. When she had to face other people at school, she could barely tolerate the rush of feeling: "The second I saw my friends, it got so much worse." Karen and Beatrice, two of Meredith's friends, tell similar stories. Karen learned about the death of her best friend's father in an instant message. She says, "It was easier to learn about it on the computer. It made it easier to hear. I could take it in pieces. I didn't have to look all upset to anyone." Beatrice reflects, "I don't want to hear bad things, but if it is just texted to me, I can stay calm."

These young women prefer to deal with strong feelings from the safe haven of the Net. It gives them an alternative to processing emotions in real time. Under stress, they seek composure above all. But they do not find equanimity. When they meet and lose composure, they find a new way to flee: often they take their phones out to text each other and friends not in the room. I see a vulnerability in this generation, so quick to say, "Please don't call." They keep themselves at a distance from their feelings. They keep themselves from people who could help.

Voices

When I first read how it is through our faces that we call each other up as human beings, I remember thinking I have always felt that way about the human voice. But like many of those I study, I have been complicit with technology in removing many voices from my life.

I had plans for dinner with a colleague, Joyce. On the day before we were to meet, my daughter got admitted to college. I e-mailed Joyce that we would have much to celebrate. She e-mailed back a note of congratulations. She had been through the college admissions process with her children and understood my relief. At dinner, Joyce said that she had thought of calling to congratulate me, but a call had seemed "intrusive." I admitted that I hadn't called her to share my good news for the same reason. Joyce and I both felt constrained by a new etiquette but were also content to follow it. "I feel more in control of my time if I'm not disturbed by calls," Joyce admitted.

Both Joyce and I have gained something we are not happy about wanting. License to feel together when alone, comforted by e-mails, excused from having to attend to people in real time. We did not set out to avoid the voice but end up denying ourselves its pleasures. For the voice can be experienced only in real time, and both of us are so busy that we don't feel we have it to spare.

Apple's visual voicemail for the iPhone was welcomed because it saves you the trouble of having to listen to a message to know who sent it. And now there are applications that automatically transcribe voicemail into text. I interview Maureen, a college freshman, who is thrilled to have discovered one of these programs. She says that only her parents send her voicemail: "I love my parents, but they don't know how to use the phone. It's not the place to leave long voice messages. Too long to listen to. Now, I can scroll through the voicemail as text messages. Great."

Here, in the domain of connectivity, we meet the narra- 35 tive of better than nothing becoming simply better. People have long wanted to connect with those at a distance. We sent letters, then telegrams, and then the telephone gave us a way to hear their voices. All of these were better than nothing when you couldn't meet face-to-face. Then, short of time, people began to use the phone instead of getting together. By the 1970s, when I first noticed that I was living in a new regime of connectivity, you were never really "away" from your phone because answering machines made you responsible for any call that came in. Then, this machine, originally designed as a way to leave a message if someone was not at home, became a screening device, our end-of-millennium Victorian calling card. Over time, voicemail became an end in itself, not the result of a frustrated telephone call. People began to call purposely when they knew that no one would be home. People learned to let the phone ring and "let the voicemail pick it up."

In a next step, the voice was taken out of voicemail because communicating with text is faster. E-mail gives you more control over your time and emotional exposure. But then, it, too, was not fast enough. With mobile connectivity (think text and Twitter), we can communicate our lives pretty much at the rate we live them. But the system backfires. We express ourselves in staccato texts, but we send out a lot and often to large groups. So we get even more back—so many that the idea of communicating with anything but texts seems too exhausting. Shakespeare might have said, we are "consumed with that which we are nourished by."[6]

I sketched out this narrative to a friend for whom it rang true as a description but seemed incredible all the same. A professor of poetry and a voracious reader, she said, "We cannot all write like Lincoln or Shakespeare, but even the least gifted among us has this incredible instrument, our voice, to communicate the range of human emotion. Why would we deprive ourselves of that?"

The beginning of an answer has become clear: in text messaging and e-mail, you hide as much as you show. You can present yourself as you wish to be "seen." And you can "process" people as quickly as you want to. Listening can only slow you down. A voice recording can be sped up a bit, but it has to unfold in real time. Better to have it transcribed or avoid it altogether. We work so hard to give expressive voices to our robots but are content not to use our own.

Like the letters they replace, e-mail, messaging, texting, and, more recently, Tweeting carry a trace of the voice. When Tara regretted that she had not called her friend Alice—on the phone she would have heard her friend's grief—she expressed the point of view of someone who grew up with the voice and is sorry to have lost touch with it. Hers is a story of trying to rebalance things in a traditional framework. Trey, her law partner, confronts something different, something he cannot rebalance.

My brother found out that his wife is pregnant and he put it on his *blog*. He didn't call me first. I called him when I saw the blog entry. I was mad at him. He didn't see why I was making a big deal. He writes his blog every day, as things happen, that's how he lives. So when they got home from the doctor—bam, right onto the blog. Actually, he said it was part of how he celebrated the news with his wife—to put it on the blog together with a picture of him raising a glass of champagne and she raising a glass of orange juice. Their idea was to celebrate on the blog, almost in real time, with the photos and everything. When I complained they made me feel like such a *girl*. Do you think I'm old-school?[7]

Trey's story is very different from Tara's. Trey's brother was not trying to save time by avoiding the telephone. His brother did not avoid or forget him or show preference to other family members. Blogging is part of his brother's intimate life. It is how he and his wife celebrated the most important milestone in their life as a family. In a very different example of our new genres of online intimacy, a friend of mine underwent a stem cell transplant. I felt honored when invited to join her family's blog. It is set up as a news feed that appears on my computer desktop. Every day, and often several times a day, the family posts medical reports, poems, reflections, and photographs. There are messages from the patient, her husband, her children, and her brother, who donated his stem cells. There is progress and there are setbacks. On the blog, one can follow this family as it lives, suffers, and rejoices for a year of treatment. Inhibitions lift. Family members tell stories that would be harder to share face-to-face. I read every post. I send e-mails. But the presence of the blog changes something in my behavior. I am grateful for every piece of information but feel strangely shy about calling. Would it be an intrusion? I think of Trey. Like him, I am trying to get my bearings in a world where the Net has become a place of intimate enclosure.

Notes

1. In the object relations tradition of psychoanalysis, an object is that which one relates to. Usually, objects are people, especially a significant person who is the object or target of another's feelings or intentions. A whole object is a person in his or her entirety. It is common in development for people to internalize part objects, representations of others that are not the whole person. Online life provides an environment that makes it easier for people to relate to part objects. This puts relationships at risk. On object relations theory, see, for example, Stephen A. Mitchell and Margaret J. Black, *Freud and Beyond: A History of Modern Psychoanalytic Thought* (New York: Basic Books, 1995).

2. See Stefana Broadbent, "How the Internet Enables Intimacy," Ted.com, www.ted.com/talks/stefana_broadbent_how_the_internet_enables_intimacy. html (accessed August 8, 2010). According to Broadbent, 80 percent of calls on cell phones are made to four people, 80 percent of Skype calls are made to two people, and most Facebook exchanges are with four to six people.

3. This mother is being destructive to her relationship with her daughter. Research shows that people use the phone in ways that surely undermine relationships with adult partners as well. In one striking finding, according to Dan Schulman, CEO of cell operator Virgin Mobile, one in five people will interrupt sex to answer their phone. David Kirkpatrick, "Do You Answer Your Cellphone During Sex?" *Fortune*, August 28, 2006, http://money.cnn.com/2006/08/25/technology/fastforward_kirpatrick.fortune/index.htm (accessed November 11, 2009).

4. See Amanda Lenhart et al., "Teens and Mobile Phones," The Pew Foundation, April 20, 2010, www.pewinternet.org/Reports/2010/Teens-and-Mobile-Phones.aspx?r=i (accessed August 10, 2010).

5. "Number of US Facebook Users over 35 Nearly Doubles in Last 60 Days," Inside Facebook, March 25, 2009, www.insidefacebookcom/2009/03/25/number-of-us-facebook-users-over-35-nearly-doubles-in-last-60-days (accessed October 19, 2009).

6. This paraphrases a line from Sonnet 73: "Consum'd with that which it was nourish'd by . . ."

7. The author of a recent blog post titled "I Hate the Phone" would not call Trey old-school, but nor would she want to call him. Anna-Jane Grossman admits to growing up loving her pink princess phone, answering machine, and long, drawn-out conversations with friends she had just seen at school. Now she

hates the phone: "I feel an inexplicable kind of dread when I hear a phone ring, even when the caller ID displays the number of someone I like. . . . My dislike for the phone probably first started to grow when I began using Instant Messenger. Perhaps phone-talking is a skill that one has to practice, and the more IMing I've done, the more my skills have dwindled to the level of a modern day 13-year-old who never has touched a landline. . . . I don't even listen to my [phone] messages any more: They get transcribed automatically and then are sent to me via e-mail or text." The author was introduced to Skype and sees its virtues; she also sees the ways in which it undermines conversation: "It occurs to me that if there's one thing that'll become obsolete because of video-chatting, it's not phones: it's natural flowing conversations with people far away." See Grossman, "I Hate the Phone."

In my experience with Skype, pauses seem long and awkward, and it is an effort not to look bored. Peggy Ornstein makes this point in "The Over-extended Family," *New York Times Magazine*, June 25, 2009, ww.nytimes.com/2009/06/28/magazine/28fob-wwln-t.html (accessed October 17, 2009). Ornstein characterizes Skype as providing "too much information," something that derails intimacy: "Suddenly I understood why slumber-party confessions always came after lights were out, why children tend to admit the juicy stuff to the back of your head while you're driving, why psychoanalysts stay out of a patient's sightline."

Joining the Conversation

1. Sherry Turkle was once optimistic about the potential for technology to improve human lives but now takes a more complex view. What does she mean here by the title, "No Need to Call"? What pitfalls does she see in our increasing reluctance to talk on the phone or face to face?

2. This reading consists mainly of stories about how people communicate on social media, on the phone, and face to face. Summarize the story about Audrey (pp. 376–81) in one paragraph.

3. According to Turkle, we "hide as much as [we] show" in text messages and email, presenting ourselves "as [we] wish to be 'seen'" (paragraph 38). Is this so different from what we do in most of our writing? How do you present yourself in your academic writing, and how does that presentation differ from what you do in text messages or email?

4. Is digital communication good or bad—or both? Read Chapter 13, which summarizes both sides of that discussion. Which side (or sides) do you come down on? Where do you think Turkle stands?

5. Turkle says she sees "a vulnerability" in those who prefer social media to phone calls or face-to-face communication: "I see a vulnerability in this generation, so quick to say, 'Please don't call'" (paragraph 30). Write an essay about your own views on communicating with social media, drawing upon this and other readings in the chapter for ideas to consider, to question, and to support your view.

I Had a Nice Time with You Tonight.
On the App.

JENNA WORTHAM

—▣—

LAST SUNDAY, I spent a lazy afternoon with my boyfriend. We chatted while I made brunch, discussed the books we were reading, laughed at some cat pictures and then settled down with dinner, before bidding each other good night.

We did all of this despite living more than 3,000 miles apart, thanks to smartphone applications and services that helped to collapse time and space. Video chat apps like Google Hangouts, FaceTime and Skype, of course, already make it possible to see and talk to one another in real time. But those formats can be awkward and require both parties to coordinate a time to talk and find someplace quiet with a decent Internet connection—a challenge with busy schedules in different time zones.

I prefer to use applications that already figure into my daily routine, like Google's instant-messaging application, Gchat, as

———

JENNA WORTHAM writes about technology for the *New York Times*. Her work also has appeared in *Bust* magazine, *Vogue*, and *Wired*, and she is a cofounder of the zine *Girl Crush*. Her Twitter handle is @jennydeluxe. This column first appeared in the *New York Times* on April 6, 2014.

well as Facebook Messenger, Twitter, Instagram and Snapchat. This way, we can talk about travel plans while I'm waiting for the train or talk about what he's making for dinner while I'm at work.

I've found that all of my conversational habits have matured beyond the static phone dates of yore. We are now in constant and continuous communication with our friends, co-workers and family over the course of a day. These interactions can help us feel physically close, even if they happen through a screen.

And because this kind of communication is less formal than 5 a phone call or an email, it feels more like the kind of casual conversation you might have over a meal or while watching television together. These conversations can also be infused with a lot more fun than a regular text message, because they often include cutesy features that let you add digital doodles to video messages, or send virtual kisses or cartoon characters.

The downside is that it can be hard to juggle all the various ways to communicate. But a modern kind of application, including one that we were experimenting with on that lazy Sunday, combines all those interactions—and is designed with couples in mind. This focus on couples is relatively new. The online and mobile dating industry has built many tools and services for single people who are looking for romantic partners and new friends. They've evolved from websites like Match.com and OKCupid to mobile apps like Tinder that let people swipe through potential dates and select the ones that pique their interest.

But in recent months, several entrepreneurs have been shifting their attention to people after they meet a mate.

"Tech entrepreneurs, long obsessed with making apps to help you find a relationship, have now begun trying to solve the problem of staying happy in one," wrote Ann Friedman on *The Cut*, a blog of *New York* magazine. Ms. Friedman points to apps like Avocado, Couple and Between as smartphone apps that "keep you close with your partner through the power of a smartphone alone."

The application that my boyfriend and I were using, called You & Me, is scheduled for public release in early May. It was created by the founders of the online dating site HowAboutWe, which initially built its business around people proposing dates— as in, "How about we go to a trivia night?"—as a means for finding matches. The original HowAboutWe dating service was started in 2010 and has attracted two million users to date.

But it had a business-model problem, said Aaron Schildkrout, 10 one of the founders of HowAboutWe. The site lost users—and potential customers—once they were in a relationship. "The couples market is huge," he said. He and his business partner were getting feedback from "couples who had met on the service but couldn't use it anymore" and decided to build an application "to facilitate communication and interaction."

The new You & Me application lets two people send photographs and voice messages and play a selfie-exchanging game called "Halfsie."

I tested an early version for a few weeks. When I described it to others, they often furrowed their brows and asked me whether people really needed yet another application to talk to people they are closest to.

Sherry Turkle, the author of *Alone Together*, says she believes that using an application in place of real-world, face-to-face interactions is having a detrimental effect on how we prioritize offline communication and, potentially, on our ability to interact even when we aren't relying on technology as a mediator.

"We've given ourselves something so gratifying that we can forget other ways we can communicate," she said. "What starts out being better than nothing becomes better than anything."

See Chapter 2 for ways to blend the author's words with your own. Ms. Turkle, who is researching the impact of technol- 15 ogy on communication, said technology-saturated types could "forget what a face-to-face interaction can do." She says she is not opposed to messaging applications, but she cautions that their most frequent users should be aware of the potential impact.

In my experience, however, I've found the opposite to be true, especially as more and more of my daily interactions with friends, colleagues and family happen through a screen. If anything, the pervasiveness of technology in my life has heightened my desire for actual one-on-one meetings.

Anyone who spends much time online and on a smartphone knows that it's no substitute for the real thing—it's just an appetizer that can delight and satisfy until the main course arrives. But that satisfaction is real. Although I am using a vast array of apps to deal with a real challenge—trying to date someone who lives on a different continent—they still hold their appeal when that distance is erased. Even when we're both in the same city for an extended time, we still use them, albeit to a lesser degree and not to the detriment of spending actual time together.

In many cases, adding the Internet to the mix can strengthen a relationship over all, because online interactions have their own kind of entertaining rapport that can coexist with their offline counterparts.

In her blog post, Ms. Friedman pointed to a February study from the Pew Research Center's Internet Research project that surveyed 2,252 adults about their digital habits in relationships. Seventy-four percent of the couples surveyed reported that the Internet had had a positive impact on their relationship. In addition, 41 percent of 18-to-29-year-olds in serious relationships said they felt closer to their partner because of online or text-message conversations.

Mr. Schildkrout, at You & Me, hopes to appeal to people 20
who want to build their relationships through the screen as well
as beyond it. Although the couples app will be free, he says, the
company may eventually add features that let their users ask
each other out on prepackaged evenings or events sold through
the application. "At the end of the day," Mr. Schildkrout said,
"technology is where some of the most beautiful interactions
happen and deepen."

The jury is still out on whether You & Me will replace the
swath of services we already use, but for what it's worth, I think
that Mr. Schildkrout is right. I've had some of my most emotionally intimate and honest conversations with friends and
romantic partners on mobile devices. And while virtual chats
and hugs will never be the same as their real-world counterparts,
they can come awfully close in a pinch.

Joining the Conversation

1. How would you summarize Jenna Wortham's attitude about
   using apps to communicate with her boyfriend and others?
   What benefits does she see, and what limitations?
2. Wortham begins her piece with a short narrative about "a lazy
   afternoon" with her boyfriend. Why is this an effective way
   to begin this essay? How else might the piece have begun?
3. So what? Who cares? Where in this piece does Wortham
   explain why her argument matters? Has she persuaded you—
   and if not, why not?

4. Sherry Turkle writes (pp. 373–92) that young women often "prefer to deal with strong feelings from the safe haven of the Net" and that doing so provides "an alternative to processing emotions in real time." What do you think Wortham would say to that?

5. What if Romeo and Juliet had to communicate using only an app? What about Samson and Delilah? Or Roosevelt and Churchill? How would the technology have affected their conversations? Write an essay developing your own argument about the larger effects of digital media, citing your experiences as well as ideas from readings in this chapter.

Small Change: Why the Revolution Will Not Be Tweeted

MALCOLM GLADWELL

—🔲—

AT FOUR-THIRTY IN THE AFTERNOON on Monday, February 1, 1960, four college students sat down at the lunch counter at the Woolworth's in downtown Greensboro, North Carolina. They were freshmen at North Carolina A. & T., a black college a mile or so away.

"I'd like a cup of coffee, please," one of the four, Ezell Blair, said to the waitress.

"We don't serve Negroes here," she replied.

The Woolworth's lunch counter was a long L-shaped bar that could seat sixty-six people, with a standup snack bar at one end. The seats were for whites. The snack bar was for blacks. Another employee, a black woman who worked at the steam

---

MALCOLM GLADWELL writes for the *New Yorker* and was named one of *Time* magazine's 100 Most Influential People in 2005. His best-selling books include *The Tipping Point: How Little Things Make a Big Difference* (2000), *Blink: The Power of Thinking without Thinking* (2005), *Outliers: The Story of Success* (2008), and *David and Goliath: Underdogs, Misfits, and the Art of Battling* (2013). This essay first appeared in the *New Yorker* on October 14, 2010.

table, approached the students and tried to warn them away. "You're acting stupid, ignorant!" she said. They didn't move. Around five-thirty, the front doors to the store were locked. The four still didn't move. Finally, they left by a side door. Outside, a small crowd had gathered, including a photographer from the Greensboro *Record.* "I'll be back tomorrow with A. & T. College," one of the students said.

By next morning, the protest had grown to twenty-seven 5 men and four women, most from the same dormitory as the original four. The men were dressed in suits and ties. The students had brought their schoolwork, and studied as they sat at the counter. On Wednesday, students from Greensboro's "Negro" secondary school, Dudley High, joined in, and the number of protesters swelled to eighty. By Thursday, the protesters numbered three hundred, including three white women, from the Greensboro campus of the University of North Carolina. By Saturday, the sit-in had reached six hundred. People spilled out onto the street. White teenagers waved Confederate flags. Someone threw a firecracker. At noon, the A. & T. football team arrived. "Here comes the wrecking crew," one of the white students shouted.

By the following Monday, sit-ins had spread to Winston-Salem, twenty-five miles away, and Durham, fifty miles away. The day after that, students at Fayetteville State Teachers College and at Johnson C. Smith College, in Charlotte, joined in, followed on Wednesday by students at St. Augustine's College and Shaw University, in Raleigh. On Thursday and Friday, the protest crossed state lines, surfacing in Hampton and Portsmouth, Virginia, in Rock Hill, South Carolina, and in Chattanooga, Tennessee. By the end of the month, there were sit-ins throughout the South, as far west as Texas. "I asked every student I met what the first day of the sitdowns had been like on his campus," the political theorist Michael Walzer wrote in *Dissent*. "The answer was always the same: 'It was like a fever. Everyone wanted to go.'" Some seventy thousand students eventually took part. Thousands were arrested and untold thousands more radicalized. These events in the early sixties became a civil-rights war that engulfed the South for the rest of the decade—and it happened without e-mail, texting, Facebook, or Twitter.

The world, we are told, is in the midst of a revolution. The new tools of social media have reinvented social activism. With Facebook and Twitter and the like, the traditional relationship between political authority and popular will has been upended, making it easier for the powerless to collaborate, coordinate, and give voice to their concerns. When ten thousand protesters took to the streets in Moldova in the spring of 2009 to protest against their country's Communist government, the action was dubbed the Twitter Revolution, because of the means by which the demonstrators had been brought together. A few months after that, when student protests rocked Tehran, the State Department took the unusual step of asking Twitter to suspend scheduled maintenance of its Web site, because the Administration didn't want such a critical organizing tool out of service at the height of the demonstrations. "Without Twitter the people of Iran would not have felt empowered and confident to stand up for freedom and democracy," Mark Pfeifle, a former national-security adviser, later wrote, calling for Twitter to be nominated for the Nobel Peace Prize. Where activists were once defined by their causes, they are now defined by their tools. Facebook warriors go online to push for change. "You are the best hope for us all," James K. Glassman, a former senior State Department official,

See Chapter 3 for tips on incorporating quotations.

Social media can't provide what social change has always required.

told a crowd of cyber activists at a recent conference sponsored by Facebook, A.T.&T., Howcast, MTV, and Google. Sites like Facebook, Glassman said, "give the U.S. a significant competitive advantage over terrorists. Some time ago, I said that Al Qaeda was 'eating our lunch on the Internet.' That is no longer the case. Al Qaeda is stuck in Web 1.0. The Internet is now about interactivity and conversation."

These are strong, and puzzling, claims. Why does it matter who is eating whose lunch on the Internet? Are people who log on to their Facebook page really the best hope for us all? As for Moldova's so-called Twitter Revolution, Evgeny Morozov, a scholar at Stanford who has been the most persistent of digital evangelism's critics, points out that Twitter had scant internal significance in Moldova, a country where very few Twitter accounts exist. Nor does it seem to have been a revolution, not least because the protests—as Anne Applebaum suggested in the *Washington Post*—may well have been a bit of stagecraft cooked up by the government. (In a country paranoid about Romanian revanchism, the protesters flew a Romanian flag over the Parliament building.) In the Iranian case, meanwhile, the people tweeting about the demonstrations were almost all in the West. "It is time to get Twitter's role in the events in Iran right," Golnaz Esfandiari wrote, this past summer, in *Foreign Policy*. "Simply put: There was no Twitter Revolution inside Iran." The cadre of prominent bloggers, like Andrew Sullivan, who championed the role of social media in Iran, Esfandiari continued, misunderstood the situation. "Western journalists who couldn't reach—or didn't bother reaching?—people on the ground in Iran simply scrolled through the English-language tweets post with tag #iranelection," she wrote. "Through it all, no one seemed to wonder why people trying to coordinate protests in Iran would be writing in any language other than Farsi."

Some of this grandiosity is to be expected. Innovators tend to be solipsists. They often want to cram every stray fact and experience into their new model. As the historian Robert Darnton has written, "The marvels of communication technology in the present have produced a false consciousness about the past—even a sense that communication has no history, or had nothing of importance to consider before the days of television and the Internet." But there is something else at work here, in the outsized enthusiasm for social media. Fifty years after one of the most extraordinary episodes of social upheaval in American history, we seem to have forgotten what activism is.

Greensboro in the early nineteen-sixties was the kind of place ₁₀ where racial insubordination was routinely met with violence. The four students who first sat down at the lunch counter were terrified. "I suppose if anyone had come up behind me and yelled 'Boo,' I think I would have fallen off my seat," one of them said later. On the first day, the store manager notified the police chief, who immediately sent two officers to the store. On the third day, a gang of white toughs showed up at the lunch counter and stood ostentatiously behind the protesters, ominously muttering epithets such as "burr-head nigger." A local Ku Klux Klan leader made an appearance. On Saturday, as tensions grew, someone called in a bomb threat, and the entire store had to be evacuated.

The dangers were even clearer in the Mississippi Freedom Summer Project of 1964, another of the sentinel campaigns of the civil-rights movement. The Student Nonviolent Coordinating Committee recruited hundreds of Northern, largely white unpaid volunteers to run Freedom Schools, register black voters, and raise civil-rights awareness in the Deep South. "No one should go *anywhere* alone, but certainly not in an automobile and certainly not at night," they were instructed. Within days of arriving in Mississippi, three volunteers—Michael Schwerner, James Chaney, and Andrew Goodman—were kidnapped and killed, and during the rest of the summer, thirty-seven black churches were set on fire and dozens of safe houses were bombed; volunteers were beaten, shot at, arrested, and trailed by pickup trucks full of armed men. A quarter of those in the program dropped out. Activism that challenges the status quo—that attacks deeply rooted problems—is not for the faint of heart.

What makes people capable of this kind of activism? The Stanford sociologist Doug McAdam compared the Freedom Summer dropouts with the participants who stayed, and discovered that the key difference wasn't, as might be expected, ideological fervor. "All of the applicants—participants and withdrawals alike—emerge as highly committed, articulate supporters of the goals and values of the summer program," he concluded. What mattered more was an applicant's degree of personal connection to the civil-rights movement. All the volunteers were required to provide a list of personal contacts— the people they wanted kept apprised of their activities—and participants were far more likely than dropouts to have close friends who were also going to Mississippi. High-risk activism, McAdam concluded, is a "strong-tie" phenomenon.

This pattern shows up again and again. One study of the Red Brigades, the Italian terrorist group of the nineteen-seventies, found that seventy per cent of recruits had at least one good friend already in the organization. The same is true of the men who joined the mujahideen in Afghanistan. Even revolutionary actions that look spontaneous, like the demonstrations in East Germany that led to the fall of the Berlin Wall, are, at core, strong-tie phenomena. The opposition movement in East Germany consisted of several hundred groups, each with roughly a dozen members. Each group was in limited contact with the others: at the time, only thirteen per cent of East Germans even had a phone. All they knew was that on Monday nights, outside St. Nicholas Church in downtown Leipzig, people gathered to voice their anger at the state. And the primary determinant of who showed up was "critical friends"—the more friends you had who were critical of the regime the more likely you were to join the protest.

So one crucial fact about the four freshman at the Greensboro lunch counter—David Richmond, Franklin McCain, Ezell Blair, and Joseph McNeil—was their relationship with one another. McNeil was a roommate of Blair's in A. & T.'s Scott Hall dormitory. Richmond roomed with McCain one floor up, and Blair, Richmond, and McCain had all gone to Dudley High School. The four would smuggle beer into the dorm and talk late into the night in Blair and McNeil's room. They would all have remembered the murder of Emmett Till in 1955, the Montgomery bus boycott that same year, and the showdown in Little Rock in 1957. It was McNeil who brought up the idea of a sit-in at Woolworth's. They'd discussed it for nearly a month. Then McNeil came into the dorm room and asked the others if they were ready. There was a pause, and McCain said, in a way that works only with people who talk late into the night with one another, "Are you guys chicken or not?" Ezell Blair worked up the courage the next day to ask for a cup of coffee because he was flanked by his roommate and two good friends from high school.

The kind of activism associated with social media isn't like this at all. The platforms of social media are built around weak ties. Twitter is a way of following (or being followed by) people you may never have met. Facebook is a tool for efficiently managing your acquaintances, for keeping up with the people you would not otherwise be able to stay in touch with. That's why 15 you can have a thousand "friends" on Facebook, as you never could in real life.

This is in many ways a wonderful thing. There is strength in weak ties, as the sociologist Mark Granovetter has observed. Our acquaintances—not our friends—are our greatest source of new ideas and information. The Internet lets us exploit the power of these kinds of distant connections with marvelous efficiency. It's terrific at the diffusion of innovation, interdisciplinary collaboration, seamlessly matching up buyers and sellers, and the logistical functions of the dating world. But weak ties seldom lead to high-risk activism.

In a new book called *The Dragonfly Effect: Quick, Effective, and Powerful Ways to Use Social Media to Drive Social Change,* the business consultant Andy Smith and the Stanford Business School professor Jennifer Aaker tell the story of Sameer Bhatia, a young Silicon Valley entrepreneur who came down with acute myelogenous leukemia. It's a perfect illustration of social media's strengths. Bhatia needed a bone-marrow transplant, but he could not find a match among his relatives and friends. The odds were best with a donor of his ethnicity, and there were few South Asians in the national bone-marrow database. So Bhatia's business partner sent out an e-mail explaining Bhatia's plight to more than four hundred of their acquaintances, who forwarded the e-mail to their personal contacts; Facebook pages and YouTube videos were devoted to the Help Sameer campaign. Eventually, nearly twenty-five thousand new people were registered in the bone-marrow database, and Bhatia found a match.

But how did the campaign get so many people to sign up? By not asking too much of them. That's the only way you can get someone you don't really know to do something on your behalf. You can get thousands of people to sign up for a donor registry, because doing so is pretty easy. You have to send in a cheek swab and—in the highly unlikely event that your bone marrow is a good match for someone in need—spend a few hours at the hospital. Donating bone marrow isn't a trivial matter. But it doesn't involve financial or personal risk; it doesn't mean spending a summer being chased by armed men in pickup trucks. It doesn't require that you confront socially entrenched norms and practices. In fact, it's the kind of commitment that will bring only social acknowledgment and praise.

The evangelists of social media don't understand this distinction; they seem to believe that a Facebook friend is the same as a real friend and that signing up for a donor registry in Silicon Valley today is activism in the same sense as sitting at a segregated lunch counter in Greensboro in 1960. "Social networks are particularly effective at increasing motivation," Aaker and Smith write. But that's not true. Social networks are effective at increasing *participation*—by lessening the level of motivation that participation requires. The Facebook page of the Save Darfur Coalition has 1,282,339 members, who have donated an average of nine cents apiece. The next biggest Darfur charity on Facebook has 22,073 members, who have donated an average of thirty-five cents. Help Save Darfur has 2,797 members, who have given, on average, fifteen cents. A spokesperson for the Save Darfur Coalition told *Newsweek*, "We wouldn't necessarily gauge someone's value to the advocacy movement based on what they've given. This is a powerful mechanism to engage this critical population. They inform their community, attend events, volunteer. It's not something you can measure by looking at a ledger." In other words, Facebook activism succeeds not by motivating people to make a real sacrifice but by motivating them to do the things that people do when they are not motivated enough to make a real sacrifice. We are a long way from the lunch counters of Greensboro.

The students who joined the sit-ins across the South during the 20 winter of 1960 described the movement as a "fever." But the civil-rights movement was more like a military campaign than like a contagion. In the late nineteen-fifties, there had been sixteen sit-ins in various cities throughout the South, fifteen of which were formally organized by civil-rights organizations like the N.A.A.C.P. and CORE. Possible locations for activism were scouted. Plans were drawn up. Movement activists held training sessions and retreats for would-be protesters. The Greensboro Four were a product of this groundwork: all were members of the N.A.A.C.P. Youth Council. They had close ties with the head of the local N.A.A.C.P. chapter. They had been briefed on the earlier wave of sit-ins in Durham, and had been part of a series of movement meetings in activist churches. When the sit-in movement spread from Greensboro throughout the South, it did not spread indiscriminately. It spread to those cities which had preexisting "movement centers"—a core of dedicated and trained activists ready to turn the "fever" into action.

The civil-rights movement was high-risk activism. It was also, crucially, strategic activism: a challenge to the establishment mounted with precision and discipline. The N.A.A.C.P. was a centralized organization, run from New York according to highly formalized operating procedures. At the Southern Christian Leadership Conference, Martin Luther King, Jr., was the unquestioned authority. At the center of the movement was the black church, which had, as Aldon D. Morris points out in his superb 1984 study, *The Origins of the Civil Rights Movement*, a carefully demarcated division of labor, with various standing committees and disciplined groups. "Each group was task-oriented and coordinated its activities through authority structures," Morris writes. "Individuals were held accountable for their assigned duties, and important conflicts were resolved by the minister, who usually exercised ultimate authority over the congregation."

This is the second crucial distinction between traditional activism and its online variant: social media are not about this kind of hierarchical organization. Facebook and the like are tools for building *networks*, which are the opposite, in structure and character, of hierarchies. Unlike hierarchies, with their rules and procedures, networks aren't controlled by a single central authority. Decisions are made through consensus, and the ties that bind people to the group are loose.

This structure makes networks enormously resilient and adaptable in low-risk situations. Wikipedia is a perfect example. It doesn't have an editor, sitting in New York, who directs and corrects each entry. The effort of putting together each entry is self-organized. If every entry in Wikipedia were to be erased tomorrow, the content would swiftly be restored, because that's what happens when a network of thousands spontaneously devote their time to a task.

There are many things, though, that networks don't do well. Car companies sensibly use a network to organize their hundreds of suppliers, but not to design their cars. No one believes that the articulation of a coherent design philosophy is best handled by a sprawling, leaderless organizational system. Because networks don't have a centralized leadership structure and clear lines of authority, they have real difficulty reaching consensus and setting goals. They can't think strategically; they are chronically prone to conflict and error. How do you make difficult choices about tactics or strategy or philosophical direction when everyone has an equal say?

The Palestine Liberation Organization originated as a net- 25 work, and the international-relations scholars Mette Eilstrup-Sangiovanni and Calvert Jones argue in a recent essay in *International Security* that this is why it ran into such trouble as it grew: "Structural features typical of networks—the absence of central authority, the unchecked autonomy of rival groups, and the inability to arbitrate quarrels through formal mechanisms—made the P.L.O. excessively vulnerable to outside manipulation and internal strife."

In Germany in the nineteen-seventies, they go on, "the far more unified and successful left-wing terrorists tended to organize hierarchically, with professional management and clear divisions of labor. They were concentrated geographically in universities, where they could establish central leadership, trust, and camaraderie through regular, face-to-face meetings." They seldom betrayed their comrades in arms during police interrogations. Their counterparts on the right were organized as decentralized networks, and had no such discipline. These groups were regularly infiltrated, and members, once arrested, easily gave up their comrades. Similarly, Al Qaeda was most dangerous when it was a unified hierarchy. Now that it has dissipated into a network, it has proved far less effective.

The drawbacks of networks scarcely matter if the network isn't interested in systemic change—if it just wants to frighten or humiliate or make a splash—or if it doesn't need to think strategically. But if you're taking on a powerful and organized establishment you have to be a hierarchy. The Montgomery bus boycott required the participation of tens of thousands of people who depended on public transit to get to and from work each day. It lasted a *year*. In order to persuade those people to stay true to the cause, the boycott's organizers tasked each local black church with maintaining morale, and put together a free alternative private carpool service, with forty-eight dispatchers and forty-two pickup stations. Even the White Citizens Council, King later said, conceded that the carpool system moved with "military precision." By the time King came to Birmingham, for the climactic showdown with Police Commissioner Eugene (Bull) Connor, he had a budget of a million dollars, and a hundred full-time staff members on the ground, divided into operational units. The operation itself was divided into steadily escalating phases, mapped out in advance. Support was maintained through consecutive mass meetings rotating from church to church around the city.

Boycotts and sit-ins and nonviolent confrontations—which were the weapons of choice for the civil-rights movement—are high-risk strategies. They leave little room for conflict and error. The moment even one protester deviates from the script and responds to provocation, the moral legitimacy of the entire protest is compromised. Enthusiasts for social media would no doubt have us believe that King's task in Birmingham would have been made infinitely easier had he been able to communicate with his followers through Facebook, and contented himself with tweets from a Birmingham jail. But networks are messy: think of the ceaseless pattern of correction and revision, amendment and debate, that characterizes Wikipedia. If Martin Luther King Jr. had tried to do a wiki-boycott in Montgomery, he would have been steamrollered by the white power structure. And of what use would a digital communication tool be in a town where ninety-eight per cent of the black community could be reached every Sunday morning at church? The things that King needed in Birmingham—discipline and strategy—were things that online social media cannot provide.

The bible of the social-media movement is Clay Shirky's *Here Comes Everybody*. Shirky, who teaches at New York University, sets out to demonstrate the organizing power of the Internet, and he begins with the story of Evan, who worked on Wall Street, and his friend Ivanna, after she left her smart phone, an expensive Sidekick, on the back seat of a New York City taxicab. The telephone company transferred the data on Ivanna's lost phone to a new phone, whereupon she and Evan discovered that the Sidekick was now in the hands of a teenager from Queens, who was using it to take photographs of herself and her friends.

When Evan e-mailed the teenager, Sasha, asking for the 30 phone back, she replied that his "white ass" didn't deserve to have it back. Miffed, he set up a Web page with her picture and a description of what had happened. He forwarded the link to his friends, and they forwarded it to their friends. Someone found the MySpace page of Sasha's boyfriend, and a link to it found its way onto the site. Someone found her address online and took a video of her home while driving by; Evan posted the video on the site. The story was picked up by the news filter Digg. Evan was now up to ten e-mails a minute. He created a bulletin board for his readers to share their stories, but it crashed under the weight of responses. Evan and Ivanna went to the police, but the police filed the report under "lost," rather than "stolen," which essentially closed the case. "By this point millions of readers were watching," Shirky writes, "and dozens of mainstream news outlets had covered the story." Bowing to the pressure, the N.Y.P.D. reclassified the item as "stolen." Sasha was arrested, and Evan got his friend's Sidekick back.

Shirky's argument is that this is the kind of thing that could never have happened in the pre-Internet age—and he's right. Evan could never have tracked down Sasha. The story of the Sidekick would never have been publicized. An army of people could never have been assembled to wage this fight. The police wouldn't have bowed to the pressure of a lone person who had misplaced something as trivial as a cell phone. The story, to Shirky, illustrates "the ease and speed with which a group can be mobilized for the right kind of cause" in the Internet age.

Shirky considers this model of activism an upgrade. But it is simply a form of organizing which favors the weak-tie connections that give us access to information over the strong-tie connections that help us persevere in the face of danger. It shifts our energies from organizations that promote strategic and disciplined activity and toward those which promote resilience and adaptability. It makes it easier for activists to express themselves, and harder for that expression to have any impact. The instruments of social media are well suited to making the existing social order more efficient. They are not a natural enemy of the status quo. If you are of the opinion that all the world needs is a little buffing around the edges, this should not trouble you. But if you think that there are still lunch counters out there that need integrating it ought to give you pause.

Shirky ends the story of the lost Sidekick by asking, portentously, "What happens next?"—no doubt imagining future waves of digital protesters. But he has already answered the question. What happens next is more of the same. A networked, weak-tie world is good at things like helping Wall Streeters get phones back from teenage girls. *Viva la revolución.*

Joining the Conversation

1. What claims about the power of social media to create large-scale social change is Malcolm Gladwell responding to? What does he say, and where in his text does he bring up the views he disagrees with?

2. What is Gladwell's view of the relationship between social media and social change? What are the main arguments he presents to support his position? How does his discussion of the Woolworth's lunch counter sit-in of 1960, which he threads through his article, fit into his argument?

3. How does Gladwell define activism? How does he distinguish between "strong tie" and "weak tie" social activism? Explain this distinction and its relevance to Gladwell's argument.

4. Read Dennis Baron's blog post on **theysayiblog.com**. How do his views compare with Gladwell's—how are they similar, and how do they differ?

5. Write an essay responding to Gladwell, drawing on your own experience using social media and framing your argument as a response to something specific that Gladwell says. (See Chapter 2 for templates for responding in this way.)

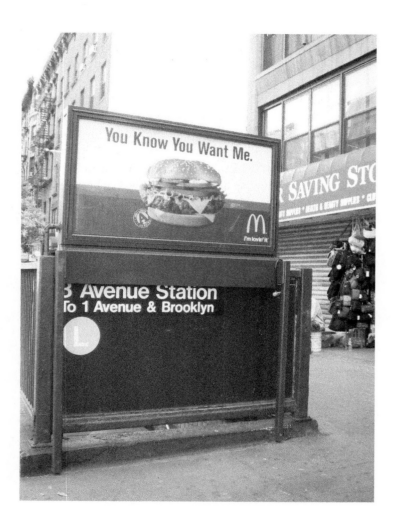

EIGHTEEN

WHAT SHOULD WE EAT?

WHAT SHOULD WE EAT? The answer may seem obvious: food, what else? But today we have more choices than ever before about what we eat. An increasing number of ethnic foods, regional dishes, and unfamiliar ingredients appear on menus in fast-food places and so-called fancy restaurants alike. TV cooking shows have never been so numerous—or so widely watched. Supermarkets have entire aisles of specialty, organic, and gluten-free foods. Recipes of all types are only a few clicks away online, typically accompanied by mouth-watering photographs.

And yet, as our food choices grow in number, we, too, are expanding. Obesity, often beginning in early childhood, has become a national concern and, with it, diabetes, high blood pressure, and hypertension. Medical costs for these illnesses are skyrocketing.

With tantalizing foods readily available, we need to learn how to make wise choices—but that can be easier said than done. Some civic leaders and public-health experts believe the government should step in to ensure that healthy foods are available for everyone, to educate us about our options, and to tax or even to outlaw the most unhealthy items, as former mayor Michael Bloomberg tried (but failed) to do in his bid to ban extra-large soft drinks in New York City. Meanwhile, civil libertarians, food and beverage producers, and those who enjoy the unhealthy items strongly oppose such governmental efforts. So, what should we eat? The readings in this chapter answer this question from various perspectives.

The chapter opens with an essay by food activist Michael Pollan outlining his rationale for ending our reliance on processed foods and moving to a diet of local, organic foods, especially vegetables. Steven Shapin, a professor of the history of science, argues that the health benefits of organic food are in many cases dubious. Mary Maxfield challenges the assumption that overeating is a social problem that needs to be fixed and suggests that Michael Pollan and other critics exaggerate its dangers. Fiction writer Jonathan Safran Foer explores his own family history to explain why he and his wife became vegetarian and are raising their children not to eat meat.

On the issue of government intervention versus personal responsibility, David Zinczenko blames the fast-food industry for the growing rate of obesity in the United States and argues that this industry should be regulated by the government. In contrast, libertarian commentator Radley Balko argues that what we eat should remain a matter of personal responsibility and that staying trim is a matter of individual willpower.

Next come two arguments about the effects of research and marketing on what we eat. Michael Moss provides a fascinating look at ways in which fast-food companies make their products difficult to resist. Similarly, professor Marion Nestle reveals how supermarkets design stores in order to maximize profits, to the detriment of customers' health and budget concerns. The chapter concludes with an essay by David H. Freedman arguing that Pollan and those who share his views should not consider fast food the enemy; rather, he suggests, fast-food companies may be the best vehicle for making millions of Americans healthier.

So read on for a wide range of opinions on food and eating today. You'll likely find plenty to agree with, and just as much to disagree with. But whatever you think, this conversation matters. The arguments in this chapter will challenge you to think about what you believe and why.

And you'll find even more readings on **theysayiblog.com**, along with a space where you respond with what you think—and literally add your own voice to the conversation.

Escape from the Western Diet

MICHAEL POLLAN

—▢—

THE UNDERTOW OF NUTRITIONISM is powerful. . . . Much nutrition science qualifies as reductionist science, focusing as it does on individual nutrients (such as certain fats or carbohydrates or antioxidants) rather than on whole foods or dietary patterns. . . . But using this sort of science to try to figure out what's wrong with the Western diet is probably unavoidable. However imperfect, it's the sharpest experimental and explanatory tool we have. It also satisfies our hunger for a simple, one-nutrient explanation. Yet it's one thing to entertain such explanations and quite another to mistake them for the whole truth or to let any one of them dictate the way you eat.

[And] many of the scientific theories put forward to account for exactly what in the Western diet is responsible for Western diseases conflict with one another. The lipid hypothesis cannot

———

MICHAEL POLLAN has written many books on food and eating, including *The Omnivore's Dilemma: A Natural History of Four Meals* (2006), *Food Rules: An Eater's Manual* (2010), *Cooked: A Natural History of Transformation* (2013), and *In Defense of Food: An Eater's Manifesto* (2008), from which this essay was excerpted. He was named one of *Time* magazine's top 100 Most Influential People in 2010 and teaches at the University of California at Berkeley.

be reconciled with the carbohydrate hypothesis, and the theory that a deficiency of omega-3 fatty acids (call it the neolipid hypothesis) is chiefly to blame for chronic illness is at odds with the theory that refined carbohydrates are the key. And while everyone can agree that the flood of refined carbohydrates has pushed important micronutrients out of the modern diet, the scientists who blame our health problems on deficiencies of these micronutrients are not the same scientists who see a sugar-soaked diet leading to metabolic syndrome and from there to diabetes, heart disease, and cancer. It is only natural for scientists no less than the rest of us to gravitate toward a single, all-encompassing explanation. That is probably why you now find some of the most fervent critics of the lipid hypothesis embracing the carbohydrate hypothesis with the same absolutist zeal that they once condemned in the Fat Boys. In the course of my own research into these theories, I have been specifically warned by scientists allied with the carbohydrate camp not to "fall under the spell of the omega-3 cult." *Cult?* There is a lot more religion in science than you might expect.

So here we find ourselves . . . lost at sea amid the cross-currents of conflicting science.

Or do we?

See pp. 84–86 for tips on introducing objections informally.

Because it turns out we don't need to declare our allegiance 5 to any one of these schools of thought in order to figure out how best to eat. In the end, they are only theories, scientific explanations for an empirical phenomenon that is not itself in doubt: People eating a Western diet are prone to a complex of chronic diseases that seldom strike people eating more traditional diets. Scientists can argue all they want about the biological mechanisms behind this phenomenon, but whichever it is, the solution to the problem would appear to remain very much the same: *Stop eating a Western diet.*

In truth the chief value of any and all theories of nutrition, apart from satisfying our curiosity about how things work, is not to the eater so much as it is to the food industry and the medical community. The food industry needs theories so it can better redesign specific processed foods; a new theory means a new line of products, allowing the industry to go on tweaking the Western diet instead of making any more radical change to its business model. For the industry it's obviously preferable to have a scientific rationale for *further* processing foods—whether by lowering the fat or carbs or by boosting omega-3s or fortifying them with antioxidants and probiotics—than to entertain seriously the proposition that processed foods of any kind are a big part of the problem.

For the medical community too scientific theories about diet nourish business as usual. New theories beget new drugs to treat diabetes, high blood pressure, and cholesterol; new treatments and procedures to ameliorate chronic diseases; and new diets organized around each new theory's elevation of one class of nutrient and demotion of another. Much lip service is paid to the importance of prevention, but the health care industry, being an industry, stands to profit more handsomely from new drugs and procedures to treat chronic diseases than it does from a wholesale change in the way people eat. Cynical? Perhaps. You could argue that the medical community's willingness to treat the broad contours of the Western diet as a given is a reflection of its realism rather than its greed. "People don't want to go there," as Walter Willett responded to the critic who asked him why the Nurses' Health Study didn't study the benefits of more alternative diets. Still, medicalizing the whole problem of the Western diet instead of working to overturn it (whether at the level of the patient or politics) is exactly what you'd expect from a health care community that is sympathetic to nutritionism as a matter of temperament, philosophy, and economics. You would not expect such a medical community to be sensitive to the cultural or ecological dimensions of the food problem—and it isn't. We'll know this has changed when doctors kick the fast-food franchises out of the hospitals.

So what would a more ecological or cultural approach to the food problem counsel us? How might we plot our escape from nutritionism and, in turn, from the most harmful effects of the Western diet? To Denis Burkitt, the English doctor stationed in Africa during World War II who gave the Western diseases their name, the answer seemed straightforward, if daunting. "The only way we're going reduce disease," he said, "is to go backwards to the diet and lifestyle of our ancestors." This sounds uncomfortably like the approach of the diabetic Aborigines who went back to the bush to heal themselves. But I don't think this is what Burkitt had in mind; even if it was, it is not a very attractive or practical strategy for most of us. No, the challenge we face today is figuring out how to escape the worst elements of the Western diet and lifestyle *without* going back to the bush.

In theory, nothing could be simpler: To escape the Western diet and the ideology of nutritionism, we have only to stop eating and thinking that way. But this is harder to do in practice, given the treacherous food environment we now inhabit and the loss of cultural tools to guide us through it. Take the question of whole versus processed foods, presumably one of the simpler distinctions between modern industrial foods and older kinds. Gyorgy Scrinis, who coined the term "nutritionism," suggests that the most important fact about any food is not its nutrient content but its degree of processing. He writes that "whole foods and industrial foods are the only two food groups I'd consider including in any useful food 'pyramid.'" In other words, instead of worrying about nutrients, we should simply avoid any food that has been processed to such an extent that it is more the product of industry than of nature.

This sounds like a sensible rule of thumb until you real- 10 ize that industrial processes have by now invaded many whole foods too. Is a steak from a feedlot steer that consumed a diet of corn, various industrial waste products, antibiotics, and hormones still a "whole food"? I'm not so sure. The steer has itself been raised on a Western diet, and that diet has rendered its meat substantially different—in the type and amount of fat in it as well as its vitamin content—from the beef our ancestors ate. The steer's industrial upbringing has also rendered its meat so cheap that we're likely to eat more of it more often than our ancestors ever would have. This suggests yet another sense in which this beef has become an industrial food: It is designed to be eaten industrially too—as fast food.

So plotting our way out of the Western diet is not going to be simple. Yet I am convinced that it can be done, and in the course of my research, I have collected and developed some straightforward (and distinctly unscientific) rules of thumb, or personal eating policies, that might at least point us in the right direction. They don't say much about specific foods—about what sort of oil to cook with or whether you should eat meat. They don't have much to say about nutrients or calories, either, though eating according to these rules will perforce change the balance of nutrients and amount of calories in your diet. I'm not interested in dictating anyone's menu, but rather in developing what I think of as eating algorithms—mental programs that, if you run them when you're shopping for food or deciding on a meal, will produce a great many different dinners, all of them "healthy" in the broadest sense of that word.

And our sense of that word stands in need of some broadening. When most of us think about food and health, we think in fairly narrow nutritionist terms—about our personal physical health and how the ingestion of this particular nutrient or rejection of that affects it. But I no longer think it's possible to separate our bodily health from the health of the environment from which we eat or the environment in which we eat or, for that matter, from the health of our general outlook about food (and health). If my explorations of the food chain have taught me anything, it's that it is a food chain, and all the links in it are in fact linked: the health of the soil to the health of the plants and animals we eat to the health of the food culture in which we eat them to the health of the eater, in body as well as mind. [So you will find rules here] concerning not only what to eat but also how to eat it as well as how that food is produced. Food consists not just in piles of chemicals; it also comprises a set of social and ecological relationships, reaching back to the land and outward to other people. Some of these rules may strike you as having nothing whatever to do with health; in fact they do.

Many of the policies will also strike you as involving more work—and in fact they do. If there is one important sense in which we do need to heed Burkitt's call to "go backwards" or follow the Aborigines back into the bush, it is this one: In order to eat well we need to invest more time, effort, and resources in providing for our sustenance, to dust off a word, than most of us do today. A hallmark of the Western diet is food that is fast, cheap, and easy. Americans spend less than 10 percent of their income on food; they also spend less than a half hour a day preparing meals and little more than an hour enjoying them.[1] For most people for most of history, gathering and preparing food has been an occupation at the very heart of daily life. Traditionally people have allocated a far greater proportion of their income to food—as they still do in several of the countries where people eat better than we do and as a consequence are healthier than we are.[2] Here, then, is one way in which we would do well to go a little native: backward, or perhaps it is forward, to a time and place where the gathering and preparing and enjoying of food were closer to the center of a well-lived life.

[I'd like to propose] three rules—*"Eat food. Not too much. Mostly plants."*—that I now need to unpack, providing some elaboration and refinement in the form of more specific guidelines, injunctions, subclauses, and the like. Each of these three main rules can serve as category headings for a set of personal policies to guide us in our eating choices without too much trouble or thought. The idea behind having a simple policy like "avoid foods that make health claims" is to make the process simpler and more pleasurable than trying to eat by the numbers and nutrients, as nutritionism encourages us to do.

So under "Eat Food," I propose some practical ways to 15 separate, and defend, real food from the cascade of foodlike products that now surround and confound us, especially in the supermarket. Many of the tips under this rubric concern shopping and take the form of filters that should help keep out the sort of products you want to avoid. Under "Mostly Plants," I'll dwell more specifically, and affirmatively, on the best types of foods (not nutrients) to eat. Lest you worry, there is, as the adverb suggests, more to this list than fruits and vegetables. Last, under "Not Too Much," the focus shifts from the foods themselves to the question of how to eat them—the manners, mores, and habits that go into creating a healthy, and pleasing, culture of eating.

NOTES

1. David M. Cutler, et al., "Why Have Americans Become More Obese?," *Journal of Economic Perspectives*, Vol. 17, No. 3 (Summer, 2003), pp. 93–118. In 1995 Americans spent twenty-seven minutes preparing meals and four minutes cleaning up after them; in 1965 the figure was forty-four minutes of preparation and twenty-one minutes of cleanup. Total time spent eating has dropped from sixty-nine minutes to sixty-five, all of which suggests a trend toward prepackaged meals.

2. Compared to the 9.9 percent of their income Americans spend on food, the Italians spend 14.9 percent, the French 14.9 percent, and the Spanish 17.1 percent.

Joining the Conversation

1. What does Michael Pollan mean when he refers to the "Western diet"? Why does he believe Americans need to "escape" from it?

2. Pollan begins with a "they say," citing a variety of scientific theories known as nutritionism. Summarize his response to these views. What is his objection to such views, and to the business and research interests that promote them?

3. If Pollan were to read Mary Maxfield's response to this article (pp. 442–47), how might he, in turn, respond to her?

4. It's likely that Pollan favors (and shops at) local farmers' markets. Go to **theysayiblog.com** and search for "Mark Bittman on Farmers' Markets." What does he say about them: who, according to Bittman, do they most benefit?

5. Write an essay that begins where Pollan's piece ends, perhaps by quoting from paragraph 14: "*Eat food. Not too much. Mostly plants.*" You'll need to explain his argument, and then respond with your own views.

What Are You Buying
When You Buy Organic?

STEVEN SHAPIN

———⌐◻⌐———

THE PLASTIC PACKAGE of Earthbound Farm baby arugula in
Whole Foods was grown without synthetic fertilizers; no toxic
pesticides or fumigants were used to control insect predators;
no herbicides were applied to deal with weeds; no genes from
other species were introduced into its genome to increase yield
or pest resistance; no irradiation was used to extend its shelf life.
It complies with the U.S. Department of Agriculture's National
Organic Program, a set of standards that came into full effect
in 2002 to regulate the commercial use of the word "organic."
So what's the problem?

———

STEVEN SHAPIN teaches at Harvard University and is the author of
several books on the history and sociology of science, including *The
Scientific Life: A Moral History of a Late Modern Vocation* (2008). He
also writes for the *London Review of Books* and the *New Yorker* and is
a fellow of the American Academy of Arts and Sciences. This essay
first appeared with the title "Paradise Sold" in the *New Yorker* on
May 15, 2006.

It all depends on what you think you're buying when you buy organic. If the word conjures up the image of a small, family-owned, local operation, you may be disappointed. Like Whole Foods, Earthbound Farm is a very big business. Earthbound's founders, Drew and Myra Goodman, Manhattanites who went to college in the Bay Area, and then started a two-and-a-half-acre raspberry-and-baby-greens farm near Carmel to produce food they "felt good about," are now the nation's largest grower of organic produce, with revenues for this year projected at more than $450 million. Their greens, including the arugula, are produced on giant farms in six different counties in California, two in Arizona, one in Colorado, and in three Mexican states. Earthbound grows more than seventy per cent of all the organic lettuce sold in America; big organic retailers like Whole Foods require big organic suppliers. (Earthbound actually dropped the "organic" specification when it started its mass-distribution program, in 1993—even though the stuff was organic—because its first client, Costco, thought it might put customers off.) By 2004, Earthbound was farming twenty-six thousand acres; its production plants in California and Arizona total four hundred thousand square feet, and its products are available in supermarkets in every state of the Union. The Carmel Valley farm stand is still there, largely for public-relations purposes, and is as much an icon of California's entrepreneurial roots as the Hewlett-Packard garage in downtown Palo Alto.

Success is not necessarily a sin, of course, and, for many people, buying organic is a way of being environmentally sensitive. Earthbound notes that its farming techniques annually obviate the use of more than a quarter of a million pounds of toxic chemical pesticides and almost 8.5 million pounds of synthetic fertilizers, which saves 1.4 million gallons

Peter Harrington grows organic vegetables on two acres at Ten Barn Farm in Ghent, New York, and sells them at farmers' markets.

of the petroleum needed to produce those chemicals. Their tractors even use biodiesel fuel.

Yet the net benefit of all this to the planet is hard to assess. Michael Pollan, who thinks that we ought to take both a wider and a deeper view of the social, economic, and physical chains that deliver food to fork, cites a Cornell scientist's estimate that growing, processing, and shipping one calorie's worth of arugula to the East Coast costs fifty-seven calories of fossil fuel. The growing of the arugula is indeed organic, but almost everything else is late-capitalist business as usual. Earthbound's compost is trucked in; the salad-green farms are models of West Coast monoculture, laser-levelled fields facilitating awesomely efficient mechanical harvesting; and the whole supply chain from California to Manhattan is only

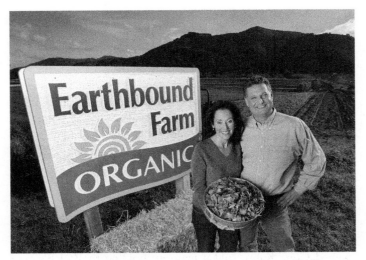

Myra and Drew Goodman began Earthbound Farm with two and half acres of raspberries and baby greens, and it's now the largest grower of organic produce in the nation.

four per cent less gluttonous a consumer of fossil fuel than that of a conventionally grown head of iceberg lettuce—though Earthbound plants trees to offset some of its carbon footprint. "Organic," then, isn't necessarily "local," and neither "organic" nor "local" is necessarily "sustainable."

Earthbound and other large-scale organic growers have 5 embraced not only the logic of capitalism but the specific logic of California agribusiness. As the geographer Julie Guthman shows in *Agrarian Dreams: The Paradox of Organic Farming in California*, ever since the gold rush, the state's growers have aimed at maximizing monetary yield per acre. First, it was wheat to feed the influx of gold miners and those dependent on the mining industry; then, after railways and refrigerated cars enabled the delivery of shining fresh produce across the country, it was orchard fruit. Later still, tract housing and mini-malls proved more profitable, which is why you'll have a hard time finding orange groves in Orange County. Guthman writes that big, concentrated, high-value organic agriculture in California is "the legacy of the state's own style of agrarian capitalism." You saw this style in action when, in 1989, a 60 *Minutes* exposé about residues of the carcinogenic pesticide Alar found on apples caused a consumer stampede to the organic-produce bins. "Don't panic, buy organic," was the mantra, and growers responded by borrowing heavily to expand their organic enterprises. When the scare subsided, supply outstripped demand, and, in the inevitable shakeout, some small-scale organic farmers had to sell out to larger players in the food industry. Washington State's Cascadian Farm was one such. Its founder, a "onetime hippie" named Gene Kahn, sold a majority holding to Welch's, and now it is a division of the $17.8 billion giant General Mills. He hasn't the least regret: "We're part of the food industry now." The investors bankrolling Big Organic have no reason to fear the vestigial hippie rhetoric: it's not so much a counterculture as a bean-counter culture.

According to the business writer Samuel Fromartz in *Organic, Inc.: Natural Foods and How They Grew*, 90 percent of "frequent" organic buyers think they're buying better "health and nutrition." They may be right. If, for any reason, you don't want the slightest pesticide residue in your salad, or you want to insure that there are no traces of recombinant bovine somatotropin hormone (rbST) in your children's milk, you're better off spending the extra money for organically produced food. But scientific evidence for the risks of such residues is iffy, as it is, too, for the benefits of the micro-nutrients that are said to be more plentiful in an organic carrot than in its conventional equivalent.

Other people are buying taste, but there's little you can say about other people's taste in carrots and not much more you can intelligibly articulate about your own. The taste of an heirloom carrot bought five years ago from the Chino family farm in Rancho Santa Fe, California, sticks indelibly in my memory, though at the time I hadn't any idea whether artificial fertilizers or pesticides had been applied to it. (I later learned that they had not.) For many fruits and vegetables, freshness, weed control, and the variety grown may be far more important to taste than whether the soil in which they were grown was dosed with ammonium nitrate. Pollan did his own taste test by shopping at Whole Foods for an all-organic meal: everything was pretty good, except for the six-dollar bunch of organic asparagus, which had been grown in Argentina, air-freighted six thousand miles to the States, and immured for a week in the distribution chain. Pollan shouldn't have been surprised that it tasted like "cardboard."

The twentieth-century origins of the organic movement can be traced to the writings of the English agronomist Sir Albert Howard, particularly his 1940 book *An Agricultural Testament*. Howard was a critic of the rise of scientific agriculture. In the mid-nineteenth century, following the work of the German chemist Justus von Liebig, it was thought that all plants really needed from the soil was the correct quantities and proportions of nitrogen, phosphorus, and potassium: the N-P-K ratios that you see on bags of garden fertilizer. For many crops, it is the availability of nitrogen that limits growth. Legumes apart, plants cannot extract nitrogen directly from the practically unlimited stores of the gas in the atmosphere, so farmers in the nineteenth century routinely enhanced soil fertility using animal manures, guano, or mined nitrates. But, just before the

First World War, the German chemist Fritz Haber and the industrialist Carl Bosch devised a way of synthesizing ammonia from atmospheric nitrogen. From there, the commercial production of enormous quantities of nitrogenous fertilizers was a relatively easy matter. The result was a technological revolution in agriculture.

But Howard had worked in India as "Imperial Economic Botanist" to the government of the Raj at Pusa, and his experiences there convinced him that traditional Indian farming techniques were in many respects superior to those of the modern West. Howard was a pragmatist—the criterion of agricultural success was what worked—but he was also a holist and a taker of the long view. The health of the soil, the health of what grew in it, and the health of those who ate what grew in it were "one great subject." To reduce this intricacy to a simple set of chemical inputs, as Liebig's followers did, was reductionist science at its worst. Soils treated this way would ultimately collapse, and so would the societies that abused them: "Artificial manures lead inevitably to artificial nutrition, artificial food, artificial animals and finally to artificial men and women," racked with disease and physically stunted. You could indeed get short-term boosts in yield through the generous application of synthetic fertilizers, but only by robbing future generations of their patrimony. Soil, Howard wrote, is "the capital of the nations which is real, permanent, and independent of everything except a market for the products of farming." We have no choice but to go "back to nature" and to "safeguard the land of the Empire from the operations of finance." The "supremacy of the West" depends upon it.

Howard's ideas reached America largely through J. I. Rodale's 10 magazine *Organic Gardening and Farming, and,* later, through a widely read essay by Wendell Berry in *The Last Whole Earth*

Catalogue. The organic movement that sprang up in America during the postwar years, manured by the enthusiasm of both the hippies and their New Age successors, supplemented Howard's ideas of soil health with the imperative that the scale should be small and the length of the food chain from farm to consumer short. You were supposed to know who it was that produced your food, and to participate in a network of trust in familiar people and transparent agricultural practices. A former nutritionist at Columbia, who went on to grow produce upstate, recalls, "When we said organic, we meant local. We meant healthful. We meant being true to the ecologies of regions. We meant mutually respectful growers and eaters. We meant social justice and equality."

There is no way to make food choices without making moral choices as well, and anthropologists have had much to say about the inevitable link between what's good to eat and what's good to think. Decisions about how we want our food produced and delivered are decisions about what counts as social virtue. One of the founding texts of modern social theory, Émile Durkheim's *The Division of Labor in Society*, drew a distinction between what he called mechanical and organic solidarity. In societies characterized by mechanical solidarity, each person knew pretty much what every other person did and each social unit encompassed pretty much all the functions it needed in order to survive. Mechanical solidarity, in Durkheim's scheme, was largely a premodern form. By contrast, organic solidarity flowed from the division of labor. Individuals depended upon one another for the performance of specialized tasks, and, as modernity proceeded, the networks of dependence that bound them together became increasingly anonymous. You didn't know who grew the food at the end of your fork, or, indeed, who made the fork. But, then, the original English sense of "organ" was an instrument or a machine made up of interdependent specialized parts, as in the musical pipe organ. The application to living things came only later, by way of analogy with machines; the eye, for example, is the "organ of seeing." And so, by semantic inversion, champions of organic farming actually seek virtue not in organic but in mechanical solidarity.

The quest for the shortest possible chain between producer and consumer is the narrative dynamic of Michael Pollan's book *The Omnivore's Dilemma: A Natural History of Four Meals*, which is cleverly structured around four meals, each representing a different network of relations between producers, eaters, and the environment, and each an attempt at greater virtue than the last. Pollan's first meal is fast food, and he follows a burger back to vast monocultural industrial blocs of Iowan corn, planted by G.P.S.-guided tractors and dosed with tons of synthetic fertilizer, whose massive runoff into the Mississippi River—as much as 1.5 million tons of nitrogen a year—winds up feeding algal blooms and depleting the oxygen needed by other forms of life in the Gulf of Mexico. Pollan then follows the corn to enormous feedlots in Kansas, where a heifer that he bought in South Dakota is speed-fattened—fourteen pounds of corn for each pound of edible beef—for which its naturally grass-processing rumen was not designed, requiring it to be dosed with antibiotics, which breed resistant strains of bacteria. Pollan would have liked to follow his heifer through the industrial slaughterhouse, but the giant beef-packing company was too canny to let him in, and so we are spared the stomach-churning details, which, in any case, were minutely related a few years ago in Eric Schlosser's *Fast Food Nation*. Pollan also follows the American mountains of industrial

See Chapter 2 for tips on summarizing what others say.

corn into factories, where the wonders of food technology transform it into the now ubiquitous high-fructose corn syrup, which sweetens the soda that, consumed in super-sized quantities across the nation, contributes to the current epidemic of type 2 diabetes. All very bad things.

The second meal is the Big Organic one that he bought at his local Whole Foods store in California, featuring an "organic" chicken whose "free-range" label was authorized by U.S.D.A. statutes, but which actually shared a shed with twenty thousand other genetically identical birds. Two small doors in the shed opened onto a patch of grass, but they remained shut until the birds were five or six weeks old, and two weeks later Pollan's "free range" chicken was a $2.99-a-pound package in his local Whole Foods. This meal was better—the corn-and-soybean chicken feed was certified organic and didn't contain antibiotics—but still not perfect. Pollan's third meal was even more virtuous. After spending several weeks doing heavy lifting on a polycultural, sustainable smallholding in the Shenandoah Valley, Pollan cooked a meal wholly made up of ingredients that he himself had a hand in producing: eggs from (genuinely) free-range, grub-eating hens, corn grown with compost from those happy birds, and, finally, a chicken whose throat he had slit himself. Very good, indeed—and no nitrogenous runoff, and no massive military machine to protect America's supplies of Middle East oil and the natural gas needed to make the synthetic fertilizer.

Finally, Pollan decides to eat a meal—"the perfect meal"—for which he had almost total personal responsibility: wild morels foraged in the Sierra foothills, the braised loin and leg of a wild pig he had shot himself in Sonoma County, a chamomile tisane made from herbs picked in the Berkeley Hills, salad greens from his own garden, cherries taken by right of usufruct from a neighbor's tree, sea salt scraped from a pond at the southern end of San Francisco Bay, and—O.K., strict perfection is unobtainable—a bottle of California Petite Sirah, presumably organic. This was not a way of eating that Pollan thinks is realistic on a routine basis, but he wanted to test what it felt like to have "a meal that is eaten in full consciousness of what it took to make it." That consciousness, for Pollan, is more religious than political—every meal a sacrament. "We eat by the grace of nature, not industry, and what we're eating is never anything more or less than the body of the world," he says.

Pollan winds up demanding that we know much more about what we're putting into our mouths: "What it is we're eating. Where it came from. How it found its way to our table. And what, in a true accounting, it really cost." The "naked lunch," William Burroughs wrote, is the "frozen moment when everyone sees what is on the end of every fork." Burroughs meant it metaphorically; Pollan means it literally. He wants to know his farmer's name, and to know that his hamburger was once part of the muscles of a particular cow. He wants to do his bit to save the planet. That means he wants to eat locally, within a network of familiarity. But, even so, the knowledge required is potentially infinite. What particular bacteria, fungi, and trace elements lurk in the soil of your sustainable community farm? Does your friendly local farmer use a tractor or a horse? If a tractor, does it use fuel made from biomass? If a horse, are the oats it eats organic? If the oats are organic, does the manure with which they were grown come from organically fed animals? How much of this sort of knowledge can you digest?

Pollan seems aware of the contradictions entailed in trying to eat in this rigorously ethical spirit, but he doesn't give much space to the most urgent moral problem with the organic ideal: how to feed the world's population. At the beginning of the twentieth century, there was a serious scare about an imminent Malthusian crisis: the world's rapidly expanding population was coming up against the limits of agricultural productivity. The Haber-Bosch process averted disaster, and was largely responsible for a fourfold increase in the world's food supply during the twentieth century. Earl Butz, Nixon's Secretary of Agriculture, was despised by organic farmers, but he might not have been wrong when he said, in 1971, that if America returned to organic methods "someone must decide which fifty million of our people will starve!" According to a more recent estimate, if synthetic fertilizers suddenly disappeared from the face of the earth, about two billion people would perish.

Supporters of organic methods maintain that total food-energy productivity per acre can be just as high as with conventional agriculture, and that dousings of N-P-K are made necessary only by the industrial scale of modern agriculture and its long-chain systems of distribution. Yet the fact remains that, to unwind conventional agriculture, you would have to unwind some highly valued features of the modern world order. Given the way the world now is, sustainably grown and locally produced organic food is expensive. Genetically modified, industrially produced monocultural corn is what feeds the victims of an African famine, not the gorgeous organic technicolor Swiss chard from your local farmers' market. Food for a "small planet" will, for the foreseeable future, require a much smaller human population on the planet.

Besides, for most consumers that Earthbound Farm organic baby arugula from Whole Foods isn't an opportunity to dismantle the infrastructures of the modern world; it's simply salad. Dressed with a little Tuscan extra-virgin olive oil, a splash of sherry vinegar, some shavings of Parmigiano Reggiano, and fleur de sel from the Camargue, it makes a very nice appetizer. To insist that we are consuming not just salad but a vision of society isn't wrong, but it's biting off more than most people are able and willing to chew. Cascadian Farm's Gene Kahn, countering the criticism that by growing big he had sold out, volunteered his opinion on the place that food has in the average person's life: "This is just lunch for most people. Just lunch. We can call it sacred, we can talk about communion, but it's just lunch."

Joining the Conversation

1. Steven Shapin focuses on Earthbound Farm and other such companies to illustrate some of the practices of organic food companies and their effects on society. What does he say about the overall impact these companies and others like them have on the environment?
2. Shapin lists the four meals Michael Pollan discusses in his book *The Omnivore's Dilemma,* ranging from factory-farm-raised fast food to a "perfect meal" for which he had "almost total personal responsibility," and notes that Pollan "wants to eat locally" and "to do his bit to save the planet." How does Shapin respond to what Pollan says?
3. Shapin claims that Earthbound Farms is not a small operation but rather "a very big business" that is no more sustainable than any other food company. With this in mind, visit **theysayiblog.com** and read Elizabeth Weiss's article "What Does 'The Scarecrow' Tell Us about Chipotle?" Do you think Shapin would characterize Chipotle in the same way?

Why or why not? Cite examples from Weiss's article to support your response.

4. Shapin concludes by suggesting that, while a small number of people may believe that eating organic arugula is a matter of great importance, for most people, "it's simply salad." What do you think he means by this statement? How might Michael Pollan (pp. 420–27) respond to this assertion?

5. Visit a grocery store, look closely at the organic foods there, and then examine the nonorganic versions of the same products. Write an essay comparing organic and nonorganic items in terms of price, calories, ingredients, packaging, location in the store, and other factors that you find significant. You might frame your essay as a response to Shapin, using something he says as a "they say."

Food as Thought:
Resisting the Moralization of Eating

MARY MAXFIELD

—▢—

How do French people eat so unhealthily—famously
indulging in cheese, cream, and wine—but stay, on average,
healthier than Americans? Journalist Michael Pollan offers
readers a simple solution: quit obsessing over this French
paradox and start obsessing over the french fry. Pointing
to what he considers the American paradox—"a notably
unhealthy population preoccupied with . . . the idea of eating
healthy" (9)—Pollan contends that our definition of healthy
eating is driven by a well-funded corporate machine. According
to Pollan, the food industry, along with nutrition science and
journalism, is capitalizing on our confusion over how to eat.

———

Mary Maxfield is a graduate student in American Studies at
Bowling Green State University. She graduated from Fontbonne
University in 2010 with a degree in creative social change and minors
in sociology, American culture studies, and women's and gender
studies. Her academic interests include bodies, gender, sexuality,
politics, and rhetoric. Read her blog at missmarymax.wordpress.com,
or follow her on Twitter @missmarymax.

While Pollan implicates his own profession in this critique, he simultaneously contributes to our cultural anxiety over food. The same critic who argues that "any and all theories of nutrition [serve] not the eater [but] the food industry," nevertheless proposes his own theory: the elimination of processed foods (141). Likewise, even after noting that the connections between diet and health that we take as gospel apparently *aren't*, Pollan nevertheless adheres to contemporary common-sense science, making assumptions about diet, health, and weight that underpin the very food industry he critiques.

Thus as he attempts to dismantle one paradox, Pollan embodies another: he's a critic of nutrition and food science who nevertheless bolsters the American investment in those industries. After publishing *In Defense of Food* (and its equally successful predecessor, *The Omnivore's Dilemma*), Pollan released *Food Rules*, a pocket-sized manual for better eating. Of course, Pollan contends that *his* guidelines function differently than the prescriptions (and proscriptions) of food scientists, because his rules See pp. 33–36 for tips on how to summarize and know where you're going. function as "eating algorithms" that "produce many different dinners" (144) rather than specifying a concrete menu. Yet no matter how many meals fit Pollan's formula—"Eat food, not too much, mostly plants" (1)—it remains a dictate provided by an expert to those who apparently can't properly nourish themselves.

Pollan and other like-minded nutrition hawks consistently back up their claims with concerns over American health. Although acknowledging that eating primarily for health represents a departure from the historical purpose of food—fuel for our bodies—these gastronomical philosophers nevertheless position themselves as protectors of health. Americans need this protection, we are told, because we're a nation stricken by heart disease, diabetes, and cancer. According to this line of thought, each of these maladies is tied to our diet and essentially to our weight. As a culture, we no longer discuss healthy eating without also discussing unhealthy weights. Linking nutrition and body type, voices like Pollan's warn us against eating too much—often without any parallel warnings against eating too little. Pollan himself insists that overeating constitutes "the greatest threat" to our survival (7), and our government concurs, pouring resources into a fight against the obesity epidemic, that plague of fatness that supposedly threatens our national health.

The problem is that our understanding of health is as based in culture as it is in fact. Despite some doubt in academic circles over connections between diet, health, and weight, common-sense reportage continues to presume that they are directly connected. Pollan, for example, twice notes that our diet of processed foods makes us "sick and fat" (10), and then—without evidence to support that claim—conflates health with weight and condemns fatness out of hand. Later, he refers to obesity as a Western disease (11)—again presuming a correlation between weight and health—and even cites statistics on eating habits from a study entitled "Why Have Americans Become More Obese?" (145).

A growing group of academics who have examined the research on obesity at length have discovered fundamental flaws behind perceptions of fatness, diet, and health. Law professor and journalist Paul Campos notes that "lies about fat, fitness, and health . . . not coincidentally serve the interests of America's $50-billion-per-year diet industry," and fat-acceptance activist Kate Harding elaborates on this point, observing that "if you scratch an article on the obesity crisis, you will almost always find a press release from a company that's developing a weight loss drug—or from a 'research group' . . . funded by such companies." Harding and Campos both belong to a school that has repeatedly challenged the validity of the body mass index (BMI), a tool that uses height and weight measurements to calculate body fat. Originally developed by a mathematician as a purely statistical tool, the BMI has become medicine's go-to means for predicting heart disease and other maladies, despite research that suggests a low BMI presents a greater mortality risk than a high one and that, in general, BMI cannot accurately predict one's health (Campos).

Culturally, however, we resist these scientific findings in favor of a perspective that considers fatness fatal and thinness immortal. Our skewed views of fatness then facilitate skewed views of food. We continue to believe in a "right" or "healthy" way of eating that involves eating less and eating differently than we instinctively would, despite evidence to the contrary provided both by scholars like Harding and Campos, and by Health at Every Size (HAES) nutritionists like Michelle Allison. HAES advocates challenge our cultural misconceptions, suggesting that—outside of specific medical conditions like celiac disease and anorexia—"what a person eats [rarely] takes primacy over how they eat it" (Allison, "Eating"). In essence, we can eat as we always have—which includes eating for emotional and social reasons—and still survive or even thrive.

Few of us, however, manage to think about eating this way. As Allison notes, "there are a lot of pressures and barriers in this world that get in our way, that confuse us, that distract us and attempt to control us in counterproductive ways" ("Rules vs. Trust"). In this context, "health" functions moralistically. It results from making decisions like choosing fresh mozzarella over spray cheese, the "right" foods over the "wrong" ones. Experts offer science to substantiate those designations, yet science—as Campos, Harding, and Allison show—does not actually support these systems. Instead, as even Pollan notes, there remains "a lot [of] religion in science" (140).

That "religion" presents itself in the moralizing of food, the attempt—in how we eat—to rise above our beastly natures. As a culture, when we imagine eating like animals, we visualize a feeding frenzy. Allison observes that when she says "Adult human beings are allowed to eat whatever and however much they want," what people actually hear is: "Go out and cram your face with Twinkies!" ("Eat Food"). (Indeed, for Pollan, the total elimination of American anxiety about food translates to a laissez-faire policy of "let them eat Twinkies" [9].) Yet Allison and other HAES nutritionists suggest that adult humans will eat in a way that is good for them, given the opportunity ("Eat Food"). When we attempt to rise above our animal nature through the moralization of food, we unnecessarily complicate the practice of eating. Food—be it french fry or granola bar, Twinkie or brown rice—isn't moral or immoral. Inherently, food is ethically neutral; notions of good and bad, healthy and unhealthy are projected onto it by culture. Staying mindful of that culture (and critical of the hidden interests that help guide it) can free us each to follow a formula we have long known but recently forgotten: Trust yourself. Trust your body. Meet your needs.

WORKS CITED

Allison, Michelle. "Eat Food. Stuff You Like. As Much As You Want." *The Fat Nutritionist*, 15 Feb. 2010, www.fatnutritionist.com/index.php/eat-food-stuff-you-like-as-much-as-you-want. Accessed 19 Jan. 2011.

———. "Eating—the WHAT or the HOW?" *The Fat Nutritionist*, 17 Aug. 2009, www.fatnutritionist.com/index.php/eating-the-what-or-the-how. Accessed 19 Jan. 2011.

_____. "Rules vs. Trust in Eating." *The Fat Nutritionist*, 15 Dec. 2009,
www.fatnutritionist.com/index.php/rules-vs-trust-in-eating. Accessed
19 Jan. 2011.

Campos, Paul. "Being Fat Is OK." *Jewish World Review*, 23 Apr. 2001,
www.jewishworldreview.com/0501/campos042301.asp. Accessed
25 Mar. 2011.

Harding, Kate. "Don't You Realize Fat Is Unhealthy?" *Shapely Prose*, 20 June
2007, kateharding.net/faq/but-dont-you-realize-fat-is-unhealthy.
Accessed 19 Jan. 2011.

Pollan, Michael. *In Defense of Food: An Eater's Manifesto.* Penguin, 2008.

Joining the Conversation

1. In what ways does Mary Maxfield disagree with Michael
   Pollan (pp. 420–27) and other critics of the Western diet?
   What is her "they say," and what does she say?

2. What supporting evidence does Maxfield offer to counter
   the views of Michael Pollan and other critics?

3. Read Jonathan Safran Foer's article (pp. 448–61), and
   compare what he says with what Maxfield says. Which of
   them is more convincing and why?

4. Maxfield concludes by offering a formula for eating: "Trust
   yourself. Trust your body. Meet your needs." This formula
   contrasts with Michael Pollan's "Eat food. Not too much.
   Mostly plants." Write an essay responding to these arguments and presenting your own formula for eating.

5. Go to **theysayiblog.com** and click on "What Should We
   Eat?" Read the article by Stuart Elliott about the ad campaign promoting Whole Foods as "America's Healthiest
   Grocery Store." How do you think Maxfield would respond
   to this message? How do you respond?

Against Meat

JONATHAN SAFRAN FOER

—⊡—

The Fruits of Family Trees

WHEN I WAS YOUNG, I would often spend the weekend at my grandmother's house. On my way in, Friday night, she would lift me from the ground in one of her fire-smothering hugs. And on the way out, Sunday afternoon, I was again taken into the air. It wasn't until years later that I realized she was weighing me.

My grandmother survived World War II barefoot, scavenging Eastern Europe for other people's inedibles: rotting potatoes, discarded scraps of meat, skins and the bits that clung to bones and pits. So she never cared if I colored outside the lines, as long as I cut coupons along the dashes. I remember hotel buffets: while the rest of us erected Golden

JONATHAN SAFRAN FOER is the author of the best-selling novels *Everything Is Illuminated* (2002) and *Extremely Loud and Incredibly Close* (2005), both of which were adapted into films. He has been named one of *Rolling Stone*'s "People of the Year" and *Esquire*'s "Best and Brightest," and his writing has appeared in the *New Yorker*'s "20 Under 40" issue, among other places. He currently teaches at New York University. This essay—adapted from his book *Eating Animals* (2009)—appeared in the *New York Times* on October 11, 2009.

Calves of breakfast, she would make sandwich upon sandwich to swaddle in napkins and stash in her bag for lunch. It was my grandmother who taught me that one tea bag makes as many cups of tea as you're serving, and that every part of the apple is edible.

Her obsession with food wasn't an obsession with money. (Many of those coupons I clipped were for foods she would never buy.)

Her obsession wasn't with health. (She would beg me to drink Coke.)

My grandmother never set a place for herself at family 5 dinners. Even when there was nothing more to be done—no soup bowls to be topped off, no pots to be stirred or ovens checked—she stayed in the kitchen, like a vigilant guard (or prisoner) in a tower. As far as I could tell, the sustenance she got from the food she made didn't require her to eat it.

We thought she was the greatest chef who ever lived. My brothers and I would tell her as much several times a meal. And yet we were worldly enough kids to know that the greatest chef who ever lived would probably have more than one recipe (chicken with carrots), and that most great recipes involved more than two ingredients.

And why didn't we question her when she told us that dark food is inherently more healthful than light food, or that the bulk of the nutrients are found in the peel or crust? (The sandwiches of those weekend stays were made with the saved ends of pumpernickel loaves.) She taught us that animals that are bigger than you are very good for you, animals that are smaller than you are good for you, fish (which aren't animals) are fine for you, then tuna (which aren't fish), then vegetables, fruits, cakes, cookies and sodas. No foods are bad for you. Sugars are great. Fats are tremendous. The fatter a child is, the fitter it is—especially if it's a boy. Lunch is not one meal, but three, to be eaten at 11, 12:30 and 3. You are always starving.

In fact, her chicken with carrots probably was the most delicious thing I've ever eaten. But that had little to do with how it was prepared, or even how it tasted. Her food was delicious because we believed it was delicious. We believed in our grandmother's cooking more fervently than we believed in God.

More stories could be told about my grandmother than about anyone else I've ever met—her otherwordly childhood, the hairline margin of her survival, the totality of her loss, her immigration and further loss, the triumph and tragedy of her assimilation—and while I will one day try to tell them to my children, we almost never told them to one another. Nor did we call her by any of the obvious and earned titles. We called her the Greatest Chef.

The story of her relationship to food holds all of the other 10 stories that could be told about her. Food, for her, is not food. It is terror, dignity, gratitude, vengeance, joy, humiliation, religion, history and, of course, love. It was as if the fruits she always offered us were picked from the destroyed branches of our family tree.

Possible Again

When I was 2, the heroes of all my bedtime books were animals. The first thing I can remember learning in school was how to pet a guinea pig without accidentally killing it. One summer my family fostered a cousin's dog. I kicked it. My father told me we don't kick animals. When I was 7, I mourned the death of a goldfish I'd won the previous weekend. I discovered that my father had flushed it down the toilet. I told my father—using other, less familial language—we don't flush animals down the toilet. When I was 9, I had a baby sitter who didn't want to hurt anything. She put it just like that when I asked her why she wasn't having chicken with my older brother and me.

"Hurt anything?" I asked.

"You know that chicken is chicken, right?"

Frank shot me a look: Mom and Dad entrusted this stupid woman with their precious babies?

Her intention might or might not have been to convert us, 15 but being a kid herself, she lacked whatever restraint it is that so often prevents a full telling of this particular story. Without drama or rhetoric, skipping over or euphemizing, she shared what she knew.

My brother and I looked at each other, our mouths full of hurt chickens, and had simultaneous how-in-the-world-could-I-have-never-thought-of-that-before-and-why-on-earth-didn't-someone-tell-me? moments. I put down my fork. Frank finished the meal and is probably eating a chicken as I type these words.

See Chapter 9 for tips on mixing formal and informal language.

What our baby sitter said made sense to me, not only because it seemed so self-evidently true, but also because it was the extension to food of everything my parents had taught me. We don't hurt family members. We don't hurt friends or strangers. We don't even hurt upholstered furniture. My not having thought to include farmed animals in that list didn't make them the exceptions to it. It just made me a child, ignorant of the world's workings. Until I wasn't. At which point I had to change my life.

Until I didn't. My vegetarianism, so bombastic and unyielding in the beginning, lasted a few years, sputtered and quietly died. I never thought of a response to our baby sitter's code but found ways to smudge, diminish and ignore it. Generally speaking, I didn't cause hurt. Generally speaking, I strove to do the right thing. Generally speaking, my conscience was clear enough. Pass the chicken, I'm starving.

Mark Twain said that quitting smoking is among the easiest things you can do; he did it all the time. I would add vegetarianism to the list of easy things. In high school I became vegetarian more times than I can now remember, most often as an effort to claim a bit of identity in a world of people whose identities seemed to come effortlessly. I wanted a slogan to distinguish my mom's Volvo's bumper, a bake-sale cause to fill the self-conscious half-hour of school break, an occasion to get closer to the breasts of activist women. (And I continued to think it was wrong to hurt animals.) Which isn't to say that I refrained from eating meat. Only that I refrained in public. Many dinners of those years began with my father asking, "Any dietary restrictions I need to know about tonight?"

When I went to college, I started eating meat more ear- 20 nestly. Not "believing in it"—whatever that would mean—but willfully pushing the questions out of my mind. It might well have been the prevalence of vegetarianism on campus that discouraged my own—I find myself less likely to give money to a street musician whose case is overflowing with bills.

But when, at the end of my sophomore year, I became a philosophy major and started doing my first seriously pretentious thinking, I became a vegetarian again. The kind of active forgetting that I was sure meat eating required felt too paradoxical to the intellectual life I was trying to shape. I didn't know the details of factory farming, but like most everyone, I knew the gist: it is miserable for animals, the environment, farmers, public health, biodiversity, rural communities, global poverty and so on. I thought life could, should and must conform to the mold of reason, period. You can imagine how annoying this made me.

When I graduated, I ate meat—lots of every kind of meat—for about two years. Why? Because it tasted good. And because more important than reason in shaping habits are the stories we tell ourselves and one another. And I told a forgiving story about myself to myself: I was only human.

Then I was set up on a blind date with the woman who would become my wife. And only a few weeks later we found ourselves talking about two surprising topics: marriage and vegetarianism.

Her history with meat was remarkably similar to mine: there were things she believed while lying in bed at night, and there were choices made at the breakfast table the next morning. There was a gnawing (if only occasional and short-lived) dread that she was participating in something deeply wrong, and there was the acceptance of complexity and fallibility. Like me, she had intuitions that were very strong, but apparently not strong enough.

People marry for many different reasons, but one that 25 animated our decision to take that step was the prospect of explicitly marking a new beginning. Jewish ritual and symbolism strongly encourage this notion of demarcating a sharp division with what came before—the most well-known example being the smashing of the glass at the end of the wedding ceremony. Things were as they were, but they will be different now. Things will be better. We will be better.

Sounds and feels great, but better how? I could think of endless ways to make myself better (I could learn foreign languages, be more patient, work harder), but I'd already made too many such vows to trust them anymore. I could also think of ways to make "us" better, but the meaningful things we can agree on and change in a relationship are few.

Eating animals, a concern we'd both had and had both forgotten, seemed like a place to start. So much intersects there, and so much could flow from it. In the same week, we became engaged and vegetarian.

Of course our wedding wasn't vegetarian, because we persuaded ourselves that it was only fair to offer animal protein to our guests, some of whom traveled from great distances to share our joy. (Find that logic hard to follow?) And we ate fish on our honeymoon, but we were in Japan, and when in Japan. . . . And back in our new home, we did occasionally eat burgers and chicken soup and smoked salmon and tuna steaks. But only whenever we felt like it.

And that, I thought, was that. And I thought that was just fine. I assumed we'd maintain a diet of conscientious inconsistency. Why should eating be different from any of the other ethical realms of our lives? We were honest people who occasionally told lies, careful friends who sometimes acted clumsily. We were vegetarians who from time to time ate meat.

But then we decided to have a child, and that was a different 30 story that would necessitate a different story.

About half an hour after my son was born, I went into the waiting room to tell the gathered family the good news.

"You said 'he'! So it's a boy?"

"What's his name?

"Who does he look like?"

"Tell us everything!" 35

I answered their questions as quickly as I could, then went to the corner and turned on my cellphone.

"Grandma," I said. "We have a baby."

Her only phone is in the kitchen. She picked up halfway into the first ring. It was just after midnight. Had she been clipping coupons? Preparing chicken with carrots to freeze for someone else to eat at some future meal? I'd never once seen or heard her cry, but tears pushed through her words as she asked, "How much does it weigh?"

A few days after we came home from the hospital, I sent a letter to a friend, including a photo of my son and some first impressions of fatherhood. He responded, simply, "Everything is possible again." It was the perfect thing to write, because that was exactly how it felt. The world itself had another chance.

Eating Animals

Seconds after being born, my son was breast-feeding. I watched 40 him with an awe that had no precedent in my life. Without explanation or experience, he knew what to do. Millions of years of evolution had wound the knowledge into him, as it had encoded beating into his tiny heart and expansion and contraction into his newly dry lungs.

Almost four years later, he is a big brother and a remarkably sophisticated little conversationalist. Increasingly the food he eats is digested together with stories we tell. Feeding my children is not like feeding myself: it matters more. It matters because food matters (their physical health matters, the pleasure they take in eating matters), and because the stories that are served with food matter.

Some of my happiest childhood memories are of sushi "lunch dates" with my mom, and eating my dad's turkey burgers with mustard and grilled onions at backyard celebrations, and of course my grandmother's chicken with carrots. Those occasions simply wouldn't have been the same without those foods— and that is important. To give up the taste of sushi, turkey or chicken is a loss that extends beyond giving up a pleasurable eating experience. Changing what we eat and letting tastes fade from memory create a kind of cultural loss, a forgetting. But perhaps this kind of forgetfulness is worth accepting—even worth cultivating (forgetting, too, can be cultivated). To remember my values, I need to lose certain tastes and find other handles for the memories that they once helped me carry.

My wife and I have chosen to bring up our children as vegetarians. In another time or place, we might have made a different decision. But the realities of our present moment compelled us to make that choice. According to an analysis of U.S.D.A. data by the advocacy group Farm Forward, factory farms now produce more than 99 percent of the animals eaten in this country. And despite labels that suggest otherwise, genuine alternatives—which do exist, and make many of the ethical questions about meat moot—are very difficult for even an educated eater to find. I don't have the ability to do so with regularity and confidence. ("Free range," "cage free," "natural" and "organic" are nearly meaningless when it comes to animal welfare.)

According to reports by the Food and Agriculture Organization of the U.N. and others, factory farming has made animal agriculture the No. 1 contributor to global warming (it is significantly more destructive than transportation alone), and one of the Top 2 or 3 causes of all of the most serious environmental problems, both global and local: air and water pollution, deforestation, loss of biodiversity. . . . Eating factory-farmed animals—which is to say virtually every piece of meat sold in supermarkets and prepared in restaurants—is almost certainly the single worst thing that humans do to the environment.

Every factory-farmed animal is, as a practice, treated in ways that would be illegal if it were a dog or a cat. Turkeys have been so genetically modified they are incapable of natural reproduction. To acknowledge that these things matter is not sentimental. It is a confrontation with the facts about animals and ourselves. We know these things matter.

Meat and seafood are in no way necessary for my family— unlike some in the world, we have easy access to a wide variety of other foods. And we are healthier without it. So our choices aren't constrained.

While the cultural uses of meat can be replaced—my mother and I now eat Italian, my father grills veggie burgers, my grandmother invented her own "vegetarian chopped liver"—there is still the question of pleasure. A vegetarian diet can be rich and fully enjoyable, but I couldn't honestly argue, as many vegetarians try to, that it is as rich as a diet that includes meat. (Those who eat chimpanzee look at the Western diet as sadly deficient of a great pleasure.) I love calamari, I love roasted chicken, I love a good steak. But I don't love them without limit.

This isn't animal experimentation, where you can imagine some proportionate good at the other end of the suffering. This is what we feel like eating. Yet taste, the crudest of our senses, has been exempted from the ethical rules that govern our other senses. Why? Why doesn't a horny person have as strong a claim to raping an animal as a hungry one does to confining, killing and eating it? It's easy to dismiss that question but hard to respond to it. Try to imagine any end other than taste for which it would be justifiable to do what we do to farmed animals.

Children confront us with our paradoxes and dishonesty, and we are exposed. You need to find an answer for every why—Why do we do this? Why don't we do that?—and often there isn't a good one. So you say, simply, because. Or you tell a story that you know isn't true. And whether or not your face reddens, you blush. The shame of parenthood—which is a good shame—is that we want our children to be more whole than we are, to have satisfactory answers. My children not only inspired me to reconsider what kind of eating animal I would be, but also shamed me into reconsideration.

And then, one day, they will choose for themselves. I don't know what my reaction will be if they decide to eat meat. (I don't 50

458

know what my reaction will be if they decide to renounce their Judaism, root for the Red Sox or register Republican.) I'm not as worried about what they will choose as much as my ability to make them conscious of the choices before them. I won't measure my success as a parent by whether my children share my values, but by whether they act according to their own.

In the meantime, my choice on their behalf means they will never eat their great-grandmother's singular dish. They will never receive that unique and most direct expression of her love, will perhaps never think of her as the greatest chef who ever lived. Her primal story, our family's primal story, will have to change.

Or will it? It wasn't until I became a parent that I understood my grandmother's cooking. The greatest chef who ever lived wasn't preparing food, but humans. I'm thinking of those Saturday afternoons at her kitchen table, just the two of us—black bread in the glowing toaster, a humming refrigerator that couldn't be seen through its veil of family photographs. Over pumpernickel ends and Coke, she would tell me about her escape from Europe, the foods she had to eat and those she wouldn't. It was the story of her life—"Listen to me," she would plead—and I knew a vital lesson was being transmitted, even if I didn't know, as a child, what that lesson was. I know, now, what it was.

Listen to Me

"We weren't rich, but we always had enough. Thursday we baked bread, and challah and rolls, and they lasted the whole week. Friday we had pancakes. Shabbat we always had a chicken, and soup with noodles. You would go to the butcher and ask for a little more fat. The fattiest piece was the best piece. It wasn't like now. We didn't have refrigerators, but we had milk and cheese. We didn't have every kind of vegetable, but we had enough. The things that you have here and take for granted. . . . But we were happy. We didn't know any better. And we took what we had for granted, too.

"Then it all changed. During the war it was hell on earth, and I had nothing. I left my family, you know. I was always running, day and night, because the Germans were always right behind me. If you stopped, you died. There was never enough food. I became sicker and sicker from not eating, and I'm not just talking about being skin and bones. I had sores all over my body. It became difficult to move. I wasn't too good to eat from a garbage can. I ate the parts others wouldn't eat. If you helped yourself, you could survive. I took whatever I could find. I ate things I wouldn't tell you about.

"Even at the worst times, there were good people, too. Some- 55 one taught me to tie the ends of my pants so I could fill the legs with any potatoes I was able to steal. I walked miles and miles like that, because you never knew when you would be lucky again. Someone gave me a little rice, once, and I traveled two days to a market and traded it for some soap, and then traveled to another market and traded the soap for some beans. You had to have luck and intuition.

"The worst it got was near the end. A lot of people died right at the end, and I didn't know if I could make it another day. A farmer, a Russian, God bless him, he saw my condition, and he went into his house and came out with a piece of meat for me."

"He saved your life."

"I didn't eat it."

"You didn't eat it?"

"It was pork. I wouldn't eat pork." 60

"Why?"

"What do you mean why?"
"What, because it wasn't kosher?"
"Of course."
"But not even to save your life?"   65
"If nothing matters, there's nothing to save."

Joining the Conversation

1. Jonathan Safran Foer spends a lot of time talking about his relationship with his grandmother and the role that her cooking and her ideas about food had in the development of his own attitudes toward food. How do you think Foer's grandmother influenced his eventual embrace of vegetarianism? Cite passages in his text to support your answer.

2. In writing about his move to vegetarianism, a topic he takes very seriously, Foer injects humor at times. How do his humorous comments affect the way you read his essay?

3. So what? Foer explains why being vegetarian matters to him. Has he convinced you that *you* should care? If so, how has he done so? If not, help him out: how could he do better?

4. Compare Foer's narrative of how and why he became a vegetarian to Mary Maxfield's essay (pp. 442–47) arguing against treating food as a moral issue. What does each author say about the role of food in our lives?

5. Write an essay about how you have developed an ethical view you hold strongly. Make clear to your readers why the issue matters to you—and why it should matter to others.

Don't Blame the Eater

DAVID ZINCZENKO

—◻—

IF EVER THERE WERE a newspaper headline custom-made for
Jay Leno's monologue, this was it. Kids taking on McDonald's
this week, suing the company for making them fat. Isn't that
like middle-aged men suing Porsche for making them get speeding tickets? Whatever happened to personal responsibility?

I tend to sympathize with these portly fast-food patrons,
though. Maybe that's because I used to be one of them.

I grew up as a typical mid-1980s latchkey kid. My parents
were split up, my dad off trying to rebuild his life, my mom
working long hours to make the monthly bills. Lunch and
dinner, for me, was a daily choice between McDonald's, Taco
Bell, Kentucky Fried Chicken or Pizza Hut. Then as now, these
were the only available options for an American kid to get an

———

DAVID ZINCZENKO, who was for many years the editor-in-chief of
the fitness magazine *Men's Health*, is president of Galvanized Brands, a
global health and wellness media company. Zinczenko is the author of
numerous best-selling books, including the *Eat This, Not That* and the
Abs Diet series. He has contributed op-ed essays to the *New York Times*,
the *Los Angeles Times*, and *USA Today* and has appeared on *Dr. Oz*,
Oprah, *Ellen*, and *Good Morning America*. This piece was first published
on the op-ed page of the *New York Times* on November 23, 2002.

affordable meal. By age 15, I had packed 21
teenage tallow on my once lanky 5-foot-10

Then I got lucky. I went to college, joined
and got involved with a health magazine
manage my diet. But most of the teenagers w... ...
did, on a fast-food diet won't turn their lives around:
They've crossed under the golden arches to a likely fate
of lifetime obesity. And the problem isn't just theirs—
it's all of ours.

For tips on saying why it matters, see Chapter 7.

Before 1994, diabetes in children was generally caused by a 5
genetic disorder—only about 5 percent of childhood cases were
obesity-related, or Type 2, diabetes. Today, according to the
National Institutes of Health, Type 2 diabetes accounts for at
least 30 percent of all new childhood cases of diabetes in this
country.

Not surprisingly, money spent to treat diabetes has skyrock-
eted, too. The Centers for Disease Control and Prevention estimate that diabetes accounted for $2.6 billion in health care costs
in 1969. Today's number is an unbelievable $100 billion a year.

Shouldn't we know better than to eat two meals a day in
fast-food restaurants? That's one argument. But where, exactly,
are consumers—particularly teenagers—supposed to find alternatives? Drive down any thoroughfare in America, and I
guarantee you'll see one of our country's more than 13,000
McDonald's restaurants. Now, drive back up the block and try
to find someplace to buy a grapefruit.

Complicating the lack of alternatives is the lack of information about what, exactly, we're consuming. There are no calorie
information charts on fast-food packaging, the way there are
on grocery items. Advertisements don't carry warning labels
the way tobacco ads do. Prepared foods aren't covered under
Food and Drug Administration labeling laws. Some fast-food

…veyors will provide calorie information on request, but even that can be hard to understand.

For example, one company's Web site lists its chicken salad as containing 150 calories; the almonds and noodles that come with it (an additional 190 calories) are listed separately. Add a serving of the 280-calorie dressing, and you've got a healthy lunch alternative that comes in at 620 calories. But that's not all. Read the small print on the back of the dressing packet and you'll realize it actually contains 2.5 servings. If you pour what you've been served, you're suddenly up around 1,040 calories, which is half of the government's recommended daily calorie intake. And that doesn't take into account that 450-calorie super-size Coke.

Make fun if you will of these kids launching lawsuits against 10 the fast-food industry, but don't be surprised if you're the next plaintiff. As with the tobacco industry, it may be only a matter of time before state governments begin to see a direct line between the $1 billion that McDonald's and Burger King spend each year on advertising and their own swelling health care costs.

And I'd say the industry is vulnerable. Fast-food companies are marketing to children a product with proven health hazards and no warning labels. They would do well to protect themselves, and their customers, by providing the nutrition information people need to make informed choices about their products. Without such warnings, we'll see more sick, obese children and more angry, litigious parents. I say, let the deep-fried chips fall where they may.

"Don't Blame the Eater." From *The New York Times*, November 23, 2002. Reprinted by permission of the author.

Joining the Conversation

1. Summarize Zinczenko's arguments (his "I say") against the practices of fast-food companies. How persuasive are these arguments?

2. One important move in all good argumentative writing is to introduce voices raising possible objections to the position being argued—what this book calls naysayers. What objections does Zinczenko introduce, and how does he respond? Can you think of other objections that he might have noted?

3. How does the story that Zinczenko tells about his own experience in paragraphs 3 and 4 support or fail to support his argument? How could the same story be used to support an argument opposed to Zinczenko's?

4. So what? Who cares? How does Zinczenko make clear to readers why his topic matters? Or, if he does not, how might he do so?

5. Write an essay responding to Zinczenko, using your own experience and knowledge as part of your argument. You may agree, disagree, or both, but be sure to represent Zinczenko's views near the beginning of your text, both summarizing and quoting from his arguments.

What You Eat Is Your Business

RADLEY BALKO

—◻—

THIS JUNE, *Time* magazine and ABC News will host a three-day summit on obesity. ABC News anchor Peter Jennings, who last December anchored the prime-time special "How to Get Fat Without Really Trying," will host. Judging by the scheduled program, the summit promises to be a pep rally for media, nutrition activists, and policy makers—all agitating for a panoply of government anti-obesity initiatives, including prohibiting junk food in school vending machines, federal funding for new bike trails and sidewalks, more demanding labels on foodstuffs, restrictive food marketing to children, and prodding the food industry into more "responsible" behavior. In other words, bringing government between you and your waistline.

———

RADLEY BALKO writes a blog about civil liberties and the criminal justice system for the *Washington Post*. He was once an editor at the *Huffington Post* and *Reason* magazine and a columnist for FoxNews.com. A self-described libertarian, Balko is the author of the book *Rise of the Warrior Cop: The Militarization of America's Police Forces* (2013). This essay was first published on May 23, 2004, on the website of the Cato Institute, which aims to promote the principles of "limited government, individual liberty, free markets, and peace."

Politicians have already climbed aboard. President Bush earmarked $200 million in his budget for anti-obesity measures. State legislatures and school boards across the country have begun banning snacks and soda from school campuses and vending machines. Senator Joe Lieberman and Oakland Mayor Jerry Brown, among others, have called for a "fat tax" on high-calorie foods. Congress is now considering menu-labeling legislation, which would force restaurants to send every menu item to the laboratory for nutritional testing.

This is the wrong way to fight obesity. Instead of manipulating or intervening in the array of food options available to American consumers, our government ought to be working to foster a sense of responsibility in and ownership of our own health and well-being. But we're doing just the opposite.

For decades now, America's health care system has been migrating toward socialism. Your well-being, shape, and condition have increasingly been deemed matters of "public health," instead of matters of personal responsibility. Our lawmakers just enacted a huge entitlement that requires some people to pay for other people's medicine. Senator Hillary Clinton just penned a lengthy article in the *New York Times Magazine* calling for yet more federal control of health care. All of the Democratic candidates for president boasted plans to push health care further into the public sector. More and more, states are preventing private health insurers from charging overweight and obese clients higher premiums, which effectively removes any financial incentive for maintaining a healthy lifestyle.

We're becoming less responsible for our own health, and 5 more responsible for everyone else's. Your heart attack drives up the cost of my premiums and office visits. And if the government is paying for my anti-cholesterol medication, what incentive is there for me to put down the cheeseburger?

This collective ownership of private health then paves the way for even more federal restrictions on consumer choice and civil liberties. A society where everyone is responsible for everyone else's well-being is a society more apt to accept government restrictions, for example—on what McDonald's can put on its menu, what Safeway or Kroger can put on grocery shelves, or holding food companies responsible for the bad habits of unhealthy consumers.

A growing army of nutritionist activists and food industry foes are egging the process on. Margo Wootan of the Center for Science in the Public Interest has said, "We've got to move beyond 'personal responsibility.'" The largest organization of trial lawyers now encourages its members to weed jury pools of candidates who show "personal responsibility bias." The title of Jennings's special from last December—"How to Get Fat Without Really Trying"—reveals his intent, which is to relieve viewers of responsibility for their own condition. Indeed, Jennings ended the program with an impassioned plea for government intervention to fight obesity.

For tips on distinguishing what you say from what others say, as Balko does here, see Chapter 5.

The best way to alleviate the obesity "public health" crisis is to remove obesity from the realm of public health. It doesn't belong there anyway. It's difficult to think of anything more private and of less public concern than what we choose to put into our bodies. It only becomes a public matter when we force the public to pay for the consequences of those choices. If policymakers want to fight obesity, they'll halt the creeping socialization of medicine, and move to return individual Americans' ownership of their own health and well-being back to individual Americans.

That means freeing insurance companies to reward healthy lifestyles, and penalize poor ones. It means halting plans to further socialize medicine and health care. Congress should also increase access to medical and health savings accounts, which give consumers the option of rolling money reserved for health care into a retirement account. These accounts introduce accountability into the health care system, and encourage caution with one's health care dollar. When money we spend on health care doesn't belong to our employer or the government, but is money we could devote to our own retirement, we're less likely to run to the doctor at the first sign of a cold.

We'll all make better choices about diet, exercise, and 10 personal health when someone else isn't paying for the consequences of those choices.

Joining the Conversation

1. What does Radley Balko claim in this essay? How do you know? What position is he responding to? Cite examples from the text to support your answer.

2. Reread the last sentence of paragraph 1: "In other words, bringing government between you and your waistline." This is actually a sentence fragment, but it functions as metacommentary, inserted by Balko to make sure that readers see his point. Imagine that this statement were not there, and reread the first three paragraphs. Does it make a difference in how you read this piece?

3. Notice the direct quotations in paragraph 7. How has Balko integrated these quotations into his text—how has he introduced them, and what, if anything, has he said to explain them and tie them to his own text? Are there any changes you might suggest? How do key terms in the quotations echo one another? (See Chapter 3 for advice on quoting, and pp. 114–16 for help on identifying key terms.)

4. Balko makes his own position about the so-called obesity crisis very clear, but does he consider any of the objections that might be offered to his position? If so, how does he deal with those objections? If not, what objections might he have raised?

5. Write an essay responding to Balko, agreeing, disagreeing, or both agreeing and disagreeing with his position. You might want to cite some of David Zinczenko's arguments (see pp. 462–65)—depending on what stand you take, Zinczenko's ideas could serve as support for what you believe or as the source of one possible objection.

The Extraordinary Science of Addictive Junk Food

MICHAEL MOSS

ON THE EVENING OF APRIL 8, 1999, a long line of Town Cars and taxis pulled up to the Minneapolis headquarters of Pillsbury and discharged 11 men who controlled America's largest food companies. Nestlé was in attendance, as were Kraft and Nabisco, General Mills and Procter & Gamble, Coca-Cola and Mars. Rivals any other day, the C.E.O.'s and company presidents had come together for a rare, private meeting. On the agenda was one item: the emerging obesity epidemic and how to deal with it. While the atmosphere was cordial, the men assembled were hardly friends. Their stature was defined by their skill in fighting one another for what they called "stomach share"—the amount

---

MICHAEL MOSS is a *New York Times* investigative reporter who won a 2010 Pulitzer Prize for "The Burger That Shattered Her Life," an article about a young dance instructor who was paralyzed after contracting an *E. coli* infection. Moss has reported for the *Wall Street Journal*, *New York Newsday*, and the *Atlanta Journal-Constitution* and taught at the Columbia University School of Journalism. This selection, adapted from his book, *Salt Sugar Fat: How the Food Giants Hooked Us* (2013), first appeared in the *New York Times Magazine* on February 24, 2013.

of digestive space that any one company's brand can grab from the competition.

James Behnke, a 55-year-old executive at Pillsbury, greeted the men as they arrived. He was anxious but also hopeful about the plan that he and a few other food-company executives had devised to engage the C.E.O.'s on America's growing weight problem. "We were very concerned, and rightfully so, that obesity was becoming a major issue," Behnke recalled. "People were starting to talk about sugar taxes, and there was a lot of pressure on food companies." Getting the company chiefs in the same room to talk about anything, much less a sensitive issue like this, was a tricky business, so Behnke and his fellow organizers had scripted the meeting carefully, honing the message to its barest essentials. "C.E.O.'s in the food industry are typically not technical guys, and they're uncomfortable going to meetings where technical people talk in technical terms about technical things," Behnke said. "They don't want to be embarrassed. They don't want to make commitments. They want to maintain their aloofness and autonomy."

A chemist by training with a doctoral degree in food science, Behnke became Pillsbury's chief technical officer in 1979 and was instrumental in creating a long line of hit products, including microwaveable popcorn. He deeply admired Pillsbury but in recent years had grown troubled by pictures of obese children suffering from diabetes and the earliest signs of hypertension and heart disease. In the months leading up to the C.E.O. meeting, he was engaged in conversation with a group of food-science experts who were painting an increasingly grim picture of the public's ability to cope with the industry's formulations—from the body's fragile controls on overeating to the hidden power of some processed foods to make people feel hungrier still. It was time, he and a handful of others felt, to warn the C.E.O.'s that their companies may have gone too far in creating and marketing products that posed the greatest health concerns.

The discussion took place in Pillsbury's auditorium. The first speaker was a vice president of Kraft named Michael Mudd. "I very much appreciate this opportunity to talk to you about childhood obesity and the growing challenge it presents for us all," Mudd began. "Let me say right at the start, this is not an easy subject. There are no easy answers—for what the public health community must do to bring this problem under control or for what the industry should do as others seek to hold it accountable for what has happened. But this much is clear: For those of us who've looked hard at this issue, whether they're public health professionals or staff specialists in your own companies, we feel sure that the one thing we shouldn't do is nothing."

As he spoke, Mudd clicked through a deck of slides—114 in all—projected on a large screen behind him. The figures were staggering. More than half of American adults were now considered overweight, with nearly one-quarter of the adult population—40 million people—clinically defined as obese. Among children, the rates had more than doubled since 1980, and the number of kids considered obese had shot past 12 million. (This was still only 1999; the nation's obesity rates would climb much higher.) Food manufacturers were now being blamed for the problem from all sides—academia, the Centers for Disease Control and Prevention, the American Heart Association and the American Cancer Society. The secretary of agriculture, over whom the industry had long held sway, had recently called obesity a "national epidemic."

Mudd then did the unthinkable. He drew a connection to the last thing in the world the C.E.O.'s wanted linked to their products: cigarettes. First came a quote from a Yale University professor of psychology and public health, Kelly Brownell, who was an especially vocal proponent of the view that the processed-food industry should be seen as a public health menace: "As a culture, we've become upset by the tobacco companies advertising to children, but we sit idly by while the food companies do the very same thing. And we could make a claim that the toll taken on the public health by a poor diet rivals that taken by tobacco."

"If anyone in the food industry ever doubted there was a slippery slope out there," Mudd said, "I imagine they are beginning to experience a distinct sliding sensation right about now."

Mudd then presented the plan he and others had devised to address the obesity problem. Merely getting the executives to acknowledge some culpability was an important first step, he knew, so his plan would start off with a small but crucial move: the industry should use the expertise of scientists—its own and others—to gain a deeper understanding of what was driving Americans to overeat. Once this was achieved, the effort could unfold on several fronts. To be sure, there would be no getting around the role that packaged foods and drinks play in overconsumption. They would have to pull back on their use of salt, sugar and fat, perhaps by imposing industrywide limits. But it wasn't just a matter of these three ingredients; the schemes they used to advertise and market their products were critical, too. Mudd proposed creating a "code to guide the nutritional aspects of food marketing, especially to children."

"We are saying that the industry should make a sincere effort to be part of the solution," Mudd concluded. "And that by doing so, we can help to defuse the criticism that's building against us."

What happened next was not written down. But according to three participants, when Mudd stopped talking, the one C.E.O. whose recent exploits in the grocery store had awed the rest of the industry stood up to speak. His name was Stephen Sanger, and he was also the person—as head of General Mills—who had the most to lose when it came to dealing with obesity. Under his leadership, General Mills had overtaken not just the cereal aisle but other sections of the grocery store. The company's Yoplait brand had transformed traditional unsweetened breakfast yogurt into a veritable dessert. It now had twice as much sugar per serving as General Mills' marshmallow cereal Lucky Charms. And yet, because of yogurt's well-tended image as a wholesome snack,

Traditional unsweetened breakfast yogurt transformed into a veritable dessert.

sales of Yoplait were soaring, with annual revenue topping $500 million. Emboldened by the success, the company's development wing pushed even harder, inventing a Yoplait variation that came in a squeezable tube—perfect for kids. They called it Go-Gurt and rolled it out nationally in the weeks before the C.E.O. meeting. (By year's end, it would hit $100 million in sales.)

According to the sources I spoke with, Sanger began by reminding the group that consumers were "fickle." (Sanger declined to be interviewed.) Sometimes they worried about sugar, other times fat. General Mills, he said, acted responsibly to both the public and shareholders by offering products to satisfy dieters and other concerned shoppers, from low sugar to added whole grains. But most often, he said, people bought what they liked, and they liked what tasted good. "Don't talk to me about nutrition," he reportedly said, taking on the voice of the typical consumer. "Talk to me about taste, and if this stuff tastes better, don't run around trying to sell stuff that doesn't taste good."

To react to the critics, Sanger said, would jeopardize the sanctity of the recipes that had made his products so successful. General Mills would not pull back. He would push his people onward, and he urged his peers to do the same. Sanger's response effectively ended the meeting.

"What can I say?" James Behnke told me years later. "It didn't work. These guys weren't as receptive as we thought they would be." Behnke chose his words deliberately. He wanted to be fair. "Sanger was trying to say, 'Look, we're not going to screw around with the company jewels here and change the formulations because a bunch of guys in white coats are worried about obesity.' "

The meeting was remarkable, first, for the insider admissions of guilt. But I was also struck by how prescient the organizers of the sit-down had been. Today, one in three adults is considered clinically obese, along with one in five kids, and 24 million Americans are afflicted by type 2 diabetes, often caused by poor diet, with another 79 million people having pre-diabetes. Even gout, a painful form of arthritis once known as "the rich man's disease" for its associations with gluttony, now afflicts eight million Americans.

The public and the food companies have known for decades now—or at the very least since this meeting—that sugary, salty, fatty foods are not good for us in the quantities that we consume them. So why are the diabetes and obesity and hypertension numbers still spiraling out of control? It's not just a matter of poor willpower on the part of the consumer and a give-the-people-what-they-want attitude on the part of the food manufacturers. What I found, over four years of research and reporting, was a conscious effort—taking place in labs and marketing meetings and grocery-store aisles—to get people hooked on foods that are convenient and inexpensive. I talked to more than 300 people in or formerly employed by the processed-food industry, from scientists to marketers to C.E.O.'s. Some were willing whistle-blowers, while others spoke reluctantly when presented with some of the thousands of pages of secret memos that I obtained from inside the food industry's operations. What follows is a series of small case studies of a handful of characters whose work then, and perspective now, sheds light on how the foods are created and sold to people who, while not powerless, are extremely vulnerable to the intensity of these companies' industrial formulations and selling campaigns.

"In This Field, I'm a Game Changer."

John Lennon couldn't find it in England, so he had cases of it shipped from New York to fuel the *Imagine* sessions. The Beach

Boys, ZZ Top and Cher all stipulated in their contract riders that it be put in their dressing rooms when they toured. Hillary Clinton asked for it when she traveled as first lady, and ever after her hotel suites were dutifully stocked.

What they all wanted was Dr Pepper, which until 2001 occupied a comfortable third-place spot in the soda aisle behind Coca-Cola and Pepsi. But then a flood of spinoffs from the two soda giants showed up on the shelves—lemons and limes, vanillas and coffees, raspberries and oranges, whites and blues and clears—what in food-industry lingo are known as "line extensions," and Dr Pepper started to lose its market share.

Responding to this pressure, Cadbury Schweppes created its first spinoff, other than a diet version, in the soda's 115-year history, a bright red soda with a very un-Dr Pepper name: Red Fusion. "If we are to re-establish Dr Pepper back to its historic growth rates, we have to add more excitement," the company's president, Jack Kilduff, said. One particularly promising market, Kilduff pointed out, was the "rapidly growing Hispanic and African-American communities."

But consumers hated Red Fusion. "Dr Pepper is my all-time favorite drink, so I was curious about the Red Fusion," a California mother of three wrote on a blog to warn other Peppers away. "It's disgusting. Gagging. Never again."

Stung by the rejection, Cadbury Schweppes in 2004 turned to a food-industry legend named Howard Moskowitz. Moskowitz, who studied mathematics and holds a Ph.D. in experimental psychology from Harvard, runs a consulting firm in White Plains, where for more than three decades he has "optimized" a variety of products for Campbell Soup, General Foods, Kraft and PepsiCo. "I've optimized soups," Moskowitz told me. "I've optimized pizzas. I've optimized salad dressings and pickles. In this field, I'm a game changer."

In the process of product optimization, food engineers alter a litany of variables with the sole intent of finding the most perfect version (or versions) of a product. Ordinary consumers are paid to spend hours sitting in rooms where they touch, feel, sip, smell, swirl and taste whatever product is in question. Their opinions are dumped into a computer, and the data are sifted and sorted through a statistical method called conjoint analysis, which determines what features will be most attractive to consumers. Moskowitz likes to imagine that his computer is divided into silos, in which each of the attributes is stacked. But it's not simply a matter of comparing Color 23 with Color 24. In the most complicated projects, Color 23 must be combined with Syrup 11 and Packaging 6, and on and on, in seemingly infinite combinations. Even for jobs in which the only concern is taste and the variables are limited to the ingredients, endless charts and graphs will come spewing out of Moskowitz's computer. "The mathematical model maps out the ingredients to the sensory perceptions these ingredients create," he told me, "so I can just dial a new product. This is the engineering approach."

• • •

I first met Moskowitz on a crisp day in the spring of 2010 at the Harvard Club in Midtown Manhattan. As we talked, he made clear that while he has worked on numerous projects aimed at creating more healthful foods and insists the industry could be doing far more to curb obesity, he had no qualms about his own pioneering work on discovering what industry insiders now regularly refer to as "the bliss point" or any of the other systems that helped food companies create the greatest amount of crave. "There's no moral issue for me," he said. "I did the best science I could. I was struggling to survive and didn't have the luxury of being a moral creature. As a researcher, I was ahead of my time."

Moskowitz's path to mastering the bliss point began in earnest not at Harvard but a few months after graduation, 16 miles from Cambridge, in the town of Natick, where the U.S. Army hired him to work in its research labs. The military has long been in a peculiar bind when it comes to food: how to get soldiers to eat more rations when they are in the field. They know that over time, soldiers would gradually find their meals-ready-to-eat so boring that they would toss them away, half-eaten, and not get all the calories they needed. But what was causing this M.R.E.-fatigue was a mystery. "So I started asking soldiers how frequently they would like to eat this or that, trying to figure out which products they would find boring," Moskowitz said. The answers he got were inconsistent. "They liked flavorful foods like turkey tetrazzini, but only at first; they quickly grew tired of them. On the other hand, mundane foods like white bread would never get them too excited, but they could eat lots and lots of it without feeling they'd had enough."

This contradiction is known as "sensory-specific satiety." In lay terms, it is the tendency for big, distinct flavors to overwhelm the brain, which responds by depressing your desire to have more. Sensory-specific satiety also became a guiding principle for the processed-food industry. The biggest hits—be they Coca-Cola or Doritos—owe their success to complex formulas that pique the taste buds enough to be alluring but don't have a distinct, overriding single flavor that tells the brain to stop eating.

Thirty-two years after he began experimenting with the bliss point, Moskowitz got the call from Cadbury Schweppes asking him to create a good line extension for Dr Pepper. I spent an afternoon in his White Plains offices as he and his vice president for research, Michele Reisner, walked me through the

Dr Pepper campaign. Cadbury wanted its new flavor to have cherry and vanilla on top of the basic Dr Pepper taste. Thus, there were three main components to play with. A sweet cherry flavoring, a sweet vanilla flavoring and a sweet syrup known as "Dr Pepper flavoring."

Finding the bliss point required the preparation of 61 subtly distinct formulas—31 for the regular version and 30 for diet. The formulas were then subjected to 3,904 tastings organized in Los Angeles, Dallas, Chicago and Philadelphia. The Dr Pepper tasters began working through their samples, resting five minutes between each sip to restore their taste buds. After each sample, they gave numerically ranked answers to a set of questions: How much did they like it overall? How strong is the taste? How do they feel about the taste? How would they describe the quality of this product? How likely would they be to purchase this product?

Moskowitz's data—compiled in a 135-page report for the soda maker—is tremendously fine-grained, showing how different people and groups of people feel about a strong vanilla taste versus weak, various aspects of aroma and the powerful sensory force that food scientists call "mouth feel." This is the way a product interacts with the mouth, as defined more specifically by a host of related sensations, from dryness to gumminess to moisture release. These are terms more familiar to sommeliers, but the mouth feel of soda and many other food items, especially those high in fat, is second only to the bliss point in its ability to predict how much craving a product will induce.

In addition to taste, the consumers were also tested on their response to color, which proved to be highly sensitive. "When we increased the level of the Dr Pepper flavoring, it gets darker and liking goes off," Reisner said. These preferences can also be cross-referenced by age, sex and race.

On page 83 of the report, a thin blue line represents the amount of Dr Pepper flavoring needed to generate maximum appeal. The line is shaped like an upside-down U, just like the bliss-point curve that Moskowitz studied 30 years earlier in his Army lab. And at the top of the arc, there is not a single sweet spot but instead a sweet range, within which "bliss" was achievable. This meant that Cadbury could edge back on its key ingredient, the sugary Dr Pepper syrup, without falling out of the range and losing the bliss. Instead of using 2 milliliters of the flavoring, for instance, they could use 1.69 milliliters and achieve the same effect. The potential savings is merely a few percentage points, and it won't mean much to individual consumers who are counting calories or grams of sugar. But for Dr Pepper, it adds up to colossal savings. "That looks like nothing," Reisner said. "But it's a lot of money. A lot of money. Millions."

The soda that emerged from all of Moskowitz's variations 30 became known as Cherry Vanilla Dr Pepper, and it proved successful beyond anything Cadbury imagined. In 2008, Cadbury split off its soft-drinks business, which included Snapple and 7-Up. The Dr Pepper Snapple Group has since been valued in excess of $11 billion.

. . .

"It's Called Vanishing Caloric Density."

At a symposium for nutrition scientists in Los Angeles on February 15, 1985, a professor of pharmacology from Helsinki named Heikki Karppanen told the remarkable story of Finland's effort to address its salt habit. In the late 1970s, the Finns were consuming huge amounts of sodium, eating on average more than two teaspoons of salt a day. As a result, the country had developed significant issues with high blood pressure, and men in the eastern part of Finland had the highest rate of fatal cardiovascular disease in the world. Research showed that this plague was not just a quirk of genetics or a result of a sedentary lifestyle—it was also owing to processed foods. So when Finnish authorities moved to address the problem, they went right after the manufacturers. (The Finnish response worked. Every grocery item that was heavy in salt would come to be marked prominently with the warning "High Salt Content." By 2007, Finland's per capita consumption of salt had dropped by a third, and this shift— along with improved medical care—was accompanied by a 75 percent to 80 percent decline in the number of deaths from strokes and heart disease.)

Karppanen's presentation was met with applause, but one man in the crowd seemed particularly intrigued by the presentation, and as Karppanen left the stage, the man intercepted him and asked if they could talk more over dinner. Their conversation later that night was not at all what Karppanen was expecting. His host did indeed have an interest in salt, but from quite a different vantage point: the man's name was Robert I-San Lin, and from 1974 to 1982, he worked as the chief scientist for Frito-Lay, the nearly $3-billion-a-year manufacturer of Lay's, Doritos, Cheetos and Fritos.

Lin's time at Frito-Lay coincided with the first attacks by nutrition advocates on salty foods and the first calls for federal regulators to reclassify salt as a "risky" food additive, which could have subjected it to severe controls. No company took this threat more seriously—or more personally—than Frito-Lay, Lin explained to Karppanen over their dinner. Three years after he left Frito-Lay, he was still anguished over his inability to effectively change the company's recipes and practices.

By chance, I ran across a letter that Lin sent to Karppanen three weeks after that dinner, buried in some files to which I had gained access. Attached to the letter was a memo written when Lin was at Frito-Lay, which detailed some of the company's efforts in defending salt. I tracked Lin down in Irvine, California, where we spent several days going through the internal company memos, strategy papers and handwritten notes he had kept. The documents were evidence of the concern that Lin had for consumers and of the company's intent on using science not to address the health concerns but to thwart them. While at Frito-Lay, Lin and other company scientists spoke openly about the country's excessive consumption of sodium and the fact that, as Lin said to me on more than one occasion, "people get addicted to salt."

Not much had changed by 1986, except Frito-Lay found 35 itself on a rare cold streak. The company had introduced a series of high-profile products that failed miserably. Toppels, a cracker with cheese topping; Stuffers, a shell with a variety of fillings; Rumbles, a bite-size granola snack—they all came and went in a blink, and the company took a $52 million hit. Around that time, the marketing team was joined by Dwight Riskey, an expert on cravings who had been a fellow at the Monell Chemical Senses Center in Philadelphia, where he was part of a team of scientists that found that people could beat their salt habits simply by refraining from salty foods long enough for their taste buds to return to a normal level of sensitivity. He had also done work on the bliss point, showing how a product's allure is contextual, shaped partly by the other foods a person is eating, and that it changes as people age. This seemed to help explain why Frito-Lay was having so much trouble selling new snacks. The largest single block of customers, the baby boomers, had begun hitting middle age. According to the research, this suggested that their liking for salty snacks—both in the concentration of salt and how much they ate—would be tapering off. Along with the rest of the snack-food industry, Frito-Lay anticipated lower sales because of an aging population, and marketing plans were adjusted to focus even more intently on younger consumers.

Except that snack sales didn't decline as everyone had projected, Frito-Lay's doomed product launches notwithstanding. Poring over data one day in his home office, trying to understand just who was consuming all the snack food, Riskey realized that he and his colleagues had been misreading things all along. They had been measuring the snacking habits of different age groups and were seeing what they expected to see, that older consumers ate less than those in their 20s. But what they weren't measuring, Riskey realized, is how those snacking habits of the boomers compared to themselves when they were in their 20s. When he called up a new set of sales data and performed what's called a cohort study, following a single group over time, a far more encouraging picture—for Frito-Lay, anyway—emerged. The baby boomers were not eating fewer salty snacks as they aged. "In fact, as those people aged, their consumption of all those segments—the cookies, the crackers, the candy, the chips—was going up," Riskey said. "They were not only eating what they ate when they were younger, they were eating more of it." In fact, everyone in the country, on average, was eating more salty snacks than they used to. The rate of consumption was edging up about one-third of a pound every year, with the average intake of snacks like chips and cheese crackers pushing past 12 pounds a year.

Riskey had a theory about what caused this surge: Eating real meals had become a thing of the past. Baby boomers, especially, seemed to have greatly cut down on regular meals. They were skipping breakfast when they had early-morning meetings. They skipped lunch when they then needed to catch up on work because of those meetings. They skipped dinner when their kids stayed out late or grew up and moved out of the house. And when they skipped these meals, they replaced them with snacks. "We looked at this behavior, and said, 'Oh, my gosh, people were skipping meals right and left,' " Riskey told me. "It was amazing." This led to the next realization, that baby boomers did not represent "a category that is mature, with no growth. This is a category that has huge growth potential."

The food technicians stopped worrying about inventing new products and instead embraced the industry's most reliable method for getting consumers to buy more: the line extension. The classic Lay's potato chips were joined by Salt & Vinegar, Salt & Pepper and Cheddar & Sour Cream. They put out Chili-Cheese-flavored Fritos, and Cheetos were transformed into 21 varieties. Frito-Lay had a formidable research complex near Dallas, where nearly 500 chemists, psychologists and technicians conducted research that cost up to $30 million a year, and the science corps focused intense amounts of resources on questions of crunch, mouth feel and aroma for each of these items. Their tools included a $40,000 device that simulated a chewing mouth to test and perfect the chips, discovering things like the perfect break point: people like a chip that snaps with about four pounds of pressure per square inch.

To get a better feel for their work, I called on Steven Witherly, a food scientist who wrote a fascinating guide for industry insiders titled, "Why Humans Like Junk Food." I brought him two shopping bags filled with a variety of chips

The industry's most reliable method for getting consumers to buy more: the line extension.

to taste. He zeroed right in on the Cheetos. "This," Witherly said, "is one of the most marvelously constructed foods on the planet, in terms of pure pleasure." He ticked off a dozen attributes of the Cheetos that make the brain say more. But the one he focused on most was the puff's uncanny ability to melt in the mouth. "It's called vanishing caloric density," Witherly said. "If something melts down quickly, your brain thinks that there's no calories in it . . . you can just keep eating it forever."

As for their marketing troubles, in a March 2010 meeting, 40 Frito-Lay executives hastened to tell their Wall Street investors that the 1.4 billion boomers worldwide weren't being neglected; they were redoubling their efforts to understand exactly what it was that boomers most wanted in a snack chip. Which was basically everything: great taste, maximum bliss but minimal guilt about health and more maturity than puffs. "They snack a lot," Frito-Lay's chief marketing officer, Ann Mukherjee, told the investors. "But what they're looking for is very different. They're looking for new experiences, real food experiences." Frito-Lay acquired Stacy's Pita Chip Company, which was started by a Massachusetts couple who made food-cart sandwiches and started serving pita chips to their customers in the mid-1990s. In Frito-Lay's hands, the pita chips averaged 270 milligrams of sodium—nearly one-fifth a whole day's recommended maximum for most American adults—and were a huge hit among boomers.

The Frito-Lay executives also spoke of the company's ongoing pursuit of a "designer sodium," which they hoped, in the near future, would take their sodium loads down by 40 percent. No need to worry about lost sales there, the company's C.E.O., Al Carey, assured their investors. The boomers would see less salt as the green light to snack like never before.

There's a paradox at work here. On the one hand, reduction of sodium in snack foods is commendable. On the other, these changes may well result in consumers eating See Chapter 4 for ways to agree and disagree simultaneously. more. "The big thing that will happen here is removing the barriers for boomers and giving them permission to snack," Carey said. The prospects for lower-salt snacks were so amazing, he added, that the company had set its sights on using the designer salt to conquer the toughest market of all for snacks: schools. He cited, for example, the school-food initiative championed by Bill Clinton and the American Heart Association, which is seeking to improve the nutrition of school food by limiting its load of salt, sugar and fat. "Imagine this," Carey said.

"A potato chip that tastes great and qualifies for the Clinton-A.H.A. alliance for schools. . . . We think we have ways to do all of this on a potato chip, and imagine getting that product into schools, where children can have this product and grow up with it and feel good about eating it."

Carey's quote reminded me of something I read in the early stages of my reporting, a 24-page report prepared for Frito-Lay in 1957 by a psychologist named Ernest Dichter. The company's chips, he wrote, were not selling as well as they could for one simple reason: "While people like and enjoy potato chips, they feel guilty about liking them. . . . Unconsciously, people expect to be punished for 'letting themselves go' and enjoying them." Dichter listed seven "fears and resistances" to the chips: "You can't stop eating them; they're fattening; they're not good for you; they're greasy and messy to eat; they're too expensive; it's hard to store the leftovers; and they're bad for children." He spent the rest of his memo laying out his prescriptions, which in time would become widely used not just by Frito-Lay but also by the entire industry. Dichter suggested that Frito-Lay avoid using the word "fried" in referring to its chips and adopt instead the more healthful-sounding term "toasted." To counteract the "fear of letting oneself go," he suggested repacking the chips into smaller bags. "The more-anxious consumers, the ones who have the deepest fears about their capacity to control their appetite, will tend to sense the function of the new pack and select it," he said.

Dichter advised Frito-Lay to move its chips out of the realm of between-meals snacking and turn them into an ever-present item in the American diet. "The increased use of potato chips and other Lay's products as a part of the regular fare served by restaurants and sandwich bars should be encouraged in a concentrated way," Dichter said, citing a string of examples:

"potato chips with soup, with fruit or vegetable juice appetizers; potato chips served as a vegetable on the main dish; potato chips with salad; potato chips with egg dishes for breakfast; potato chips with sandwich orders."

In 2011, *The New England Journal of Medicine* published 45 a study that shed new light on America's weight gain. The subjects—120,877 women and men—were all professionals in the health field, and were likely to be more conscious about nutrition, so the findings might well understate the overall trend. Using data back to 1986, the researchers monitored everything the participants ate, as well as their physical activity and smoking. They found that every four years, the participants exercised less, watched TV more and gained an average of 3.35 pounds. The researchers parsed the data by the caloric content of the foods being eaten, and found the top contributors to weight gain included red meat and processed meats, sugar-sweetened beverages and potatoes, including mashed and French fries. But the largest weight-inducing food was the potato chip. The coating of salt, the fat content that rewards the brain with instant feelings of pleasure, the sugar that exists not as an additive but in the starch of the potato itself—all of this combines to make it the perfect addictive food. "The starch is readily absorbed," Eric Rimm, an associate professor of epidemiology and nutrition at the Harvard School of Public Health and one of the study's authors, told me. "More quickly even than a similar amount of sugar. The starch, in turn, causes the glucose levels in the blood to spike"—which can result in a craving for more.

If Americans snacked only occasionally, and in small amounts, this would not present the enormous problem that it does. But because so much money and effort has been invested over decades in engineering and then relentlessly selling these products, the effects are seemingly impossible to unwind. More than 30 years have passed since Robert Lin first tangled with Frito-Lay on the imperative of the company to deal with the formulation of its snacks, but as we sat at his dining-room table, sifting through his records, the feelings of regret still played on his face. In his view, three decades had been lost, time that he and a lot of other smart scientists could have spent searching for ways to ease the addiction to salt, sugar and fat. "I couldn't do much about it," he told me. "I feel so sorry for the public."

"These People Need a Lot of Things, But They Don't Need a Coke."

The growing attention Americans are paying to what they put into their mouths has touched off a new scramble by the processed-food companies to address health concerns. Pressed by the Obama administration and consumers, Kraft, Nestlé, Pepsi, Campbell and General Mills, among others, have begun to trim the loads of salt, sugar and fat in many products. And with consumer advocates pushing for more government intervention, Coca-Cola made headlines in January by releasing ads that promoted its bottled water and low-calorie drinks as a way to counter obesity. Predictably, the ads drew a new volley of scorn from critics who pointed to the company's continuing drive to sell sugary Coke.

One of the other executives I spoke with at length was Jeffrey Dunn, who, in 2001, at age 44, was directing more than half of Coca-Cola's $20 billion in annual sales as president and chief operating officer in both North and South America. In an effort to control as much market share as possible, Coke extended its aggressive marketing to especially poor or vulnerable areas of the U.S., like New Orleans—where people were drinking twice as much Coke as the national average—or Rome, Georgia, where the per capita intake was nearly three Cokes a day. In Coke's headquarters in Atlanta, the biggest consumers were referred to as "heavy users." "The other model we use was called 'drinks and drinkers,' " Dunn said. "How many drinkers do I have? And how many drinks do they drink? If you lost one of those heavy users, if somebody just decided to stop drinking Coke, how many drinkers would you have to get, at low velocity, to make up for that heavy user? The answer is a lot. It's more efficient to get my existing users to drink more."

One of Dunn's lieutenants, Todd Putman, who worked at Coca-Cola from 1997 to 2001, said the goal became much larger than merely beating the rival brands; Coca-Cola strove to outsell every other thing people drank, including milk and water. The marketing division's efforts boiled down to one question, Putman said: "How can we drive more ounces into more bodies more often?" (In response to Putman's remarks, Coke said its goals have changed and that it now focuses on providing consumers with more low- or no-calorie products.)

In his capacity, Dunn was making frequent trips to Brazil, 50 where the company had recently begun a push to increase consumption of Coke among the many Brazilians living in [the slums known as] *favelas*. The company's strategy was to repackage Coke into smaller, more affordable 6.7-ounce bottles, just 20 cents each. Coke was not alone in seeing Brazil as a potential boon; Nestlé began deploying battalions of women to travel poor neighborhoods, hawking American-style processed foods door to door. But Coke was Dunn's concern, and on one trip, as he walked through one of the impoverished areas, he had an epiphany. "A voice in my head says, 'These people need a lot of things, but they don't need a Coke.' I almost threw up."

Dunn returned to Atlanta, determined to make some changes. He didn't want to abandon the soda business, but he did want to try to steer the company into a more healthful mode, and one of the things he pushed for was to stop marketing Coke in public schools. The independent companies that bottled Coke viewed his plans as reactionary. A director of one bottler wrote a letter to Coke's chief executive and board asking for Dunn's head. "He said what I had done was the worst thing he had seen in 50 years in the business," Dunn said. "Just to placate these crazy leftist school districts who were trying to keep people from having their Coke. He said I was an embarrassment to the company, and I should be fired." In February 2004, he was.

Dunn told me that talking about Coke's business today was by no means easy and, because he continues to work in the food business, not without risk. "You really don't want them mad at you," he said. "And I don't mean that, like, I'm going to end up at the bottom of the bay. But they don't have a sense of humor when it comes to this stuff. They're a very, very aggressive company."

When I met with Dunn, he told me not just about his years at Coke but also about his new marketing venture. In April 2010, he met with three executives from Madison Dearborn Partners, a private-equity firm based in Chicago with a wide-ranging portfolio of investments. They recently hired Dunn to run one of their newest acquisitions—a food producer in the San Joaquin Valley. As they sat in the hotel's meeting room, the men listened to Dunn's marketing pitch. He talked about giving the product a personality that was bold and irreverent, conveying the idea that this was the ultimate snack food. He went into detail on how he would target a special segment of the 146 million Americans who are regular snackers—mothers, children, young professionals—people, he said, who "keep their snacking ritual fresh by trying a new food product when it catches their attention."

He explained how he would deploy strategic storytelling in the ad campaign for this snack, using a key phrase that had been developed with much calculation: "Eat 'Em Like Junk Food."

After 45 minutes, Dunn clicked off the last slide and thanked 55 the men for coming. Madison's portfolio contained the largest Burger King franchise in the world, the Ruth's Chris Steak House chain and a processed-food maker called AdvancePierre whose lineup includes the Jamwich, a peanut-butter-and-jelly contrivance that comes frozen, crustless and embedded with four kinds of sugars.

The snack that Dunn was proposing to sell: carrots. Plain, fresh carrots. No added sugar. No creamy sauce or dips. No salt. Just baby carrots, washed, bagged, then sold into the deadly dull produce aisle.

"We act like a snack, not a vegetable," he told the investors. "We exploit the rules of junk food to fuel the baby-carrot conversation. We are pro-junk-food behavior but anti-junk-food establishment."

The investors were thinking only about sales. They had already bought one of the two biggest farm producers of baby carrots in the country, and they'd hired Dunn to run the whole operation. Now, after his pitch, they were relieved. Dunn had figured out that using the industry's own marketing ploys would work better than anything else. He drew from the bag of tricks that he mastered in his 20 years at Coca-Cola, where he learned one of the most critical rules in processed food: The selling of food matters as much as the food itself.

Later, describing his new line of work, Dunn told me he was doing penance for his Coca-Cola years. "I'm paying my karmic debt," he said.

Joining the Conversation

1. Michael Moss provides three examples of scientific research on junk food and its effects. What common denominator links these examples? What makes the science of addictive junk food so extraordinary?

2. Moss opens this essay by describing a meeting that the leaders of several major food companies held to discuss the obesity epidemic and how to respond to it. Why do you think he begins with this story? How does it set the stage for the rest of the piece?

3. Moss is able to present complex technical information so that nonscientists can understand it. One way he does this is by using colloquial language to explain technical terms such as "product optimization," "bliss point," and "sensory-specific satiety." This technique helps us understand his topic, but how also does it make his argument interesting—and persuasive?

4. Moss reports that the major food companies hire experts to make their products as appealing as possible. Similarly, on pp. 496–505, Marion Nestle discusses ways that psychologists and marketing specialists help supermarkets arrange items to increase their appeal and boost sales. Now that you know about these tactics, what are some specific actions you can take to guard against manipulation when you shop for food?

5. If Jeffrey Dunn could turn carrots into "the ultimate snack food" (paragraph 53) what other healthy foods could be similarly transformed? Beets? Kale? What else? Write an essay proposing such a product. Use the "they say/I say" format, perhaps quoting or summarizing something said in Moss's essay as your "they say."

The Supermarket: Prime Real Estate

MARION NESTLE

—▢—

A VISIT TO A LARGE SUPERMARKET can be a daunting experience: so many aisles, so many brands and varieties, so many prices to keep track of and labels to read, so many choices to make. No wonder. To repeat: An astonishing 320,000 edible products are for sale in the United States, and any large supermarket might display as many as 40,000 of them. You are supposed to feel daunted—bewildered by all the choices and forced to wander through the aisles in search of the items you came to buy. The big companies that own most supermarkets want you to do as much searching as you can tolerate. It is no coincidence that one supermarket is laid out much like another: breathtaking amounts of research have gone into designing these places.

———

MARION NESTLE teaches in the department of nutrition, food studies, and public health at New York University. She writes a monthly column on food for the *San Francisco Chronicle* and blogs at foodpolitics.com. Her many books include *Food Politics: How the Food Industry Influences Nutrition and Health* (2003) and *What to Eat: An Aisle-by-Aisle Guide to Savvy Food Choices and Good Eating* (2006), from which this essay is taken.

There are precise reasons why milk is at the back of the store and the center aisles are so long. You are forced to go past thousands of other products on your way to get what you need.

Supermarkets say they are in the business of offering "choice." Perhaps, but they do everything possible to make the choice theirs, not yours. Supermarkets are not social service agencies providing food for the hungry. Their job is to sell food, and more of it. From their perspective, it is *your* problem if what you buy makes you eat more food than you need, and more of the wrong kinds of foods in particular.

And supermarket retailers know more than you could possibly imagine about how to push your "buy" buttons. Half a century ago, Vance Packard revealed their secrets in his book *The Hidden Persuaders*. His most shocking revelation? Corporations were hiring social scientists to study unconscious human emotions, not for the good of humanity but to help companies manipulate people into buying products. Packard's chapter on supermarket shopping, "Babes in Consumerland," is as good a guide as anything that has been written since to methods for getting you—and your children—to "reach out, hypnotically . . . and grab boxes of cookies, candies, dog food, and everything else that delights or interests [you]."

More recent research on consumer behavior not only confirms his observations but continues to be awe-inspiring in its meticulous attention to detail. Your local library has entire textbooks and academic journals devoted to investigations of consumer behavior and ways to use the results of that research to sell products. Researchers are constantly interviewing shoppers and listening carefully to what they are told. Because of scanners, supermarkets can now track your purchases and compare what you tell researchers to what you actually buy. If you belong to a supermarket discount "shoppers club," the store gains your loyalty but gets to track your personal buying habits in exchange. This research tells food retailers how to lay out the stores, where to put specific products, how to position products on shelves, and how to set prices and advertise products. At the supermarket, you exercise freedom of choice and personal responsibility every time you put an item in your shopping cart, but massive efforts have gone into making it more convenient and desirable for you to choose some products rather than others.

As basic marketing textbooks explain, the object of the game is to "maximize sales and profit consistent with customer convenience." Translated, this means that supermarkets want to expose you to the largest possible number of items that you can stand to see, without annoying you so much that you run screaming from the store. This strategy is based on research proving that "the rate of exposure is

See Chapter 3 for tips on how to frame quotations.

5

directly related to the rate of sale of merchandise." In other words, the more you see, the more you buy. Supermarkets dearly wish they could expose you to every single item they carry, every time you shop. Terrific as that might be for your walking regimen, you are unlikely to endure having to trek through interminable aisles to find the few items you came in for—and retailers know it. This conflict creates a serious dilemma for the stores. They have to figure out how to get you to walk up and down those aisles for as long as possible, but not so long that you get frustrated. To resolve the dilemma, the stores make some compromises—but as few as possible. Overall, supermarket design follows fundamental rules, all of them based firmly on extensive research.

- Place the highest-selling food departments in the parts of the store that get the greatest flow of traffic—the periphery. Perishables—meat, produce, dairy, and frozen foods—generate the most sales, so put them against the back and side walls.
- Use the aisle nearest the entrance for items that sell especially well on impulse or look or smell enticing—produce, flowers, or freshly baked bread, for example. These must be the first things customers see in front or immediately to the left or right (the direction, according to researchers, doesn't matter).
- Use displays at the ends of aisles for high-profit, heavily advertised items likely to be bought on impulse.
- Place high-profit, center-aisle food items sixty inches above the floor where they are easily seen by adults, with or without eyeglasses.
- Devote as much shelf space as possible to brands that generate frequent sales; the more shelf space they occupy, the better they sell.

- Place store brands immediately to the right of those high-traffic items (people read from left to right), so that the name brands attract shoppers to the store brands too.
- Avoid using "islands." These make people bump into each other and want to move on. Keep the traffic moving, but slowly.
- Do not create gaps in the aisles that allow customers to cross over to the next one unless the aisles are so long that shoppers complain. If shoppers can escape mid-aisle, they will miss seeing half the products along that route.

Additional principles, equally well researched, guide every other aspect of supermarket design: product selection, placement on shelves, and display. The guiding principle of supermarket layout is the same: products seen most sell best. Think of the supermarket as a particularly intense real estate market in which every product competes fiercely against every other for precious space. Because you can see products most easily at eye level, at the ends of aisles, and at the checkout counters, these areas are prime real estate. Which products get the prime space? The obvious answer: the ones most profitable for the store.

But store profitability is not simply a matter of the price charged for a product compared to its costs. Stores also collect revenue by "renting" real estate to the companies whose products they sell. Product placement depends on a system of "incentives" that sometimes sound suspiciously like bribes. Food companies pay supermarkets "slotting fees" for the shelf space they occupy. The rates are highest for premium, high-traffic space, such as the shelves near cash registers. Supermarkets demand and get additional sources of revenue from food companies in "trade allowances," guarantees that companies will buy local advertising for the products for which they pay slotting fees. The local advertising, of course, helps to make sure that products in prime real estate sell quickly.

This unsavory system puts retail food stores in firm control of the marketplace. They make the decisions about which products to sell and, therefore, which products you buy. This system goes beyond a simple matter of supply and demand. The stores *create* demand by putting some products where you cannot miss them. These are often "junk" foods full of cheap, shelf-stable ingredients like hydrogenated oils and corn sweeteners, made and promoted by giant food companies that can afford slotting fees, trade allowances, and advertising. This is why entire aisles of prime supermarket real estate are devoted to soft drinks, salty snacks, and sweetened breakfast cereals, and why you can always find candy next to cash registers. Any new product that comes into a store must come with guaranteed advertising, coupons, discounts, slotting fees, and other such incentives.

Slotting fees emerged in the 1980s as a way for stores to cover the added costs of dealing with new products: shelving, tracking inventory, and removing products that do not sell. But the system is so corrupt and so secret that Congress held hearings about it in 1999. The industry people who testified at those hearings were so afraid of retribution that they wore hoods and used gadgets to prevent voice recognition. The General Accounting Office, the congressional watchdog agency (now called the Government Accountability Office), was asked to do its own investigation but got nowhere because the retail food industry refused to cooperate.

The defense of the current system by both the retailers who 10 demand the fees and the companies that agree to pay them comes at a high cost—out of your pocket. You pay for this system in at least three ways: higher prices at the supermarket;

taxes that in part compensate for business tax deductions that food companies are allowed to take for slotting fees and advertising; and the costs of treating illnesses that might result from consuming more profitable but less healthful food products.

In 2005, supermarkets sold more than $350 billion worth of food in the United States, but this level of sales does not stop them from complaining about low after-tax profit margins— just 1 to 3 percent of sales. One percent of $350 billion is $3.5 billion, of course, but by some corporate standards that amount is too little to count. In any case, corporations have to grow to stay viable, so corporate pressures on supermarkets to increase sales are unrelenting. The best way to expand sales, say researchers, is to increase the size of the selling area and the number of items offered. Supermarkets do both. In the last de cade, mergers and acquisitions have turned the top-ranking supermarkets—Kroger, Albertsons, and Safeway— into companies with annual sales of $56, $40, and $36 billion, respectively. Small chains, like Whole Foods and Wegmans, have sales in the range of just $4 billion a year.

But sales brought in by these small chains are peanuts compared to those of the store that now dominates the entire retail food marketplace: Wal-Mart. Wal-Mart sold $284 billion worth of goods in 2005. Groceries accounted for about one-quarter of that amount, but that meant $64 billion, and rising. Many food companies do a third of their business with this one retailer. Wal-Mart does not have to demand slotting fees. If a food company wants its products to be in Wal-Mart, it has to offer rock-bottom prices. Low prices sound good for people without much money, but nutritionally, there's a catch. Low prices encourage everyone to buy more food in bigger packages. If you buy more, you are quite likely to eat more. And if you eat more, you are more likely to gain weight and become less healthy.

Food retailers argue that if you eat too much it is your problem, not theirs. But they are in the business of encouraging you to buy more food, not less. Take the matter of package size and price. I often talk to business groups about such matters and at a program for food executives at Cornell University, I received a barrage of questions about where personal responsibility fits into this picture. One supermarket manager insisted that his store does not force customers to buy Pepsi in big bottles. He also offers Pepsi in 8-ounce cans. The sizes and prices are best shown in a Table.

PRICE OF PEPSI-COLA, P&C MARKET,
ITHACA, NEW YORK, JULY 2005

Container Size	Total Ounces	Price	Price per Quart
2-liter bottle	67	$1.49	$0.71
24-ounce bottles (6-pack)	144	$3.00*	$0.67
16-ounce bottles (6-pack)	96	$2.99	$1.00
12-ounce cans (12-pack)	144	$4.49	$1.00
8-ounce cans (6-pack)	48	$2.25	$1.50

*This is with a P&C store membership "Wild Card."

In this store, the 2-liter container and the special-for-members 6-pack of 24-ounce bottles were less than half the cost of the equivalent volume in 8-ounce cans. Supermarket managers tell me that this kind of pricing is not the store's problem. If you want smaller sizes, you should be willing to pay more for them. But if you care about how much you get for a price, you are likely to pick the larger sizes. And if you buy the larger sizes, you are likely to drink more Pepsi and take in more calories; the 8-ounce cans of Pepsi contain 100 calories each, but the 2-liter bottle holds 800 calories.

Sodas of any size are cheap because they are mostly water 15
and corn sweeteners—water is practically free, and your taxes

pay to subsidize corn production. This makes the cost of the ingredients trivial compared to labor and packaging, so the larger sizes are more profitable to the manufacturer and to the stores. The choice is yours, but anyone would have a hard time choosing a more expensive version of a product when a cheaper one is right there. Indeed, you have to be strong and courageous to hold out for healthier choices in the supermarket system as it currently exists.

You could, of course, bring a shopping list, but good luck sticking to it. Research says that about 70 percent of shoppers bring lists into supermarkets, but only about 10 percent adhere to them. Even with a list, most shoppers pick up two additional items for every item on it. The additions are "in-store decisions," or impulse buys. Stores directly appeal to your senses to distract you from worrying about lists. They hope you will:

- Listen to the background music. The slower the beat, the longer you will tarry.
- Search for the "loss leaders" (the items you always need, like meat, coffee, or bananas, that are offered at or below their actual cost). The longer you search, the more products you will see.
- Go to the bakery, prepared foods, and deli sections; the sights and good smells will keep you lingering and encourage sales.
- Taste the samples that companies are giving away. If you like what you taste, you are likely to buy it.
- Put your kids in the play areas; the longer they play there, the more time you have to walk those tempting aisles.

If you find yourself in a supermarket buying on impulse and not minding it a bit, you are behaving exactly the way store managers want you to. You will be buying the products they have worked long and hard to make most attractive and convenient for you—and most profitable for them.

Joining the Conversation

1. The title of this essay tells us the topic: supermarkets. The subtitle adds some metacommentary, telling us Nestle's main point. What is the main point?
2. Why, according to Nestle, do supermarket chains invest so heavily in consumer research? What does she claim are the results of this research? Give two or three examples from her text.
3. Writers often use metacommentary to explain something they've said, to elaborate on an idea, or to offer other such guidance. Paragraph 5 includes two examples of metacommentary, in the second and fourth sentences. What purposes do these sentences serve? Find several other instances of metacommentary in this essay and explain their purposes. See Chapter 10 for more on metacommentary.
4. According to Nestle, food retailers say that if we eat too much, it's our problem, "not theirs." What do you think David Zinczenko would say to that (pp. 462–65)?
5. Reread Nestle's article and then do some of your own field research. Visit a supermarket and see if Nestle's observations hold true: what's the first thing you see? What products are at the end of the aisles? Which ones are at eye level? Is there music with a slow beat—and if so, does it make you linger? Then write an essay agreeing, disagreeing, or both agreeing and disagreeing with Nestle. If you agree, you'll still need to bring something new to the conversation, drawing from your own observations or insights.

How Junk Food Can End Obesity

DAVID H. FREEDMAN

—◻—

Demonizing processed food may be dooming many to obesity and disease. Could embracing the drive-thru make us all healthier?

LATE LAST YEAR, in a small health-food eatery called Cafe Sprouts in Oberlin, Ohio, I had what may well have been the most wholesome beverage of my life. The friendly server patiently guided me to an apple-blueberry-kale-carrot smoothie-juice combination, which she spent the next several minutes preparing, mostly by shepherding farm-fresh produce into machinery. The result was tasty, but at 300 calories (by my rough calculation) in a 16-ounce cup, it was more than my diet could regularly absorb without consequences, nor was I about to make a habit of $9 shakes, healthy or not.

———

DAVID H. FREEDMAN is the author of *Wrong: Why Experts Keep Failing Us—and How to Know When Not to Trust Them* (2010) and the coauthor, with Eric Abrahamson, of *A Perfect Mess: The Hidden Benefits of Disorder* (2007). He is a contributing editor at the *Atlantic* and *Inc.* magazines and is widely published on issues relating to science, technology, and health care. He blogs at fatandskinner.org. This essay first appeared in the July/August 2013 issue of the *Atlantic*.

Inspired by the experience nonetheless, I tried again two months later at L.A.'s Real Food Daily, a popular vegan restaurant near Hollywood. I was initially wary of a low-calorie juice made almost entirely from green vegetables, but the server assured me it was a popular treat. I like to brag that I can eat anything, and I scarf down all sorts of raw vegetables like candy, but I could stomach only about a third of this oddly foamy, bitter concoction. It smelled like lawn clippings and tasted like liquid celery. It goes for $7.95, and I waited 10 minutes for it.

I finally hit the sweet spot just a few weeks later, in Chicago, with a delicious blueberry-pomegranate smoothie that rang in at a relatively modest 220 calories. It cost $3 and took only seconds to make. Best of all, I'll be able to get this concoction just about anywhere. Thanks, McDonald's!

If only the McDonald's smoothie weren't, unlike the first two, so fattening and unhealthy. Or at least that's what the most-prominent voices in our food culture today would have you believe.

An enormous amount of media space has been dedicated 5 to promoting the notion that all processed food, and only processed food, is making us sickly and overweight. In this narrative, the food-industrial complex—particularly the fast-food industry—has turned all the powers of food-processing science loose on engineering its offerings to addict us to fat, sugar, and salt, causing or at least heavily contributing to the obesity crisis. The wares of these pimps and pushers, we are told, are to be universally shunned.

Consider the *New York Times*. Earlier this year, the *Times Magazine* gave its cover to a long piece based on Michael Moss's about-to-be-best-selling book, *Salt Sugar Fat: How the Food Giants Hooked Us*. Hitting bookshelves at about the same time was the former *Times* reporter Melanie Warner's *Pandora's Lunchbox: How Processed Food Took Over the American Meal*, which addresses more or less the same theme. Two years ago the *Times Magazine* featured the journalist Gary Taubes's "Is Sugar Toxic?," a cover story on the evils of refined sugar and high-fructose corn syrup. And most significant of all has been the considerable space the magazine has devoted over the years to Michael Pollan, a journalism professor at the University of California at Berkeley, and his broad indictment of food processing as a source of society's health problems.

"The food they're cooking is making people sick," Pollan has said of big food companies. "It is one of the reasons that we have the obesity and diabetes epidemics that we do. . . . If you're going to let industries decide how much salt, sugar and fat is in your food, they're going to put [in] as much as they possibly can. . . . They will push those buttons until we scream or die." The solution, in his view, is to replace Big Food's engineered, edible evil—through public education and regulation—with fresh, unprocessed, local, seasonal, *real* food.

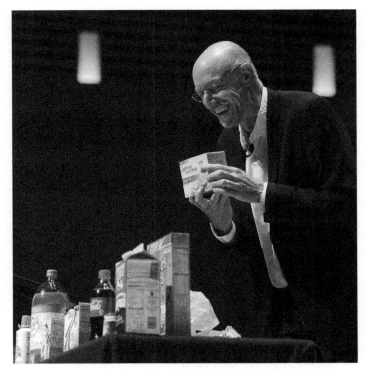

Michael Pollan

Pollan's worldview saturates the public conversation on healthy eating. You hear much the same from many scientists, physicians, food activists, nutritionists, celebrity chefs, and pundits. *Foodlike substances,* the derisive term Pollan uses to describe processed foods, is now a solid part of the elite vernacular. Thousands of restaurants and grocery stores, most notably the Whole Foods chain, have thrived by answering the call to reject industrialized foods in favor of a return to natural, simple, nonindustrialized—let's call them "wholesome"—foods.

The two newest restaurants in my smallish Massachusetts town both prominently tout wholesome ingredients; one of them is called the Farmhouse, and it's usually packed.

A new generation of business, social, and policy entrepreneurs is rising to further cater to these tastes, and to challenge Big Food. Silicon Valley, where tomorrow's entrepreneurial and social trends are forged, has spawned a small ecosystem of wholesome-friendly venture-capital firms (Physic Ventures, for example), business accelerators (Local Food Lab), and Web sites (Edible Startups) to fund, nurture, and keep tabs on young companies such as blissmo (a wholesome-food-of-the-month club), Mile High Organics (online wholesome-food shopping), and Wholeshare (group wholesome-food purchasing), all designed to help reacquaint Americans with the simpler eating habits of yesteryear.

In virtually every realm of human existence, we turn to technology to help us solve our problems. But even in Silicon Valley, when it comes to food and obesity, technology—or at least food-processing technology—is widely treated as if it *is* the problem. The solution, from this viewpoint, necessarily involves turning our back on it.

If the most-influential voices in our food culture today get their way, we will achieve a genuine food revolution. Too bad it would be one tailored to the dubious health fantasies of a small, elite minority. And too bad it would largely exclude the obese masses, who would continue to sicken and die early. Despite the best efforts of a small army of wholesome-food heroes, there is no reasonable scenario under which these foods could become cheap and plentiful enough to serve as the core diet for most of the obese population—even in the unlikely case that your typical junk-food eater would be willing and able to break lifelong habits to embrace kale and yellow beets. And many of the dishes glorified by the wholesome-food movement are, in any case, as caloric and obesogenic as anything served in a Burger King.

Through its growing sway over health-conscious consumers and policy makers, the wholesome-food movement is impeding the progress of the one segment of the food world that is actually positioned to take effective, near-term steps to reverse the obesity trend: the processed-food industry. Popular food producers, fast-food chains among them, are already applying various tricks and technologies to create less caloric and more satiating versions of their junky fare that nonetheless retain much of the appeal of the originals, and could be induced to go much further. In fact, these roundly demonized companies could do far more for the public's health in five years than the wholesome-food movement is likely to accomplish in the next 50. But will the wholesome-food advocates let them?

Michael Pollan Has No Clothes

Let's go shopping. We can start at Whole Foods Market, a critical link in the wholesome-eating food chain. There are three Whole Foods stores within 15 minutes of my house—we're big on real food in the suburbs west of Boston. Here at the largest of the three, I can choose from more than 21 types of tofu, 62 bins of organic grains and legumes, and 42 different salad greens.

Much of the food isn't all that different from what I can get in any other supermarket, but sprinkled throughout are items that scream "wholesome." One that catches my eye today, sitting prominently on an impulse-buy rack near the checkout counter, is Vegan Cheesy Salad Booster, from Living Intentions, whose package emphasizes the fact that the food is enhanced with spirulina, chlorella, and sea vegetables. The label also proudly lets me know that the contents are raw—no processing!—and that they don't contain any genetically modified ingredients. What the stuff does contain, though, is more than three times the fat content per ounce as the beef patty in a Big Mac (more than two-thirds of the calories come from fat), and four times the sodium.

After my excursion to Whole Foods, I drive a few minutes 15 to a Trader Joe's, also known for an emphasis on wholesome foods. Here at the register I'm confronted with a large display of a snack food called "Inner Peas," consisting of peas that are breaded in cornmeal and rice flour, fried in sunflower oil, and then sprinkled with salt. By weight, the snack has six times as much fat as it does protein, along with loads of carbohydrates. I can't recall ever seeing anything at any fast-food restaurant that represents as big an obesogenic crime against the vegetable kingdom. (A spokesperson for Trader Joe's said the company does not consider itself a "'wholesome food' grocery retailer." Living Intentions did not respond to a request for comment.)

This phenomenon is by no means limited to packaged food at upscale supermarkets. Back in February, when I was at Real Food Daily in Los Angeles, I ordered the "Sea Cake" along with my green-vegetable smoothie. It was intensely delicious in a way that set off alarm bells. RFD wouldn't provide precise information about the ingredients, but I found a recipe online for "Tofu 'Fish' Cakes," which seem very close to what I ate. Essentially, they consist of some tofu mixed with a lot of refined carbs (the RFD version contains at least some unrefined carbs) along with oil and soy milk, all fried in oil and served with a soy-and-oil-based tartar sauce. (Tofu and other forms of soy are high in protein, but per 100 calories, tofu is as fatty as many cuts of beef.) L.A. being to the wholesome-food movement what Hawaii is to Spam, I ate at two other mega-popular wholesome-food restaurants while I was in the area. At Café Gratitude

I enjoyed the kale chips and herb-cornmeal-crusted eggplant parmesan, and at Akasha I indulged in a spiced-lamb-sausage flatbread pizza. Both are pricey orgies of fat and carbs.

I'm not picking out rare, less healthy examples from these establishments. Check out their menus online: fat, sugar, and other refined carbs abound. (Café Gratitude says it uses only "healthy" fats and natural sweeteners; Akasha says its focus is not on "health food" but on "farm to fork" fare.) In fact, because the products and dishes offered by these types of establishments tend to emphasize the healthy-sounding foods they contain, I find it much harder to navigate through them to foods that go easy on the oil, butter, refined grains, rice, potatoes, and sugar than I do at far less wholesome restaurants. (These dishes also tend to contain plenty of sea salt, which Pollanites hold up as the wholesome alternative to the addictive salt engineered by the food industry, though your body can't tell the difference.)

One occasional source of obesogenic travesties is the *New York Times Magazine's* lead food writer, Mark Bittman, who now rivals Pollan as a shepherd to the anti-processed-food flock. (*Salon,* in an article titled "How to Live What Michael Pollan Preaches," called Bittman's 2009 book, *Food Matters,* "both a cookbook and a manifesto that shows us how to eat better—and save the planet.") I happened to catch Bittman on the *Today* show last year demonstrating for millions of viewers four ways to prepare corn in summertime, including a lovely dish of corn sautéed in bacon fat and topped with bacon. Anyone who thinks that such a thing is much healthier than a Whopper just hasn't been paying attention to obesity science for the past few decades.

That science is, in fact, fairly straightforward. Fat carries more than twice as many calories as carbohydrates and proteins do per gram, which means just a little fat can turn a serving of food into a calorie bomb. Sugar and other refined carbohydrates,

Mark Bittman demonstrates cooking on the *Today* show.

like white flour and rice, and high-starch foods, like corn and potatoes, aren't as calorie-dense. But all of these "problem carbs" charge into the bloodstream as glucose in minutes, providing an energy rush, commonly followed by an energy crash that can lead to a surge in appetite.

Because they are energy-intense foods, fat and sugar and other problem carbs trip the pleasure and reward meters placed in our brains by evolution over the millions of years during which starvation was an ever-present threat. We're born enjoying the stimulating sensations these ingredients provide, and exposure strengthens the associations, ensuring that we come to crave them and, all too often, eat more of them than we should. Processed food is not an essential part of this story: recent examinations of ancient human remains in Egypt, Peru, and elsewhere have repeatedly revealed hardened arteries, suggesting that pre-industrial diets, at least of the affluent, may not have been the epitome of healthy eating that the Pollanites

20

make them out to be. People who want to lose weight and keep it off are almost always advised by those who run successful long-term weight-loss programs to transition to a diet high in lean protein, complex carbs such as whole grains and legumes, and the sort of fiber vegetables are loaded with. Because these ingredients provide us with the calories we need without the big, fast bursts of energy, they can be satiating without pushing the primitive reward buttons that nudge us to eat too much.

(A few words on salt: Yes, it's unhealthy in large amounts, raising blood pressure in many people; and yes, it makes food more appealing. But salt is not obesogenic—it has no calories, and doesn't specifically increase the desire to consume high-calorie foods. It can just as easily be enlisted to add to the appeal of vegetables. Lumping it in with fat and sugar as an addictive junk-food ingredient is a confused proposition. But let's agree we want to cut down on it.) See Chapter 6 for ways to anticipate objections.

To be sure, many of Big Food's most popular products are loaded with appalling amounts of fat and sugar and other problem carbs (as well as salt), and the plentitude of these ingredients, exacerbated by large portion sizes, has clearly helped foment the obesity crisis. It's hard to find anyone anywhere who disagrees. Junk food is bad for you because it's full of fat and problem carbs. But will switching to wholesome foods free us from this scourge? It could in theory, but in practice, it's hard to see how. Even putting aside for a moment the serious questions about whether wholesome foods could be made accessible to the obese public, and whether the obese would be willing to eat them, we have a more immediate stumbling block: many of the foods served up and even glorified by the wholesome-food movement are themselves chock full of fat and problem carbs.

Some wholesome foodies openly celebrate fat and problem carbs, insisting that the lack of processing magically renders them healthy. In singing the praises of clotted cream and lard-loaded cookies, for instance, a recent *Wall Street Journal* article by Ron Rosenbaum explained that "eating basic, earthy, fatty foods isn't just a supreme experience of the senses—it can actually be good for you," and that it's "too easy to conflate eating fatty food with eating industrial, oil-fried junk food." That's right, we wouldn't want to make the same mistake that all the cells in our bodies make. Pollan himself makes it clear in his writing that he has little problem with fat—as long as it's not in food "your great-grandmother wouldn't recognize."

Television food shows routinely feature revered chefs tossing around references to healthy eating, "wellness," and farm-fresh ingredients, all the while spooning lard, cream, and sugar over everything in sight. (A study published last year in the *British Medical Journal* found that the recipes in the books of top TV chefs call for "significantly more" fat per portion than what's contained in ready-to-eat supermarket meals.) Corporate wellness programs, one of the most promising avenues for getting the population to adopt healthy behaviors, are falling prey to this way of thinking as well. Last November, I attended a stress-management seminar for employees of a giant consulting company, and listened to a high-powered professional wellness coach tell the crowded room that it's okay to eat anything as long as its plant or animal origins aren't obscured by processing. Thus, she explained, potato chips are perfectly healthy, because they plainly come from potatoes, but Cheetos will make you sick and fat, because what plant or animal is a Cheeto? (For the record, typical potato chips and Cheetos have about equally nightmarish amounts of fat calories per ounce; Cheetos have fewer carbs, though more salt.)

The Pollanites seem confused about exactly what benefits [25] their way of eating provides. All the railing about the fat, sugar, and salt engineered into industrial junk food might lead one to infer that wholesome food, having not been engineered, contains substantially less of them. But clearly you can take in obscene quantities of fat and problem carbs while eating wholesomely, and to judge by what's sold at wholesome stores and restaurants, many people do. Indeed, the more converts and customers the wholesome-food movement's purveyors seek, the stronger their incentive to emphasize foods that light up precisely the same pleasure centers as a 3 Musketeers bar. That just makes wholesome food stealthily obesogenic.

Hold on, you may be thinking. Leaving fat, sugar, and salt aside, what about all the nasty things that wholesome foods do not, by definition, contain and processed foods do? A central claim of the wholesome-food movement is that wholesome is healthier because it doesn't have the artificial flavors, preservatives, other additives, or genetically modified ingredients found in industrialized food; because it isn't subjected to the physical transformations that processed foods go through; and because it doesn't sit around for days, weeks, or months, as industrialized food sometimes does. (This is the complaint against the McDonald's smoothie, which contains artificial flavors and texture additives, and which is pre-mixed.)

The health concerns raised about processing itself—rather than the amount of fat and problem carbs in any given dish—are not, by and large, related to weight gain or obesity. That's important to keep in mind, because obesity is, by an enormous margin, the largest health problem created by what we eat. But even putting that aside, concerns about processed food have been magnified out of all proportion.

Some studies have shown that people who eat wholesomely tend to be healthier than people who live on fast food and other processed food (particularly meat), but the problem with such studies is obvious: substantial nondietary differences exist between these groups, such as propensity to exercise, smoking rates, air quality, access to health care, and much more. (Some researchers say they've tried to control for these factors, but that's a claim most scientists don't put much faith in.) What's more, the people in these groups are sometimes eating entirely different foods, not the same sorts of foods subjected to different levels of processing. It's comparing apples to Whoppers, instead of Whoppers to hand-ground, grass-fed-beef burgers with heirloom tomatoes, garlic aioli, and artisanal cheese. For all these reasons, such findings linking food type and health are considered highly unreliable, and constantly contradict one another, as is true of most epidemiological studies that try to tackle broad nutritional questions.

The fact is, there is simply no clear, credible evidence that any aspect of food processing or storage makes a food uniquely unhealthy. The U.S. population does not suffer from a critical lack of any nutrient because we eat so much processed food. (Sure, health experts urge Americans to get more calcium, potassium, magnesium, fiber, and vitamins A, E, and C, and eating more produce and dairy is a great way to get them, but these ingredients are also available in processed foods, not to mention supplements.) Pollan's "foodlike substances" are regulated by the U.S. Food and Drug Administration (with some exceptions, which are regulated by other agencies), and their effects on health are further raked over by countless scientists who would get a nice career boost from turning up the hidden dangers in some common food-industry ingredient or technique, in part because any number of advocacy groups and journalists are ready to pounce on the slightest hint of risk.

The results of all the scrutiny of processed food are hardly 30 scary, although some groups and writers try to make them appear that way. The Pew Charitable Trusts' Food Additives Project, for example, has bemoaned the fact that the FDA directly reviews only about 70 percent of the ingredients found in food, permitting the rest to pass as "generally recognized as safe" by panels of experts convened by manufacturers. But the only actual risk the project calls out on its Web site or in its publications is a quote from a *Times* article noting that bromine, which has been in U.S. foods for eight decades, is regarded as suspicious by many because flame retardants containing bromine have been linked to health risks. There is no conclusive evidence that bromine itself is a threat.

In *Pandora's Lunchbox*, Melanie Warner assiduously catalogs every concern that could possibly be raised about the health threats of food processing, leveling accusations so vague, weakly supported, tired, or insignificant that only someone already convinced of the guilt of processed food could find them troubling. While ripping the covers off the breakfast-cereal conspiracy, for example, Warner reveals that much of the nutritional value claimed by these products comes not from natural ingredients but from added vitamins that are chemically synthesized, which must be bad for us because, well, they're *chemically synthesized*. It's the tautology at the heart of the movement: processed foods are unhealthy because they aren't natural, full stop.

In many respects, the wholesome-food movement veers awfully close to religion. To repeat: there is no hard evidence to back any health-risk claims about processed food—evidence, say, of the caliber of several studies by the Centers for Disease Control and Prevention that have traced food poisoning to raw milk, a product championed by some circles of the wholesome-food movement. "Until I hear evidence to the contrary, I think it's reasonable to include processed food in your diet," says Robert Kushner, a physician and nutritionist and a professor at Northwestern University's medical school, where he is the clinical director of the Comprehensive Center on Obesity.

There may be other reasons to prefer wholesome food to the industrialized version. Often stirred into the vague stew of benefits attributed to wholesome food is the "sustainability" of its production—that is, its long-term impact on the planet. Small farms that don't rely much on chemicals and heavy industrial equipment may be better for the environment than giant industrial farms—although that argument quickly becomes complicated by a variety of factors. For the purposes of this article, let's simply stipulate that wholesome foods are environmentally superior. But let's also agree that when it comes to prioritizing among food-related public-policy goals, we are likely to save and improve many more lives by focusing on cutting obesity—through any available means—than by trying to convert all of industrial agriculture into a vast constellation of small organic farms.

The impact of obesity on the chances of our living long, productive, and enjoyable lives has been so well documented at this point that I hate to drag anyone through the grim statistics again. But let me just toss out one recent dispatch from the world of obesity-havoc science: a study published in February in the journal *Obesity* found that obese young adults and middle-agers in the U.S. are likely to lose almost a decade of life on average, as compared with their non-obese counterparts. Given our obesity rates, that means Americans who are alive today can collectively expect to sacrifice 1 billion years to obesity. The study adds to a river of evidence suggesting that for the first time in modern history—and in spite of many health-related improvements in our environment, our health care, and our nondietary habits—our health prospects are worsening, mostly because of excess weight.

By all means, let's protect the environment. But let's not rule 35 out the possibility of technologically enabled improvements to our diet—indeed, let's not rule out *any* food—merely because we are pleased by images of pastoral family farms. Let's first pick the foods that can most plausibly make us healthier, all things considered, and then figure out how to make them environmentally friendly.

. . .

The Food Revolution We Need

The one fast-food restaurant near a busy East L.A. intersection otherwise filled with bodegas was a Carl's Jr. I went in and saw that the biggest and most prominent posters in the store were pushing a new grilled-cod sandwich. It actually looked pretty good, but it wasn't quite lunchtime, and I just wanted a cup of coffee. I went to the counter to order it, but before I could say anything, the cashier greeted me and asked, "Would you like to try our new Charbroiled Atlantic Cod Fish Sandwich today?" Oh, well, sure, why not? (I asked her to hold the tartar sauce, which is mostly fat, but found out later that the sandwich is normally served with about half as much tartar sauce as the notoriously fatty Filet-O-Fish sandwich at McDonald's, where the fish is battered and fried.) The sandwich was delicious. It was less than half the cost of the Sea Cake appetizer at Real Food Daily. It took less than a minute to prepare. In some ways, it was the best meal I had in L.A., and it was probably the healthiest.

We know perfectly well who within our society has developed an extraordinary facility for nudging the masses to eat certain foods, and for making those foods widely available in cheap and convenient forms. The Pollanites have led us to conflate the industrial processing of food with the adding of fat and sugar in order to hook customers, even while pushing many faux-healthy foods of their own. But why couldn't Big Food's processing and marketing genius be put to use on genuinely healthier foods, like grilled fish? Putting aside the standard objection that the industry has no interest in doing so—we'll see later that in fact the industry has plenty of motivation for taking on this challenge—wouldn't that present a more plausible answer to America's junk-food problem than ordering up 50,000 new farmers' markets featuring locally grown organic squash blossoms?

According to Lenard Lesser, of the Palo Alto Medical Foundation, the food industry has mastered the art of using in-store and near-store promotions to shape what people eat. As Lesser and I drove down storied Telegraph Avenue in Berkeley and into far less affluent Oakland, leaving behind the Whole Foods Markets and sushi restaurants for gas-station markets and barbecued-rib stands, he pointed out the changes in the billboards. Whereas the last one we saw in Berkeley was for fruit juice, many in Oakland tout fast-food joints and their wares, including several featuring the Hot Mess Burger at Jack in the Box. Though Lesser noted that this forest of advertising may simply reflect Oakland residents' preexisting preference for this type of food, he told me lab studies have indicated that the more signs you show people for a particular food product or dish, the more likely they are to choose it over others, all else being equal.

We went into a KFC and found ourselves traversing a maze of signage that put us face-to-face with garish images of various fried foods that presumably had some chicken somewhere deep inside them. "The more they want you to buy something, the bigger they make the image on the menu board," Lesser explained. Here, what loomed largest was the $19.98 fried-chicken-and-corn family meal, which included biscuits and cake. A few days later, I noticed that McDonald's places large placards showcasing desserts on the trash bins, apparently calculating that the best time to entice diners with sweets is when they think they've finished their meals.

Trying to get burger lovers to jump to grilled fish may already 40 be a bit of a stretch—I didn't see any of a dozen other customers buy the cod sandwich when I was at Carl's Jr., though the cashier said it was selling reasonably well. Still, given the food industry's power to tinker with and market food, we should not dismiss its ability to get unhealthy eaters—slowly, incrementally—to buy better food.

That brings us to the crucial question: Just how much healthier could fast-food joints and processed-food companies make their best-selling products without turning off customers? I put that question to a team of McDonald's executives, scientists, and chefs who are involved in shaping the company's future menus, during a February visit to McDonald's surprisingly bucolic campus west of Chicago. By way of a partial answer, the team served me up a preview tasting of two major new menu items that had been under development in their test kitchens and high-tech sensory-testing labs for the past year, and which were rolled out to the public in April. The first was the Egg

White Delight McMuffin ($2.65), a lower-calorie, less fatty version of the Egg McMuffin, with some of the refined flour in the original recipe replaced by whole-grain flour. The other was one of three new Premium McWraps ($3.99), crammed with grilled chicken and spring mix, and given a light coating of ranch dressing amped up with rice vinegar. Both items tasted pretty good (as do the versions in stores, I've since confirmed, though some outlets go too heavy on the dressing). And they were both lower in fat, sugar, and calories than not only many McDonald's staples, but also much of the food served in wholesome restaurants or touted in wholesome cookbooks.

In fact, McDonald's has quietly been making healthy changes for years, shrinking portion sizes, reducing some fats, trimming average salt content by more than 10 percent in the past couple of years alone, and adding fruits, vegetables, low-fat dairy, and oatmeal to its menu. In May, the chain dropped its Angus third-pounders and announced a new line of quarter-pound burgers, to be served on buns containing whole grains. Outside the core fast-food customer base, Americans are becoming more health-conscious. Public backlash against fast food could lead to regulatory efforts, and in any case, the fast-food industry has every incentive to maintain broad appeal. "We think a lot about how we can bring nutritionally balanced meals that include enough protein, along with the tastes and satisfaction that have an appetite-tiding effect," said Barbara Booth, the company's director of sensory science.

Such steps are enormously promising, says Jamy Ard, an epidemiology and preventive-medicine researcher at Wake Forest Baptist Medical Center in Winston-Salem, North Carolina, and a co-director of the Weight Management Center there. "Processed food is a key part of our environment, and it needs to be part of the equation," he explains. "If you can reduce fat and calories by only a small amount in a Big Mac, it still won't be a health food, but it wouldn't be as bad, and that could have a huge impact on us." Ard, who has been working for more than a decade with the obese poor, has little patience with the wholesome-food movement's call to eliminate fast food in favor of farm-fresh goods. "It's really naive," he says. "Fast food became popular because it's tasty and convenient and cheap. It makes a lot more sense to look for small, beneficial changes in that food than it does to hold out for big changes in what people eat that have no realistic chance of happening."

According to a recent study, Americans get 11 percent of their calories, on average, from fast food—a number that's almost certainly much higher among the less affluent over-weight. As a result, the fast-food industry may be uniquely positioned to improve our diets. Research suggests that calorie counts in a meal can be trimmed by as much as 30 percent without eaters noticing—by, for example, reducing portion sizes and swapping in ingredients that contain more fiber and water. Over time, that could be much more than enough to literally tip the scales for many obese people. "The difference between losing weight and not losing weight," says Robert Kushner, the obesity scientist and clinical director at Northwestern, "is a few hundred calories a day."

Which raises a question: If McDonald's is taking these sorts 45 of steps, albeit in a slow and limited way, why isn't it more loudly saying so to deflect criticism? While the company has heavily plugged the debut of its new egg-white sandwich and chicken wraps, the ads have left out even a mention of health, the reduced calories and fat, or the inclusion of whole grains. McDonald's has practically kept secret the fact that it has also begun substituting whole-grain flour for some of the less healthy refined flour in its best-selling Egg McMuffin.

The explanation can be summed up in two words that surely strike fear into the hearts of all fast-food executives who hope to make their companies' fare healthier: McLean Deluxe.

Among those who gleefully rank such things, the McLean Deluxe reigns as McDonald's worst product failure of all time, eclipsing McPasta, the McHotdog, and the McAfrica (don't ask). When I brought up the McLean Deluxe to the innovation team at McDonald's, I faced the first and only uncomfortable silence of the day. Finally, Greg Watson, a senior vice president, cleared his throat and told me that neither he nor anyone else in the room was at the company at the time, and he didn't know that much about it. "It sounds to me like it was ahead of its time," he added. "If we had something like that in the future, we would never launch it like that again."

Introduced in 1991, the McLean Deluxe was perhaps the boldest single effort the food industry has ever undertaken to shift the masses to healthier eating. It was supposed to be a healthier version of the Quarter Pounder, made with extra-lean beef infused with seaweed extract. It reportedly did reasonably well in early taste tests—for what it's worth, my wife and I were big fans—and McDonald's pumped the reduced-fat angle to the public for all it was worth. The general reaction varied from lack of interest to mockery to revulsion. The company gamely flogged the sandwich for five years before quietly removing it from the menu.

The McLean Deluxe was a sharp lesson to the industry, even if in some ways it merely confirmed what generations of parents have well known: if you want to turn off otherwise eager eaters to a dish, tell them it's good for them. Recent studies suggest that calorie counts placed on menus have a negligible effect on food choices, and that the less-health-conscious might even use the information to steer clear of low-calorie fare—perhaps assuming that it tastes worse and is less satisfying, and that it's worse value for their money. The result is a sense in the food industry that if it is going to sell healthier versions of its foods to the general public—and not just to that minority already sold on healthier eating—it is going to have to do it in a relatively sneaky way, emphasizing the taste appeal and not the health benefits. "People expect something to taste worse if they believe it's healthy," says Charles Spence, an Oxford University neuroscientist who specializes in how the brain perceives food. "And that expectation affects how it tastes to them, so it actually *does* taste worse."

Thus McDonald's silence on the nutritional profiles of its new menu items. "We're not making any health claims," 50

Watson said. "We're just saying it's new, it tastes great, come on in and enjoy it. Maybe once the product is well seated with customers, we'll change that message." If customers learn that they can eat healthier foods at McDonald's without even realizing it, he added, they'll be more likely to try healthier foods there than at other restaurants. The same reasoning presumably explains why the promotions and ads for the Carl's Jr. grilled-cod sandwich offer not a word related to healthfulness, and why there wasn't a whiff of health cheerleading surrounding the turkey burger brought out earlier this year by Burger King (which is not yet calling the sandwich a permanent addition).

If the food industry is to quietly sell healthier products to its mainstream, mostly non-health-conscious customers, it must find ways to deliver the eating experience that fat and problem carbs provide in foods that have fewer of those ingredients. There is no way to do that with farm-fresh produce and wholesome meat, other than reducing portion size. But processing technology gives the food industry a potent tool for trimming unwanted ingredients while preserving the sensations they deliver.

I visited Fona International, a flavor-engineering company also outside Chicago, and learned that there are a battery of tricks for fooling and appeasing taste buds, which are prone to notice a lack of fat or sugar, or the presence of any of the various bitter, metallic, or otherwise unpleasant flavors that vegetables, fiber, complex carbs, and fat or sugar substitutes can impart to a food intended to appeal to junk-food eaters. Some 5,000 FDA-approved chemical compounds—which represent the base components of all known flavors—line the shelves that run alongside Fona's huge labs. Armed with these ingredients and an array of state-of-the-art chemical-analysis and testing tools, Fona's scientists and engineers can precisely control flavor perception. "When you reduce the sugar, fat, and salt in foods, you change the personality of the product," said Robert Sobel, a chemist, who heads up research at the company. "We can restore it."

For example, fat "cushions" the release of various flavors on the tongue, unveiling them gradually and allowing them to linger. When fat is removed, flavors tend to immediately inundate the tongue and then quickly flee, which we register as a much less satisfying experience. Fona's experts can reproduce the "temporal profile" of the flavors in fattier foods by adding edible compounds derived from plants that slow the release of flavor molecules; by replacing the flavors with similarly flavored compounds that come on and leave more slowly; or by enlisting "phantom aromas" that create the sensation of certain tastes even when those tastes are not present on the tongue. (For example, the smell of vanilla can essentially mask reductions in sugar of up to 25 percent.) One triumph of this sort of engineering is the modern protein drink, a staple of many successful weight-loss programs and a favorite of those trying to build muscle. "Seven years ago they were unpalatable," Sobel said. "Today we can mask the astringent flavors and eggy aromas by adding natural ingredients."

I also visited Tic Gums in White Marsh, Maryland, a company that engineers textures into food products. Texture hasn't received the attention that flavor has, noted Greg Andon, Tic's boyish and ebullient president, whose family has run the company for three generations. The result, he said, is that even people in the food industry don't have an adequate vocabulary for it. "They know what flavor you're referring to when you say 'forest floor,' but all they can say about texture is 'Can you make it more creamy?'" So Tic is inventing a vocabulary, breaking textures down according to properties such as "mouth coating" and "mouth clearing." Wielding an arsenal of some 20 different "gums"—edible ingredients mostly found in tree sap, seeds, and other plant matter—Tic's researchers can make low-fat foods taste, well, creamier; give the same full body that sugared drinks offer to sugar-free beverages; counter chalkiness and gloopiness; and help orchestrate the timing of flavor bursts. (Such approaches have nothing in common with the ill-fated Olestra, a fat-like compound engineered to pass undigested through the body, and billed in the late 1990s as a fat substitute in snack foods. It was made notorious by widespread anecdotal complaints of cramps and loose bowels, though studies seemed to contradict those claims.)

Fona and Tic, like most companies in their industry, won't 55 identify customers or product names on the record. But both firms showed me an array of foods and beverages that were under construction, so to speak, in the name of reducing calories, fat, and sugar while maintaining mass appeal. I've long hated the taste of low-fat dressing—I gave up on it a few years ago and just use vinegar—but Tic served me an in-development version of a low-fat salad dressing that was better than any I've ever had. Dozens of companies are doing similar work, as are the big food-ingredient manufacturers, such as ConAgra, whose products are in 97 percent of American homes, and whose whole-wheat flour is what McDonald's is relying on for its breakfast sandwiches. Domino Foods, the sugar manufacturer, now sells a low-calorie combination of sugar and the nonsugar sweetener stevia that has been engineered by a flavor company to mask the sort of nonsugary tastes driving many consumers away from diet beverages and the like. "Stevia has a licorice note we were able to have taken out," explains Domino Foods CEO Brian O'Malley.

High-tech anti-obesity food engineering is just warming up. Oxford's Charles Spence notes that in addition to flavors and textures, companies are investigating ways to exploit a stream of insights that have been coming out of scholarly research about the neuroscience of eating. He notes, for example, that candy companies may be able to slip healthier ingredients into candy bars without anyone noticing, simply by loading these ingredients into the middle of the bar and leaving most of the fat and sugar at the ends of the bar. "We tend to make up our minds about how something tastes from the first and last bites, and don't care as much what happens in between," he explains. Some other potentially useful gimmicks he points out: adding weight to food packaging such as yogurt containers, which convinces eaters that the contents are rich with calories, even when they're not; using chewy textures that force consumers to spend more time between bites, giving the brain a chance to register satiety; and using colors, smells, sounds, and packaging information to create the belief that foods are fatty and sweet even when they are not. Spence found, for example, that wine is perceived as 50 percent sweeter when consumed under a red light.

Researchers are also tinkering with food ingredients to boost satiety. Cargill has developed a starch derived from tapioca that gives dishes a refined-carb taste and mouthfeel, but acts more like fiber in the body—a feature that could keep the appetite from spiking later. "People usually think that processing leads to foods that digest too quickly, but we've been able to use processing to slow the digestion rate," says Bruce McGoogan, who heads R&D for Cargill's North American food-ingredient business. The company has also developed ways to reduce fat in beef patties, and to make baked goods using half the usual sugar and oil, all without heavily compromising taste and texture.

Other companies and research labs are trying to turn out healthier, more appealing foods by enlisting ultra-high pressure, nanotechnology, vacuums, and edible coatings. At the University of Massachusetts at Amherst's Center for Foods for Health and Wellness, Fergus Clydesdale, the director of the school's Food Science Policy Alliance—as well as a spry 70-something who's happy to tick off all the processed food in his diet—showed me labs where researchers are looking into possibilities that would not only attack obesity but also improve health in other significant ways, for example by isolating ingredients that might lower the risk of cancer and concentrating them in foods. "When you understand foods at the molecular level," he says, "there's a lot you can do with food and health that we're not doing now."

The Implacable Enemies of Healthier Processed Food

What's not to like about these developments? Plenty, if you've bought into the notion that processing itself is the source of the unhealthfulness of our foods. The wholesome-food movement is not only talking up dietary strategies that are unlikely to help most obese Americans; it is, in various ways, getting in the way of strategies that could work better.

The Pollanites didn't invent resistance to healthier popular foods, as the fates of the McLean Deluxe and Olestra demonstrate, but they've greatly intensified it. Fast food and junk food have their core customer base, and the wholesome-food gurus have theirs. In between sit many millions of Americans—the more the idea that processed food should be shunned no matter what takes hold in this group, the less incentive fast-food joints will have to continue edging away from the fat- and problem-carb-laden fare beloved by their most loyal customers to try to broaden their appeal.

Pollan has popularized contempt for "nutritionism," the idea behind packing healthier ingredients into processed foods. In his view, the quest to add healthier ingredients to food isn't a potential solution, it's part of the problem. Food is healthy not when it contains healthy ingredients, he argues, but when it can be traced simply and directly to (preferably local) farms. As he resonantly put it in *The Times* in 2007: "If you're concerned about your health, you should probably avoid food products that make health claims. Why? Because a health claim on a food product is a good indication that it's not really food, and food is what you want to eat."

In this way, wholesome-food advocates have managed to pre-damn the very steps we need the food industry to take, placing the industry in a no-win situation: If it maintains the status quo, then we need to stay away because its food is loaded with fat and sugar. But if it tries to moderate these ingredients, then it is deceiving us with nutritionism. Pollan explicitly counsels avoiding foods containing more than five ingredients, or any hard-to-pronounce or unfamiliar ingredients. This rule eliminates almost anything the industry could do to produce healthier foods that retain mass appeal—most of us wouldn't get past xanthan gum—and that's perfectly in keeping with his intention.

By placing wholesome eating directly at odds with healthier processed foods, the Pollanites threaten to derail the reformation of fast food just as it's starting to gain traction. At McDonald's, "Chef Dan"—that is, Dan Coudreaut, the executive chef and director of culinary innovation—told me of the dilemma the movement has caused him as he has tried to make the menu healthier. "Some want us to have healthier food, but others want us to have minimally processed ingredients, which can mean more fat," he explained. "It's becoming a balancing act for us." That the chef with arguably the most influence in the world over the diet of the obese would even consider adding fat to his menu to placate wholesome foodies is a pretty good sign that something has gone terribly wrong with our approach to the obesity crisis.

Many people insist that the steps the food industry has already taken to offer less-obesogenic fare are no more than cynical ploys to fool customers into eating the same old crap under a healthy guise. In his 3,500-word *New York Times Magazine* article on the prospects for healthier fast food, Mark Bittman lauded a new niche of vegan chain restaurants while devoting just one line to the major "quick serve" restaurants' contribution to better health: "I'm not talking about token gestures, like the McDonald's fruit-and-yogurt parfait, whose calories are more than 50 percent sugar." Never mind that 80 percent of a farm-fresh apple's calories come from sugar; that almost any obesity expert would heartily approve of the yogurt parfait as a step in the right direction for most fast-food-dessert eaters; and that many of the desserts Bittman glorifies in his own writing make the parfait look like arugula, nutrition-wise. (His recipe for corn-and-blueberry crisp, for example, calls for adding two-thirds of a cup of brown sugar to a lot of other problem carbs, along with five tablespoons of butter.)

Bittman is hardly alone in his reflexive dismissals. No sooner 65 had McDonald's and Burger King rolled out their egg-white sandwich and turkey burger, respectively, than a spate of articles popped up hooting that the new dishes weren't healthier because they trimmed a mere 50 and 100 calories from their standard counterparts, the Egg McMuffin and the Whopper. Apparently these writers didn't understand, or chose to ignore, the fact that a reduction of 50 or 100 calories in a single dish places an eater exactly on track to eliminate a few hundred calories a day from his or her diet—the critical threshold needed for long-term weight loss. Any bigger reduction would risk leaving someone too hungry to stick to a diet program. It's just the sort of small step in the right direction we should be aiming for, because the obese are much more likely to take it than they are to make a big leap to wholesome or very-low-calorie foods.

Many wholesome foodies insist that the food industry won't make serious progress toward healthier fare unless forced to by regulation. I, for one, believe regulation aimed at speeding the replacement of obesogenic foods with appealing healthier foods would be a great idea. But what a lot of foodies really want is to ban the food industry from selling junk food altogether. And that is just a fantasy. The government never managed to keep the tobacco companies from selling cigarettes, and banning booze (the third-most-deadly consumable killer after cigarettes and food) didn't turn out so well. The two most health-enlightened, regulation-friendly major cities in America, New York and San Francisco, tried to halt sales of two of the most horrific fast-food assaults on health—giant servings of sugared beverages and kids' fast-food meals accompanied by toys, respectively—and neither had much luck. Michelle Obama is excoriated by conservatives for asking schools to throw more fruits and vegetables into the lunches they serve. Realistically, the most we can hope for is a tax on some obesogenic foods. The research of Lisa Powell, a University of Illinois professor, suggests that a 20 percent tax on sugary beverages would reduce consumption by about 25 percent. (As for fatty foods, no serious tax proposal has yet been made in the U.S., and if one comes along, the wholesome foodies might well join the food industry and most consumers in opposing it. Denmark did manage to enact a fatty-food tax, but it was deemed a failure when consumers went next door into Germany and Sweden to stock up on their beloved treats.)

Continuing to call out Big Food on its unhealthy offerings, and loudly, is one of the best levers we have for pushing it toward healthier products—but let's call it out intelligently, not reflexively. Executives of giant food companies may be many things, but they are not stupid. Absent action, they risk a growing public-relations disaster, the loss of their more affluent and increasingly health-conscious customers, and the threat of regulation, which will be costly to fight, even if the new rules don't stick. Those fears are surely what's driving much of the push toward moderately healthier fare within the industry today. But if the Pollanites convince policy makers and the health-conscious public that these foods are dangerous by virtue of not being farm-fresh, that will push Big Food in a different direction (in part by limiting the profit potential it sees in lower-fat, lower-problem-carb foods), and cause it to spend its resources in other ways.

Significant regulation of junk food may not go far, but we have other tools at our disposal to prod Big Food to intensify and speed up its efforts to cut fat and problem carbs in its offerings, particularly if we're smart about it. Lenard Lesser points out that government and advocacy groups could start singling out particular restaurants and food products for praise or shaming—a more official version of "eat this, not that"—rather than sticking to a steady drumbeat of "processed food must go away." Academia could do a much better job of producing and highlighting solid research into less obesogenic, high-mass-appeal foods, and could curtail its evidence-light anti-food-processing bias, so that the next generation of social and policy entrepreneurs might work to narrow the gap between the poor obese and the well-resourced healthy instead of inadvertently widening it. We can keep pushing our health-care system to provide more incentives and support to the obese for losing weight by making small, painless, but helpful changes in their behavior, such as switching from Whoppers to turkey burgers, from Egg McMuffins to Egg White Delights, or from blueberry crisp to fruit-and-yogurt parfaits.

And we can ask the wholesome-food advocates, and those who give them voice, to make it clearer that the advice they sling is relevant mostly to the privileged healthy—and to start getting behind realistic solutions to the obesity crisis.

Joining the Conversation

1. Early in this essay, David Freedman explicitly lays out a "they say" that frames his argument. Summarize the position that he then sets out to refute.
2. What is Freedman's argument, and how does he support it? Why do you think he cites his own personal experiences? What do they contribute to his argument—and to his essay as a whole?
3. Paragraphs 30 and 31 introduce opinions that differ from Freedman's views. How fairly does he represent these opposing views, and how persuasively does he respond to what they say?
4. Freedman is particularly critical of the views of Michael Pollan (pp. 420–27). What are his specific criticisms? How do you think Pollan might respond?
5. What do you think? Could "embracing the drive-thru make us all healthier"? Write an essay responding to Freedman, saying what *you* think—and why. Draw from your own experience as well as from information in his essay in arguing for what you say.

NINETEEN

WHAT'S UP WITH
THE AMERICAN DREAM?

—⌐回⌐—

WHAT IS MORE FUNDAMENTAL to most Americans than the belief that we are the authors of our own fate—that we are in control, particularly when it comes to our economic success? We go to school, study, get jobs, and work hard, all with the assumption that doing so will allow us to achieve financial security, rise up the economic ladder, and perhaps even achieve great wealth. This faith in the American Dream, in the United States as a land of opportunity, was alive and well in 1867 when Horatio Alger Jr. published his first "rags-to-riches" novel featuring Ragged Dick, a penniless young man who works his way up from poverty to a position of respectability. But in recent times, many have wondered whether the American Dream is still achievable. Consider the image on the facing page, which originally accompanied "Of the 1%, by the 1%, for the 1%," an *Atlantic Monthly* article by the Nobel Prize–winning economist Joseph Stiglitz. Would Ragged Dick be able to work his way up into the larger of the two houses today?

Political scientist Robert Putnam wrote in 2013, "My hometown—Port Clinton, Ohio, population 6,050—was in the 1950s a passable embodiment of the American Dream, a place that offered decent opportunity for the children of bankers and factory workers alike. But a half-century later, wealthy kids park BMW convertibles in the Port Clinton High School lot next to decrepit 'junkers' in which homeless classmates live. The American Dream has turned into a split-screen nightmare." His critique and those of others raise the question of whether or not the American Dream, which has sustained us for so long, is truly in trouble.

Several of the writers in this chapter echo Putnam's concerns: in their view, the American Dream has been undermined by a combination of global economic developments and government policies that have perilously widened the gulf between the very rich and the rest of us. Paul Krugman, a Nobel Prize–winning economist, expresses a classic *liberal* position, highlighting the fact that the incomes of the wealthiest Americans have increased greatly in recent decades while middle-class incomes have remained stagnant, and offers policy recommendations to increase opportunities for all. Journalist Monica Potts looks at studies showing a significant recent decrease in life expectancy among white women lacking high-school degrees in order to raise questions about economic prospects among the rural poor. Edward McClelland examines the role of industrial decline in the loss of middle-class American jobs. Though several of these writers question whether the dream of equal opportunity ever delivered for most Americans in the way that Alger and others suggested, they all argue that the last two decades have so shifted the balance of wealth and power to large corporations and the privileged few that even the humble financial security that average Americans dream about is becoming just that: a dream with little chance of realization.

Other writers in this unit take a more *conservative* position, suggesting that alarmist critiques are unwarranted and that the American Dream is alive and well. Tim Roemer, a former U.S.

congressman and ambassador to India, points out that count-less people still wish to come to this country, expecting—and finding—a chance at prosperity for themselves and their fami-lies. Entrepreneur Shayan Zadeh, one such immigrant who built a successful business here, argues that immigration laws should be changed to allow entrepreneurs to more easily enter the country and start businesses. Student Brandon King argues that opportunities for advancement still exist in the United States and that the economic situation of the average person would improve if taxes were lowered and government support for Wall Street increased. Finally, economists Gary S. Becker (also a Nobel Prize winner) and Kevin M. Murphy concede the existence of income inequality but assert that such inequality is actually good for the economy as a whole.

While these two camps argue over possibilities for upward mobility, others take a middle-ground position. *New York Times* economics writer David Leonhardt takes a balanced view, argu-ing that while the income gap is widening in the United States, the potential for increasing broad-based prosperity still exists and can be realized with a few straightforward shifts in eco-nomic policy. And a Pew Research report discusses the pes-simism many Americans feel concerning progress made toward racial equality, along with persistent disparities among the races in terms of income, education, and other measures of "well-being and civic engagement."

As you read this chapter, you will have a chance to make your own contribution to this ongoing discussion.

Inequality Has Been Going on Forever ... but That Doesn't Mean It's Inevitable

DAVID LEONHARDT

—◻—

WE HAVE BEEN LIVING with rising income inequality for so long—in good times and bad, under Republican presidents and Democratic ones—that it has come to seem inevitable. It is no longer news that the affluent did better than everyone else during the booms of the 1980s and '90s and through the mediocre growth of this century's first years. Or that the rich have recovered from the financial crisis far better than the rest of country.

But with exquisite timing, one of the most ambitious (and best-reviewed) books on the subject in years—Thomas Piketty's "Capital in the Twenty-First Century"—appeared

———

DAVID LEONHARDT is the managing editor of *The Upshot*, a *New York Times* site that "presents news, analysis and data visualization about politics and policy." He won the 2011 Pulitzer Prize for commentary for his columns about economic issues for the *Times*, where he served as Washington bureau chief. He is also the author of an e-book, *Here's the Deal: How Washington Can Solve the Deficit and Spur Growth* (2013). This article first appeared in the *New York Times Magazine* on May 4, 2014.

this spring to argue that rising inequality wasn't merely a feature of our times. It has been the historical norm, writes Piketty, a professor at the Paris School of Economics. Inequality has risen throughout much of modern history, he writes, with the notable exceptions of wars, depressions and their aftermath, when everyone was forced to rebuild from a more equal place. And inequality is likely to continue increasing for decades, he says. Ultimately, we could end up with a society in which the rich separate themselves from everyone else, perpetuating their wealth from one generation to the next, as nobility of past centuries did.

See Chapter 2 for tips on summarizing an argument.

That prospect sounds depressing, but it doesn't necessarily have to turn out that way. To say that something is likely, or even natural, is not to say that it is inevitable. Not so long ago, the rich owned a much smaller share of this country's resources and made a smaller share of its income than many of their predecessors. Perhaps more important, even though inequality has risen abroad, it has done so far less rapidly. Other developed economies . . . are not more equal simply because they lack success stories, like Warren Buffett, or have fewer investment bankers or hedge-fund executives. Instead, their middle class and poor have enjoyed more aggressively rising incomes, all while their economies grow as rapidly as this country's in recent years. A more equal society does not mean a less dynamic one. (Germany is notably alone among wealthy European countries in having broad-based income trends nearly as weak as the United States.)

Inequality, then, is less an inevitability than a choice. Just as societies have conquered many of the challenges of the natural world—making childbirth safe for women or beating back common illnesses that once were frequent killers—we can alter the course of inequality, too.

For all of the clarity of Piketty's historical analysis, I emerged 5 from the book not quite grasping the mechanics of rising inequality. What is it about market economies that typically cause the assets and incomes of the rich to rise more rapidly than those of everyone else? So I called Piketty at his office in Paris, and he agreed to walk me through it.

He suggested imagining a hypothetical village from centuries ago in which neither the population nor the economy was growing. Every year, the village produced the same amount of goods for the same number of people to divide—a reality that was typical before the Enlightenment, when material living standards and human longevity barely rose. (The peasants of the 15th century were not better off than peasants in ancient Rome.) Even in a zero-growth society, however, assets that helped people produce goods—also known as capital—had value. Capital, Piketty told me, counts as anything "useful, any kind of equipment. Basic tools. Stones in prehistorical times." Anything, in other words, that "makes people more productive."

In our hypothetical village, a large farm might produce $10,000 worth of crops in a year and yield $1,000 in profit for its owner. A small farm might have the same 10 percent rate of return: $1,000 in annual crop sales, yielding $100 in profit. If the large farmer and small farmer each spent all of their money every year, the situation could continue ad infinitum, Piketty said, and the rate of inequality in the village would not change.

But one of capital's great advantages is that its owners can make enough income to spend some of their money and sock the rest of it away. If the large farmer saved $500 of that $1,000 profit, he could buy more capital, which would bring more profit. Perhaps a few owners of smaller farms had debts to pay, and one of the large farmers bought them out. Eventually, the owner of the expanding farm might find himself owning land that yielded $1,500 or $2,000 in annual profit, allowing him to put aside more and more for future capital acquisitions. Less-stylized versions of this story have been playing out for centuries.

I have come to think of this idea as Piketty's First Law of Inequality. The fact that the rich earn enough money to save money allows them to make investments that other people simply cannot afford. And investments—whether stones, land, corporate stock or education—tend to bring a positive return. Piketty describes the relationship formally as r > g: the rate of return on capital usually exceeds economic growth.

Piketty, however, notes that certain things can disrupt this 10 relationship. When a war destroys farms, the big farmers are no longer much richer than anyone else. A depression can play the same role. When income or wealth is taxed at high rates, the rich are not able to save and accumulate as much. It's no accident that in the decades after World War II, when middle-class incomes were rising even more rapidly than the incomes of the rich, the top marginal income-tax rates were exceptionally high. In the 1950s, the top rate exceeded 90 percent. Today, it is 39.6 percent, and only because President Obama finally won a yearslong battle with Republicans in early 2013 to increase it from 35 percent.

Piketty advocates a global wealth tax aimed more directly at capital inequality than income taxes currently are. It would apply to anyone with more than about $1.4 million in net worth and become steeper on higher fortunes than moderate ones. It's an interesting idea, but it has little, if any, chance of passing the current legislative environment. Yet Piketty mentions another, more politically plausible force that can disrupt his first law of inequality: education. When a society becomes more educated, many of its less-wealthy citizens quickly acquire an ephemeral but nonetheless crucial form of capital—knowledge—that can bring enormous returns. They learn to make objects and accomplish tasks more efficiently, and they sometimes create entirely new objects (or services). They become those children in the small village who attended school, went off to work in a factory, became managers and made bigger economic leaps above their parents than those of the large farmer did.

The great income gains for the American middle class and poor in the mid-to-late 20th century came after this country made high school universal and turned itself into the most educated nation in the world. As the economists Claudia Goldin and Lawrence Katz have written, "The 20th century was the American century because it was the human-capital century." Education continues to pay today, despite the scare stories to the contrary. The pay gap between college graduates and everyone else in this country is near its all-time high. The countries that have done a better job increasing their educational attainment, like Canada and Sweden, have also seen bigger broad-based income gains than the United States.

Yet the debate over our schools and colleges tends to exist in a separate political universe from our debate over inequality. Liberals often shy away from making the connection because they worry it holds the struggling middle class and poor responsible for their plight and distracts from income redistribution. Many conservatives fear the implicit government spending involved. And so, our once-large international lead in educational attainment has vanished, and our lead in inequality has grown.

There are some reasons for optimism in education. Charter schools and school systems that have tried to introduce more accountability offer some lessons about what works and doesn't in K–12. The total number of college graduates has begun rising again. That said, the changes in education—not to mention the tax code—are not nearly large enough to counteract the forces pushing in the other direction. A true attack on inequality would require that the country move the issue to the center of every political debate: how we tax wealth, how we tax the income of the middle class and poor (often stealthily through the payroll tax), how we finance schools and measure their results, how we tolerate income-sapping waste in health care, how we build roads, transit systems and broadband networks. These are precisely the sort of policies pursued by countries with better recent middle-class income growth than the United States.

The closest thing to an antihero in Piketty's book is an 15 economist named Simon Kuznets, who argued in the decades after World War II that inequality was destined to decline. His soothing prediction grew out the experience of the previous few decades, but he and many others confused a trend with destiny. We are now making that same mistake in the opposite direction. Rising inequality is a trend, but it is one we have helped create and one we can still change.

Joining the Conversation

1. The first two paragraphs of this essay offer a "they say" on the subject of inequality. What is the argument that David Leonhardt wants to discuss, and what is his "I say" in the remainder of the essay?

2. Leonhardt discusses the views of French economist Thomas Piketty throughout this piece. In one paragraph, summarize Piketty's views.

3. Leonhardt published this piece in the *New York Times* and thus could assume that many of his readers were generally informed about his topic. How might he have written it differently for an audience of first-year college students?

4. Monica Potts's essay (pp. 591–609) examines the effects of poverty, lack of education, and scarce job opportunities on rural Americans. How might some of the material discussed in her essay be incorporated in Leonhardt's essay to help him support his argument about inequality?

5. In paragraph 14, Leonhardt suggests policies that could reduce inequality: "how we tax wealth, how we tax the income of the middle class and poor (often stealthily through the payroll tax), how we finance schools and measure their results, how we tolerate income-sapping waste in health care, how we build roads, transit systems and broadband networks . . . precisely the sort of policies pursued by countries with better recent middle-class income growth than the United States." Write an essay in which you first quote or summarize and explain what he means and then present your own views on this subject, drawing from readings in this chapter.

RIP, the Middle Class: 1946–2013

EDWARD McCLELLAND

I KNOW I'M DATING MYSELF by writing this, but I remember the middle class.

I grew up in an automaking town in the 1970s, when it was still possible for a high school graduate—or even a high school dropout—to get a job on an assembly line and earn more money than a high school teacher.

"I had this student," my history teacher once told me, "a real chucklehead. Just refused to study. Dropped out of school, a year or so later, he came back to see me. He pointed out the window at a brand-new Camaro and said, 'That's my car.' Meanwhile, I was driving a beat-up station wagon. I think he was an electrician's assistant or something. He handed light bulbs to an electrician."

EDWARD McCLELLAND is a journalist and the author of several books, including *Nothin' But Blue Skies: The Heyday, Hard Times, and Hopes of America's Industrial Heartland* (2013) and *Young Mr. Obama: Chicago and the Making of a Black President* (2010). His articles have appeared in the *Los Angeles Times*, the *New York Times*, and *Slate*—and you can follow him on Twitter @tedmcclelland. This article first appeared on September 20, 2013, in *Salon*, an online news site that often publishes "fearless commentary and criticism."

In our neighbors' driveways, in their living rooms, in their backyards, I saw the evidence of prosperity distributed equally among the social classes: speedboats, Corvette Stingrays, waterbeds, snowmobiles, motorcycles, hunting rifles, RVs, CB radios. I've always believed that the '70s are remembered as the Decade That Taste Forgot because they were a time when people without culture or education had the money to not only indulge their passions, but flaunt them in front of the entire nation. It was an era, to use the title of a 1975 sociological study of a Wisconsin tavern, of blue-collar aristocrats.

That all began to change in the 1980s. The recession at the 5 beginning of that decade—America's first Great Recession— was the beginning of the end for the bourgeois proletariat. Steelworkers showed up for first shift to find padlocks on mill gates. Autoworkers were laid off for years. The lucky ones were transferred to plants far from home. The unlucky never built another car.

See p. 25 for more ways to introduce something implied or assumed.

When I was growing up, it was assumed that America's shared prosperity was the natural endpoint of our economy's development, that capitalism had produced the workers paradise to which Communism unsuccessfully aspired. Now, with the perspective of 40 years, it's obvious that the nonstop economic expansion that lasted from the end of World War II to the Arab oil embargo of 1973 was a historical fluke, made possible by the fact that the United States was the only country to emerge from that war with its industrial capacity intact. Unfortunately, the middle class—especially the blue-collar middle class—is also starting to look like a fluke, an interlude between Gilded Ages that more closely reflect the way most societies structure themselves economically. For the majority of human history—and in the majority of countries today— there have been only two classes: aristocracy and peasantry.

It's an order in which the many toil for subsistence wages to provide luxuries for the few. Twentieth century America temporarily escaped this stratification, but now, as statistics on economic inequality demonstrate, we're slipping back in that direction. Between 1970 and today, the share of the nation's income that went to the middle class—households earning two-thirds to double the national median—fell from 62 percent to 45 percent. Last year, the wealthiest 1 percent took in 19 percent of America's income—their highest share since 1928. It's as though the New Deal and the modern labor movement never happened.

Here's the story of a couple whose working lives began during the Golden Age of middle-class employment, and are ending in this current age of inequality. Gary Galipeau was born in Syracuse, N.Y., in the baby boom sweet spot of 1948. At age 19, he hired in at his hometown's flagship business, the Carrier Corp., which gave Syracuse the title "Air-Conditioning Capital of the World." Starting at $2.37 an hour, Galipeau worked his way into the skilled trades, eventually becoming a metal fabricator earning 10 times his original wage.

"Understand," he said, "in the mid-'60s, you could figuratively roll out of bed and find a manufacturing job."

Voss joined Carrier after dropping out of Syracuse University, and getting laid off from an industrial laundry.

"It was 1978," she said. "You could still go from factory to factory. One day, a friend and I were looking for a job. We saw this big building. We said, 'Must be jobs in there.' In those days, you could fill out an application and get an interview the same day. I was offered a job within three or four days, making window units. I sprayed glue on fiberglass insulation, stuck it inside units—400 a day, nearly one a minute. I was told, 'After five years, you'll have a job for life. You'll be golden.'"

Galipeau and Voss, who met working at Carrier, lost their jobs in 2004, when the company moved the last of its Syracuse manufacturing operations to Singapore. There, even the most skilled workers were paid half the $27 an hour Galipeau had earned as a metalworker. The corporation they'd expected to spend their careers with divorced them in middle age, and now they had to bridge the years until Social Security and Medicare. Eligible for Trade Adjustment Assistance, because her job had moved overseas, Voss earned a two-year degree in health information technology—"a fancy way of saying medical records."

Even with the degree, Voss couldn't find decent-paying work in healthcare, so she took a job with a sump pump manufacturer, for $12.47 an hour—a substantial drop from Carrier, but decent money for Central New York in the A.D. of A/C. (The No. 1 employer of ex-Carrier workers is an Iroquois casino.) Less than two weeks into the new job, a thread on Voss' work glove wrapped itself around a drill press, taking Voss' finger with it. The digit was torn off at the first knuckle. When Voss returned to work, two months later, she found the factory so distressing that she soon took a medical records job in a hospital, paying $2.50 an hour less.

After earning a degree in human resources management, Galipeau found that 56 was too old to start a new career. Fortunate enough to draw a full pension from Carrier, Galipeau took a part-time job at a supermarket meat counter, for the health insurance. Syracuse's leading vocations are now education and medicine—the training of the young and the preservation of the old. Where nothing is left for the middle-aged, or the middle class, it's difficult to be both.

The shrinking of the middle class is not a failure of capitalism. It's a failure of government. Capitalism has been doing exactly what it was designed to do: concentrating wealth in the ownership class, while providing the mass of workers with just enough wages to feed, house and clothe themselves. Young people who graduate from college to $9.80 an hour jobs as sales clerks or data processors are giving up on the concept of employment as a vehicle for improving their financial fortunes: In a recent survey, 24 percent defined the American dream as "not being in debt." They're not trying to get ahead. They're just trying to get to zero.

That's the natural drift of the relationship between capital and labor, and it can only be arrested by an activist government that chooses to step in as a referee. The organizing victories that founded the modern union movement were made possible by the National Labor Relations Act, a piece of New Deal legislation guaranteeing workers the right to bargain collectively. The plotters of the 1936–37 Flint Sit Down Strike, which gave birth to the United Auto Workers, tried to time their action to coincide with the inauguration of Frank Murphy, Michigan's newly

15

elected New Deal governor. Murphy dispatched the National Guard to Flint, but instead of ordering his guardsmen to throw the workers out of the plants, as he legally could have done, he ordered them to ensure the workers remained safely inside. The strike resulted in a nickel an hour raise and an end to arbitrary firings. It guaranteed the success of the UAW, whose high wages and benefits set the standard for American workers for the next 45 years. (I know a Sit Down Striker who died on September 17, at 98 years old, an age he might not have attained without the lifetime health benefits won by the UAW.)

The United States will never again be as wealthy as it was in the 1950s and '60s. Never again will 18-year-olds graduate directly from high school to jobs that pay well enough to buy a house and support a family. (Even the auto plants now demand a few years in junior college.) That was inevitable, due to the recovery of our World War II enemies, and automation that enables 5,000 workers to build the same number of cars that once required 25,000 hands. What was not inevitable was the federal government withdrawing its supervision of the economy at the precise moment Americans began to need it more than at any time since the Great Depression.

The last president who had a plan for protecting American workers from the vicissitudes of the global economy was Richard Nixon, who was in office when foreign steel and foreign cars began seriously competing with domestic products. The most farsighted politician of his generation, Nixon realized that America's economic hegemony was coming to an end, and was determined to cushion the decline by (a) preventing foreign manufacturers from overrunning our markets and (b) teaching Americans to live within their new limits. When the United States began running a trade deficit, Nixon tried to reverse the trend with a 10 percent tariff on imported products. After the 1973 Arab Oil Embargo suddenly increased the price of gasoline from 36 cents to 53 cents a gallon (and just as suddenly increased the demand for fuel-efficient German and Japanese cars), Nixon lowered the speed limit to 55 miles an hour and introduced the Corporate Average Fuel Economy law, which gave automakers until 1985 to double their fleetwide fuel efficiency to 27.5 miles per gallon.

Had Nixon survived Watergate, he might have set the nation on a course that emphasized government regulation of the economy, and trade protection as a response to globalism. We might also have preserved more of the manufacturing base necessary for a strong middle class. But his successors dismantled that vision, beginning with Jimmy Carter, an economically conservative Southern planter. Nixon's answer to inflation had been wage and price controls, an intrusion into the free market that would be unimaginable today. Carter deregulated the airline, rail and trucking industries, hoping that competition would result in lower prices. It didn't, but it gave the newly liberated companies more leverage against their unions. When inflation nonetheless reached 14 percent, Carter's hand-picked Federal Reserve Board chairman, Paul Volcker, responded by tightening the money supply, raising interest rates so high that Americans could not afford loans for cars or houses. Ronald Reagan also chose low prices over employment, refusing to free up money until inflation declined. Car sales hit a 20-year low. In the fall of 1982, the national unemployment rate was 10.8 percent, the highest since the Great Depression. Walter Mondale accused Reagan of turning the Midwest into "a rust bowl"—a term reformulated to Rust Belt. Buffalo, Cleveland, Flint and Detroit still haven't recovered. Neither has the middle class.

"You can't grow an economy, grow a middle class, without making things, producing stuff," says Mike Stout, a steelworker who lost his job when Pennsylvania's Homestead Works closed in 1986. "It's just impossible. I haven't seen it anywhere."

Reagan also fired the striking members of the Professional 20 Air Traffic Controllers Organization [PATCO]. He argued that he was simply trying to end an illegal strike by public employees, but his action encouraged private employers to use the same tactic. Once workers realized they could lose their jobs by joining a picket line, the number of strikes dropped tenfold, from 300 a year before 1981, to 30 a year today.

Pre-PATCO, 21 percent of workers belonged to unions (still down from the all-time high of 30 percent). Now, fewer than 12 percent do. Union membership is at 14.7 million, the lowest total since just before World War II. There's a well-known graph that shows middle-class income share declining along the same axis as unionization.

Bill Clinton continued down the same deregulatory path, signing the North American Free Trade Agreement and the repeal of the Glass-Steagall Act, which prohibited commercial banks from owning investment firms.

NAFTA, which resulted in hundreds of small manufacturers moving to Mexico, was passed over the vehement objections of labor.

In 1994, Rep. Glenn Poshard of Illinois tried to persuade the Labor Department to intervene in a lockout at the A.E. Staley Mfg. Co., a Decatur corn starch manufacturer that had been bought by Tate and Lyle, a London-based food conglomerate. Poshard considered the dispute the "flashpoint" for the new economic globalism of the 1990s, but when he took a group of workers to meet Labor Secretary Robert Reich, the secretary gave no indication the federal government would try to settle the matter.

After two-and-a-half years, the union capitulated, settling 25 for a third of its pre-lockout jobs.

Only in 2008, after the bubble of false prosperity created by easy credit and inflated housing values blew up, did two presidents finally take an active role in the economy. George W. Bush decided he didn't want to be remembered as the president who allowed American automakers to fall apart, and sent them $17.4 billion of the $700 billion Wall Street bailout money. Barack Obama finished the job, setting up an auto task force to guide General Motors and Chrysler through bankruptcy. (He did so over the objections of his house Clintonite, Chief of Staff Rahm Emanuel. Emanuel's response to the prospect of tens of thousands of autoworkers losing their jobs: "Fuck the UAW"). Even so, new autoworkers now start at $14 an hour—hardly a middle-class wage.

Obama also passed the Affordable Care Act, the most significant piece of social welfare legislation since the Great Society, but author Peter Beinart still thinks Obama belongs to the modern tradition of small government presidents, calling his politics "pro-capitalist, anti-bureaucratic, Reaganized liberalism."

The lesson of the last 40 years is that we can't depend on the free market to sustain a middle class. It's not going to happen without government intervention. Even when American industry dominated the world, one reason workers prospered was that the economy operated on New Deal underpinnings, which included legal protections for labor unions, government regulation of industry and high marginal income tax rates.

It's time to declare an end to the deregulatory experiment that has resulted in the greatest disparity between the top earners and the middle earners in nearly a century. Now that the New Deal has been vanquished—a goal conservatives have cherished since before Robert Taft went extinct—we need a Newer Deal that will raise the minimum wage, reduce obstacles to union organizing, levy higher taxes on passive wealth such as investments and inheritances, and provide benefits for workers unable to obtain it at their jobs, perhaps by lowering Medicaid eligibility or instituting a single-payer health system. The demand for such reforms is brewing. We heard from the middle class during the Occupy movement of 2011, and from the lower class in this year's fast food strikes.

Not long ago, I was in Flint, Michigan, to meet with its new congressman, Dan Kildee. No American city has suffered more during the Age of Deregulation than Flint. In 1978, Flint had 80,000 automaking jobs, and the highest per capita income in the nation. Today, it has 6,000 automaking jobs, and the highest murder rate in the English-speaking world. Instead of Corvettes and speedboats, the yards are filled with mean dogs, "This Property Protected by Smith & Wesson" signs, and weeds. So far, Kildee's biggest achievement has been securing federal funding to tear down 2,000 abandoned houses. In Flint, where the average home sale price is $15,000, eliminating blight increases property values. Having seen the consequences of government indifference, Kildee wants to return to the days of government activism. As county treasurer, he founded a public land bank that helped revive downtown Flint by purchasing and renovating a hotel that had sat empty since 1973.

"It is a myth that there is any market that is not supported or affected by the structure of government in one way or another," he said. "We're picking winners and losers right now, and we're picking the wrong ones. We're making matters worse by not intervening in these communities. It's not fine for Flint to be one of the losers, as far as I'm concerned."

As far as I'm concerned, it's not fine for the middle class to be one of the losers, either.

Joining the Conversation

1. Edward McClelland opens this article with a discussion of the industrial heyday of the United States, from the late 1940s through the 1970s, when blue-collar workers had their choice of well-paying jobs. What evidence does he give for this period of "shared prosperity"? What exactly does he mean by this term? Why, in his view, did the prosperity end, and what steps are required to bring it back?

2. This selection comes from *Salon*, a progressive online news site that boasts of publishing "fearless commentary and criticism." Where in the article do you find evidence of such writing, and of the author's own political position? Cite specific examples from the text.

3. McClelland offers a lot of evidence for his own views, but he does not say much about any other viewpoints. What objections might be raised to what he says, and where would you introduce them in his essay? How would doing so improve his argument?

4. Brandon King, in his essay on the American Dream (pp. 610–17), argues that "supporting the richest sectors of the American economy will bring economic stability and a full recovery." How might McClelland respond to King? What evidence might he provide to prove King wrong?

5. Develop an argument of your own that responds to McClelland's argument about the decline of the American middle class, agreeing with him, disagreeing, or both. However you choose to argue, be sure to consider other positions in addition to your own, including those of other authors in this chapter.

Confronting Inequality

PAUL KRUGMAN

———🔲———

THE AMERICA I GREW UP IN was a relatively equal middle-class society. Over the past generation, however, the country has returned to Gilded Age levels of inequality. In this chapter I'll outline policies that can help reverse these changes. I'll begin with the question of values. Why should we care about high and rising inequality?

One reason to care about inequality is the straightforward matter of living standards. The lion's share of economic growth in America over the past thirty years has gone to a small, wealthy minority, to such an extent that it's unclear whether the typical family has benefited at all from technological progress and the rising productivity it brings. The lack of clear economic progress for lower- and middle-income families is in itself an important reason to seek a more equal distribution of income.

———

PAUL KRUGMAN teaches economics at Princeton and the City University of New York and writes an op-ed column in the *New York Times*. He was awarded the Nobel Prize in Economics in 2008. Krugman is the author of many books, most recently *End This Depression Now!* (2012). "Confronting Inequality" is a chapter from his 2007 book, *The Conscience of a Liberal*.

Beyond that, however, is the damage extreme inequality does to our society and our democracy. Ever since America's founding, our idea of ourselves has been that of a nation without sharp class distinctions—not a leveled society of perfect equality, but one in which the gap between the economic elite and the typical citizen isn't an unbridgeable chasm. That's why Thomas Jefferson wrote, "The small landholders are the most precious part of a state."[1] Translated into modern terms as an assertion that a broad middle class is the most precious part of a state, Jefferson's statement remains as true as ever. High inequality, which has turned us into a nation with a much-weakened middle class, has a corrosive effect on social relations and politics, one that has become ever more apparent as America has moved deeper into a new Gilded Age.

The Costs of Inequality

One of the best arguments I've ever seen for the social costs of inequality came from a movement conservative trying to argue the opposite. In 1997 Irving Kristol, one of the original neoconservative intellectuals, published an article in the *Wall Street Journal* called "Income Inequality Without Class Conflict." Kristol argued that we shouldn't worry about income inequality, because whatever the numbers may say, class distinctions are, in reality, all but gone. Today, he asserted,

> income inequality tends to be swamped by even greater social equality. . . . In all of our major cities, there is not a single restaurant where a CEO can lunch or dine with the absolute assurance that he will not run into his secretary. If you fly first class, who will be your traveling companions? You never know. If you go to Paris, you will be lost in a crowd of young people flashing their credit cards.[2]

By claiming that income inequality doesn't matter because we have social equality, Kristol was in effect admitting that income inequality *would* be a problem if it led to social inequality. And here's the thing: It does. Kristol's fantasy of a world in which the rich live just like you and me, and nobody feels socially inferior, bears no resemblance to the real America we live in.

See p. 60 on using someone else's evidence to support your position.

Lifestyles of the rich and famous are arguably the least important part of the story, yet it's worth pointing out that Kristol's vision of CEOs rubbing shoulders with the middle class is totally contradicted by the reporting of Robert Frank of the *Wall Street Journal*, whose assigned beat is covering the lives of the wealthy. In his book *Richistan* Frank describes what he learned:

> Today's rich had formed their own virtual country. . . . [T]hey had built a self-contained world unto themselves, complete with their own health-care system (concierge doctors), travel network (Net Jets, destination clubs), separate economy. . . . The rich weren't just getting richer; they were becoming financial foreigners, creating their own country within a country, their own society within a society, and their own economy within an economy.[3]

The fact is that vast income inequality inevitably brings vast social inequality in its train. And this social inequality isn't just a matter of envy and insults. It has real, negative consequences for the way people live in this country. It may not matter much that the great majority of Americans can't afford to stay in the eleven-thousand-dollar-a-night hotel suites popping up in luxury hotels around the world.[4] It matters a great deal that millions of middle-class families buy houses they can't really afford, taking on more mortgage debt than they can safely handle, because they're desperate to send their children to a good school—and intensifying inequality means that the desirable school districts are growing fewer in number, and more expensive to live in.

Elizabeth Warren, a Harvard Law School expert in bankruptcy, and Amelia Warren Tyagi, a business consultant, have studied the rise of bankruptcy in the United States. By 2005, just before a new law making it much harder for individuals to declare bankruptcy took effect, the number of families filing for bankruptcy each year was five times its level in the early 1980s. The proximate reason for this surge in bankruptcies was that families were taking on more debt—and this led to moralistic pronouncements about people spending too much on luxuries they can't afford. What Warren and Tyagi found, however, was that middle-class families were actually spending *less* on luxuries than they had in the 1970s. Instead the rise in debt mainly reflected increased spending on housing,

A couple and their two dogs board a private jet in Aspen, Colorado.

largely driven by competition to get into good school districts. Middle-class Americans have been caught up in a rat race, not because they're greedy or foolish but because they're trying to give their children a chance in an increasingly unequal society.[5] And they're right to be worried: A bad start can ruin a child's chances for life.

Americans still tend to say, when asked, that individuals can make their own place in society. According to one survey 61 percent of Americans agree with the statement that "people get rewarded for their effort," compared with 49 percent in Canada and only 23 percent in France.[6] In reality, however, America has vast inequality of opportunity as well as results. We may believe that anyone can succeed through hard work and determination, but the facts say otherwise.

There are many pieces of evidence showing that Horatio Alger stories are very rare in real life. One of the most striking comes from a study published by the National Center for

Crowds of passengers at O'Hare International Airport in Chicago.

Education Statistics, which tracked the educational experience of Americans who were eighth graders in 1988. Those eighth graders were sorted both by apparent talent, as measured by a mathematics test, and by the socioeconomic status of their parents, as measured by occupations, incomes, and education.

The key result is shown in Table 1. Not surprisingly, both getting a high test score and having high-status parents increased a student's chance of finishing college. But family status mattered more. Students who scored in the bottom fourth on the exam, but came from families whose status put them in the top fourth—what we used to call RDKs, for "rich dumb kids," when I was a teenager—were more likely to finish college than students who scored in the top fourth but whose parents were in the bottom fourth. What this tells us is that the idea that we have anything close to equality of opportunity is clearly a fantasy. It would be closer to the truth, though not the whole truth, to say that in modern America, class—inherited class—usually trumps talent.

Isn't that true everywhere? Not to the same extent. International comparisons of "intergenerational mobility," the extent to which people can achieve higher status than their parents, are tricky because countries don't collect perfectly comparable

TABLE I. PERCENTAGE OF
1988 EIGHTH GRADERS FINISHING COLLEGE

	Score in Bottom Quartile	Score in Top Quartile
Parents in Bottom Quartile	3	29
Parents in Top Quartile	30	74

Source: National Center for Education Statistics, *The Condition of Education 2003*, 47.

data. Nonetheless it's clear that Horatio Alger has moved to someplace in Europe: Mobility is highest in the Scandinavian countries, and most results suggest that mobility is lower in the United States than it is in France, Canada, and maybe even Britain. Not only don't Americans have equal opportunity, opportunity is less equal here than elsewhere in the West.

It's not hard to understand why. Our unique lack of universal health care, all by itself, puts Americans who are unlucky in their parents at a disadvantage: Because American children from low-income families are often uninsured, they're more likely to have health problems that derail their life chances. Poor nutrition, thanks to low income and a lack of social support, can have the same effect. Life disruptions that affect a child's parents can also make upward mobility hard—and the weakness of the U.S. social safety net makes such disruptions more likely and worse if they happen. Then there's the highly uneven quality of U.S. basic education, and so on. What it all comes down to is that although the principle of "equality of opportunity, not equality of results" sounds fine, it's a largely fictitious distinction. A society with highly unequal results is, more or less inevitably, a society with highly unequal opportunity, too. If you truly believe that all Americans are entitled to an equal chance at the starting line, that's an argument for doing something to reduce inequality.

America's high inequality, then, imposes serious costs on our society that go beyond the way it holds down the purchasing power of most families. And there's another way in which inequality damages us: It corrupts our politics. "If there are men in this country big enough to own the government of the United States," said Woodrow Wilson in 1913, in words that would be almost inconceivable from a modern president, "they are going to own it."[7] Well, now there are, and they do.

Not completely, of course, but hardly a week goes by without the disclosure of a case in which the influence of money has grotesquely distorted U.S. government policy.

As this book went to press, there was a spectacular example: 15 The way even some Democrats rallied to the support of hedge fund managers, who receive an unconscionable tax break. Through a quirk in the way the tax laws have been interpreted, these managers—some of whom make more than a billion dollars a year—get to have most of their earnings taxed at the capital gains rate, which is only 15 percent, even as other high earners pay a 35 percent rate. The hedge fund tax loophole costs the government more than $6 billion a year in lost revenue, roughly the cost of providing health care to three million children.[8] Almost $2 billion of the total goes to just twenty-five individuals. Even conservative economists believe that the tax break is unjustified, and should be eliminated.[9]

Yet the tax break has powerful political support—and not just from Republicans. In July 2007 Senator Charles Schumer of New York, the head of the Democratic Senatorial Campaign Committee, let it be known that he would favor eliminating the hedge fund loophole only if other, deeply entrenched tax breaks were eliminated at the same time. As everyone understood, this was a "poison pill," a way of blocking reform without explicitly saying no. And although Schumer denied it, everyone also suspected that his position was driven by the large sums hedge funds contribute to Democratic political campaigns.[10]

The hedge fund loophole is a classic example of how the concentration of income in a few hands corrupts politics. Beyond that is the bigger story of how income inequality has reinforced the rise of movement conservatism, a fundamentally undemocratic force. Rising inequality has to an important extent been caused by the rightward shift of our politics, but the causation also runs the other way. The new wealth of the rich has increased their influence, sustaining the institutions of movement conservatism and pulling the Republican Party even further into the movement's orbit. The ugliness of our politics is in large part a reflection of the inequality of our income distribution.

More broadly still, high levels of inequality strain the bonds that hold us together as a society. There has been a long-term downward trend in the extent to which Americans trust either the government or one another. In the sixties, most Americans agreed with the proposition that "most people can be trusted"; today most disagree.[11] In the sixties, most Americans believed that the government is run "for the benefit of all"; today, most believe that it's run for "a few big interests."[12] And there's convincing evidence that growing inequality is behind our growing cynicism, which is making the United States seem increasingly like a Latin American country. As the political scientists Eric Uslaner and Mitchell Brown point out (and support with extensive data), "In a world of haves and have-nots, those at either end of the economic spectrum have little reason to believe that 'most people can be trusted' . . . social trust rests on a foundation of economic equality."[13]

The Arithmetic of Equalization

Suppose we agree that the United States should become more like other advanced countries, whose tax and benefit systems do much more than ours to reduce inequality. The next question is what that decision might involve.

In part it would involve undoing many of the tax cuts for the wealthy that movement conservatives have pushed through since 1980. Table 2 shows what has happened to three tax rates that strongly affect the top 1 percent of the U.S. population,

TABLE 2. THREE TOP RATES (PERCENTAGE)

	Top Tax on Earned Income	Top Tax on Long-Term Capital Gains	Top Tax on Corporate Profits
1979	70	28	48
2006	35	15	35

Source: Urban-Brookings Tax Policy Center <http://taxpolicycenter.org/taxfacts/tfdb/tftemplate.cfm>.

while having little effect on anyone else. Between 1979 and 2006 the top tax rate on earned income was cut in half; the tax rate on capital gains was cut almost as much; the tax rate on corporate profits fell by more than a quarter. High incomes in America are much less taxed than they used to be. Thus raising taxes on the rich back toward historical levels can pay for part, though only part, of a stronger safety net that limits inequality.

The first step toward restoring progressivity to the tax system is to let the Bush tax cuts for the very well off expire at the end of 2010, as they are now scheduled to. That alone would raise a significant amount of revenue. The nonpartisan Urban-Brookings Joint Tax Policy Center estimates that letting the Bush tax cuts expire for people with incomes over two hundred thousand dollars would be worth about $140 billion a year starting in 2012. That's enough to pay for the subsidies needed to implement universal health care. A tax-cut rollback of this kind, used to finance health care reform, would significantly reduce inequality. It would do so partly by modestly reducing incomes at the top: The Tax Policy Center estimates that allowing the Bush tax cuts to expire for Americans making more than two hundred thousand dollars a year would reduce the aftertax incomes of the richest 1 percent of Americans by about 4.5 percent compared with what they would be if the Bush tax cuts were made permanent. Meanwhile middle- and lower-income Americans would be assured of health care—one of the key aspects of being truly middle class.[14]

Another relatively easy move from a political point of view would be closing some of the obvious loopholes in the U.S. system. These include the rule described earlier that allows financial wheeler-dealers, such as hedge fund managers, to classify their earnings as capital gains, taxed at a 15 percent rate rather than 35 percent. The major tax loopholes also include rules that let corporations, drug companies in particular, shift recorded profits to low-tax jurisdictions overseas, costing billions more; one recent study estimates that tax avoidance by multinationals costs about $50 billion a year.[15]

Going beyond rolling back the Bush cuts and closing obvious loopholes would be a more difficult political undertaking. Yet there can be rapid shifts in what seems politically realistic. At the end of 2004 it seemed all too possible that Social Security, the centerpiece of the New Deal, would be privatized and effectively phased out. Today Social Security appears safe, and universal health care seems within reach. If universal health care can be achieved, and the New Deal idea that government can be a force for good is reinvigorated, things that now seem off the table might not look so far out.

Both historical and international evidence show that there is room for tax increases at the top that go beyond merely rolling back the Bush cuts. Even before the Bush tax cuts, top tax rates in the United States were low by historical standards—the tax rate on the top bracket was only 39.6 percent during the Clinton years, compared with 70 percent in the seventies and 50 percent even *after* Reagan's 1981 tax cut. Top U.S. tax rates are also low compared with those in European countries. For example, in Britain, the top income tax rate is 40 percent, seemingly equivalent to the top rate of the Clinton years. However, in Britain employers also pay a social insurance tax— the equivalent of the employer share of FICA* here—that applies to all earned income. (Most of the U.S. equivalent is levied only on income up to a maximum of $97,500.) As a result very highly paid British employees face an effective tax rate of almost 48 percent. In France effective top rates are even higher. Also, in Britain capital gains are taxed as ordinary income, so that the effective tax rate on capital gains for people with high income is 40 percent, compared with 15 percent in the United States.[16] Taxing capital gains as ordinary income in the United States would yield significantly more revenue, and also limit the range of tax abuses like the hedge fund loophole.

Also, from the New Deal until the 1970s it was considered normal and appropriate to have "super" tax rates on very-high-income individuals. Only a few people were subject to the 70 percent top bracket in the 70s, let alone the 90 percent-plus top rates of the Eisenhower years. It used to be argued that a surtax on very high incomes serves no real purpose other than punishing the rich because it wouldn't raise much money, but that's no longer true. Today the top 0.1 percent of Americans, a class with a minimum income of about $1.3 million and an average income of about $3.5 million, receives more than 7 percent of all income—up from just 2.2 percent in 1979.[17] A surtax on that income would yield a significant amount of revenue, which could be used to help a lot of people. All in all, then, the

*FICA   Federal Insurance Contributions Act, an employment tax that helps fund Social Security and Medicare.

next step after rolling back the Bush tax cuts and implementing universal health care should be a broader effort to restore the progressivity of U.S. taxes, and use the revenue to pay for more benefits that help lower- and middle-income families.

Realistically, however, this would not be enough to pay for social expenditures comparable to those in other advanced countries, not even the relatively modest Canadian level. In addition to imposing higher taxes on the rich, other advanced countries also impose higher taxes on the middle class, through both higher social insurance payments and value-added taxes— in effect, national sales taxes. Social insurance taxes and VATs are not, in themselves, progressive. Their effect in reducing inequality is indirect but large: They pay for benefits, and these benefits are worth more as a percentage of income to people with lower incomes.

As a political matter, persuading the public that middle-income families would be better off paying somewhat higher taxes in return for a stronger social safety net will be a hard sell after decades of antitax, antigovernment propaganda. Much as I would like to see the United States devote another 2 or 3 percent of GDP* to social expenditure beyond health care, it's probably an endeavor that has to wait until liberals have established a strong track record of successfully using the government to make peoples' lives better and more secure. This is one reason health care reform, which is tremendously important in itself, would have further benefits: It would blaze the trail for a wider progressive agenda. This is also the reason movement conservatives are fiercely determined not to let health care reform succeed.

*GDP Gross domestic product. One measure of income and output for a country's economy.

Reducing Market Inequality

Aftermarket policies can do a great deal to reduce inequality. But that should not be our whole focus. The Great Compression* also involved a sharp reduction in the inequality of market income. This was accomplished in part through wage controls during World War II, an experience we hope won't be repeated. Still, there are several steps we can take.

The first step has already been taken: In 2007 Congress passed the first increase in the minimum wage within a decade. In the 1950s and 1960s the minimum wage averaged about half of the average wage. By 2006, however, the purchasing power of the minimum wage had been so eroded by inflation that in real terms it was at its lowest point since 1955, and was only 31 percent of the average wage. Thanks to the new Democratic majority in Congress, the minimum is scheduled to rise from its current $5.15 an hour to $7.25 by 2009. This won't restore all the erosion, but it's an important first step.

There are two common but somewhat contradictory 30 objections often heard to increasing the minimum wage. On one hand, it's argued that raising the minimum wage will reduce employment and increase unemployment. On the other it's argued that raising the minimum will have little or no effect in raising wages. The evidence, however, suggests that a minimum wage increase will in fact have modest positive effects.

On the employment side, a classic study by David Card of Berkeley and Alan Krueger of Princeton, two of America's best labor economists, found no evidence that minimum wage increases in the range the United States has experienced led to job losses.[18] Their work has been furiously attacked both

*See paragraph 40.

because it seems to contradict Econ 101 and because it was ideologically disturbing to many. Yet it has stood up very well to repeated challenges, and new cases confirming its results keep coming in. For example, the state of Washington has a minimum wage almost three dollars an hour higher than its neighbor Idaho; business experiences near the state line seem to indicate that, if anything, Washington has gained jobs at Idaho's expense. "Small-business owners in Washington," reported the *New York Times*, "say they have prospered far beyond their expectation. . . . Idaho teenagers cross the state line to work in fast-food restaurants in Washington."

All the empirical evidence suggests that minimum wage increases *in the range that is likely to take place* do not lead to significant job losses. True, an increase in the minimum wage to, say, fifteen dollars an hour would probably cause job losses, because it would dramatically raise the cost of employment in some industries. But that's not what's on—or even near—the table.

Meanwhile minimum wage increases can have fairly significant effects on wages at the bottom end of the scale. The Economic Policy Institute estimates that the worst-paid 10 percent of the U.S. labor force, 13 million workers, will gain from the just-enacted minimum wage increase. Of these, 5.6 million are currently being paid less than the new minimum wage, and would see a direct benefit. The rest are workers earning more than the new minimum wage, who would benefit from ripple effects of the higher minimum.

The minimum wage, however, matters mainly to low-paid workers. Any broader effort to reduce market inequality will have to do something about incomes further up the scale. The most important tool in that respect is likely to be an end to the thirty-year tilt of government policy against unions.

The drastic decline in the U.S. union movement was not, 35 as is often claimed, an inevitable result of globalization and increased competition. International comparisons show that the U.S. union decline is unique, even though other countries faced the same global pressures. Again, in 1960 Canada and the United States had essentially equal rates of unionization, 32 and 30 percent of wage and salary workers, respectively. By 1999 U.S. unionization was down to 13 percent, but Canadian unionization was unchanged. The sources of union decline in America lie not in market forces but in the political climate created by movement conservatism, which allowed employers to engage in union-busting activities and punish workers for supporting union organizers. Without that changed political climate, much of the service economy—especially giant retailers like Wal-Mart—would probably be unionized today.

A new political climate could revitalize the union movement—and revitalizing unions should be a key progressive goal. Specific legislation, such as the Employee Free Choice Act, which would reduce the ability of employers to intimidate workers into rejecting a union, is only part of what's needed. It's also crucial to enforce labor laws already on the books. Much if not most of the antiunion activity that led to the sharp decline in American unionization was illegal even under existing law. But employers judged, correctly, that they could get away with it.

The hard-to-answer question is the extent to which a newly empowered U.S. union movement would reduce inequality. International comparisons suggest that it might make quite a lot of difference. The sharpest increases in wage inequality in the Western world have taken place in the United States and in Britain, both of which experienced sharp declines in union membership. (Britain is still far more unionized than

America, but it used to have more than 50 percent unionization.) Canada, although its economy is closely linked to that of the United States, appears to have had substantially less increase in wage inequality—and it's likely that the persistence of a strong union movement is an important reason why. Unions raise the wages of their members, who tend to be in the middle of the wage distribution; they also tend to equalize wages among members. Perhaps most important, they act as a countervailing force to management, enforcing social norms that limit very high and very low pay even among people who aren't union members. They also mobilize their members to vote for progressive policies. Would getting the United States back to historical levels of unionization undo a large part of the Great Divergence? We don't know—but it might, and encouraging a union resurgence should be a major goal of progressive policy.

A reinvigorated union movement isn't the only change that could reduce extreme inequalities in pay. A number of other factors discouraged very high paychecks for a generation after World War II. One was a change in the political climate: Very high executive pay used to provoke public scrutiny, congressional hearings, and even presidential intervention. But that all ended in the Reagan years.

Historical experience still suggests that a new progressive majority should not be shy about questioning private-sector pay when it seems outrageous. Moral suasion was effective in the past, and could be so again.

Another Great Compression?

The Great Compression, the abrupt reduction in economic 40 inequality that took place in the United States in the 1930s and 1940s, took place at a time of crisis. Today America's state is troubled, but we're not in the midst of a great depression or a world war. Correspondingly, we shouldn't expect changes as drastic or sudden as those that took place seventy years ago. The process of reducing inequality now is likely to be more of a Great Moderation than a Great Compression.

Yet it is possible, both as an economic matter and in terms of practical politics, to reduce inequality and make America a middle-class nation again. And now is the time to get started.

NOTES

1. Thomas Jefferson, letter to James Madison, 28 Oct. 1785 <http://press-pubs.uchicago.edu/founders/documents/v1ch15s32.html>.

2. Irving Kristol, "Income Inequality Without Class Conflict," *Wall Street Journal* 18 Dec. 1997: A22.

3. Robert Frank, *Richistan: A Journey Through the American Wealth Boom and the Lives of the New Rich* (Crown, 2007) 3–4.

4. "Suites for the Sweet," *Newsweek International* July 2–9 <http://www.msnbc.msn.com/id/19388720/site/newsweek>, part of a special report on "Secret Habits of the Super Rich."

5. Elizabeth Warren and Amelia Warren Tyagi, "What's Hurting the Middle Class," *Boston Review* (Sept./Oct. 2005) <http://bostonreview.net/BR30.5/warrentyagi.html>.

6. Tom Hertz, *Understanding Mobility in America* (Center for American Progress, 2006) <http://www.americanprogress.org/issues/2006/04/b1579981.html>.

7. Woodrow Wilson, *The New Freedom* (Doubleday, 1913), Project Gutenberg <http://www.gutenberg.org/files/14811/14811-h/14811-h.htm>.

8. "Tax Breaks for Billionaires," Economic Policy Institute Policy Memorandum no. 120 <http://www.epi.org/content.cfm/pm120>.

9. See, for example, Jessica Holzer, "Conservatives Break with GOP Leaders on a Tax Bill," *The Hill* 18 July 2007 <http://thehill.com/leading-the-news/conservatives-break-with-gop-leaders-on-a-tax-bill-2007-07-18.html>.

10. "In Opposing Tax Plan, Schumer Supports Wall Street Over Party," *New York Times* 30 July 2007: A1.

11. Eric M. Uslaner and Mitchell Brown, "Inequality, Trust, and Civic Engagement," *American Politics Research* 33.6 (2005): 868–94.

12. *The ANES Guide to Public Opinion and Electoral Behavior*, table 5A.2 <http://electionstudies.org/nesguide/toptable/tab5a_2.htm>.

13. Uslaner and Brown, "Inequality, Trust, and Civic Engagement."

14. Tax Policy Center, "Options to Extend the 2001–2006 Tax Cuts, Static Impact on Individual Income and Estate Tax Liability and Revenue ($ billions), 2008–17," Table T07-0126 <http://taxpolicycenter.org/TaxModel/tmdb/Content/PDF/T07-0126.pdf>.

15. Kimberly A. Clausing, "Multinational Firm Tax Avoidance and U.S. Government Revenue" (working paper, Wellesley College, Wellesley, MA, 2007).

16. OECD Tax Database <http://www.oecd.org/ctp/taxdatabase>.

17. Piketty and Saez, 2005 preliminary estimates <http://elsa.berkeley.edu/<saez/TabFig2005prel.xls>.

18. David Card and Alan B. Krueger, "Minimum Wages and Employment: A Case Study of the Fast-Food Industry in New Jersey and Pennsylvania," *American Economic Review* 84.4 (1994): 772–93.

Joining the Conversation

1. Paul Krugman begins by asking the "so what?" question in paragraph 1: "Why should we care about high and rising inequality?" How does he answer this question?

2. What evidence does Krugman provide for the prevalence of economic inequality in U.S. society? How convincing is this evidence to you?

3. Notice how many direct quotations Krugman includes. Why do you think he includes so many? What, if anything, do the quotations contribute that a summary or paraphrase would not?

4. In paragraph 4 Krugman quotes someone whose views he does not agree with, but then uses those views to support his own argument. How do you know he is quoting a view that he disagrees with?

5. Write an essay responding to Krugman, agreeing with him on some points and disagreeing with him on others. Start by summarizing his arguments before moving on to give your own views. See guidelines on pp. 64–66 that will help you to agree and disagree simultaneously.

The Upside of Income Inequality

GARY S. BECKER AND KEVIN M. MURPHY

INCOME INEQUALITY in China substantially widened, particularly between households in the city and the countryside, after China began its rapid rate of economic development around 1980. The average urban resident now makes 3.2 times as much as the average rural resident, and among city dwellers alone, the top 10 percent makes 9.2 times as much as the bottom 10 percent.[1] But at the same time that inequality rose, the number of Chinese who live in poverty fell—from 260 million in 1978 to 42 million in 1998.[2] Despite the widening gap in incomes, rapid economic development dramatically improved the lives of China's poor.

GARY S. BECKER (1930–2014), a Nobel laureate in economics, taught at the University of Chicago and wrote a column for *BusinessWeek*. KEVIN M. MURPHY, a professor at the University of Chicago, was the recipient of a 2005 MacArthur "genius" fellowship. Together, Becker and Murphy wrote *Social Economics: Market Behavior in a Social Environment* (2001). This article first appeared in the May/June 2007 issue of the *American*, the magazine of the American Enterprise Institute, a group "committed to expanding liberty, increasing individual opportunity, and strengthening free enterprise."

Politicians and many others in the United States have grown concerned that earnings inequality has increased among Americans. But as the example of China—or India, for that matter—illustrates, the rise in inequality does not occur in a vacuum. In the case of China and India, the rise in inequality came along with an acceleration of economic growth that raised the standard of living for both the rich and the poor. In the United States, the rise in inequality accompanied a rise in the payoff to education and other skills. We believe that the rise in returns on investments in human capital is beneficial and desirable, and policies designed to deal with inequality must take account of its cause.

To show the importance to inequality of the increased return to human capital, consider Figure 1, which shows the link between earnings and education by displaying the wage premium received by college-educated workers compared with high school graduates. In 1980, an American with a college degree earned about 30 percent more than an American who

FIGURE I. HIGHER EDUCATION EQUALS
MUCH HIGHER WAGES

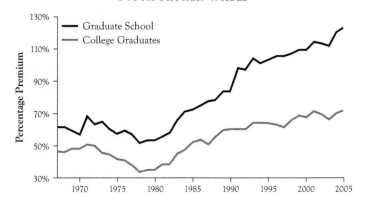

stopped education at high school. But, in recent years, a person with a college education earned roughly 70 percent more. Meanwhile, the premium for having a graduate degree increased from roughly 50 percent in 1980 to well over 100 percent today. The labor market is placing a greater emphasis on education, dispensing rapidly rising rewards to those who stay in school the longest.

This trend has contributed significantly to the growth in overall earnings inequality in the United States. And just as in China and India, this growing inequality gap is associated with growing opportunity—in this case, the opportunity to advance through education. The upward trend in the returns to education is not limited to one segment of the population. Education premiums for women and African Americans have increased as much as, or more than, the premiums for all workers.

Figure 2 shows that the growth in returns to education for women has paralleled that for men over the past 25 years, but has remained at a somewhat higher level. Figure 3 shows that returns for blacks have increased as much as those for whites. As these two figures show, the potential to improve one's labor-market prospects through higher education is greater now than at any time in the recent past, and this potential extends across gender and racial lines.

The growth in returns to college has generated a predictable response: as the education earnings gap increased, a larger fraction of high school graduates went on to college. As Figure 4 shows, the proportion of men and women ages 20 to 25 who attended college jumped by about half over the past 40 years, tracking the rise in the wage premium. When returns fell in the 1970s, the fraction going on to college declined. The rise in returns since 1980 has been accompanied by a significant rise in the fraction going on to college.[3]

FIGURE 2. WOMEN GAIN MORE FROM COLLEGE . . .

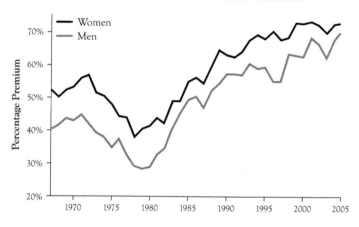

FIGURE 3. . . . AND SO DO AFRICAN AMERICANS

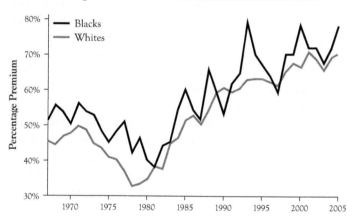

FIGURE 4. AS COLLEGE OFFERS HIGHER WAGES,
MORE AMERICANS ATTEND

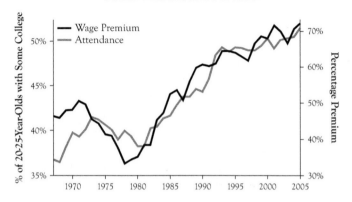

This increase in the proportion of persons going on to higher education is found among all racial and ethnic groups, but it is particularly important for women, who, in 2004, outnumbered men as students in degree-granting institutions of higher education by 33 percent.

Women have also shifted toward higher-earnings fields, such as business, law, and medicine: the number of women in graduate schools rose 66 percent between 1994 and 2004, while the number of men rose just 25 percent.[4] And the greater education achievement of women compared to men is particularly prominent among blacks and Latinos: the proportion of black women who attend colleges and universities jumped from 24 percent to 43 percent between 1974 and 2003, while the proportion of white men rose only from 41 percent to 49 percent.[5]

The potential generated by higher returns to education extends from individuals to the economy as a whole. Growth in the education level of the population has been a significant source of rising wages, productivity, and living standards over the past century. Higher returns to education will accelerate growth in living standards as existing investments have a higher return, and additional investments in education will be made in response to the higher returns. Gains from the higher returns will not be limited to GDP and other measures of economic activity; education provides a wide range of benefits not captured in GDP, and these will grow more rapidly as well due to the additional investments in schooling.

Why is the earnings gap widening? Because the demand for educated and other skilled persons is growing. That is hardly surprising, given developments in computers and the Internet, advances in biotechnology, and a general shift in economic activity to more education-intensive sectors, such as finance and professional services. Also, globalization has encouraged the importing of products using relatively low-skilled labor from abroad. At the same time, world demand has risen for the kinds of products and services that are provided by high-skilled employees.

When calculating the returns to education, we look at the costs of education as well. And even accounting for the rise in university tuition (it more than doubled, on average, in constant dollars between 1980 and 2005), overall returns to college and graduate study have increased substantially. Indeed, it appears that the increases in tuition were partly induced by the greater return to college education. Pablo Peña, in a Ph.D. dissertation in progress at the University of Chicago, argues convincingly that tuition rose in part because students want to invest more in the quality of their education, and increased spending per student by colleges is partly financed by higher tuition levels.[6] More investment in the quality and quantity of schooling will benefit both individuals and society.

This brings us to our punch line. Should an increase in earnings inequality due primarily to higher rates of return on

The Upside of Income Inequality

education and other skills be considered a favorable rather than an unfavorable development? We think so. Higher rates of return on capital are a sign of greater productivity in the economy, and that infer-

See p. 137 for other ways to guide readers to your main point.

ence is fully applicable to human capital as well as to physical capital. The initial impact of higher returns to human capital is wider inequality in earnings (the same as the initial effect of higher returns on physical capital), but that impact becomes more muted and may be reversed over time as young men and women invest more in their human capital.

We conclude that the forces raising earnings inequality in the United States are beneficial to the extent that they reflect higher returns to investments in education and other human capital. Yet this conclusion should not produce complacency, for the response so far to these higher returns has been disturbingly limited. For example, why haven't more high school graduates gone on to a college education when the benefits are so apparent? Why don't more of those who go to college finish a four-year degree? (Only about half do so.)[7] And why has the proportion of American youth who drop out of high school, especially African-American and Hispanic males, remained fairly constant?

The answers to these and related questions lie partly in the breakdown of the American family, and the resulting low skill levels acquired by many children in elementary and secondary school—particularly individuals from broken households. Cognitive skills tend to get developed at very early ages while, as our colleague James Heckman has shown, noncognitive skills—such as study habits, getting to appointments on time, and attitudes toward work—get fixed at later, although still relatively young, ages. Most high school dropouts certainly appear to be seriously deficient in the noncognitive skills that would enable them to take advantage of the higher rates of return to education and other human capital.

So instead of lamenting the increased earnings gap caused by education, policymakers and the public should focus attention on how to raise the fraction of American youth who complete high school and then go on for a college education. Solutions are not cheap or easy. But it will be a disaster if the focus remains so much on the earnings inequality itself that Congress tries to interfere directly with this inequality rather than trying to raise the education levels of those who are now being left behind.

For many, the solution to an increase in inequality is to make the tax structure more progressive—raise taxes on high-income households and reduce taxes on low-income households. While this may sound sensible, it is not. Would these same individuals advocate a tax on going to college and a subsidy for dropping out of high school in response to the increased importance of education? We think not. Yet shifting the tax structure has exactly this effect.

A more sensible policy is to try to take greater advantage of the opportunities afforded by the higher returns to human capital and encourage more human capital investment. Attempts to raise taxes and impose other penalties on the higher earnings that come from greater skills could greatly reduce the productivity of the world's leading economy by discouraging investments in its most productive and precious form of capital—human capital.

Notes

1. Dexter Roberts, "China's Widening Income Gap," *BusinessWeek*, February 16, 2007.

2. "China: Two Decades of Poverty Reduction," *Overcoming Human Poverty: UNDP Poverty Report 2000*, United Nations Development Programme, 2000.

3. U.S. Department of Education, National Center for Education Statistics.

4. Ibid.

5. "Postsecondary Participation Rates by Sex and Race/Ethnicity: 1974–2003," *Issue Brief*, March 2005, National Center for Education Statistics.

6. Pablo A. Peña, "What is the Effect of Colleges' Wealth on Tuition Fees?" Introduction to "Tuition and Wealth at American Colleges," University of Chicago, 2006.

7. Associated Press, "U.S. College Drop-out Rate Sparks Concern," September 27, 2006.

Joining the Conversation

1. Why, according to Gary Becker and Kevin Murphy, has income inequality in the United States increased significantly since 1980? In what ways do they believe that this change is "beneficial and desirable"?

2. According to the authors, "Growth in the education level of the population has been a significant source of rising wages, productivity, and living standards over the past century" (paragraph 9). Which groups have benefited from these developments, and which ones have not? What do Becker and Murphy say about what can be done to improve the situation of the less advantaged?

3. This article appeared in a magazine published by an institute "committed to expanding liberty, increasing individual opportunity, and strengthening free enterprise." What aspects of the authors' argument seem consistent with those goals? What other views do they mention, and how persuasively do they respond? What other objections could be raised?

4. Paul Krugman offers a different perspective on economic inequality (pp. 561–80). How might he respond to Becker and Murphy's argument that earnings inequality should be considered "a favorable rather than an unfavorable development"?

5. Becker and Murphy conclude by saying that "Attempts to raise taxes and impose other penalties on the higher earnings that come from greater skills could greatly reduce the productivity of the world's leading economy by discouraging investments in its most productive and precious form of capital—human capital." Summarize this conclusion in your own words, and see if you can think of some examples that would help demonstrate what they're saying.

6. Go to **theysayiblog.com** and read "Of the 1%, by the 1%, for the 1%" by Joseph Stiglitz, a Nobel-winning economist who does *not* believe that inequality in the United States is at all "beneficial." Imagine that Stiglitz wrote his article for the kind of politically conservative audience in favor of free enterprise that Becker and Murphy were writing for. How might Stiglitz have developed his argument differently to appeal to such readers? Consider his title, for example, and suggest a title that would be more likely to appeal to such an audience. What in Becker and Murphy's article might he quote as a "they say"—and what then might he say?

What's Killing Poor White Women?

MONICA POTTS

—⊡—

*For most Americans, life expectancy continues to rise—
but not for uneducated white women. They have lost five
years, and no one understands why.*

ON THE NIGHT OF MAY 23, 2012, which turned out to be
the last of her life, Crystal Wilson baby-sat her infant grand-
daughter, Kelly. It was how she would have preferred to spend
every night. Crystal had joined Facebook the previous year,
and the picture of her daughter cradling the newborn in the
hospital bed substituted for a picture of herself. Crystal's entire
wall was a catalog of visits from her nieces, nephews, cousins'
kids, and, more recently, the days she baby-sat Kelly. She was

————

MONICA POTTS writes for the *American Prospect*, a magazine whose
website says, "We're liberal, progressive, lefty—call it what you want,
we're proud of it." Her work also has appeared in the *Connecticut
Post*, the *Stamford Advocate*, and the *New York Times*. She blogs at
postbourgie.com. This article first appeared in the July/August 2013
issue of the *American Prospect*.

a mother hen, people said of Crystal. She'd wanted a house full of children, but she'd only had one.

The picture the family chose for her obituary shows Crystal and her husband holding the infant. Crystal leans in from the side, with dark, curly hair, an unsmiling round face, and black eyebrows knit together. She was 38 and bore an unhealthy heft, more than 200 pounds. Crystal had been to the doctor, who told her she was overweight and diabetic. She was waiting to get medicine, but few in her family knew it, and no one thought she was near death.

Crystal's 17-year-old daughter, Megan, split her time between her parents' house in Cave City, Arkansas, and that of her boyfriend, Corey, in nearby Evening Shade. Megan made sure that each set of grandparents could spend time with the baby. The night before Crystal's death, Megan and Corey were moving with his parents to a five-acre patch near Crystal. Megan and Corey were running late, so they didn't pick the baby up until 11 P.M. Crystal seemed fine. "You couldn't tell she was sick," Megan says. "She never felt sick." They went back home, and Megan got a text from her mom around midnight. "She said she loved me, give Kelly kisses, and give Corey hugs and tell him to take care of her girls and she'd see me in the morning. I was supposed to drop Kelly off at ten o'clock and finish moving."

Instead, at around 9:30 the next morning, when Megan was getting ready to leave, Corey's grandfather called and said Crystal was dead. Megan didn't believe him. If one of her parents passed, it had to be her dad. "I thought it was my dad that died because he was always the unhealthy one." Megan left Kelly with her mother-in-law and raced with Corey and his dad in the truck, hazards on, laying on the horn, and pulled into the dirt driveway outside her parents' tan-and-brown single-wide trailer. "Daddy was sitting there in the recliner crying,"

Megan says. "It was Momma gone, not him." Crystal had died in her bed early in the morning.

Just after 10 A.M., nearly every relative Crystal had was 5 in the rutted driveway in front of the trailer. Crystal was the last of six children and considered the baby of the family. She was the third sibling to die. Her brother Terry, the "Big Man," who hosted all the holiday dinners and coached the family softball team, had died three months earlier at age 47, and her sister Laura, whom everybody called Pete, died at age 45 in 2004. The police—dozens, it seemed, from the county and from the town—had arrived and blocked off the bedroom where she lay and were interviewing people to figure out what had killed her.

The coroner arrived and pronounced Crystal dead at 11:40. Her body was rolled out on a gurney and shipped to the state lab in Little Rock. One of the officers, Gerald Traw, later told me an autopsy is routine when someone dies without a doctor present. "We like to know why somebody died," he says.

Everything about Crystal's life was ordinary, except for her death. She is one of a demographic—white women who don't graduate from high school—whose life expectancy has declined dramatically over the past 18 years. These women can now expect to die five years earlier than the generation before them. It is an unheard-of drop for a wealthy country in the age of modern medicine. Throughout history, technological and scientific innovation have put death off longer and longer, but the benefits of those advances have not been shared equally, especially across the race and class divides that characterize 21st-century America. Lack of access to education, medical care, good wages, and healthy food isn't just leaving the worst-off Americans behind. It's killing them.

The journal *Health Affairs* reported the five-year drop last August. The article's lead author, Jay Olshansky, who studies human longevity at the University of Illinois at Chicago, with a team of researchers looked at death rates for different groups from 1990 to 2008. White men without high-school diplomas had lost three years of life expectancy, but it was the decline for women like Crystal that made the study news. Previous studies had shown that the least-educated whites began dying younger in the 2000s, but only by about a year. Olshansky and his colleagues did something the other studies hadn't: They isolated high-school dropouts and measured their outcomes instead of lumping them in with high-school graduates who did not go to college.

The last time researchers found a change of this magnitude, Russian men had lost seven years after the fall of the Soviet Union, when they began drinking more and taking on other risky behaviors. Although women generally outlive men in the U.S., such a large decline in the average age of death, from almost 79 to a little more than 73, suggests that an increasing number of women are dying in their twenties, thirties, and forties. "We actually don't know the exact reasons why it's happened," Olshansky says. "I wish we did."

Most Americans, including high-school dropouts of other races, are gaining life expectancy, just at different speeds. Absent a war, genocide, pandemic, or massive governmental collapse, drops in life expectancy are rare. "If you look at the history of longevity in the United States, there have been no dramatic negative or positive shocks," Olshansky says. "With the exception of the 1918 influenza pandemic, everything has been relatively steady, slow changes. This is a five-year drop in an 18-year time period. That's dramatic."

Researchers had known education was linked to longer life since the 1960s, but it was difficult to tell whether it was a proxy for other important factors—like coming from a wealthy family or earning a high income as an adult. In 1999, a Columbia economics graduate student named Adriana Lleras-Muney decided to figure out if education was the principal cause. She found that each additional year of schooling added about a year of life. Subsequent studies suggested the link was less direct. Education is strongly associated with a longer life, but that doesn't mean that every year of education is an elixir. "It is the biggest association, but it is also the thing that we measure about people the best," Lleras-Muney says. "It is one of those things that we can collect data on. There could be other things that matter a lot more, but they're just very difficult to measure."

As is often the case when researchers encounter something fuzzy, they start suggesting causes that sound decidedly unscientific. Their best guess is that staying in school teaches people to delay gratification. The more educated among us are better at forgoing pleasurable and possibly risky behavior because we've learned to look ahead to the future. That connection isn't new, however, and it wouldn't explain why the least-educated whites like Crystal are dying so much younger today than the same group was two decades ago.

Cave City gives itself the low-stakes title of "Home of the World's Sweetest Watermelons." Beneath the ground, the Crystal River carves out the caverns that lend the town its name. Above it, 1,900 people live in single-wides in neighborhoods dotted with fenced lawns or along spindly red-dirt trails off the main highway. In this part of Arkansas, the Ozark Plateau flattens to meet the Mississippi embayment, and the hills give way to rice paddies. About 17,000 people live in Sharp County, a long string of small towns with Cave City at the bottom and the Missouri border at the top. Most of the residents are white—96 percent—with a median household income of $29,590. Nearly a quarter live in poverty, and Crystal was among them; for most of her married life, she relied on income from her husband's disability checks.

For work, people drive to the college town of Batesville, about 20 minutes south, which has a chicken-processing plant that periodically threatens to close and an industrial bakery with 12-hour shifts that make it hard for a mother to raise children. Less than 13 percent of county residents have a bachelor's degree. Society is divided into opposites: Godly folk go to church and sinners chase the devil, students go to college and dropouts seek hard labor, and men call the shots and women cook for them.

Crystal's parents, Junior and Martha Justice, had moved to 15 the area when her three oldest siblings were still toddlers. "My aunt told my dad that he could make better money up here, but it wasn't so," says Linda Holley, one of Crystal's sisters. Junior farmed, which fed his family and brought in a little money. He found a piece of land on a country road called Antioch and bought a prefabricated home from the Jim Walters company. It was on this land they had their next three children. Crystal, born July 6, 1973, was the sixth and youngest.

Their life was old-school country. They raised chickens and goats and grew their own vegetables. The house was small, with only three bedrooms. Crystal's closest sibling, Terry, was 7 years older. Linda was a full 15 years older than Crystal, which made her more like a second mom than a sister. When Crystal was two, Linda's twin sister, Pete, began having children and, fleeing a string of abusive relationships, turned over custody to her parents. Having four slightly younger nieces and nephews in the house gave Crystal playmates her own age.

It was Linda, the doting older sister and aunt, who would take all the kids to Dogpatch, a creaky little Ozarks amusement park based on the comic strip, with actors playing Daisy Mae and Li'l Abner. Linda keeps Polaroids of Crystal from that time. They show her with long, curly blond hair and often half-clothed, happy, covered in clay and mud. "Grandpa used to call her his little Shirley Temple," says Crystal's niece, Lori.

When Crystal was starting out in elementary school, the family moved to a trailer to be closer to town. Her dad worked occasionally for lumber companies, and the proximity made jobs easier to find. Crystal was well behaved in school, and teachers would ask Lori, only two years behind, "Why aren't you like her, she was so quiet and shy?" Crystal loved basketball and, especially, softball, which she played in summer clubs even as an adult. As she got older, her hair darkened and she became stocky and muscular. She played ball like a bulldozer and was aggressive on the field and mouthy off. The whole family would play and bicker and joke. Crystal would smack people across the butt with the bat if they weren't moving fast enough.

"It wasn't until we got in high school that I realized she was struggling so bad in school," Lori says. "I was in the seventh grade, and she was in the ninth, and I wasn't really smart myself. But I could help her do some of her work." In 1988, Junior died from lung cancer at age 55. Both he and Martha were smokers. The next year Crystal met Carl Wilson, whom everybody called Possum. He was related to a cousin through marriage and, at 28, was 12 years her senior. They kept their relationship secret for a few months. "He came up to see her at the school," Lori says. "So I pretty much put two and two together. I was the one that told my grandmother." Lori thought that would put an end to it; instead, Martha let them marry. According to Linda, Martha had one admonition for Possum: "Momma said, 'As long as you take care of her and don't hit her, you have my permission.' He done what he could do for her. They was mates."

Possum moved in with the family in the trailer. He and 20
Crystal had one room, Martha another, and the four nephews
and nieces shared two bunk beds in the third. Crystal dropped
out in the tenth grade because she had married. That was the
way things were. None of Crystal's siblings finished high school.
Instead, they became adults when they were teenagers. Crystal
would spend the rest of her years as a housewife to a husband
who soon became ill and as a mother to a daughter who would
grow up as fast as she did.

Researchers have long known that high-school dropouts like
Crystal are unlikely to live as long as people who have gone
to college. But why would they be slipping behind the generation before them? James Jackson, a public-health researcher at
the University of Michigan, believes it's because life became
more difficult for the least-educated in the 1990s and 2000s.
Broad-scale shifts in society increasingly isolate those who don't
finish high school from good jobs, marriageable partners, and
healthier communities. "Hope is lowered. If you drop out of
school, say, in the last 20 years or so, you just had less hope
for ever making it and being anything," Jackson says. "The
opportunities available to you are very different than what they
were 20 or 30 years ago. What kind of job are you going to get
if you drop out at 16? No job."

In May, Jennifer Karas Montez of the Harvard University
Center for Population and Development Studies co-authored
the first paper investigating why white women without high-
school diplomas might be dying. Most research has looked at
which diseases are the cause of death, but Montez and her co-
author wanted to tease out quality of life: economic indicators
like employment and income, whether women were married
and how educated their spouses were, and health behaviors

like smoking and alcohol abuse. It is well known that smoking shortens life; in fact, smoking led to the early deaths of both of Crystal's parents and her sister and brother. Crystal, though, never smoke or drank. But the researchers discovered something else that was driving women like her to early graves: Whether the women had a job mattered, and it mattered more than income or other signs of financial stability, like homeownership. In fact, smoking and employment were the only two factors of any significance.

At first, Montez and her co-author suspected that women who are already unhealthy are less able to work and so are already more likely to die. When they investigated that hypothesis, however, it didn't hold up. Jobs themselves contributed something to health. But what? It could be, the authors suggested, that work connects women to friends and other social networks they otherwise wouldn't have. Even more squishy sounding, Montez wrote that jobs might give women a "sense of purpose."

Better-educated women are the most likely to work and to achieve parity with men: Seventy-two percent are in the workforce, compared with 81 percent of their male counterparts. Women without high-school diplomas are the least likely to work. Only about a third are in the workforce, compared to about half of their male counterparts. If they do find work, women are more likely than men to have minimum-wage jobs. They account for most workers in the largest low-paying occupations—child-care providers, housecleaners, food servers. Even if they do have minimum-wage jobs, this group of women is more likely to leave the labor force to take care of young children because child care is prohibitively expensive.

Montez's joblessness study, however, raised more questions. 25 Would any job do? What does giving women a "sense of purpose" mean? And why would joblessness hit white women harder than other groups? Overall, men lost more jobs during the Great Recession. Why are women losing years at a faster rate?

Cave City life revolves around its rivers, thick with runoff from the mountains and barreling toward the Mississippi. Crystal loved the area, but she also didn't know anything else. She hunted squirrels and rabbits in the fall, but spring was filled with what she loved most. School ends, and softball season begins. It is a brief, lovely time, before humidity and mosquitoes, when the world smells of wildflowers and dirt and storms. Every year, one of Crystal's brothers made sure she had a fishing license for the spring-swollen White River and the less touristy Black River, where they had better hauls. People come from around the state to float lazily, drunkenly down the rivers in canoes and rafts. Songbirds come too—buntings, mockingbirds, whippoorwills, woodpeckers—settling in for the season near the quieter streams, ponds, and water-filled rice paddies. Deer fill the kudzu-covered woods. Copperhead snakes awakened from hibernation nest in muddy puddles.

Crystal wanted to start a family as soon as she was married but couldn't. Her first three pregnancies, in the early '90s, ended in miscarriages. The first two occurred so late she gave the babies names, Justin and Crystal; the last was a set of twins. None of her relatives knew if she ever went to a doctor to find out why she miscarried. "I just thought maybe it was one of those things, you know, some people can have them and carry them and some can't," Lori says. Megan said her mother had had "female cancer," a catchall phrase for cervical cancer and the infections and dysplasia leading up to it.

When Lori's son was born, Crystal teased her about stealing him. She was always volunteering to baby-sit the kids in the family. When Crystal finally got pregnant with Megan, no one was sure she would make it, least of all Crystal and Possum. "They ended up just praying for me," Megan says. She was born July 20, 1994, and became the center of Crystal's world.

By the time Megan was born, Crystal and Possum were living in their own trailer but were struggling financially. Possum had worked the first four years of their marriage at the chicken-processing plant before quitting for good because of health problems. An accident on an oil rig when he was a teenager had left him with a plate in his skull. Chicken-processing plants are tough places to work, and besides, he qualified for disability. Crystal spent her life taking him to specialists—he was covered by Medicaid—but the problems piled up. He had a congenital heart condition and a bad back. A young-old man.

When Megan was 12, Crystal worked for a brief spell as a housekeeper at a nursing home in Cave City, where Linda and Lori worked. Mostly, though, she stayed home to take care of Possum and Megan. Baby-sitting brought in small amounts of cash, but she and Possum relied on disability, which was about $1,000 a month. Outside of a brief trip to Texas after Megan was born to show her off to Possum's family, and a trip to a small town near St. Louis to visit a niece after one of the trailers they lived in burned down, Crystal passed her entire life in Cave City.

Crystal spent what money she had on Megan. She gave her any new toy she wanted and, later, name-brand clothes, a four-wheeler, a laptop, and a phone. When Megan started playing softball, Crystal spent money on shoes, gloves, and club fees. "Crystal was a super mom," says Steve Green, the school superintendent and Megan's softball coach. "They didn't have a lot of revenue, but they put everything they had into Megan."

Crystal and Possum made it to every practice and every game, even if it meant driving for an hour, deep into the mountains. They brought snacks and sports drinks for Megan's teammates. Crystal would watch her nieces, nephews, and cousins' kids play, and she still played for her family team in Batesville. Crystal went with Linda to a missionary Baptist church near the family road in Antioch, but she and Possum weren't every-Sunday Christians—it was the softball field her spring weekends revolved around. But when Terry was diagnosed with cancer in 2009, the family stopped playing, and Crystal lost her favorite activity.

When her relatives look back, they think Crystal was probably lonely. Her mother had died three years after Megan was born. Although she and Possum had a Ford Contour, Crystal seldom drove, relying on relatives to come by to take her to the grocery store. It was a chance to visit. When Linda's daughter took her truck-driver husband to pick up his 18-wheeler for his next haul, Crystal would always want to go with them. She would call her family members throughout the day, gossiping. She didn't stir up trouble, but she reveled in drama. Crystal would often go to Linda's for homemade biscuits and gravy for breakfast, and she'd ask Linda to buy her liter bottles of Dr Pepper whenever she ran out. She was addicted to Dr Pepper. Sometimes, relatives paid for Possum's medicine; Linda's daughter remembers paying as much as $64 in one visit. Crystal's nieces and nephews had gotten older and started their own families, and now she relied on them as much as she had her older siblings.

Another mystery emerged from the lifespan study: Black women without a high-school diploma are now outliving their white counterparts.

As a group, blacks are more likely to die young, because the factors that determine well-being—income, education, access to health care—tend to be worse for blacks. Yet blacks on the whole are closing the life–expectancy gap with whites. In a country where racism still plays a significant role in all that contributes to a healthier, longer life, what could be affecting whites more than blacks?

One theory is that low-income white women smoke and 35 drink and abuse prescription drugs like OxyContin and street drugs like meth more than black women. Despite Crystal's weight and diabetes, those problems are more common among black women and usually kill more slowly. Meth and alcohol kill quickly. It could be that white women, as a group, are better at killing themselves.

Still, why would white women be more likely to engage in risky behaviors? Another theory is that the kind of place people live in, who is around them, and what those neighbors are doing play a central role. Health is also a matter of place and time.

In March, two researchers from the University of Wisconsin reported that women in nearly half of 3,140 counties in the United States saw their death rates rise during the same time period that Olshansky studied. The researchers colored the counties with an increase in female mortality a bright red, and the red splashed over Appalachia, down through Kentucky and Tennessee, north of the Cotton Belt, and across the Ozarks—the parts of the South where poor white people live. Location seemed to matter more than other indicators, like drug use, which has been waning. The Wisconsin researchers recommended more studies examining "cultural, political, or religious factors."

Something less tangible, it seems, is shaping the lives of white women in the South, beyond what science can measure. Surely these forces weigh on black women, too, but perhaps they are more likely to have stronger networks of other women.

Perhaps after centuries of slavery and Jim Crow, black women are more likely to feel like they're on an upward trajectory. Perhaps they have more control relative to the men in their communities. In low-income white communities of the South, it is still women who are responsible for the home and for raising children, but increasingly they are also raising their husbands. A husband is a burden and an occasional heartache rather than a helpmate, but one women are told they cannot do without. More and more, data show that poor women are working the hardest and earning the most in their families but can't take the credit for being the breadwinners. Women do the emotional work for their families, while men reap the most benefits from marriage. The rural South is a place that often wants to remain unchanged from the 1950s and 1960s, and its women are now dying as if they lived in that era, too.

Crystal's world was getting smaller and smaller and more sedentary. Everyone was worried about Possum, but Crystal's own health was bad. She'd had a cystic ovary removed when Megan was 13, and about a year before her death she had a hysterectomy. The surgery was necessary after Crystal had started hemorrhaging, which was brought on by another miscarriage—something her family didn't know about until the autopsy. It's unclear when she learned she was a diabetic. Megan thinks her mom might have heard it for the first time when she was pregnant with her, but Crystal never had regular medical care because she didn't qualify for Medicaid as Possum did.

Megan started spending more time away from her mom in the tenth grade, when Corey and his family moved to town. Crystal consented to their high-school romance, though she warned Corey that if he ever hit her daughter, she'd put him in the ground herself. Within a year of going out with Corey,

Megan was pregnant. She swears she didn't know it until she was seven and a half months along, when Corey's mother made her take a pregnancy test. They had a short time to prepare for Kelly's birth in February 2012, but Crystal was happy about the new baby. It was a way for her to have another child. But after Kelly's birth, Crystal and Megan argued; Megan was worried her mother would spoil Kelly. Because Corey's father worked, his family had a bit more money, and they bought more baby clothes than Crystal could, which only made her feel worse.

In the final months of her life, Crystal complained of chest 40 aches, but when she went to the emergency room, the doctors assured her it wasn't a heart attack. She said that she felt like she had the flu or allergies. In hindsight, it was after Terry's death—he died a week after Kelly was born—when Crystal really began to suffer. He had been the linchpin of the family, and now they were breaking apart. After he died, Crystal would call Linda's daughter and say, "I wish God would have took me instead of Terry." Crystal posted regularly about Terry on her Facebook page. Crystal had stopped coming to Linda's for breakfast, too, because Possum was growing sicker and had started falling when he tried to walk on his own. He was diagnosed with cancer about a week before Crystal's death. "I couldn't help but wonder if maybe some of it might have been attributed to her system just being drug down from having to take care of Carl and Megan," says Steve Green, the school superintendent. "Just everyday stress."

The night before she died, Crystal made herself a peanut-butter-and-jelly sandwich for dinner. After Megan took Kelly home, she went to bed and fell asleep, but Possum said she woke up at 1 A.M., said she was thirsty, and went to the kitchen. She was a fitful sleeper, and she returned to bed. When Crystal wasn't up before him the next morning, it struck Possum as odd, but he let her sleep. Crystal usually called her relatives around 6 or 7 A.M. to see what their plans were for the day. They wondered if something was wrong when their phones didn't beep. Finally, Possum sent in his brother, who'd been staying with them, to wake Crystal up; they were always going after each other, and he thought the teasing would spur her out of bed.

Crystal's funeral was small, mostly attended by family, and held at the funeral home in Cave City. They buried her in a tiny graveyard next to a little white chapel on Antioch Road, near the land where Crystal was born. Megan went to stay with Corey's family, and they offered to buy Possum a prefabricated barn so he could come live near them, but there was no need. He spent most of the next four weeks in and out of the hospital, until he died of massive heart failure on June 22. Possum was buried right beside Crystal. Both graves are marked with temporary notices. Linda has promised Megan she will help buy tombstones.

The medical examiner's investigation into Crystal's death was closed because it was determined she died of natural causes. The police report lists no official cause. With untreated, unmanaged diabetes, her blood would have been thick and sticky—the damage would have been building for years—and it could have caused cardiac arrest or a stroke. Linda has her own explanation: "Her heart exploded." And, in a way, it had.

After her mom's death, Megan was 17, hitched, and living on the same land where Crystal had given birth to her. Was it going to be the same life over again?

At school, a number of administrators and teachers stepped in to make sure Megan felt supported; one of them was the technology coordinator for the Cave City schools, Julie Johnson. With big gray eyes and a neat gray bob, she seems younger than

46. When I visited the school this spring, Julie showed me a picture of Megan with Kelly, Corey, and his family that Megan copied and gave to her. They became close last winter when Julie walked into one of Megan's classrooms and the teacher asked, "Have you congratulated Megan?" Julie turned to her and said, "What have you done, sister?" Megan told her that she'd given birth only a week before but that she'd wanted to come back to school. Julie said, "Dang, you're tough!"

Julie has seen a lot of teen mothers. Arkansas ranks No. 1 in the country in teenage births. About a month before Megan gave birth to Kelly, another young woman from the school had gotten married and had a baby, then died mysteriously. Nobody knew what had caused it, and the girl, Bethany, was in the back of Julie's mind when she saw Megan. "I've been in education for 25 years. I kind of got a good eye and sensed where she was coming from. And I was troubled because, as I kept thinking, OK, if a teacher here at school has a baby, they have a big shower for her, and if somebody at church has a baby, they have a shower for her, but if you have a child as a child, we don't do anything."

She prayed on what to do, and prayed some more. It led her to start the Bethany Project, a donation program that would give Megan and other young mothers baby clothes, school supplies, and community support. Megan was only in the spring of her junior year when she had Kelly. Megan told Julie she'd promised her mother she'd stay in school—Megan told me Crystal wanted her to have a good job so she could take care of Kelly and spoil her rotten—and Julie thinks Megan's mother-in-law helped her uphold her promise. "Corey's mother, I think she would have fought the devil to make sure those two finished school." They did. Megan and Corey finished school on May 3 of this year, were married eight days later on May 11, and then graduated on May 18, just a few days shy of the anniversary of Crystal's death. Megan found a job at Wendy's and plans to enroll in the community college in Batesville. Finishing college would give her the best chance to escape her mother's fate.

Julie knows a lot of young women who will never break the cycle. She has her own thoughts about what might be dragging down their life expectancy. "Desperation," she says. "You look at the poverty level in this county—I love this place. It's where I'm from. I don't want you to think I'm being negative about it." But she gestures toward the highway and notes how little is there: a few convenience stores, a grocery, and a nursing home. You have to drive north to the county seat in Ash Flat for a Walmart, or you can negotiate traffic in Batesville, where you might get a job at the chicken plant or a fast-food restaurant. "If you are a woman, and you are a poorly educated woman, opportunities for you are next to nothing. You get married and you have kids. You can't necessarily provide as well as you'd like to for those kids. Oftentimes, the way things are, you're better off if you're not working. You get more help. You get better care for your kids if you're not working. It's a horrible cycle.

"You don't even hear about women's lib, because that's come and gone. But you hear about glass ceilings, and I think girls, most especially girls, have to be taught that just because they're girls doesn't mean they can't do something. That they are just as smart, that they are just as valuable as males. And we have to teach boys that girls can be that way, too. They all need the love, nurturing, and support from somebody from their family or who's not their family. Somebody who's willing to step up. There has to be something to inspire kids to want more, to want better. And they have to realize that they're going to have to work hard to get it. I don't know how you do that.

"It's just horrible, you know? I don't know if 'horrible' is the 50 right word." Julie puts her face into her hands. "The desperation of the times. I don't know anything about anything, but that's what kills them."

Joining the Conversation

1. Monica Potts concludes by quoting a school administrator in rural Arkansas: "The desperation of the times . . . that's what kills them." Based on what you've learned in this article, what factors might she be referring to when she talks about "desperation"?

2. This article appeared in the *American Prospect*, a political magazine whose editors say, "We're liberal, progressive, lefty—call it what you want, we're proud of it." In what respects does Potts's article reflect this political perspective?

3. So what? Who cares? How does Potts show us why this topic matters? How might she make that point even more persuasively?

4. How do you think Potts would respond to Radley Balko's argument (pp. 466–70) that choices about eating, lifestyle, and health are largely matters of personal responsibility and should not be considered the government's responsibility?

5. This article is written primarily as a narrative about the life and death of Crystal Wilson. Rewrite the article as an argument about creating more government programs to help people like Crystal. You can write in favor of such programs, against them, or both, but be sure to consider arguments other than your own.

The American Dream:
Dead, Alive, or on Hold?

BRANDON KING

— ◻ —

WHAT IS THE TRUE STATE of the so-called "American Dream" today? Is it still around, waiting to be achieved by those who work hard enough, or is it effectively dead, killed off by the Great Recession and the economic hardships that many Americans have come to face? Statistics reveal alarming facts, including trillions of dollars lost in the stock market (Paradis, 2009). While these losses, combined with admittedly high unemployment in the past few years, have contributed to seemingly dismal prospects for prosperity in the United States, I believe that the ideals and values of the American Dream are still very much alive. In fact, the original term "American Dream" was coined during the Great Depression by James Truslow Adams, who wrote that the American dream "is that dream of a land in which life should be better and richer and fuller for everyone, with opportunity for each according to ability

———

BRANDON KING is a law student at Indiana University. He majored in political science at the University of Cincinnati. He has always enjoyed writing on the topics of economic inequality and political structures in the United States and wrote this essay in 2011, for this book.

and achievement, regardless of social class or circumstances of birth" (1931). I would redefine the American Dream today as the potential to work for an honest, secure way of life and save for the future. Many liberal economists and activists say that the American Dream is dead, but I say that it's more alive and important than ever—and that it is the key to climbing out of the Great Recession, overcoming inequality, and achieving true prosperity.

Despite the harshness of the Great Recession, a 2009 *New York Times* survey found that 72 percent of Americans still believed it was possible to start poor, work hard, and become rich in America (Seelye, 2009). In the same survey, Americans were also asked questions about what they believed constituted being "successful," with the majority naming things such as a steady job, financial security for the future, being able to retire without struggling, and having a secure place of residence. Less common were responses about owning a home or car and being able to buy other expensive goods, implying a subtle shift from the American Dream of the past to a more modest one today. In many ways, the American Dream of today is a trimmed down version of its former self. The real sign of success in our society used to be owning expensive items, namely cars and homes, and acquiring more material wealth. Living the American Dream meant going from dirt poor to filthy rich and becoming more than you could have ever imagined. Today, most people do not strive for a rags-to-riches transition, and instead prefer a stable, middle-class lifestyle, one in which they can focus on saving money for the future and having secure employment. For example, more and more people now rent their homes instead of buying; a recent study showed a decrease in home ownership from 69% in 2005 to about 66.5% in 2010, and an increase in renter households of 1.1 million (Hoak, 2011). Americans are scrutinizing their spending habits more intensely, as shown in a survey completed in 2009 showing that approximately two-thirds of Americans have permanently changed their spending habits as a result of the Great Recession and that one-fourth hope to save more money for the future (Frietchen, 2009).

Looking at the fragile economy today, it is tempting to focus on the unevenness of the recovery: the stock market has made impressive rebounds in recent months, but the unemployment rate remains high. Thanks to bailouts for large corporations and stimulus measures intended to generate growth, economic activity seems to be on its way towards pre-recession levels, but the economy remains fragile. Weak national real estate markets, sluggish job growth, and the slow recovery of liquid assets lost during the recession are obstacles to a full recovery.

To many, the most worrisome problem is inequality: that wealth is concentrated into the hands of a rich minority. One economist, Robert Reich, even says that "As long as income and wealth keep concentrating at the top, and the great divide between America's have-mores and have-lesses continues to widen, the Great Recession won't end, at least not in the real economy" (Reich, 2009). The essence of Reich's argument is that Wall Street will effectively deter any meaningful recovery on Main Street. Another economist, Paul Krugman, holds a similar position, writing that "The lion's share of economic growth in America over the past thirty years has gone to a small, wealthy minority," and that "the lack of clear economic progress for lower and middle income families is in itself an important reason to seek a more equal distribution of income" (2007). Krugman believes that the American Dream is no longer possible for most Americans, and that the government should enact policies to close the income gap.

We may have genuine inequality issues and a sizable divide 5 between the rich and poor, and we might have an economy that is recovering too slowly for public interest. The American Dream, however, is based on perception, on the way some-one *imagines* how to be successful. How can anyone claim that because there are more poor people than rich, or more power and wealth concentrated at the top, that the entire premise of the American Dream is dead? In fact, the safeguards of the welfare system, including the minimum wage and unemploy-ment benefits, were long ago put in place to protect the poorest Americans. During the Great Recession, the federal government decided that raising the minimum wage would stimulate worker productivity and help close the income gap. In reality, however, it has done little to make the poor richer. In fact, raising the minimum wage, which makes labor more expensive, could force companies to cut back and hire fewer workers.

With a different approach to fixing the economy, some economists and politicians argue that supporting the richest sectors of the American economy will bring economic stability and a full recovery. They claim that a sizable income gap does not necessarily prevent individuals in the lower and middle classes from achieving the American Dream. I agree: govern-ment funding for Wall Street and struggling businesses makes the economy healthier. I believe that we should keep in mind the ways in which large businesses and financial insti-tutions enable many others to attain economic stability and security. For example, providing money to businesses may encourage them to hire more people, thereby increasing job opportu-nities. Just last year, President Obama presented a proposal, later passed by Congress, establishing a $33 billion tax credit to provide incentives for businesses to hire more workers and increase existing wages (Gomstyn, 2010). Increased support for Wall Street could in this way make the overall economy healthier so that everyone has increased opportunities.

Some, however, argue that raising taxes on the rich and on America's wealthy businesses is an effective means of closing the income gap. For *New York Times* columnist Bob Herbert, our economic problems are the result of bad policy decisions that have led to the rapid migration of American jobs overseas, the degradation of the American education system, and continuous costly wars. His primary point in a recent *New York Times* column was that America "does not have the common sense to raise taxes," his solution to solving inequality issues and achieving greater economic security (2010). Robert Reich and Paul Krugman concur with Herbert's analysis and recommend raising taxes (Krugman, 2007). My question for Herbert is, "Given the Great Recession and the tough economic climate that we continue to live in, would raising taxes still be the prudent thing to do?" Maybe Herbert believes that higher taxes for the rich would help solve the issue of inequality, but in reality, it would not help people achieve the American Dream at all. According to writer Dana Golden (2009), the more wealth the rich accumulate, the more they will spend it, thereby stimulating the economy. She also points out that the creation of wealth and its subsequent use is one way jobs are created, even in difficult economic times. Taxing the rich only decreases their spending potential and thus their ability to stimulate the economy.

See Chapter 5 for tips on distinguishing what you say from what they say.

In contrast to Herbert's bleak view, economist Cal Thomas responds to arguments about inequality issues by arguing that "The rules for achieving the American Dream may no longer be taught and supported by culture, but that doesn't mean that they don't work" (2010). Indeed, the media inundate us with countless images and stories of struggling workers and the growing ranks of the poor while suggesting that the American Dream is simply beyond the grasp of the vast majority of Americans. Thomas's response is that only because of "unrestrained liberalism" are the true means of realizing the American Dream being more and more eroded in our society. Despite the recent recession, Thomas and others like him have faith that as long as people believe they have a chance of becoming better off than they are today, then the American Dream is intact. Instead of trying to interfere with the enterprise that creates jobs and growth, we should rely on the values of the American Dream: that anybody can climb out of hardship and achieve success. Only then will the American Dream remain alive for future generations.

Just last year, a newspaper editor in Atlanta stated that, "the Great Recession didn't kill the American Dream. But the promise of a good life in exchange for hard, honest work has been bruised and frayed for millions of middle class Americans" (Chapman, 2010). The idea of the American Dream has in fact suffered in recent years, although it is my belief that this is not new. As a nation, we have dealt with economic downturns in the past, and the American Dream has faced trials and tests before. The economic panics of the late 1970s and after the 9/11 terrorist attacks are both prime examples. Even since the height of the Great Recession, however, we have adapted the values contained within the American Dream to meet new challenges. Of course, some will be quick to say that these changes have only come about as a result of the greed and corruption of the rich and powerful. Like laissez-faire economists and Wall Street supporters, however, I believe that it is necessary and imperative to continue supporting the business mechanisms that sustain our economy. The American Dream will continue to exist as part of the American psyche, not artificially stimulated by government regulations to change income distribution. If the Great Recession has taught us anything, it is that planning for the future by saving more and enacting policies that sustain economic growth are what will keep the American Dream alive.

References*

Adams, J. T. (1931). *Epic of America*. Boston: Little, Brown.

Chapman, D. (2010, December 10). American dream deferred, not dead. *Atlanta Journal-Constitution*. Retrieved from http://www.ajc.com/

Frietchen, C. (2009, October 24). Imagining yourself post-recession: Survey shows spending-habit changes [Web log post]. *Productopia: A World Without Buyer's Remorse*. Retrieved from http://www.consumersearch. com/blog/imagining-yourself-post-recession-survey-shows-spending-habit-changes#

Golden, D. (2009, January 10). The economy, credit and trickle down economics (the ripple effect). *EzineArticles*. Retrieved from http://ezinearticles.com/?The-Economy,-Credit-and-Trickle-Down-Economics-(The-Ripple-Effect)&id=1865774

Gomstyn, A. (2010, January 29). Obama announces $33B hiring tax credit. *ABC News*. Retrieved from http://abcnews.go.com/

Herbert, B. (2010). Hiding from reality. *The New York Times*. Retrieved from http://www.nytimes.com/

Hoak, A. (2011, February 8). More people choosing to rent, not buy, their home. *MarketWatch*. Retrieved from http://www.marketwatch.com/

Krugman, P. (2007). *The conscience of a liberal*. New York, NY: Norton.

Paradis, T. (2009, October 10). The statistics of the great recession. *Huffington Post*. Retrieved from http://www.huffingtonpost.com/

Reich, R. (2009, December 27). 2009: The year Wall Street bounced back and Main Street got shafted. *Huffington Post*. Retrieved from http://www.huffingtonpost.com/

Seelye, K. (2009, May 7). What happens to the American Dream in a recession? *The New York Times*. Retrieved from http://www.nytimes.com/

*Based on the APA style of documentation.

The American Dream: Dead, Alive, or on Hold?

Thomas, C. (2010, November 23). Is the American Dream over? *Townhall.* Retrieved from http://townhall.com/columnists/CalThomas/2010/11/23 /is_the_american_dream_over

Joining the Conversation

1. How does Brandon King redefine the American Dream? How does the redefinition affect his argument?
2. Summarize King's argument in this essay. What reasons and evidence does he use to support his views? How persuasive do you find his argument?
3. How does King connect the various parts of his essay? Look in particular at the beginnings and endings of paragraphs. What sorts of transitions and other connecting devices does King use? If you find places where he needs a transition or other device, supply it and explain why you think it improves the essay.
4. How well does King introduce and explain Paul Krugman's views on inequality and taxation (pp. 561–80)? How thoroughly does he respond?
5. Write an essay responding to King's argument about the American Dream from your own perspective—as a student, as a worker, or both.

America Remains the World's Beacon of Success

TIM ROEMER

WHEN I WENT TO SERVE as U.S. ambassador to India in 2009, I hoped to learn more about that country's vibrant democracy and our shared values. I gained an additional benefit while overseas: I learned that America is still deeply admired around the world and the place where many people want to live out their dreams. Consequently, I have been appalled by the gloom of those predicting that America's greatest days are behind us. These sentiments seep through our society, from pundits to parents at my daughter's basketball game, as people complain they are "despondent" and "depressed" that our children will be left behind by the United States' "decline."

Frustration at current conditions is understandable. Millions of Americans are out of work. Our trade deficit runs about

TIM ROEMER served in Congress as a Democrat from Indiana and as ambassador to India from 2009 to 2011. He also has been a scholar at the Mercatus Center, a conservative think tank at George Mason University, and served on the 9/11 Commission. He has written extensively on policy issues for publications such as the *New York Times*, *Time* magazine, and the *Wall Street Journal*. This essay first appeared as an op-ed in the *Washington Post* on January 20, 2012.

$44 billion per month. The news is filled with stories of greed and corruption. Congress is paralyzed by partisanship. Meanwhile, we hear that India and China are outpacing us in infrastructure, technology and manufacturing capability, and investment.

But living overseas, I saw that ours is not the only country facing profound challenges. Most major powers are experiencing similar or bigger problems. True, we feel the pain of our setbacks and fear that we are losing ground. Yet when I met Indian students at schools or living in slums, they consistently told me America is the place where they most want to study. Rather than underselling our historical record and natural resiliency, we must build on these assets.

The United States has the largest and most technologically powerful economy in the world, a per capita gross domestic product of $47,200 and a gross national purchasing power that equals those of China and Japan. Our national economy is bigger than those of Russia, Britain, Brazil, France and Italy combined.

Our huge GDP is no accident. We have a market-oriented ⁵ economy where most decisions are made independently by individuals and individual businesses. From Robert Fulton to Thomas Edison to Bill Gates and Steve Jobs, inventions spring from our labs, universities and garages, and eventually propel world growth. Meanwhile, in China, government still peers over the shoulder of inventors and ordinary Internet users. India still fights a legacy of corruption in too many places, at too many levels. In Europe, red tape has stifled many small businesses.

During a meeting in Mumbai with three dozen business millionaires in their twenties and thirties, I asked a simple question: Which market would you most like to access?

Almost unanimously, the answer was the United States. U.S. companies remain world leaders in information technology, bioscience, nanotechnology and aerospace. The evidence is clear not only in the development of products such as the iPad and iPhone but also in new patents. Last year, U.S. firms captured more than 50 percent of all U.S. patents; they received twice as many corporate patents as Japan, which came in second.

Yes, our high schools need to do better, as reading and math scores and dropout rates show. But when it comes to higher education, we remain a beacon of success. Four of the world's top five universities, and seven of the top 10, listed in last year's Times Global Higher Education Rankings are in the United States. Americans have won 333 Nobel prizes, almost triple the number of Britons, the runner-up. In the past three years, Americans have won Nobel prizes in such critical fields as economics, physics, medicine and chemistry.

Here's a "yes, but" move— see p. 65.

Even immigration, a topic of some tension, continues to enhance our competitiveness. Highly capable and legal immigrants flock to our country—aiming not for Ellis Island but Silicon Valley and the Research Triangle Park. As researchers at Duke and the University of California at Berkeley showed in 2007, 25 percent of U.S. tech and engineering start-ups between 1995 and 2005 had one or more immigrant key founders, whose companies collectively generated an estimated $52 billion in 2005 sales and created nearly 450,000 jobs.

Since the time of railroads and canals, our often-maligned federal government has invested in vital research in early phases for developing technologies, such as the Internet and energy technology, helping build a head start for the next generation of U.S. industry.

Other advantages include our positive demographic growth 10 pattern, our environmental protections of water and natural resources, and, as demonstrated by the smooth operation that took out Osama bin Laden, incredible military skill.

This country faces real challenges, including a growing deficit, crumbling infrastructure and unsustainable entitlement spending. Addressing these issues will require leadership to meet the times, as happened during the Civil War, the Great Depression, World War II and the civil rights era. Leaders need to exhibit the spirit captured by Theodore Roosevelt when he reminded us that "aggressive fighting for the right is the noblest sport the world affords."

My experience in India reinforced the perspective of America's image as a country of tomorrow. We should be heartened, not distressed, by the Tea Party and Occupy Wall Street movements. These activists remind us our country is worth fighting for. During this election year, we have the renewed opportunity to channel our feelings about country—love, fear, anger and hope—into action to transform problems into solutions and move closer toward a more perfect union.

Joining the Conversation

1. In this article, Tim Roemer focuses primarily on the strengths and potential of the United States today. Which positive factors in particular does he emphasize, and why do you think he chooses these as opposed to other factors?
2. Roemer is careful to acknowledge some possible objections to his views. Name three objections that he mentions, and explain how he attempts to answer them.
3. What's Roemer's main point, and how well do you think he argues for it?

4. Roemer states that he has "been appalled by the gloom of those predicting that America's greatest days are behind us" (paragraph 1). He might have been talking about Edward McClelland, the author of "RIP, the Middle Class: 1946–2013" (pp. 549–60). Compare the arguments and evidence that each writer provides. What, if anything, do they agree about?

5. Write an essay summarizing the arguments made by Roemer and McClelland and then saying what *you* think—and why.

Bring on More Immigrant Entrepreneurs

SHAYAN ZADEH

—🔲—

My response to the claim that immigrants drain the economy? I've created 150 new jobs.

AMERICAN CITIZENS MAY FIND it hard to imagine having to sneak into Canada to get permission to study in another country, or being told you can't start your own business because you weren't born within particular borders. But this has been my reality for 13 years—and it is the reality faced by untold numbers of would-be American entrepreneurs.

I was born in Urmia, Iran, to a Kurdish middle-class family. Because my hometown sits at the border of Turkey and Iraq, I was exposed to instability and war from an early age. I dreamed of moving away and doing something great with my life.

When I was 17 years old, I moved to Tehran to study computer science at the well-respected Sharif University of Technology, where I met my friend and future business partner

———

SHAYAN ZADEH is the cofounder and CEO of Zoosk, an online dating website, and an investor in and adviser to startup companies. Previously, he was a program manager and software engineer for Microsoft. This essay first appeared as an opinion piece in the *Wall Street Journal* on November 6, 2013.

Alex Mehr. We both aspired to be academics, and we were both accepted to Ph.D. programs in mechanical engineering and computer science at the University of Maryland.

There was only one obstacle: We had to obtain F1 visas to attend the school we'd worked so hard to get into.

In another country, this might mean a trip to the American 5 Embassy, but the U.S. does not have an embassy in Iran. The closest embassy was in Turkey, but there were no flights at the time because of political tensions. So we took buses, walked and hitchhiked into Ankara to get visas. It made the college application process look like a breeze by comparison.

While we were at Maryland, Alex and I changed our minds about becoming academics. Instead, we wanted to create a company using our technical skills. Our goal would have to be put on hold: The Office of International Affairs at the University of Maryland told us that they didn't think it was possible to start a business on a student visa. The university referred us to a lawyer in Washington, D.C., who confirmed that we couldn't move forward, and added that any company we founded as nonpermanent residents could not sponsor an H1B work visa for us. He suggested that if we wanted to create Zoosk, our online dating site, we should build it in another country.

Alex and I considered ourselves American, and we wanted access to the talent, financial backing and opportunities that the U.S. provides. So we decided to postpone our entrepreneurial dreams and try to become citizens. By going to work for Microsoft instead, I learned a great deal about building a technology company, and I became a permanent resident in 2008, a process that took over five years. Shortly after, I left my job at Microsoft, drove a U-Haul to Berkeley to meet up with Alex, and we founded Zoosk.

During the 13 years that I was in immigration limbo, I was consistently discouraged from accepting professional opportunities that could set back my bid for citizenship. While working for Microsoft, the company's immigration legal team and outside counsel regularly advised me not to change roles within the company while my Labor Certificate was in progress, since this would lead to a restart of the more than two-year long process. I was warned against traveling internationally, even for prestigious conferences, because the company feared I would not be granted re-entry because I am from Iran.

At Zoosk, we continue to face such issues. Of our 150 employees, dozens are not American, and we have sponsored them for visas, shepherding them through the same, frustrating immigration process.

My story has a happy ending: I finally became a U.S. citi- 10 zen in April. But it also shows how easy it is to lose skilled talent to other countries. I chose to stay and put up with the restrictions because there is nowhere better to build a tech company. But many young, educated and ambitious friends of mine decided it was too difficult here, especially when countries like Canada and United Kingdom welcomed their expertise. It's not a surprise that Microsoft and Google have set up offices in Vancouver to work around U.S. visa quotas.

We hear a lot from some quarters about the fear that immigrants will take jobs from Americans, or drain the U.S. economy. Nonsense. Granting legal status to illegal immigrants alone would create 121,000 jobs per year over the next 10 years according to the Center for American Progress. The U.S. economy would grow by $1.4 trillion over the next 20 years if the Senate's proposed immigration-reform legislation was adopted, according to the Congressional Budget Office.

See Chapter 6 for more ways to introduce objections.

As an American by choice, I am proud of our country's history of welcoming the tired, the poor and the "huddled masses" who were starving or persecuted and came here create a better life. But I'm baffled by the fact that we are turning away the skilled masses that are hungry only for work, even as our economy remains stagnant.

Joining the Conversation

1. Shayan Zadeh tells the story of how he, an immigrant to this country, was able to overcome significant obstacles, including some that resulted from U.S. laws, to become a successful entrepreneur and employer here. What's his point, and how does the story he relates support that point?

2. This article appeared as an opinion piece in the *Wall Street Journal*, a national newspaper focusing on business and the economy. Why do you think Zadeh chose to publish his piece in this particular newspaper? What are two or three ways in which the text is specifically geared for the *Wall Street Journal*'s audience?

3. Most op-ed pieces are relatively short. If you were revising this one to be a longer essay, which strategies taught in this book could help? What naysayers might you include? Where would you add metacommentary? How would you say more explicitly than Zadeh does why the argument matters?

4. Tim Roemer's op-ed (pp. 618–22) argues that this country is still viewed around the world as a land of opportunity. How does Zadeh's piece relate to Roemer's? How could Roemer incorporate Zadeh's story into his own text? Write a paragraph telling Zadeh's story as support for Roemer's argument.

5. Write a short response to Zadeh's op-ed in which you give your own reasons for supporting his argument, opposing it, or both.

King's Dream Remains an Elusive Goal;
Many Americans See Racial Disparities

PEW RESEARCH TEAM

FIVE DECADES AFTER Martin Luther King's historic "I Have a Dream" speech in Washington, D.C., a new survey by the Pew Research Center finds that fewer than half (45%) of all Americans say the country has made substantial progress toward racial equality and about the same share (49%) say that "a lot more" remains to be done.

Blacks are much more downbeat than whites about the pace of progress toward a color-blind society. They are also more likely to say that blacks are treated less fairly than whites by police, the courts, public schools and other key community institutions.

———

THE PEW RESEARCH CENTER is a nonpartisan think tank in Washington, D.C., that "conducts public opinion polling, demographic research, media content analysis and other empirical social science research." This report was written collaboratively by thirteen members of the staff of Pew's Social & Demographic Trends Project and the Pew Research Center for the People & the Press. This excerpt is the overview to the report, which was published on August 22, 2013.

DESPITE PROGRESS, MANY SAY RACIAL EQUALITY
STILL NOT A REALITY

How much progress toward Martin Luther King's dream of racial equality do you think the U.S. has made over the last 50 years? % saying . . .

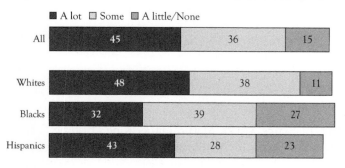

How much more needs to be done in order to achieve racial equality? % saying . . .

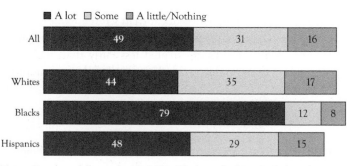

Notes: Based on full sample, N=2,231. Blacks and whites include only non-Hispanics. Hispanics may be of any race.

Source: Pew Research Center Race Survey conducted Aug. 1–11, 2013. Unless otherwise noted, survey findings in this report are from this poll.

While these differences by race are large, significant minorities of whites agree that blacks receive unequal treatment when dealing with the criminal justice system.

For example, seven-in-ten blacks and about a third of whites (37%) say blacks are treated less fairly in their dealings with the police.

Similarly, about two-thirds of black respondents (68%) and ₅ a quarter of whites (27%) say blacks are not treated as fairly as whites in the courts.

The survey also finds that large majorities of blacks (73%) and whites (81%) say the two races generally get along either "very well" or "pretty well."

How Well Do Racial and Ethnic Groups Get Along These Days

% saying these groups get along ...

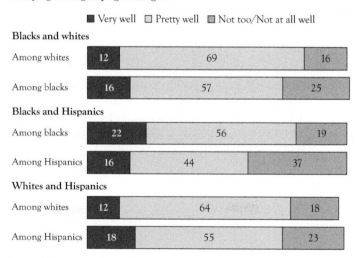

Notes: "Don't know/Refused" responses not shown.

Similarly, large majorities of Hispanics and whites say the same thing about relations between their groups (74% and 77%, respectively). A substantial majority of blacks (78%) and smaller share of Hispanics (61%) say their groups get along.

Still, about a third of all blacks (35%) say they had been discriminated against or treated unfairly because of their race in the past year, as do 20% of Hispanics and 10% of whites.

The nationally representative survey of 2,231 adults, including 376 blacks and 218 Hispanics, was conducted by telephone Aug. 1–11.

50 Years of Change

The mixed views on progress toward racial equality found in 10 the survey results are echoed in the findings of a Pew Research Center analysis of U.S. government data on indicators of well-being and civic engagement, including personal finance, life expectancy, educational attainment and voter participation. These data look at equality of outcomes rather than equality of opportunity.

The analysis finds that the economic gulf between blacks and whites that was present half a century ago largely remains.

See Chapter 13 for tips on analyzing data. When it comes to household income and household wealth, the gaps between blacks and whites have widened. On measures such as high school completion and life expectancy, they have narrowed. On other measures, including poverty and homeownership rates, the gaps are roughly the same as they were 40 years ago.

Finances

Between 1967 and 2011 the median income of a black household of three rose from about $24,000 to nearly $40,000.[1]

WHERE GAPS HAVE WIDENED

Median Household Income
Household of three, in 2012 dollars

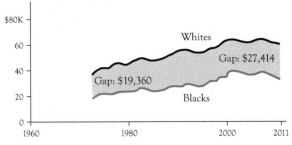

Marriage Rate
Ages 18 and older

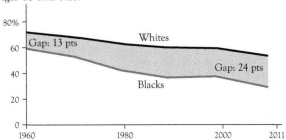

Median Household Wealth
In 2012 dollars

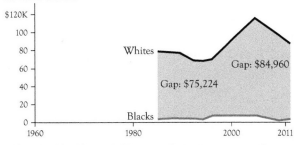

Source: Based on Pew Research Center analysis of government data.

Expressed as a share of white income, black households earn about 59% of what white households earn, a small increase from 55% in 1967. But when expressed as dollars, the black-white income gap widened, from about $19,000 in the late 1960s to roughly $27,000 today. The race gap on household wealth has increased from $75,224 in 1984 to $84,960 in 2011.

Other indicators of financial well-being have changed little in recent decades, including homeownership rates and the

WHERE GAPS ARE LITTLE CHANGED

Above Poverty Line

Homeownership

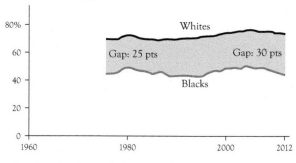

Source: Based on Pew Research Center analysis of government data.

share of each race that live above the poverty line. The black unemployment rate also has consistently been about double that of whites since the 1950s.

Education

High school completion rates have converged since the 1960s, and now about nine-in-ten blacks and whites have a high school diploma. The trend in college completion rates tell a more nuanced story. Today, white adults 25 and older are significantly more likely than blacks to have completed at least a bachelor's degree (34% vs. 21%, a 13 percentage point difference). Fifty years ago, the completion gap between whites and blacks was about 6 percentage points (10% vs. 4%). But expressed a different way, the black completion rate as a percentage of the white rate has improved from 42% then to 62% now.

Family Formation

The analysis finds growing disparities in key measures of family formation. Marriage rates among whites and blacks have declined in the past 50 years, and the black-white difference has nearly doubled. Today about 55% of whites and 31% of blacks ages 18 and older are married. In 1960, 74% of whites and roughly six-in-ten blacks (61%) were married. The share of births to unmarried women has risen sharply for both groups; in 2011, more than seven-in-ten births to black women were to unmarried mothers, compared with about three-in-ten births to white women (72% vs. 29%). 15

Incarceration

Black men were more than six times as likely as white men in 2010 to be incarcerated in federal and state prisons, and

Where Gaps Have Narrowed

High School Completion
Ages 25 and older

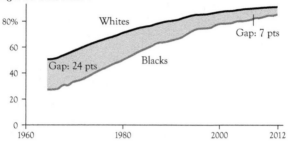

Life Expectancy
At birth

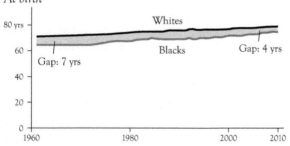

Voter Turnout
In presidential election years

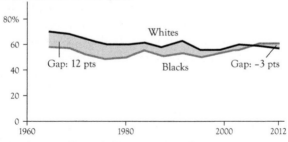

Source: Based on Pew Research Center analysis of government data.

local jails, the last year complete data are available. That is an increase from 1960, when black men were five times as likely as whites to be incarcerated.

Voter Turnout

Participation rates for blacks in presidential elections has lagged behind those of whites for most of the past half century but has been rising since 1996. Buoyed by the historic candidacies of Barack Obama, blacks nearly caught up with whites in 2008 and surpassed them in 2012, when 67% of eligible blacks cast ballots, compared with 64% of eligible whites.

Life Expectancy

The gap in life expectancy rates among blacks and whites has narrowed in the past five decades from about seven years to four.

Looking Back Five Years

While demographic change happens slowly, attitudes can change quickly. The Pew Research Center survey finds that since 2009, there has been a fading of the heightened sense of progress that blacks felt immediately after Obama's election in 2008.

Today, only about one-in-four African Americans (26%) say 20 the situation of black people in this country is better now than it was five years ago, down sharply from the 39% who said the same in a 2009 Pew Research Center survey.

Among whites, the share that sees improvement in situation of blacks also fell, from 49% to 35%, in the last four years.

For both blacks and whites, the latest finding on this question is returning to the levels recorded in a Pew Research Center poll in 2007 on the eve of the Great Recession.

Sense of Black Progress Down Sharply from 2009

Percentage saying the situation of black people is better today, compared with five years ago

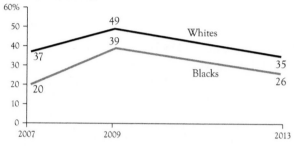

In the latest survey, opinions about black progress vary considerably by educational attainment among blacks, a change from the 2009 survey when there was no gap by education among blacks.

In the current poll, only 22% of blacks who have attended at least some college say the situation of black people in this country is better today than it was five years ago. Among those with a high school education or less, roughly one-third say things are better.

Note

1. 1967 and 2011 median household income figures expressed in 2012 dollars.

Joining the Conversation

1. The Pew researchers examined white, black, and Hispanic Americans' views on racial equality and then looked at what the actual economic data show on the subject. What are their main findings, and how closely do people's perceptions appear to match the realities?

2. The Pew Research Center describes itself as "a nonpartisan fact tank that informs the public about the issues, attitudes, and trends shaping America and the world." What audience(s) do you think would be most interested in a report such as this one? How is the information the report provides relevant for you and for others who are not policymakers?

3. This report includes many charts to show research findings. Study one such chart and then read what the authors say to explain its findings. Which is easier to understand, the chart or the author's explanation?

4. Given his argument about increasing the economic disparities in the United States (pp. 561–80), how do you think Paul Krugman would interpret the results of the Pew report?

5. This document does not take a position on the findings it reports, but the data could certainly be used in an argumentative essay. Write an argument about some aspect of the current state of the American Dream, using the data in this report as well as your own observations and experiences to support your points.

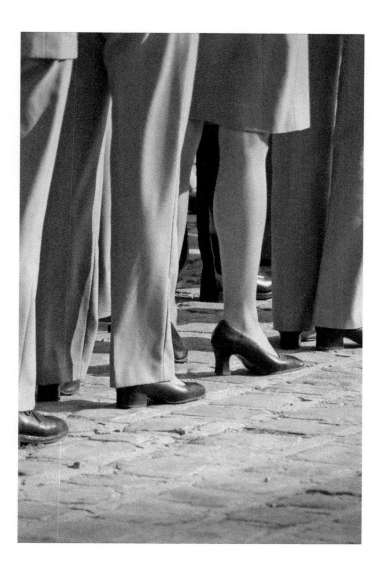

TWENTY

WHAT'S GENDER GOT
TO DO WITH IT?

—⌐回⌐—

WHAT'S GENDER GOT TO DO WITH IT? Everything—or so it might seem. Gender, in the words of Kate Gilles, a policy analyst at the Population Reference Bureau, "is a social construct—that is, a society's assumptions about the way a man or woman should look and behave." Gender roles in our society have changed considerably in recent decades: there are more women in the workforce, many doing jobs once held exclusively or primarily by men, and a growing number of men who choose to stay home with the kids while their partner works outside the home.

Still, many writers in this chapter argue that while women have made substantial progress in the United States, serious obstacles remain. Anne-Marie Slaughter, a former government official, observes that women who aspire to rise to the top of their fields find it difficult to also raise children—and that it's not possible to really "have it all." Computer programmer Ellen Ullman further discusses gender inequities, reminding us that women in her field are underrepresented and "held to higher standards" than their male counterparts.

Facebook executive Sheryl Sandberg, while acknowledging the gender discrimination that Slaughter and Ullman describe, urges young women to "lean in" by actively pursuing leadership roles and dividing home responsibilities with their partners. Meanwhile, feminist writer bell hooks, while agreeing that women should aspire to positions of leadership, questions Sandberg's focus on wealthy, privileged women and urges women not to replicate what she calls "imperialist white supremacist capitalist patriarchy" but instead work for equality and opportunity for all.

In response to such critiques, others argue that the situation for American men is in many ways just as problematic. Journalist, husband, and father Richard Dorment writes about the increasing difficulty men have in balancing work and home life. And business executive Saul Kaplan raises concerns about the growing achievement gap among young people, with girls now outpacing boys in both school and the workplace.

But discussions of gender take place outside the confines of an office and beyond the walls of a family's home. On a daily basis, pressure still exists for people, particularly children, to maintain traditional gender roles—for males, playing sports, acting tough, and not showing emotion; and for females, maintaining their physical appearance, being sensitive to other people's feelings, and not acting "too aggressive."

Stephen Mays, a student at the University of Georgia, finds that gender stereotypes are often present in same-sex relationships as well, and he argues against these limiting stereotypes. Dennis Baron, a linguist who regularly blogs on issues of language and society, considers Facebook's recent decision to allow users the opportunity to select from fifty-eight different terms for gender identification, while still offering the same "three tired pronouns" to refer to those they identify. And Penelope Eckert and Sally McConnell-Ginet, scholars of language and gender, describe the ways parents, teachers, and even doctors in the delivery room reinforce gender distinctions in ways that steer children into what societies deem as normal gender roles.

Gender is personal, part of everyone's developing identity and web of relationships, but it is also political, related to questions of equity, fairness, and civil rights. As you read this chapter, you will encounter a range of perspectives and perhaps be challenged to consider or reconsider your own views—and have the opportunity to add your voice to an important conversation that affects all members of society.

Lean In:
What Would You Do If You
Weren't Afraid?

SHERYL SANDBERG

My grandmother Rosalind Einhorn was born exactly fifty-two years before I was, on August 28, 1917. Like many poor Jewish families in the boroughs of New York City, hers lived in a small, crowded apartment close to their relatives. Her parents, aunts, and uncles addressed her male cousins by their given names, but she and her sister were referred to only as "Girlie."

During the Depression, my grandmother was pulled out of Morris High School to help support the household by sewing fabric flowers onto undergarments that her mother could resell for a tiny profit. No one in the community would have considered taking a boy out of school. A boy's education was

---

Sheryl Sandberg is the chief operating officer of Facebook and the first woman member of its board of directors. She has also served as a vice president at Google and as chief of staff for the U.S. Secretary of the Treasury. This selection is the first chapter of her book *Lean In: Women, Work, and the Will to Lead* (2013).

the family's hope to move up the financial and social ladder. Education for girls, however, was less important both financially, since they were unlikely to contribute to the family's income, and culturally, since boys were expected to study the Torah while girls were expected to run a "proper home." Luckily for my grandmother, a local teacher insisted that her parents put her back into school. She went on not only to finish high school but to graduate from U.C. Berkeley.

After college, "Girlie" worked selling pocketbooks and accessories at David's Fifth Avenue. When she left her job to marry my grandfather, family legend has it that David's had to hire four people to replace her. Years later, when my grandfather's paint business was struggling, she jumped in and took some of the hard steps he was reluctant to take, helping to save the family from financial ruin. She displayed her business acumen again in her forties. After being diagnosed with breast cancer, she beat it and then dedicated herself to raising money for the clinic that treated her by selling knockoff watches out of the trunk of her car. Girlie ended up with a profit margin that Apple would envy. I have never met anyone with more energy and determination than my grandmother. When Warren Buffett talks about competing against only half of the population, I think about her and wonder how different her life might have been if she had been born half a century later.

When my grandmother had children of her own—my mother and her two brothers—she emphasized education for all of them. My mother attended the University of Pennsylvania, where classes were coed. When she graduated in 1965 with a degree in French literature, she surveyed a workforce that she believed consisted of two career options for women: teaching or nursing. She chose teaching. She began a Ph.D. program, got married, and then dropped out when she became pregnant with me. It was thought to be a sign of weakness if a husband needed his wife's help to support their family, so my mother became a stay-at-home parent and an active volunteer. The centuries-old division of labor stood.

Even though I grew up in a traditional home, my parents 5 had the same expectations for me, my sister, and my brother. All three of us were encouraged to excel in school, do equal chores, and engage in extracurricular activities. We were all supposed to be athletic too. My brother and sister joined sports teams, but I was the kid who got picked last in gym. Despite my athletic shortcomings, I was raised to believe that girls could do anything boys could do and that *all* career paths were open to me.

When I arrived at college in the fall of 1987, my classmates of both genders seemed equally focused on academics. I don't remember thinking about my future career differently from the male students. I also don't remember any conversations about someday balancing work and children. My friends and I assumed that we would have both. Men and women competed openly and aggressively with one another in classes, activities, and job interviews. Just two generations removed from my grandmother, the playing field seemed to be level.

But more than twenty years after my college graduation, the world has not evolved nearly as much as I believed it would. Almost all of my male classmates work in professional settings. Some of my female classmates work full-time or part-time outside the home, and just as many are stay-at-home mothers and volunteers like my mom. This mirrors the national trend. In comparison to their male counterparts, highly trained women are scaling back and dropping out of the workforce in high numbers. In turn, these diverging percentages teach institutions

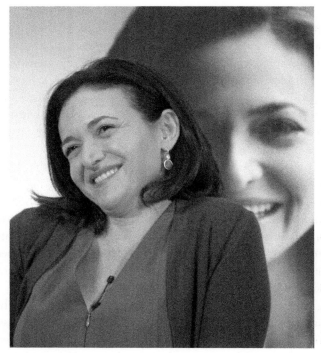

Sheryl Sandberg

and mentors to invest more in men, who are statistically more likely to stay.

Judith Rodin, president of the Rockefeller Foundation and the first woman to serve as president of an Ivy League university, once remarked to an audience of women my age, "My generation fought so hard to give all of you choices. We believe in choices. But choosing to leave the workforce was not the choice we thought so many of you would make."

So what happened? My generation was raised in an era of increasing equality, a trend we thought would continue.

In retrospect, we were naïve and idealistic. Integrating professional and personal aspirations proved far more challenging than we had imagined. During the same years that our careers demanded maximum time investment, our biology demanded that we have children. Our partners did not share the housework and child rearing, so we found ourselves with two full-time jobs. The workplace did not evolve to give us the flexibility we needed to fulfill our responsibilities at home. We anticipated none of this. We were caught by surprise.

If my generation was too naïve, the generations that have followed may be too practical. We knew too little, and now girls know too much. Girls growing up today are not the first generation to have equal opportunity, but they are the first to know that all that opportunity does not necessarily translate into professional achievement. Many of these girls watched their mothers try to "do it all" and then decide that something had to give. That something was usually their careers.

There's no doubt that women have the skills to lead in the workplace. Girls are increasingly outperforming boys in the classroom, earning about 57 percent of the undergraduate and 60 percent of the master's degrees in the United States. This gender gap in academic achievement has even caused some to worry about the "end of men." But while compliant, raise-your-hand-and-speak-when-called-on behaviors might be rewarded in school, they are less valued in the workplace. Career progression often depends upon taking risks and advocating for oneself—traits that girls are discouraged from exhibiting. This may explain why girls' academic gains have not yet translated into significantly higher numbers of women in top jobs. The pipeline that supplies the educated workforce is chock-full of women at the entry level, but by the time that same pipeline is filling leadership positions, it is overwhelmingly stocked with men.

There are so many reasons for this winnowing out, but one important contributor is a leadership ambition gap. Of course, many individual women are as professionally ambitious as any individual man. Yet drilling down, the data clearly indicate that in field after field, more men than women aspire to the most senior jobs. A 2012 McKinsey survey of more than four thousand employees of leading companies found that 36 percent of the men wanted to reach the C-suite, compared to only 18 percent of the women. When jobs are described as powerful, challenging, and involving high levels of responsibility, they appeal to more men than women. And while the ambition gap is most pronounced at the highest levels, the underlying dynamic is evident at every step of the career ladder. A survey of college students found that more men than women chose "reaching a managerial level" as a career priority in the first three years after graduating. Even among highly educated professional men and women, more men than women describe themselves as "ambitious."

There is some hope that a shift is starting to occur in the next generation. A 2012 Pew study found for the first time that among young people ages eighteen to thirty-four, more young women (66 percent) than young men (59 percent) rated "success in a high-paying career or profession" as important to their lives. A recent survey of Millennials found that women were just as likely to describe themselves as ambitious as men. Although this is an improvement, even among this demographic, the leadership ambition gap remains. Millennial women are less likely than Millennial men to agree that the statement "I aspire to a leadership role in whatever field I ultimately work" describes them very well. Millennial women were also less likely than their male peers to characterize themselves as "leaders," "visionaries," "self-confident," and "willing to take risks."

Since more men aim for leadership roles, it is not surprising that they obtain them, especially given all the other obstacles that women have to overcome. This pattern starts long before they enter the workforce. Author Samantha Ettus and her husband read their daughter's kindergarten yearbook, where each child answered the question "What do you want to be when you grow up?" They noted that several of the boys wanted to be president. None of the girls did. (Current data suggest that when these girls become women, they will continue to feel the same way.) In middle school, more boys than girls aspire to leadership roles in future careers. At the top fifty colleges, less than a third of student government presidents are women.

Professional ambition is expected of men but is optional—or worse, sometimes even a negative—for women. "She is *very* ambitious" is not a compliment in our culture. Aggressive and hard-charging women violate unwritten rules about acceptable social conduct. Men are continually applauded for being ambitious and powerful and successful, but women who display these same traits often pay a social penalty. Female accomplishments come at a cost.

And for all the progress, there is still societal pressure for women to keep an eye on marriage from a young age. When I went to college, as much as my parents emphasized academic achievement, they emphasized marriage even more. They told me that the most eligible women marry young to get a "good man" before they are all taken. I followed their advice and throughout college, I vetted every date as a potential husband (which, trust me, is a sure way to ruin a date at age nineteen).

When I was graduating, my thesis advisor, Larry Summers, suggested that I apply for international fellowships. I rejected the idea on the grounds that a foreign country was not a likely place to turn a date into a husband. Instead, I moved to Washington, D.C., which was full of eligible men. It worked. My first year out of college, I met a man who was not just eligible, but also wonderful, so I married him. I was twenty-four and convinced that marriage was the first—and necessary—step to a happy and productive life.

It didn't work out that way. I was just not mature enough to have made this lifelong decision, and the relationship quickly unraveled. By the age of twenty-five, I had managed to get married . . . and also divorced. At the time, this felt like a massive personal *and* public failure. For many years, I felt that no matter what I accomplished professionally, it paled in comparison to the scarlet letter D stitched on my chest. (Almost ten years later, I learned that the "good ones" were not all taken, and I wisely and very happily married Dave Goldberg.)

Like me, Gayle Tzemach Lemmon, deputy director of the Council on Foreign Relations' Women and Foreign Policy Program, was encouraged to prioritize marriage over career. As she described in *The Atlantic*, "When I was 27, I received a posh fellowship to travel to Germany to learn German and work at the *Wall Street Journal*. . . . It was an incredible opportunity for a 20-something by any objective standard, and I knew it would help prepare me for graduate school and beyond. My girlfriends, however, expressed shock and horror that I would leave my boyfriend at the time to live abroad for a year. My relatives asked whether I was worried that I'd never get married. And when I attended a barbecue with my then-beau, his boss took me aside to remind me that 'there aren't many guys like that out there.'" The result of these negative reactions, in Gayle's view, is that many women "still see ambition as a dirty word."

Many have argued with me that ambition is not the problem. 20 Women are not less ambitious than men, they insist, but more enlightened with different and more meaningful goals. I do not dismiss or dispute this argument. There is far more to life than climbing a career ladder, including raising children, seeking personal fulfillment, contributing to society, and improving the lives of others. And there are many people who are deeply committed to their jobs but do not—and should not have to—aspire to run their organizations. Leadership roles are not the only way to have profound impact.

I also acknowledge that there are biological differences between men and women. I have breast-fed two children and See p. 89 for tips on making concessions while still standing your ground. noted, at times with great disappointment, that this was simply not something my husband was equipped to do. Are there characteristics inherent in sex differences that make women more nurturing and men more assertive? Quite possibly. Still, in today's world, where we no longer have to hunt in the wild for our food, our desire for leadership is largely a culturally created and reinforced trait. How individuals view what they can and should accomplish is in large part formed by our societal expectations.

From the moment we are born, boys and girls are treated differently. Parents tend to talk to girl babies more than boy babies. Mothers overestimate the crawling ability of their sons and underestimate the crawling ability of their daughters. Reflecting the belief that girls need to be helped more than boys, mothers often spend more time comforting and hugging infant girls and more time watching infant boys play by themselves.

Other cultural messages are more blatant. Gymboree once sold onesies proclaiming "Smart like Daddy" for boys and "Pretty like Mommy" for girls. The same year, J. C. Penney marketed a T-shirt to teenage girls that bragged, "I'm too pretty to do homework so my brother has to do it for me." These things did not happen in 1951. They happened in 2011.

Even worse, the messages sent to girls can move beyond encouraging superficial traits and veer into explicitly discouraging leadership. When a girl tries to lead, she is often labeled bossy. Boys are seldom called bossy because a boy taking the role of a boss does not surprise or offend. As someone who was called this for much of my childhood, I know that it is not a compliment.

The stories of my childhood bossiness are told (and retold) 25 with great amusement. Apparently, when I was in elementary school, I taught my younger siblings, David and Michelle, to follow me around, listen to my monologues, and scream the word "Right!" when I concluded. I was the eldest of the neighborhood children and allegedly spent my time organizing shows that I could direct and clubs that I could run. People laugh at these accounts, but to this day I always feel slightly ashamed of my behavior (which is remarkable given that I have now written an entire book about why girls should not be made to feel this way, or maybe this partially explains my motivation).

Even when we were in our thirties, pointing out this behavior was still the best way for my siblings to tease me. When Dave and I got married, David and Michelle gave a beautiful, hilarious toast, which kicked off with this: "Hi! Some of you think we are Sheryl's younger siblings, but really we were Sheryl's first employees—employee number one and employee number two. Initially, as a one-year-old and a three-year-old, we were worthless and weak. Disorganized, lazy. We would just as soon spit up on ourselves as read the morning paper. But Sheryl could see that we had potential. For more than ten years, Sheryl took us under her wing and whipped us into shape." Everyone laughed. My siblings continued, "To the best of our knowledge Sheryl never actually *played* as a child, but really just organized other children's play. Sheryl supervised adults as well. When our parents went away on vacation, our grandparents used to babysit. Before our parents left, Sheryl protested, 'Now I have to take care of David and Michelle *and*

Grandma and Grandpa too. It's not fair!'" Everyone laughed even louder.

I laughed too, but there is still some part of me that feels it was unseemly for a little girl to be thought of as so . . . domineering. *Cringe.*

From a very early age, boys are encouraged to take charge and offer their opinions. Teachers interact more with boys, call on them more frequently, and ask them more questions. Boys are also more likely to call out answers, and when they do, teachers usually listen to them. When girls call out, teachers often scold them for breaking the rules and remind them to raise their hands if they want to speak.

I was recently reminded that these patterns persist even when we are all grown up. Not long ago, at a small dinner with other business executives, the guest of honor spoke the entire time without taking a breath. This meant that the only way to ask a question or make an observation was to interrupt. Three or four men jumped in, and the guest politely answered their questions before resuming his lecture. At one point, I tried to add something to the conversation and he barked, "Let me finish! You people are not good at listening!" Eventually, a few more men interjected and he allowed it. Then the only other female executive at the dinner decided to speak up—and he did it again! He chastised her for interrupting. After the meal, one of the male CEOs pulled me aside to say that he had noticed that only the women had been silenced. He told me he empathized, because as a Hispanic, he has been treated like this many times.

The danger goes beyond authority figures silencing female 30 voices. Young women internalize societal cues about what defines "appropriate" behavior and, in turn, silence themselves. They are rewarded for being "pretty like Mommy" and encouraged to be nurturing like Mommy too. The album *Free to Be . . . You and*

Me was released in 1972 and became a staple of my childhood. My favorite song, "William's Doll," is about a five-year-old boy who begs his reluctant father to buy him a traditional girl's toy. Almost forty years later, the toy industry remains riddled with stereotypes. Right before Christmas 2011, a video featuring a four-year-old girl named Riley went viral. Riley paces in a toy store, upset because companies are trying to "trick the girls into buying the pink stuff instead of stuff that boys want to buy, right?" Right. As Riley reasons, "Some girls like superheroes, some girls like princesses. Some boys like superheroes, some boys like princesses. So why do all the girls have to buy pink stuff and all the boys have to buy different color stuff?" It takes a near act of rebellion for even a four-year-old to break away from society's expectations. William still has no doll, while Riley is drowning in a sea of pink. I now play *Free to Be . . . You and Me* for my children and hope that if they ever play it for *their* children, its message will seem quaint.

The gender stereotypes introduced in childhood are reinforced throughout our lives and become self-fulfilling prophesies. Most leadership positions are held by men, so women don't *expect* to achieve them, and that becomes one of the reasons they don't. The same is true with pay. Men generally earn more than women, so people *expect* women to earn less. And they do.

Compounding the problem is a social-psychological phenomenon called "stereotype threat." Social scientists have observed that when members of a group are made aware of a negative stereotype, they are more likely to perform according to that stereotype. For example, stereotypically, boys are better at math and science than girls. When girls are reminded of their gender before a math or science test, even by something as simple as checking off an M or F box at the top of the test, they perform worse. Stereotype threat discourages girls and women from entering technical fields and is one of the key reasons that so few study computer science. As a Facebook summer intern once told me, "In my school's computer science department, there are more Daves than girls."

The stereotype of a working woman is rarely attractive. Popular culture has long portrayed successful working women as so consumed by their careers that they have no personal life (think Sigourney Weaver in *Working Girl* and Sandra Bullock in *The Proposal*). If a female character divides her time between work and family, she is almost always harried and guilt ridden (think Sarah Jessica Parker in *I Don't Know How She Does It*). And these characterizations have moved beyond fiction. A study found that of Millennial men and women who work in an organization with a woman in a senior role, only about 20 percent want to emulate her career.

This unappealing stereotype is particularly unfortunate since most women have no choice but to remain in the workforce. About 41 percent of mothers are primary breadwinners and earn the majority of their family's earnings. Another 23 percent of mothers are co-breadwinners, contributing at least a quarter of the family's earnings. The number of women supporting families on their own is increasing quickly; between 1973 and 2006, the proportion of families headed by a single mother grew from one in ten to one in five. These numbers are dramatically higher in Hispanic and African-American families. Twenty-seven percent of Latino children and 52 percent of African-American children are being raised by a single mother.

Our country lags considerably behind others in efforts to 35 help parents take care of their children and stay in the workforce. Of all the industrialized nations in the world, the United States is the only one without a paid maternity leave policy.

As Ellen Bravo, director of the Family Values @ Work consortium, observed, most "women are not thinking about 'having it all,' they're worried about losing it all—their jobs, their children's health, their families' financial stability—because of the regular conflicts that arise between being a good employee and a responsible parent."

For many men, the fundamental assumption is that they can have both a successful professional life and a fulfilling personal life. For many women, the assumption is that trying to do both is difficult at best and impossible at worst. Women are surrounded by headlines and stories warning them that they cannot be committed to both their families and careers. They are told over and over again that they have to choose, because if they try to do too much, they'll be harried and unhappy. Framing the issue as "work-life balance"—as if the two were diametrically opposed—practically ensures work will lose out. Who would ever choose work over life?

The good news is that not only can women have both families and careers, they can *thrive* while doing so. In 2009, Sharon Meers and Joanna Strober published *Getting to 50/50*, a comprehensive review of governmental, social science, and original research that led them to conclude that children, parents, and marriages can all flourish when both parents have full careers. The data plainly reveal that sharing financial and child-care responsibilities leads to less guilty moms, more involved dads, and thriving children. Professor Rosalind Chait Barnett of Brandeis University did a comprehensive review of studies on work-life balance and found that women who participate in multiple roles actually have lower levels of anxiety and higher levels of mental well-being. Employed women reap rewards including greater financial security, more stable marriages, better health, and, in general, increased life satisfaction.

It may not be as dramatic or funny to make a movie about a woman who loves both her job and her family, but that would be a better reflection of reality. We need more portrayals of women as competent professionals and happy mothers—or even happy professionals and competent mothers. The current negative images may make us laugh, but they also make women unnecessarily fearful by presenting life's challenges as insurmountable. Our culture remains baffled: *I don't know how she does it.*

Fear is at the root of so many of the barriers that women face. Fear of not being liked. Fear of making the wrong choice. Fear of drawing negative attention. Fear of overreaching. Fear of being judged. Fear of failure. And the holy trinity of fear: the fear of being a bad mother/wife/daughter.

Without fear, women can pursue professional success and 40 personal fulfillment—and freely choose one, or the other, or both. At Facebook, we work hard to create a culture where people are encouraged to take risks. We have posters all around the office that reinforce this attitude. In bright red letters, one declares, "Fortune favors the bold." Another insists, "Proceed and be bold." My favorite reads, "What would you do if you weren't afraid?"

In 2011, Debora Spar, president of Barnard College, an all-women's liberal arts school in New York City, invited me to deliver its commencement address. This speech was the first time I openly discussed the leadership ambition gap. Standing on the podium, I felt nervous. I told the members of the graduating class that they should be ambitious not just in pursuing their dreams but in aspiring to become leaders in their fields. I knew this message could be misinterpreted as my judging women for not making the same choices that I have. Nothing could be farther from the truth. I believe that choice means choice for all of us. But I also believe that we need to do more to encourage women to reach for leadership roles. If we can't tell women to aim high at a college graduation, when can we?

As I addressed the enthusiastic women, I found myself fighting back tears. I made it through the speech and concluded with this:

> You are the promise for a more equal world. So my hope for everyone here is that after you walk across this stage, after you get your diploma, after you go out tonight and celebrate hard—you then will lean way in to your career. You will find something you love doing and you will do it with gusto. Find the right career for you and go all the way to the top.
>
> As you walk off this stage today, you start your adult life. Start out by aiming high. Try—and try hard.
>
> Like everyone here, I have great hopes for the members of this graduating class. I hope you find true meaning, contentment, and passion in your life. I hope you navigate the difficult times and come out with greater strength and resolve. I hope you find whatever balance you seek with your eyes wide open. And I hope that you—yes, you—have the ambition to lean in to your career and run the world. Because the world needs you to change it. Women all around the world are counting on you.
>
> So please ask yourself: What would I do if I weren't afraid? And then go do it.

As the graduates were called to the stage to collect their diplomas, I shook every hand. Many stopped to give me a hug. One young woman even told me I was "the baddest bitch" (which, having checked with someone later, actually did turn out to be a compliment).

I know my speech was meant to motivate them, but they actually motivated me. In the months that followed, I started thinking that I should speak up more often and more publicly about these issues. I should urge more women to believe in themselves and aspire to lead. I should urge more men to become part of the solution by supporting women in the workforce and at home. And I should not just speak in front of friendly crowds at Barnard. I should seek out larger, possibly less sympathetic audiences. I should take my own advice and be ambitious.

Joining the Conversation

1. Sheryl Sandberg argues that women are on the whole still raised to be less ambitious than men and that they should be encouraged to aim more for leadership roles. What evidence does she provide for this so-called "leadership ambition gap"? What factors does she say cause this gap?
2. Sandberg mentions her grandmother, who was a successful businesswoman, as well as her mother, who dropped out of a Ph.D. program to be a "stay-at-home parent." How do these personal details support her argument?
3. According to Sandberg, the media stereotype of a working woman is "rarely attractive" (paragraph 33). Do you agree? Think of some examples of successful working women in movies and television. How do these examples support or contradict Sandberg's claim?
4. How do you think Sandberg might respond to Saul Kaplan's argument in "The Plight of Young Males" (pp. 732–35)?
5. According to Sandberg, most American girls are led to have modest career expectations and to focus more on having a family, while boys are typically raised to aim for leadership positions. Has this been your experience? Write an essay responding to what she says, drawing from your own experience and the readings in this chapter as support for what you say.

Dig Deep: Beyond Lean In

BELL HOOKS

—▣—

A YEAR AGO, few folks were talking about Sheryl Sandberg.
Her thoughts on feminism were of little interest. More
significantly, there was next-to-no public discussion of feminist
thinking and practice. Rarely, if ever, was there any feminist
book mentioned as a bestseller and certainly not included on
the *New York Times* Best Seller list. Those of us who have
devoted lifetimes to teaching and writing theory, explaining to
the world the ins and outs of feminist thinking and practice,
have experienced that the primary audience for our work is an
academic sub-culture. In recent years, discussions of feminism
have not evoked animated passion in audiences. We were far
more likely to hear that we are living in a post-feminist society

BELL HOOKS is an author and activist who teaches at Berea College, in
Kentucky. She has written numerous books, including *Feminism Is for
Everybody: Passionate Politics* (2000), *Teaching to Transgress: Education
as the Practice of Freedom* (1994), and *Ain't I a Woman: Black Women
and Feminism* (1981). Born Gloria Jean Watkins, she changed her
name to honor her mother and grandmother. She says she chose not
to capitalize the name because "it is the substance of my books, not
who is writing them, that is important." This essay, a response to
Sheryl Sandberg's book *Lean In*, appeared on the blog *The Feminist
Wire* on October 28, 2013.

than to hear voices clamoring to learn more about feminism. This seems to have changed with Sandberg's book *Lean In*, holding steady on the *Times* bestseller list for more than sixteen weeks.

No one was more surprised than long-time advocates of feminist thinking and practice to learn via mass media that a new high priestess of feminist movement was on the rise. Suddenly, as if by magic, mass media brought into public consciousness conversations about feminism, reframing the scope and politics through an amazing feat of advertising. At the center of this drama was a young, high-level corporate executive, Sheryl Sandberg, who was dubbed by Oprah Winfrey and other popular culture pundits as "the new voice of revolutionary feminism." *Forbes Magazine* proclaimed Sandberg to be one of the most influential women in the world, if not the most. *Time Magazine* ranked her one of a hundred of the most powerful and influential world leaders. All over mass media, her book Lean In has been lauded as a necessary new feminist manifesto.

Yet Sandberg confesses to readers that she has not been a strong advocate of feminist movement; that like many women of her generation, she hesitated when it came to aligning herself with feminist concerns. She explains:

> I headed into college believing that the feminists of the sixties and seventies had done the hard work of achieving equality for my generations. And yet, if anyone had called me a feminist I would have quickly corrected that notion. . . . On one hand, I started a group to encourage more women to major in economics and government. On the other hand, I would have denied being in any way, shape, or form a feminist. None of my college friends thought of themselves as feminists either. It saddens me to admit that we did not see the backlash against women around us. . . . In our defense, my friends and I truly, if naively, believed that the world did not need feminists anymore.

bell hooks

Although Sandberg revised her perspective on feminism, she did not turn towards primary sources (the work of feminist theorists) to broaden her understanding. In her book, she offers a simplistic description of the feminist movement based on women gaining equal rights with men. This construction of simple categories (women and men) was long ago challenged by visionary feminist thinkers, particularly individual black women/women of color. These thinkers insisted that everyone acknowledge and understand the myriad ways race, class, sexuality, and many other aspects of identity and difference made explicit that there was never and is no simple homogenous gendered identity that we could call "women" struggling to be equal with men. In fact, the reality was and is that privileged white women often experience a greater sense of solidarity with men of their same class than with poor white women or women of color.

Sandberg's definition of feminism begins and ends with the 5
notion that it's all about gender equality within the existing
social system. From this perspective, the structures of imperialist
white supremacist capitalist patriarchy need not be challenged.
And she makes it seem that privileged white men will eagerly
choose to extend the benefits of corporate capitalism to white
women who have the courage to "lean in." It almost seems as if
Sandberg sees women's lack of perseverance as more the problem than systemic inequality. Sandberg effectively uses her race
and class power and privilege to promote a narrow definition
of feminism that obscures and undermines visionary feminist
concerns.

Contrast her definition of feminism with the one I offered
more than twenty years ago in *Feminist Theory From Margin To
Center* and then again in *Feminism Is For Everybody*. Offering
a broader definition of feminism, one that does not conjure up
a battle between the sexes (i.e. women against men), I state:
"Simply put, feminism is a movement to end sexism, sexist
exploitation, and oppression." No matter their standpoint, anyone who advocates feminist politics needs to understand the
work does not end with the fight for equality of opportunity
within the existing patriarchal structure. We must understand
that challenging and dismantling patriarchy is at the core of
contemporary feminist struggle—this is essential and necessary
if women and men are to be truly liberated from outmoded
sexist thinking and actions.

Ironically, Sandberg's work would not have captured the
attention of progressives, particularly men, if she had not
packaged the message of "lets go forward and work as equals
within white male corporate elites" in the wrapping paper
of feminism. In the "one hundred most influential people in
the world" issue of *Time Magazine*, the forty-three-year old

Facebook COO was dubbed by the doyen of women's liberation movement Gloria Steinem in her short commentary with the heading "feminism's new boss." That same magazine carried a full page ad for the book *Lean In: Women, Work, and The Will to Lead* that carried the heading "Inspire the Graduate in Your Life" with a graduating picture of two white females and one white male. The ad included this quote from Sandberg's commencement speech at Barnard College in 2011: "I hope that you have the ambition to lean in to your career and run the world. Because the world needs you to change it." One can only speculate whether running the world is a call to support and perpetuate first world imperialism. This is precisely the type of feel good declaration Sandberg makes that in no way clarifies the embedded agenda she supports.

Certainly, her vision of individual women leaning in at the corporate table does not include any clear statements of which group of women she is speaking to and about, and the "lean in" woman is never given a racial identity. If Sandberg had acknowledged that she was primarily addressing privileged white women like herself (a small group working at the top of the corporate hierarchy), then she could not have portrayed herself as sharing a message, indeed a life lesson, for *all* women. Her basic insistence that gender equality should be important to all women and men is an insight that all folks involved in feminist movement agree is a central agenda. And yes, who can dispute the facts Sandberg offers as evidence; despite the many gains in female freedom, implicit gender bias remains the norm throughout our society. Patriarchy supports and affirms that bias. But Sandberg offers readers no understanding of what men must do to unlearn sexist thinking. At no point *In Lean In* does she let readers know what would motivate patriarchal white males in a corporate environment to change their belief system or the structures that support gender inequality.

Readers who only skim the surface of Sheryl Sandberg's book *Lean In* will find much they can agree with. Very few if any professional women will find themselves at odds with a fellow female who champions the cause gender equality, who shares with us all the good old mother wisdom that one of the most important choices any of us will make in life is who we will partner with. And she shares that the best partner is one who she tells readers will be a helpmeet—one who cares and shares. Sandberg's insistence that men participate equally in parenting is no new clarion call. From its earliest inception, the feminist movement called attention to the need for males to participate in parenting; it let women and men know that heteronormative relationships where there was gender quality not only lasted but were happier than the sexist norm.

Sandberg encourages women to seek high-level corporate 10 jobs and persevere until they reach the top. For many individual women, Sandberg telling them that they would not be betraying family if they dedicated themselves to work was affirming. It is positive in that it seemed to be a necessary response to popular anti-feminist backlash, which continually suggests that the feminist push to place more women in the workforce was and is a betrayal of marriage and family.

Unfortunately her voice is powerful, yet Sandberg is for the most part not voicing any new ideas. She is simply taking old ideas and giving them a new twist. When the book *Lean In* began its meteoric rise, which continues to bring fame and notoriety to Sandberg, many prominent feminists and/or progressive women denounced the work, vehemently castigating Sandberg. However, there was just one problematic issue at the core of the anti-Sandberg movement; very few folks attacking the work had actually read the book. Some of them had heard sound bites on television or had listened to her Ted Talk presentation. Still others had seen her interviewed. Many of these older female feminist advocates blatantly denounced the work and boldly announced their refusal to read the book.

As a feminist cultural critic, I found the eagerness with which Sandberg was viciously attacked disheartening. These critiques seem to emerge from misplaced rage not based solely on contempt for her ideas, but a rage bordering on envy. The powerful white male-dominated mass media was giving her and those ideas so much attention. There was no in-depth discussion of why this was the case. In the book Sandberg reminds readers that, "men still run the world." However, she does not discuss white male supremacy. Or the extent to which globalization has changed the makeup of corporate elites. In Mark Mizruchi's book *The Fracturing of the American Corporate Elite*, he describes a corporate world that is made up of a "more diverse crowd," one that is no longer white and male "blue chip dudes." He highlights several examples: "The CEO of Coca-Cola is Muhtar Kent, who was born in the United States but raised in Turkey; PepsiCo is run by Indra Nooyi, an Indian woman who came to America in her twenties. Burger King's CEO is Brazilian, Chrysler's CEO is Italian, and Morgan Stanley's CEO is Australian. Forget about influencing policy; many of today's leading US CEO's can't even vote here." Perhaps, even in the corporate world, imperialist white supremacist capitalist patriarchy is ready to accept as many white women as necessary to ensure white dominance. Race is certainly an invisible category in Sandberg's corporate fantasy world.

Sandberg is most seductive when sharing personal anecdotes. It is these true-life stories that expose the convenient lies underlying most of her assertions that as more women are at the top, all women will benefit. She explains: "Conditions for all women will improve when there are more women in leadership roles giving strong and powerful voice to their needs and concerns." This unsubstantiated truism is brought to us by a corporate executive who does not recognize the needs of pregnant women until it's happening to her. Is this a case of narcissism as a potential foundation for female solidarity? No behavior in the real world of women relating to women proves this to be true. In truth, Sandberg offers no strategies for the building of feminist solidarity between women.

She makes light of her ambivalence towards feminism. Even though Sandberg can humorously poke fun at herself and her relationship to feminism, she tells readers that her book "is not a feminist manifesto." Adding as though she is in a friendly conversation with herself, "okay, it is sort of a feminist manifesto." This is just one of the "funny" folksy moments in the book, which represent her plain and ordinary approach— she is just one of the girls. Maybe doing the book and talking about it with co-writer Nell Scovell provides the basis for the conversational tone. Good humor aside, cute quips and all, it is when she is talking about feminism that many readers would have liked her to go deeper. How about just explaining what she means by "feminist manifesto," since the word implies "a full public declaration of intentions, opinions or purposes." Of course, historically the best feminist manifestos emerged from collective consciousness raising and discussion. They were not the voice of one individual. Instead of creating a space of female solidarity, Sandberg exists as the lone queen amid millions of admirers. And no one in her group dares to question how she could be heralded as the "voice of revolutionary feminism."

How feminist, how revolutionary can a powerful rich woman 15 be when she playfully admits that she concedes all money management and bill paying to her husband? As Sandberg confesses, she would rather not think about money matters when she could be planning little Dora parties for her kids. This anecdote, like many others in the book, works to create the personal image of Sandberg. It is this "just plain folks" image that has been instrumental in her success, for it shows her as vulnerable.

This is not her only strategy. When giving filmed lectures, she wears clothes with sexy deep V-necks and stiletto heels and this image creates the aura of vulnerable femininity. It reminds one of the popular television advertisement from years ago wherein a sexy white woman comes home and dances around singing: "I can bring home the bacon, fry it up in the pan and never let you forget you're a man . . . cause I'm a w-o-m-a-n!" Sandberg's constructed image is not your usual sexist misogynist media portrayal of a feminist. She is never depicted as a man-hating ball-busting feminist nag.

Instead, she comes across both in her book and when performing on stages as a lovable younger sister who just wants to play on the big brother's team. It would be more in keeping with this image to call her brand of women's liberation *faux feminism*. A billionaire, one of the richest women in the world, Sandberg deflects attention from this reality. To personify it might raise critical questions. It might even have created the conditions for other women to feel threatened by her success. She solves that little problem by never speaking of money in *Lean In*; she uses the word once.

See pp. 114–16 for ways to repeat key terms and phrases.

And if that reality does not bring to her persona enough I'M EVERYWOMAN appeal, she tells her audiences: "I truly believe that the single most important career decision that a woman makes is whether she will have a life partner or who that partner is." Even though most women, straight or gay, have not seen choosing a life partner as a "career decision," anyone who advocates feminist politics knows that the choice of a partner matters. However, Sandberg's convenient use of the word partner masks the reality that she is really speaking about heteronormative partnerships, and even more specifically marriages between white women and white men. She shares: "Contrary to the popular notion that only unmarried women can make it to the top, the majority of the more successful female business leaders have partners." Specifically, though not directly, she is talking about white male husbands. For after telling readers that the most successful women at the top are partnered, she highlights the fact that "of the twenty-eight women who have served as CEO's of Fortune 500 companies, twenty-six were married, one was divorced and only one was never married." Again, no advocates of feminism would disagree with the notion that individual women should choose partners wisely. Good partners as defined by old style women's liberation movement and reiterated by Sandberg (who makes it seem that this is a new insight) are those who embrace equality, who care and share. One of the few radical arguments in Lean In is that men should come to the table—"the kitchen table." This is rarely one of the points Sandberg highlights in her media performances.

Of course, the vast majority of men in our society, irrespective of race, embrace patriarchal values; they do not embrace a vision or practice of gender equality either at work or in the domestic household. Anyone who acts as though women just need to make right choices is refusing to acknowledge the reality that men must also be making the right choice. Before females even reach the stage of life where choosing partners is important, we should all be developing financial literacy, preparing ourselves to manage our money well, so that we need not rely on finding a sharing partner who will manage our finances fairly.

According to *More Magazine*, American women are expected to control 23 trillion dollars by the end of the decade, which is "nearly twice the current amount." But what will this control mean if women lack financial literacy? Acquiring money and managing money are not the same actions. Women need to confront the meaning and uses of money on all levels. This is knowledge Sandberg the Chief Operating Officer possesses even if she coyly pretends otherwise.

In her 2008 book *The Comeback*, Emma Gilbey Keller exam- 20 ines many of the issues Sandberg addresses. Significantly, and unlike Sandberg, she highlights the need for women to take action on behalf of their financial futures. One chapter in the book begins with the epigram: "A woman's best production is a little money of her own." Given the huge amounts of money Sandberg has acquired, ostensibly by paying close attention to her financial future, her silence on the subject of money in *Lean In* undermines the call for genuine equality. Without the ability to be autonomous, in control of self and finances, women will not have the strength and confidence to "lean in."

Mass media (along with Sandberg) is telling us that by sheer strength of will and staying power, any woman so inclined can work hard and climb the corporate ladder all the way to the top. Shrewdly, Sandberg acknowledges that not all women desire to rise to the top, asserting that she is not judging women who make different choices. However, the real truth is that she is making judgments about the nature of women and work—that is what the book is fundamentally about. Her failure to confront the issue of women acquiring wealth allows her to ignore concrete systemic obstacles most women face inside the workforce. And by not confronting the issue of women and wealth, she need not confront the issue of women and poverty. She need not address the ways extreme class differences make it difficult for there to be a common sisterhood based on shared struggle and solidarity.

The contemporary feminist movement has not concentrated meaningful attention on the issue of women and wealth. Rightly, however, the movement highlighted the need for gender equity in the workforce—equal pay for equal work. This economic focus exposed the reality that race was a serious factor over-determining women's relationship to work and money. Much feminist thought by individual visionary women of color (especially black women thinkers) and white female allies called for a more accurate representation of female identity, one that would consider the reality of intersectionality. This theory encouraged women to see race and class as well as gender as crucial factors shaping female destiny. Promoting a broader insight, this work lay the groundwork for the formation of genuine female solidarity—a solidarity based on awareness of difference as well as the all-too-common gendered experiences women share. It has taken many years of hard work to create basic understandings of female identity; it will take many more years for solidarity between women to become reality.

It should surprise no one that women and men who advocate feminist politics were stunned to hear Sandberg promoting her trickle-down theory: the assumption that having more women at the top of corporate hierarchies would make the work world better for all women, including women on the bottom. Taken at face value, this seems a naive hope given that the imperialist white supremacist capitalist patriarchal corporate world Sandberg wants women to lean into encourages competition over cooperation. Or as Kate Losse, author of *Boy Kings: A Journey into the Heart of the Social Network*, which is an insider look at the real gender politics of Facebook, contends: "By arguing that women should express their feminism by remaining in the workplace at all costs, Sandberg encourages women to maintain a commitment to the work place without encouraging the workplace to maintain a commitment to them." It is as though Sandberg believes a subculture of powerful elite women will emerge in the workplace, powerful enough to silence male dominators.

Yet Sandberg spins her seductive fantasy of female solidarity as though comradely support between women will magically occur in patriarchal work environments. Since patriarchy has no gender, women "leaning in" will not automatically think in terms of gender equality and solidarity. Like the issue of money, patriarchy is another subject that receives little attention in Sandberg's book and in her many talks. This is ironic, since the vision of gender quality she espouses is most radically expressed when she is delineating what men need to do to work for change. It is precisely her avoidance of the difficult questions (like how will patriarchal thinking change) that empowers her optimism and the overall enthusiastic spirit she exudes. Her optimism is so affably intense, it encourages readers to bypass the difficulties involved in challenging and changing patriarchy so that a just moral and ethical foundation for gender equality would become the norm.

Women, and our male allies in struggle, who have been 25 on the frontlines of feminist thinking and practice, see clearly the fairytale evocation of harmonious solidarity is no easy task. Given all the forces that separate women and pit us against one another, solidarity is not an inevitable outcome. Sandberg's refusal to do anything but give slight mention to racialized class differences undercuts the notion that she has a program that speaks to and for all women. Her unwillingness to consider a vision that would include all women rather than white women from privileged classes is one of the flaws in the representation of herself as a voice for feminism. Certainly she is a powerful mentor figure for fiscally conservative white female elites. The corporate infusion of gender equality she evokes is a "whites only" proposition.

To women of color young and old, along with anti-racist white women, it is more than obvious that without a call to challenge and change racism as an integral part of class mobility she is really investing in top level success for highly educated women from privileged classes. The call for gender equality in the corporate American is undermined by the practice of exclusivity, and usurped by the heteronormative white supremacist bonding of marriage between white women and men. Founded on the principles of white supremacy and structured to maintain it, the rites of passage in the corporate world mirror this aspect of our nation. Let it be stated again and again that race, and more importantly white supremacy, is a taboo subject in the world according to Sandberg.

At times Sandberg reminds readers of the old stereotypes about used car salesmen. She pushes her product and she pushes it well. Her shpiel is so good, so full of stuff that is obviously true, that one is inclined to overlook all that goes unspoken, unexplained. For example, she titles a chapter "You Can't Have It All," warning women that this idea is one of the most dangerous concepts from the early feminist movement. But the real deal is that Sandberg has it all, and in a zillion little ways she flaunts it. Even though she epitomizes the "have it all kinda girl"—white, rich, and married to a wonderful husband (like the television evangelist Joyce Meyer, Sandberg is constantly letting readers know how wonderful her husband is lest we forget)—she claims women can't have it all. She even dedicated the book to her husband "for making everything possible"—what doesn't she have? Sandberg confesses that she has a loving family and children, more helpers in daily life than one can count. Add this to the already abundant list, she is deemed by the larger conservative media to be one of "the most influential," most powerful women in the world. If this is not another version of the old game show "queen for a day," what is? Remember that the women on the show are puppets and white men behind the scenes are pulling the strings.

Even though many advocates of feminist politics are angered by Sandberg's message, the truth is that alone, individually she was no threat to feminist movement. Had the conservative white male dominated world of mass media and advertising not chosen to hype her image, this influential woman would not be known to most folks. It is this patriarchal male dominated re-framing of feminism, which uses the body and personal success of Sheryl Sandberg, that is most disturbing and yes threatening to the future of visionary feminist movement. The model Sandberg represents is all about how women can participate and "run the world." But of course the kind of world we would be running is never defined. It sounds at times like benevolent patriarchal imperialism. This is the reason it seemed essential for feminist thinkers to respond critically, not just to Sandberg and her work, but to the conservative white male patriarchy that is using her to let the world know what kind of woman partner is acceptable among elites, both in the home and in the workplace.

Feminism is just the screen masking this reframing. Angela McRobbie offers an insightful take on this process in her book, *The Aftermath of Feminism: Gender, Culture, and Social Change*, explaining: "Elements of feminism have been taken into account and have been absolutely incorporated into political and institutional life. Drawing on a vocabulary that includes words like 'empowerment' and 'choice,' these elements are then converted into a much more individualistic discourse and they are deployed in this new guise, particularly in media and popular culture, but also by agencies of the state, as a kind of substitute for feminism. These new and seemingly modern ideas about women and especially young women are then disseminated more aggressively so as to ensure that a new women's movement will not re-emerge." This is so obviously the strategy Sandberg and her supporters have deployed. McRobbie then contends that "feminism is instrumentalized. It is brought forth and claimed by Western governments, as a signal to the rest of the world that this is a key part of what freedom now means. Freedom is revitalized and brought up to date with this faux feminism." Sandberg uses feminist rhetoric as a front to cover her commitment to western cultural imperialism, to white supremacist capitalist patriarchy.

Clearly, Sandberg, with her website and her foundation, [30] has many female followers. Long before she was chosen by conservative mass media as the new face of faux feminism, she had her followers. This is why I chose to call my response "dig deep," for it is only as we place her in the overall frame of female cultural icons that we can truly unpack and understand why she has been chosen and lifted up in the neoliberal marketplace. Importantly, whether feminist or not, we all need to remember that visionary feminist goal which is not of a women running the world as is, but a women doing our part to change the world so that freedom and justice, the opportunity to have optimal well-being, can be equally shared by everyone—female and male.

Joining the Conversation

1. This essay is a response to Sheryl Sandberg's book *Lean In* (excerpted here on pp. 642–58), which encourages women to aim for positions of leadership and power. What is bell hooks's overall assessment of that book, both positive and negative?
2. What does hooks mean by her title, "Dig Deep: Beyond *Lean In*"? The subtitle tells us that the essay is about *Lean In*; what does "Dig Deep" add, and why do you think hooks phrased it that way?
3. Even as hooks quotes and summarizes Sandberg and others, she makes her own views clear. How does she signal when she's asserting her own views and when she's summarizing those of someone else? (See Chapter 5 for this book's advice on distinguishing what you say from what others say.)
4. According to hooks, "Sandberg uses feminist rhetoric as a front to cover her commitment to western cultural imperialism, to white-supremacist capitalist patriarchy" (paragraph 29). What exactly does she mean by these criticisms? How do you think Sandberg would respond to these charges?
5. Write an essay summarizing briefly the arguments made by Sheryl Sandberg and bell hooks and then saying what you think and why.

Why Women Still Can't Have It All

ANNE-MARIE SLAUGHTER

Redefining the Arc of a Successful Career

EIGHTEEN MONTHS INTO MY JOB as the first woman director of policy planning at the State Department, a foreign-policy dream job that traces its origins back to George Kennan, I found myself in New York, at the United Nations' annual assemblage of every foreign minister and head of state in the world. On a Wednesday evening, President and Mrs. Obama hosted a glamorous reception at the American Museum of Natural History. I sipped champagne, greeted foreign dignitaries, and mingled. But I could not stop thinking about my 14-year-old son, who had started eighth grade three weeks earlier and was already resuming what had become his pattern of skipping homework,

ANNE-MARIE SLAUGHTER is the president and CEO of the New America Foundation, "a nonprofit, nonpartisan public policy institute," according to its website. In the past, she has taught at Princeton University and Harvard Law School and worked as director of policy planning for the U.S. State Department. She is also the author and editor of several books, most recently *The Idea That Is America: Keeping Faith with Our Values in a Dangerous World* (2007). This essay first appeared in the July/August 2012 issue of the *Atlantic*.

disrupting classes, failing math, and tuning out any adult who tried to reach him. Over the summer, we had barely spoken to each other—or, more accurately, he had barely spoken to me. And the previous spring I had received several urgent phone calls—invariably on the day of an important meeting—that required me to take the first train from Washington, D.C., where I worked, back to Princeton, New Jersey, where he lived. My husband, who has always done everything possible to support my career, took care of him and his 12-year-old brother during the week; outside of those midweek emergencies, I came home only on weekends.

As the evening wore on, I ran into a colleague who held a senior position in the White House. She has two sons exactly my sons' ages, but she had chosen to move them from California to D.C. when she got her job, which meant her husband commuted back to California regularly. I told her how difficult I was finding it to be away from my son when he clearly needed me. Then I said, "When this is over, I'm going to write an op-ed titled 'Women Can't Have It All.'"

She was horrified. "You *can't* write that," she said. "You, of all people." What she meant was that such a statement, coming from a high-profile career woman—a role model—would be a terrible signal to younger generations of women. By the end of the evening, she had talked me out of it, but for the remainder of my stint in Washington, I was increasingly aware that the feminist beliefs on which I had built my entire career were shifting under my feet. I had always assumed that if I could get a foreign-policy job in the State Department or the White House while my party was in power, I would stay the course as long as I had the opportunity to do work I loved. But in January 2011, when my two-year public-service leave from Princeton University was up, I hurried home as fast as I could.

A rude epiphany hit me soon after I got there. When people asked why I had left government, I explained that I'd come home not only because of Princeton's rules (after two years of leave, you lose your tenure), but also because of my desire to be with my family and my conclusion that juggling high-level government work with the needs of two teenage boys was not possible. I have not exactly left the ranks of full-time career women: I teach a full course load; write regular print and online columns on foreign policy; give 40 to 50 speeches a year; appear regularly on TV and radio; and am working on a new academic book. But I routinely got reactions from other women my age or older that ranged from disappointed ("It's such a pity that you had to leave Washington") to condescending ("I wouldn't generalize from your experience. *I've* never had to compromise, and my kids turned out great").

The first set of reactions, with the underlying assumption 5 that my choice was somehow sad or unfortunate, was irksome enough. But it was the second set of reactions—those implying that my parenting and/or my commitment to my profession were somehow substandard—that triggered a blind fury. Suddenly, finally, the penny dropped. All my life, I'd been on the other side of this exchange. I'd been the woman smiling the faintly superior smile while another woman told me she had decided to take some time out or pursue a less competitive career track so that she could spend more time with her family. I'd been the woman congratulating herself on her unswerving commitment to the feminist cause, chatting smugly with her dwindling number of college or law-school friends who had reached and maintained their place on the highest rungs of their profession. I'd been the one telling young women at my lectures that you *can* have it all and do it all, regardless of what field you are in. Which means I'd been part, albeit unwittingly, of making millions of women feel that *they* are to blame if they cannot manage to rise up the ladder as fast as men and also have a family and an active home life (and be thin and beautiful to boot).

Last spring, I flew to Oxford to give a public lecture. At the request of a young Rhodes Scholar I know, I'd agreed to talk to the Rhodes community about "work-family balance." I ended up speaking to a group of about 40 men and women in their mid-20s. What poured out of me was a set of very frank reflections on how unexpectedly hard it was to do the kind of job I wanted to do as a high government official and be the kind of parent I wanted to be, at a demanding time for my children (even though my husband, an academic, was willing to take on the lion's share of parenting for the two years I was in Washington). I concluded by saying that my time in office had convinced me that further government service would be very unlikely while my sons were still at home. The audience was rapt, and asked many thoughtful questions. One of the first was from a young woman who began by thanking me for "not giving just one more fatuous 'You can have it all' talk." Just about all of the women in that room planned to combine careers and family in some way. But almost all assumed and accepted that they would have to make compromises that the men in their lives were far less likely to have to make.

The striking gap between the responses I heard from those young women (and others like them) and the responses I heard from my peers and associates prompted me to write this article. Women of my gen-eration have clung to the feminist credo we were raised with, even as our ranks have been steadily thinned by unresolvable tensions between family and career, because we are determined not to drop the flag for the next generation. But when many members of the younger generation have stopped listening, on

See p. 136 for tips on indicating the importance of a claim.

the grounds that glibly repeating "you can have it all" is simply airbrushing reality, it is time to talk.

I still strongly believe that women can "have it all" (and that men can too). I believe that we can "have it all at the same time." But not today, not with the way America's economy and society are currently structured. My experiences over the past three years have forced me to confront a number of uncomfortable facts that need to be widely acknowledged— and quickly changed.

Before my service in government, I'd spent my career in academia: as a law professor and then as the dean of Princeton's Woodrow Wilson School of Public and International Affairs. Both were demanding jobs, but I had the ability to set my own schedule most of the time. I could be with my kids when I needed to be, and still get the work done. I had to travel frequently, but I found I could make up for that with an extended period at home or a family vacation.

I knew that I was lucky in my career choice, but I had 10 no idea how lucky until I spent two years in Washington within a rigid bureaucracy, even with bosses as understanding as Hillary Clinton and her chief of staff, Cheryl Mills. My workweek started at 4:20 on Monday morning, when I got up to get the 5:30 train from Trenton to Washington. It ended late on Friday, with the train home. In between, the days were crammed with meetings, and when the meetings stopped, the writing work began—a never-ending stream of memos, reports, and comments on other people's drafts. For two years, I never left the office early enough to go to any stores other than those open 24 hours, which meant that everything from dry cleaning to hair appointments to Christmas shopping had to be done on weekends, amid children's sporting events, music lessons, family meals, and conference calls. I was entitled to four hours of vacation per pay period, which came to one day of vacation a month. And I had it better than many of my peers in D.C.; Secretary Clinton deliberately came in around 8 a.m. and left around 7 p.m., to allow her close staff to have morning and evening time with their families (although of course she worked earlier and later, from home).

In short, the minute I found myself in a job that is typical for the vast majority of working women (and men), working long hours on someone else's schedule, I could no longer be both the parent and the professional I wanted to be—at least not with a child experiencing a rocky adolescence. I realized what should have perhaps been obvious: having it all, at least for me, depended almost entirely on what type of job I had. The flip side is the harder truth: having it all was not possible in many types of jobs, including high government office—at least not for very long.

I am hardly alone in this realization. Michèle Flournoy stepped down after three years as undersecretary of defense for policy, the third-highest job in the department, to spend more time at home with her three children, two of whom are teenagers. Karen Hughes left her position as the counselor to President George W. Bush after a year and a half in Washington to go home to Texas for the sake of her family. Mary Matalin, who spent two years as an assistant to Bush and the counselor to Vice President Dick Cheney before stepping down to spend more time with her daughters, wrote: "Having control over your schedule is the only way that women who want to have a career and a family can make it work."

Yet the decision to step down from a position of power—to value family over professional advancement, even for a time—is directly at odds with the prevailing social pressures on career professionals in the United States. One phrase says it all about current attitudes toward work and family, particularly among elites. In Washington, "leaving to spend time with your family" is a euphemism for being fired. This understanding is so ingrained that when Flournoy announced her resignation last December, *The New York Times* covered her decision as follows:

> Ms. Flournoy's announcement surprised friends and a number of Pentagon officials, but all said they took her reason for resignation at face value and not as a standard Washington excuse for an official who has in reality been forced out. "I can absolutely and unequivocally state that her decision to step down has nothing to do with anything other than her commitment to her family," said Doug Wilson, a top Pentagon spokesman. "She has loved this job and people here love her."

Think about what this "standard Washington excuse" implies: it is so unthinkable that an official would *actually* step down to spend time with his or her family that this must be a cover for something else. How could anyone voluntarily leave the circles of power for the responsibilities of parenthood? Depending on one's vantage point, it is either ironic or maddening that this view abides in the nation's capital, despite the ritual commitments to "family values" that are part of every political campaign. Regardless, this sentiment makes true work-life balance exceptionally difficult. But it cannot change unless top women speak out.

Only recently have I begun to appreciate the extent to which many young professional women feel under assault by women my age and older. After I gave a recent speech in New York, several women in their late 60s or early 70s came up to tell me how glad and proud they were to see me speaking as a foreign-policy expert. A couple of them went on, however, to contrast my career with the path being traveled by "younger women today." One expressed dismay that many younger women "are just not willing to get out there and do it." Said another, unaware of the circumstances of my recent job change: "They think they have to choose between having a career and having a family."

A similar assumption underlies Facebook Chief Operating 15 Officer Sheryl Sandberg's widely publicized 2011 commencement speech at Barnard, and her earlier TED talk, in which she lamented the dismally small number of women at the top and advised young women not to "leave before you leave." When a woman starts thinking about having children, Sandberg said, "she doesn't raise her hand anymore . . . She starts leaning back." Although couched in terms of encouragement, Sandberg's exhortation contains more than a note of reproach. We who have made it to the top, or are striving to get there, are essentially saying to the women in the generation behind us: "What's the matter with you?"

They have an answer that we don't want to hear. After the speech I gave in New York, I went to dinner with a group of 30-somethings. I sat across from two vibrant women, one of whom worked at the UN and the other at a big New York law firm. As nearly always happens in these situations, they soon began asking me about work-life balance. When I told them I was writing this article, the lawyer said, "I look for role models and can't find any." She said the women in her firm who had become partners and taken on management positions had made tremendous sacrifices, "many of which they don't even seem to realize. . . . They take two years off when their kids are young but then work like crazy to get back on track professionally, which means that they see their kids when they are toddlers but not teenagers, or really barely at all." Her friend nodded, mentioning the top professional women she knew, all of whom essentially relied on round-the-clock nannies. Both were very clear that they did not want that life, but could not figure out how to combine professional success and satisfaction with a real commitment to family.

I realize that I am blessed to have been born in the late 1950s instead of the early 1930s, as my mother was, or the beginning of the 20th century, as my grandmothers were. My mother built a successful and rewarding career as a professional artist largely in the years after my brothers and I left home—and after being told in her 20s that she could not go to medical school, as her father had done and her brother would go on to do, because, of course, she was going to get married. I owe my own freedoms and opportunities to the pioneering generation of women ahead of me—the women now in their 60s, 70s, and 80s who faced overt sexism of a kind I see only when watching *Mad Men*, and who knew that the only way to make it as a woman was to act exactly like a man. To admit to, much less act on, maternal longings would have been fatal to their careers.

But precisely thanks to their progress, a different kind of conversation is now possible. It is time for women in leadership positions to recognize that although we are still blazing trails and breaking ceilings, many of us are also reinforcing a falsehood: that "having it all" is, more than anything, a function of personal determination. As Kerry Rubin and Lia Macko, the authors of *Midlife Crisis at 30*, their cri de coeur for Gen-X and Gen-Y women, put it:

> What we discovered in our research is that while the empowerment part of the equation has been loudly celebrated, there has been very little honest discussion among women of our age about the real barriers and flaws that still exist in the system despite the opportunities we inherited.

I am well aware that the majority of American women face problems far greater than any discussed in this article. I am writing for my demographic—highly educated, well-off women who are privileged enough to have choices in the first place. We may not have choices about whether to do paid work, as dual incomes have become indispensable. But we have choices about the type and tempo of the work we do. We are the women who could be leading, and who should be equally represented in the leadership ranks.

Millions of other working women face much more difficult life [20] circumstances. Some are single mothers; many struggle to find any job; others support husbands who cannot find jobs. Many cope with a work life in which good day care is either unavailable or very expensive; school schedules do not match work schedules; and schools themselves are failing to educate their children. Many of these women are worrying not about having it all, but rather about holding on to what they do have. And although women as a group have made substantial gains in wages, educational attainment, and prestige over the past three decades, the economists Justin Wolfers and Betsey Stevenson have shown that women are less happy today than their predecessors were in 1972, both in absolute terms and relative to men.

The best hope for improving the lot of all women, and for closing what Wolfers and Stevenson call a "new gender gap"—measured by well-being rather than wages—is to close the leadership gap: to elect a woman president and 50 women senators; to ensure that women are equally represented in the ranks of corporate executives and judicial leaders. Only when women wield power in sufficient numbers will we create a society that genuinely works for all women. That will be a society that works for everyone.

· · ·

Rediscovering the Pursuit of Happiness

One of the most complicated and surprising parts of my journey out of Washington was coming to grips with what I really wanted. I had opportunities to stay on, and I could have tried to work out an arrangement allowing me to spend more time at home. I might have been able to get my family to join me in Washington for a year; I might have been able to get classified technology installed at my house the way Jim Steinberg did; I might have been able to commute only four days a week instead of five. (While this last change would have still left me very little time at home, given the intensity of my job, it might have made the job doable for another year or two.) But I realized that I didn't just *need* to go home. Deep down, I *wanted* to go home. I wanted to be able to spend time with my children in the last few years that they are likely to live at home, crucial years for their development into responsible, productive, happy, and caring adults. But also irreplaceable years for me to enjoy the simple pleasures of parenting—baseball games, piano recitals, waffle breakfasts, family trips, and goofy rituals. My older son is doing very well these days, but even when he gives us a hard time, as all teenagers do, being home to shape his choices and help him make good decisions is deeply satisfying.

The flip side of my realization is captured in Rubin and Macko's ruminations on the importance of bringing the different parts of their lives together as 30-year-old women:

> If we didn't start to learn how to integrate our personal, social, and professional lives, we were about five years away from morphing into the angry woman on the other side of a mahogany desk who questions her staff's work ethic after standard 12-hour workdays, before heading home to eat moo shoo pork in her lonely apartment.

Women have contributed to the fetish of the one-dimensional life, albeit by necessity. The pioneer generation of feminists walled off their personal lives from their professional personas to ensure that they could never be discriminated against for a lack of commitment to their work. When I was a law student in the 1980s, many women who were then climbing the legal hierarchy in New York firms told me that they never admitted to taking time out for a child's doctor appointment or school performance, but instead invented a much more neutral excuse.

Today, however, women in power can and should change 25 that environment, although change is not easy. When I became dean of the Woodrow Wilson School, in 2002, I decided that one of the advantages of being a woman in power was that I could help change the norms by deliberately talking about my children and my desire to have a balanced life. Thus, I would end faculty meetings at 6 p.m. by saying that I had to go home for dinner; I would also make clear to all student organizations that I would not come to dinner with them, because I needed to be home from six to eight, but that I would often be willing to come back after eight for a meeting. I also once told the Dean's Advisory Committee that the associate dean would chair the next session so I could go to a parent-teacher conference.

After a few months of this, several female assistant professors showed up in my office quite agitated. "You *have* to stop talking about your kids," one said. "You are not showing the gravitas that people expect from a dean, which is particularly damaging precisely because you are the first woman dean of the school." I told them that I was doing it deliberately and continued my practice, but it is interesting that gravitas and parenthood don't seem to go together.

Ten years later, whenever I am introduced at a lecture or other speaking engagement, I insist that the person introducing me mention that I have two sons. It seems odd to me to list degrees, awards, positions, and interests and *not* include the dimension of my life that is most important to me—and takes an enormous amount of my time. As Secretary Clinton once said in a television interview in Beijing when the interviewer asked her about Chelsea's upcoming wedding: "That's my real life." But I notice that my male introducers are typically uncomfortable when I make the request. They frequently say things like "And she particularly wanted me to mention that she has two sons"—thereby drawing attention to the unusual nature of my request, when my entire purpose is to make family references routine and normal in professional life.

This does not mean that you should insist that your colleagues spend time cooing over pictures of your baby or listening to the prodigious accomplishments of your kindergartner. It does mean that if you are late coming in one week, because it is your turn to drive the kids to school, that you be honest about what you are doing. Indeed, Sheryl Sandberg recently acknowledged not only that she leaves work at 5:30 to have dinner with her family, but also that for many years she did not dare make this admission, even though she would of course make up the work time later in the evening. Her willingness to speak out now is a strong step in the right direction.

Seeking out a more balanced life is not a women's issue; balance would be better for us all. Bronnie Ware, an Australian blogger who worked for years in palliative care and is the author of the 2011 book *The Top Five Regrets of the Dying*, writes that the regret she heard most often was "I wish I'd had the courage to live a life true to myself, not the life others expected of me." The second-most-common regret was "I wish I didn't work so hard." She writes: "This came from every male patient that I nursed. They missed their children's youth and their partner's companionship."

Juliette Kayyem, who several years ago left the Department of Homeland Security soon after her husband, David Barron, left a high position in the Justice Department, says their joint decision to leave Washington and return to Boston sprang from their desire to work on the "happiness project," meaning quality time with their three children. (She borrowed the term from her friend Gretchen Rubin, who wrote a best-selling book and now runs a blog with that name.)

It's time to embrace a national happiness project. As a daughter of Charlottesville, Virginia, the home of Thomas Jefferson and the university he founded, I grew up with the Declaration of Independence in my blood. Last I checked, he did not declare American independence in the name of life, liberty, and professional success. Let us rediscover the pursuit of happiness, and let us start at home.

Innovation Nation

As I write this, I can hear the reaction of some readers to many of the proposals in this essay: It's all fine and well for a tenured professor to write about flexible working hours, investment intervals, and family-comes-first management. But what about the real world? Most American women cannot demand these things, particularly in a bad economy, and their employers have little incentive to grant them voluntarily. Indeed, the most frequent reaction I get in putting forth these ideas is that when the choice is whether to hire a man who will work whenever and wherever needed, or a woman who needs more flexibility, choosing the man will add more value to the company.

In fact, while many of these issues are hard to quantify and measure precisely, the statistics seem to tell a different story. A seminal study of 527 U.S. companies, published in the *Academy of Management Journal* in 2000, suggests that "organizations with more extensive work-family policies have higher perceived firm-level performance" among their industry peers. These findings accorded with a 2003 study conducted by Michelle Arthur at the University of New Mexico. Examining 130 announcements of family-friendly policies in *The Wall Street Journal*, Arthur found that the announcements alone significantly improved share prices. In 2011, a study on flexibility in the workplace by Ellen Galinsky, Kelly Sakai, and Tyler Wigton of the Families and Work Institute showed that increased flexibility correlates positively with job engagement, job satisfaction, employee retention, and employee health.

This is only a small sampling from a large and growing literature trying to pin down the relationship between family-friendly policies and economic performance. Other scholars have concluded that good family policies attract better talent, which in turn raises productivity, but that the policies themselves have no impact on productivity. Still others argue that results attributed to these policies are actually a function of good management overall. What is evident, however, is that many firms that recruit and train well-educated professional women are aware that when a woman leaves because of bad work-family balance, they are losing the money and time they invested in her.

Even the legal industry, built around the billable hour, is taking notice. Deborah Epstein Henry, a former big-firm litigator, is now the president of Flex-Time Lawyers, a national consulting firm focused partly on strategies for the retention of female attorneys. In her book *Law and Reorder*, published by the

American Bar Association in 2010, she describes a legal profession "where the billable hour no longer works"; where attorneys, judges, recruiters, and academics all agree that this system of compensation has perverted the industry, leading to brutal work hours, massive inefficiency, and highly inflated costs. The answer—already being deployed in different corners of the industry—is a combination of alternative fee structures, virtual firms, women-owned firms, and the outsourcing of discrete legal jobs to other jurisdictions. Women, and Generation X and Y lawyers more generally, are pushing for these changes on the supply side; clients determined to reduce legal fees and increase flexible service are pulling on the demand side. Slowly, change is happening.

At the core of all this is self-interest. Losing smart and motivated women not only diminishes a company's talent pool; it also reduces the return on its investment in training and mentoring. In trying to address these issues, some firms are finding out that women's ways of working may just be better ways of working, for employees and clients alike.

Experts on creativity and innovation emphasize the value of encouraging nonlinear thinking and cultivating randomness by taking long walks or looking at your environment from unusual angles. In their new book, *A New Culture of Learning: Cultivating the Imagination for a World of Constant Change*, the innovation gurus John Seely Brown and Douglas Thomas write, "We believe that connecting play and imagination may be the single most important step in unleashing the new culture of learning."

Space for play and imagination is exactly what emerges when rigid work schedules and hierarchies loosen up. Skeptics should consider the "California effect." California is the cradle of American innovation—in technology, entertainment, sports, food, and lifestyles. It is also a place where people take leisure as seriously as they take work; where companies like Google deliberately encourage play, with Ping-Pong tables, light sabers, and policies that require employees to spend one day a week working on whatever they wish. Charles Baudelaire wrote: "Genius is nothing more nor less than childhood recovered at will." Google apparently has taken note.

No parent would mistake child care for childhood. Still, seeing the world anew through a child's eyes can be a powerful source of stimulation. When the Nobel laureate Thomas Schelling wrote *The Strategy of Conflict*, a classic text applying game theory to conflicts among nations, he frequently drew on child-rearing for examples of when deterrence might succeed or fail. "It may be easier to articulate the peculiar difficulty of constraining [a ruler] by the use of threats," he wrote, "when one is fresh from a vain attempt at using threats to keep a small child from hurting a dog or a small dog from hurting a child."

The books I've read with my children, the silly movies I've watched, the games I've played, questions I've answered, and people I've met while parenting have broadened my world. Another axiom of the literature on innovation is that the more often people with different perspectives come together, the more likely creative ideas are to emerge. Giving workers the ability to integrate their non-work lives with their work— whether they spend that time mothering or marathoning—will open the door to a much wider range of influences and ideas.

Enlisting Men

Perhaps the most encouraging news of all for achieving the sorts of changes that I have proposed is that men are joining the cause. In commenting on a draft of this article, Martha Minow, the dean of the Harvard Law School, wrote me that one change she has observed during 30 years of teaching law at Harvard is that today many young men are asking questions about how they can manage a work-life balance. And more systematic research on Generation Y confirms that many more men than in the past are asking questions about how they are going to integrate active parenthood with their professional lives.

Abstract aspirations are easier than concrete trade-offs, of course. These young men have not yet faced the question of whether they are prepared to give up that more prestigious clerkship or fellowship, decline a promotion, or delay their professional goals to spend more time with their children and to support their partner's career.

Yet once work practices and work culture begin to evolve, those changes are likely to carry their own momentum. Kara Owen, a British foreign-service officer who worked a London job from Dublin, wrote me in an e-mail:

> I think the culture on flexible working started to change the minute the Board of Management (who were all men at the time) started to work flexibly—quite a few of them started working one day a week from home.

Men have, of course, become much more involved parents over the past couple of decades, and that, too, suggests broad support for big changes in the way we balance work and family. It is noteworthy that both James Steinberg, deputy secretary of state, and William Lynn, deputy secretary of defense, stepped down two years into the Obama administration so that they could spend more time with their children (for real).

Going forward, women would do well to frame work-family 45 balance in terms of the broader social and economic issues that affect both women and men. After all, we have a new generation of young men who have been raised by full-time working mothers. Let us presume, as I do with my sons, that they will understand "supporting their families" to mean more than earning money.

I have been blessed to work with and be mentored by some extraordinary women. Watching Hillary Clinton in action makes me incredibly proud—of her intelligence, expertise, professionalism, charisma, and command of any audience. I get a similar rush when I see a front-page picture of Christine Lagarde, the managing director of the International Monetary Fund, and Angela Merkel, the chancellor of Germany, deep in conversation about some of the most important issues on the world stage; or of Susan Rice, the U.S. ambassador to the United Nations, standing up forcefully for the Syrian people in the Security Council.

These women are extraordinary role models. If I had a daughter, I would encourage her to look to them, and I want a world in which they are extraordinary but not unusual. Yet I also want a world in which, in Lisa Jackson's* words, "to be a strong woman, you don't have to give up on the things that define you as a woman." That means respecting, enabling, and indeed celebrating the full range of women's choices. "Empowering yourself," Jackson said in a speech at Princeton, "doesn't have to mean rejecting motherhood, or eliminating the nurturing or feminine aspects of who you are."

I gave a speech at Vassar last November and arrived in time to wander the campus on a lovely fall afternoon. It is a place infused with a spirit of community and generosity, filled with

---

*Jackson From 2009 until 2013, Administrator of the United States Environmental Protection Agency.

benches, walkways, public art, and quiet places donated by alumnae seeking to encourage contemplation and connection. Turning the pages of the alumni magazine (Vassar is now coed), I was struck by the entries of older alumnae, who greeted their classmates with *Salve* (Latin for "hello") and wrote witty remembrances sprinkled with literary allusions. Theirs was a world in which women wore their learning lightly; their news is mostly of their children's accomplishments. Many of us look back on that earlier era as a time when it was fine to joke that women went to college to get an "M.R.S." And many women of my generation abandoned the Seven Sisters as soon as the formerly all-male Ivy League universities became coed. I would never return to the world of segregated sexes and rampant discrimination. But now is the time to revisit the assumption that women must rush to adapt to the "man's world" that our mothers and mentors warned us about.

I continually push the young women in my classes to speak more. They must gain the confidence to value their own insights and questions, and to present them readily. My husband agrees, but he actually tries to get the young men in his classes to act more like the women—to speak less and listen more. If women are ever to achieve real equality as leaders, then we have to stop accepting male behavior and male choices as the default and the ideal. We must insist on changing social policies and bending career tracks to accommodate *our* choices, too. We have the power to do it if we decide to, and we have many men standing beside us.

We'll create a better society in the process, for *all* women. ₅₀ We may need to put a woman in the White House before we are able to change the conditions of the women working at Walmart. But when we do, we will stop talking about whether women can have it all. We will properly focus on how we can help all Americans have healthy, happy, productive lives, valuing the people they love as much as the success they seek.

Joining the Conversation

1. According to Anne-Marie Slaughter, women can "'have it all.' . . . But not today, not with the way America's economy and society are currently structured" (paragraph 8). Summarize her "I say," noting the reasons and evidence she gives to support her claims.
2. In paragraph 19, Slaughter entertains a possible objection to her argument, saying that she is "well aware that a majority of American women face problems far greater than any discussed in this article." How does she answer this objection?
3. This essay consists of four sections: Redefining the Arc of a Successful Career, Rediscovering the Pursuit of Happiness, Innovation Nation, and Enlisting Men. Summarize each section in a sentence or two. Put yourself in Slaughter's shoes; your summary should be true to what she says. (See pp. 31–33 for guidance in writing this kind of summary.)
4. Slaughter claims that most young men today have not yet had to decide between accepting a promotion or other professional opportunity and delaying their own goals "to spend more time with their children and to support their partner's career" (paragraph 42). What would Richard Dorment (pp. 697–717) say to that?
5. Write a paragraph stating your own thoughts and perceptions on mixing family and career. Given Slaughter's arguments, how do you think she'd respond to what you say?

Why Men Still Can't Have It All

RICHARD DORMENT

———⌖———

*Lately, the raging debate about issues of "work-life balance" has
focused on whether or not women can "have it all." Entirely
lost in this debate is the growing strain of work-life balance on
men, who today are feeling the competing demands of work and
home as much or more than women. And the truth is as shocking as it is obvious: No one can have it all. Any questions?*

THE BABY HAS A HEARTBEAT. The ultrasound shows ten
fuzzy fingers and ten fuzzy toes and a tiny crescent-moon mouth
that will soon let out the first of many wails. We have chosen
not to find out the gender, and when the question comes, as it
does every day, we say we have no preference. Ten fingers, ten
toes. A wail in the delivery room would be nice. But in private,
just us, we talk. About the pros and cons of boys versus girls,
and about whether it would be better, more advantageous, to

———

RICHARD DORMENT is an editor at *Esquire* magazine. He has been
a guest on television and radio programs including the *Today Show*,
CNN Newsroom, *Here and Now*, and *Upfront and Straightforward*. This
essay first appeared in the June/July 2013 issue of *Esquire*.

be born a boy or a girl right now. It's a toss-up, or maybe just a draw—impossible to say that a boy *or* a girl born in America in 2013 has any conspicuous advantages because of his or her gender.

Consider the facts: Nearly 60 percent of the bachelor's degrees in this country today go to women. Same number for graduate degrees. There are about as many women in the workforce as men, and according to Hanna Rosin's 2012 book, *The End of Men*, of the fifteen professions projected to grow the fastest over the coming years, twelve are currently dominated by women. Per a 2010 study by James Chung of Reach Advisors, unmarried childless women under thirty and with full-time jobs earn 8 percent more than their male peers in 147 out of 150 of the largest U. S. cities. The accomplishments that underlie those numbers are real and world-historic, and through the grueling work of generations of women, men and women are as equal as they have ever been. Adding to that the greater male predisposition to ADHD, alcoholism, and drug abuse, women have nothing but momentum coming out of young adulthood— the big mo!—and then . . .

Well, what exactly? Why don't women hold more than 15 percent of *Fortune* 500 executive-officer positions in America? Why are they stalled below 20 percent of Congress? Why does the average woman earn only seventy-seven pennies for every dollar made by the average man? Childbirth plays a role, knocking ambitious women off their professional stride for months (if not years) at a time while their male peers go chug-chug-chugging along, but then why do some women still make it to the top while others fall by the wayside? Institutional sexism and pay discrimination are still ugly realities, but with the millions in annual penalties levied on offending businesses . . . they have become increasingly, and thankfully, uncommon.

College majors count (women still dominate education, men engineering), as do career choices, yet none of these on their own explains why the opportunity gap between the sexes has all but closed yet a stark achievement gap persists.

For a fuller explanation, the national conversation of late has settled on a single issue—work-life balance—with two voices in particular dominating: The first belongs to former State Department policy chief Anne-Marie Slaughter, whose essay "Why Women Still Can't Have It All" was the most widely read story ever on the *Atlantic*'s web site and landed her a book deal and spots on *Today* and *Colbert*. Slaughter's twelve-thousand-word story relies on personal anecdotes mixed with wonk talk: "I still strongly believe that women can 'have it all' (and that men can too). I believe that we can 'have it all at the same time.' But not today, not with the way America's economy and society are currently structured." The scarcity of female leaders to effect public and corporate change on behalf of women; the inflexibility of the traditional workday; the prevalence of what she calls "'time macho'—a relentless competition to work harder, stay later, pull more all-nighters, travel around the world and bill the extra hours that the international date line affords you." All these factors conspire to deprive women of "it all." (The "it" in question being like Potter Stewart's definition of pornography: You know it when you have it.)

The second, and altogether more grown-up, voice belongs 5 to Facebook COO Sheryl Sandberg, whose "sort of feminist" manifesto *Lean In* urges women to command a seat at any table of their choosing. Like Slaughter, Sandberg references the usual systemic challenges, but what it really boils down to, Sandberg argues, is what Aretha Franklin and Annie Lennox prescribed back in the eighties: Sisters Doin' It for Themselves. Sandberg encourages women to negotiate harder, be more assertive, and forget about being liked and concentrate instead on letting 'er rip. She believes that women can, and should, determine the pace and scope of their own careers, and for her audacity in assigning some agency to the women of America, her critics (Slaughter among them) say she blames women for their failure to rise farther, faster, rather than the real culprits: society, corporations, and men (which is to say: men, men, and men). Commenting on the *Lean In* debate in a blog for *The New York Times*, Gail Collins asked, "How do you give smart, accomplished, ambitious women the same opportunities as men to reach their goals? What about universal preschool and after-school programs? What about changing the corporate mind-set about the time commitment it takes to move up the ladder? What about having more husbands step up and take the major load?"

Her questions echo a 2010 *Newsweek* cover story, "Men's Lib," which ended with an upper: "If men embraced parental leave, women would be spared the stigma of the 'mommy track'—and the professional penalties (like lower pay) that come along with it. If men were involved fathers, more kids might stay in school, steer clear of crime, and avoid poverty as adults. And if the country achieved gender parity in the workplace—an optimal balance of fully employed men and women—the gross domestic product would grow by as much as 9 percent. . . . Ultimately, [it] boils down to a simple principle: in a changing world, men should do whatever it takes to contribute their fair share at home and at work."

Two men wrote that, incidentally, which must make it true, and among those who traffic in gender studies, it is something of a truth universally acknowledged: Men are to blame for pretty much everything. And I freely admit, we do make for a compelling target. Men have oppressed their wives and sisters and daughters for pretty much all of recorded history, and now women are supposed to trust us to share everything 50-50?

Allow me to paint another picture. One in which women are asked to make the same personal sacrifices as men past and present—too much time away from home, too many weekends at the computer, too much inconvenient travel—but then claim some special privilege in their hardship. One in which universal preschool and after-school programs would be a boon to all parents (and not, as Collins suggests, simply to women). In which men spend more time with their children, and are more involved with their home lives, than ever before. In which men work just as hard at their jobs, if not harder, than ever before. In which men now report higher rates of work-life stress than women do. In which men are tormented by the lyrics of "Cat's in the Cradle." In which men are being told, in newspapers and books, on web sites and TV shows, that they are the problem, that they need to help out, when, honestly folks, they're doing the best they can. In which men like me, and possibly you, open their eyes in the morning and want it all—*everything!*—only to close their eyes at night knowing that only a fool could ever expect such a thing.

My wife makes more money than I do. We majored in the same thing at the same college at the same time, and when I chose to go into journalism, she chose to go to law school. She works longer hours, shoulders weightier responsibilities, and faces greater (or at least more reliable) prospects for long-term success, all of which are direct results of choices that we made in our early twenties. She does more of the heavy lifting with our young son than I do, but I do as much as I can. (Someone else watches him while we are at work.) I do a lot of cooking and cleaning around our house. So does she. I don't keep score (and she says she doesn't), and it's hard to imagine how our life would work if we weren't both giving every day our all.

According to a study released in March by the Pew Research 10 Center, household setups like ours are increasingly the norm: 60 percent of two-parent homes with kids under the age of eighteen are made up of dual-earning couples (i.e., two working parents). On any given week in such a home, women put in more time than men doing housework (sixteen hours to nine) and more time with child care (twelve to seven). These statistics provoke outrage among the "fair share" crowd, and there is a sense, even among the most privileged women, that they are getting a raw deal. (In April, Michelle Obama referred to herself as a "single mother" before clarifying: "I shouldn't say single— as a busy mother, sometimes, you know, when you've got a husband who is president, it can feel a little single." Because really: The president should spend more time making sure the First Lady feels supported.)

But the complete picture reveals a more complex and equitable reality.

Men in dual-income couples work outside the home eleven more hours a week than their working wives or partners do (forty-two to thirty-one), and when you look at the total weekly workload, including paid work outside the home and unpaid work inside the home, men and women are putting in roughly the same number of hours: fifty-eight hours for men and fifty-nine for women.

How you view those numbers depends in large part on your definition of work, but it's not quite as easy as saying men aren't pulling their weight around the house. (Spending eleven fewer hours at home and with the kids doesn't mean working dads are freeloaders any more than spending eleven fewer hours at work makes working moms slackers.) These are practical accommodations that reflect real-time conditions on the ground, and rather than castigate men, one might consider whether those extra hours on the job provide the financial cover the family needs so that women can spend more time with the kids.

Also, according to women in the Pew study, it seems to be working out well. Working mothers in dual-earning couples are more likely to say they're very or pretty happy with life right now than their male partners are (93 percent to 87 percent); if anything, it's men who are twice as likely to say they're unhappy. (Pew supplied *Esquire* with data specific to dual-income couples that is not part of its published report. There is plenty of data relating to other household arrangements—working father and stay-at-home mom; working mother and stay-at-home dad; same-sex households—but since the focus of Slaughter, Sandberg, et al. is on the struggles of working mothers, and most working mothers are coupled with working fathers, the dual-income data set seems most relevant to examine here.)

Ellen Galinsky has been studying the American workplace 15 for more than thirty years. A married mother of two grown kids with a background in child education and zero tolerance for bullshit, she cofounded the Families and Work Institute in part to chart how the influx of women in American offices and factories would affect family dynamics. "In 1977," she says, "there was a Department of Labor study that asked people, 'How much interference do you feel between your work and your family life?' and men's work-family conflict was a lot lower than women's." She saw the numbers begin to shift in the late 1990s, and "by 2008, 60 percent of fathers in dual-earning couples were experiencing some or a lot of conflict compared to about 47 percent of women. I would go into meetings with business leaders and report the fact that men's work-family conflict was higher than women's, and people in the room—who were so used to being worried about women's advancement—couldn't believe it."

What they couldn't believe was decades of conventional wisdom—men secure and confident in the workplace, women somewhat less so—crumbling away as more and more fathers began to invest more of their time and energy into their home lives. Though they still lag behind women in hours clocked at the kitchen sink, men do more than twice as much cooking and cleaning as they did fifty years ago, which probably comes as a shock to older women who would famously come home from work to a "second shift" of housework. In reporting her book, *Big Girls Don't Cry*, a study of women's roles in the 2008 election, Rebecca Traister interviewed dozens of high-achieving women who were in the thick of second-wave feminism and encountered the generation gap for herself. "I remember one day, right before Thanksgiving, a woman who had grown children said something like 'I would love to keep talking to you but

I have to start my two-day slog to Thanksgiving.' And I said very lightly, 'Oh, my husband does the cooking in our house.' This woman then got very serious, as if she had never heard of such a thing. For people [in their thirties], isn't it totally normal for guys to do a lot of cooking? In fact it's one of the things about today—dudes love food, right? But it was so foreign to her."

In speaking with a variety of men for this article, I found that most men say they share responsibilities as much as circumstances allow. One of the men who spoke with me, Dave from Atherton, California, runs a successful business, and both he and his wife (a fellow technology executive) say that they split their family duties 50-50. "We have a Google calendar that we share so that everyone is on the same page, and on the weekend, we plan out our week: who's doing what, who's driving the kids which day, what dinner looks like each night during the week."

Yet Dave still considers himself an anomaly. "There is still this expectation that women are going to do the majority of the housework, and deal with schools and stuff, while men can just make it home for dinner and show up at sporting events and be like, 'Wow, I'm being a great father.' It is a real issue, and it is something you really have to work at. You have to try and make sure that you're doing the other stuff around the house in a way that's fair and equal."

He makes a valid point, and in trying to figure out why men don't do more around the house, we could discuss any number of factors—men generally spend more time at work, out of the home, than women do, so they don't have as much time for chores; women are inherently more fastidious; men are lazy and/or have a higher threshold for living in filth—but the most compelling argument comes from writer Jessica Grose in *The New Republic*. "Women are more driven to keep a clean house because they know they—before their male partners—will be judged for having a dirty one." Rather than confront or ignore paternalistic expectations, some women seem willing to cede to them, and this whiff of put-upon-ness recalls something Slaughter acknowledged in an online chat with readers following her article's publication: "SO MUCH OF THIS IS ABOUT WHAT WE FEEL, or rather WHAT WE ARE MADE TO FEEL by the reactions of those around us." Between the all-caps (hers) and the sentiments expressed, this writing wouldn't be out of place on a teenage blog, and as anyone who's ever argued with a teenager knows, it's hard to reason with feelings.

However, I will try. The *validation of one's feelings* is the language of therapy, which is to say that it is how we all talk now. This is not to denigrate the language or the feelings; it is only to say that to use one's feelings as evidence of an injury is no way to advance a serious cause. And to imply that one has been *made* to feel any way at all— well, no grown man has ever won that argument before.

See p. 135 for ways to ward off potential misunderstandings.

A final point about housework: It is not always as simple as men volunteering to do what needs to be done. To give a small, vaguely pitiful example from my own life: We share laundry duty in my house, and yet whenever I'm through folding a pile of clothes, my wife will then refold everything, quietly and without comment. This used to annoy me—why do I even bother? or, conversely, Is this the Army?—but now it mostly amuses me. When I press her on it, she tells me that I'm doing it wrong, and this too used to annoy me, until I realized that it wasn't really about me. "If I've talked to one group of people about this, I've talked to hundreds," says Galinsky. "Women will say 'Support me more,' and men will say 'But you're telling me I'm doing it wrong.' I wouldn't say it's biological, because I'm not a biologist, but it feels biological to me in that it's very hard to let someone else do something different, because it might mean that the way you're doing it isn't right." When I asked Galinsky if this could explain why a wife would refold a pile of laundry that her husband had just done a perfectly good job folding, she laughed. "Exactly."

What you're about to read is a passage from "Why Women Still Can't Have It All," and though it's long and windy, I feel the need to quote from as much of it as possible. You will understand why:

> The proposition that women can have high-powered careers as long as their husbands or partners are willing to share the parenting load equally (or disproportionately) assumes that most women will *feel* as comfortable as men do about being away from their children, as long as their partner is home with them. . . . From years of conversations and observations . . . I've come to believe that men and women respond quite differently when problems at home force them to recognize that their absence is hurting a child, or at least that their presence would likely help. I do not believe fathers love their children any less than mothers do, but men do seem more likely to choose their job at a cost to their family, while women seem more likely to choose their family at a cost to their job.

(Dr. Slaughter, you had me at "I do not believe fathers love their children any less than mothers do. . . .")

Since Slaughter doesn't provide any evidence to support her claim, it's impossible to say whether the men she's referring to are the sole breadwinners in the family (meaning: the ones who feel the intense weight and pressure of being what one writer described as "one job away from poverty") or are in two-income households, or what, but it's worth keeping in mind that this comes from a person whose husband, by her own admission, sacrificed much in his own academic career to do the heavy lifting with their children, all so she could pursue her dream job and then complain about it, bitterly, in the pages of a national magazine.

The trouble with probing men's and women's emotional relationships with their children is that the subject is fraught with stereotypes and prone to specious generalities (see above), but here goes: In my own experience as both son and father, I've learned that one parent's relationship with a child (and vice versa) isn't inherently richer or deeper than the other parent's. It's just different, and with more and more fathers spending more and more time with their kids today—nearly three times as much as they did in 1965—that has become more true than ever. "There is a dramatic cultural shift among millennial and Gen X-ers in wanting to be involved fathers," says Galinsky. "And I don't just think it's just women who are telling men they need to share. Men want a different relationship with their children than men have had in the past. . . . They don't want to be stick figures in their children's lives. They don't want it on their tombstone how many hours they billed. That 'Cat's Cradle' song is very much alive and well in the male psyche."

"Men are being judged as fathers now in a way that I think 25 they never have been before," says Traister, and just as women are historically new to the workplace, men are new to the car-pool and negotiating these fresh expectations (their own and others') as they go along. Not only do working fathers from dual-income homes spend just as much time at work as their fathers and grandfathers did (all while putting in many, many more hours with kids and chores), they also spend more time at work than non-fathers. Seven hours more a week, according to Pew, a trend that Galinsky has noticed in her own research and that she attributes to the unshakable, if often illusory, sense of being the breadwinner. "There are these expectations, even among men whose wives bring in 45 percent of family income, that they were still responsible for the family."

There is the matter of guilt and whether women find it harder than men to be away from their children—which, if that's the case, would mean that women looking to advance in the workplace would have heavier emotional baggage than their male peers. Any husband who's watched his wife cry before taking a business trip (and wondering—silently, I hope—to himself, why?) will tell you that men and women have different ways of experiencing and expressing ambivalence, frustration, and, yes, guilt. "I have no idea if it's societal or genetic or whatever," says Dave, the California businessman, "but it's certainly real that I think my wife feels more guilty than I do when she's gone from the kids. There's no question." I can't claim to speak for Men Everywhere, but in the interviews I conducted for this article, nearly every subject admitted to missing his kids on late nights at the office or aching for home while on a business trip, yet they couch any guilt or regret in the context of sacrifice. Chalk this up to social conditioning (men are raised to be the providers, so it's easier for them to be absent) or genetic predisposition (men are not naturally nurturing) or emotional shallowness (men aren't as in touch with their feelings), but there is the sense, down to the man, that missing their kids is the price of doing business.

And so we all do the best we can. Dave and his wife make weekends sacrosanct and family dinners a priority. "My wife famously said she leaves her office at 5:30 so we can be home at 6:00 for dinner, and I do the same thing, though we're both back online doing work after the kids go to bed."

(Dave's last name, by the way, is Goldberg, and his wife is Sheryl Sandberg, and thanks to *Lean In*, she is famous. Goldberg is the CEO of a company named SurveyMonkey, which provides interactive survey tools for the masses, and he helped build it from a twelve-person operation to a staff of more than two hundred and a $1.35 billion valuation. All while splitting parenting responsibilities 50-50 with a really busy wife. They have the means, certainly, but more importantly, the will.)

Speaking of: In her commencement speech for Harvard Business School in 2012, Sandberg addressed an issue that comes up often—men need to do more to support women in the workplace. "It falls upon the men who are graduating today just as much or more than the women not just to talk about gender but to help these women succeed. When they hear a woman is really great at her job but not liked, take a deep breath and ask why. We need to start talking openly about the flexibility all of us need to have both a job and a life."

Among the various ways men can help women, paternity 30 leave is sometimes mentioned as a good place to start, the idea being that if more men took a few weeks off following the birth of a child, they would help remove the professional stigma surrounding maternity leave and level the playing field. Anyone who has watched any woman, much less one with a full-time job, endure third-term pregnancy, delivery, and the long, lonely nights of postpartum life would tell you how necessary a national paid maternity-leave policy is. Expectant and new mothers are put through the physical and emotional ringer, and they need that time to heal without worrying about losing their job or paying the bills. There are really no two ways about it.

Dads, however, are a different and more complicated story. In California, the first state to fund up to six weeks of paid leave for new moms and dads, only 29 percent of those who take it are men, and there have been numerous studies lately exploring why more men aren't taking greater advantage of the ability to stay home. The general consensus is reflected in a paper out of Rutgers University: "Women who ask for family leave are behaving in a more gender normative way, compared with men who request a family leave. . . . Because the concept of work-life balance is strongly gendered, men who request a family leave may also suffer a *femininity stigma*, whereby 'acting like a woman' deprives them of masculine agency (e.g., competence and assertiveness) and impugns them with negative feminine qualities (e.g., weakness and uncertainty)." This is some paleolithic thinking here, starting, for instance, with the idea that "acting like a woman" means anything at all, much less weakness and uncertainty.

I'm lucky enough to work for a company that provides paid paternity leave, but a few days after my son was born, I was back in the office. It's not because I was scared about appearing weak to my mostly male coworkers or employers, and it's not because I was any more wary of losing my job than usual. At work, I had a purpose—things needed to be done, people needed me to do them. At home, watching my wife feed and swaddle our son and then retreat to our bed to get some sleep of her own, I learned what many first-time fathers learn: assuming an absence of any health issues related to child or mother, the first six weeks of a child's life are fairly uneventful for men. A baby eats (with about 80 percent of women today choosing to breast-feed); he poops; he sleeps. There is potential for valuable bonding time, and a new mother could almost certainly use another pair of hands, but a man's presence is not strictly necessary. Baby book after baby book warns parents that new fathers typically feel "left out," and there's a reason for that: because they are typically left out. More and more companies offer paid and unpaid paternity leave, and a man should feel proud to exercise that option if that's what is best for him and his family. Maybe with the next baby I will. Maybe I won't. But when the doctor delivers a newborn to my exhausted, elated wife, I won't kid myself thinking that I, of all people, really deserve a little time off.

In her Harvard speech, Sandberg also evoked the specter of good old-fashioned sexism by claiming that ambitious, assertive women are generally less well liked than ambitious, assertive men. (In her book, she cites a now famous study conducted by a team of Columbia and NYU professors in which two groups were asked to assess two hard-charging executives, a man named Howard and a woman named Heidi, who were identical in every way except their names. Howard was considered the Man. Heidi, the Shrew.) It's a compelling and convincing study, and Sandberg is persuasive when she argues that too many women too often get an eye roll when they open their mouths. Two things I would hasten to add, though. One: Productivity, profitability, drive, and talent trump all. (I'm reminded of Tina Fey's defense of Hillary Clinton in 2008: "She is [a bitch]. So am I. . . . Bitches get stuff done.") Women might suspect that men don't like assertive, confrontational women, which is only half the truth, leading to my next point: that nobody wants to work with a nightmare of either gender. While the Howard-Heidi problem suggests that some men may get a longer leash than some women, the workplace is not every man's for the shitting all over.

"Advertising is a very small world and when you do something like malign the reputation of a girl from the steno pool on her first day, you make it even smaller. Keep it up, and even if you do get my job, you'll never run this place. You'll die in that corner office, a midlevel executive with a little bit of hair who women go home with out of pity. Want to know why? 'Cause no one will like you." Don Draper said that. Not me. And the wisdom he drops on Pete Campbell in the pilot of *Mad Men* shows that men can be just as vulnerable to office politics as women.

Finally, there is the issue of flex time, with some suggesting 35 that men should demand more options for when and where they can do their work so that women alone aren't penalized for requesting it. It has never been easier to work remotely for many professionals, yet many jobs—and in particular the top jobs, the leadership roles that history (men) has deprived women of in the past—don't have much give to them. Marissa Mayer at Yahoo was dragged into the flex-time debate when she decided that in order to save a struggling business with abysmal morale, she would do away with the company's generous work-from-home policy and require her employees to show up to an office. She was immediately painted as elitist and antiwoman, and it's easy to see why. Even though men and women are equally likely to telecommute, they typically don't place the same value on being able to do so. According to the Pew study, 70 percent of working mothers say a flexible schedule is extremely important to them, compared with just 48 percent of working fathers, and for many of those women (including my wife, who often works well past midnight at a crowded desk in our bedroom), the opportunity to do some work from home is the critical difference between a life that works and one that doesn't. That's what Mayer was messing with when she ordered all hands on deck, and it's what any employer faces when trying to balance family-friendly policies with the sometimes soul-destroying demands of a competitive marketplace.

When Barack Obama entered the White House, he talked about how he wanted his administration to be family-friendly, offering up Sasha and Malia's swing set to staffers so they could bring their own kids to work on the weekends. Rahm Emanuel famously assured him that it would be—"family-friendly to your family."

It was classic Obama—well-meaning, forward-thinking, mindful of the struggles of the common man—undermined by classic Emanuel, which is to say reality. The White House staff would be working at the highest levels of government, investing their love and labor into what can only be described as dream jobs at a time that can only be described as a national nightmare, and if that meant kids and partners had to take the backseat for a year or two, so be it. Man, woman, whoever: Get a shovel and start digging.

Slaughter, a tenured professor at Princeton, came on board as Hillary Clinton's head of policy planning at State, and in her *Atlantic* piece, she describes her grueling workweek in D.C., her weekend commute back to New Jersey, and her ultimate conclusion that "juggling high-level government work with the needs of two teenage boys was not possible." She talked about her struggles to a fellow wonk, Jolynn Shoemaker of Women in International Security, and Shoemaker offered her two cents on high-level foreign-policy positions: "Inflexible schedules, unrelenting travel, and constant pressure to be in the office are common features of these jobs." Slaughter acknowledges that it needn't be as difficult as all that: "Deputy Secretary of State James Steinberg, who shares the parenting of his two young daughters equally with his wife, made getting [secured access to confidential material] at home an immediate priority so that he could leave the office at a reasonable hour and participate in important meetings via videoconferencing if necessary. I wonder how many women in similar positions would be afraid to ask, lest they be seen as insufficiently committed to their jobs."

Slaughter makes an important point here, though probably not the one she intended to make. Steinberg did what he had to do to make a difficult situation work better for him; Slaughter's contention that a woman wouldn't feel as comfortable making the same request may or may not be true, but it doesn't matter. The option was apparently on the table. Fight for it, don't fight for it—it's entirely up to the individual. But don't complain that you never had a choice.

In the end, isn't this what feminism was supposed to be 40 about? Not equality for equality's sake—half of all homes run by men, half of all corporations run by women—but to give each of us, men and women, access to the same array of choices and then the ability to choose for ourselves? And who's to say, whether for reasons biological or sociological, men and women would even want that? When the Pew Research Center asked working mothers and fathers to picture their ideal working situation, 37 percent of women would opt for full time; 50 percent part time; and 11 percent wouldn't have a job at all. (Compare this with men's answers: 75 percent say full time, 15 percent say part time, and 10 percent wouldn't work at all.) Assuming that women had all the flexibility in the world, one of every two working mothers would choose to work part time. Perhaps with guaranteed paid maternity leave, universal daycare, and generous after-school programs, more women would be freed from the constraints of child care and would want to work full time. Or, possibly, they're just happy working part time, one foot in the workplace and one foot in the home. Hard to say.

"I can't stand the kind of paralysis that some people fall into because they're not happy with the choices they've made. You live in a time when there are endless choices. . . . Money certainly helps, and having that kind of financial privilege goes a long way, but you don't even have to have money for it. But you have to work on yourself. . . . Do something!"

Hillary Clinton said that. Not me. And while she wasn't referring to Slaughter in her interview with *Marie Claire*, she offers valuable advice to anyone who's looking to blame someone, or something, for the challenges they face in life. Getting ahead in the workplace is really hard. Getting to the top is really, really hard. And unless you are very fortunate indeed, there will always be somebody smarter, faster, tougher, and ready and willing to take a job if you're not up to the task. It's a grown-up truth, and it bites the big one, but for anyone to pretend otherwise ignores (or simply wishes away) what generations of working men learned the hard way while their wives did the backbreaking work of raising kids and keeping house. Hearing Gail Collins grumble about changing the corporate mind-set (as if competition weren't the soul of capitalism, and capitalism weren't the coin of the realm) or reading Slaughter complain that our society values hard work over family (as if a Puritan work ethic weren't in our national DNA) makes me feel like channeling Tom Hanks in *A League of Their Own*: There's no crying in baseball! If you don't want a high-pressure, high-power, high-paying job that forces you to make unacceptable sacrifices in the rest of your life, don't take the job. Or get another job that doesn't require those sacrifices. And if you can't get another job, take comfort knowing that the guy who sits across from you, the one with kids the same age as yours and a partner who's busting his or her ass to make it work, is probably in the very same boat. We are all equals here.

Then again, I would say that. I'm a man, with a working wife and a busy schedule and a little boy and another baby on the way, and I live with the choices that I've made. That is all I've ever asked for, and it is all I will ever need.

Joining the Conversation

1. Why, in Richard Dorment's view, can men still not "have it all"? What in particular does he mean by "it all," and what evidence does he provide to support his position?
2. This article is a response to Anne-Marie Slaughter's "Why Women Still Can't Have It All" (pp. 676–96), and Dorment summarizes and quotes from that piece extensively. How fairly do you think he represents Slaughter's views? Cite specific examples from his article in your answer.
3. Dorment published this article in *Esquire*, which calls itself "the magazine for men." How can you tell that he has written his article primarily for a male audience? How might he revise the article, keeping the same basic argument, to appeal to an audience of women?
4. Imagine you have a chance to speak with Dorment about this article. Write out what you'd say, remembering to frame your statement as a response to what he has said. (See Chapter 12 for advice on entering class discussions.)
5. Dorment's writing is quite informal—colorful and in places even irreverent. How does this informality suit his audience and purpose? How does it affect your response? Choose a paragraph in his article and dress it up, rewriting it in more formal, academic language. Which version do you find more appealing, and why?

What about Gender Roles in Same-Sex Relationships?

STEPHEN MAYS

———⌐回⌐———

Imposing gender roles on gay couples is even more ridiculous than doing so with straight couples.

I RECENTLY OVERHEARD someone comment to her friend about a gay male couple walking ahead of them on the sidewalk. The girl said, "Who do you think is the girl in the relationship?" I couldn't help but frown at the girl and shake my head. As clear as you would think it is to see, I'll spell it out for you: neither of them is the girl. They're both boys.

Not to say that traditional ideas of gender roles don't play a part in a gay relationship, but they're a little more diluted, I would say. A gay man may show effeminate qualities, but that doesn't make him the "woman" of the relationship. Just like the muscled, bearded gay man doesn't have to be the "man" of the relationship.

———

STEPHEN MAYS is a student at the University of Georgia, majoring in English and journalism. He is the editor in chief of the *Red & Black*, an independent, student-run newspaper covering campus news and *Ampersand Magazine*, a UGA lifestyle magazine. This piece appeared in the *Red & Black* on September 24, 2013.

One huge aspect of the gay male relationship that I appreciate is the more leveled playing field that we have. We're both men. If one of us opens the door for the other on a whim of affection or chivalry, it wasn't expected because he was the "man." It was simply a nice gesture. If one of us cooks dinner once, or every night for that matter, it isn't because he's the "woman" of the relationship. He's probably just better at it than his partner.

I have noticed, however, here in the South that a good number of gay men claim to be seeking "masc" or "masculine" partners. They want a boyfriend who likes the outdoors, is in good physical condition, plays sports and all those other standard characteristics for "men." I have no idea why this is, other than perhaps personal preference, because there's nothing wrong with the guys who like wearing skinny jeans, putting highlights in their hair, or shopping all the time. We simply associate certain actions with very classic ideas of masculinity or femininity. There are few actions or characteristics that classify as gender-neutral.

Why does caring about your appearance, cooking dinner, or 5 enjoying shopping for new clothes have to be considered feminine? Why does hiking, playing football, or working out a lot have to be considered masculine? When it boils down to it, all of us, gay and straight alike, comprise many characteristics—some are considered masculine, and some are considered feminine.

Chapter 4 shows ways to agree and disagree simultaneously.

Despite sexual orientation, some people simply demonstrate more masculine qualities or more feminine qualities. In the case of a gay male relationship, however, the key point is that neither of us is the girl of the relationship, no matter which side of the scale we fall on. We're both boys. Neither sexual preferences in the bedroom nor our daily characteristics have any effect on that biology.

Joining the Conversation

1. Stephen Mays begins by literally quoting what someone said, which he then uses as a way to launch what he says in response. He could have summarized what was said; why do you think he quoted it instead? What argument does he offer in response?

2. Mays obviously cares a lot about this topic, but does he explain why we should care? If not, do it for him. Write a paragraph—perhaps it could be a new concluding paragraph—discussing explicitly why this topic matters and who should care. (See Chapter 7 for guidance.)

3. This short piece was written as a newspaper column. What strategies in this book could Mays use to revise his article as an academic essay? (See the tips in Chapter 11 for using the templates to revise.)

4. Read Eckert and McConnell-Ginet's essay (pp. 736–46) on the ways that society inscribes and enforces gender distinctions. How does their argument relate to Mays's views on gender roles in same-sex relationships?

5. Mays critiques various gender stereotypes, including ones affecting gay people and straight people, both men and women. What do you think? Write an essay in which you agree, disagree, or both with what he says.

Facebook Multiplies Genders but Offers Users the Same Three Tired Pronouns

DENNIS BARON

—▢—

FOR YEARS Facebook has allowed users to mark their relationship status as "single," "married," and "it's complicated." They could identify as male or female or keep their gender private. Now, acknowledging that gender can also be complicated, the social media giant is letting users choose among male, female, and 56 additional custom genders, including *agender, cis, gender variant, intersex, trans person,* and *two-spirit.*

Facebook users now have so many gender choices that a single drop-down box can't hold them all. And they're free to pick more than one. But to refer to this set of 58 genders Facebook offers only three tired pronouns: *he, she,* and *they.*

———

DENNIS BARON teaches at the University of Illinois at Urbana-Champaign. He has written numerous books and articles on language, literacy, and the technologies of communication, most recently *A Better Pencil: Reading, Writing, and the Digital Revolution* (2009). Baron has been a commentator for CNN, BBC, National Public Radio, and other television and radio shows discussing issues of language use. He is a regular blogger on language topics on his website, *The Web of Language,* where the piece included here was first published in February 2014.

A Facebook user can now identify as a genderqueer, neutrois, cis male, androgynous other, but Facebook friends can only wish him, her, or them a happy birthday.

The persons at Facebook are enlightened enough to acknowledge gender as fluid, but when it comes to grammar, their thinking rigidifies into masculine, feminine, and neuter. Mess with gender words and Facebook might get a few emails from bible thumpers reminding them about Adam and Eve or from godless humanists complaining, "Hey, you left my gender out." But deploy a string of invented pronouns to match the new genders and at best there's a Distributed Denial of Service attack, at worst the server is struck by thunderbolts from the grammar gods, because gender may be socially constructed, but grammar is sacred.

Chapter 9 has tips on using colloquial language in academic writing.

The linguist Mark Liberman lists Facebook's new custom gender options on LanguageLog, and I copy them below:

Agender, Androgyne, Androgynous, Bigender, Cis, Cis Female, Cis Male, Cis Man, Cis Woman, Cisgender, Cisgender Female, Cisgender Male, Cisgender Man, Cisgender Woman, Female to Male, FTM, Gender Fluid, Gender Nonconforming, Gender Questioning, Gender Variant, Genderqueer, Intersex, Male to Female, MTF, Neither, Neutrois, Non-binary, Other, Pangender, Trans, Trans Female, Trans Male, Trans Man, Trans Person, Trans Woman, Trans*, Trans* Female, Trans* Male, Trans* Man, Trans* Person, Trans* Woman, Transfeminine, Transgender, Transgender Female, Transgender Male, Transgender Man, Transgender Person, Transgender Woman, Transmasculine, Transsexual, Transsexual Female, Transsexual Male, Transsexual Man, Transsexual Person, Transsexual Woman, Two-spirit.

But where are all the pronouns? Facebook may play fast and ⁵
loose with our private parts, but they're reluctant to tinker with
the parts of speech. Fortunately, grammarians have no such
scruples. They have repeatedly proposed new pronouns to fill
linguistic gaps. They even beat Facebook in the race for new
genders.

In 1792 the Scottish grammarian James Anderson argued
that English would be better served if we sorted our words
into more than the traditional *masculine, feminine,* and *neuter.*
Anderson added ten new genders: *indefinite, imperfect* (or
soprana), *matrimonial, masculine imperfect, feminine imperfect,*
mixt imperfect, masculine mixt, feminine mixt, united, and
universally indefinite.

And that's not all. Currently only the third person singular
English pronouns have gender: *he, she,* and *it.* Anderson wanted
all of our first and second person pronouns, both singular and
plural, and the third person plural, to express all of the thirteen genders (so, seventy-eight pronouns instead of the current
eight), and he preferred each pronoun to have two alternates,
for the times when the same pronoun must refer to different
people. For example, the first male referred to would be *he,* the
second, *hei,* the third, *ho.* That makes 234 pronouns (and that's
just counting the nominative case; if you add the possessives
and accusatives, which every pronoun needs, well, you do the
math).

Anderson thought up some minor genders as well, but fortunately he kept them to himself "to avoid the appearance of
unnecessary refinement."

Anderson also suggested that we need a true common-
gender pronoun, one equivalent to *he or she, his or her, him*
or her. But he offered no examples. Other grammarians have
been less reticent. Some eighty common-gender pronouns have

been coined between 1850 and the present. Two of them, *thon* and *hesh*, even made it into dictionaries. Subtracting duplicates coined multiple times by different people, the list shrinks to fifty-five:

> ae, alaco, de, e, E, em, en, et, ey, fm, ghach, ha, han, hann, he'er, heesh, herm, hes, hesh, heshe, hey, hi, hir, hizer, ho, hse, ip, ir, ith, j/e, jhe, le, mef, na, ne, one, ons, po, s/he, sap, se, shem, sheme, shey, shis, ta, tey, thir, thon, ton, ve, ws, xe, z, ze.

But if we add the current *he, she,* and *they* to the fifty-five coinages above, we get one pronoun for every Facebook gender. 58 genders, 58 pronouns. It's uncanny. It's irresistible. It's pictures of cats. Of course, Facebook could go in the opposite direction and slash the pronoun choices down to one. Sometimes it's better to simplify language than complicate it.

But whatever Facebook does about pronouns—and my guess 10 is it will do nothing in order to avoid those grammar-god-hurled thunderbolts—I'm keeping my Facebook gender private, and my pronoun choice is *thon*. Or maybe *ip*. Or *E*. I don't know. It's complicated.

Joining the Conversation

1. Why, according to Dennis Baron, does Facebook now provide a list of fifty-eight terms for gender but still limit its use of pronouns to three?
2. This piece was written for Baron's blog, *The Web of Language*, a "go-to site for language and technology in the news" followed by linguists and others interested in those topics. With that context in mind, what do you think his point is? How can you tell?
3. Baron quotes and discusses a proposal by an eighteenth-century Scottish grammarian to add many new pronouns to the English language. What does this example add to Baron's argument?
4. Read "Learning to Be Gendered," by Penelope Eckert and Sally McConnell-Ginet (pp. 736–46). What do you think Eckert and McConnell-Ginet would have to say about Facebook's policy on gender terms?
5. Consider Baron's statement that "gender may be socially constructed, but grammar is sacred" (paragraph 3). What do you think he means by this statement? Write a short essay summarizing what Baron says in his blog post and then responding with your own views.

How to Be a "Woman Programmer"

ELLEN ULLMAN

—⌐—

I WAS AN ORDINARY COMPUTER PROGRAMMER. I wrote code that ran at the levels between flashy human interfaces and the deep cores of operating systems, like the role of altos in a chorus, who provide the structure without your taking much notice of their melodic lines. I made realistic schedules and met my deadlines. Those were decent accomplishments.

But none of it qualified me as extraordinary in the great programmer scheme of things. What seems to have distinguished me is the fact that I was a "woman programmer." The questions I am often asked about my career tend to concentrate not on how one learns to code but how a woman does.

Let me separate the two words and begin with what it means to become a programmer.

———

ELLEN ULLMAN is a computer programmer and the author of the novels *By Blood* (2012) and *The Bug* (2003) and a memoir, *Close to the Machine: Technophilia and Its Discontents* (2001), which describes her experiences as one of the few female programmers in the 1980s. She has been a technology commentator for NPR's *All Things Considered* and written for *Harper's*, *Wired*, and *Salon*. This essay first appeared as an op-ed column in the *New York Times* on May 19, 2013.

The first requirement for programming is a passion for the work, a deep need to probe the mysterious space between human thoughts and what a machine can understand; between human desires and how machines might satisfy them.

The second requirement is a high tolerance for failure. 5 Programming is the art of algorithm design and the craft of debugging errant code. In the words of the great John Backus, inventor of the Fortran programming language: "You need the willingness to fail all the time. You have to generate many ideas and then you have to work very hard only to discover that they don't work. And you keep doing that over and over until you find one that does work."

Now to the "woman" question.

I broke into the ranks of computing in the early 1980s, when women were just starting to poke their shoulder pads through crowds of men. There was no legal protection against "hostile environments for women." I endured a client—a sweaty man with pendulous earlobes—who stroked my back as I worked to fix his system. At any moment I expected him to snap my bra. I considered installing a small software bomb but understood, right then, what was more important to me than revenge: the desire to create good systems.

I had a boss who said flatly, "I hate to hire all you girls but you're too damned smart." By "all" he meant three but, at the time, it was rare to find even one woman in a well-placed technical position. At a meeting, he kept interrupting me to say, "Gee, you sure have pretty hair." By then I realized he was teaching me a great deal about computing. It would be a complicated professional relationship, in which his occasional need for male dominance would surface.

So, on that day of my pretty hair, I leaned to one side and said, "I'm just going to let that nonsense fly over my shoulder."

The meeting went on. We discussed the principles of relational databases, which later led me to explore deeper reaches of programming, closer to operating systems and networks, where I would find my real passion for the work. My leaning to one side, not confronting him, letting him be the flawed man he was, changed the direction of my technical life.

Over the 20 years that followed, I found that being a woman 10 put me at one remove from the general society of programmers. I resented that distance, but I liked to think that it was in some way fortunate—that my standing back gave me a clearer view of our profession and its effects on society at large.

According to the Bureau of Labor Statistics, women comprise 29.4 percent of people working in "Computer and Software," a subcategory of "Commercial Equipment." Since this broad (and vague) designation might include everyone from system designers to office assistants, it tells us nothing about the participation of women at the deeper technical and theoretical levels. By "deeper" I mean computer science, hardware and software engineering, the creation of operating systems and deep algorithms—in short, the levels at which the future of technology is being defined.

To elaborate on a previous idea, see p. 135.

I touched those fundamental levels as a software engineer but never plumbed their depths. Yet I could see that, at the deeper reaches, it was as if some plague had specialized in the killing of females. I looked around and wondered, "Where are all the other women?" We women found ourselves nearly alone, outsiders in a culture that was sometimes boyishly puerile, sometimes rigorously hierarchical, occasionally friendly and welcoming. This strange illness meanwhile left the female survivors with an odd glow that made them too visible, scrutinized too closely, held to higher standards. It placed upon them the terrible burden of being not only good but the best.

Women today face a new, more virile and virulent sexism. The definition of success has somehow become running your own start-up. And venture capitalists decide who will get funding, who will get a chance for that success. Venture capitalists are all but explicit in their search: they want a couple of guys who can write an app over a weekend.

If hired by start-ups, younger women find themselves sorely underrepresented. One woman told me that in her growing, 24-person company there were four women, which is "considered a good ratio." And, as always, our ranks thin at the deeper technical levels. We get stalled at marketing and customer support, writing scripts for Web pages. Yet coding, looking into the algorithmic depths, getting close to the machine, is the driver of technology; and technology, in turn, is driving fundamental changes in personal, social and political life.

The question is how we react to this great prejudice against women. The rule of law and social activism certainly are crucial. But no matter how strong the social structure, there is always that cheek-slapped moment when you are alone with the anti-woman prejudice: the joke, the leer, the disregard, the invisibility, the inescapable fact that the moment you walk through the door you are seen as lesser, no matter what your credentials.

I have no guidance for women who want to rise through the ranks into technical management. I have led a peripatetic life, moving on when a project was done or the next thing intrigued me.

And I am not advising younger women (or any woman) to tough it out. You can lash back, which I have done too often and which has rarely served me well. You can quit and look for other jobs, which is sometimes a very good idea.

But the prejudice will follow you. What will save you is tacking into the love of the work, into the desire that brought you there in the first place. This creates a suspension of time, opens a spacious room of your own* in which you can walk around and consider your response. Staring prejudice in the face imposes a cruel discipline: to structure your anger, to achieve a certain dignity, an angry dignity.

room of your own An allusion to an essay by Virginia Woolf arguing for the need to make space for women writers in a literary field dominated by men.

Joining the Conversation

1. In the first two paragraphs of this essay, Ellen Ullman characterizes her accomplishments as a programmer as "ordinary" and says that what most distinguished her was the fact that she was "a woman programmer." How does she assess the nature of opportunities for women in the programming world? What impediments does she say still exist? What advice does she offer for women interested in going into that field?

2. According to Ullman, women today "face a new, more virile and virulent sexism" (paragraph 13). What does she mean by this strong claim, and what evidence does she provide to support it? What other supporting points might strengthen her argument?

3. Ullman does not include any viewpoints other than her own. How might adding other perspectives, even those of naysayers, improve her argument? Name two or three objections she might have considered.

4. This op-ed was written shortly after the publication of Sheryl Sandberg's *Lean In*, a best-seller that encourages women to aim for leadership positions. In paragraph 9, when Ullman writes about "leaning to one side" rather than confronting a "flawed" boss, do you think she was referring to that book (excerpted here on pp. 642–58)? How do you think Ullman might respond to Sandberg's advice, with regard to the field of programming, and what might Sandberg say to Ullman?

5. This essay appeared in the *New York Times*. How would you advise Ullman to revise her text to make the same basic argument to an audience of undergraduate computer science majors, both men and women? Make a list of ways you think she could better appeal to such an audience.

The Plight of Young Males

SAUL KAPLAN

—◻—

I AM PROUD OF MY BONA FIDES on supporting the advancement of women. It angers me to think how slow executive suites and boardrooms are to welcome more qualified females. Stubborn gender wage gaps for comparable work are unacceptable and must be closed.

However, with all of the attention and focus on supporting equal opportunities for women, we have taken our eyes off an alarming trend. Young men in the United States are in trouble by any measure of educational attainment. It's a big deal and, for reasons of political correctness, we aren't talking enough about this growing national problem.

I refuse to believe the support of young Americans' progress is a zero-sum game—that somehow if we call attention to the

———

SAUL KAPLAN is the founder of the Business Innovation Factory, which designs and tests new business models, and the author of *The Business Model Innovation Factory: How to Stay Relevant When the World Is Changing* (2012). He blogs at *It's Saul Connected*. This essay first appeared on the *Harvard Business Review* blog on March 9, 2011, and included a link to a trailer with information about the work done by the Business Innovation Factory.

problem and take a different approach to improve the experience and outcomes of boys it would come at the expense of celebrating and enabling continued advancement of girls. We can and must recognize the unique challenges of young men and we had better start doing something about it now.

Have you taken a stroll on a college campus recently? Where have the men gone? In the latest census, males comprise 51% of the total U.S. population between the ages of 18–24. Yet, just over 40% of today's college students are men. In fact, in each year since 1982, more American women than men have received bachelor's degrees. Over the last decade two million more women graduated from college than men. And the gap continues to grow. Michael Thompson, author of *Raising Cain*, a great book on the plight of young males, illustrates the path we are going down with a startling extrapolation. He notes that if today's trends continue unaltered, the last young man in the US to get a college degree will do so in 2068. Scary stuff.

See Chapter 8 for tips on how to transition within a paragraph.

The gender achievement gap is astounding. The average 11th grade boy writes at the level of the average 8th grade girl. Men are significantly underperforming women. According to a recent NBC news report, women dominate high school honor rolls and now make up more than 70% of class valedictorians.

Again, I am happy to see women succeeding. But can we really afford for our country's young men to fall so far behind? A growing education attainment gap has profound consequences for the economy.

It mattered far less during the industrial era when young men in this country could find good high-wage jobs in the manufacturing sector without a college degree or post-secondary credential. In a post-industrial economy, the social contract has changed. The deal used to be that college was only for a narrow segment of our population. Everyone else willing to work hard could make enough money to raise a family and achieve the American dream of owning a home, without higher education. With the disappearance of those industrial era jobs, the rug got pulled out from under that assumption. We replaced it with a new social contract by which a college degree, or at least some form of post-secondary credential, was a necessity for anyone hoping to make a decent living. The numbers on this are clear. According to census data, annual earnings for high-school dropouts average $18,900; for high-school graduates, $25,900; for college graduates, $45,400. Add up those numbers over a lifetime and the importance of education comes into focus.

And that's if there is a job at all. Take a look at how hard the current recession has hit men. Of the jobs lost over the last four years 78% of them were held by men. That leaves 20% of working age men out of work. These jobs are not coming back and men are ill prepared for the 21st century workplace.

If you dig deeper and examine these trends for young men of color, it will make you cry. At the Business Innovation Factory, our team has been working with the College Board to explore the experience of young men of color in the United States. The statistics are staggering. Only 26% of African American, 18% of Latino American, and 24% of Native American and Pacific Islander young men ages 24–34 have attained at least an Associates Degree. BIF and the College Board are bringing the voice and experience of young men of color to the center of an innovation conversation on how to turn these disturbing trends around.

We think equal progress will only come when the United States 10 has transformed its education system from a one-size-fits-all pipeline responding to the learning needs of all young men and women in the same way to an individualized approach where every student can find his or her own pathway. We must go from a system geared toward enrollment to one designed around the goal of completion.

In some way, we must turn schools into places that recognize the specific learning needs of young men and help them prepare for 21st century jobs—and we must do so urgently, or leave an entire generation foundering.

Joining the Conversation

1. What exactly is Saul Kaplan arguing in this essay, and what evidence does he provide to support his argument? What are his credentials for making this argument?

2. When Kaplan posted this article on the *Harvard Business Review* blog, he included a link to the Business Innovation Factory website so that readers could learn more about what the company has been doing "to turn these disturbing trends around" (paragraph 9). Why do you think he chose this venue for publication? What has motivated him to write this article?

3. Kaplan cares about the future of young men, but does he convince you that you should care as well? Why, or why not? What, if anything, might he add or change to make his point more powerfully?

4. Like Kaplan, Edward McClelland (pp. 549–60) laments the dramatic loss of industrial jobs that do not require a college degree—but he discusses the effects of these job losses on both men and women. Consider both arguments. Which one do you find more persuasive, and why?

5. Kaplan paints a bleak picture of the situation many young males face in the United States today, implying that young women are doing much better. Write a letter to the editor of the *Harvard Business Review* responding to this essay from the perspective of a women's rights advocate.

Learning to Be Gendered

PENELOPE ECKERT

AND SALLY McCONNELL-GINET

—⊡—

IN THE FAMOUS WORDS of Simone de Beauvoir,* "women are not born, they are made." The same is true of men. The making of a man or a woman is a never-ending process that begins before birth—from the moment someone begins to wonder if the pending child will be a boy or a girl. And the ritual announcement at birth that it is in fact one or the other instantly transforms an "it" into a "he" or a "she" (Butler 1993), standardly assigning it to a lifetime as a male or as a female.[1] This attribution is further made public and lasting through the linguistic event of naming. In some times and places, the state

---

*Simone de Beauvoir (1908–86)   French philosopher and novelist. Beauvoir's 1953 book, *The Second Sex*, explores women's need for independence.

———

PENELOPE ECKERT is a professor of linguistics and anthropology at Stanford University. Her books include *Jocks and Burnouts* (1989) and *Linguistic Variation as Social Practice* (2003). SALLY McCONNELL-GINET is an emeritus professor of linguistics at Cornell University. This selection comes from *Language and Gender* (2013), a book that Eckert and McConnell-Ginet coauthored.

or religious institutions disallow sex-ambiguous given names. Finland, for example, has lists of legitimate female and legitimate male names that must be consulted before the baby's name becomes official. In English-speaking societies, not all names are sex-exclusive (e.g., *Chris, Kim, Pat*) and sometimes names change their gender classification. For example, *Evelyn* was available as a male name in Britain long after it had become an exclusively female name in America, and *Whitney*, once exclusively a surname or a male first name in America, is now bestowed on baby girls. But these changes do nothing to mitigate the fact that English names are gendered.

Thus the dichotomy of male and female is the ground upon which we build selves from the moment of birth. These early linguistic acts set up a baby for life, launching a gradual process of learning to be a boy or a girl, a man or a woman, and to see all others as boys or girls, men or women as well. There are currently no other readily available ways to think about ourselves and others—and we will be expected to pattern all kinds of things about ourselves as a function of that initial dichotomy. In the beginning, adults will do the child's gender work, treating it as a boy or as a girl, and interpreting its every move as that of a boy or of a girl. Then over the years, the child will learn to take over its part of the process, doing its own gender work and learning to support the gender work of others. The first thing people want to know about a baby is its sex, and social convention provides a myriad of props to reduce the necessity of asking—and it becomes more and more important, as the child develops, not to have to ask. At birth, many hospital nurseries provide pink caps for girls and blue caps for boys, or in other ways provide some visual sign of the sex that has been assigned to the baby. While this may seem quite natural to members of the society, in fact this color coding points out no difference that has any bearing on the medical treatment of the infants. Go into a store in the United States to buy a present for a newborn baby, and you will immediately be asked "boy or girl?" Overalls for a girl may be OK (though they are "best" if pink or flowered or in some other way marked as "feminine") but gender liberalism goes only so far. You are unlikely to buy overalls with vehicles printed on them for a girl, and even more reluctant to buy a frilly dress with puffed sleeves or pink flowered overalls for a boy. And if you're buying clothing for a baby whose sex you do not know, sales people are likely to counsel you to stick with something that's plain yellow or green or white. Colors are so integral to our way of thinking about gender that gender attributions have bled into our view of the colors, so that people tend to believe that pink is a more "delicate" color than blue (and not just any blue, but baby blue). This is a prime example of the naturalization of what is in fact an arbitrary sign. In America in the late nineteenth and early twentieth centuries, Anne Fausto-Sterling (2000) reports, blue was favored for girls and bright pink for boys.

If gender flowed naturally from sex, one might expect the world to sit back and simply allow the baby to become male or female. But in fact, sex determination sets the stage for a life-long process of gendering, as the child becomes, and learns how to be, male or female. Names and clothing are just a small part of the symbolic resources used to support a consistent ongoing gender attribution even when children are clothed. That we can speak of a child growing up *as a girl* or *as a boy* suggests that initial sex attribution is far more than just a simple observation of a physical characteristic. *Being a girl* or *being a boy* is not a stable state but an ongoing accomplishment, something that is actively *done* both by the individual so categorized and by those who interact with it in the various communities to which it belongs. The newborn initially depends on others to *do* its gender, and they come through in many different ways, not just as individuals but as part of socially structured communities that link individuals to social institutions and cultural ideologies. It is perhaps at this early life stage that it is clearest that gender is a collaborative affair—that one must learn to perform as a male or a female, and that these performances require support from one's surroundings.

Indeed, we do not know how to interact with another human being (or often members of other species), or how to judge them and talk about them, unless we can attribute a gender to them. Gender is so deeply engrained in our social practice, in our understanding of ourselves and of others, that we almost cannot put one foot in front of the other without taking gender into consideration. People even, it seems, apply gender stereotypes to computer-generated speech depending on whether they perceive the computer's voice as male or female (Nass et al. 1997). Although most of us rarely notice this overtly in everyday life, most of our interactions are colored by our performance of our own gender, and by our attribution of gender to others.

From infancy, male and female children are interpreted differently, and interacted with differently. Experimental evidence suggests that adults' perceptions of babies are affected by their beliefs about the babies' sex. John and Sandra Condry (1976) found that adults watching a film of a crying infant were more likely to hear the cry as angry if they believed the infant was a boy, and as plaintive or fearful if they believed the infant was a girl. In a similar experiment, adults judged a 24-hour-old baby as bigger if they believed it to be a boy, and finer-featured if they believed it to be a girl (Rubin et al. 1974). Such judgments then enter into the way people interact with infants and small children. People handle infants more gently when they believe them to be female, more playfully when they believe them to be male.

And they talk to them differently. Parents use more diminutives (*kitty, doggie*) when speaking to girls than to boys (Gleason et al. 1994), they use more inner state words (*happy, sad*) when speaking to girls (Ely et al. 1995), and they use more direct prohibitives (*don't do that!*) and more emphatic prohibitives (*no! no! no!*) to boys than to girls (Bellinger & Gleason 1982). Perhaps, one might suggest, the boys need more prohibitions because they tend to misbehave more than the girls. But Bellinger and Gleason found this pattern to be independent of the actual nature of the children's activity, suggesting that the adults and their beliefs about sex difference are far more important here than the children's behavior.

With differential treatment, boys and girls do learn to *be* different. Apparently, male and female infants cry the same amount (Maccoby & Jacklin 1974), but as they mature, boys cry less and less. There is some evidence that this difference emerges primarily from differential adult response to the crying. Qualitative differences in behavior come about in the same way. A study of 13-month-old children in day care (Fagot et al. 1985) showed that teachers responded to girls when they talked, babbled, or gestured, while they responded to boys when they whined, screamed, or demanded physical attention. Nine to eleven months later, the same girls talked more than the boys, and the boys whined, screamed, and demanded attention more than the girls. Children's eventual behavior, which seems to look at least statistically different across the sexes, is the product of adults' differential responses to ways of acting that are in many (possibly most) cases very similar indeed. The kids do indeed learn to *do* gender for themselves, to produce sex-differentiated behavior—although even with considerable differential treatment they do not end up with dichotomizing behavioral patterns.

Voice, which we have already mentioned, provides a dramatic example of children's coming to perform gender. At the ages of four to five years, in spite of their identical vocal apparatus, girls and boys begin to differentiate the fundamental frequency of their speaking voice. Boys tend to round and extend their lips, lengthening the vocal tract, whereas girls are tending to spread their lips (with smiles, for example), shortening the vocal tract. Girls are raising their pitches, boys lowering theirs. It may well be that adults are more likely to speak to girls in a high-pitched voice. It may be that they reward boys and girls for differential voice productions. It may also be that children simply observe this difference in older people, or that their differential participation in games (for example playacting) calls for different voice productions. Elaine Andersen (1990, pp. 24–25), for example, shows that children use high pitch when using baby talk or "teacher register" in role play. Some children speak as the other sex is expected to and thus, as with other aspects of doing gender, there is not a perfect dichotomization in voice pitch (even among adults, some voices are not consistently classified). Nonetheless, there is a striking production of mostly different pitched voices from similar vocal equipment.

See p. 25 for ways to introduce an ongoing debate.

There is considerable debate among scholars about the extent to which adults actually do treat boys and girls differently, and many note that the similarities far outweigh the differences. Research on early gender development—in fact the research in general on gender differences—is almost exclusively done by psychologists. As a result, the research it reports on largely involves observations of behavior in limited settings—whether in a laboratory or in the home or the preschool. Since these studies focus on limited settings and types of interaction and do not follow children through a normal day, they quite possibly miss the cumulative effects of small differences across many different situations. Small differences here and there are probably enough for children to learn what it means in their community to be male or female.

The significance of the small difference can be appreciated 10 from another perspective. The psychological literature tends to treat parents, other adults, and peers as the primary socializing agents. Only relatively recently have investigators begun to explore children's own active strategies for figuring out the social world. Eleanor Maccoby (2002) emphasizes that children have a very clear knowledge of their gender (that is, of whether they are classified as male or female) by the time they are three years old. Given this knowledge, it is not at all clear how much differential treatment children need in order to learn how to do their designated gender. What they mainly need is the message that male and female are supposed to be different, and that message is everywhere around them.

It has become increasingly clear that children play a very active role in their own development. From the moment they see themselves as social beings, they begin to focus on the enterprise of growing up. And to some extent, they probably experience many of the gendered developmental dynamics we discuss here not so much as gender-appropriate, but as *grown-up*. The greatest taboo is being "a baby," but the developmental imperative is gendered. Being grown-up, leaving babyhood, means very different things for boys than it does for girls. And the fact that growing up involves gender differentiation is encoded in the words of assessment with which progress is monitored— kids do not behave as good or bad people, but as *good boys* or *good girls*, and they develop into *big boys* and *big girls*.[2] In other words, they do not have the option of growing into just people, but into boys or girls. This does not mean that they see what they're doing in strictly gendered terms. It is probable that when boys and girls alter the fundamental frequency of their voices they are not trying to sound like *girls* or like *boys*, but that they are aspiring for some quality that is itself gendered—cuteness, authority. And the child's aspiration is not simply a matter of reasoning, but a matter of desire—a projection of the self into desired forms of participation in the social world. Desire is a tremendous force in projecting oneself into the future—in the continual remaking of the self that constitutes growing up.

Until about the age of two, boys and girls exhibit the same play behaviors. After that age, play in boys' and girls' groups begins to diverge as they come to select different toys and engage in different activities, and children begin to monitor each other's play, imposing sanctions on gender-inappropriate play. Much is made of the fact that boys become more agonistic than girls, and many attribute this to hormonal and even evolutionary differences (see Maccoby 2000 for a brief review of these various perspectives). But whatever the workings of biology may be, it is clear that this divergence is supported and exaggerated by the social system. As children get older, their play habits are monitored and differentiated, first by adults, and eventually by peers. Parents of small children have been shown to reward their children's choice of gender-appropriate toys (trucks for boys, dolls for girls) (Langlois & Downs 1980). And while parents' support of their children's gendered behavior is not always and certainly not simply a conscious effort at gender socialization, their behavior is probably more powerful than they think. Even parents who strive for gender equality, and who believe that they do not constrain their children's behavior along gender lines, have been observed in experimental situations to do just that.

Notes

1. Nowadays, with the possibility of having this information before birth, wanting to know in advance or not wanting to know can become ideologically charged. Either way, the sex of the child is frequently as great a preoccupation as its health.
2. Thorne (1993) and others have observed teachers urging children to act like "big boys and girls." Very rarely is a child told "don't act like a baby—you're a big kid now."

References*

Andersen, E. S. (1990). *Speaking with style: The sociolinguistic skills of children.* London: Routledge.

Bellinger, D., & Gleason, J. B. (1982). Sex differences in parental directives to young children. *Journal of Sex Roles, 8*, 1123–1139.

Butler, J. (1993). *Bodies that matter: On the discursive limits of sex.* New York and London: Routledge.

Condry, J., and Condry, S. (1976). Sex differences: a study in the eye of the beholder. *Child Development, 47*, 812–819.

Ely, R., Gleason, J. B., Narasimhan, B., & McCabe, A. (1995). Family talk about talk: Mothers lead the way. *Discourse Processes, 9* (2), 201–218.

Fagot, B. I., Hagan, R., Leinbach, M. D., & Kronsberg, S. (1985). Differential reactions to assertive and communicative acts of toddler boys and girls. *Child Development, 56*, 1499–1505.

Fausto-Sterling, A. (2000). *Sexing the body: Gender politics and the construction of sexuality.* New York: Basic Books.

Gleason, J. B., Perlmann, R. Y., Ely, D., & Evans, D. (1994). The baby talk register: Parents' use of diminutives. In J. L. Sokolov & C. E. Snow (Eds.), *Handbook of research in language development using CHILDES* (pp. 50–76). Hillsdale; NJ: Lawrence Erlbaum.

Langlois, J. H., & Downs, A. C. (1980). Mothers, fathers, and peers as socialization agents of sex-typed play behaviors in young children. *Child Development, 62*, 1217–1247.

*Based on the APA style of documentation.

Maccoby, E. E. (2000). Perspectives on gender development. *International Journal of Behavioural Development, 24*(4), 398–406.

Maccoby, E. E. (2002). Gender and social exchange: A developmental perspective. *New Directions for Child and Adolescent Development, 2002*(95), 87–106.

Maccoby, E. E., and Jacklin, C. N. (1974). *The psychology of sex differences.* Stanford, CA: Stanford University Press.

Nass, C., Moon, Y., and Green, N. (1997). Are machines gender neutral? Gender-stereotypic responses to computers with voices. *Journal of Language and Social Psychology, 27,* 864–876.

Rubin, J. Z., Provenzano, F. J., & Luria, Z. (1974). The eye of the beholder: Parents' view on sex of newborns. *American Journal of Orthopsychiatry, 44,* 512–519.

Joining the Conversation

1. This selection opens by saying that women "are not born, they are made"—and that "the same is true for men." How, according to Penelope Eckert and Sally McConnell-Ginet, does language contribute to our gender identities, and what evidence do they provide to support their argument?

2. The authors start by quoting Simone de Beauvoir. How do they then frame the quotation? In other words, how do they explain whose words these are, what the quotation means, and how it relates to their own text?

3. Notice how these authors handle gender references in their own writing: they don't use "he" to refer to both males and females, nor do they use the often awkward "he or she." What do they do instead? Cite some specific examples from their text in your answer.

4. Read the short op-ed by Stephen Mays on pp. 718–20. How do you think Mays would respond to this piece on learning to be gendered?

5. Write an essay on the topic of gender in which you consider your own masculine and/or feminine personality traits and behaviors. What memories do you have of your own gender formation? You might start with this sentence from Eckert and McConnell-Ginet as a "they say": "*Being a girl* or *being a boy* is not a stable state but an ongoing accomplishment, something that is actively *done* both by the individual . . . and by those . . . in the various communities to which it belongs" (paragraph 3).

CREDITS

TEXT

Liz Addison: "Two Years Are Better Than Four." From *The New York Times*, September 2, 2007. Copyright © 2007 The New York Times. All rights reserved. Used by permission and protected by the Copyright Laws of the United States. The printing, copying, redistribution, or retransmission of this Content without express written permission is prohibited.

Radley Balko: "What You Eat Is Your Business." The Cato Institute, May 23, 2004. Reprinted by permission of the publisher.

Dennis Baron: "Facebook multiplies genders but offers users the same three tired pronouns," by Dennis Baron. From The Web of Language Blog, February 28, 2014. Used by permission of the author.

Gary Becker and Kevin Murphy: "The Upside of Income Inequality," by Gary Becker and Kevin Murphy. From *The American*, May/June 2007. Reprinted with permission of the American Enterprise Institute, Washington, D.C.

Nicholas Carr: "Is Google Making Us Stupid?" by Nicholas Carr. From *The Atlantic*, July/August 2008. Copyright © 2008 The Atlantic Media Co., as first published in The Atlantic Magazine. All rights reserved. Distributed by Tribune Content Agency, LLC.

Richard Dorment: "Why Men Still Can't Have It All," by Richard Dorment. From *Esquire*, June/July 2013. Used by permission of *Esquire* Magazine.

Penelope Eckert and Sally McConnell-Ginet: Excerpts from *Language and Gender, 2nd Edition*. Copyright © 2013 by Penelope Eckert and Sally McConnell-Ginet. Reprinted with the permission of Cambridge University Press.

Credits

Credits

Sanford J. Ungar: Originally published as "7 Major Misconceptions about the Liberal Arts," *The Chronicle of Higher Education*, March 5, 2010. Reprinted with the permission of the author.

Jenna Wortham: "I Had a Nice Time with You Tonight. On the App," by Jenna Wortham. From *The New York Times*, April 6, 2014. © 2014 The New York Times. All rights reserved. Used by permission and protected by the Copyright Laws of the United States. The printing, copying, redistribution, or retransmission of this Content without express written permission is prohibited.

Shayan Zadeh: "Bring on More Immigrant Entrepreneurs," by Shayan Zadeh. From The *Wall Street Journal*, November 6, 2013. Used by permission of the author.

David Zinczenko: "Don't Blame the Eater." From *The New York Times*, November 23, 2002. Reprinted by permission of the author.

PHOTOGRAPHS

Chapter 16: p. 204: iStock/Getty Images; pp. 273, 278: Photo courtesy of Mike Rose; p. 286: Chip Somodevilla/Getty Images. **Chapter 17:** p. 296: iStock/Getty Images; p. 302: SIPA USA/Rethink Robotics via Sipa USA/Newscom; p. 314: Courtesy of The Everett Collection; p. 318 (left): Gustav Schultze, Naumburg, 1882/Wikimedia Commons; p. 318 (right): akg images/Newscom; p. 322: Midvale Company Photographs (1883–1953)/Flickr; https://creativecommons.org/licenses/by/2.0; p. 324: Sebastian Bergmann/Wikimedia Commons; pp. 330–38: from *The Influencing Machines* by Brooke Gladstone, W. W. Norton, 2012; p. 341: Foto Marburg/Art Resource, NY; p. 345: AP Photo; p. 378: Creatista/Shutterstock; p. 402: Seymour Chwast. **Chapter 18:** p. 416: Marilyn Moller; p. 430: Marilyn Moller; p. 431: AP Photo/Tony Avelar; p. 451:Tim Hill/Alamy; p. 452 Predrage/Getty Images; p. 475: iStockphoto; p. 487: Shutterstock; p. 497: Shutterstock; p. 507: iStock/Getty Images; p. 509: Jahi Chikwendiu/The Washington Post via Getty Images; p. 513: Peter Kramer/NBC/NBC NewsWire via Getty Images; p. 521: iStock/Getty Images; p. 524: AP Photo/Reed Saxon. **Chapter 19:** p. 538: © 2012 Doyle Partners; p. 550: iStock/Getty Images; p. 563: Michael Brands/The New York Times/Redux; p. 564: AP Photo. **Chapter 20:** p. 638: Getty Images; p. 645: Partha Sarkar Xinhua/Eyevine/Redux; fig. p. 661: Margaret Thomas/The Washington Post/Getty Images; p. 669: Thodoris Tibilis/Shutterstock.

ACKNOWLEDGMENTS

LIKE THE PREVIOUS TWO EDITIONS, this one would never have seen print if it weren't for Marilyn Moller, our superb editor at Norton, and the extraordinary job she has done of inspiring, commenting on, rewriting (and then rewriting and rewriting again) our many drafts. Our friendship with Marilyn is one of the most cherished things to have developed from this project.

Our thanks go as well to Ariella Foss, associate editor, for offering a wealth of helpful suggestions throughout; to Rebecca Homiski, Andy Ensor, and Kurt Wildermuth for managing the editing and production of this edition; and to Michal Brody, Cliff Landesman, and Claire Wallace for curating and producing the fabulous blog that accompanies this book, **theysayiblog.**

We thank John Darger, our Norton representative, who offered early encouragement to write this book, to Debra Morton Hoyt for her excellent work on the cover—and give special thanks to Lib Triplett and all the Norton travelers for the superb work they've done on behalf of our book.

Thanks to Lisa Ampleman, a prize-winning poet and doctoral graduate in English from the University of Cincinnati, for her invaluable aid in finding effective readings for the book and for writing the instructor's notes that accompany the book.

We owe special thanks to our colleagues in the English department at the University of Illinois at Chicago: Mark Canuel, our former department head, for supporting our earlier efforts overseeing the university's Writing in the Disciplines requirement; Walter Benn Michaels, our current department head; and Ann Feldman, former Director of University Writing Programs, for encouraging us to teach first-year composition courses at UIC in which we could try out ideas and drafts of our manuscript; Tom Moss, Diane Chin, Vainis Aleksa, and Matt Pavesich, who have also been very supportive of our efforts; and Matt Oakes, our former research assistant. We are also grateful to Ann, Diane, and Mark Bennett for bringing us into their graduate course on the teaching of writing, and to Lisa Freeman, John Huntington, Walter Benn Michaels, and Ralph Cintron, for inviting us to present our ideas in the keynote lecture at UIC's 2013 "Composition Matters" conference.

We are also especially grateful to Steve Benton and Nadya Pittendrigh, who taught a section of composition with us using an early draft of this book. Steve made many helpful suggestions, particularly regarding the exercises. We are grateful to Andy Young, a lecturer at UIC who has tested our book in his courses and who gave us extremely helpful feedback. And we thank Vershawn A. Young, whose work on code-meshing influenced our argument in Chapter 9, and Hillel Crandus, whose classroom handout inspired the chapter on "Entering Classroom Discussions."

We are grateful to the many colleagues and friends who've let us talk our ideas out with them and given extremely helpful responses. UIC's former dean, Stanley Fish, has been central in this respect, both in personal conversations and in his incisive articles calling for greater focus on form in the teaching of writing. Our conversations with Jane Tompkins have also been integral to this book, as was the composition course that Jane co-taught with Gerald entitled "Can We Talk?" Lenny Davis, too, offered both intellectual insight and emotional support, as did

Heather Arnet, Jennifer Ashton, Janet Atwill, Kyra Auslander, Noel Barker, Jim Benton, Jack Brereton, Tim Cantrick, Marsha Cassidy, David Chinitz, Lisa Chinitz, Pat Chu, Duane Davis, Bridget O'Rourke Flisk, Steve Flisk, Judy Gardiner, Howard Gardner, Rich Gelb, Gwynne Gertz, Jeff Gore, Bill Haddad, Ben Hale, Scott Hammerl, Patricia Harkin, Andy Hoberek, John Huntington, Joe Janangelo, Paul Jay, David Jolliffe, Nancy Kohn, Don Lazere, Jo Liebermann, Steven Mailloux, Deirdre McCloskey, Maurice J. Meilleur, Alan Meyers, Greg Meyerson, Anna Minkov, Chris Newfield, Jim Phelan, Paul Psilos, Bruce Robbins, Charles Ross, Eileen Seifert, Evan Seymour, David Shumway, Herb Simons, Jim Sosnoski, David Steiner, Harold Veeser, Chuck Venegoni, Marla Weeg, Jerry Wexler, Joyce Wexler, Virginia Wexman, Jeffrey Williams, Lynn Woodbury, and the late Wayne Booth, whose friendship we dearly miss.

We are grateful for having had the opportunity to present our ideas to a number of schools: University of Arkansas at Little Rock, Augustana College, Brandeis University, Brigham Young University, Bryn Mawr College, Case Western University, Columbia University, Community College of Philadelphia, California State University at Bakersfield, California State University at Northridge, University of California at Riverside, University of Delaware, DePauw University, Drew University, Duke University, Duquesne University, Elmhurst College, Emory University, Fontbonne University, Furman University, Gettysburg College, Harper College, Harvard University, Haverford College, Hawaii Office of Secondary School Curriculum Instruction, Hunter College, University of Illinois College of Medicine, Illinois State University, John Carroll University, Kansas State University, Lawrence University, the Lawrenceville School, University of Louisiana at Lafayette, MacEwan University, University of Maryland at College Park,

Massachusetts Institute of Technology, University of Memphis, Miami University, University of Missouri at Columbia, New Trier High School, State University of New York at Geneseo, State University of New York at Stony Brook, North Carolina A&T University, University of North Florida, Northern Michigan University, Norwalk Community College, Northwestern University Division of Continuing Studies, University of Notre Dame, Ohio Wesleyan University, Oregon State University, University of Portland, University of Rochester, St. Ambrose University, St. Andrew's School, St. Charles High School, Seattle University, Southern Connecticut State University, South Elgin High School, University of South Florida, University of Southern Mississippi, Swarthmore College, Teachers College, University of Tennessee at Knoxville, University of Texas at Arlington, Tulane University, Union College, Ursinus College, Wabash College, Washington College, University of Washington, Western Michigan University, Westinghouse/ Kenwood High Schools, University of West Virginia at Morgantown, Wheaton Warrenville English Chairs, and the University of Wisconsin at Whitewater.

We particularly thank those who helped arrange these visits and discussed writing issues with us: Jeff Abernathy, Herman Asarnow, John Austin, Greg Barnheisel, John Bean, Crystal Benedicks, Joe Bizup, Sheridan Blau, Dagne Bloland, Chris Breu, Mark Brouwer, Joan Johnson Bube, John Caldwell, Gregory Clark, Irene Clark, Dean Philip Cohen, Cathy D'Agostino, Tom Deans, Gaurav Desai, Lisa Dresdner, Kathleen Dudden-Rowlands, Lisa Ede, Alexia Ellett, Emory Elliott, Anthony Ellis, Kim Flachmann, Ronald Fortune, Rosanna Fukuda, George Haggerty, Donald Hall, Joe Harris, Gary Hatch, Elizabeth Hatmaker, Harry Hellenbrand, Nicole Henderson, Donna Heiland, Doug Hesse, Van Hillard, Andrew Hoberek,

Acknowledgments

Michael Hustedde, Sara Jameson, T. R. Johnson, David Jones, Ann Kaplan, Don Kartiganer, Linda Kinnahan, Dean Georg Kleine, Albert Labriola, Craig Lawrence, Lori Lopez, Tom Liam Lynch, Hiram Maxim, Michael Mays, Thomas McFadden, Sean Meehan, Connie Mick, Joseph Musser, Margaret Oakes, John O'Connor, Gary Olson, Tom Pace, Les Perelman, Emily Poe, Dominick Randolph, Clancy Ratliff, Monica Rico, Kelly Ritter, Jack Robinson, Warren Rosenberg, Laura Rosenthal, Dean Howard Ross, Deborah Rossen-Knill, Paul Schacht, Petra Schatz, Evan Seymour, Rose Shapiro, Mike Shea, Cecilia M. Shore, Erec Smith, Nancy Sommers, Stephen Spector, Timothy Spurgin, Ron Strickland, Trig Thoreson, Josh Toth, Judy Trost, Aiman Tulamait, Charles Tung, John Webster, Robert Weisbuch, Sandi Weisenberg, Karin Westman, Martha Woodmansee, and Lynn Worsham.

We also wish to extend particular thanks to two Chicago area educators who have worked closely with us: Les Lynn of the Chicago Debate League and Eileen Murphy of CERCA. Lastly, we wish to thank two high school teachers for their excellent and inventive adaptations of our work: Mark Gozonsky in his YouTube video clip, "Building Blocks," and Dave Stuart, Jr., in his blog, "Teaching the Core."

For inviting us to present our ideas at their conferences we are grateful to John Brereton and Richard Wendorf at the Boston Athenaeum; Wendy Katkin of the Reinvention Center of State University of New York at Stony Brook; Luchen Li of the Michigan English Association; Lisa Lee and Barbara Ransby of the Public Square in Chicago; Don Lazere of the University of Tennessee at Knoxville; Dennis Baron of the University of Illinois at Urbana-Champaign; Alfie Guy of Yale University; Irene Clark of the California State University at Northridge; George Crandell and Steve Hubbard, co-directors of the

ACETA conference at Auburn University; Mary Beth Rose of the Humanities Institute at the University of Illinois at Chicago; Diana Smith of St. Anne's Belfield School and the University of Virginia; Jim Maddox and Victor Luftig of the Bread Loaf School of English; Jan Fitzsimmons and Jerry Berberet of the Associated Colleges of Illinois; and Rosemary Feal, Executive Director of the Modern Language Association.

We are very grateful to those who reviewed the new readings for this third edition. Our thanks go to Elias Dominguez Barajas (University of Arkansas), Christine Berni (Austin Community College), Wanda Fries (Somerset Community College), Leigh Hancock (Germanna Community College), Jennie Joiner (Keuka College), Elizabeth Kalbfleisch (Southern Connecticut State University), Jeanne McDonald (Waubonsee Community College), Roxanne Munch (Joliet Junior College), Michael O'Connor (Onondaga Community College), Kelly Ritter (University of Illinois, Urbana-Champaign), Gail Suberbielle (Baton Rouge Community College), Eleanor Welsh (Chesapeake College), and Debbie J. Williams (Abilene Christian University).

A very special thanks goes to those who reviewed materials for the third edition: Carrie Bailey (Clark College); Heather Barrett (Boston University); Amy Bennett-Zendzian (Boston University); Seth Blumenthal (Boston University); Ron Brooks (Oklahoma State University); Jonathan Cook (Durham Technical Community College); Tessa Croker (Boston University); Perry Cumbie (Durham Technical Community College); Robert Danberg (Binghamton University); Elias Dominguez Barajas (University of Arkansas); Nancy Enright (Seton Hall University); Jason Evans (Prairie State College); Ted Fitts (Boston University); Karen Gaffney (Raritan Valley Community College); Karen Gardiner (University of Alabama);

Acknowledgments

Stephen Hodin (Boston University); Michael Horwitz (University of Hartford); John Hyman (American University); Claire Kervin (Boston University); Melinda Kreth (Central Michigan University); Heather Marcovitch (Red Deer College); Christina Michaud (Boston University); Marisa Milanese (Boston University); Theresa Mooney (Austin Community College); Roxanne Munch (Joliet Junior College); Sarah Quirk (Waubonsee Community College); Lauri Ramey (California State University, Los Angeles); David Shawn (Boston University); Jennifer Sia (Boston University); Laura Sonderman (Marshall University); Katherine Stebbins McCaffrey (Boston University); K. Sullivan (Lane Community College); Anne-Marie Thomas (Austin Community College at Riverside); Eliot Treichel (Lane Community College); Rosanna Walker (Lane Community College); Mary Erica Zimmer (Boston University).

A very special thanks goes to those who reviewed materials for the second edition: Kathy Albertson (Georgia Southern University); Joseph Aldinger (State University of New York, Buffalo); Nicolette Amann (Humboldt State University); Sonja Andrus (Collin College); Gail Arnoff (John Carroll University); Lisa Siefker Bailey (Indiana University-Purdue University Indianapolis); John Berteaux (California State University, Monterey Bay); Sonya Blades (University of North Carolina, Greensboro); Elyse Blankley (California State University, Long Beach); Andrew Bodenrader (Manhattanville College); Rachel Bowman (University of North Carolina, Greensboro); Eric Branscomb (Salem State College); Harryette Brown (Eastfield College); Elena Brunn (Borough of Manhattan Community College/City University of New York); Rita Carey (Clark College); Julie Cassidy (Borough of Manhattan Community College); Catherine Chaterdon (The University of Arizona); Amy Lea Clemons (Francis Marion University);

ACKNOWLEDGMENTS

Tracey Clough (University of Texas, Arlington); Julie Colish (University of Michigan, Flint); Matt Copeland (San Diego State University); Christopher Cowley (State University of New York, Buffalo); Angela Crow (Georgia Southern University); Susie Crowson (Del Mar College); Sean Curran (California State University, Northridge); Kate Dailey (Bowling Green State University, Firelands); Jill Darley-Vanis (Clark College); Virginia Davidson (Mount Saint Mary College); Page Delano (Borough of Manhattan Community College); Elisabeth Divis (University of Michigan); Will Dodson (University of North Carolina, Greensboro); Patricia Dowcett (Quinnipiac University); Laura Dubek (Middle Tennessee State University); William Duffy (University of North Carolina, Greensboro); Gary Eberle (Aquinas College); Alycia Ehlert (Darton College); Sarah Farrell (University of Texas, Arlington); Joseph Fasano (Manhattanville College); Benjamin Fischer (Northwest Nazarene University); Joan Forbes (Kean University); Courtney Fowler (California State University, Long Beach); Caimeen Garrett (American University); William Griswold (California State University, Long Beach); Deborah Greenhut (New Jersey City University); Charles Guy-McAlpin (University of North Carolina, Greensboro); Katalin Gyurian (Kean University); Jami Hemmenway (Eureka College); Jane Hikel (University of Hartford); Erin Houlihan (University of North Carolina, Greensboro); Erik Hudak (University of Texas, Arlington); Chris Hurst (State University of New York, Buffalo); Kristopher Jansma (Manhattanville College); Michael Jauchen (Colby-Sawyer College); Jeanine Jewell (Southeast Community College); Antonnet Johnson (University of Arizona); Donald Johnson (Santa Monica College); Lou Ann Karabel (Indiana University Northwest); Rod Kessler (Salem State College); Kristi Key (Newberry College); Kelly Kinney (Binghamton

University); Francia Kissel (Indiana University-Purdue University Indianapolis); Geoff Klock, Debra S. Knutson (Shawnee State University); Morani Kornberg-Weiss (State University of New York, Buffalo); David LaPierre (Central Connecticut State University); Ann-Gee Lee (St. Cloud State University); Jerry Lee (University of Arizona); Jessica Lee (University of Arizona); Eric Leuschner (Fort Hays State University); Brian Lewis (Century College); Damon Kraft (Missouri Southern State University); Amy Losi (Hamburg Central School District); Aimee Lukas (Central Connecticut State University); Jaclyn Lutzke (Indiana University-Purdue University Indianapolis); John McBratney (John Carroll University); Heather McPherson (University of Minnesota); Cruz Medina (University of Arizona); Dawn Mendoza (Dean College); Rae Ann Meriwether (University of North Carolina, Greensboro); Catherine Merritt (University of Alabama); Gina Miller (Alaska Pacific University); Tomas Q. Morin (Texas State University); Jenny Mueller (McKendree University); Matt Mullins (University of North Carolina, Greensboro); Roxanne F. Munch (Joliet Junior College); Charles Nelson (Kean University); Pauline Newton (Southern Methodist University); Pat Norton (University of Alabama); Marsha Nourse (Dean College); Anne-Marie Obilade (Alcorn State University); Adair Olson (Black Hills State University); Nancy Pederson (University of Minnesota, Morris); Christine Pipitone-Herron (Raritan Valley Community College); D. Pothen (Multnomah University); Sarah A. Quirk (Waubonsee Community College); Clancy Ratliff (University of Louisiana, Lafayette); Kelly Ritter (University of North Carolina, Greensboro); Stephanie Roach (University of Michigan, Flint); Jeffrey Roessner (Mercyhurst College); Scott Rogers (Weber State University); Suzanne Ross (St. Cloud State University); Keidrick

Roy; Myra Salcedo (University of Texas, Arlington); Ronit Sarig (California State University, Northridge); Samantha Seamans (Central Connecticut State University); Rae Schipke (Central Connecticut State University); Michael Schoenfeldt (University of Michigan); Pat Sherbert (National Math and Science Initiative); Joyce Shrimplin (Miami University of Ohio); Leticia Slabaugh (Texas A&M, Galveston); Lars Soderlund (Purdue University); Summar Sparks (University of North Carolina, Greensboro); David Squires (State University of New York, Buffalo); Alice Stephens (Oldenburg Academy of the Immaculate Conception); Mary Stroud (The University of Arizona); Kimberly Sullivan (Clark College); Doug Swartz (Indiana University Northwest); William Tate (Covenant College); James Tolan (Borough of Manhattan Community College); Dawn Trettin-Moyer (University of Washington, Oshkosh); Clementina Verge (Central Connecticut State University); Norma Vogel (Dean College); Nhu Vu (Seattle Central Community College); Christie Ward (Central Connecticut State University); Stephanie Wardrop (Western New England College); Rachael Wendler (University of Arizona); Cara Williams (University of North Carolina, Greensboro); Todd Williams (Kutztown University); Robert Wilson (Cedar Crest College); Courtney Wooten (University of North Carolina, Greensboro); Chuck Venegoni (John Hersey High School); William Younglove (California State University, Long Beach).

We also thank those who reviewed materials for the first edition: Marie Elizabeth Brockman (Central Michigan University); Ronald Clark Brooks (Oklahoma State University); Beth Buyserie (Washington State University); Michael Donnelly (University of Tampa); Karen Gardiner (University of Alabama); Greg Glau (Northern Arizona University); Anita

Helle (Oregon State University); Michael Hennessy (Texas State University); Asao Inoue (California State University at Fresno); Sara Jameson (Oregon State University); Joseph Jones (University of Memphis); Amy S. Lerman (Mesa Community College); Marc Lawrence MacDonald (Central Michigan University); Andrew Manno (Raritan Valley Community College); Sylvia Newman (Weber State University); Carole Clark Papper (Hofstra University); Eileen Seifert (DePaul University); Evan Seymour (Community College of Philadelphia); Renee Shea (Bowie State University); Marcy Taylor (Central Michigan University); Rita Treutel (University of Alabama at Birmingham); Margaret Weaver (Missouri State University); Leah Williams (University of New Hampshire); and Tina Žigon (State University of New York at Buffalo).

Finally, a special thank you to David Bartholomae for suggesting the phrase that became the subtitle of the book.

INDEX OF TEMPLATES

—▢—

INTRODUCING WHAT "THEY SAY"
(p. 23)

▸ A number of _____ have recently suggested that
_____.

▸ It has become common today to dismiss _____.

▸ In their recent work, Y and Z have offered harsh critiques of
_____ for _____.

INTRODUCING "STANDARD VIEWS"
(pp. 23–24)

▸ Americans today tend to believe that _____.

▸ Conventional wisdom has it that _____.

▸ Common sense seems to dictate that _____.

▸ The standard way of thinking about topic X has it that _____.

▸ It is often said that _____.

▸ My whole life I have heard it said that _____.

▸ You would think that _____.

▸ Many people assume that _____.

INDEX OF TEMPLATES

MAKING WHAT "THEY SAY" SOMETHING *YOU* SAY
(pp. 24–25)

▸ I've always believed that _____ .

▸ When I was a child, I used to think that _____ .

▸ Although I should know better by now, I cannot help thinking that _____ .

▸ At the same time that I believe _____ , I also believe _____ .

INTRODUCING SOMETHING IMPLIED OR ASSUMED
(p. 25)

▸ Although none of them have ever said so directly, my teachers have often given me the impression that _____ .

▸ One implication of X's treatment of _____ is that _____ .

▸ Although X does not say so directly, she apparently assumes that _____ .

▸ While they rarely admit as much, _____ often take for granted that _____ .

INTRODUCING AN ONGOING DEBATE
(pp. 25–28)

▸ In discussions of X, one controversial issue has been _____ . On the one hand, _____ argues _____ . On the other hand, _____ contends _____. Others even maintain _____. My own view is _____.

▸ When it comes to the topic of _____, most of us will readily agree that _____. Where this agreement usually ends, however, is on the question of _____. Whereas some are convinced that _____, others maintain that _____.

▸ In conclusion, then, as I suggested earlier, defenders of _____ can't have it both ways. Their assertion that _____ is contradicted by their claim that _____.

CAPTURING AUTHORIAL ACTION
(pp. 38–40)

▸ X acknowledges that _____.

▸ X agrees that _____.

▸ X argues that _____.

▸ X believes that _____.

▸ X denies/does not deny that _____.

▸ X claims that _____.

▸ X complains that _____.

▸ X concedes that _____.

▸ X demonstrates that _____.

▸ X deplores the tendency to _____.

▸ X celebrates the fact that _____.

▸ X emphasizes that _____.

- ▸ X insists that _____.

- ▸ X observes that _____.

- ▸ X questions whether _____.

- ▸ X refutes the claim that _____.

- ▸ X reminds us that _____.

- ▸ X reports that _____.

- ▸ X suggests that _____.

- ▸ X urges us to _____.

INTRODUCING QUOTATIONS
(p. 46)

- ▸ X states, "_____."

- ▸ As the prominent philosopher X puts it, "_____."

- ▸ According to X, "_____."

- ▸ X himself writes, "_____."

- ▸ In her book, _____, X maintains that "_____."

- ▸ Writing in the journal _____, X complains that "_____."

- ▸ In X's view, "_____."

- ▸ X agrees when she writes, "_____."

- ▸ X disagrees when he writes, "_____."

- ▸ X complicates matters further when he writes, "_____."

Index of Templates

EXPLAINING QUOTATIONS

(pp. 46–47)

▸ Basically, X is saying _____.

▸ In other words, X believes _____.

▸ In making this comment, X urges us to _____.

▸ X is corroborating the age-old adage that _____.

▸ X's point is that _____.

▸ The essence of X's argument is that _____.

DISAGREEING, WITH REASONS

(p. 60)

▸ I think X is mistaken because she overlooks _____.

▸ X's claim that _____ rests upon the questionable assumption that _____.

▸ I disagree with X's view that _____ because, as recent research has shown, _____.

▸ X contradicts herself/can't have it both ways. On the one hand, she argues _____. On the other hand, she also says _____.

▸ By focusing on _____, X overlooks the deeper problem of _____.

AGREEING—WITH A DIFFERENCE
(pp. 61–64)

▶ I agree that _____ because my experience _____ confirms it.

▶ X surely is right about _____ because, as she may not be aware, recent studies have shown that _____ .

▶ X's theory of _____ is extremely useful because it sheds insight on the difficult problem of _____ .

▶ Those unfamiliar with this school of thought may be interested to know that it basically boils down to _____ .

▶ I agree that _____ , a point that needs emphasizing since so many people believe _____ .

▶ If group X is right that _____ , as I think they are, then we need to reassess the popular assumption that _____ .

AGREEING AND DISAGREEING SIMULTANEOUSLY
(pp. 64–66)

▶ Although I agree with X up to a point, I cannot accept his overall conclusion that _____ .

▶ Although I disagree with much that X says, I fully endorse his final conclusion that _____ .

▶ Though I concede that _____ , I still insist that _____ .

▶ Whereas X provides ample evidence that _____ , Y and Z's research on _____ and _____ convinces me that _____ instead.

▸ X is right that _____, but she seems on more dubious ground when she claims that _____.

▸ While X is probably wrong when she claims that _____, she is right that _____.

▸ I'm of two minds about X's claim that _____. On the one hand, I agree that _____. On the other hand, I'm not sure if _____.

▸ My feelings on the issue are mixed. I do support X's position that _____, but I find Y's argument about _____ and Z's research on _____ to be equally persuasive.

SIGNALING WHO IS SAYING WHAT
(pp. 71–73)

▸ X argues _____.

▸ According to both X and Y, _____.

▸ Politicians _____, X argues, should _____.

▸ Most athletes will tell you that _____.

▸ My own view, however, is that _____.

▸ I agree, as X may not realize, that _____.

▸ But _____ are real and, arguably, the most significant factor in _____.

▸ But X is wrong that _____.

▸ However, it is simply not true that _____.

▸ Indeed, it is highly likely that _____.

▸ X's assertion that _____ does not fit the facts.

INDEX OF TEMPLATES

▶ X is right that _____.

▶ X is wrong that _____.

▶ X is both right and wrong that _____.

▶ Yet a sober analysis of the matter reveals _____.

▶ Nevertheless, new research shows _____.

▶ Anyone familiar with _____ should agree that _____.

EMBEDDING VOICE MARKERS
(pp. 74–75)

▶ X overlooks what I consider an important point about _____.

▶ My own view is that what X insists is a _____ is in fact a _____.

▶ I wholeheartedly endorse what X calls _____.

▶ These conclusions, which X discusses in _____, add weight to the argument that _____.

ENTERTAINING OBJECTIONS
(p. 82)

▶ At this point I would like to raise some objections that have been inspired by the skeptic in me. She feels that I have been ignoring _____. "_____," she says to me, "_____."

▶ Yet some readers may challenge the view that _____.

▶ Of course, many will probably disagree with this assertion that _____.

NAMING YOUR NAYSAYERS

(pp. 83–84)

▸ Here many _____ would probably object that _____.

▸ But *social* _____ would certainly take issue with the argument that _____.

▸ _____, of course, may want to question whether _____.

▸ Nevertheless, both followers and critics *of* _____ will probably argue that _____.

▸ Although not all _____ think alike, some of them will probably dispute my claim that _____.

▸ _____ are so diverse in their views that it's hard to generalize about them, but some are likely to object on the grounds that _____.

INTRODUCING OBJECTIONS INFORMALLY

(pp. 84–85)

▸ But is my proposal realistic? What are the chances of its actually being adopted?

▸ Yet is it always true that _____? Is it always the case, as I have been suggesting, that _____?

▸ However, does the evidence I've cited prove conclusively that _____?

▸ "Impossible," some will say. "You must be reading the research selectively."

MAKING CONCESSIONS WHILE STILL
STANDING YOUR GROUND (p. 89)

▶ Although I grant that _____ , I still maintain that _____ .

▶ Proponents of X are right to argue that _____ . But they exaggerate when they claim that _____ .

▶ While it is true that _____ , it does not necessarily follow that _____ .

▶ On the one hand, I agree with X that _____ . But on the other hand, I still insist that _____ .

INDICATING WHO CARES
(pp. 95–96)

▶ _____ used to think _____ . But recently [or within the past few decades] _____ suggests that _____ .

▶ These findings challenge the work of earlier researchers, who tended to assume that _____ .

▶ Recent studies like these shed new light on _____ , which previous studies had not addressed.

▶ Researchers have long assumed that _____ . For instance, one eminent scholar of cell biology, _____ , assumed in _____ , her seminal work on cell structures and functions, that fat cells _____ . As _____ herself put it, "_____ " (2012). Another leading scientist, _____ , argued that fat cells "_____ " (2011). Ultimately, when it came to the nature of fat, the basic assumption was that _____ .

But a new body of research shows that fat cells are far more complex and that _____.

▸ If sports enthusiasts stopped to think about it, many of them might simply assume that the most successful athletes _____. However, new research shows _____.

▸ These findings challenge neoliberals' common assumptions that _____.

▸ At first glance, teenagers appear to _____. But on closer inspection _____.

ESTABLISHING WHY YOUR CLAIMS MATTER
(pp. 98–99)

▸ X matters/is important because _____.

▸ Although X may seem trivial, it is in fact crucial in terms of today's concern over _____.

▸ Ultimately, what is at stake here is _____.

▸ These findings have important consequences for the broader domain of _____.

▸ My discussion of X is in fact addressing the larger matter of _____.

▸ These conclusions/This discovery will have significant applications in _____ as well as in _____.

▸ Although X may seem of concern to only a small group of _____, it should in fact concern anyone who cares about _____.

COMMONLY USED TRANSITIONS
(pp. 108–10)

ADDITION

also	in fact
and	indeed
besides	moreover
furthermore	so too
in addition	

ELABORATION

actually	to put it another way
by extension	to put it bluntly
in short	to put it succinctly
that is	ultimately
in other words	

EXAMPLE

after all	for instance
as an illustration	specifically
consider	to take a case in point
for example	

CAUSE AND EFFECT

accordingly	since
as a result	so
consequently	then
hence	therefore
it follows, then	thus

Index of Templates

COMPARISON

along the same lines

in the same way

likewise

similarly

CONTRAST

although

but

by contrast

conversely

despite

even though

however

in contrast

nevertheless

nonetheless

on the contrary

on the other hand

regardless

whereas

while

yet

CONCESSION

admittedly

although it is true that

granted

I concede that

of course

naturally

to be sure

CONCLUSION

as a result

consequently

hence

in conclusion, then

in short

in sum, then

it follows, then

so

the upshot of all this is that

therefore

thus

to sum up

to summarize

ADDING METACOMMENTARY

(pp. 131–37)

- In other words, _____.

- What _____ really means by this is _____.

- Ultimately, my goal is to demonstrate that _____.

- My point is not _____, but _____.

- To put it another way, _____.

- In sum, then, _____.

- My conclusion, then, is that, _____.

- In short, _____.

- What is more important, _____.

- Incidentally, _____.

- By the way, _____.

- Chapter 2 explores _____, while Chapter 3 examines _____.

- Having just argued that _____, let us now turn our attention to _____.

- Although some readers may object that _____, I would answer that _____.

INTRODUCING GAPS IN THE EXISTING RESEARCH

(p. 191)

▸ Studies of X have indicated _____ . It is not clear, however, that this conclusion applies to _____ .

▸ _____ often take for granted that _____ . Few have investigated this assumption, however.

▸ X's work tells us a great deal about _____ . Can this work be generalized to _____ ?

INDEX OF AUTHORS AND TITLES

GERALD GRAFF, a professor of English and education at the University of Illinois at Chicago and the 2008 president of the Modern Language Association of America, has had a major impact on teachers through such books as *Professing Literature: An Institutional History, Beyond the Culture Wars: How Teaching the Conflicts Can Revitalize American Education,* and, most recently, *Clueless in Academe: How Schooling Obscures the Life of the Mind.*

CATHY BIRKENSTEIN is a lecturer in English at the University of Illinois at Chicago and co-director of the Writing in the Disciplines program. She has published essays on writing, most recently in *College English,* and, with Gerald Graff, in *The Chronicle of Higher Education, Academe,* and *College Composition and Communication.* She has also given talks and workshops with Gerald at numerous colleges and is currently working on a study of common misunderstandings surrounding academic discourse.

RUSSEL DURST, who edited the readings in this book, is a professor of English at the University of Cincinnati, where he teaches courses in composition, writing pedagogy and research, English linguistics, and the Hebrew Bible as literature. A past president of the National Conference on Research in Language and Literacy, he is the author of several books, including *Collision Course: Conflict, Negotiation, and Learning in College Composition.*